This is number two hundred and eight in the
second numbered series of the
Miegunyah Volumes
made possible by the
Miegunyah Fund
established by bequests
under the wills of
Sir Russell and Lady Grimwade.

'Miegunyah' was Russell Grimwade's home
from 1911 to 1955
and Mab Grimwade's home
from 1911 to 1973.

EMPERORS IN LILLIPUT

CLEM CHRISTESEN of *Meanjin* & STEPHEN MURRAY-SMITH of *Overland*

JIM DAVIDSON

THE MIEGUNYAH PRESS

THE MIEGUNYAH PRESS
An imprint of Melbourne University Publishing Limited
Level 1, 715 Swanston Street, Carlton, Victoria 3053, Australia
mup-contact@unimelb.edu.au
www.mup.com.au

First published 2022

Cover design by Design by Committee
Typeset in Adobe Garamond Pro 11.5/14.5pt by Cannon Typesetting

Printed and bound in Malaysia for Imago

NATIONAL LIBRARY OF AUSTRALIA
A catalogue record for this book is available from the National Library of Australia

9780522877403 (hardback)
9780522877410 (ebook)

Contents

Introduction

THERE'S NOTHING SO dead as last week's newspapers—and that was true even before they began appearing on the internet. But literary magazines, broadly conceived, are quite different. Many of us may have picked up an old one, lying in a corner, and been surprised by its quality. Indeed, sometimes there are sleepers, articles or authors whose time has not quite come when they first appear, but who acquire the full force of established reputation to validate a retrospective glance. One begins to understand the remark of Schopenhauer, that he never read anything unless it was a hundred years old.

Clem Christesen used to say that he was preparing the journal for posterity—laying out the wares of the present for future examination. Even when most depressed about *Meanjin*'s prospects, he never lost sight of how it presented to the future. In a sense he was right. Every effective literary magazine is also a time capsule.

'The great editor', Fintan O'Toole remarked of Bob Silvers of the *New York Review of Books*, 'is a chimerical creature, combining contrary qualities in one mind: assertive and self-effacing, commanding and sensitive, infinitely curious and sharply focused, patient and fearfully demanding, wide-angle and close-up.'[1] Our men qualify. This book examines the nature and context of two great editorships, and how their magazines, *Meanjin* and *Overland*, responded to the times. The remark of Michael Ondaatje (recycling Stendhal) that 'A novel is a mirror walking down the road' applies even more to literary magazines.

Emperors in Lilliput focuses on the personae of Christesen and Murray-Smith, extending to their personalities as expressed in their editorial work and beyond, taking the reader behind the scenes. For a time I toyed with the title '34 × 2': not a formula, but the thirty-four years each edited the journals they founded. Despite this correlation (only twenty years were shared) the style of their magazines and editorships were very different.

They were colleagues as well as rivals. Each (particularly Clem) had a strong sense of their magazine's role; each (particularly Stephen) a sense of the particular public their magazines were trying to reach. Both magazines came out of the University of Melbourne—*Meanjin* officially, *Overland* almost under cover. (The university administration chided Stephen for using its internal mail system to distribute copies to academic subscribers.) A good many people subscribed to both magazines; writers, eager for publication, happily wrote for both of them. In effect they functioned conjointly, like a 'W'. Each provides a different model of magazine editorship. It therefore seemed a good idea to tell their story within one set of covers. It would be all the richer for the contrast.

A good deal of the subject matter has been traversed before, but there are huge gaps. The most exhaustive treatment is by Lynne Strahan: her *Just City and the Mirrors: Meanjin Quarterly and the Intellectual Front 1940–1965* (1984) covers Clem Christesen's first twenty-five years at *Meanjin*. There has been no published account of the complete editorship. Judith Armstrong's *The Christesen Romance* (1996) is structured as much around the life of Nina, Clem's wife and head of the University of Melbourne's Russian Department, as it is around Clem. Accordingly, it doesn't explore the contents of the magazine. Mention should also be made of the anthology, with extensive commentary, edited by then *Meanjin* editor Jenny Lee (with Philip Mead and Gerald Murnane), *The Temperament of Generations* (1990). The life and work of Stephen Murray-Smith has been much less explored, but he is one of the three figures examined in John McLaren's study *Free Radicals of the Left in Postwar Melbourne* (2003).

The material in the archives relating to the two editorships is vast, between them amounting to nearly a thousand boxes. Here the challenge has been to capture something of the essence of the two magazines, and of the two men as editors. Of necessity, omissions—and cuts—have had to be made. The emphasis has been on the phases of each magazine, highlighting particular preoccupations and episodes, and giving cameos of various writers. This approach provides guide ropes across two vast mosaics. Otherwise the book would be a recital of articles, a kind of catalogue aria.

The first two chapters trace the lives first of Clem, then of Stephen, to the point where their magazines fully emerged. Interestingly, both could be said to have had a false start. *Meanjin*'s first four years were in Brisbane (the name being derived from the Indigenous name for the 'spike' on which the city is built), before it moved south at the invitation of the University of Melbourne. Similarly, *Overland* emerged after two years from the *Realist Writer*, a publication associated with the Communist Party.

Little magazine editors are usually made, not born—it may be quite otherwise with old-style newspaper editors. The question of how somebody evolves into one, sometimes involuntarily, is therefore a crucial biographical question. Since both men were around thirty when this happened, the gradual channelling of their energies and enthusiasms into this calling takes up a considerable portion of this book.

The next two chapters (3 and 4) are again matching chapters, showing how each magazine found form. *Meanjin* as it emerged in the fifteen years after its arrival in Melbourne remained, in essentials, the template for the journal as Clem continued to edit it into the 1970s. The same is true of *Overland* (although less so), which is less surprising as by comparison it was edited on the run (or more accurately, sometimes on the train).

Chapter 5, 'All those wonderful cultural renaissances we're having nowadays …', discusses the two magazines as they were in the 1960s, when creating an Australian high culture was seen as crucial to the national project. At this stage, despite a greater populism, and a much greater accessibility, *Overland* ran the risk of becoming *Meanjin*-lite. Meanwhile its senior contemporary became, rather grandly, *Meanjin Quarterly*. For Clem it was his best decade.

The next chapter, 'The Little Magazine Nexus', discusses how the magazines were funded, published and distributed. The editorial styles are discussed, including support, and relations with the University of Melbourne and the Commonwealth Literary Fund (later the Literature Board of the Australia Council). Their respective outreach and ambience is also described.

In 'Power Struggle in the Clemlin', Chapter 7, I switch modes. The question of the succession to an editorship of an essentially private venture is often difficult. It was shaping up to be so even for Stephen, despite there being a collectivist impulse at the heart of *Overland*. With Clem, conscious of himself as a one-man band, it was much more fraught. And so it is in the first person that I have told the story of how I came to be his successor. I couldn't see how I could fairly enter this territory any other way.

Chapter 8 (the last before an Afterword) is focused on Stephen—once he could claim to be the 'senior literary editor', as he did from 1974. Clem makes an appearance in these pages, but it was Stephen's time: he wrote some significant books, while his magazine had never been better. His very full diaries for most of this period enable this chapter to be given unusual depth.

Writing this book has been an education. I have developed more respect for Stephen, and more sympathy for Clem.

Emperors in Lilliput can also be seen as the third book of a loose trilogy. The first two explored the lives and careers of two expatriates—WK Hancock, the historian, working across the world, and Louise Hanson-Dyer, a patron and musical activist, centred particularly on Paris. Those earlier people felt that, with their cultural concerns, they had to leave Australia—Hancock juxtaposed 'country' and 'calling' (as choices) in the title of his autobiography. This book explores how two figures from a subsequent time sought to advance the cultural front at home in Australia.

Acknowledgements

Researching and writing this book was enabled by a Senior Fellowship from the Literature Board of the Australia Council, a Redmond Barry Fellowship awarded jointly by the State Library of Victoria and the University of Melbourne, and a Visiting Fellowship from the National Library of Australia. I thank these bodies, in particular the National Library, as I was able to spend a happy and profitable time in Canberra reading manuscript sources. I would also like to thank various staff members of these institutions, and of the National Archives of Australia. And—closer to home—of the Baillieu Library at the University of Melbourne.

I am particularly indebted to the family of Stephen Murray-Smith, especially his son David. The late Ray Marginson was always supportive, as was the late Stuart Macintyre. I am indebted, professionally—though also much more than that—to John Timlin, Phillipa McGuinness and Sophie Garrett. Among those who have helped at various stages have been Paul Adams, John Arnold, Ian Britain, Patricia Excell, Diana Georgeff, Claire Grady, Andrew Green, Barry Jones, Vane Lindesay, Humphrey McQueen, Robert Newton, Leonie Sandercock, Peter Skewes, Alex Skutenko, Sara Schneider, Jamie Serle and John Thompson—together with the people who agreed to be interviewed and share a slice of their lives. Chapter 7 was run past the late Ray Marginson and John Poynter. I would also like to thank my friends Stephen and Valsa Foster, Legh and Helen Davis, and Seán Deany. And recall my English teacher, John Anwyl, who, in addition to providing much needed stimulation at Mentone Grammar School, would occasionally refer to a strangely titled magazine, and (as is known to me now) go off in the evenings to sort out its accounts.

To which must be added my thanks to the people at Melbourne University Publishing.

I

CLEM

TRANSCENDING THE PRISON HOUSE OF SELF

1911–1945

Lost Eden

When, deep in retirement, Clem Christesen began work on the autobiography he had long been contemplating—much of it destroyed in a house fire—the image that loomed at the beginning was of an island across the sea. This island, just across the water from the Townsville beach where the child used to play (often by himself) became a way of reading the humours of the world. At midday it would shimmer in the heat; in the slanting rays of the sun become a luminous orange; and occasionally, in squally weather or low cloud, disappear altogether. In the morning the child would rush down to the beach to reassure himself it was still there.

Yet when he reflected on his life, and admitted the word 'obsessions', Clem was aware of the paradox that everything in his early life suggested order, security and stasis:

> People around me did not change, the environment of ocean beach and tropical garden did not change. Tides moved, the seasons moved, but they did not really change. The sea remained, waves breaking against beach in regular rhythm. The trees did not shed their leaves in what passed for winter; birds flew away but always returned, as did

the sun and stars; flowers withered but bloomed again. There were no uncertainties, no doubts, no anxieties.

In the fullness of time Clem's Townsville childhood had become a lost Eden: its brilliant colours and scents and birdsong, framed by the sea, would always infuse much of his writing. His sense of expulsion was real, if unadmitted: fully one-third of the projected autobiography would have been devoted to those first seven years (and their antecedents). Indeed the young Clem was unusually responsive to his environment, and seems to have inwardly recorded it.

But rather than being static, there seem to have been more than the usual dramas of childhood. Clem was born on 28 October 1911. Even reading the newspaper at table could make his mother cry, for by then the war was on, and the young Clem was taken to see Townsville's first contingent sail away. Later he would visit, with the maid, the army camps: he was inspired to conscript a young Aboriginal girl (who also lived in the house) into an army of two, and drilled her—casting himself as Lord Kitchener. She was his closest friend. One night Dolly suggested they sneak away to the beach, as she wanted to show him Torres Strait Islanders holding a corroboree. Clem was impressed, and tried to master the movements; he soon got four of his mates to join in as they proceeded in crocodile-file down the street. But there were also terrifying incidents, such as the cyclone that hit Townsville when Clem was four. Or the nightmares he had following sermons preaching hellfire, in which the devil was a real presence. He was an impressionable child.[1]

Clem has left us the image of his looking up at his mother as she read to him, in a favourite spot under an enormous weeping fig, immaculate, beautiful, her fine and sweeping black hair fashionably piled on top of her head. A spirited woman, Susan Byrne had been a journalist, and still wrote occasionally for the Catholic press. Later she would edit the *Elector*, the paper of the Queensland Women's Electoral League, and run the campaign for the election of Irene Longman, Queensland's first female member of parliament. Two of Susan's brothers were socialists, one indeed a Communist: they were alive to a family tradition of dissent that could be traced back to Hugh Vesty Byrne, a man stirred up by the Wexford rebellion of 1798, who subsequently left Ireland for more promising prospects in Australia. But for all her drive and flair, Susan was essentially conservative, her observations laced with sarcasm. There were political arguments with the brothers: Susan, conscious of her pastoral relatives, was more concerned to maintain the social order. The infant Clem would go to the convent school, where she taught.[2]

While the original Christesen to come to Queensland was a Dane, and therefore probably Lutheran, his son had married an Irish girl, and so Clem's father, Patrick, had been brought up Catholic. Patrick saw himself primarily as an outdoors man, although he topped the public service entrance examinations; he was a champion rifle shot. Conservative by temperament, his caution was evident in careful betting as he followed the horses. Usually he wore a three-piece suit as well as the standard hat, and worked in Queensland's Department of Justice. Patrick shared the pro-British, king-and-country attitude of Susan, and also something of her aspirations. He was desperate to acquire a country property, and just missed out on getting one in a land ballot scheme.

'That attempt to acquire a country property did interfere with my schooling quite considerably,' Clem reflected. He travelled with his father out west—later drawing on these experiences for short stories—and seems to have changed schools frequently. Addresses changed too, since Patrick was loath to buy anything on terms, including a house. This constant change made it hard for Clem to make real friends of other boys. Moreover, when they moved to Brisbane, his parents also brought an infant son, who to some degree displaced him in their affections.

For Clem, the problem was exacerbated by the way the relationship with each of his parents had become fractured. Susan felt that Patrick should be 'more pally with the lad', exercise more patience, show an interest in his activities. Instead of which Patrick seemed content basically to sail through life on what he had learned at school, his horizons enlarged only by concerns at work. But Susan was scarcely the ideal mother. Feeling checked by her marriage, she was demanding, explosive, intractable. She went through servants like Clem would later go through printers. Aware that he was indebted to her for literary encouragement, Clem was always trying to placate her. But his sudden decision at the age of twelve to discard Catholicism, as he grew impatient waiting to go into confession, seems to have placed a permanent wedge between them. Difficult relations with each of his parents would leave their mark: because Clem had never been given enough emotional support by them, from others he would always expect too much.[3]

A checkered apprenticeship

Attending East Brisbane State School, Clem was appointed school captain and topped the school in the scholarship exams for secondary level. In 1927 he moved on to Brisbane State High, which he left at the end of second term the following year. Despite asthma, and nasal and ear trouble, it was in sport and athletics that he distinguished himself: 'Christesen has been consistent in his broad jumping,' reported the school magazine, 'having never been beaten so far.' One particular feat became legendary as 'Christesen's jump'; he won the Queensland championship three years in a row. He was also a dashing football player, and was shaping up as a champion sprinter when he injured his knee. But a photograph shows him detached, sad even, a long neck sustaining an air of defensive haughtiness.

As an athlete Clem knew that this was one way of pleasing his father. Not long after leaving school—wanting in confidence—he fell in with the idea of going to the Queensland Wool College. Clem became an expert wool classer, and took trips to various stations. There he was paid £25 a week (some $2000 in today's money) with all found; he wore silk shirts as he dined at squatters' tables. It was while staying at a homestead of the Leslie brothers, an old pioneering family, that he first attempted a novel.[4]

Suddenly, while he was on holiday, a telegram arrived from Clem's mother saying that the editor of the Brisbane *Courier* was offering work. Susan had used the little influence she had as an occasional contributor to maximum effect. Clem jumped at the chance, and while the first year or two were difficult, things eased when it was realised he had real skills as a feature writer and sub-editor. Soon he transferred to another paper, the *Telegraph*, persuading the editor to give him a column of his own. Here he commented, sometimes humorously, on literary and current affairs.[5]

Clem now decided to begin a university course. He enrolled part-time in Arts (Journalism), intending to be an evening student and do one or two subjects a year. But he could never settle down to it; other things kept getting in the way. Later he claimed he was 'uninspired … so managed to escape from being indoctrinated by traditional conservatism'. There was a succession of fails and no-shows over ten years. Clem passed only one subject, English, but gave up the course only the year he founded *Meanjin*. This bruising encounter with academe did not, as it might have done, lead him to reject it; rather, it left him with an exaggerated respect for those with formal qualifications and learned publications. He envied them their cultural certainties.

Nonetheless Clem's time at the University of Queensland (then located in Brisbane's Old Government House) was not fruitless. He continued with his athletics, becoming a university blue and state champion. He contributed poetry to the university magazine, *Galmahra*, and became one of its editors. In 1934 Clem won the Thomas Morrow Prize for an essay: the topics were historical that year, and most likely he chose the Queensland sugar industry. He also chose to be a resident at King's College, the Methodist residential college centred on a colonial mansion at Kangaroo Point. Why he decided to go there remains a mystery; it possibly arose from sporting contacts, while its Protestantism was a declaration of independence from his mother. Apart from being twenty-one, Clem had had enough of the quarrelsome household, and of always having to cope with his mother's manipulativeness. 'Your sentiments are swamped by your Ego', she wrote on one occasion, telling him he would never write good love-letters. 'Remember,' she enjoined, 'I love you in spite of your undutiful and unnatural behaviour towards me which has made me very unhappy and aged me considerably.'

To escape entailed a pyrrhic victory: at King's there was no drink, no dancing, not even Sunday games (a prohibition that included billiards, because of their association with gambling). The students made up for this by organising social activities elsewhere. Some of these Clem must have participated in, for he retained an affection for King's to the end of his life. Among other things, discussions there may have pushed him towards radicalism.[6]

Meanwhile Clem had lost his job at the *Telegraph*, but managed (as the Depression deepened) still to get casual work on newspapers. He used the time that had become available to secrete himself in the parliamentary library, where he worked on a book called *Queensland Journey*. His response to nature now went into overdrive: 'Glorious sandy beaches drenched and soaked and quivering in pagan sunshine,' he wrote of the Gold Coast, 'azurite ridges of sea water, white plumed, charging shoreward, curling and breaking in long foamy lines.' The manuscript was shown to the premier, W Forgan Smith, who was keen to promote the state as a tourist destination. Distressingly, Clem's manuscript, while taken up, was drastically trimmed and published with advertisements; but Clem himself got a job as government publicist. He churned out more tourist literature, and also prepared speeches, wrote for periodicals and produced radio scripts.[7]

Clem was developing a radio presence of his own, as 'Chris Byrne'. (The name was probably chosen to differentiate it from official activities.) His voice, refined by his exacting mother, was described in a press release as 'eminently suited for radio', while another press release promoted him as 'infusing into every one of his narrations—whether humorous, horrific, or historical—an element of dramatic intensity that is highly satisfying and convincing to the listener'.[8]

Probably thinking it a case of now or never, in mid-1939 Clem took leave and sailed to Europe. Although he took letters of introduction (including one from the premier), in England these served to open few doors for him. It may be that the only notables he encountered were the actors Lewis Casson and Sybil Thorndike; he went backstage after a performance, and they greeted him warmly, since they had met in Brisbane. Otherwise, while he was able to get work subediting on a number of papers including *The Times*, he seems to have been very much the outsider. A car trip to Scotland seems to have been a highlight, visiting an Australian balladist and relatives of the pastoral Leslie family. But generally Clem was dismissive: he felt businessmen were narrowly pursuing their own interests—even selling arms abroad in this time of peril—and that, together with sympathy for fascism in high places, there was no sign of 'Democracy … about to be rejuvenated'. It was a mess: 'I feel there is no hope for England if & when she is put to the test.' And that, he noted in a journal, carried a corollary: 'the decline—or rather, fall, of the British Empire. Not very happy today'.

Clem was responding to Britain after having visited Germany. He was drawn there partly because his family, while of Danish stock, were from Schleswig-Holstein and had become German. He caught up with a great-uncle in Hamburg—and also had a brief romance there. Clem had also been curious to experience the new Germany at firsthand. But his diary is not very illuminating about his impressions, except to reveal that he found Vienna unaccountably 'stagnant', whereas Berlin was brisk, its streets full of people in uniform. One day the sirens went and he was ordered into an air-raid shelter, where he found himself stared at.

Back in England, in the countdown to the outbreak of war, Clem covered the windows of his flat, got himself a gas mask, and saw little children being evacuated at Waterloo. Sandbags were in place in shops in The Strand. He 'sensed a heightened feeling of excitement, urgency—for the first time'. Without any sense of contradiction Clem found the idea of 'deserting London at such an interesting period … almost unbearable', yet, after some difficulty, once he had secured a berth on a ship sailing across the Atlantic, he declared himself 'glad to be leaving the Old World for the New; leaving behind diseased and al[l]ergic-to-itself Europe, strife-ridden and decadent, for that "new Britannia" in the Antipodes, with its friendly climate and friendly people'. The ship he was originally booked on had been torpedoed; his obituary appeared in a Brisbane newspaper. But no, he had survived, although shaken by the desperation of people trying to get onto the vessel when it docked at Cherbourg. They had clung to the gangplank as it was being pulled away, and some had fallen into the sea.[9]

Towards *Meanjin*

Clem made his way home via America. (Little survives of his time there.) But Brisbane awaited him, much the same as it had been before:

> The long sweep of the afternoon
> finds the river with his tired arm round
> a captured breast of land.

Clem would turn that into a spike: he had already noted the name Mee-an-jin, or Meeginchin as 'the native name for the settlement'.

Despite Brian Vrepont's hopeful pointing to Brisbane's having seven hills—like Rome—in many ways it had subsided into subtropical torpor, its wooden and often dilapidated dwellings the corollary of the branch offices lining its main streets. Although the population was not much over 300,000, the class and sectarian divide was sharp, with the state government long in the hands of a breezily corrupt Labor oligarchy. There was little stir for change: the assumptions of public opinion were isolationist and conservative. And now the war had brought a cultural shutdown.

Brisbane was, Clem wrote, 'from a cultural aspect the least fortunate of the Australian capitals. There are some, indeed,' he added, 'who would say that it was culturally bankrupt.' Tellingly, he crossed out that second sentence: perhaps the very backwardness of the place meant there was also opportunity. Clem drew heart from the existence of earlier poets such as Essex Evans and Brunton Stephens; and, while young poets might refer to the members of the Queensland Authors and Artists Association as 'the Arthurs and Marthas', nonetheless it was a pioneering writers organisation in Australia. Queensland could always surprise: a few years later, the government would pay for a string quartet to tour and give concerts in schools, helping to found school orchestras. It was a place where someone as multi-talented as Clem, who could write poetry, turn out short stories, act, broadcast and paint, could relatively easily advance his interests across a broad front. Soon he became secretary of the QAAA, and was the most high-powered they had known. He diversified its activities and quadrupled the membership, bringing it up to almost a hundred.[10]

Clem first thought of producing an annual in 1938, one that would include not only poems and stories but also art and literary criticism. It was conceived (almost as a counterpart to his tourism writings) as 'an exclusively Queensland production'. He got as far as producing a dummy, but there was scarcely any local interest. The idea was shelved. When he went overseas he must have encountered literary magazines, but they seem to have made little impression on him. He does not appear to have sought out editors or taken notes.

Although not evident yet in the bookshops, in recent years a literary quickening in Australia had been underway. In Adelaide the *Jindyworobak Review*, with its stress on environmental values and the Aboriginal precedent, first appeared in 1938, while *Southerly*—the name an indication of where it stood in relation to Britain—began appearing the following year from the English Department at the University of Sydney. Nineteen forty, the year of *Meanjin*, also saw *Angry Penguins* emerge from Adelaide.

Clem had been struck by Walter Jago's attempt to start a national literary magazine: he had come to Brisbane selling £10 debentures in order to put its finances on a sound footing, but there and elsewhere the response was poor and the venture failed. Then one evening after dinner in the home of his good friend the university lecturer Dr Robinson (president of the QAAA), Clem found a copy of the American JR Lowell's *The Biglow Papers*. Although almost a century old, they aroused his interest as one of the first renderings of Yankee dialect. On handling the volume, the title stood out. 'Quite suddenly', Clem recalled, 'I had the idea of publishing a series of Papers instead of the usual kind of literary journal.' A … *Brisbane Papers*? (He was not quite there yet.) Since it was wartime, the idea of an occasional series rather than a regular monthly or quarterly had an obvious attraction, particularly as paper would be a problem. To give it a tight focus, he would concentrate on poetry—Queensland poetry.[11]

The most respected figure in this milieu was James Devaney, who had trained as a Marist brother and retained a clerical sense of composure. This was despite a taxing marriage; people found him friendly, dignified and a great listener. As a young man recovering from a sinus operation, Clem was sent to stay with him and his wife at Mt Tambourine, and there explored a different landscape from the one he had known as a boy. Devaney was an expert guide, since he wrote a nature column in the *Courier*. He also introduced him to the delicate lyrics of Shaw Neilson, awakening in Clem 'a serious interest in the literature of my own country'. He showed the older man his verse, and was strongly encouraged: poetry was 'right in your blood', Devaney told him. Initially open-minded about free verse, the older man saw it as getting away from conventional poetry 'with its sentiment, its prettiness'. But the trouble was it could lead to a 'cutting out of personality', and of the emotions—something far removed from his own rather old-fashioned lyric poetry, usually centred on a response to Nature. Devaney's reservations would grow; he was also sceptical that a literary magazine would draw sufficient support. Nonetheless he remained on hand to provide advice and support whenever Clem required it.[12]

Three other poets would become more directly involved with *Meanjin*: 'Picot, Grano and Vrepo', as somebody dubbed them. Brian Vrepont was nearing sixty when Clem first met him. He was a six-footer (183 cm) when that was rare, and a man of slim build; his silvery hair topped a suntanned face, notable for its deep-set eyes and fine forehead. Clem felt that if he were 'dressed in a toga, he would look like a Roman patrician'. But usually Vrepont appeared in a tweed sports jacket and an old tweed hat, with a knapsack on his back, for he was an inveterate walker. A musician who had taught violin, Vrepont had a deeply resonant voice and a courtly manner. But subservience was not his style so much as insistent independence. He was a freethinker, a pantheist. 'This earth of ours is a singing universe', he told Clem, and the only way forward was to live 'a true life of harmonic spirituality—from industrial complex to pagan simplicity'. Clem—half his age—later regretted he had not sought him out more often, but Vrepont was something of a mystery man. He never spoke of his past. He answered to Brian, but Vrepont was a Frenchified confection; his real name was Benjamin Truebridge. Between odd jobs ranging from fruit picking and gold fossicking to being a masseur and trading in antiques, he wrote poetry when he could. Clem admired 'the fresh lyrical quality' of much of it.

When Clem's magazine duly appeared, it was Vrepont who would provide its cornerstone: his poem 'The Apple Tree'—which seemed to occlude Shaw Neilson's 'The Orange Tree'—began the first issue. It was a shrewd choice: Vrepont could be a 'difficult' poet, but was already familiar. He was a bridging figure, 'perhaps the only link' between the 'Romantic faith of our older writers', Clem believed, and the enthusiasm of youth for TS Eliot and free verse. Vrepont would become a mainstay of *Meanjin*, publishing more verse there than any other of the founding poets.[13]

Sometime in 1939, Brian Vrepont began to hold joint readings with another poet, James Picot. He introduced him to Clem, but they had met before. Soon Picot—who had had a poem commended in the *London Poetry Review*—was urging him on to launch his magazine. 'I don't think I would have had the courage to go ahead if it had not been for his strong enthusiasm,' Clem would later say.[14]

When Picot was reading his poetry, his hair would persistently get in the way; but his features were neat and intense, with, thought Clem, 'a steady Norman cast of countenance.' Picot had been shipped out to Queensland as a seventeen year-old. As his long-dead mother was French, and he had gone to school in Guernsey, the Channel Islands became a mystic homeland for him. Deeply spiritual, he had begun studying for the Anglican priesthood; but his early years in the bush, often living off the land, instilled an ease in vagrancy. Literature became his calling; material things, and practical matters, were quite foreign to him. He got around in hand-me-downs. As a friend put it, 'A man seeing visions does not bother about food or clothes.' But he had a kindly manner, usually charmed the Arthurs and Marthas, and with his ready wit and well-stocked mind spoke with a natural authority. James Devaney said, 'He was a fellow we all loved'—Clem not least.[15]

In poetry, Picot told Clem, 'I started as the most orthodox of Romantics', but, understanding life as a journey, his approach was changed by exposure to TS Eliot and also Freud. Originally Picot's verse had been markedly nostalgic. 'As a poet', Paul Grano thought, 'he fought against the impact of his adopted country, clinging with all his strength to British sources.' Then one day he announced, 'Paul, I have accepted Australia.' To shed the old perspective and symbols (such as the nightingale) took a little longer, but by the time Picot met Clem he was producing verse with a sheeny surface that included telling re-creations of Australian country speech. Picot was a work in progress; Clem thought him the local poet with 'the surest application of colour and tone of words'. Then off he went to war, sending back letters that seemed tamed by dislocation as well as by censorship; poetical concerns had been replaced by plain eagerness.[16]

The third poet to be involved in *Meanjin* was Paul Grano. Like Vrepont, Grano was a Victorian, a law graduate of the University of Melbourne, but he had been knocked about by life and had tried his hand at various jobs and been on the dole; he was now a tally clerk with the Queensland Main Roads Commission—an undemanding daytime occupation for a poet. Grano was a late starter: he had published his first book of verse at the age of thirty-nine, and on the strength of that and another quickly following, in 1934 was taken up by the Catholic *Advocate*. While literary editor there he helped found a Catholic Poetry Society, less religious in objectives than concerned that Irish Australians should contribute to an emerging national culture. They produced a magazine, of which he was proud, but the CPS crumbled 'under the pre-war tensions'.

Grano still had hopes of producing a publication, cyclostyled if necessary, when he heard yet another rumour about Christesen starting a magazine. They already knew each other; Grano had taken an instinctive dislike to Clem 'from our first meeting, before I knew anything about him'. One day they met in the street. Grano mentioned his cyclostyled magazine. 'Don't do that,' said Clem; 'I'm about to bring one out.' And as they talked, Grano became aware of his own shortcomings, and agreed to hold his venture over:

> his idea was far more ambitious far more worthwhile and if successful of far greater import. In short he had a vision—I had a view. It turned out that he also had the lasting enthusiasm of the visionary, the tenacity and courage, the organisational and directional ability and the flair for editorship necessary to bring his vision successfully into reality.[17]

Meanjin had crystallised when Clem found an old man with a small platen press who could hand set and print 250 copies of an eight-page magazine (a 'handsel', Clem would uniquely call it, a foretaste). 'I might be able to increase the size gradually if it caught on', he calculated; the outlay had been £4/10/-. Even so he lost money on it, and he hadn't much. It was a difficult birth: Clem was laid up in hospital with an injured knee, and even when discharged could not easily get about to promote his publication. *Meanjin Papers* was priced at two shillings, which was not cheap. Only one bookseller in Brisbane took the pamphlet, half a dozen copies. Fortunately the response interstate was better.

Something of Clem's ambition can be seen in the Foreword to the first issue, which appeared in December 1940. It was headed 'Traditionalist Number'—a way of ensuring the widest readership, at the same time indicating that more would follow, sometimes of a different kind. The country was at war, conceded, but:

> We believe that it would be a grave error to suppose the nation can drop its mental life, its intellectual and aesthetic activities for three

> or five or more years, neglecting them and those trained to minister to them, and then pick everything up again as though nothing had happened. Literature and art, poetry and drama do not spring into being at the word of command. Their life is a continuous process growing within itself, and its suppression is death.[18]

'Contemporary Queensland verse' proclaimed the cover, which now seems quaint. But at the time it was a realistic theatre of operations. FT Macartney, visiting Brisbane in 1940, said 'we really have a separate poetical literature in each state of this country'. In consequence, HM Green was particularly concerned to include Queensland poets in his anthology; 'disappointed' when initially he could find no poem 'good enough' to include. Moreover, there was a notably strong tradition of landscape and nature poetry in Queensland, sometimes tinged with a repudiation of the softnesses down south.[19]

For his magazine Clem had deliberately chosen a name that was distinctive: 'Decision' was a contender for a time. Instinctively he felt what Lawrence Durrell would later say, that 'the important determinant of any culture is … the spirit of place'. The spike of Meanjin would become a prodding metaphor, while the adoption—it would not have been seen as appropriation—of the Indigenous name was a gesture towards continuity. The cover, sand-coloured with four footprints (each poet putting only his best foot forward) was a strong nativist statement. 'Four naked black feet …' objected the *Bulletin*. Inside, there were just eight pages of verse, two pieces from each poet. (Prose was promised later.) There were Vrepont and Picot, plus Grano with a particularly fine lyric, together with two from Clem himself. In all, Devaney wrote in his review, 'They are far better work than much of what we see in the best magazines or in book form.'[20]

One of Clem's poems, 'By Lantern Light', was singled out by a lot of people 'who are slating us in the suburbs', wrote Picot, as '"the only poem" in *Meanjin*'. When this was said to him it made Clem—who wanted to publish more work in the class of Vrepont and Grano—'as wild as anything'. Years later, Clem said his appearance in the first *Meanjin* with the other poets was 'a mistake, for mine were pretty awful'. His critical faculty always impeded his capacity for production, and it may be for this reason, after an initial flourish, he published no more of his own poetry in *Meanjin* itself for fifteen years. Instead he used its imprint to publish two separate booklets, *North Coast* (1943) and *South Coast* (1944).

In his poetry Clem was sometimes eager to display his sophistication: to provide a cosmopolitan counterpoint to his nativist impulses. 'O Milhaud, O Darius, shatter me with music!' he had exclaimed in 'Paul Pentecost and the Mocking-Bird', invoking somewhat improbably the perky French composer. But it was also characteristic of him that he would turn, editorially, on his own children, and in a later version that verse went. More usually, he was an accomplished lyrical poet, drawn first to the sea, but increasingly absorbed in the voluptuous tropical landscape. The two met, like male and female, at the foreshore, in Clem's poetry the prime site of sexual possibility—and realisation. In the early poems, dappled light and birdsong were unusually present; he had a strong identification with birds, and thought of Grano (tall and thin) as a 'lone brolga'. One poem unites many of these characteristics, with a girl in a glade by a stream communing with nature. The picture (alas) is complete—and accepted by the poet with humorous resignation.[21]

Clem meets Nina

In the meantime Clem, who was tiring of being 'a dashing Best Man at cobbers' weddings', had found a muse of his own. On his return to Brisbane, for whatever reason, he wanted to learn German. On asking around he was told that the best person available was a Miss Maximov, who despite her Russian accent was a proficient language teacher. Clem got in touch, but got nowhere at first, since Nina was busy; but a little while later she became available, and took him on. He was already known to her, from his acting and radio work and activities as a journalist. Clem, although he did not then realise it, had for a short time shared a class with Nina in primary school, and remembered the way that, rather than submit to unjust physical punishment, she had with great dignity gone back to her desk, removed her books, and left the room. (The class rioted in approval.) There was a touch of gravity about this woman, a quiet steadiness of purpose, but also a sweetness and daintiness. ('Is she ravishingly beautiful, as everyone tells me?' asked AD Hope.) For her part Nina saw a tall handsome young journalist, with, she recalled in old age, 'a lot of good hair, big, blue eyes, and big eyebrows'. After some hesitancy on her part, they fell in love.

Nina Maximov had been in Australia for fourteen years: she had been born, a few months after Clem, near the Amur River on the Manchurian frontier. Her father was a sea captain, and came from a military family devoted to the Tsar. When the revolution broke out, they had not been troubled at first, and the little Nina, embedded in a loving family, would retain happy memories of St Petersburg glistening in snow and sunshine. But her expulsion from Eden was to be more dramatic than Clem's: when it became apparent that it would be wise to leave, Mrs Maximov decided to join the captain in the Russian Far East. They had trouble getting on the packed train; reservations counted for nothing, particularly with soldiers. There were constant halts and disruptions; sometimes, owing to military activity further down the line, they travelled backwards and forwards. The journey, which should have taken two weeks, took a torrid three months. Eventually the destination was reached, and the family decided to settle in Harbin, then very much a Russian city over the border in Manchuria. It had a fine Russian school, and there Nina was soundly educated; her mother simultaneously developed a taste for literature by introducing her to novels from the world beyond, including English and American novels.

Nina arrived in Queensland with her family as a fourteen-year-old, and they found conditions difficult. Ventures on the land were not successful; despite their best efforts with cotton-growing, circumstances (including drought) conspired against them. Russian men found work hard to get: there were language barriers, and the inscrutable ways of Australian unionism. Despair encouraged them to stick together, clustering around the Orthodox Church, hoping for the day—surely not far off—when they would return to Mother Russia. But the women found they could always get menial work, and so while still at school Nina would iron, scrub floors, wash dishes, and acted as a maid in a federal minister's home. On leaving high school (attendance made possible by a scholarship) she became a typist in a lawyer's office—and kept her age down so that she could retain her job as a 'junior'. Another scholarship, to university, she was not able to take up as it required full-time study; the family was too desperately in need of money for it to be considered. So Nina became an evening student. On graduating, she was appointed senior mistress at St Aidan's Church of England School for Girls, and in the course of her seven years there became president of the Secondary School Mistresses Association. It was there that she learned German; a group of girls had approached her, asking her to teach it. They learned it together—at lunchtimes—with results that were conspicuously successful.[22]

The university registrar, in recommending Nina to Clem, was wiser than he knew. She had, as it happened, been exposed to Australian literature when at school. 'Displaced by the Revolution', she later reflected, 'I did not find adaptation to another culture particularly difficult; rather it was enriching.' From the very beginning Nina was interested in Clem's venture, and supported it to the utmost. (Perhaps the great nineteenth-century Russian literary reviews were an influence here.) His vision—in this raw country—was one of the things about him that appealed to her deeply. 'I somehow think you will keep some of your idealism till the end of your days,' she told him. For Nina, who had a strong sense of life's contingencies, Clem offered a grand project, and access to an interesting milieu. More emotionally independent than him, she could accept that from time to time 'my second wife', as Clem came to think of *Meanjin*, would take priority.

Clem and Nina began living together a few weeks after *Meanjin* appeared, and married just over a year later. Theirs was a passionate relationship; in addition, they made such an excellent fit in complementarity of temperament and interests, that theirs was a sufficiently buttressed relationship even should there be any loss of ardour. Later, Nina not only turned a blind eye to Clem's amorous adventures, but seems to have facilitated them. Yet the first irregularity may well have been hers, more or less with his blessing. It seems odd that Clem's *Dirge and Lyrics* of 1945, recalling Picot, should be 'For Nina, in memory of Jim'. But a conversation with Tim Burstall, almost ten years later, revealed that she had been in love with Picot when he had, with a poet's urgency, gone and enlisted when the Germans occupied his beloved Channel Islands. Clem accepted the responsibility of looking after her should anything happen to him, for she was with child. But Nina began bleeding; an operation was necessary, and the child was lost. She would be unable to have another. The presence of Jim now lingered for them both; but Clem's happiness was real. Nina became his rock. Two years later, he concluded his first booklet of verse with:

> My love is a golden bough
> Whereon a bird is nesting
> Break heart, crack doom,
> Here is my resting.[23]

Meanjin: context and course

Clem's political attitudes were slow to emerge and, while they were emphatic, did not always have clarity. An early influence on Clem (as independently on Nina) had been a lecturer in modern languages, HG Tommerup. Born in Europe—of Danish parents—Tommerup was a cultivated man with claims to aristocracy; he took a keen interest in the arts, extending to literary magazines, and in Germany. He had, on occasion, strongly expressed pro-Nazi views. But Clem's attachment to him was real. On Tommerup's death in 1943, he remarked that 'I would dearly like to have had him as a father'. Subsequently he came close to expunging the link, as a possible source of embarrasment.[24]

Nonetheless, there are also indications that Clem enthusiastically accepted the organic/eugenic discourse of the day, which did not then necessarily entail a right-wing position. Later, in Germany—no doubt because of its conspicuous absence in Australia—he 'was nearly bowled off my feet by the pulsating waves of the Great Dynamic'. He could also express—in a diary—anti-Semitic sentiments, again at a time when they were likely to turn up anywhere across the political spectrum. Returning to England, Clem saw a 'vile collection' of Jewish refugees sitting on the quayside, 'Monstrosities of people', he thought them, 'jabbering incessantly in foreign tongues'.

He had picked up more from Tommerup and Germany than he realised. But it was part of the mix; at that time he also declared himself strongly in favour of a multicultural future for Australia. Clem was not concerned about consistency; at this stage he could be branded a Communist, yet by the Communists be thought 'a very Fascist-minded young man'. For Clem it was always important to have a view—which should be stated, even if he had nothing particularly original to say.

In this there was something of the newspaperman, combining with his self-perception that he was someone who 'won't go with the herd'.[25]

Plotting a trajectory for the new magazine was not easy. There would be some difficulty in treading a path between contending cultural movements, while simultaneously creating a distinct nexus for *Meanjin*. First there were the activities of PR Stephensen. For most of his life Clem had been aware of this fellow Queenslander, probably holding the older man (who also had a Danish grandfather) in awe. 'Inky' had been a Rhodes Scholar—even when a Communist—and had then published the first English translation of Lenin's *Imperialism*. He also made his mark in the world of small presses and little magazines. In England Stephensen had worked with Jack Lindsay, DH Lawrence, Aldous Huxley (and Aleister Crowley); in Australia, in addition to pioneering publishing ventures, he worked largely as ghost writer for the travelling accountant Frank Clune. Stephensen's real achievement here was the brilliant polemic *The Foundations of Culture in Australia* (1936). Originally appearing in instalments, it prefigured Stephensen's descent into fascism—but for Clem usefully crystallised the key role of place in determining a national culture.

Stephensen welcomed *Meanjin*. But he felt that Queensland poetry should be 'hot, rich in colour, tropic or sub-tropic in atmosphere', rather than echo 'the cold neurosis of English experimentalists'. This might yet happen if 'the *Meanjin* modernists will let themselves go a bit'. Meanwhile Clem's mother turned up at Stephensen's office, and on seeing the latest issue of *Meanjin Papers*, immediately declared that she thought the venture had taken her son 'off the track'. For his part Stephensen—a man driven to extremes by having the temper of a revolutionary (perfectly capable of taking up any cause)—was beginning to see himself primarily as a political activist rather than a man of letters. The name of his party, Australia First, seemed to signify, even in wartime, an understandable objective; but its milieu was racist, elitist and anti-Semitic, perhaps collaborationist.

Clem was targeted not only as a supporter, but possibly also as the nucleus of a developing Queensland group. It was difficult. Planning his Nationality Number (6), Clem wanted Stephensen in it: if he were not, as Inky remarked, it could be like *Hamlet* without the prince. Stephensen—vigorously arguing for intense localism in 'Queensland culture'—duly submitted his article, if that's the verb, for he was adamant that not a word or a comma be touched. When a misprint appeared in the proofs, Stephensen was furious; he was also annoyed over an attack on his ally the poet Ian Mudie, concluding in an article that *Meanjin* could be welcomed only on the principle that something was better than nothing. Clem asked around. Xavier Herbert, one of the many who had had unsatisfactory business dealings with him, remembered Stephensen's wooden face and toothbrush moustache. He told Clem to forget the 'Sydney Führer … he has no forgiveness, no friendliness, no humanity, in his little heart'. Some said Clem should sue after a published attack, but he had no wish to mix 'poeticals and politicals'.[26]

Second, there was the group of poets emerging in Adelaide, to whom Stephensen had acted as godfather. Stephensen's *Foundations* had encouraged Rex Ingamells, poet and schoolteacher, to publish his *Conditional Culture* two years later. Here the word 'Jindyworobak', recuperated by James Devaney, was applied to a specific program: the term, meaning to annexe or join, could be taken as joining up the dots as white people were encouraged to think through the cultural consequences of living in Australia. Instead of Stephensen's exaltation of place, Ingamells propounded environmental values, and (with the particularity of a poet) demonstrated how descriptive language must be made more responsive to Australia: it must rely less on formulations handed down from England. Indeed, a fundamental break from English culture was necessary. Equally striking was Ingamells' intense respect for Indigenous culture, which he saw as not only being primeval, but, as white Australia moved beyond the colonial, joining it in the culture of a modern Australia.

'Jindyworobak', Humphrey McQueen has written, 'is probably the most misunderstood and misrepresented aspect of Australia's cultural past.' Some of the early programmatic poetry of the movement, going out of its way to include Indigenous words, helped to make it so. Moreover, Jindy's preoccupation with 'the surface features of the landscape', as Geoffrey Serle pointed out, 'unwittingly reflected the English Georgian poets they so vigorously condemned'. But as the ideas of the movement foreshadowed key contemporary cultural values in Australia, some reappraisal is underway.[27]

Clem had been impressed by *Conditional Culture*, and once he decided on a 'Nationality Number', approached Ingamells in Adelaide to write an introduction. 'Surely', he enthused, 'we can both strengthen and amplify each other—the northern and southern points of the Southern Cross.' Ingamells responded in kind, saying in his piece that the two ventures were complementary, but *Meanjin* uniquely spoke for new forces operating on the Australian people both at home and from abroad. Clem was gratified, and spoke of *Meanjin* coordinating with Jindy, which, while a club, now produced only an annual: there was space in between. While rejecting Ingamells' verse, he was—to his credit—relatively indifferent as to whether his own was accepted (or altered) for the Jindy anthology. As *Meanjin* groped its way forward—'meanjeering', as a colleague described it—Clem came to respond more and more to Ingamells' sympathetic intelligence and warmth, and to share some of his concerns with him. When Ingamells' letters were not forthcoming, he experienced what can only be termed withdrawal symptoms.

For his part Ingamells began to find this correspondence demanding. Clem lectured him about PR Stephensen, whom he admired. Clem had concluded (correctly) that his unbalanced behaviour could cause people to be suspicious of 'the whole cultural nationalist movement … He's dangerous'. Then a gratuitous phrase in a review by RG Howarth, the editor of the newly founded *Southerly*, caused Ingamells great offence. As Howarth's poems appeared quite frequently in Clem's magazine, increasingly Ingamells discerned a nexus between *Southerly*, the *Bulletin* and *Meanjin*, with himself and Jindy on the outer. He also came to suspect that Clem quite often printed one thing, and said another: the literary world in Australia was 'a vast whispering gallery', and he simply wanted to get on with his own work. Ingamells also felt that Clem may not have been quite straight in his dealings with Jindy: he had come down brutally on a young man in Melbourne who had offered to help him, but when it became plain he was deeply involved with Jindy as well, Clem virtually dismissed him for having served two masters.[28]

Third, another group had appeared centred on Max Harris. When a promising Adelaide schoolboy, Harris had been published by Ingamells, and for a time was secretary to the Jindyworobak Club. But his trajectory was so clear—Harris would become a national figure while still an undergraduate—that the generous Ingamells could be philosophical about the way the young man had 'outgrown Jindy'. He became rather less equable when Harris wrote an article attacking his poetry in

Meanjin—which further cooled relations with Clem. Meanwhile Clem told Harris 'your work is so interesting and so important'—something he did not really need to be told. His magazine, *Angry Penguins*, proclaimed itself 'the only literary publication in Australia which is alive; contemporaneous in spirit and idiom'.

It quickly moved from being a vehicle for Harris's verse to becoming a bridgehead not only for modernist poetry but also an advocate for contemporary art. An alliance was forged with the innovative patrons John and Sunday Reed in Melbourne, and soon work by Sidney Nolan, Albert Tucker and Arthur Boyd began appearing in its pages. *Angry Penguins* became the most sumptuous literary magazine in the country. Increasingly it was broadening its scope, including significant international authors—Dylan Thomas, Robert Penn Warren, Kenneth Rexroth—as well as attracting material from regular *Meanjin* contributors. Soon there was a scratchy exchange: a measured but sardonic review in Clem's magazine had not helped. But Australia being a small place, Clem felt it was best that 'we should try to make more than a passing attempt to keep the peace'. He wanted Harris's respect, but was given short rations. The inescapable fact was that *Angry Penguins* was the only competition worth bothering about.[29]

There were others who found Harris insufferable, not least in his shameless self-promotion. One afternoon in Victoria Barracks, Melbourne, the poets James McAuley and Harold Stewart launched what Robert Hughes has described as '*the* literary hoax of the twentieth century'. They randomly slung together a group of poems, aping surrealist techniques while drawing on their real poetic skills to produce an *oeuvre* for one Ern Malley. Ern, alas, was an honest working-class lad now dead, and it was his 'sister', Ethel, who sent the manuscripts off to *Angry Penguins*, innocently enquiring whether they would be of any interest. Harris swallowed the bait, hook, line and sinker. A special issue of *Angry Penguins*, with a cover by Nolan based on one of the poems, appeared in June 1944.[30]

It caused a sensation, since the hoax was revealed almost immediately. Clem had been in the know for some time, but not as long as AD Hope, who had been planning a mischief of his own before being asked to stay his hand by the perpetrators. Knowing what was coming, Hope couldn't resist saying—after Clem asked him to review Harris's novel

The Vegetative Eye—'Here is Maxie's head on a charger'. A savage review became, under the circumstances, a merciless one. Harris felt it to be an 'utter injustice'.[31]

Meanwhile saner voices were saying that Stewart and McAuley had written better than they knew, perhaps 'more forcefully and [with] more purpose than they have ever done before'. *Meanjin*'s reviewer (an American) said much the same thing. As he had repeatedly referred to *Meanjin* as an 'experiment', Clem had little difficulty in agreeing with the hoaxers that the escapade too was a 'serious literary experiment'. It also lifted him above the ruck. The continuing controversy made it hard for Clem to square the circle, his preferred editorial mode; he may have also thought, there but for the grace of God go I. Clem wanted to give Ern a 'decent burial', but there was no chance of that. The affair was given a second wind—a foul one—when Harris was prosecuted in an Adelaide court for publishing 'indecent' literature. Clem thought it had all gone far enough. He engineered a motion of support from the QAAA, and published an amusing and insightful account of the trial.

After a pause, Harris would contribute to *Meanjin* once again, but the legacy of Ern Malley hovered for years. Dorothy Green foresaw that it would have a deleterious effect on the reception of modernism in Australia. During the trial, Harris had been shouted at in the street, had things thrown at him. The hoax, Les Murray said later, prolonged 'the life of some pretty lousy anti-artistic attitudes here'.[32]

The Brisbane *Meanjin*

Given the contending cultural impulses, there was a shrewdness (beyond a shepherding of scarce resources) in restricting *Meanjin*'s ambit initially to Queensland—a geographical unit rather than a particular school. Similarly it made sense to focus on poetry, which had an unusual importance in Australia at that time. People learned poetry by heart and recited it publicly, even competitively; it was also identified as central to the national project. (It was here that talk of a 'canon', seen as helping to forge a national identity, first emerged.) In the present circumstances, some believed poetry was the literary form 'best adapted to distilling the desperation of war'; certainly good poems might be produced anywhere. Clem believed that poets—after all, he was one—were endowed with an 'intuitive understanding of life and the conditions around them. For that reason modern poetry may be said to be the most accurate guide to the psychology of contemporary life'.

That involved experimentation. 'Traditional verse', said Brian Vrepont, 'is escapism from actuality.' Clem saw this, but was not entirely comfortable with it, being essentially a traditional versifier himself. Rather speedily he retreated from the stand taken in the first two issues, to produce an 'Everyman's Number', containing poetry with 'a more pronounced singing quality'. Reaching beyond the Jindies and the Angry Penguins, whose work he included, he was keen to find new, original voices. One was Harry Hooton, the anarchist poet. More significantly, *Meanjin* appeared at the same time as major new poets emerged, people who would dominate Australian poetry for a generation. Clem published James McAuley before and after Ern Malley, and also AD Hope, whose scabrous poem 'Australia' would have surprised *Meanjin* readers. In early issues, Judith Wright was also a powerful presence. With *protégés*, Clem was less successful: while a *Meanjin* poetry prize went to 'Jael Paris', who turned out to be the young Dorothy Hewett, the Meanjin Press he founded to publish booklets of verse was slow to make a name for itself in the Brisbane years. While Clem published a volume of early poems by Hugh McCrae, the two other poets published failed to secure a reputation.[33]

Initially appearing bimonthly, it was not till its fifth issue that *Meanjin* showed signs of branching out from its focus on poetry. Even then, a dialogue on individualism was disguised as a discussion between Apollo and Marsyas, while Vance Palmer's 'Note on Randolph Bedford' was occasioned by the writer's recent death. It would be the first of many tributes. But that issue also saw the first 'Letter to Tom Collins' (the pseudonym of Joseph Furphy), a series that would run for some years. The conceit of writing to Furphy asserted an ongoing nativist tradition, the issues raised by a variety of authors increasingly trenching on broader cultural questions.

Subsequent achievement disguises the fact that Clem, for all his natural aptitude, was a journeyman editor who had to learn his craft on the job. He was a newspaperman busy turning himself into a literary figure. For a while he held clerihew competitions (with dismal results), and spoke of literary sketches or short stories showing how Australia was coping with 'this Crisis'. He edged his way forward: cultural comment was hinted at early on, but did not become a major component till the sixth issue. Similarly, it was not till its thirteenth issue that *Meanjin* began to publish short stories; for a time they were undistinguished. But then, as Miles Franklin wrote to Clem, 'Another Ern Malley is needed to rescue our short story from different but equally deleterious vapours.' Perhaps he felt, as a feature writer, insecure in his judgement; poetry more clearly removed itself from hackwork.

Following a radio talk in 1942, Clem published an article on 'The Meanjin "School"'. As those double quotes suggest, he was uncomfortable about the term—not least because, after some hesitation, he had decided from the beginning of 1942 to accept contributions from all over the country. *Meanjin*, the editor emphasised, was essentially experimental, a 'workshop'. Rather than seeking to found a school, the magazine intended to 'mark out a meeting ground'. This extended to including prose pieces by religious writers, 'though the editor is opposed to religiosity'. The magazine also hoped to maintain continuity between the past and the present, and 'provide a connecting link with the future, the post-war years'. As he put it in another radio talk, 'The culture of a country is the essence of nationality, the permanent element of a nation.' If he could, Clem wanted to sidestep 'literary politics', even while asserting poetry acted as 'an interpreter of the urgent problems confronting society today'. But in likening poems to 'blue-prints', Clem drew fire from those suspicious of instrumentalism. AD Hope remembered an earlier *Meanjin* call for poetry that would assist in 'the development of a strong and virile Australian culture'. But poets were not civil servants. 'A poet no more sets out to produce culture', Hope declared, 'than a pig sets out to produce bacon.'[34]

Meanjin in these years advanced from the original dozen pages to thirty-two at the end of 1941, to sixty-four by the end of 1943, while almost a year later its last Brisbane issue ran to eighty pages. The notes to contributors similarly underwent amplification. By January 1942 poetry was still prioritised, but the war had induced an awareness of 'writers-at-arms' who might submit pieces. At this stage, Clem stated that *Meanjin* was prepared to publish 'second rate' material, even by local standards, if it encouraged new writers, or raised new issues. The important thing was 'genuineness'. A concern with Australian culture also entailed a respect for its past—'In that respect *Meanjin* may be termed traditional'. In 1943 appeared a special Furphy centenary issue. Clem wanted articles on 'our literature, art, philosophy, ethics, modes of conduct, and the mentality that lies behind these cultural systems in Australia and abroad'. By 1944 he was focusing on the need for 'sound critical discussion' and pieces on 'social-consciousness'. Although primarily concerned with Australian culture, Clem insisted that *Meanjin* was not 'confined by any narrow chauvinistic outlook'. And, he thundered, 'Political pressure from any direction will not be tolerated.' This was a private venture, of the broadest scope. Soon he was calling for articles on Australia in world affairs, and the postwar problems of the Pacific Basin. He even toyed with the idea of a *Pacific Review* of literature.[35]

While the trajectory outlined above suggests confidence, in fact *Meanjin* was buffeted a good deal by circumstances and criticism. Famously Randolph Bedford had denounced the first issue as a waste of ink, by poets who should be out 'digging post holes'. Others sent back their copies, and in not buying pleaded wartime conditions, higher taxation and diminished resources. A few, such as Firmin McKinnon of the *Courier-Mail*, believed that in wartime it was simply a misplaced venture of little value. One woman added that the 'wandering footsteps on the cover are going nowhere in particular, though they incline slightly to the *left* I notice!!' Then there were many people who did not take to modernism—providing a further incentive for editorial pluralism.[36]

But there was also growing enthusiasm. Frederick Macartney was not the only one in Sydney to comment, 'You folk up there do strike me as being "live" in a way we here don't seem to be.' By mid-1942 the critic WA Amiet was writing that the magazine's variety of talent and its eminence was beginning to make Brisbane 'the centre of gravity of Australia's cultural effort'. About the same time Rex Ingamells congratulated Clem on his 'strongly established' magazine, noting that the policy of 'not being too doctrinaire' had been 'vindicated'. But Clem saw *Meanjin* as 'not being of much account yet', to which Ingamells replied: 'balls'! For the more measured AR Chisholm, *Meanjin* had become 'the sanest and sturdiest little magazine in Australia'. Nonetheless from time to time people mistook its openness, grumbling about an insufficient sense of direction.[37]

The turning point had come after two special issues, a 'Nationality Number' (Summer 1941) and a 'Crisis Number' (March 1942). The war had suddenly reached Australia's shores: Pearl Harbor had been raided in December 1941, Singapore fell the following February, with Darwin being bombed almost immediately. In May–June 1942, midget Japanese submarines attacked Sydney, killing twenty-one sailors. In Melbourne, Nettie Palmer, wondering what to save in the face of possible enemy action, decided she would bury a trove of Bernard O'Dowd's letters. Clem had always been one to thrive on challenge, which he construed as crisis: now it was all around him. Urgency would ramp up his journalistic capacity to editorialise and direct. Recently, in the Brisbane Repertory's production of Shaw's *Pygmalion*, he had taken the role of Henry Higgins. Now Australia could be cast as the cockney girl Eliza, and taught by him to enunciate a national culture of its own.[38]

Meanjin's character

'So much talk about Australian Kulchewer', wrote Max Harris after reading a pile of *Meanjin*s. But Clem had struck a nerve. People who had taken Australia's identity for granted now began to consider what it might mean, since at that moment there was a real risk of losing it. *Meanjin*'s Nationality Number, with its half dozen articles led off by Ingamells on Australianism, included Stephensen's piece on Queensland literature and another by WA Amiet on Australian literary history that, with its acute judgements and direct style, anticipates the better known *Meanjin* critic AA (Arthur) Phillips. Poetry retained its strong presence, with the Jindies Flexmore Hudson and Ian Mudie present; the latter's fine poem 'Here Strike Our Roots' usefully advanced the theme—a *Meanjin* technique—in another key. With articles discussing other matters (including a recent enactment by the Queensland government, stacking the University Senate with its nominees), the number set its preoccupation in a wider field, foreshadowing the style of future issues.

Four months later, following the pattern of its Nationality predecessor, there appeared a Crisis Number. Vance Palmer provided the keynote in a piece called 'Battle': how Australia as we knew it could disappear, leaving little trace; how there was, nonetheless, 'an Australia of the spirit', sardonic, idealist, ready to fight the invader every inch of the way. 'I believe', he concluded, 'that what is significant in us will survive; that we will come out of this struggle battered, stripped to the bone, but spiritually sounder than we went in, surer of our essential character'. The tone was stoic; Clem, by contrast, seemed to relish the prospect of 'the roar and bark and thunder' of battle on Australian soil. He became a Banana-bender Savonarola: flailing Australia for its lack of a 'dominating dynamic spirit', its 'disunity of purpose', and for the most part having 'roots … embedded in shallow sand and rubbish'.[39]

Discussion, in this issue and others, tried to diagnose what would be involved as an incipient Australian nationalism (often unwittingly framed by the assumptions of Empire) coped with the challenge of the modern world at war. Australia was adolescent, a 'nation in name only', said some. It lacked an activating spirit. The reason, said Vance Palmer, is that people had always been predatory towards the land. 'Australia was a colony: you exploit colonies: you draw material but not spiritual nourishment from them.' Somehow the impetus of an emerging literature in the 1890s had spluttered out; perhaps mateship could be reconfigured. Australian culture generally had become drip-fed from London, giving rise to what Clem termed 'the incredibly great mass of un-Australian ignorant colonial thought'. Manning Clark, in a characteristic note of desolation, was driven to ask whether we belonged here at all.[40]

A more spirited response had come from the Jindyworobaks. But the disjunction from Indigenous culture was profound, and as well as emulation there was louche appropriation. 'Beauty hoarded for centuries', wrote Gina Ballantyne, a poet often published in *Meanjin*, 'is now in the possession of a white race whose poets should be encouraged to interpret it, bringing to that interpretation all the power of our civilised art.' Ingamells himself was more level-headed: in a letter to Clem (making a point the editor took up), he said that one day, 'when we're a truly healthy people, our Australianism and our cosmopolitanism will both be so natural that to hot-house either will be superfluous and silly'.[41]

Not everyone took to this soul-searching and prognostication. A *Meanjin* editorial had referred to 'the pitifully negative prejudices of the uneducated masses', and certain articles were attacked for their elitism—what the poet Neil Smith termed 'intellectual class consciousness'. Meanwhile, AD Hope pointed out that 'small appendage countries like Australia do not decide their own destinies'; trying to promote national consciousness was all very well, but there must be a party promoted and a position taken. 'Otherwise it is the kind of vague gesture of good will that anyone can make, raising your hat when the hearse goes past.' A little later, as Clem detected the stirrings of postwar possibility, Donald Horne in Sydney read aloud a *Meanjin* editorial to some friends, and 'they just laughed'.[42]

When the war was still on, Clem's sense of crisis had extended far beyond the military challenge and nationality. The editorial for the Crisis Number was headed 'War on the Intellectual Front'. 'There is sufficient reason to speak of a crisis of modern thought and knowledge', Clem believed, 'so violent and so far-reaching as can hardly be found in any known period of history.' The evils were everywhere—regimentation of thought, 'capitalistic commercialism' strangling cultural life, even the growing estrangement from basic religious values. In a later issue he would complain that, now the 'bourgeois revolution' had come to a dead end, culture had gone obscurantist, politics become more totalitarian; there was a 'New Failure of Nerve'. But, he averred, '*Meanjin* is for enthusiasm over cynicism', and, switching focus to the magazine, declared it to be 'an Idea—and we're damned if you can wring the neck of an Idea'. In the end, it was all about embattlement: cultural, national, and personal.[43]

Clem was a born editor. 'I feel you have the gifts and approach of a sort of liaison officer in literary life,' Nettie Palmer told him. (He was none too happy with the designation.) 'Mr Christesen seems to excel in mixtures,' said one reviewer of the early *Meanjin*s. The critic JK Ewers, unaware of the editor's craft, declared himself puzzled at Clem's ability to get authors to combine to produce work on a particular theme. Yet difficulties there were. Sometimes writers approached were suspicious, as though *Meanjin* was a front for some sort of subversive activity. Nonetheless—although he thought some of the authors were not up to the subjects they tackled—AD Hope remarked that 'As a poet Mr Christesen leaves me cold, but as an editor he is the apple of my eye.'[44]

Clem was a great encourager. Partly this arose from his sense of conducting a collective enterprise—if a voice was distinctive, but the talent slight, the author might still make a 'contribution'. (The word is telling.) At least that was the case at the beginning, when a sense of

Queensland community was strong, and Clem had not yet taken the national stage. But he remained encouraging to the young—young female poets took his fancy—and while the prognosticators were predominantly male, something approaching a gender balance could be struck in the magazine's poetry. While he did not take up Vrepont's suggestion to establish poetry workshops—an almost literal *Meanjin* school—he was persuaded by the precocious Barrie Reid and Laurie Collinson, teenage editors of a magazine specifically aimed at youth, to give young poets a special page in the magazine. Clem looked benignly on their publication, *Barjai*, and gave them the considerable sum of £2 in order that it could be upgraded to letterpress production. He was capable of sudden generosity; usefully, its quixotic nature could stun the recipient, inducing a wary support.[45]

The way Clem's relations with other people often broke down was a source of puzzlement to him. Only someone who had not met him could gush, as Kate Baker did, 'What a beautiful name! Christ (his) son, and Clement befitting it so.' Clem was unusually self-absorbed, and at times this assumed comic proportions. Getting Harris's novel reviewed had been difficult, he told Max, as 'Two jokers have let me down'—they had been called up for the army at short notice. (There was a war on.) Clem would pour his frustrations into a sympathetic ear, such as Nettie Palmer's, using the word 'disappointing' frequently, and even apply it to himself. 'No doubt you found me, frankly, disappointing: that I had little to say of an original nature …' He then referred to some verse he had been too shy to show her. Other people were likely to get the full whinge, or Clemmiad as it might be styled (his own jeremiad or lamentation, both distinctive and ritual): that he was not receiving sufficient support, and that he was losing money—'both true', conceded Paul Grano, 'but rather tiring in reiteration', particularly as he showed no gratitude for such support as he was given.

Often the passing remark of a third person was enough to launch a Clemmiad. The poet Victor Kennedy was surprised to receive a letter containing half a dozen minor grievances. 'I suppose I should make some frail effort to address the jury', he stated in reply, and systematically rebutted the charges. That more or less did the job of placating Clem, who nonetheless insisted on fingering the cracks they were papering over. But then Kennedy, in the next letter, referred to *Minjie*. 'Sorry for the levity,' he immediately added: 'it slipped out'. Clem now had a fresh grievance.[46]

Clem was torn between editorial duties and the tug of his own creativity—without quite having the confidence that he could produce material at a high level. Devaney told him he should prioritise his writing, and organise his time so that he got some done; Ingamells that he was 'academicizing' himself in *Meanjin*. On a number of occasions Clem thought of giving it up, perhaps handing over to a known writer. He had toyed with involving the other founding poets, mainly to get them involved in editorial work, because he wished to stay on as publisher—and proprietor. Not surprisingly, 'Nothing doing'. The rumour went round that he was going to Caloundra for a year, to write a novel; he would stay in a flat owned by the Palmers. But this did not happen. Word of a new literary magazine, based in Sydney and financed by the Commonwealth Literary Fund, fired him up once again: he was not going to vacate the field for a newcomer. Perhaps all this talk was a way of drawing reaffirmation from interlocutors, a vote of confidence. He could be cheered up, momentarily, and was capable of a grim jest: he called the second, Everyman's Number, the 'Appeasement Issue'. But when he did not hear from correspondents, he never considered the context of their own busy lives, and habitually construed it as neglect.[47]

Clem was certainly under pressure. There was the job at the *Courier-Mail*, which, when handling cables, involved night work; for a time his secretaryship with the QAAA; and then the work with *Meanjin*, attending to authors, contributors, printers and distribution. It wore him down. Sinus attacks came back, with asthma, and then persisting trouble with his knee. But walking down a city street—passing men dressed in shorts and sandals—he cut quite a figure with 'his measured stride, brooding face', his customary hat, tortoise-shell glasses, smart suit and quality shoes. Bravado was less apparent in the office. One visitor credited him with 'the sensitive face of an intellectual', but noted the beginnings of a stoop and a bumper bar of a moustache, 'designed to ward off critics and disgruntled contributors'. Liverish by temperament and combative by instinct, Clem had tried to enlist; he was rejected on health grounds, three times by the RAAF, and twice by the AIF.

The magazine constantly offered Clem a chance to recreate himself anew. The rhythms of editing, and the sudden switches from acceptance to assertion, from receptivity to dominance, could accommodate the rollercoaster of his personality. He was galvanised, perhaps integrated, by putting the world in order. 'Want to say so very much,' he told Ingamells in connection with his creative writing, 'but somehow lack the ability'. He would organise others, and speak through them.[48]

No-one would completely understand, but one day everyone might see. In the third issue Clem devoted two pages to comments on the new magazine. The first general index, the contents of issues one to eight, appeared in Number Nine; another was prepared, anticipating Marjorie Tipping's comprehensive index for the twenty-fifth anniversary. There was always an element of monumentalism about the *Meanjin* project. Arrangements for bound sets were offered early. Somewhat unexpectedly, Clem also had a strong sense of documentation. Before long, in addition to seeing the magazine as 'a medium for the interpretation of the varied phenomena underlying the imaginative life', he was also describing it as 'a literary documentation of experience during these critical years'. The impulse went further: he made a point of keeping correspondence and other materials, in the hope of building a significant archive. If control of the present was impossible, one might go a considerable way towards controlling the past.[49]

Aboriginality, the Americans and Dr Duhig

One aspect of the past remained problematic for Clem, and that was Aboriginality. The impulse to connect was there, given his naming of the magazine; but there was no hope of making the kind of connection the Greek poet Cavafy could effect, reaching from the modern Alexandria across the Arab centuries to the city's classical past. A cutesy woodcut of a boy advancing with a dead goanna in one hand, and a boomerang labelled 'Meanjin Papers' in the other, became the magazine's colophon.

Did Clem ever think, when toying with Aboriginality, of Dolly, his childhood friend? Her constant presence, as a subordinate, had given his childhood the flavour of an African colonial one—habituating him to the notion that there would always be somebody following him about, enlarging his sense of self. But now he was searching for a basis for respect, and anthropology seemed to give it. Indeed he saw Aboriginality as providing, with Australian history in the broadest sense, and 'Australian books so far', the foundations for an Australian literary culture.

AP Elkin was at hand to educate *Meanjin* readers on 'Steps into the Dream-time' (a word that had only recently sharpened to this form), explicating the footprints on the magazine's cover. (Clem had come across the notion somewhere, and had made the first rough sketch himself.) Elkin explained that the tracks were crucial to Indigenous ritual, as the site for re-enactment of the past of a cult hero; but they also enabled the supplicant to 'pre-enact' a desired future along the same lines, the ceremony giving him the necessary courage. All of this, as Elkin pointed out, provided a blueprint for white Australia's moving away from a culture of transplantation: we would have to develop appropriate, continuing myths of our own. 'We cannot fly with borrowed plumes nor run with artificial legs.' Clem must have felt he could not have put it better.[50]

The issue Elkin's article appeared in was a significant one, despite its lack of designation. The frontispiece was by Margaret Preston: *Aboriginal Hunt Design*; the short story 'Last of the Tribe'. Clem was making Indigenous people the cornerstone of an issue that, while wide-ranging, opened with 'Three Polynesian Ceremonies' (poetry) and included an article on China as 'Australia's opportunity'. The war—and what might follow—had given Clem a conspicuous regional consciousness. He quoted Wendell Willkie: 'Perhaps the most significant fact in the world today is the awakening that is going on in East Asia.'

Some were encouraging him to make *Meanjin* not only represent Australia to Australians, but also internationally. 'Australia its axis,' suggested Kate Baker, 'the World its circumference?' Clem had sent copies to Britain, but the response had been poor, both from writers and institutions. But suddenly the world came to him. In July 1942 General MacArthur established Allied headquarters in Brisbane.[51]

Along with the wave of Coca-Cola, cigarettes in new brands, and nylons, came African-Americans—and poets. Prominent among them was Karl Shapiro, who contributed his dissonant 'Troop Train' to the first issue for 1943; he enjoyed the 'fiery warmth' of the Christesens' hospitality a few months later. Shapiro was publishing steadily and had just produced a book in Melbourne; he would shortly win the Pulitzer Prize. Another poet, Harry Roskolenko, also made contact and published in *Meanjin*, but his links with *Angry Penguins* were stronger. Significantly, this new dimension helped change the way Clem thought about the magazine. *Meanjin*'s first quarterly issue was the one that included 'Troop Train', and a screed from the time indicates Clem's ambition to publish poems from writers in America itself; the magazine might 'serve as a link between the two countries'. He was delighted when *Meanjin* received notice in the *Christian Science Monitor*, and that every mail from America brought interesting correspondence. American university and public libraries began to subscribe; as an encouragement, Clem began to highlight a special American rate when listing subscription details. The ripples of *Meanjin* were widening, from Queensland to Australia as a whole, and then outwards to the world.[52]

Clem now felt emboldened to number its pages consecutively through the year; but the growing success of the magazine underscored its need for financial stability. Someone prepared to underwrite it now stepped forward: JV Duhig (nephew of Brisbane's Catholic archbishop), a pathologist who had recently been appointed to a chair at the university. But Duhig's interests were much more extensive than that: actively interested in all the arts, he was a founder of the Brisbane Repertory Theatre Society (which is probably how Clem came into contact with him), and had himself written plays. He was also a prominent Rationalist, a keen art collector and a promoter of radical causes. Duhig was concerned about the state of Australian culture, believed writers should be paid a salary (as in Russia), and saw the sceptical prognostications of academics on Australian literature as nothing but harmful. There was a real convergence of interest.[53]

Clem had to be prodded by Vrepont to go and see Duhig, and activate the doctor's interest. The upshot was that Duhig provided secretarial help from his office, in particular the handling of accounts, and agreed to guarantee Clem against loss with the journal. This took the form of his paying the printing bills, with Clem passing on the money from subscriptions and sales as it came to hand. *Meanjin* was 'the best thing of its kind in Australia', Duhig believed, but he may have become a bit alarmed at Clem's constant itch to expansionism. Duhig's original thought had been one of helping poetry; and, while he was happy to publish three articles in the expanded *Meanjin*, he felt some check should be placed on Clem's plans. There should be a trust, he believed, with fortnightly meetings, and the 'journal' should appear regularly. He was

***Meanjin* 1/1940**
Contemporary Queensland Verse

Traditionalist Number
Two poems each from four poets

Brian Vrepont	The Apple Tree
	The Heron
Paul L. Grano	For These Are Gracious Things
	Pray Pity for Bill Smith
James Picot	Australia to a War
	Variation on a Theme of John Keats
CB Christesen	Morning Bound
	By Lantern Light

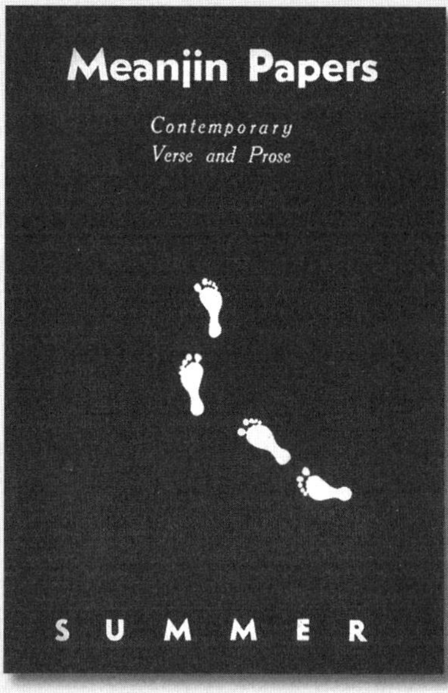

Meanjin 3/1944
Contemporary Verse and Prose, vol 3, no 3

The editorial of this last Brisbane number to appear spoke of the need 'to strive to arrest the anti-life forces, to reaffirm the idea of balance within the community and the personality.' The 'personalist' theme is addressed by philosopher A Boyce Gibson, and in a socialist and writerly context by Len Fox. CR Badger writes 'In Search of a National Idea' ('politically and socially, we still lack boldness and initiative'), while Nettie Palmer pleads for a greater connection with New Zealand. Brian Elliott attends the *Angry Penguins* obscenity trial ('Probably no other work of Australian literary invention has ever received such close and extensive analysis.'), while Miles Franklin, in her 'Letter to Tom Collins', castigates the many who are chary of Australian creativity and seek refuge in the imitative. RG Howarth writes a centenary piece on Gerard Manley Hopkins, emphasising his inventiveness. The issue contains a score of poets, among them Judith Wright, Harry Roskolenko, Barrie Reid and Alex Comfort. There are two stories, one from Vance Palmer, the other from the front in New Guinea. The books reviewed are mainly poetry, with some fiction.

not concerned about expenditure as such, he explained, so much as having a hand in planning that could lead to deficits. Nonetheless, the magazine should aim ultimately to be self-supporting.[54]

Clem claimed that Duhig proved 'unbearably arrogant', and that was why he broke with him. Paul Grano, looking on, thought Duhig 'as self-opinionated & as dictatorial as Clem himself'. Certainly, while it was professed that Clem had full editorial independence, Duhig was capable of writing to people and asking them to submit articles that would be published if they were up to scratch. Increasingly Clem felt pressured, and expected to show his gratitude—something that did not come easily to him at the best of times. When Duhig's secretary hinted that she might have to give up *Meanjin* work the following year, he began to think of retreat. Initially proposing that some of the work be transferred to an accountant, Clem came and collected the subscription cards for his own perusal—and then took them to the new man too. The secretary felt tricked, and hurt, and received another letter from Clem—so full of self-justification that it scarcely read as the intended apology. Clem and Duhig parted, after a flaming row. Subsequently the patron was simply excised from the narrative. Sixteen years later an article he submitted was rejected by *Meanjin*, a secretary writing the letter. 'I hope your paper can get along without me,' rejoined Duhig. 'Once upon a time it couldn't. It would have died. I wish it had.'[55]

Enter Dorothy Green, enter—and exit—Judith Wright

One day a short story arrived from a young woman in Sydney; Clem advised that she should consider writing criticism for the journal. That would become her forte as Dorothy Green, but Dorothy Auchterlonie would first become known to the literary world as a poet. In 1943 she turned up in Brisbane, brisk and businesslike, the first woman news reporter for the ABC. Given the presence of General MacArthur, it was an important position, requiring much resourcefulness from this detached woman sitting in the Christesens' living room.

There was more to Dorothy than met the eye. A fine singer—lack of money prevented her from going overseas for training, a lasting cause for regret—she had a passionate nature that had been crimped by isolation. Having been brought to Australia as a child of twelve, she had bridled at the excessive discipline that led to children being strapped when they got their sums wrong. It left her with a powerful impulse to challenge injustice. Dorothy's father had died when she was quite young, but recently she had lost both her mother and her brother (of whom she was fond), missing in action at sea. At twenty-eight she felt quite alone.

She had requested the transfer to Brisbane, to help reorient herself; the friendship with the Christesens, which would be lifelong, played an important part in this. With Clem she shared a commitment to literature and to progressive causes; with Nina, to whom she was closer, a love of Russian literature and social values informed, in the manner of Tolstoy, by Christianity. But suddenly Dorothy decided to return to Sydney. It seemed that she had made up her mind: the university librarian and respected literary figure HM Green, a handsome man, had been pursuing her. She reciprocated his feelings, but there were problems. Green was thirty-four years older, and married with two grown-up daughters. There would have to be a divorce—not common then, and almost unthinkable for a high church Anglican such as Dorothy. But she would go for broke.[56]

Dorothy had no sooner vacated her flat than it was occupied by Judith Wright. It was a 'little windowless slice of a room', but, given the pressures of accommodation in wartime Brisbane, Judith was grateful. Clem had much more reason to be appreciative of her. By the time she arrived Judith had already sent a number of poems, which he was glad to publish. The first, 'The Company of Lovers', had appeared eighteen months earlier: her verse not only had the elements of lyricism that always appealed to him, but a rare emotional intensity and moral engagement. And she was sympathetic. In her initial letter Judith expressed admiration for the work being done by 'you and your staff'—little realising that one day she would be it. She gave money, troubled a little that since she wished to publish in the magazine, it might not be quite right—but this hesitation was ignored by Clem. She listened to his plaint, expressing regret that she was too far away to help.

When Judith learned that an issue might not appear, she volunteered to come to Brisbane to assist. Although becoming aware of the spiritual sustenance she drew from New England, Judith was finding life on the family property tough: her brothers were away at the war, so there was much hard work to be done. Moreover, warmth and light were restricted in the gloomy homestead, and following a drought the cold was bitter.

Judith was desperate to get away as soon as her brothers returned. Not quite knowing how to respond, and hoping at one point that he might be able to meet Judith and talk to her (however briefly) from a train as it passed through Armidale, Clem was silent. But she prodded him into frankness, and some time afterwards, in 1944, she came.

As the train steamed into Brisbane, the response of this woman sitting in her carriage in prewar clothes was positive. Brisbane, she would later write, 'if corrupt was cheerful, if dirty was warm. It was disposed to enjoy life, and its flamboyant vegetables and flowers, the electric-blue of morning glories scrambling over unpainted fences ... disguised its sins.' Although hard of hearing, Judith brought with her some practical experience: in Sydney (where she did not want to resettle) she had taken a business course, become a fast typist, and worked for an advertising agency. Along the way she had learned how to give a boss hints about improving office efficiency or business methods, 'but never to remind him that you had made the suggestion in the first place'—skills that unexpectedly came into play at *Meanjin*.[57]

Judith's real job, a paid one, was as a clerk with the Universities Commission; at *Meanjin* she was an after-hours volunteer who hoped to be included in editorial discussions. But this did not happen. The rising poet of her generation was regarded just as a secretary. Working in the Christesens' home in Dutton Park, she did meet the young poets of *Barjai*, who often dropped in to borrow books from Clem's extensive library. And one day, having been introduced to the freelance philosopher Jack McKinney, she was surprised when he followed her into the kitchen to help with the dishes.

McKinney and Wright had read each other's work in *Meanjin*, and been impressed, but Judith was not expecting to be listened to with such respect. McKinney, trim and fit, had spent much of his time trying to scratch a living from the land; he had written in his spare time, as much as poor health allowed. His family life was in ruins, and eventually he would leave his wife and take to the road with his bike, a battered tent, and a few possessions. He was determined to devote the rest of his life to philosophy.

McKinney believed that Western philosophy had become derailed by its progressive analysis not of the world, but of our shared world picture. It was important to find an alternative, since that approach had contributed substantially to the crisis in Western civilisation. Judith was predisposed to accept this idea, for it paralleled a truth she was working towards:

> The language and culture I was brought up in … had nothing to do with the land my relatives had taken. It was wholly imported, a second skin that never fitted, no matter how we pulled and dragged it over the landscape that we lived in. Nor, of course, did we ourselves fit. That fact was growing more obvious as the land changed under our hands.

Jack's quicksilver mind, his accessibility and humour, naturally complemented Judith's moral earnestness and the deliberativeness of the deaf. Jack was slow to declare himself, but the pair were a natural fit. Much of the poetry Judith was then writing 'arose directly out of attempts to translate ideas into images and language as we talked'. Before long she saw it as her task to help this untutored man, clearly in need of support, proclaim his ideas to the world.[58]

Clem did not take kindly to the suspected closeness between his secretary and McKinney. Seeing himself as a mentor, he felt displaced by this trim greyhead with keen blue eyes; a charmer, yes, but possibly a fraud, certainly an amateur. Besides, having recently failed to write a novel himself, Clem was involuntarily hostile to a man with a big idea. Nonetheless he accepted Jack's manuscript, 'Towards the Future', for the Meanjin Press, pushed along by the enthusiasm of Mrs Hamlyn-Harris, who—while wishing to pepper it with references to astrology and the pyramids—was prepared to underwrite it. Clem had published articles by McKinney, but his misgivings persisted, abetted by the sceptical response of academic philosophers. Eventually Clem declared the work did not 'satisfy' him: Judith believed that once he had an eye on moving *Meanjin* to the University of Melbourne, the nature of the work became an embarrassment. And yet … some of Jack's ideas accorded with those of Lewis Mumford, whom Clem admired. So he procrastinated, then reported further negative academic advice. Jack (who would later win academic respect) withdrew the manuscript.

When the move to Melbourne was in the offing, Clem asked Judith to go with him as *Meanjin*'s paid secretary. But there were no details as to wage and salary (he did not have them), and a profound disinclination on her part to comply. Much as she loved Nina Christesen, she had always found good relations with Clem to be difficult, given his 'unpredictable mixture of self-esteem and self-distrust'. This, she felt, could only increase in the new setting. Judith was not sure either that the job would last, realised her deafness would limit other job opportunities, and dreaded Melbourne's cold. Besides, she had grown to love Jack McKinney, and in consequence was angered by the way 'the detestable Clement' was treating him. As a token of appreciation, Clem sent her money, and later apologised gruffly for his 'bad blunders while you were helping me in Brisbane.' But Judith's attitude had hardened. 'I wouldn't trust him any further than a snake under the house,' she told Jack.[59]

Increasing difficulties

With the knowledge that Jim Picot was—at best—living the life of a prisoner of the Japanese, Clem was aware that, of the founding four poets, he alone was still involved with *Meanjin*. Brian Vrepont, after being helpful assessing manuscripts, faded away, since (a natural aristocrat), he did not like literary politics or being subjected to a Clemmiad. Vrepont then moved to Sydney: for a time Clem lost touch. With Paul Grano, his relations were never easy. Given to sardonic remarks, Grano was notoriously moody and becoming more consciously Catholic: he had begun compiling an anthology of Australian religious verse. Although he approved the *Meanjin* project, Grano knew that his own verse had little appeal for Clem and that, given his trajectory, it would come to have less. He pulled out abruptly.

A year later, when PR Stephensen was interned along with the other leaders of Australia First, Grano's house was raided by the police. Not long after, he turned up at Clem's office, violently abusive with (false) accusations that Clem had spread stories about the raid. He 'could scarcely talk, he was so excited'. But Grano subsided, and cordial relations were resumed. Important here was Nina, who would send him poetry. As Nettie Palmer remarked, 'your other problems remain, my dear sir'; but Nina, who drew universal approval, was there to help him face them. 'She's a pearl!' Nina's sagacity was needed: Clem was 'very resentful against his "friends"', noted Jim Devaney. Clem had persuaded him, against his better judgement, to read poetry submissions. 'Am more than ever convinced', Devaney told Grano, 'that Clem and I will clash badly'.[60]

There were also continual problems with production. First was paper: as *Meanjin* had come into existence since the war began, it was refused a licence, and therefore a quota. Numerous visits to government offices got Clem nowhere, despite the small amount of paper involved. 'I was always being threatened', he recalled, 'by Paper Control with imprisonment for using paper without authority.' Once typeset, copy had to be approved by the censor. Then there were the printers, from whom Clem forever after carried stigmata. Errors were numerous, often the result of carelessness; sometimes a whole issue would have to be reprinted. One printer came to his rescue, telling Clem not to worry as he could get machine-finished paper, and he did. But he was inclined to run his business from the pub next door. Clem moved *Meanjin* to *Truth* newspapers, but they stole an anthology of short stories he had prepared and, using newsprint, distributed it for sale under their own imprint among the troops. Later, Paul Grano ascertained that Clem had been through five printers in the Brisbane years: even the alcoholic had had enough, and told him to go. True, he was a perfectionist, but his demands were less important than his way of being unpleasantly emphatic. He simply wore people out.[61]

Clem was running out of associates, and out of printers. Meanwhile it was plain, by mid-1944, that MacArthur was about to move north. The Afro-Americans, the jazz, the street fights and the snatches of passion would largely disappear with him. Brisbane would be returned to its sluggish self: a place where the premier still had not seen Clem after a year of having kept him waiting. Indeed the premier, along with the minister for education and his director-general, plus the two archbishops, had been sent *Meanjin*; they either said they never read poetry, or could not understand the poems that had been printed, or—nothing. There was not much interest at the university, either. The place could do with a Max Harris, Clem decided, to produce an *Angry Turtle*.[62]

In addition, at the QAAA there was the feeling that *Meanjin* had grown 'too big for its Queensland boots'. The society had given £10 to the magazine in 1942, but was not happy with the result. The worthy efforts of its members seemed increasingly pushed aside to make way for writers from the southern states. 'You are moving over from the younger and un-established to the older and established', a local poet told Clem.

Since the rift with Duhig, Clem was feeling anything but established. How would he finance the growing journal? He told (Sir) Keith Murdoch that he could see the answer might have to be a move to either Sydney or Melbourne. While pondering his situation, Clem was caught up in a tram smash, bore a minor injury, and experienced further ill-health.[63]

As early as the Summer issue of 1941 Clem had seen *Meanjin* in national terms, though a 'cultural sapling … tended by Queensland writers'. By mid-1944—perhaps building on a suggestion of AD Hope—there was a national committee of consultants, one from each state. Queensland, relatively small in population and with a low educational base, could not sustain a magazine of *Meanjin*'s ambition. In one of the big cities there would be greater opportunities, not least for influence. Clem longed, Judith Wright recalled, 'for a hand in the making of the new national and international cultural renaissance which he believed was on the way'.[64]

For a time it seemed Sydney might be *Meanjin*'s new home. RG Howarth had always been sympathetic—'a friend to *Meanjin*', as Clem would say. He had just arranged for *Southerly* to be taken over by Angus & Robertson, which had drawn an immediate response from Clem, outlining *Meanjin*'s difficulties. Howarth urged Clem to come to Sydney and encouraged him to go into book publishing 'in a big way', since he had 'an absolute genius for it'. Douglas Stewart, too, was keen for him to come—and Clem's inclination at first had been towards the harbour city. He may even have had an offer of financial assistance. Meanwhile Vrepont wrote a chirpy letter, saying that he was keeping an eye out for a suitable house or flat.

But it did not happen. In Melbourne lived the encouraging Nettie Palmer, and Vance, and Percival Serle, and soon a proposal came that he had scarcely thought possible. The last issue for 1944 was cancelled, 'As a result of unavoidable publishing delays'. A number of articles, listed as forthcoming on a previous back cover, never eventuated. The Christesens were about to strike camp, and take the magazine to Victoria.[65]

2

STEPHEN

CASTING OFF THE CHRYSALIS OF CONSERVATISM

1922–1954

ONCE WHEN IN the city I bumped into Stephen Murray-Smith, carrying a sack. We were standing outside the GPO. After we'd been talking a few minutes, he said (as senior to junior), 'Come with me as I collect the *Overland* mail.' So in we went, around a corner to a large post office box at the bottom of a wall of them. Stephen bent down, scooping out an impressive batch of letters into his sack, then hoisted it over his shoulders. Like a bleached Santa Claus he then proceeded, with me in attendance, across the vast space. 'I like to think of my grandfather being in this hall', he said, which with its steady assurance (and his steady step) brought to mind a host of hyphenated glories.

Beyond the hyphenation

But it was not like that. Stephen's father was the first hyphenation, devised (at his bride's suggestion) by placing it behind his last given name. Although born in Glasgow, his family had come from an obscure island in the Hebrides. William Murray-Smith—generally known as Murray—was dour like many Scots, and with a temperament that elided easily into conservatism. Murray served in the First World War, as a lieutenant in the AIF. He was active in the paramilitary organisations that sprang up shortly afterwards—to man the bridges of the Yarra and defend the wealthy suburbs from working-class hordes, if need be. He was also stingy; while his womenfolk, to whom he was devoted, were free to bedeck themselves with finery, he stuck to the same suit for twenty years. Murray's most striking characteristic was his exceptional honesty, so marked that it impeded his career as a retailer. But since it came with a distinct chill, domestically it added to his remoteness: Stephen later recalled his father's 'touching attempt to make contact with his children'. He later came to realise that his personality had been scarred and sealed by terrible experiences on the Western Front.

Murray had found his niche shortly after he married Alice Margrett, when he joined his father-in-law Steve in his horse-trading business. This was quite distinctive, even prestigious, supplying the Indian Army with mounts from Australian farms—'walers', the horses were called, as they were identified with New South Wales. It has been described as the longest haul on which livestock was regularly carried in the nineteenth century (and after), and Steve Margrett was at the centre of it. Although the thirty-first(!) child of a Cheltenham baker—born insignificant in a snooty English spa town—Steve's dapper style, charm and business acumen took him to the heights of society in Calcutta, where, owing to his military bearing, he was known as 'the Colonel'. Towards the end of his life he would boast that he had not missed Christmas dinner in Calcutta or a Viceroy's Cup in forty-five years. Grandmother Maud would recall those occasions with pleasure, regaling the young Stephen with stories of their 'absolutely marvellous' social life.

Stephen's mother Alice was also cognisant of antecedents, less distinguished, including pub owners and poor farmers on the western fringe of Melbourne: she put up the barriers almost as keenly as her husband would have defended them. Conservative, sceptical and articulate, Alice was a woman of great flair, superbly turned out in taffeta gowns from Le Louvre; these were sometimes sprinkled with the ash she dropped everywhere, for she was a chain smoker. Practical and kindly, Alice could turn her hand to surprising things. When the family fortunes took a turn for the worse, she began making and marketing ingenious felt toys. But she was an overbearing parent, particularly to her daughter Barbara, and on occasion to 'My darling only son Stephen'.

'Bibury', designed by a fashionable architect and built alongside Alice's mother's house in Macquarie Road, Toorak, was peopled by a cook and a nursemaid as well as the family; outside there was a gardener. Alice threw lots of bridge parties, particularly when Murray was away, as he often was—in addition to business trips that took him to country properties, he was absent for four months each year in India. To pass the time, she endlessly read middlebrow fiction borrowed from libraries. But for Stephen, who at first did not recall this, theirs was a 'bookless two-storeyed brick house on a Toorak hill'. It sounds lifeless, and in a measure it was, since for him there was a double absence. First there was his father being so often away, and then the family absorption with India—over at his grandmother's prints of British life there lined the walls—augmenting a loose imperial consciousness. (For a time it was personalised in an Indian servant, Makbul, while at an early age Stephen was taught to count to twelve in Hindustani.) Despite the apparent solidity, there was little in this setting that could be called distinctively Australian. Increasingly for Stephen this would feel like another absence.[1]

The education of young Stephen

Born in 1922, Stephen was just twelve when he was sent to Geelong Grammar School, 'the Eton of Australia', located with its playing fields on the shores of Corio Bay. From his prep school Glamorgan Stephen brought home reports of being 'inclined to be pugilistic', and his need to become more considerate. Now he found himself bullied. Hating boarding school at first, Stephen announced he would run away. Soon he found a more acceptable form of escapism and began reading voraciously—largely middlebrow novels (like his mother). At home he had read Mary Grant Bruce and Ethel Turner, but practically none of this new material was Australian.

Stephen was failing to distinguish himself at school, when suddenly there was a crisis. He was at home that day in 1938 when a cable arrived, saying that no further horses would be required; the Indian Army was to become fully mechanised. Years later he recalled the look on his parents' faces as they contemplated ruin, or something like it; the signs had been plain, but Murray had persuaded himself that good horses would always be needed, not least because of the roughness of the country. There was an interview with the headmaster, because it seemed Stephen would have to leave school; but JR Darling saw promise in the boy, his grandfather was induced to come to the rescue, and a way was found to keep him on.[2]

JR Darling was probably the greatest headmaster Australia has seen. He once stated that everybody in the school was good at something, and that it was the school's job to find out what it was. An admirable educational precept—sadly unrealisable in most schools. Darling was a brilliant entrepreneur—the bold stroke of launching the bush school Timbertop solved a number of problems at once—and, for all his high principle, a gifted tactician. In order to build greater awareness and appreciation of the arts, he organised mass plays in which the whole school would participate. His prefect system was more controversial, and when in later life Stephen pointed out that some of those chosen had not had notable careers, he was simply told that you don't choose boys to run a school because you think they will be leaders in later life. As an enlightened Englishman, Darling believed in *noblesse oblige*, in community, and in self-sacrificing leadership by the privileged. He once said that the school would not be doing its job until it was sending Labor members to parliament. 'He was the first and incomparably the most humane, liberal, and best employer I had,' recalled the radical historian Russel Ward; Manning Clark was employed by him, too. Darling saw 'problem boys' as a challenge, and while Stephen was not in that category, he was idiosyncratic, slow to find himself, and needed guidance.[3]

To some extent he got it from EWH Pinner, his housemaster at Cuthbertson, a laconic Australian who understood that (following occupational best practice) there should always be a margin between what he knew and what he decided to act upon. But Darling's endorsement of Stephen as someone worthy of support resulted in a sudden spurt of engagement. In class, he was reported as being less pedantic, showing more humour, and also greater patience with difficulties. But a couple of teachers thought, in history, he was prone to regurgitating the views he thought were required. Otherwise, it was noted in his final year, he was unusually opinionated. In history, 'His work is thorough & conscientious. I imagine his mind will mature late ...' It was difficult to judge his ability right then.

Beyond the classroom, Stephen became a presence in the school. He was on the library committee, the students representative council, and became secretary of the Public Affairs Society, where he worked to Russel

Ward. He was involved in bringing speakers from Melbourne—including Ralph Gibson, the state secretary of the Communist Party. Once they were addressed by their own Manning Clark, who gave his impressions of Europe: Stephen noted that he 'dwelt on international "atmosphere" and psychology rather than actual facts'. In the meantime he was assisting with the production of Shakespeare's *Henry V*—phase two of Darling's cultural consciousness raising—with himself cast in the title role. That was no mean achievement, since he had tended to slur his speech and had had to work hard on it. Now, with the 'English' dressed in school cadet corps uniforms, and with the 'French' in borrowed Melbourne Grammar navy blues, Stephen stood forth 'smothered in a glory of red tape', and 'rendered the part of King Henry with characteristic vigour'.

Geelong Grammar gave Stephen Murray-Smith much, a scholarship to study 'at any British university' not the least of it. The Darling ambience—as his son David recognises—gave him the courage to go against the herd. Although 'forced into being a premature rebel', Stephen was made to feel it was quite acceptable to be oppositional towards family and school. In the fullness of time, Darling became a personal friend, while the headmaster's characteristic mix—radicalism by temperament blended with conservatism in taste—would gradually become his own.[4]

The whole of Stephen's last year at Corio was overshadowed by the Second World War. Manning Clark later recalled his first day at the school, and how Stephen approached him 'carrying an armful of books, and with the expression of a troubled man on his face, the fretful expression of a young man who wanted answers'. They would elude him all through his first year of adult life. Earlier a vocational guidance counsellor had recommended that Stephen study commerce, with a view to becoming a company secretary. Something of this sober purpose remained when he enrolled in the combined Arts/Law course at the University of Melbourne.

He was not at all clear what he wanted. The education he had been given was a traditional English one: in middle school, a steady diet of Latin, maths, and German. In later life Stephen would scarcely draw on the first two; more immediately he would fail first-year German. He had an acute sense of vacuum. School had been boarding school; Stephen later said he did not know anything about the student union or clubs. He hung around mainly with Geelong Grammar friends, notably Tim Burstall and the daredevil, stylish bohemian Denison Deasey. In escapist mode, he wrote to his friend Rob Hamilton, saying after the war, let's go exploring. Yet while yearning for new horizons, Stephen maintained a close connection with his school. It had been an integrating agent: Darling's program of 'national service' had taken Stephen into slums, prisons and factories, giving him a real and unsettling view of how the other half lived.[5]

Outwardly he was still Tory. Rob Hamilton chided him for believing what appeared in the conservative Melbourne daily the *Argus*. He would do so even more heavily when Stephen was silly enough to assert, once Germany invaded the Soviet Union, that perhaps Nazism was more truly socialist, and that the Soviets were more imperialist than defensive. Confronted by these loose remarks, his friend remarked, 'I feel the world to crumble about my ears.'

At this time Stephen was still reading widely, although much of it stolidly middlebrow material, overwhelmingly English. In the three years to the end of 1941, he read some 314 books; only one was of Australian interest, *Flying Fox and Drifting Sand*—written by the Englishman Francis Ratcliffe. A childhood gift of a two-volume edition of Henry Lawson remained unopened for more than ten years. Stephen did sell copies of *Angry Penguins* in Melbourne, but this stemmed from doing his friend Rob (now in Adelaide) a favour, rather than from any cultural radicalism. Although this period was marked by indirection, some characteristic attitudes were emerging: a desire to beat the system, and an anti-war position derived from the English essayist CE Montague.

If pacifist by recent conviction, Stephen's pugnacity nonetheless found satisfaction at school when firing a Vickers gun. But his first action was unintended. He and the Hamilton boys stole away from school and clambered on board a four-masted schooner, lit a camp fire, and to their horror read in the paper next day that the vessel had been burnt to the waterline. Once the war began, Stephen was keen to join up. The family was opposed to his enlisting in the AIF, probably thinking him immature, or at least inexperienced in the ways of the world. But by July 1941 Stephen had received three separate offers, placing him either in the

AIF or the militia. He discussed these matters with Rob, who suggested that they wait till his brother Jim emerged from Duntroon, take a holiday together, and then join up with him. There was plenty of time, Stephen believed; 'the war's got another good five years, perhaps thirty'. In the event Stephen and Rob did join up together, in December 1941.[6]

The war and New Guinea

Stephen's war began with two months training in guerrilla warfare around Wilsons Promontory, and as a member of the Fifth Independent Company he sailed to New Guinea. Action began almost as soon he got to Port Moresby: Japanese bombers would swoop over the army barracks on their daily raids, and Stephen, to the surprise of other soldiers, once opened up on them from Bren guns mounted on the hillside. His only war injury was sustained here, when bits of shrapnel flew up from a round of ammunition someone mistakenly threw on a fire.

Then it was northwards, into the jungle, his company joining the New Guinea Volunteer Rifles to form Kanga Force. The detachment functioned as commandos, reconnoitring the area and harassing 'the Japs'. Stephen took part in an important action at Heath's Plantation, blowing up a bridge, and in a number of raids. In January 1943 he was present at the battle of Wau—which the Japanese, expecting an easy victory, lost. Stephen saw the reddened sky following the burning of four adjacent towns by the Australians. Kanga Force was disbanded, so Stephen became a medical orderly. Later he worked in the Intelligence Section of Signals.

The crucial experience was the year or more spent in the jungle, generally in a patrol of half a dozen (compared with the Japanese fifty or sixty). The Australians were constantly aware of the Japanese, and had to duck out of sight from reconnaissance planes. It was Stephen's boast that they were not surprised once. But there were moments when the gravity of the situation pressed heavily: on guard duty came the realisation that there was 'no-one at all between you and the Japanese … that one was the ultimate outpost of the army, the spearhead of the whole Pacific War'. At any moment it all might suddenly end. That tommy gun kar-r-r-ack: enemy action, or branches falling in the jungle? That whirring noise: the characteristic sound of the hornbill, or a low-flying Japanese plane?

All that could be done was to hold one's ground and try not to cough or rustle, for up to five hours on end.

The army, Stephen later reflected, consolidated two important lessons from boarding school: 'how to stay alive under difficulties, and the idiocy of authority'. What was new was the constant high state of alert, punctuated by moments of real terror. Stephen's heart was in his mouth when, having volunteered with Rob Hamilton to blow up the bridge at Heath's, a match failed to ignite—three times. In this operation he was traumatised by seeing his commanding officer shot. He was also sobered by seeing a slit trench having taken a direct bomb hit: he had occupied it the day before.

As he stumbled forward in night advances, perhaps over a slippery, treacherous bridge, Stephen owned to being frightened. His father's whistle from the Great War, worn around his neck, became a real comfort. Sometimes the days were little better. On occasion the unit was so deep in the jungle that they could not see the sun; instead, set off by the faint smell of decay, weird phosphorescent fungi, 'gleaming evilly'. Patrols were tense, and physically exhausting; soldiers had to cope with the heat, drizzle and mosquitoes. After a while Stephen didn't notice the bites. Malaria—which laid him low half a dozen times—could come as a relief.

At the same time, Stephen found a kind of fulfilment in New Guinea. He had always wanted to explore rough country, and see if he could rise to the challenges, physical and mental. He did, although it slimmed him down from 90 to some 60 kilograms in the process. He grew a beard—useful for saving razor blades, for camouflage, and for providing some protection from mosquitoes. Gradually Stephen came to see that 'The jungle was our friend, not our enemy, and through necessity we learned to conceal ourselves, how to feed ourselves, how to treat the [natives]', talking pidgin. In fact the men of 2/5th Independent Company seemed to have been almost forgotten by headquarters in Port Moresby: months went by without food and other supplies being forwarded. The isolation fed into the men's interdependence, as they became relaxed with each other: at night, under the soft glow of the lamps, they would play pontoon for stakes that in the end were reduced to a single matchstick.

In other ways, too, New Guinea was transformative. The experience of being a commando was in some respects deracinating: home, for which they all longed, 'had lost its meaning'. They were in thoroughly bad shape, having survived for months on poor food and scant shelter. For Stephen there was now a greater sense of detachment. He felt a witness to great events, while his elite education gave him the confidence to feel that one day he could play a public role. (At one point, he jotted down weight details, adding they might be 'of interest to some future biographer'.) For the moment his experiences, particularly as a medical orderly, left him with the memory of soldiers' groans and cries, and a deep distaste for the smell of old blood.

He began keeping a detailed diary. He was proud of it, revised and expanded it after discharge from the army, but never quite got the account to publishable standard. Even so, it contains vividly written passages and is a useful account of the company's activities. For Stephen it served as a way of learning how to write, as well as to record. Already there are signs of the characteristic range, and the capacity to identify clues to a broader meaning arising from events taking place in front of him. Moreover, Stephen's diaries are conspicuously alert, and reveal a capacity to question received opinion. He was struck by the fact that the (white) New Guinea Volunteer Rifles were often spoken of lightly—they had been civilians, had no uniforms, were men of all ages, were short of guns and sometimes lacked military experience. But, Stephen noted, they were far from being ramshackle and useless. As scouts they were highly valuable, for they knew the country intimately; their signallers had been first-class amateur wireless men in peacetime; and their medical orderlies were already experienced, as plantation men, in recognising and treating a wide variety of tropical diseases. Don't judge a book by its cover, Stephen was implicitly saying, showing a characteristic appreciation of human diversity that would grow in him.[7]

When Stephen considered the future of the land he had come to know, his identification with the settler interest was complete. More forcefully than most, he articulated a lot of common assumptions. In a pair of papers written towards the end of the war, he saw the territory as more really Australian once hostilities ended, part of our 'heritage' as a consequence of blood sacrifice. We would be fools, he believed, if we did not 'exploit' New Guinea—but it could be done to the maximum advantage of the natives. The big, exploitative companies should be kept out. Ex-servicemen should be at the vanguard, in a broader form of 'trying to shepherd sulky natives', as Stephen once described dealing with porters. The country could in effect have two administrations; in addition the white settlers—whom he saw as reaching up to 200,000—could send members to the Australian House of Representatives. 'We will not offer the natives the franchise,' he wrote, 'and we will not educate them. We will only cause unhappiness and strife.' Instinctively an educationist, Stephen began to modify that constraint immediately. Quite soon his attitude to Papua New Guinea would undergo radical transformation, while his attachment to the country would become an abiding one.[8]

The university and the Labor Club

While still in New Guinea Stephen received the news, brought by a 'native runner', that he had been given a place in an Arts course at the University of Melbourne. He would be able to attend thanks to the Commonwealth Reconstruction Training Scheme, which among other things enabled ex-servicemen to study full-time at university. The effect was transformative: while Stephen was one of 356 such students at Melbourne in 1945, by 1947 there were more than 4000 of them, amounting to half of student numbers. The beginning of Commonwealth funding of individual students, the scheme broadened the student body considerably. Just as the slit trenches between Wilson Hall and the Engineering school were now filled with water and rubbish, so too the ex-soldiers were eager to put the war behind them. They worked hard and played hard, stealing a march on the students just out of school when it came to dealing with the world—and with women, inevitably drawn to them by their greater experience (of all kinds). In tutorials, they could intimidate fellow students by superior knowledge, or by uttering blunt certitudes. Many were quite conservative.[9]

But a significant segment were not, and they were more in tune with the times. As the nature of Nazi oppression and the enormity of the Holocaust were gradually revealed, it had sharpened a sense of the democratic values the Allies were fighting for. It would be impossible to return, at war's end, to a simple as-you-were position. The university's urbane vice-chancellor, the Englishman John Medley, had caused a flutter when he stated this in 1940. There was, Ken Gott later recalled, 'an unprecedented fervour for social change', soon evident in the ousting of Churchill as Labour was voted into power in Britain. In Queensland, a Communist member of parliament had been elected the year before.

By virtue of the Russian victories against Hitler, Communism was given the benefit of the doubt. Local Communists became almost respectable. In Melbourne, when the Soviet Friendship League acquired a multistorey building, their headquarters were officially opened by the lord mayor.

Stephen, unwittingly, exemplified this tug to the left. In the space of one year he joined three political parties. Indeed, when he first returned from New Guinea, he acquiesced in his father's signing him up in the Frankston branch of the Liberal Party. Later, Stephen was persuaded by Geoff Serle to join the Labor Party; shortly afterwards he explored the possibility of contesting the seat of Flinders as the ALP candidate. That did not happen, and he again moved left, joining the Communist Party. 'I was politically unawakened, rather than conservative,' he later explained. But around that time he also returned to Corio for a stint of teaching. There he befriended the young Rupert Murdoch, providing a real (if short-lived) radical influence. Perhaps for Stephen the return to Corio acted as a clarifier. Others, too, had difficulty in locating themselves politically in those heady times. Manning Clark told of one talented young man who, in the space of one month, moved from being a theological student to membership of the Communist Party, and then became a leader of the university's Conservative Club.[10]

Stephen's political shifts are less surprising given the functional overlapping of left-wingers in the University Labor Club. In the postwar years the club was 450 strong, including some 110 members of the Communist Party, whose membership was, as a matter of policy, secret—not from choice, it was claimed, but for fear of victimisation. Public identification was largely limited to selling copies of the party newspaper the *Guardian* outside the Union building. For the three years immediately after the war, there were no major policy differences between Labor and the Communists. Content with building up a presence, the Party underplayed its hand, and deliberately did *not* seek majorities on all student committees. Moreover, since many democratic socialists were Christian, the Party frowned upon comrades joining the Free Thought Society. It was happy to use the Labor Club as a sphere of influence, a catchment area for likely members.

The Labor Club prided itself on being a United Left front, capable of accommodating a variety of progressive positions, ranging from Communist to members of the Student Christian Movement and even Catholics—so long as their religious values could accommodate socialism. Apart from legitimate student issues, all the more pressing given the influx of ex-servicemen, there was a convergence between Christian concern and socialist action on many issues, such as racism, slum clearance and working-class advancement. Capitalism was in crisis, it was believed; socialism clearly offered the most rational form of social organisation: 'The facts are on our side.' In the Labor Club the emphasis was as much on true freedom of the individual—which extended to a stated belief that members should not be pressed to join a political party if they did not feel ready.[11]

As a result, the Labor Club had something of the aspect of a vast, left-wing jamboree. It is significant that one stalwart could not remember any figure of the left from this time who went into politics—unlike the conservatives on campus. 'It seemed not so much a club as a way of life,' recalled Ken Gott. With the judgmental distance of middle age, Stephen was inclined to dismiss the Labor Club as practising 'a borrowed radicalism', founded on assumptions and earlier achievements overseas.

But this is too severe. The Labor Club sustained an impressive range of activity. There were the debates with opponents in the Public Lecture Theatre, weekly lunchtime meetings, study groups and play-readings, and also hikes and vacation conferences in bayside or mountain guest houses. These had an earnest core: reading lists were issued, and there were sessions on political economy and political theory as well as those on the questions of the day. An impressive array of speakers (which might include the Communist Ralph Gibson on fascism, or the patron John Reed on the artist and society) would give papers and lead discussion. The conversations that followed could continue till the small hours; there were also gatherings around the campfire, and dances. There was not much promiscuity—when a delegation from Sydney turned up at the first NUAUS conference in Tasmania early in 1947, some Labor Club people were rather shocked by their cynicism and sophistication. The Melbourne style was, as Ray Marginson recalled, 'Presbyterian free love'. A number of feisty women attached themselves to a man quite early in their undergraduate careers, and rarely strayed from his side—or (if not quite so unswervingly) he from theirs.[12]

These activities had as a soundtrack the jazz band of Graeme Bell, then emerging with a distinctive sound. Stephen, who had taken up the bassoon, did not share this enthusiasm; but he threw himself into much else. Believing that effective music helped to augment solidarity, he proceeded, with Edgar Waters, to produce a Labor Club song book, *Rebel Songs*. Interestingly, Stephen rarely wrote at this stage, and when he did contribute to *Melbourne University Magazine* it would be a co-authored venture with Nita Bluthal, translating and introducing the Jewish-Australian writer Pinchas Goldhar. But he had been heavily involved in theatre on his return to Melbourne—a way of finding himself, through other roles—first in the National Theatre, and then at the university. An army friend was prompted to comment, 'You always did remind me of Orson Welles.' Later (political commitment having increased) he took to the boards only in Labor Club revues, producing one and writing a song for another to the tune of *The Red Flag*:

> The old school tie, we proudly wear
> Above our coats, beneath our hair—
> What else is found between these twain?
> It may be fluff, it isn't brain.

Stephen was severing himself from his past, and it was fun. The emerging assurance of early adulthood was blending enjoyably with the bright youth the war had postponed. 'I draw my inspiration from the twin founts of anarchy and romanticism,' he wrote in a fanciful moment.[13]

Active in the Labor Club were two people already known to him, who would remain significant figures throughout Stephen's life. Both had been encountered in New Guinea. One was Peter Ryan, who, while a secretary of the Labor Club, stood as an Independent Labor candidate in Toorak in 1947. (Australian intelligence services at one stage had thought him a future Communist leader.) The other was Geoff Serle, whom he had met by chance at the end of a day's march near Port Moresby, when Stephen went up to a tent and asked if there was room for one more inside. A firm friendship emerged, based on a conversation that went on for the best part of a day, exchanging stories and enunciating hopes and aspirations. Hartley Grattan's recent account of Australia, which Serle passed to Murray-Smith, was its sheet anchor: 'Pity a bloody Yank had to write it!' Serle commented. The book would influence both of them, but Serle most.

Before he went to the war, Geoff Serle had lived a rather circumscribed life in Hawthorn, supplemented by Ormond College. He came from a cultivated household: his mother, Dora, was a well-known painter and his father, Percival Serle, had abandoned his profession as an accountant once he had saved sufficiently to enable him to live the life of a literary scholar. Unlike Stephen, who grew up in an intellectual vacuum, Serle was familiar with most of the literary figures of the day—as a boy he had gone to the front door and let them in at home. At Scotch College, Serle had shone as a keen sportsman, particularly in hockey and cricket; solid application rather than brilliance had marked his intellectual style. Looking back, he realised he had been 'incurious … with a fairly closed mind'. The war changed that. He had been seriously wounded, but bore that lightly.

More lastingly, like Stephen, Serle discovered that mateship could be a functional reality; it helped him to reach another self, more laid-back and laconic. It also spun his Melbourne groundedness into cultural nationalism. Despite his implicit elitism, Serle always retained something of the manner of an older Australia. His cheery blokey style, together with his level-headedness and a strong sense of civic responsibility, made him an adroit student politician: he practised an idealism that was, in his own words, 'quite tough and open-eyed'. Capable of being both tolerant and tactical, Serle was president of the Labor Club in 1945 (to be succeeded by Stephen), and drew sustenance from its existence as a broad progressive front, united primarily in a hostility to the machinations of the right. As Percival Serle noted approvingly in his diary, 'Geoff … is a good chap & very sensible about his Socialism'.[14]

Coming to the Party

Stephen had no intention of being sensible about his. Following his father's attempt to capture him for the Liberal Party, he increasingly felt a need to move out. After a brief period in the student hostel in Brunswick Street, Stephen found the perfect place. A scattering of students lived around the university, but Stephen found a loft at the back of a house almost directly opposite. 'The Loft', as it was generally known—'I think I may boast that mine was the only one with the definite article'—was entered through a trapdoor. Furniture was basic, showers had in

Union House across the way, while down the ladder and across the yard was a dunny. Stephen had only a toaster and a kettle, but there were plenty of cheap eateries in the city as well as nearer to hand.

'The Loft' functioned as headquarters, conveniently just off campus. Small meetings were held there, and a list of Communist Party members secreted in a gap between loose bricks. (Australian security fantasised that a map of Moscow was pinned to the wall.) Everyone knew where the key was. It was a place of trysts and parties: people noticed the floor, sticky with beer. There was no contradiction in this: as Ian Turner put it, 'We worked and struggled together, certainly—but we also talked and studied and ate and drank and slept and lived together.' It was an intenser version of the Labor Club: almost an 'inner Party' like the one Orwell was fictionalising at the time. (As Stephen later recalled, 'we all thought of ourselves as future leaders of a Communist Australia'.) People from the club who joined the Party and went along to the weekly university branch meetings, held in dingy rooms off Russell Street, were surprised to find how much they determined—by debating whom they would support and who not—the shape of student politics.

There was a joke that Communists never left the Party willingly: they either died or were expelled. Feeling themselves beleaguered, Party members had the compensation of a camaraderie that extended interstate, or even to people in Colombo and Bombay they could link up with if passing through on a steamship. People lived their entire lives within the Party—particularly if they came to see their life's work (as some did) in becoming an activist. There was a writers group (with which Stephen would later become involved), an artists group, and a Marx School to discuss theory, which Stephen periodically attended: it was held that theory became 'a material Force when it grips the masses'. The extensive social activities had as their defining points the screening of Soviet films, or attending the Up Town Club on Friday nights to listen and dance to Graeme Bell's band. The Eureka Youth League had endorsed Hot Jazz as 'People's Art'.

In addition to 'the Loft', Stephen secured his place at the heart of things by getting hold of a baby Austin, ferrying up to seven other people—if necessary—to one function or another. The friends he made in this period were crucial to him, augmenting a sense of self when he had gone a long way towards renouncing family and class.

Although thinned out—the universally popular Noel Ebbels died young in a road accident—they were still a formidable cohort at the time of Stephen's death in 1988. Not all were Communists: there was Geoff Serle and Ray Marginson—a keen jazz man and book collector—and his girlfriend Betty Reilly, a notable student politician. In the Party was Ray's brother Max, professionally a biochemist but active in theatre. Among a number of brilliant women were the feisty Amirah Gust and the Noye sisters. One of them, Beth, would marry Ken Gott, chairman of the Party's university branch. Gott showed a flair for journalism early, and edited a notable issue of *Melbourne University Magazine* with Serle in 1947; he became close to Stephen, and helped persuade him to join the Party.[15]

Gradually the foremost among them became Ian Turner. Turner, too, had had an indecisive year at university before being conscripted, and although his war service was largely on the Australian mainland, army experience was a common bond with Stephen. A country boy, Turner came from Nhill, where his father was a stock-and-station agent; his mother could never quite forget her connections with Scottish landed gentry, and increasingly disapproved of the activities of her son. Sent to Geelong College as a boarder, Turner came to exercise an easy ascendancy there; he discovered jazz and socialism—and, to his regret, that he was not a natural sportsman.

Even so, he was (as they said then) a man's man: 'All the machines are marvellous,' he remarked of Whyalla. 'I love machinery, especially when it's enormous.' Recently he had been with the Army Education Service, where a group of left-wingers and Communists—including Frank Hardy and Vane Lindesay—were producing the magazine *Salt*. Turner, with his pronounced interest in the visual arts, had already moved in bohemian circles, reading fiction widely, exploring film, and became an early champion of Sidney Nolan and the avant-garde. 'The individualism and anarchism of radical art,' he came to believe, 'are needed to temper the collectivism and authoritarianism of radical politics.'

At university Turner made an immediate impression—not in a medical course, as his mother had hoped, given those 'surgeon's hands', nor in the law course he just managed to scrape through—but as a campus personality. 'Ian, when I met him,' Amirah Inglis recalled as she looked past his death and their failed marriage, 'was a handsome man of twenty-three, with a fine strong head, twinkling eyes … a romantic figure who powerfully attracted men and women.' A party animal, he exuded sexuality and a chaster charisma. With his quick intelligence and ready wit, together with debating skills and a talent for negotiation, Turner became a successful student politician—drawing support, from time to time, even from those who were his opponents.

He co-edited *Farrago*, the student newspaper, and was secretary of the Students Representative Council, then president. A gifted orator, he clarified even as he harangued. One of the reasons he was so popular was that he gave the impression that with him—beyond the projection of power (and, later, the almost calculated scruffy image) and that harsh public voice—there lay a hint of something beyond the evident toughness. Turner was notably courteous in debate, even under provocation, and—since he knew despair himself—was capable of signalling good cheer to an opponent if he were down. Consideration, even respect, was reciprocated: later his adversary Frank Knopfelmacher would write warmly in support of Turner being granted a visa to enter the United States. More immediately, Turner knew he needed discipline, and found it both in his History honours course—which he did subsequently to Law, gaining first class honours—and in the Party.

It was as a student of Manning Clark, then offering his course on Australian History for the first time, that Turner would have first encountered Stephen. (Geoff Serle was also in that class.) Stephen had little to do with the SRC (having stood once, unsuccessfully), or *Farrago*, but in the Labor Club they were drawn to each other; they came to have long talks late at night about the future of Australia, and the Communist Party's role in it. It was Turner who probably persuaded Stephen to join. Gradually they would have become aware of a deep complementarity. Stephen was already exhibiting a much greater intellectual breadth, having an instinctive sense of how things fitted into the great world. He also had drive, and a keenness to organise others; Turner was more lackadaisical, even unorganised. But he was the greater Marxist ideologue, a stiffener for Stephen's latitudinarianism. The foundations were being laid for a close alliance. Stephen would later describe Turner as 'the best man of his generation', a claim Amirah considered just.[16]

Stephen had slid into the Communist Party. By the time he reflected on his life in a series of lectures given more than thirty years later, he wondered how, having experienced boarding school and then the army, he should once 'again set myself on a path towards becoming a rebellious subordinate within a rigid and demented authoritarian system'. (Stephen himself struck many contemporaries as having been something of a bully.) In those lectures, the Party years are passed over as if a scorched-earth zone.

In fact, the university comrades had hoped their branch would be an 'independent, self-governing unit', but it was soon made plain to them that no such thing was possible in a democratic-centralist party. With Stephen, a large part of the attraction of the Party was not so much the need for radical social equality, or a confident assertion of the scientific nature of Marxism, so much as a sense of the tide of history. In a 1947 speech to the university branch, Stephen addressed a number of challenges, but almost immediately spoke of the necessity to fight for peace, extending to 'colonial independence for our northern neighbours'. American influence in Australia also needed to be countered, he argued. At the same time, the feeling against 'aliens', and anti-Semitism, should be fought vigorously; students needed to be made more internationally minded.

A good Communist was a good student, it was maintained; but, unlike Ian Turner after his switch to history, Stephen was too much the individualist to wholly submit to the dictates of the course. It is said that he made a late entrance to a first class just as Professor Crawford was calling the roll, sitting down at the table and plonking a small suitcase in front of him. 'Smith', called the professor; '*Murray*-Smith', corrected the burly figure in masterly tones. Tutorials Stephen found boring. He responded to the elegance of the lectures given by Katie Fitzpatrick, as well as to the prognostications of Manning Clark. But he had already encountered him at school, and so was almost as impressed with Max Crawford as with Clark when they gave their pioneering course in Australian History.

'They gave me a sense of place,' Stephen wrote, 'while the Communist Party gave me a sense of purpose.' Exposure to Lawson and Furphy, and the configuring of an Australian culture, took deep root in him. As a son of empire, Stephen had come back from the war wanting to connect more deeply with Australia—and particularly with ordinary

Australians, who in the army had been almost confronting in their authenticity. A set of lectures by HS Canby, 'How American Writing became American Literature: The Growth of a National Culture', may also have been important. Then since returning to Melbourne, Stephen had begun collecting books; a new interest in Australiana now gave it particular point. A second, long-term enthusiasm also arose from the History Department: Stephen participated in archaeological expeditions to Phillip Island and, during the summer of 1945–46, to Flinders Island. There he found significant remains of an Indigenous camp in a creek bed, undisturbed for 7000 years; on return he supported the idea of a museum of ethnographic and primitive art at the university. This did not eventuate, but the attachment Stephen formed to the islands of Bass Strait would prove lifelong.

Stephen's personality was such that tedium was never to be endured, but avoided; on the other hand, his capacity for enthusiasm served to fire up organisational skills, so that enthusiasm became commitment. But since the fruits of his study of history did not follow the contours of the course, Stephen's results were an unimpressive lower second class honours. He wasn't particularly troubled, feeling that he was on the *side* of history. More, that he was helping to make it: at the time he spoke of the need for a history of the university branch, and proposed to Gott that they write a history of the Labor Club for Melbourne University Press. Meanwhile he had begun taking Russian lessons. Stephen saw himself as being in the vanguard, but partly because of this poor result, 'Ten very hard and difficult years were to follow.'[17]

Marriage and Mother Country

By his side, as she would remain, was Nita. Other women acknowledged at the start that Nita Bluthal was 'a husky-voiced and sexy beauty'; Stephen, going to the cinema one evening, saw Nita enter with an old friend, Geelong Grammarian Tim Burstall. They sat down in the row behind; attraction was instant. Nita wondered who the 'marvellous-looking creature' was; Burstall introduced them. For Stephen Nita never lost her allure, saying she was like a mistress to him.

Born in Poland, Nita had come to Australia in 1938, when she was eleven; she had no English. In Galicia the family had been prosperous millers; Nita's grandmother, through her work with the Jewish Red Cross, had been granted an audience with the Austro-Hungarian emperor. Propelled by the rise of Hitler to Melbourne, Nita's father was in the rag trade; her mother (who read Thomas Mann) was educated and captivating. Once Ken Gott, reluctantly calling at their home to collect a parcel, stayed a couple of hours talking to her about politics and religion. Meanwhile Nita, having got to university, slowed down her course—partly because she was not confident in writing English, and partly because she wanted to be more effective as an activist for the Communist Party. She helped put together the branch cyclostyled newsletter, *Antidote*, and was involved with the New Theatre. She too had appeared in plays, sometimes in the same production as Stephen.[18]

By the beginning of 1946, three months or so after Stephen had joined the Party, they were going steady. A crisis in their relationship had eventually served to confirm it, emboldening Stephen to hold fast with regards to his family. He left home in 'a disgraceful outburst of temper', as his father put it, and could not be lured back. That was scarcely surprising, as Stephen was banned from bringing Labor or Communist friends (and documents) back to Mt Eliza. Worst of all, he was expected to give an 'assurance' that that the friendship with Nita would not 'lead to anything more serious'. By this stage Stephen had found The Loft, originally thought of just as a pied-à-terre. It became his home. Nita did not move in—too bold a step for the times—but such was her notoriety that the school where she taught later refused to give her a reference.

But there were greater difficulties closer to home. As Beth Gott put it pithily, 'Nita's family didn't approve of him because he wasn't Jewish, and Stephen's family didn't approve of her because she was.' His mother, Alice, was also appalled by the fact that the prospective in-laws had a stall at Victoria Market. To be fair, she was concerned that Stephen's marrying a D.P. (displaced person) would damage his career prospects, while Stephen's communism—which she hoped would become an episode—could only be confirmed by Nita's. In fact Stephen joined the Party without telling Nita, who, once she got over her annoyance, followed him a few months later.

There was less opposition from Nita's parents, but even so she thought it expedient that they should get married while her father was away on holidays. (She had just turned twenty-one.) In the event, the only member of either family present at the civil wedding in February 1948 was Nita's actor brother John. Stephen, under relentless pressure from his mother, looked tired and drawn—and forgot the ring. Nita, secure in the relationship, was deeply moved nonetheless. They planned to go overseas, which would give them needed space. It also applied pressure in the other direction: as departure day neared, Alice came round. Eventually the two women would become close friends.[19]

With his first real publication being the short essay on the writer Pinchas Goldhar, Stephen was beginning to become familiar with a Jewish ambience. In addition to Nita, there were some high-spirited Jewish girls active in the Party and the Labor Club. A number of other men in the circle (notably Ian Turner with Amirah Gust) would make Jewish marriages, sharing, as Stephen put it, 'the good fortune to marry out of Old Australia into the New'. Stephen's marriage helped him to see that Australia's dominant monoculture was just one of many, and one rather derivative in form; other cultures had deeper roots, and had evolved to encounter more profound questions. Later in life, after a visit to Auschwitz, and thinking of Nita's relatives (gassed in the Holocaust), Stephen was left 'with the feeling, which in some ways came to overlay and subdue my radical nationalism, that there are bigger moral issues … than the level of Commonwealth grants to education, or the number of artists who can dance on the head of an opera house pin.'[20]

The time came to leave—Australian security had picked up that their original goal was the Soviet Union, but the Russians didn't want them. Otherwise Stephen projected a sense of his invincible right to advance. 'We needed a marshal', Ian Turner would wryly write, saying that Stephen was missed at the Melbourne May Day procession. Even the English customs officers seemed a little intimidated, for when the Murray-Smiths arrived with a lordly twenty pieces of luggage, they omitted to examine them. And once they got to St Pancras Station, Stephen threw himself into the arms of Beth Noye and Geoff Serle—which led them all to feel a little embarrassed.

London overwhelmed him at first—crawling around it, 'you feel like a humiliated ant'. But the sights were given a mixed report, with

Westminster Abbey declared 'disappointing'. Seeing Queen Mary coming out of a theatre, Stephen told his mother as one agreeably surprised—and adopted a more censorious tone when mentioning it to Comrade Gott. He caught up with other Australians—Serle he now found 'an old man in many ways'. Stephen chided him for his belief in majority rule (rather than the majority of the workers), and did not share his despondency (as many did) that there would be another war, with England caught in the middle. On going to Oxford, Stephen met Hugh Stretton, 'a charming sitter on all possible fences'. Soon the Murray-Smiths found an airy flat in Battersea, where they were joined by the newly married Gotts. Ken, who had been alarmed by the 'sudden flare-ups' between Stephen and Nita, soon got used to their adjustive scrapping.[21]

Briskly using introductions (especially the one from JR Darling), Stephen got a teaching job within ten days of landing. Nita got one as a supply (substitute) teacher—involving harder, temporary work—and, he soon discovered, she 'likes teaching more than I do'. He was surprised to find it quite common for teachers to 'boast of the antiquity of their ramshackle schools': his, a partly Anglican school in Chelsea, certainly qualified. The rugged stone structure was so solid it had been used as a mortuary during the war. Stephen discovered that discipline was poor—partly the result of dislocations and evacuations. The headmaster found that his strong personality and breezy manner made it easy for him to get along with colleagues, and become popular with the boys. But Stephen's heart was not in it.[22]

Meanwhile, Stephen and Nita transferred their Communist Party membership to the British Party. He was put on the Dominions Committee (its styling concealed a concern with 'the crisis in British imperialism') but he would have preferred other work. He was offered a job as co-secretary of the (British) Student Labour Federation, on the strength of his having been secretary of the Australian one; but it would have involved a massive salary cut. Stephen was unimpressed with the British Communist Party: he found its publicity excellent—literate—but its organisation poor, especially in trade unions.

There was at the time an ideological difference with the Communist Party of Australia—which felt that the view taken that the Labour Party would lead Britain into socialism was too soft. Comments from Australia and Australians were not appreciated—there was, Stephen detected, something of the bourgeois view that 'criticism cannot be accepted from a *colonial* party'. But there were many meetings, speakers and occasions like May Day. While he found that in some respects less impressive than Melbourne's—since there were fewer bands and floats—it won out because of the presence of veterans of the International Brigade from the Spanish Civil War, and various famous marchers.[23]

Nita 'gets a big kick out of the culture here', Stephen declared, being 'more European by temperament'. (She had assimilated so completely in Melbourne he had forgotten that she wasn't born there.) She loved theatre, but Stephen was exploring film, and delighting in meeting Malays and Chinese who seemed happy to accept Australia as part of their home region. But despite 'the general thrill of living here for a while, at the hub of so much', Stephen was restless. He wanted to move on, and sought posts in Hungary and West Germany. For the *Guardian* at home he wrote newsletters for a time; nearer at hand was the BBC. Although he failed to get a job there, they did take one script and included him in a discussion on migration. There was a problem with disgruntled returnees: the difficulty, Stephen said, is that Australia is neither a better nor a worse country than Britain; simply different. 'All of us in Australia are immigrants in a sense.' But he was annoyed with the BBC when they turned down a script, 'Is there an Australian Literature?'[24]

Nothing made him more conscious that there was than a particular issue of *Meanjin* that turned up. Stephen hadn't been overly impressed with the earlier issues of the year, but that of September 1948 was 'a humdinger, a breath of burning gum leaves which managed to overcome the barrier of the London cold', he told Clem; a model of what he had always wanted the magazine to be. Stephen then wrote that he was very depressed about England, particularly the literary scene. There were no outstanding left-wing writers, as in Australia, to give a constructive lead. (Orwell's *1984* was about to burst upon the world, but it was the exact opposite of what Stephen wanted.) *Meanjin* was 'a surge of floodwater into this foetid billabong of English literary decadence'. He had shown it to John Manifold, whose response was, 'Doesn't it make the English literary magazines look silly!' Stephen's desire to return home was quickened. 'I languish for home; I don't want to feel a foreigner too long.' He had been haunted by Australian landscapes—the Alps, the Prom. Now these were complemented by a growing sense of cultural possibility.[25]

The month before Stephen and Nita had hitchhiked for a month around England and Scotland, more than 3000 kilometres. They quickly found that '"Australian" is a password everywhere'. Brighton was an early destination, where they saw the Royal Pavilion. Stephen, never the cut-out Communist, owned to 'a sentimental and inexplicable regard for Prinny', its builder, the elegant and utterly self-indulgent George IV. He was more censorious about Bath, the Georgian spa town. Ugly and grey, it was 'a breeding ground for hypochondriac dowagers and spleen-aged colonels, full of expensive hotels and snobbish antique shops'. The Roman baths—now used only by goldfish—were well worth visiting 'for those who had an eye to picture the pot-bellied proconsuls lolling in the hot water and sneering at the English ... The hot water is still administered to the same types, but upstairs in the Pump Room and internally, not externally.'[26]

Indolent Roman imperialists had readily come to mind because Stephen, building on his friendships with Asian activists, had become a member of the Party's Far Eastern Committee. 'More and more I am convinced that South East Asia is the vital area in the world today,' he wrote to Rob Hamilton. Even some English bourgeois historians were capable of seeing Munich as possibly the last time 'world events hinged solely on European decisions. The democratic victory in China will perhaps be the most important event of our lifetimes.' He had 'always been conscious of Australia's extraordinary geopolitical position'—at school, pessimistically—but 'now I look forward to the constructive role we can play in the East'. 'Colonialism is a state of war,' he declared at a peace congress. 'In fighting, the colonial peoples are not fighting against Peace, but for it.'[27]

Czechoslovakia, not bohemia

Communism was advancing across the Eurasian double continent: Australia must wait. The place that increasingly beckoned was Czechoslovakia. Alone among the satellite countries, its non-Communist government had been treated as a wartime ally by Stalin. And, because he was intent on ethnically cleansing the Sudetenland of Germans (and might need support), President Beneš was prepared to be remarkably accommodating. When he moved his government back to Prague, Beneš increased its Communist component. Czechoslovakia's government was widely seen as an experiment—a kind of Melbourne University Labor Club writ large. Serle found it appealing: 'That's the place to go, boy, every one raves about it.' But in February 1948 increasing political tensions resulted in a Communist coup. There was a sense of betrayal in the West, a reinforcement of the belief that Stalin could not be trusted: the Cold War entered a new phase. It was precisely at this moment, with characteristic pugnacity, that Stephen decided to go to Prague.

Stephen first went to a peace congress in Paris—he was one of half a dozen Australian delegates—and was struck by the big-name speakers, the flags, the headphones with simultaneous translations, and an Englishman declaring, 'Anyone who drops an atom bomb on his fellow is a cad.' For the journey to Prague Stephen was warned to take not only food on the train, but also a towel and soap: 'you get soot all over you'. He went equipped with functional German, widely spoken in Bohemia; Nita, who soon joined him, from the base of her native Polish had already begun to pick up Czech and Russian. (She also had Yiddish and some German.) For Stephen it would be challenging: he soon told Clem, 'It is like jumping into a cold swimming pool to live in a completely foreign country.' Moreover, defining relationships would also be pushed to snapping point. After some months went by, his family 'suggested that I stay in Europe and not return'. Similarly Rob Hamilton, having joined the Department of External Affairs, warned that while Stephen was at his present address, any view expressed by either of them in correspondence would be viewed with suspicion. The friendship ended.

The Murray-Smiths arrived in Prague in June 1949. After London, the Czech capital had an 'intimate atmosphere rather reminiscent of Melbourne'; the police, he thought, were dressed rather like British colonels, and didn't behave like police at all. The people were well-dressed, the place festive with bunting for the Communist Party congress. There were still a few wistful reminders of the Hapsburg era, and 'apparently gentle methods of the govt yet … progress obviously made'. In fact the government was popular; from May 1945 the Communist Party had swelled from a mere 50,000 members to well over a million by the beginning of 1948. Apart from an extraordinarily high number of people in transport and industry already working in state enterprises, much of the economy—including banks, mines insurance companies and steel works—had already been taken over by the state before the coup. The Communist government would cut some slack, for a time.[28]

Earlier it had seemed that Stephen might land a job at the International Union of Students (IUS) headquarters, but they needed somebody who could speak Czech. The Murray-Smiths decided to chance it. There was a knot of Australian expats in Prague, while the IUS was the centre of a stimulating milieu: even a Russian there could manage an ironic expression when he dismissed an article on Leonardo as 'good, but too objective'. There were engaging Latin Americans inventive in their obscenities, some people traumatised by the war, but increasingly eastern European hatchet men. The IUS, like Czechoslovakia, was being transformed. The Soviet bloc had the numbers, and was increasingly turning this and correlative organisations into anti-Western propaganda agencies; the Western affiliates then withdrew. They would then be denounced as 'bogus', or 'unrepresentative', and some pro-Communist faction from that country invited to replace them. Meanwhile Stephen declared that the Prague head office had 'by normal standards the efficiency of an Australian brothel'.

Telepress—the Eastern Bloc equivalent of Reuters—wanted to employ Stephen, but first there were bureaucratic requirements that had to be satisfied. In the interim he was able to do limited work for them, supplementing this by freelance writing—for Czech publications appearing in English. (He became particularly interested in Czech education, thinking he might get a book out of it.) But it was tough—he and Nita were forced to sell clothes at one point. Then there were the shortages—of such things as razor blades, pipe tobacco, jam and coffee. And, although they never complained, as winter approached the Murray-Smiths had to get used to nights when the temperature could drop to minus 25. The job with Telepress came through, and things looked up: Stephen was responsible for putting out news material on Asia and the Pacific. Nita soon found a job teaching at a school for the children of diplomats, where she was, she admitted years later, 'a bit of a spy'. Meanwhile events in Australia, where the Labor government was moving against the coalminers, excited expatriates. The Communist Lance Sharkey had recently been jailed for seditious utterances; now eight trade union leaders were jailed as well. 'Doesn't the above news about

Australia,' wrote Stephen, 'make you want to get the first boat home to work against the bastards?'[29]

In March 1951 the Murray-Smiths left Prague. Stephen had been increasingly disconcerted by the growing Soviet control of the IUS, and when the opportunity presented would say so to friends. He would not have been impressed, either, with the then Russian claims to have invented radio, cars and aeroplanes. On the other hand, Stephen's patrician manner and his imperturbability in themselves would have caused offence, quite apart from his tendency to regard the Party as being as arbitrary as the army in its irksome minor disciplines. Just after he formally bade farewell to the head of Telepress, she was heard to remark, 'I wonder if I shouldn't have had him arrested after all.' But it was too late.[30]

Stephen as Party activist

Back in Australia in May 1951, Stephen and Nita took a while to unpack fully. Almost immediately there was the distraction provided by someone who had travelled out on the same ship, Gloria Foley, a violinist who 'was brought back to Australia solely to spread slanders about the CSR [Czechoslovak Republic]'. In counter-attack Stephen wrote letters to the paper, made broadcasts, and set off on a national tour up the east coast: at the Bondi-Waverley School of Arts his set piece on 'The Truth about the Peoples Democracies' was shared with documentary films and a Charlie Chaplin. Elsewhere he spoke to wharfies and factory workers, at public and street meetings, as well as giving Party 'cottage lectures' in private homes. He was discovering new aspects of his own country; it was, he told a Czech friend, 'a most educational trip'. Before the year was out, he went to Queensland again, speaking 'in houses at Mareeba, under the mangoes at Bowen … and on the Ipswich coal-fields'. At home in Melbourne he was so effective addressing construction workers, the men at the Swan Street bridge invited him back for three consecutive lunch hours. Meanwhile he wrote a pamphlet, *There Is no Iron Curtain*, later in life dismissing it as 'a whitewash pamphlet'.[31]

As often the case on resettling after a long absence overseas, it was a bumpy return. For a time it looked as though Stephen might be directed to live in Sydney, 'a city where you can't buy at the moment butter, sugar, milk, salt, pepper, onions, potatoes, canned goods, cereals, fish, margarine, matches or candles'. Sometimes it seemed that in Prague they had 'lived in the future'. The Murray-Smiths didn't move anywhere much, for a time. They lived with Nita's parents, since money became increasingly short: Stephen still wrote for Telepress, but payment was erratic and eventually he learned that when the organisation was closed down, secret policemen had been sent to seal its doors. There was nothing for it but to teach again. At Essendon High he was a success with the students, speaking to them after school in an adult tone, and surprising them by the frankness with which he said he didn't want to be a teacher. It was as well: ASIO saw to it that he would not be given a permanent position.[32]

Stephen turned to the Party: at the end of 1952 he was appointed organising secretary of the Australian Peace Council. Since he had to raise his own salary, he had to continue with subediting work at the *Age,* and kept an eye out for a regular job. But Stephen did now have a sense of high purpose. In addition, relations with his parents had improved markedly; soon they gave the young couple a block of land at Mt Eliza, not far from their own home. Drawing on the well-known Small Homes section in the *Age*, Stephen secured a war services loan on the customary generous terms, and began building. While drawing on a little additional money, the house would be a modest timber dwelling of two bedrooms, for a time not even painted. But a new home of their own it was. 'We are terribly happy to be back in Australia and to renew our roots', Stephen wrote. Soon they would begin a family.

Stephen had been attracted to peace activism for some time. He had seen, particularly as a medical orderly in New Guinea, what war could do, even before he had gone to a battle-scarred Europe. Moreover, the peace movement—precisely because it articulated the anxiety of the general public—was the prime Communist front. In Melbourne, no less than three clergymen, the reverends Alfred Dickie, Victor James and Frank Hartley, spearheaded the council; they brought out Dr Hewlett Johnson, the 'Red Dean' of Canterbury, to address a Peace Congress in Melbourne the year before Stephen returned. Twice he drew crowds of 10,000 to the Exhibition Buildings.

People knew there was deep Communist involvement in the Australian Peace Council, but the involvement of churchmen helped the cause become a mass movement all the same. The Soviets themselves still had considerable capital in these matters. It was known (if not always remembered) that they had borne the brunt of the war against Germany, and that, given a history stretching back to Western intervention after the revolution, the Russians had some reason to cry 'encirclement'. Even if it could be said that the United States had the atomic bomb first and used it first, the fact that both major powers now had it put the world in dire peril of nuclear war. Peace and disarmament had become matters of urgency.

Stephen's role as organising secretary involved speaking, travelling, writing, putting out a newsletter and maintaining international contacts, 'as well as more involved questions of strategy, tactics, [and] the means of broadening our influence in the community'. Fund-raising was important: there were four full-time office workers. Stephen's resourcefulness as an organiser was soon apparent. In 1953, for (Korean) Cease Fire Week—centred on a World Peace Council meeting in Budapest, the call locally was for the 'biggest concerted effort ever'. Stephen gave tips on how to be effective. Hold a preliminary meeting, set specific goals; nominate particular people to be seen, and focus on clergymen (particularly Methodist), showing them the resolution of the peace conference. Then, in capitals: 'ASK FOR THEIR IDEAS BEFORE YOU GIVE YOURS'. He organised a big meeting in the Assembly Hall (church property), and to boost morale had barometers installed in the Peace Council office showing the number of letters sent and money raised.

As a veteran of the massive Youth Carnivals for Peace and Friendship the Party organised in Europe, Stephen was involved in the big one held in Sydney in March 1952. It was 'just like seeing Budapest or Berlin in Australia', he told Nita. Twelve thousand people attended; 8000 marched. Established writers such as Dame Mary Gilmore, Walter Murdoch and Alan Marshall took part in the Literature section. But the authorities, viewing the whole thing as an exercise in pro-Soviet propaganda, did their best to frustrate the carnival at every turn: sponsors found halls were suddenly unavailable, police delayed delegates arriving in cars and broke up meetings, and the minister for immigration refused a visa to a troupe of Chinese acrobats. When the New Zealand delegation arrived and were asked by customs how many they were, there was a dry response: '28 delegates and four policemen!' Even the film of the carnival was cut by the censor.[33]

Given his various activities, it is not surprising that Stephen found that any thought of editing a literary magazine had 'receded'. At the back of his mind he hoped one day, when less busy, to do some writing—short stories or a novel, and began collecting material for one on the liberation struggle in Malaya. Literature had remained an enthusiasm all through: half the books he had taken to Czechoslovakia were Australian. Becoming a member of the Realist Writers Group, he now began to think of resuscitating his Czech project of compiling a short-story anthology.[34]

But there was a more immediate enthusiasm. 'In Australia and in England,' Stephen told Ralph Gibson, 'we sing too few songs in the Labour movement.' He now tried to publish *Rebel Songs* in England; but since it contained words only, when aimed at that surprisingly musically literate country it did not get very far. So when Ken Tolhurst at the IUS said he needed a songbook produced for the forthcoming Youth Festival in Budapest, something Stephen could edit as 'a sideline' when he got to Prague, he jumped at the chance. Once there, Stephen worked hard at it, seeking to include songs from South Africa, Ceylon and the West Indies. Prepared to make himself 'thoroughly unpopular' around the IUS, he insisted every effort must be made to have the handsome booklet appear in time for the festival; it did. Already his mind was turning to more research on the people's songs in Australia. The activist folksinger Pete Seeger encouraged him, noting that Aussie soldiers had done far more singing during the war than the Yanks.[35]

Back in Australia, Stephen worked with Edgar Waters on an expanded version of *Rebel Songs*. John Manifold, when asked to contribute, was scathing about a songbook without music—'as silly as the *Oxford Book of Ballads*, for the same reason'. Stephen explained that in university Labor clubs—for which it was being compiled—there was a tradition of certain people in each club being supplied with the music, to teach the rest of the members. Of course there would be incorrect words, wrong notes;

but the songs would be treated as 'healthy, living things'. All of this was in line with Stephen's view that songs and stories kept alive the memory of the people's past struggles, and emboldened them to fight new battles.

Driving this concern was an awareness that as the consumer society advanced with its mass culture, cultural activity would be replaced by cultural passivity: creators would become consumers, particularly of American popular culture. It was vital to establish independent cultural networks. Having first thought of the idea in exile, Stephen moved to establish a People's Music Association at the 1952 Sydney Youth Carnival. Then he was instrumental in establishing a (short-lived) company, Wallaby Recordings, to record and market the old songs of the Bush—alongside instructive discs of people's music from other countries. Greater familiarity with Australian culture would go hand in hand with a greater understanding of the culture of other countries. But Wallaby lacked the resources to make much impact, and once again songs were often reduced to availability in words only. Some existed only in this form.[36]

Stephen occasionally went out, with Nita, talking to old-timers and collecting songs. It connected him to something local and authentic, something greatly undervalued. One old fellow, Phil Shirley, had worked as a lad in the Glenrowan district, and could remember when they caught the Kellys. Coaxed by Stephen, his high-pitched voice laboured in recalling the verses of Kate Kelly's song. He paused, mentioning contemporaries. 'They're old-timers ... that's what you want?' 'Yes!' came the emphatic reply.

In these activities Stephen was very much a man of his time. Vance Palmer had published a collection of folksongs, 'restored' by the composer Margaret Sutherland. Then the musical *Reedy River*, incorporating old bush songs augmented by new tunes in the same mould, was a hit with the Left when it opened at Melbourne's New Theatre in 1953. (By the time it moved on to Sydney a small orchestra was replaced by 'the prototype bush band'.) It was, as advertising made clear, 'something that Hollywood could not make'. In all, 450,000 people paid to see it.

Reedy River was a romance about the shearers' strike of 1891, an airing of the Legend of the Nineties: whitefella dreaming. Beyond its immediate appeal, drawing on nostalgic nationalism and historic class warfare, was the belief articulated by Maxim Gorky, that folklore was a true reflection of the outlook of the working people: its very anonymity conferred authenticity. As Graeme Davison has put it, folklore would become 'the lingua franca of international Communism'. Thus Stephen's loose liking for music was refocused, and turned into activism. Similarly, his love of Australian literature would also be energised into commitment, providing new forums for its articulation and development.[37]

Frank Hardy, and the *Realist Writer*

A force in Party circles at the time, a man whom Stephen had not previously met, was Frank Hardy. He was a hero: for his vigorous denunciation of corruption and capitalism in *Power Without Glory*, and even more—once John Wren laid charges for criminal libel—when he emerged from the notorious court case as the victor. Hardy was a fighter, and literature his 'weapon'. Growing up in Bacchus Marsh, then a rural community beyond the western fringe of Melbourne, he had to leave school at fourteen to help support his large family. Hardy's father had been a militant socialist and a well-known spinner of yarns, even giving 'concerts' of them. Frank also liked a good story, got into gambling and on the grog, and became, in the eyes of English journalist Malcolm Muggeridge, 'the most Australian Australian'. Hardy abandoned the country for the city and, at the outbreak of war, joined the Communist Party. Crucially, his expanded sense of the world—literature, politics, economics—was both made available and filtered by this primal commitment. Literature, as he understood and practised it, was inseparable from the class struggle.[38]

While in *Power Without Glory* Hardy had drawn on the techniques of progressive American writers such as Theodore Dreiser, his views generally followed the cue given at the Soviet Writers Congress of 1934. There Gorky had made his views known as he named and promoted Socialist Realism, a doctrine later more vigorously expounded by Zhdanov. It was partly a response to literary modernism as a decadent elaboration of bourgeois culture. In contrast, Socialist Realism would be centrally concerned to promote 'revolutionary romanticism', expressing in literature 'the very soul of the proletariat, its passion and its love'. It would advance the struggle for socialism, seek to abolish exploitation and wage slavery, and articulate the aspirations of all the oppressed—extending from male workers to 'woman, whom we are making into a comrade', and the 'coloured' races. Writers themselves should be proletarians, said Hardy; indeed only working-class writers and Marxist-Leninist intellectuals allied with them 'can produce significant works of literature'. Moreover, bourgeois ideas of high and low art had to be discarded. Hardy attacked writers who sought conventional public recognition and reward from established publishers; also those middle-class comrades who disdained factory bulletins and other art forms workers used. There should be more faith, he urged, in 'the creative powers of the working class'. The Party, Hardy believed, should 'develop worker readers, worker critics and worker writers'.[39]

Hardy did not act as the Australian party's cultural commissar—others stepped up to do that, among them Jack Beasley, who dismissed *Power Without Glory* as lacking the necessary element of Socialist Realism. But Hardy was a seminal cultural influence, particularly in Melbourne: *Power Without Glory* had placed him as the captain of the flagship of Communist resistance, at the very time when the Menzies government's attempt to implement the Communist Party Dissolution Bill was being challenged in the High Court.

While still writing the novel, Hardy had enlisted several researchers to assist in compiling the necessary material, and—given its controversial nature—spoke of forming a special printing company and a publishing company to distribute it. The book did come to be published underground, and when it came to distribution, Hardy worked through the Party and the trade union movement. Then there were the high-profile activities of the Frank Hardy Defence Committee (chaired by Clem), at the time of the trial. In not much more than six months it organised more than 200 functions, many of them in private homes, but primarily with factory and union meetings. There were even two floats in the 1951 May Day march. All of this activity demonstrated what could be done for a cultural-political cause. This degree of mobilisation should not be allowed to fade away.[40]

A Realist Writers Group had already loosely formed, and authors had given spasmodic readings of short stories in factories. Some had published in trade union journals: primarily the Group offered a venue where writers could see and hear each other's work and take part in discussion groups. It was a time when reading was still a common leisure pursuit—people had never read so much as in flat periods during the war. Private lending libraries existed beyond middle-class suburbs, and now there was an additional taste for progressive literature articulating workers' experience and aspirations. To build a community of socialist readers and writers—potential mobilisers—would advance Party objectives across a broader front: in addition, the arts represented a 'passive transmission belt' for the cause. Moreover, since Commonwealth Literary Fund grants were rare, and now less likely to be given to left-wing writers, the development of infrastructure for writers and readers made sense. Two initiatives therefore arose from the context of Hardy's *cause célèbre*, both crystallising in March 1952.[41]

First was the registration of the Australasian Book Society (ABS). The initial meeting to discuss such a venture had been urged by the 'legal' distributor of *Power Without Glory* some time before the court case; George Seelaf of the Meat Industry Employees' Union was keen too. The aim was to publish books by realist writers regularly, making them available to workers and the interested public. Hardy suggested that the example of the prewar Left Book Club in England should be followed, with people subscribing and in effect paying for their books in instalments. Later he elaborated a scheme that included establishing factory libraries, and having more readings in factories to fuel discussion groups. The ABS would become an instrument of consciousness-raising. Yet it would not be an exclusively Party venture, could not be: as Ian Turner remarked, selling leftist novels was 'just as difficult as publishing them'. Moreover, there was a convergence with liberal nationalists such as AA Phillips, Leonard Mann and Alan Marshall, who joined the committee. But when the Party intervened to insist on the publication of Hardy's book on his travels in the Soviet Union, they resigned.

Stephen thought the book could have been better written, but he was impressed with Hardy ('the life and spirit of the Book Society'), and joined the committee. He admired his 'energy, vision and political acumen', and found him 'delightful' to work with. And although people had said that Hardy's Soviet book would lead to a fall off in interest, precisely the opposite happened. Hundreds of subscriptions were sold to workers—Hardy's work more than anyone's—and by October 1953 there were 1500 members, with the promise of more once a campaign was launched interstate. But the society would need at least twice as many members to be effective. Stephen joined others in going out and setting up ABS groups, and, finding that people were often shy about participating in discussion in front of real writers, he reached for bush ballads and shearers songs to loosen them up. Stephen was fired up by the prospect of publishing his short-story anthology, and another of the 'most revolutionary' of Henry Lawson's writings. The ABS 'really is something very big', he wrote to a friend, 'and I'm proud and happy to be associated with it'.[42]

Parallel to the founding of the Australasian Book Society was the appearance of the first issue of the *Realist Writer*. 'The old order', it proclaimed, 'is dying and the old literature, the old journalism with it. We aim to assist in the birth of a new order and its new literature.' Stephen contributed a manifesto, 'In Defence of Australia's Culture and Freedom'. There was a pattern, he averred: America 'sees Australia as the provider of cannon fodder to be thrown against the Asian people', while the country would become a dumping ground for American manufactures and agricultural surpluses. Stephen ran with an idea aired at a recent conference: our lads were to be militarised, and 'militarization and Americanization cannot be divorced'.

Wherever one looked, Americanisation was on the advance. The rollcall proceeded through film, radio and music, areas where Australia 'has already all but lost its national independence', to syndicated printed material and so to comics (a particular *bête noire* of intellectuals at the time). It was important that people appreciate that the 'Australian cultural crisis' did not exist in isolation, but was a 'very important section of the whole fight of the Australian people for real independence today'.

The *Realist Writer* began so tentatively (despite the confident vol. 1, no. 1) that each article was paginated separately. It was typewritten and cyclostyled, not typeset; on the cover, like flowers on wallpaper, was the word 'Peace' ('the dominant issue' of our time.) The plan was to have it appear monthly, commenting on social and political events, and publishing work by members of the group. In addition to Hardy, 'our group' included Ralph de Boissière, who provided the ABS with its first novel for publication (set in Trinidad, but outstandingly good); Walter Kaufmann, who had just completed one, and a recent newcomer, David Martin, together with various poets. Eric Lambert in Sydney, whose novel-in-progress was said to be even better than his previous success *The Twenty Thousand Thieves*, was also a presence. Nonetheless, the paper declared, 'we shall be looking for written down experiences of men on the job and in the struggle, applying standards of realism and strength rather than of literary style'.

Indeed literary style as such it despised: Cyril Connolly was scorned for his remark about a writer being judged 'by the quality of his despair', which was simply indicative of the breakdown of the capitalist system. The 'detailed probing' of stream-of-consciousness writers 'had no more important purpose than to show indecision, futility, boredom, escape'. Socialist Realism was the way, because instead of pessimism its leading authors 'understood the processes of history and they know that the future is with the people'.[43]

Frank Hardy hoped that the *Realist Writer*, through discussion of socialist realism and other cultural issues, would become 'a minor *Novy Mir*'. There were more general hopes that writing would be published by promising workers; as Hardy saw it, writers ideally were 'worker-writers'. But the *Realist Writer* was not conspicuous in doing either of these things. A lot of the writing submitted was dire.

Bill Wannan edited the *Realist Writer* at first, and—as a man concerned with Australian folklore—was keen that the ABS should put out a more populist magazine. He was well aware that it would need many more members before it could do that. Wannan, concerned with getting the ABS up and running, seems to have gradually withdrawn, so that Stephen was effectively running the paper from the third issue (September 1952). It functioned basically as a bulletin board for the Realist Writers Group; sometimes with shades of the *Bulletin*. From the very first issue there was a column called 'Swag'. There were also statements by writers about their work. Poems appeared, too, most notably by John Manifold, Laurence Collinson and David Martin. The poems were often purposive. The English writer Alex Comfort said of Martin: 'People will sing poems and songs like that—they are like fists.' But most of the paper was taken up with news items, including pieces relating to the ABS, the Commonwealth Literary Fund, censorship issues, peace activities, McCarthyism, progressive theatre and the progress of writers, in Australia and abroad. Readers would have learned that by early 1953 *Power Without Glory* had appeared in 15 languages, and sold 200,000 copies worldwide.[44]

Stephen's broader approach to Australia's past—a militant sense of history, which gave a sense of inevitability to the people's struggle—advanced as he ran the *Realist Writer*. Discovering extra depth in Australia's history excited him: he delighted in learning, from a reprint of Alexander Harris's *Settlers and Convicts* (1847), that anti-authoritarianism—and even the epithet 'crawler'—were well established in New South Wales by the early nineteenth century. But to connect with the past, with an embodiment of the Australian tradition, was even more exciting. In 1952 he went with a small group of writers to see the poet Bernard O'Dowd:

> how that creative, rebel Irish blood surged in his old veins that afternoon! Asked to read from *The Bush*, he was helped unsteadily to his feet. Despite doctor's warnings, he would not sit to recite his own verse. His unwithered sincerity forbade it. After a few lines his voice gathered resonance, his stance stiffened, his black boot thumped the floor in time to his own verse: he was back making his testimony … singing in unwearied stanzas, tremulous as a heat-filled noon-day in the bush, of the great inspiration to be won by Australians from their own country … The vision, as O'Dowd puts it, of 'the great Australia yet to be' … is the continuing and dominant note in our literature and thought. The more we study our yesterday, the more we will grasp the significance of this, the undying note now stronger than ever and reinforced by a thousand harmonies.[45]

Writers in particular needed to know Australian authors, both famous and less recognised. They should follow contemporary Australian writing, simultaneously making themselves familiar with the theoretical works of socialist realism, and regularly read publications like *Soviet Literature*. The aim should be to develop a literature 'national in form, but socialist in content.' There was no conflict; to the contrary, a reassuring congruency. Stephen regularly quoted AA Phillips' observation that to this day no Australian writer has identified so completely with proletarian subject matter as did Lawson and Furphy.[46]

Others were unable to countenance any such synthesis or accommodation. For them literature existed to adumbrate political action: in the words of Comrade Stalin, writers were 'the engineers of human souls'. Following this line of thinking, and in search of documentation, Eric Lambert went looking for a jailable offence, and Kylie Tennant, gathering material on the lives of prostitutes, managed to get herself arrested for soliciting. As workers, they accepted that they were subject to the same Party rules as anybody else.

The socialist realist ideal was to represent the 'typical'—not the average, but 'the individual who combines the best characteristic qualities of the general type', advanced as a 'positive hero'. There was no place here for a free play of the imagination. The Party operative JB Miles could not understand why Katharine Susannah Prichard would not submit her manuscripts for Communist Party approval before publication. Also writing in Western Australia was the poet Vic Williams. A waterside worker, his best work was on industrial subjects: girded by a confident rhyming structure, his poems displayed a lightly tamed rawness. He did not like the way the *Realist Writer* seemed to be heading.

When Stephen started a Comment feature in the paper, Williams was one of the first to write in, stating that he had consciously set out to write about the economic struggles of the people: 'to the extent I have succeeded I am better than most other Australian writers'. In the same issue Stephen cautioned that 'We must learn to know, not idealise, the workers.' In private he would deliver a more stinging rebuke. He referred to Williams' 'infantile leftism', of a kind abandoned in the Soviet Union in the 1950s, and how his attitude was one 'of almost lunatic self-satisfaction', exhibiting a 'proletarian arrogance long since hammered out of our writers over here'. His poetry paid for it: yes, there was a real feeling for cadences and rhythm and words, but it was written to appeal to militants. There was no sense of the 'warmth & richness & *potential flowering*' of the people. Stephen was also angry with the way that, because 'I happened to be born in the wrong suburb', he was regarded as being not quite kosher in his socialism. Moreover, 'the liberation of the working class is *not* the task of the working class alone.'

Stephen's involvement in the peace movement, which was not always amenable to Party control, led him to think about the 'broad masses' of the people rather than simply the proletariat. Realist Writers Group members should think about how they related to them: should they seek to differentiate themselves, by their political program, or should they try to articulate 'what is common to us and our traditions'? This was Stephen's preference; instead, he was increasingly aware of the narrowness of 'a group which sticks to itself, refusing to take any active part in important broad organisations'. The 'truths of Marxist science' were important, and people should be led to them; instead, there was an ever tighter sectarianism, centred in Sydney. Recent discussion of ABS publications in *Tribune*, the Sydney Communist newspaper, not only assumed Party ownership of the society, but was marked by a condemnation of 'all books not written as they would write'. *Tribune,* Stephen argued, 'seeks to narrow the base, rather than broaden it. Think of how it would review *Such Is Life*.'[47]

A real magazine, as distinct from a writers bulletin, had been on the agenda of the Realist Writers Group for quite some time. That had been as a separate publication, but Stephen began to feel that the *Realist Writer* might provide the basis for the broader venture. The cosiness John Manifold discerned in the paper would have to be transcended, cast off with the narrowness. Even a Party official had asked Stephen why did it have to 'read so much like a *Communist* journal'? The new journal Stephen had in mind would not be addressed exclusively to the working class, but also to sections of 'other classes' who were 'determined to join with us in defence of peace & national independence'. A vigorous battle must be fought on the middle-class intellectual front, he told Vic Williams. The Realist Writers Group approved the new, expanded journal; they were aware of a number of left-wing writers who might be drawn in. Stephen, to ensure control of the transformation, used a simple device: he went out and registered a new name. *Overland* would be his.[48]

3

CLEM

MEANJIN FINDS FORM

1945–c. 1960

The place of little and literary magazines

Clem would have been aware of the *Little Review*, the avant-garde magazine that had started in Chicago, drew Ezra Pound to become its guiding spirit, published extracts from *Ulysses* and then found itself in court. Little magazines—the name an implicit homage to the *Little Review*—were valued by Clem: he understood they were part of the modernist project, arose from writerly urgencies, were 'exploratory, stimulating, useful to the health and growth of contemporary literature'. But for all their gadfly characteristics, they were usually fugitive—money was always a big problem, and circulation (if not influence) invariably small. Moreover, they lacked '*continuity* of publication', and were not big enough to publish the longish story or the 'full-dress' critical essay. The latter was one of his favourite terms, and a key to Clem's aspirations.

Meanjin had been a little magazine—a showcase for Queensland poets—and had emerged tentatively. But it had broadened in content, and it is likely that the idea of a literary review had always lurked in the background. Nina, aware as she was of the Russian 'thick journals', may have helped to check Clem's impulsiveness: one step at a time. Meanwhile Clem was gradually moving towards the view that 'a magazine devoted to literature cannot be completely literary'. In his first Melbourne Notes to Contributors, he restated that new creative work was sought that 'accept[ed] the challenge of the Australian environment', endeavouring 'to integrate today's imagination and thought in prose and verse'. He declared that '*Meanjin* is particularly anxious to develop a core of sound literary criticism', for '*Meanjin* wishes to learn much of the modern mind—but even more so of the continuing mind'. Any tension between the two could be productive, since Clem believed that 'the true creative artist accepts tradition and enriches it', changing it in the process. Consideration of the broader social and political context was therefore essential.

Whereas the little magazine addressed a coterie, the literary review sought to reach an educated public. Clearly the role of the editor—ideally urbane, cultivated, liberal in the best sense—was crucial in this project, as he sought to publish material of 'quality', ultimately resting on his personal choice. Usually this would be drawn from the centre-left, but by definition could extend to a broader range of political and social assumptions. Brought into being by his directive hand, and eclipsing when not extinguishing his own creative writing, *Meanjin* would become Clem's great Work in Progress.[1]

Sitting in his study at Melbourne University, Clem must have felt he had been placed in the box seat: later there were times when he slipped into dating the magazine from its relocation there. His and *Meanjin*'s position were seen by many as the ideal one for a literary editor and his magazine. In England, a questionnaire sent to readers of *Horizon* had exposed real resistance to the idea of state support for writers, on the grounds of loss of autonomy. It was the universities that were seen as a possible 'new kind of postwar patron'. In America there was sometimes a measure of support for literary ventures, but the association often turned out to be disappointing. Even quarterlies like the *Kenyon Review* were not securely funded by the host institution, despite spreading their name far and wide.

America provided much of the inspiration for *Meanjin*'s broadened horizons. Following on from the contact with American soldier-poets during the war, Clem was much taken by the lectures given in 1945 by the visiting HS Canby on how American writing became American literature, effectively creating a national culture. In writing to Canby, he traced the considerable American literary influence here, not least because it was *homely*. American writing, coming from another 'new' country, shared everyday assumptions that were similar to our own. 'On the other hand, fiction from England', Clem wrote, 'depicted life which was relatively foreign to us.' He had, as we have seen, been unimpressed by England on his visit there in 1939. A number of significant literary magazines were folding at the time.

Yet it was England, rather than America, that showed him how to do it. He would have seen copies of John Lehmann's *New Writing*, notable not for its modernism but for a radical sense of contemporary engagement. (It may have contributed to Clem's keen sense of documenting the present.) Of Lehmann, too, it has been said that he 'viewed editorship as a higher form of authorship'. Similarly, Clem's reiteration of the need for 'quality' may have come from Cyril Connolly: his *Horizon* began in the same year as *Meanjin*, and was seen explicitly as a cultural marshalling yard during the war.

Even Connolly was prepared to acknowledge that in contemporary literature American was superior to English, which was Clem's instinct. One American magazine he did follow closely, though hardly ever mentioned, was *Partisan Review*. (Perhaps it became a trade secret.) Originally associated with the Communist Party, and adopting the viewpoint of 'the revolutionary working class', by the late 1930s *PR* had become anti-Stalinist and would move towards a non-affiliated radicalism. Its growing sense of preserving a literary tradition from the effects of mass culture was also congenial to Clem—as would be the increasing penchant for nonfiction over creative work.[2]

With the move to a university setting, 'Contemporary Verse and Prose' was no longer the subtitle of *Meanjin Papers*; instead it proclaimed itself to be 'A Quarterly of Literature'. But the road to an increase in size was bumpy; wartime restrictions were still in force. The 1945 issues still appeared on newsprint. Nonetheless, given the context of national reconstruction spearheaded by a Labor government, the prospects were good. 'No Australian concerned with art and literature', wrote Clem in his first Melbourne editorial, 'can fail to feel that something new is stirring throughout the country ... This alertness, this heightened consciousness, is evident also in the cultural field.' The new drive was coming, Clem believed, 'mainly from the younger people ... largely untouched by the between-wars disillusionment'. Aware of the corrosive effects of capitalism, their idealism, applied to politics, culture and art, would fire the national imagination. Now there was encouraging talk of a national cultural council, and a national film board; and while Clem welcomed that, he pointed to the dangers of political interference.

The issue opened with a hyper-enthusiastic piece by Lloyd Ross—the originator of the idea of a cultural council—which spoke of building up a national, democratic culture from well-stocked community centres. But this did not happen. While Clem became an activist for the cultural council, that idea did not materialise either. The concept was still far ahead of its time. Indeed, renowned British director Tyrone Guthrie, advising Chifley, recommended a national theatre, or company—in London, so that young actors and directors could be properly trained.[3]

Melbourne calling

The University of Melbourne was headed by the urbane John Medley, an Englishman (as a number of people holding important educational posts then still were). More than most intellectuals, Medley had given some thought to the Australia that would emerge after the war. He had plans to develop theatre, fine arts and architecture at the university; and with Colin Badger, the director of the university's Extension Board (which carried out adult education in Melbourne), Medley had been following *Meanjin*'s rising star. They were alarmed by its difficulties and Clem's declarations that the magazine might have to close.

Also working at the Extension Board was Donovan Clarke. A footloose bohemian character, Clarke knew the Christesens, having visited them when he was in the army camp at Kanungra. He submitted material regularly to the magazine. Some of it was published, some rejected, but he accepted that with good grace. In July 1944 Clem received a letter from Clarke that must have caused alarm: Clarke, it seems, had been approached to found a literary quarterly in Melbourne—something 'more academic than *Meanjin*, and more creative than the *Australian Quarterly*': a famous Parisian heavyweight was the precedent in mind, capable of publishing a long short story or a critical piece that might run to 30,000 words. Clarke enjoined secrecy—not even the Palmers knew—after all, nothing might come of it. He was telling Clem only as an indication that he was conscious of his interests, and that nothing would be done underhand.

Just how much he bore Clem in mind was apparent in another letter that arrived three weeks later. Previously Clarke had written to say that he might, for a number of reasons, move back to Queensland, not least to help with *Meanjin*. Perhaps it was he who (switching into reverse) came up with the suggestion, now made to Clem, that *Meanjin* should come to Melbourne. The scheme for a Melbourne magazine would be dropped, he said; 'instead we would enlarge *Meanjin*'. Clem would be guaranteed a salary, and have to accept a small editorial board. Again he was asked to be discreet: at this stage, not even the vice-chancellor knew about the proposal.

On the same day as Clarke's letter arrived—and to Clem's great surprise—a second, more substantive one came from Colin Badger. He noted *Meanjin*'s track record, and as a professional involved in adult education, applauded the way the magazine made a real contribution to raising standards of taste and judgement in the community. Badger's hope was that, in association with the University of Melbourne, *Meanjin* might become 'the real literary periodical for the country'. At the same time he showed what Clem would have seen as a rare understanding of his difficulties. 'Success is usually the undoing of all such ventures', Badger cooed, meaning that they came to require more than a spare-time commitment, while at the same time offering little prospect of sufficient financial return. This Badger thought he could provide—at least to the extent of £250. Melbourne University Press would publish the magazine, and should be able to cover printing and some administrative costs from sales and advertisements. So said Gwyn James, its manager.

Soon after, Clem was flown to Melbourne—and was so keen to move he thought of sending down material for his current issue to be typeset, sidestepping pesky Brisbane printers. Staying in Badger's flat, he was 'tense and nervous': among the various meetings, there was one scheduled with the suave vice-chancellor, alone. He had been told that Medley backed the idea strongly, believing that a Melbourne *Meanjin* would help members of the arts faculty reach a broader audience. Shortly afterwards the Extension Board approved the venture, 'doing ourselves honour', said the professor of philosophy, 'by trying to help such a good show'. There was further good news: the Extension Board could offer Nina a job as tutor organiser, a post that involved visiting various locations to set up and launch discussion groups. Her salary was higher than Clem's honorarium; she would hold the position for some years, with distinction.

Clem's meeting with Medley had been a success. He could say that he had been invited by the vice-chancellor to bring *Meanjin* to the University of Melbourne; but there was no documentation. Various points had been raised, but Clem was a supplicant, 'sensitive about my lack of formal education', easily neutralised by the swish of high-powered affability. A letter he did receive, from the Extension Board, was more notable for its caveats: the £250 grant was to be paid for one year, and 'in no way' was the board committed to extending it beyond 1945; 'the University … incurs no obligation or liability beyond this offer'. The presumption was that it would; Badger had hoped that the term of the offer would be for five years. But this commitment had been overruled.

Clem was guaranteed full editorial control and management of the magazine, but the concomitant became that the university felt it should be troubled by *Meanjin* as little as possible. The registrar shrugged it off as one of 'Medley's follies'. The promise of secretarial assistance was never fully realised, while talk of additional funding melted into air. Clem's anchorage, the Extension Board, was—as Badger himself recognised—'the least important of all the departments', with very little influence around the university. So Clem had little leverage. The basic fact was that *Meanjin* remained on annual funding for the whole of his editorship—and beyond. Not only was the commitment minimal; there was always the risk its terms could be changed.[4]

Publishing *Meanjin* with Melbourne University Press was part of the original proposal. MUP would handle distribution (including subscriptions), and other matters including publicity, which would free Clem from a great deal of routine work. He welcomed that: more than 75 per cent of his time was taken up with such matters, he claimed. On his initial sortie to Melbourne, Clem had found Gwyn James 'helpful, business-like, considerate'. But he was horrified to receive, some weeks after his return to Brisbane, a letter from James discussing the future relationship with the press. It might take the form of a ten-year contract, with Clem remaining as proprietor; or that Clem should 'assign' *Meanjin* to the press, and then be offered a contract—in effect becoming a press employee. This was the favoured option of the MUP board. 'What the hell is going on, Colin?' Clem wrote to Badger, who was himself surprised at the idea. James said that he had been instructed to put the proposition by his board, and wasn't surprised by Clem's firm rejection of it. But Clem remained apprehensive: he did not want control of *Meanjin* slipping from his hands.

As an issue had failed to appear before he left Brisbane, Clem was relieved, once he got to Melbourne, to find James 'exceedingly helpful, and as keen as mustard'. A former history lecturer, James had printer's ink in his veins. He was good at his job, if 'complaining and procrastinating': he could alternate enthusiasm with sudden stubbornness. At MUP he still had to cope with paper shortages, while there were serious long-term problems. The press doubled as printer to the university, a service department, and was expected to be financially self-sustaining. James—no less than Clem—had ambitions of his own: to become 'University Publisher', augmented by a university printer and sustained by a full-time sales representative and overseas agents. Instead—as Clem would later come to feel with *Meanjin*—he had to contend with 'Certain sections of the University … almost hostile' to the press.

Clem was becoming alarmed as *Meanjin*'s circulation was visibly shrinking. There was a general decline in book sales in the immediate postwar period, since people seemed to be reading less; but *Meanjin*'s 4000 copies dropped to 3000 at the end of 1945, and then—after another final issue for the year had failed to appear—to 2000 copies in 1946. One cause was that Robertson & Mullens, booksellers and publishers, had slashed their order by 850 copies; the impending association with MUP threw into relief the piles of *Meanjin* they were not moving. More immediately, since MUP handled subscriptions, Clem often found himself without the money on hand to pay printers' bills. He had to make up the shortfall himself. He was not happy. Clem felt 'rather like a patient who is being kept "alive" by small injections of a drug—and yet is slowly dying'.

For his part James found that 'Every time we offer an inch in concessions, a yard is seized as a first instalment.' He had increased, gradually, the amount of money Clem was to be paid from £50 an issue to £135. In his plans for new plant and equipment, he delayed production of new 'pocket editions' (paperbacks), so that *Meanjin* would have 'No 1 priority'. But Clem had taken the magazine to Specialty Press, which, in James' view, produced a shoddy product—bearing the MUP imprint. Clem was unappreciative of the efforts being made, particularly with publicity, and the way things were going, *Meanjin* would cause the press to 'lose heavily'. While James had indicated as late as November 1945 that a final number for that year would appear, in fact it slipped away. James could see no urgency about a quarterly.

Meanwhile Clem, always feeling besieged, responded as would any resourceful general, by opening up another front. When James pointed out the necessity of cutting back the size of the magazine, Clem immediately countered with talk of producing not four smaller issues a year, but six. (Quite correctly, he pointed out that for a quarterly too small a size would have neither balance nor scope.) Another scheme was to bring out a cultural monthly magazine—since there was a clear gap in commentary: *Angry Penguins Broadsheet* was showing signs of filling it, drawing in authors and topics Clem had already lined up for *Meanjin*. (Meanwhile he began a Broadsheet of his own, consisting of poetry and practical criticism, to assist young writers and students.) He was also, to James' considerable annoyance, involving himself more directly in publishing—with the Meanjin Press, with other publishers—and resisting definition of his role in connection with MUP. Relations deteriorated; Clem boycotted the press building.[5]

For some time Clem had been developing his relations with Ted Harris, the publisher at Georgian House. Harris had been handling a number of Meanjin Press titles, with some success. Clem had produced other manuscripts for Harris, who declared an interest in distributing *Meanjin*—Clem's greatest problem. His terms were more favourable than MUP's—much more favourable, as he would guarantee at least £50 an issue, whether the copies were sold or not. Harris was prepared to do that for the prestige involved, and told Clem that even a loss of £200 a year would be a good investment.[6]

Harris could offer no guarantee beyond a year; but then, with the basic grant, the Extension Committee offered no more either. The challenge for Clem was to extricate himself from MUP without severing the university connection: this was done, but not without damage. The university had scaled down the grant, and now the limited secretarial help was withdrawn. The council would come in with a special grant of £50, but this was for the specific purpose of *Meanjin* publishing contributions from members of the modern language departments. Once the Commonwealth Literary Fund provided an emergency grant, as it did in 1946, the university felt less compelled to sustain the magazine. There had been no formal agreement with the press, but Badger had assured Clem that none was necessary to receive the subsidy, yet there was no overall statement of the university's commitment. *Meanjin* was, as AR Chisholm, the professor of French put it, 'nobody's baby, and did not even have a birth certificate'. The university would offer support, but of a limited kind—premises, and the restricted annual grant.[7]

So Clem took *Meanjin* to Georgian House, which worked for a while, but it was a small firm with enough challenges of its own. He took back the distribution (amicably), decided to pay for secretarial help, and looked elsewhere for some work. There was book reviewing, other journalism, broadcasting, lecturing for the Extension Board on Australian literature (which helped to make him a campus personality), and his later position as representative for the English publisher Heinemann. Clem did not want to return fully to newspaper work: apart from anything else, it would then be difficult to meet the growing demands of *Meanjin*. The move south had certainly broadened opportunity, but the correlative problems had become more complex.

The Palmers: a Queensland beachhead

In Melbourne were Australia's most famous literary couple of the day, Vance and Nettie Palmer. Their influence on Clem cannot be overestimated. Vance, a handsome man of little more than average height, usually sported a bow tie over regular blue shirts, which suited him; otherwise he dressed in neat, brown, casual clothes, which went well with his 'customary shade of mahogany'. And, answering a question that was on everyone's lips, he had served overseas—even if the Armistice had been declared in 1918 before he saw action. He had, in fact, already been to Europe twice, the second time moving in the circle of AR Orage and the *New Age*. Here he had rubbed shoulders with people such as Katherine Mansfield, Wyndham Lewis and Ezra Pound, among others. More importantly, Vance had imbibed guild socialist ideas of community, craftsmanship and folk culture, sustaining a lifelong detestation of cities, industrial society and mass culture.

A determined writer—who had been prepared to write pulp fiction to support himself—Vance Palmer would come to be praised for the wide social range of his serious fiction, Jack Lindsay even pointing to an 'affinity with Tolstoy'. A greater influence, as Nettie pointed out, was Turgenev—which can be seen in the anaemic pages of Vance's one novel set in Melbourne, *The Swayne Family*. AD Hope spoke of his having the 'vision of a poet', but others like Christina Stead said that Vance could not write. Certainly Palmer's prose can be clogged, his plots insubstantial, while intensities are usually dodged: Jack Lindsay noted that he 'shrinks unduly at various intimacies and contacts, emotional and physical'. In person, despite 'a slow, easy, generous smile', Vance always held himself in reserve. There was always urbanity, but he struck some as being a cold fish.[8]

By the time Clem first met him Vance had returned to Queensland subjects for his fictional material. His earlier novel *The Passage* (1930) had already indicated a strong regressive streak. For Vance the novel—inspired by Caloundra, where the Palmers lived for a time—was a form of dreaming. Certain themes revealingly come to the fore. The main character, modelled on a fisherman they knew, is presented as a sturdy figure 'who drew power from the earth beneath him'. He sustains the family, even a flash brother who returns to the settlement; so too does his first love, returning after unsuccessfully venturing abroad as an artist. Back they come to an enclosed world; the implication is that you leave it at your peril.

'We are a bush people', Vance once wrote: the Australia beyond the cities remained for him the most authentic. And as David Walker put it, 'Palmer felt that if Australia was not socialist in reality, then it showed signs of a socialist disposition.' That the place had been isolated had provided—might still provide—a real opportunity to build up culture and community, and to reconfigure mateship. He had recently stated that the writer had a role as 'a co-ordinating force … a means by which people get to know themselves'. In Vance's view, the production of masterpieces was less important than the way 'literature opened fresh windows to life'. But one important point he truly grasped: 'local colour to be true and real must emanate from the subconscious, having been previously absorbed'.[9]

Nettie was a good six inches (15cm) shorter than Vance, a metaphor for the way she always placed herself second. To some extent her emotional needs were unmet by him, since by nature he was undemonstrative and withheld. ('Mate', they called each other.) Perhaps as a consequence Nettie increasingly became indifferent to her personal appearance, and wore dowdy clothes. Her face became more severe. But her eyes sparkled even before she spoke, for Nettie was vivacious, loved repartee, and would return phrases by giving them an ironic twist. And so she wrote: 'skittish highbrowism', Arthur Phillips initially thought it. AD Hope was nearer the mark when, while noting her 'intellectual toughness', he described it as 'good talk', the 'style at once feminine, Australian and civilised'. But Nettie was no dilettante. Her French was so good she read Proust in it, so effortlessly that she couldn't remember which volumes she had read in that language first. And she learned Spanish—partly to read South American literature, for the comparative light it might shed on Australia's.

Nettie's stiff-backed deportment (a trademark of the Presbyterian Ladies College) at once reminded any visitor that she was of the Melbourne establishment. She was the niece of the famous judge and radical Henry Bournes Higgins (and would write his biography). Her own radicalism went further: she and Vance were civil liberties activists, while Nettie took part in the famous debate at Melbourne University on the Spanish Civil War. (The Palmers had been living in Spain when the war broke out.) In Melbourne, Nettie became president of the Spanish relief organisation—just as later she would work for Jewish refugees from Nazism.

Apart from her extensive reviewing, Nettie was a great encourager. She ran the Palmer secretariat: Dymphna Cusack said that although she met the Palmers only twice in twenty years, she felt they were friends. The interest extended to male writers: after the appearance of his first novel, Leonard Mann was invited to come and stay. For Nettie, Australian authors did not constitute a club so much as a vanguard.

At the centre of it, always, was Vance. Significantly, Nettie stopped writing and publishing poetry—the necessary cultivation of an individual sensibility could not be maintained. Instead, she subordinated her voice to his, even writing some of Vance's radio scripts. Believing him to be 'better and greater than I am in every way', his success became increasingly important to her. Meanwhile she ran the household.[10]

Vance had been approached by Clem for an introduction to his *Queensland Journey*; shortly afterwards, he called on Christesen in his spacious government office. For Clem, Vance was 'the most representative of Australian writers': he enticed him into *Meanjin* by asking him to write a tribute to Randolph Bedford. By 1944 he would write, 'I was IMMENSELY pleased and gratified with Vance's article,' he told Nettie. 'When I first read it I felt that the four years of battling … were well worth it—comment which was EXACTLY the sort of thing which I've been wanting *Meanjin* to carry.'

Nettie, above all others, became Clem's confidant. She constantly made suggestions or comments as to contributors, articles and tactics—even though her casual description of Clem as a 'literary liaison officer' was constantly thrown in her teeth. 'If you say that *Meanjin*'s neglected, dying … [people] won't want to help', she told him—particularly when its expanding size pointed the other way. 'Forgive my grandmotherly tone', she wrote, as she fussed over his health: Clem was annoyed that Nettie seemed more concerned to discuss that, when she came to Brisbane, than meet a group for 'a *Meanjin* yabba'. Nor would she hear his grievances, or comment on his difficulties with the other founding poets. He hadn't shouldered them out, he countered, when she hinted at what was being said around the traps. 'I never wished to be editor,' he expostulated; 'all I wanted was … to get the publication going, and let them run it editorially.' Repeatedly he talked of closing the journal down. But if you do that, said Nettie, who would replace you? For, as the author of a pioneering account of Australian literature, Nettie was well aware of the importance of continuity. Too often it was difficult to find out what had been thought and done here before. As she complained to Rex Ingamells, 'It is as if we had no past.' So she joined Clem's national committee for *Meanjin*, but came to chide him for his letters. Surely he could be more systematic in his approach? Not appreciating that an outpouring was the essence of the Clemmiad (even Clem referred to them as 'winges' [*sic*]), she pointed out they must only exhaust him further. And they were 'darned hard to answer'.[11]

On their intermittent visits, the Palmers may have implanted in Clem the idea of moving away from Brisbane. He complained to Nettie how 'Most of the work I receive from Qld writers is just punk.' If it were not for her and Vance's support, and those of others 'in the south …

Meanjin simply cld not exist'. And then he felt isolated, removed from the national conversation. 'I have a terrible feeling of impotence.' Once the *Angry Penguins* case blew up, Clem found it extremely difficult to comment, 'unless I am fed with material'. He needed to be nearer the centre of things.[12]

The Palmers had been quietly lobbying on Clem's behalf, and Nettie wrote to Clem saying it was 'awfully good news' that *Meanjin* was likely to come to Melbourne. 'There isn't much of a spike in our free-flowing Yarra', she warned him; 'you will have to find a foothold for yourself.' The place, she had decided long ago, was 'stiffish, and rather philistine in its genteel, detached way'. Vance, who probably still thought of himself as a Queenslander, had similar sentiments. But he was sympathetic to Clem, not least because twenty years earlier he had been involved in a stillborn venture rather like *Meanjin*.

Once in Melbourne, Clem would soon have been made aware of the sharp divide between the Palmers' writing lives and their public activities. The family circle, which included two intellectual daughters, accounted for some of it. They entertained, sparingly. But now Vance's projection was national. Apart from his occasional journalism, his 'distinctive, dry voice' could be heard on the ABC, discussing new books every Sunday. And having been a force in the Victorian branch of the Fellowship of Australian Writers, he was now a member of the Advisory Board of the Commonwealth Literary Fund, and would become its chair. With Nettie the overly willing helpmate, Vance had matured into a literary statesman: Australia's archetypal writer. People spoke of his integrity, and at his funeral AA Phillips recalled 'the splendid serenity of his presence'. But the price was beginning to be exacted: Nettie had recently had a coronary thrombosis, and her first stroke. Vance's first heart attack would come a few years later. There would be limits to the degree they could be leant on.[13]

Clem and *Meanjin* had to be supported, Nettie believed: 'its existence is a symbolic triumph'. But she soon found that her loyal attachment would often be tested, and that her own involvement was not enough. Clem wanted Vance to be an *explicit* supporter of *Meanjin*, lending his name. Yet when Vance did make suggestions for the magazine, Clem was inclined to contest them, one by one. For some months there was a rift: Nina acted as peacemaker. Relations were resumed, but Nettie noticed that in his difficulties Clem always managed to blame someone else. 'Very gloomy letter from Clem', she jotted; 'gloomy in more directions at once than anyone else can be.' And—partly because he was short of money, and did not want to go back to newspaper work, Clem always had an eye out for a possible job—even overseas. Once he spoke of the opportunities for journalists suddenly available in Japan. But such ideas were sheer escapism, because the problem, as Nettie discerned, was more basic. His 'impossibly restless mind' arose from his keenness to write fiction: editing was not enough. 'Clem', she noted in her diary, is 'attacked by feelings of inadequacy mixed with immortal longings.'[14]

The Palmers had taken up a joint project about the time Clem and Nina moved to Melbourne. This was the preparation of extracts from the diaries Nettie had been keeping. By late 1947 Vance and Nettie were fully taken up with *Fourteen Years*: when they first mentioned it to Clem, he published a sample and suggested a publisher. But gradually the idea emerged that it should be published by the Meanjin Press. Although Clem was going cold on his auxiliary venture, he could see that, since the Palmers wanted to be fully involved in the book's production, his press could provide the means. In effect he turned it over to them: they would meet all production costs, as well as paying him a consultant's fee.

But it was not quite as simple as that, for the *Meanjin* office handled all payments and other transactions. Payments jointly for the book and for *Meanjin* caused complications; despatching copies overloaded the system. It was 'a fine ruddy mess', Clem noted, directing his anger away from the Palmers towards his secretary and the printer. He begged them to find some other distributor, but Nettie refused. Their relations again became strained for a time. For Clem, the experience confirmed his feeling that he could no longer 'kid myself' about the Meanjin Press. It had been a failure: 'I sought the prestige,' he confessed to Vance. 'I *could not* succeed without risking a fairly substantial sum of money.' But the Palmers had reason to be satisfied. Even though not all the copies printed of *Fourteen Years* came to be bound as books, they made some money on the venture.

Nettie's 'Extracts from a Private Journal', as *Fourteen Years* was subtitled, is a very writerly book. Hence despite the greater critical attention feminism has brought to Nettie in recent years, the work remains far less known than it should. Appearing in 1948, *Fourteen Years* discreetly concludes in 1939, as the world is drifting towards war. The range is impressive. The book opens in Queensland: the glimpses of fishermen and Indigenous sailors are sharp and sympathetic. But Nettie's impressions of particular works and extracts from letters of other writers increasingly come to the fore, along with focused descriptions of them. Projected is a sense of a full Australian literary life. For contrast, there are passages on London, Paris and life in a Spanish village—with telling glimpses of André Gide, the Left Bank figures Sylvia Beach and Adrienne Monnier, and even the sexologist Havelock Ellis.[15]

Enter AA Phillips; the cause of Aust. Lit.

Among the people who were there to greet Clem and Nina on their arrival in Melbourne in 1945 was AA (Arthur Angel) Phillips. Arthur had just had his first article accepted for publication in the journal—it would appear in the first Melbourne issue, beginning an association that would last right through to the 1980s. Arthur was primarily a schoolmaster, at Wesley College; as a young man he had graduated from Melbourne and gone on to Oxford, but found it an anti-climax. He was not the only one in that student generation to have found Melbourne more stimulating. But he was prompted by the experience to contemplate the ways Australian culture was different. Years later, I put it to him that being Jewish in gentile society perhaps predisposed him towards articulating Australian distinctiveness within the Anglosphere: though surprised by the idea, he readily agreed.

Given his school teaching—his preoccupation as well as his occupation—Phillips made reviewing and the short critical essay his métier. Although drawn to the theatre, and hopeful one day of producing a book on George Bernard Shaw, it was the Australian tradition—the label itself provocative then, as most believed Australia had none—that engaged his attention. Vance Palmer, too, was intrigued by what he termed *The Legend of the Nineties.* Phillips, focusing on the writers of the period, saw their significance (extending beyond Australia) as being the first to have 'broken out of the cage of the middle class', writing about ordinary folk for a broader audience. Pugnaciously democratic, their work helped to sustain humane values; they should become the cornerstone of an Australian tradition. Phillips did not care for social realism, feeling that its principles and self-conscious aesthetic got in the way of the writing. Nor did he care for Martin Boyd—too much the Anglophile. As for the Jindies, 'they don't inspire me to anything much', he told Clem, 'except spleen at their self-importance & bad writing'.

But there was a convergence between Christesen's aims and those of Phillips. Arthur thought *Southerly* 'maidenly', in its careful avoidance of politics and its reticence in cultural nationalism. Christesen, on the other hand, had an 'earnest sense of what needed to be done', giving *Meanjin* 'bite and vitality'. Their political opinions could diverge, but the two men shared, as Arthur put it, 'an almost obsessive hope to see … the emergence of Australian arts of vigorous confidence and increasing maturity'.

AA Phillips' most famous contribution to *Meanjin* was the short essay 'The Cultural Cringe', published in 4/1950. The expression would, a generation later, enter the language; is now sometimes used in England; and has on occasion in Australia come to be misapplied to people adopting a mildly nationalist position. But as Phillips carefully diagnosed it seventy years ago, the term was a protest against the insidious influence that instamatic comparison with metropolitan achievement could have, particularly on readers. Any sense of high cultural possibility was thereby weakened, leading to the 'denaturalised' Australian intellectual. 'The core of the difficulty', Phillips wrote, 'is … that, in the back of the Australian mind, there sits a minatory Englishman.' The fear was of mediocrity, rather than engaging with authenticity. At least writers, in the past twenty years, had progressed in becoming 'unself-consciously ourselves'. But much was still to be done: the cringe was culturally crippling, worse than the traditional isolation. Ideally one day there would be, as he put it, not an overcompensating strut, but 'a relaxed erectness of carriage'.

Clem didn't think much of 'the Cultural Cringe': perhaps he thought it too much a Melbourne view, as some did. But following a good reader response, he changed his tune. It was as well, for at a time when the universities gave Australian literature scant recognition, *Meanjin* needed Arthur's rigour. Acute in judgement, his style was as plain as it was perceptive: in person, his slowness of speech made it all the more effective. He could be quirkily humorous, and blunt. One day on the way to school, a boy pranced up to him with a cheery 'Good morning, sir!' A pause. 'Shut up!' came the unexpected reply. The boy slumped away.

Clem was also subjected to such bluntness. Arthur was inclined to recommend plain-speaking all round: shown an early editorial, he remarked that the terser sentences 'suit you better', and 'convey your sense of urgency'. Later he told Clem that a trailer he had written on public schools was 'hooey', and sent a rejoinder. Clem accepted this, for he had come to rely on Phillips' assessment of manuscripts, as well as his utility as a man who with apparent ease could write about Australian culture, past or present. But Arthur challenged him over some snide comments made in connection with emerging journals, overplaying his hand—'You are, in yourself, often a bloody fool and perhaps inclined to invent injuries …' Furious, Clem composed a long letter in reply, but wisely decided not to send it. Instead, he consoled himself with the knowledge that this Clemmiad would remain in the files. For two years, all correspondence with Phillips was delegated to his assistant editor. Clem could never quite accept that Arthur was a busy man, literature being only part of his life; twice he had come to see him, as requested, only for nothing substantial to emerge at the meeting. Thus even when Phillips volunteered a 'Tribute to *Meanjin*' in *Overland*, Clem could not resist (when thanking him) quarrelling over some of the remarks, and raking over long-dead coals. By this stage Arthur had more or less decided to retreat, as he had forewarned, 'to a level of polite distance'. He was secure in the high regard of the literary community—including much younger writers, such as Helen Garner. Years later, Clem had the grace to write, 'Whatever reputation the journal achieved was due largely to your contributions and your pervasive influence.'[16]

Australian writers felt as though they were 'trying to breathe in a vacuum', observed AA Phillips: no wonder, as others noted, they could be surprisingly gauche at social occasions. It was a factor helping to impel Phillips towards criticism, for even Judah Waten declared (when reviewing *Meanjin*), 'Without a body of creative literary criticism, Australian literature cannot advance.' Clem, having given a series of lectures and seminars through the university Extension Board shortly after arriving in Melbourne, sought to advance the cause wherever he could. He would always tend to circle round Vance Palmer and the 'socially conscious' writers, for he was mindful of the remark of the recurrently visiting American Australianist Hartley Grattan: the literary tradition here was 'a compound of sound learning, rebelliousness, ardent faith in the common man, and an even more ardent faith in the Australian future'. Clem was eager to plug the gaps, to redress the neglect that arose from a discontinuous tradition and a small or erratic readership. In January 1950 Clem told Phillips that he was planning 'full-length' essays on Marjorie Barnard, Flora Eldershaw, Katharine Susannah Prichard, Frank Dalby Davison, Kylie Tennant and Eleanor Dark. But this was easier said than done: only half were to reach fruition.[17]

The problem was that there was as yet little interest in Australian literature in the universities. (There would have been even less but for the lectures funded by the Commonwealth Literary Fund.) It was the author Marjorie Barnard, rather than any academic, who wrote a pioneering analysis of Patrick White's fiction. (White's gratitude was expressed not only to her, but also by letting *Meanjin* publish a segment from his forthcoming *Voss*.) What is needed, Clem declared from his Uneasy Chair, was '*a different attitude of mind*'. Scholarship, criticism and literature should be brought together, in the interests of the country at large. 'The Australian scholar has failed the Australian reader time and time again,' he thundered. In 1954 Clem invited discussion on the matter in *Meanjin*. It became plain that even someone professing to espouse Australian literature, such as Allan Edwards in Perth, still regarded it as a junior branch of the trade, to be treated as something not needing formal recognition as a subject on its own. Sydney University was the most advanced, with all staff members having written or broadcast on Australian Literature, and with a high proportion of graduate students working in it.

But Melbourne! Clem had been agitating for Aust. Lit. courses to be established there when Ian Maxwell—misty-eyed from journeying into the sagas—was appointed professor. He would become chairman of the *Meanjin* board, but no further progress was made. Generally, Clem found historians more sympathetic to the project than English departments. But the Melbourne contribution to the *Meanjin* discussion came from outside the university, from Vance Palmer—who may have been the first to advocate, and name, a broader 'Australian Studies'. As Geoffrey Serle acknowledged years later, creative writers 'had much more to say about

Australia in the ideas [then] being floated … than the historians or any other commentators'.

The series began with a statement by AD Hope: from his standing as both a poet and a rising academic, he crisply wrote that even if it were conceded that Australian literature had deficiencies—it did—unquestionably it should be studied in its home country. (Hope himself would write appreciatively of Steele Rudd and Henry Lawson.) Yet not one of the eight teaching universities had so far established a course in Aust. Lit. He intended to introduce one at the Canberra University College—once his Melbourne boss Ian Maxwell permitted him. Yet even this course was initially envisaged as being undertaken only by people already trained in English or other advanced literatures. Nonetheless, Clem could justly claim that the *Meanjin* discussion had been significant: 'The arguments in favour broke the universities' reluctance to touch the subject.' In 1962 Sydney—acknowledging *Meanjin*'s role as a prompt—established a full chair in Aust. Lit. By 1975 it was taught as a full course in six of the eighteen universities—or as a significant segment of a course in virtually all of them.[18]

Clem and the creative writers

For all Clem's concern to establish Australian literature in the universities, it was the new, raw material for such a discipline that excited him most. Usually the postwar *Meanjin* led with a short story; he would have liked, Clem would say, to have a whole issue devoted to fiction. But the material at hand was usually disappointing. AA Phillips complained in *Meanjin*'s pages of the way many short stories were 'not so much continuing an Australian tradition as stuck in an Australian rut', following the tracks of the pioneers—'who followed no man's tracks'. The point was elaborated by Tim Burstall. Most published short stories were short, trite, and poorly written, avoided contemporary issues, and were set in remote places. Contributions from overseas—Clem ruefully observed—could sometimes save the day.[19]

In the issues from the decade following *Meanjin*'s coming to Melbourne, there are many short-story writers who appeared in the journal only once. The recurring names are those firmly in the Australian social-realist tradition: Tom Hungerford, Eric Lambert—each to a limited extent—then Alan Marshall and Judah Waten. Dal Stivens—who pirouetted on it fancifully, with humour and tall tales—was also a particular favourite. Another was Esme Gollschewsky, whose stories drew Clem back to fishermen and the Queensland seashore. Katharine Susannah Prichard, while firm in her support, appeared only once; Vance Palmer appeared less than might have been expected. By far the most published author was John Morrison, who—unlike many novelists—wrote short stories with ease.

Morrison had grown up in the English shipbuilding town of Sunderland, and worked as a wharfie—among other things—after emigrating to Australia as a young man in 1923. He never quite lost his sense of wonder at being here, something fed by his everyday occupation as a gardener. He passed on tips—and seeds—when he visited the Christesens at Eltham. Modest in manner and his requirements, Morrison wrote that he was content to 'keep a roof over my head, by pushing drums of chemicals around, and write at odd times what I want to write just for the Hell of it. In short, only the muscle is for sale.' The dozen or so stories Clem published are marked by a studied delicacy, all the more striking for their usually rough male settings; carefully rendered dialogue, with its pauses, often comes as a contrast to the alertly moving prose. Yet Morrison was, in every sense, a realist: he knew that short-story collections were not popular (compared with novels), but also believed that popular taste—debauched by romances—could be improved. A yen was there. Morrison told of stories of his—some of them reprints from *Meanjin*—that had been the most popular among, say, textile workers. So he was supportive of Clem: '*Meanjin* is the only bright life left for the Australian short story writer,' he wrote in 1951; 'for Christ's sake keep it burning.'[20]

Clem was keen to find bridges linking Australia with Europe wherever he could. So he was partial to stories by the Greek Australian James Galanis—a Newcastle businessman—in particular for their strong visual imagery and 'poetic atmosphere'. But he rejected more than he published. Quite otherwise were his dealings with David Martin. Martin, born in Hungary, had lived in a number of European countries and participated in the Spanish Civil War. He had arrived in Australia, via India, and was wondering whether he should stay here when he happened upon a copy of *Meanjin* in the Mitchell Library—and was excited to get home and tell his wife that here was 'a magazine which was NOT provincial … it could be worthwhile working in Australia after all'.

For his part Clem was so impressed with Martin that, when they made contact, he suggested that he should write reviews, essays, even a guest editorial. It was a common pattern with him, of falling over a new contributor as if a gift from the gods; the high expectations inevitably led to disappointment. Here was a genuine European intellectual, committed, setting about discovering his new country. But right from the start Martin made it plain that he was 'bursting with eagerness to write stories and poems'. The stories Martin placed in *Meanjin* were wide-ranging, versatile, and looked at rural Australia with fresh eyes. Nevertheless Clem tugged, wanting him to write essays and reviews—even suggesting a piece on Miles Franklin, which Martin felt he could not tackle. He did not know enough. It was not until he had been in the country for ten years that he confidently took up Australian literary subjects.

Martin was happy enough to review books occasionally—it was the kind of thing a professional writer must do—to maintain a regular connection with the magazine. Admiring his 'strong editing', Martin was careful to write to Clem about the latest issue as soon as it appeared—knowing that editors receive far less comment than the public imagines. He also came up with suggestions for increasing the magazine's subscriber base. But it took some years for there to be a strong personal relationship: 'Sorry', he wrote; 'I'm better to know by letter.' Clem grumbled that it was much the same with him.[21]

Meanjin's poetry in the ten years or so following the move to Melbourne was generally more distinguished than its short stories. A high proportion of those published were names still recognised today—such as Harold Stewart, AD Hope, Geoffrey Dutton, Rosemary Dobson, Dame Mary Gilmore, RD FitzGerald, Chris Wallace-Crabbe and Gwen Harwood. Other regulars have now faded, such as Alex Craig and Peter Hopegood (whom AD Hope thought good). But two of the strongest presences were Judith Wright and James McAuley: one issue carried Wright's famous 'Woman to Man' opposite McAuley's impressive 'The True Discovery of Australia'.

Clem's publication of McAuley, whose verse was originally often cast in a Drydenesque mode, persisted even after it took a religious turn. It was part of his insistence on quality as the prime determinant for publication in *Meanjin*. Even after McAuley founded *Quadrant*, Clem was glad to take his poems. But there were no further essays from McAuley, and their correspondence, once light-hearted, was twice suspended. After a longer gap, McAuley submitted a final poem in 1969, puzzlingly signing himself—for the very first time—'Jim'.

Better, if spasmodic, relations were had with a greater neo-classicist, AD Hope—despite his preference for avoiding the contemporary world with its compromising convergences and conformities. (Clem published Hope's mischievously witty 'Sonnet on First Looking into Gerard Manley Hopkins': retreat into intense nature poetry was not the answer.) Most characteristic of Hope was his playfully amorous verse—appreciative of women (although objectifying them), and remarkable for its elegance. Clem could not get enough of it. But Hope, apprehensive about prosecution after Robert Close's punitive treatment over *Love Me, Sailor*, had withdrawn a book (already at the printers) that Clem had been going to publish. This created a rift, which was not healed when Hope took up his chair in Canberra.

Hope assumed a position of lofty isolation; Clem felt left behind. But when a fire destroyed Hope's house and contents, Clem prompted Melbourne friends to send a cheque. There was a seven-year stretch in which Hope submitted no poems at all, and wrote few reviews. At the time of the Petrov affair he came closer, in sympathy, and contributed poems and articles to the magazine. When Hope now corresponded—as increasingly he did—he offered comfort and support (extending to lobbying), as well as applying his cool judgement when providing detailed advice on *Meanjin*'s problems. 'I like your guts and good luck to you,' he had told Clem. He held to this opinion.[22]

Clem's former assistant Judith Wright was now invaluable as a contributor, frequently sending Clem poems well into the 1950s. Wright's poems—among her best—were notable for their awareness of Indigenous and ecological issues, even then; elsewhere they addressed issues of love and death with a particular intensity (and sometimes a primal twist of savagery). A few years after the move from Brisbane, Wright asked Clem whether he still wanted to publish 'that collection of mine'. Yes, he did. Right from the beginning Judith insisted on businesslike arrangements for *The Moving Image*; 'Poets should not, I know, be businesslike, but my father brought me up strict, and my solicitors are carrying on the process.'

Clem didn't care for this at all, and dragged his feet. When eventually he did send the contract, she found that he had not deleted the option clause, as requested, for this would leave the choice of future publishers open. So she pointed this out. 'He fairly chewed his moustache to ribbons,' Wright surmised to Jack McKinney, 'so crossed the clause out very crossly and returned the contracts for signing without a Word. I'm enjoying returning it without a word.' Later she was even more firm with her old boss, particularly for complaining about her publishing a poem elsewhere that he had passed over. Then she proposed a new collection for the Meanjin Press—but said it had better appear without undue delay, that it would struggle to break even, and 'I wouldn't take it on myself'. Given these disclaimers, plus a new disconcerting rock-solid 'Judy', Clem procrastinated, his indecision prolonged by a firm belief in the value of her work. Judith endured six weeks of 'strong silence', then placed the collection with Angus & Robertson, which published it as *Woman to Man*. Relations were repaired, but never fully resumed.[23]

Meanwhile in *Meanjin*'s pages there was the sombre, lingering presence of James Picot. Around this time came news of Picot's death: 'I never had a mate except Jim,' Clem began a threnody. In difficult patches with the magazine, Clem had told himself he would keep it going so Jim could take it over on his return, or edit it with him; indeed Picot had already described himself as 'one editor of *Meanjin Papers*'. Clem desperately wanted to know what had happened to Picot, and set about gathering testaments of his time as a Japanese prisoner of war on the Burma–Thailand railway. Thus he learned of Jim's exemplary resilience, the way he had mastered Japanese, and so sometimes had been able to resolve misunderstandings between prisoners and guards. Since he always had the knack of raising morale, Picot seems to have elicited much the same love and solicitousness in the army as he had in Brisbane. As a way of making him live, Clem searched far and wide for lost poems. Eventually he would publish not only these but tributes and other pieces in *Meanjin*. He also gathered Picot's verse in a book, *With a Hawk's Quill*. In his review, RD FitzGerald declared the poet 'a romantic in spite of himself'.

For Clem, nothing could stanch the open wound, 'a loss from which I have never truly recovered'.[24]

One local ally Clem had in these years was Vincent Buckley, whom he first encountered—and impressed—when Buckley was editing the campus newspaper *Farrago*. Years later Buckley would recall him as 'a focal point and unifying presence', for in those days—having had an early curiosity about Marxism—Buckley was quite left-wing. In 1952 his first poem appeared in 'the cherished *Meanjin*', as well as his first critical essay. Buckley had just joined Melbourne's English Department as a tutor. Given the prevailing departmental indifference to literature being created—let alone by colleagues—some convergence of views arose between the acolyte and the editor. Nonetheless Buckley was playing a straight bat: he went off to Cambridge, impressed leading literary scholars there, and modulated an intended further degree into an acclaimed book of criticism, *Poetry and Morality* (1959). The Melbourne English Department were keen to have him back—and to use funding from the Lockie Bequest to do it.

Nevertheless, in being both a Cambridge-credentialed English Department member and someone keen to advance the cause of Australian literature—not least by teaching it—Buckley might be a useful ally to *Meanjin*. 'Beneath a seminarian's testiness', David Martin recalled, 'he had the naughty charm of a Renaissance princeling.' Less apparent was the way that Buckley's radicalism (which for a time saw him involved in the *Catholic Worker*) would gradually weaken, as it came to be eclipsed by a virulent anti-communism. Similarly, his concern with Catholicism—and major involvement in the Apostolate, which enabled people at the university to live their secular lives within an enlightened Catholic framework—would also become looser, more mystical, eventually even *post*-Catholic. By then Buckley's attachment to Ireland was becoming primal: it would complete, he fondly believed, the spiritually truncated Irish environment he had known in his boyhood in central Victoria. But that, too, would fail him in the end. He came to see the Irish themselves, after 800 years of English occupation, as riddled with the timidity of the colonised. Buckley's was, as John McLaren recognised in the title of his biography, a *Journey without Arrival*.

In addition to Buckley's poetry—its tone always distinctive, right from the initial 'Responsary', which managed at once to be calm, invocatory and slightly sinister—Clem was eager to publish a number of critical articles by him. 'He may be said', Clem wrote commending the young man, 'to be pioneering in this country a form of literary criticism ... based on a humanism conceived in spiritual terms and resting on scrupulous textual analysis for its conclusion.' This, he believed, was 'absolutely necessary if our literature is to develop as a spiritual and a cultural force'. In one extended article, Buckley wrote convincingly of the ailments affecting contemporary poetry in England, together with the challenges it faced in Australia. Here, he maintained, it still tended to be surfacey; what was needed was 'a calm acceptance of it as a source of communion between men, based on the presentation of the human mystery in fully human terms'. In *Meanjin* he placed convincing pieces on Kenneth Slessor, the emerging novelists Stow and Koch, and Xavier Herbert. But the production line would cease.[25]

Shortly after he had published Buckley on the need for Australian literature to be taught in universities, Clem expressed his irritation with the activities of Buckley in his other role, as co-editor of the quarterly *Prospect*. He was still waiting, he wrote, for him 'to place evidence on my desk' confirming allegations Buckley had made in conversations and in print about the pro-Communist stance of *Meanjin*. If he couldn't support the charges, then he should print an apology in *Prospect*. Reluctantly Buckley put the case, 'formally only because you challenged me to do so'. He would have preferred the matter to have remained at the level of 'a relatively disinterested comment'. But ... here goes. From 1949 to 1956 in particular, *Meanjin* 'had the air of a typical fellow-travelling journal'. It presented a world 'threatened by America and Americanism', and while its editorial policy was to attack McCarthyist tendencies—'laudable' enough, if not overdone—the 'effect was to endorse the local Communist Party line and Soviet foreign policy'. There was never a word of criticism voiced editorially of the Soviet bloc, Communism, or of any Communist tactic, official or writers.

Moreover, the journal seemed to give a privileged position to Communist writers, and to books produced by the Communist-run Australasian Book Society. Buckley conceded that many of these articles were not objectionable on their own, but—particularly for the period up to 1956—'almost all the politically relevant material in *Meanjin* is from Communist or fellow-travelling sources'. He accepted that the issues of the past three years were not pro-Communist, but they could not be viewed on their own. Indeed, *Meanjin*'s politics 'seem to me now to be in a stage of transition'—Buckley ventured in a skewering insight—'from a kind of fellow-travelling to an uneasy and ambiguous emotional sympathy for its own past'.

Clem mulled upon the letter—after all, it closed with an assurance of abiding good will—and immediately turned to Brian Fitzpatrick for advice. Fitzpatrick drafted a sagacious reply, but Clem could not bring himself to send it. After nearly three months he managed a more or less gracious one, explaining that he didn't have the time to respond fully. Buckley meanwhile continued to send pieces to *Meanjin*, but the continuing silence congealed his position. He remembered that Clem had told him that the rejoinder to one of his poems being attacked by Elizabeth Vassilieff would have to wait for three issues before publication, whereupon he had withdrawn it. This may have become a grudge. Buckley's last appearance in Clem's *Meanjin* was in 1961; not even the full-dress critical treatment eight years later (complete with interview) could winkle fresh work out of him. Poems, just then, did not come easily. He remained aloof but respectful. Years later, Buckley explained his views to Lynne Strahan. She protested vigorously (and would tellingly rebut them in *Just City and the Mirrors*). Subsequently Buckley seems to have had second thoughts; in his memoir *Cutting Green Hay*, he declared that Clem 'could not justly be called a fellow-traveller'.[26]

One person Clem was keen to publish was Dorothy Auchterlonie, the poet, who would become better known as the critic Dorothy Green. He had been struck by her moral force and capacity for deep attachment since she had helped out as *Meanjin*'s secretary in Brisbane; then suddenly Dorothy had returned to Sydney to marry the university librarian HM Green, a man many years her senior. Things were not easy for her, running a household with two small children while earning a living: teaching was put aside for freelance journalism. When the opening came, Dorothy took the Green family to Warwick in Queensland, where she shared the duties of headmistress at the Presbyterian Girls College. But the cost was high: she found herself becoming a drudge, her ideas slipping away because she didn't have the time to put them on paper. Clem did get one article from her in these years, on the position of the artist in society. Dorothy—well aware that 'There are too many phoney ones'—thought there should be less talk of artists' *rights* and more of their *obligations*.

Dorothy's moral earnestness acted as a stiffener for Clem, since she shared his pessimism: around 1950 she repeatedly wrote that 'the Dark Ages are upon us once more'. For this reason (as pressures mounted), he must do nothing to imperil the existence of *Meanjin*. Fully aware of Clem's difficulties, she nonetheless couldn't understand his tetchiness: surely he could take 'immense pride' in his achievement. 'I think you are to be envied, not consoled', she told him. Instead—since there was an undercurrent of rivalry for Dorothy's affections—Clem became more niggardly in his dealings with her husband HM Green. In 1959—after he had rejected a commissioned article—this exploded into a full-scale row. Dorothy, always close to Nina, wrote of her neglect, and accused them both of mouthing the sentiments of friendship while really not giving a damn. Clem's reply was masterly, and revealed him at his very best. He conceded much, and reassured Dorothy where it most counted—that in the event of some misfortune overtaking her, the Christesens would always honour their promise of looking after her children.[27]

Reaching out: painting, and press

Even in the Brisbane years, *Meanjin* had carried occasional glossy-paper art supplements, but now Clem was intent on a more thorough inclusion of the visual arts. Apart from literature, these were his other great interest: he was a dab hand at painting in oils—which seemed to calm him—and would sometimes set up his easel alongside the well-known artist 'Jock' Frater. Moreover, he saw an opportunity here, as there was no existing venue for serious discussion of them. First he counted on the rising critic Bernard Smith. But he could never accept that *Meanjin*, while regarded by Smith as a worthy cause (even essential), was often marginal to his own clear plans: on the contrary, Clem tended to cast him as an ingrate, insufficiently thankful for having 'come up' through its pages.

In 1950 he appointed Alan McCulloch, the art critic of the *Herald*, as art editor; McCulloch also painted. *Meanjin* would carry a reproduction of McCulloch's impressive *Palio of Siena*—rendered rather like an agitated eye, amid the pronounced verticals of Sienese towers. But it was an impossible task, McCulloch found. He could not afford the necessary travel, found the task politicised by his newspaper criticism, and did not have enough space. At most he had a segment of articles—recurrently on European art movements (rather than individual artists), previous Australian painters, with the discussion of contemporary work generally restricted to that associated with the major prizes. It was a pirouette, insufficient to sustain Clem's expectations. When money became short, the illustrated inserts on quality paper went. Meanwhile the artists did not come. As Bernard Smith had warned, no journal or paper depending upon artists 'is critically worth a tinker's cuss … you couldn't turn *Meanjin* into a successful art journal without destroying much of its character as "a magazine of ideas"'. Clem bleakly concluded—from a stray remark of McCulloch's—that 'All my efforts to build up the art side of *Meanjin* seemingly resulted in "virtually nothing".' He was puzzled, given the effort put into it.[28]

More understandable—although no less frustrating—were the difficulties associated with the Meanjin Press. Clem had started the venture in Queensland, encouraging young poets as well as putting out his own verse in book form; in Melbourne he was optimistic it could be expanded. But there were difficulties when he was associated with Melbourne University Press, while later at Heinemann he was debarred from any publishing activity beyond the magazine. (In the gap he produced his notably successful anthology *Australian Heritage*.) Subsequently Clem approached the Commonwealth Literary Fund for support, but found the arrangements made to be unsatisfactory. The Meanjin Press produced fifteen titles in the twelve years to 1953: they ranged from Vance Palmer writing on Louis Esson to verse by Hugh McCrae and translations from Pushkin and Chinese poetry. Its one palpable hit was Judith Wright's *The Moving Image*, which was reprinted and became a steady seller. The great disappointment there, which rocked him, was James Picot's *With a Hawk's Quill.* Clem lost interest in the press soon after.[29]

This is the best juncture at which to discuss *Meanjin*'s approach to the visual arts in general. Clem showed a predilection in the magazine for small woodcuts, contributing to the sought-after elegant appearance. Line drawings by various artists appeared too, but irregularly. The covers—not least for their colour—were what stood out most. These included work by Danila Vassilieff, Leonard French, Arthur Boyd and Roger Kemp; the impact of an early Fred Williams was blunted by the adjacent strips of red. A surprise was a light and gaily coloured cover by Picasso, showing a bunch of flowers being presented. (It was the poster from the current Stockholm Peace Congress.) More stark—his style more adaptive to magazine requirements—were a couple of covers by Eric Thake. One is apparently of an Indigenous person eating a witchetty grub, metaphorically the feast for *Meanjin*'s tenth anniversary. A traditional 'Aboriginal drawing' was the elegant dancing woman of 1951, which Clem would use again—this time fessing up that it was actually the work of a white man. But a 1961 cover duly carried an Arnhem Land bark painting in full-colour reproduction.

As if centred on an Indigenous camp fire was Alan McCulloch's memorable design for the covers for the Melbourne Olympics year 1956. Two arty types (as people would have seen them then), one bearded, one with glasses, look up from a map of Australia to an Olympic athlete (with torch) high above, the bearded man extending his arm in wonderment. Many things could be read into this image—the ultimate triumph of sport in Australia, or the remoteness of the country as it reached out to the world.

The two artists most associated with *Meanjin* were Louis Kahan and Stan[islaw] Ostoja-Kotkowski. Kahan, born in Vienna, had made his way as an artist in Parisian bohemian circles (and into the French Foreign Legion). It was probably McCulloch who introduced him to Clem, with the result that his sketches of various luminaries appeared in most issues for fourteen years. The best are very good: the historians Manning Clark and Geoffrey Serle (after a second try), but the poets tend to be seraphic. While some of the sketches are drawn lightly, and tellingly, in the manner of Matisse, other subjects are worried at with lines that almost obscure their features. To be Kahanised was to be admitted to *Meanjin*'s own academy.

Clem was much taken with the Polish-born Ostoja-Kotkowski, who had settled in Adelaide. Indeed Ostoja-Kotkowski's career can be traced on his thirty-odd covers for *Meanjin*, notably more than from any other artist. The most striking are the set produced for the year 1966, with their 'electronic painting', each of them a still, 'chords isolated from longer pieces'. Increasingly, Ostoja-Kotkowski would move into multimedia, pioneering the use of lasers. Clem had followed him into the theatre, publishing an insert of his stage designs, and would continue to turn to him for cover designs well after Ostoja-Kotkowski had seemingly lost interest. Meanwhile there was his stand-by designer Douglas Annand, whom Clem had known since Queensland days. Annand had the modernist itch to appropriate Indigenous images, no doubt seeing himself as interpreting them. Annand too was frequently used to the end, on the way providing *Meanjin*'s most unforgettable set of covers, the paranoid emu of 1965.[30]

Brian Fitzpatrick, gentleman radical

At Clem's right hand was Brian Fitzpatrick, whose influence upon him, he said at a testimonial dinner, 'has been greater than any other man's'. Fitzpatrick's parents had been country schoolteachers, but it was his brother returning from the war who sought to impose rigorous discipline—from which Fitzpatrick was in flight for the rest of his life. The country boy was soon sandpapered when he took up residence in the Anglican Trinity College—improbably the place where Fitzpatrick and others founded the Melbourne University Labor Club in 1925. A prodigious worker, he was an equally enthusiastic drinker. As a young man, Fitzpatrick frequented pubs, including bohemian haunts and gateways to the underworld: later he would settle on the Swanston Family Hotel, the watering hole of Melbourne's artists and intellectuals. In this setting, as elsewhere, people were struck by a courtliness about him. He would insist on no swearing, and, after a brief stint in England, for a short time affected a cane. It was the life of a writer he wanted: he published verse, wrote a novel, and became a journalist. For a time he was spoken of as being groomed by Keith Murdoch as a future newspaper editor.

Murdoch had noted Fitzpatrick's sense of purpose, manifested in his two great contributions to Australian historiography, *British Imperialism and Australia, 1788–1833* (1939) and *The British Empire in Australia* (1941). These books provided, for the first time, a sustained left-wing interpretation of Australian history: Fitzpatrick saw it primarily as a contest between 'the organised rich and the organised poor', the latter being cast as those working for greater social justice. He believed that 'The history of the Australian past is best written from an intimate knowledge of the Australian present'; such writing needed to be energised, connected with the world around us. In effect he turned the tables. Rather than assuming (as many had done) that we shared the glories of imperial Britain, Fitzpatrick was more inclined to show how the British were even more privileged to share in the profits of Australia. As Geoffrey Blainey noted, he brought to history-writing some of the spirit that had entered Australian fiction half a century earlier.

Fitzpatrick did not last long in the Labor Party; he was not a party man. He called himself a socialist, but was really a libertarian, a romantic anarchist. 'The proper end of government', he wrote, 'is to order *things*, rather than men.' Rather than develop a systemic program for society, Fitzpatrick addressed particular issues, or cases. Involved from its foundation with the Australian Council for Civil Liberties (an organisation he would later dominate), he worked for refugees, against censorship, and against all oppressive legislation—attacking what he termed 'influential oafs' encroachments on common rights'.

He was, in consequence, repeatedly attacked—if not as an outright Communist, then as a fellow-traveller. But the ruling class were simply using Communism as a distraction from their own reactionary ends, Fitzpatrick maintained. As the Cold War developed, he shifted his focus from Britain to America: 'our independence is as nominal as our freedom'. He was indefatigable, propagating his views through influential (roneoed) newsletters, a column in the popular press, and regular appearances on 3XY—a Liberal Party radio station—which increasingly set him aside for the trots. Not even his close friends knew all that he was doing.

Although a lobbyist, Fitzpatrick was a man, it was said after his death, 'of almost childlike integrity'. A portrait by Graeme Inson captures him: fit, combative, but relaxed. There's a hint of exasperation about his expression, but also a suggestion of good humour. As Tim Burstall said of him, Fitzpatrick 'somehow manages to look sensitive and brutal at the same time'. It was 'the *human* tone of all his writings and lectures and discussions which perhaps strikes us first', Clem declared. Invariably he managed to assume the tone of someone rising above the fray (even as he relished it). Quoting the liberal British jurist AV Dicey, Fitzpatrick believed that 'circumstance is the arbiter of men's opinions, and [so held] malice towards none'. Revealingly, his favourite piece of music was Beethoven's overture *The Consecration of the House*, notable for the confident serenity of its opening; so composed, Fitzpatrick would advance to face public debate—doubling the declaratory martial theme that follows.

Clem probably met Fitzpatrick through the Palmers. Apart from their general political stance, they had a lot in common. They would at once have recognised the element of courtliness in each other, and perhaps eventually come to see that the other had a contradictory, romantic view of himself as carrying forward a family tradition of Irish rebelliousness. But rather than go at things like a bull at a gate, Fitzpatrick strove to understand the workings of society: he became an expert lobbyist and behind-the-scenes man. Increasingly he put his skills as a master tactician at Clem's service. When Clem went abroad for most of 1957, he took up the slack when Geoff Serle was appointed acting editor. Unexpectedly, Fitzpatrick strove to make *Meanjin* apolitical, 'on my part a careful policy of lulling university and Commonwealth Literary Fund cowards to unsuspicious sleep'. Deliberately he published (good) pieces by 'lilywhite academics'.

Fitzpatrick was not only fighting the good fight, but (with a young family) struggling to find employment. There he was, the author of pioneering, significant histories—books that provided the groundwork for many academics—working as a mail sorter at the post office and a 'bulldog' (invigilator) at exams in the Exhibition Buildings. While he received occasional grants, suitable employment in universities repeatedly eluded him. Fitzpatrick prided himself on never complaining: Clem, sympathetic given his own difficulties with the university, admired his stoicism—and probably envied him his equanimity. So Fitzpatrick never received a full, accusatory Clemmiad—although this did not preclude an occasional recital of Clem's and *Meanjin*'s difficulties. For his part, Fitzpatrick was inclined to treat Clem with a measure of distancing dignity: right to the very end, all his letters were signed complete with surname.

Fitzpatrick took a while to come into *Meanjin*, given that it united bohemianism with his politics. Yet he came to see it as central, as he placed himself in the tradition of the great English polemicists. *Meanjin* enabled him to write as if for the *Quarterly Review* (London) or the

Edinburgh Review; he developed a style at once formal and colloquial—with flashes of wit, and mischief. He would have seen the journal as an engine for 'civilising Australia', as he put it. In its pages he wrote on a wide variety of subjects, including the need for full Indigenous rights, while one piece speculated on the rise of the professional, technical and managerial classes.

Fitzpatrick gave *Meanjin* unstinting service: he would propose ideas, read manuscripts, and come to the office for lunch with Clem and his assistant editor—and listen. He would take up most suggestions made for articles, especially when they involved a clutch of books to be reviewed. He subjected issues of the magazine to exhaustive technical analysis, providing detailed lists of typographical errors and variations in inking and spacing. Clem, appreciative of the way Fitzpatrick had helped to run the journal while he had been away, sent him an unexpected cheque for £50. It was Christmas, and Fitzpatrick as usual was in dire need. Nonetheless he returned it, 'moved by your generous thought of me'. He was well aware of what *Meanjin* cost Clem personally.[31]

Clem, Heinemann and Red herrings

Clem once remarked he could never be an official: his sense of being a free agent was too strongly developed. But he was a member of a number of organisations. In 1950 he was co-opted by Fitzpatrick as a vice-president of the Australian Council for Civil Liberties. He was also involved in the Australian Peace Council—later claiming to have set up the first peace committee in Melbourne—as well as the Peace Action Council, the Democratic Rights Council, the Release Sharkey Council, plus the APC Writers Auxiliary. He was a vice-president of the Fellowship of Australian Writers. Poor health would compel Clem to prune some of these commitments, but that one would stay—for a time. He chaired the committee for the Hardy Defence Fund, when the novelist was charged with criminal libel in connection with *Power Without Glory*. From the time when Robert Close was jailed in 1948 for obscenity in *Love Me, Sailor*, Clem was constantly involved in censorship battles.

In 1948 Clem was appointed Australian manager of the English firm William Heinemann Ltd. He applied his energies to the task, cutting back on other journalistic and literary commitments. Operations were conducted from a separate down-town office, piled up with travellers' parcels: he trebled sales, made it the biggest publishing venture in the country. But there were a number of tensions. One of them arose almost at the beginning, when he published in *Meanjin* a hostile review of an anthology the firm published, of poetry drawn from across the English-speaking world. This resulted in Heinemann suspending his contract. But since (after initial refusal) Clem published an agreed-upon apology in the magazine, Heinemann was disposed to re-employ him. Clem took up his job fully again, and collected back pay.

But there were other, more serious problems: first, although Clem was expected to 'watch for authors of promise', Heinemann were not really interested in publishing Australian titles, unless they could be bestsellers: for them this country existed simply as one of the best markets for British books. Clem was also chafed by his status, the way he was often referred to in the trade simply as Heinemann's 'publicity officer'. Moreover, there was pressure from the firm concerning *Meanjin*: they expected total commitment (to them) and vanilla politics. Then there were problems with the printers, Specialty Press, whose manager branded all Australian writers as 'Red', and hinted that Clem must be a Communist.

Here and elsewhere Clem detected the hand of the Catholic right: he had attacked Catholic Action (which was mobilising in the unions, and would provide the core of the Democratic Labor Party), and had incurred the enmity of Paul McGuire, its chief publicist. McGuire had had considerable success with his Heinemann books, and was on friendly terms with the English directors. One of them came to Melbourne, announced a restructure, and the appointment of McGuire to the board: Clem would lose all editorial direction. He cut up rough, believing McGuire had shown the Heinemann chair a batch of press cuttings demonstrating that Clem was 'a Red'. He was to be given notice—but seems to have got in first and resigned. Bruised but intact, Clem laid low at Eltham for a time, reading, painting, taking gardening jobs—and still producing *Meanjin*.[32]

Some months later, in August 1952, in the course of the debate on the estimates, federal parliament noted Vance Palmer's sixty-seventh birthday. The opportunity was taken by the right-wing Labor member Stan Keon, a friend and associate of McGuire in Catholic Action, to launch an attack on the Commonwealth Literary Fund, of which Palmer was chair. Keon spoke of a 'deliberate and concerted attempt' to restrict grants to either 'well-known Communists or active workers for the Communist Party'. It was the height of the Cold War: Menzies, six months earlier, had instructed that the names of all CLF applicants should be subject to clearance by ASIO.

But in parliament he assumed the mantle of the cultivated liberal, rising to defend Palmer and firmly rebut the charges. They were, of course, baseless: there were Communist writers who had been supported by the fund, but six of the seven were well-known authors. The basic problem was that conservatives were out of sympathy with the Australian realist tradition—which, insofar as Australian writing was appreciated—enjoyed most popularity. For his part Clem discussed the matter calmly in *Meanjin*, even devoting more space to Keon's simultaneous assault on the Australian National University. But he pointed out that such 'political and sectarian heresy-hunting' would lead to a situation where 'conformity becomes the only morality'. Meanwhile he heard reports that Keon could be heard in a restaurant boasting, after the assault on the CLF, 'Now for Christesen and *Meanjin*'.[33]

The corollary of the crusade being fought by Keon and others was that Clem (and Nina) were fighting a series of rear-guard actions. Even before the Menzies victory at the polls in December 1949, a royal commission into the Communist Party had been sitting in Victoria; commendably forensic in its deliberations, its existence nonetheless contributed to the general air of suspicion. Altogether more serious was the attempt—modelled on the new Suppression of Communism Act by South Africa's apartheid regime—to ban the Communist Party in 1951. After the High Court rejected the legislation, the Menzies government took it to a referendum, where the proposal was narrowly defeated.

The political climate did not change, and Nina, as head of the Russian Department, would feel the brunt of it. A lecturer, Boris Christa, appointed on inflated references, had proved incompetent; Nina decided in 1952 that she would not recommend his being given tenure. Christa appealed: he wrote to the chancellor (Lowe, chairing the royal commission) that the Russian Department 'directed by Mrs Christesen is an instrument of Soviet propaganda'. Other smears and hostile documents were quietly circulated. The university then not only overturned

Nina's decision, but inserted Professor AR Chisholm as chairman over her while she remained departmental head. It was, in effect, a censure. Fortunately Chisholm was courteous and tactful, but these leading strings remained in place for three years.[34]

Given the earlier attack on the Commonwealth Literary Fund—augmented by another when a fellowship had been awarded to the Communist Judah Waten, to enable him to write *The Unbending*—Clem expected more trouble once the novel appeared. He was so concerned that in mid-1954 he wrote to the secretary of the CLF stating that if there were more attacks in the House, and they were not rebutted effectively, he might have to consider … not receiving any more assistance from the fund. Writers were beginning to fear being the subject of indiscriminate parliamentary attacks. In preparation for the onslaught, Clem set up a discussion in *Meanjin* on Waten's novel.

Vance Palmer, who had become ill and had resigned as chair of the CLF Advisory Board, penned a rather weary summary: he made the point that the hinge of *The Unbending* was the way the Kochansky family had fled the persecutions of Russia to find a safe haven here, only to find the storms surrounding conscription and the Industrial Workers of the World (IWW) involving them willy-nilly. Chisholm, the professor of French and a First World War veteran, liked the novel not one little bit, but conceded it had 'real power'. Katharine Susannah Prichard also contributed, while Brian Fitzpatrick pointed out that the severity of the repression of IWW members had not been exaggerated, the 'Wobblies' having been scapegoated—rather like the Chartists in England almost a century earlier. In the event, despite some hostility expressed in the press, a fresh parliamentary attack was not made. But Clem was not out of the woods yet.[35]

The Petrov affair

In April 1954 prime minister Menzies announced the defection of the third secretary at the Embassy of the Soviet Union to Australia. Vladimir Petrov was head of Soviet espionage in Australia; the case immediately attracted international interest, since Canberra was privy to secret information passed on by its senior allies. (There had been leaks before, RG Casey going so far as to describe the public service as 'a nest of traitors'.) Shortly after, the image of Mrs Petrov, dragging her feet as she was hustled by Soviet officials towards a waiting plane, was flashed around the world. Australia would have (as Canada had) a royal commission into espionage—initially with bipartisan support. It began sitting a month later—and less than a fortnight before a general election. Menzies told his rank and file that they should not refer directly to the Petrov affair, but they certainly could campaign against Communism. He knew full well that in the public mind they were interchangeable.

In November Clem was contacted by Security, and subsequently interviewed in his office. It went well enough, but was unsettling. He consulted about what tactics to adopt, not least with Brian Fitzpatrick (who was advising Dr Evatt, the leader of the Opposition). Fearing that word of the interview would get out, Clem adopted a low public profile. 'We are already nervous ... We even imagine looks of inquiry on the faces of friends. This is absurd, I know; but the thing is real.' Clem was trying to avoid being subpoenaed: appearance before the commissioners could have dire consequences for the standing of *Meanjin*, let alone damage his own reputation. Even his interlocutor had conceded that some mud might stick. While generally satisfied, and courteous, he had pointed out that the decision to call Clem, or not, rested with the commissioners. Each day the morning newspaper brought extensive fresh accounts of the proceedings. Max Marginson thought it expedient to burn all the correspondence between the university branch and the Central Committee of the Communist Party. Meanwhile a general diversion was the first sponsored Round Australia car rally: a joke went the rounds that the papers were full of Redex, and ex-Reds.

One night a black car silently approached Clem's home. Out got two security men; Nina was alone at the time, but invited them in: they served a subpoena. When Clem arrived some time later, the Holden was still there, at the bottom of the drive; it slowly followed him up to the house. Quickly ascertaining what it was about, he did not invite the pair in—and declined payment for the fares for the hearing in Sydney in a few days' time.

On 17 January 1955 Clem and Nina found themselves before the commissioners at Darlinghurst. Their advocate, James Meagher, had asked that they be not called: surely a statutory declaration would be sufficient? The chairman thought otherwise. There was a strong security presence in the room: Petrov had again been examined that day, through an interpreter. Clem had wanted to make a statement of protest, but Meagher had managed to dissuade him. Examined first, he was asked whether the name *Meanjin* meant 'spike' or 'spite'? 'I assure you it is spike,' he replied, before finding himself at the sharp end of three particular lines of inquiry. One concerned lists—he had appeared on an MVD (Soviet Ministry of Internal Affairs) list, under the codename 'Crab'. In themselves codenames signified little: they were a kind of diplomatic shorthand. The document was no more than a scrap of paper, drawn up by Petrov's predecessor. Another list was produced, and handed first to Clem, then to Nina. Could they identify these people, and see … any common purpose linking them? No: of the seven, Nina scored two and Clem one. They were instructed not to read out the names (for then they would have been recorded in the transcript). They were surnames only. There was also much concern about dealings with the TASS representative, Nasov: they had met at a party, which was followed by the two married couples dining together. This had occurred partly because Clem and Nina were not in the habit of attending official Soviet functions on the national day.

Clem was asked, as expected, Was he a Communist? He found it 'an offensive question'; stated that he had never belonged to either the Liberal Party, the Labor Party or the Communist Party, but (being the independent he was) 'it was not a simple question to answer'. The commissioners failed to see why. Clem's tetchiness became more apparent when the examination moved on to an article he had published by Ian Milner. Milner, a political scientist who joined the Department of External [Foreign] Affairs, seems to have been one of two people who leaked documents to Moscow, which led directly to the establishment of ASIO by the Chifley government in 1949.

Clem had published a piece by him, sent from Prague (where he now lived), which was simply a rebuttal of an earlier article by Andrew Fabinyi that had appeared in *Meanjin*. It drew attention to the surprisingly wide range of English-language literature, particularly the classics, available in Czechoslovakia, and was honest in indicating its political assumptions. But the commissioners, alert to plot and conspiracy, would not take it at face value. They had difficulty believing that Clem would publish a piece like this without checking the credentials of the writer. Not surprisingly, the commissioners had no idea how much an editor could rely on the bounty of the mailbag. Instead, they probed him concerning the timing and the nature of the correspondence, and would have had some read out for the transcript, until Clem's advocate requested that it should be shown instead. (An editor writing to a contributor was to be regarded as something like what we would now call 'commercial in confidence'.) Clem, seeking exoneration, was agitated: 'Mr Christesen,' said the chairman, 'I think you have been treated with complete courtesy. There is no need to get worked up about these things.'

Clem might have said, as he wrote some time after, 'I myself am a Socialist, on moral grounds … I have never published any party political article in *Meanjin*. All you can say is that there has been a "Leftist tone" about some issues of the journal.' Few writers were active in party politics—but they were concerned with broad social and political issues. As was *Meanjin*, 'particularly when assaults are made on civil liberties and academic freedoms'.

Nina's answers—in a briefer examination—were shorter and considered. Yes, she taught Russian—her school was 'supposed to be the third largest in the British Empire', and yes, she had called at the Russian embassy to collect Russian language books (so briskly that once she went with AD Hope). She had met a few more Soviet officials than Clem had, and had once provided a translation for titles to children's paintings, without payment. She had not taken the bait. There was no case to answer. Nina had been a British subject for more than twenty years, and was not political. 'I avoid politics. I do not want to worry my parents for one thing, and also I am simply not political by nature.' Her father had been a tsarist naval officer, and remained a strong monarchist—so much so that she thought that was the reason she had been refused a visa to visit the Soviet Union five years earlier.

Not long after a letter arrived from Clem's mother, Susan, calling them 'mugs … dupes', and saying that Clem had 'flirted' with Communists, and was 'not well-balanced'. It was too much for Nina, who, while piously addressing 'my dear Mother', penned a letter in cold fury. How abusive and unappreciative of her son Susan had always been, she wrote: 'to me it seems unbelievable that you should continue, year by year, to chastise your elder son in this extraordinarily offensive manner … as though he were a little wayward boy'. If she had shown 'some understanding and some appreciation', Nina told her, Clem might not have had 'these emotional reactions that sometimes exhaust and exasperate people, most of all himself'. Susan had 'invariably been wrong', and was blind to Clem's achievement—Dr Evatt spoke of the 'national service' he performed with *Meanjin*. Even if it were to fold immediately, Nina correctly perceived, 'it would live in Australia's history, as … JF Archibald or AG Stephens will continue to be remembered'. But Susan was intransigent, sending Nina's letter back to her with combative marginalia—'Commo tripe'. Further vituperative correspondence followed. But relations never completely broke down, and within a matter of months Susan was writing once again to 'My dear girl', and offering them accommodation.

Clem was inclined to make light of the ordeal at first—particularly as there was much support in the university community, extending to a surprise party. But the university itself had not supported him, failing to send along someone from the law faculty to witness the interview in his office; the vice-chancellor (himself a lawyer) compounded the offence with a bland letter saying that ultimately the commissioners had a job to do and yes, some of the charge would stick … In fact the royal commission, in its report, declared there was 'nothing to suggest that either Christesen or his wife ever participated in any way in espionage'.

The fact that *Meanjin* had even published RG Menzies a few months earlier (on management) counted for nothing. Unfortunately, while Clem was no Communist and his wife's political milieu could be said to have been tsarist, people tended to blur categories: he was a 'fellow-traveller', she the head of the *Russian* Department. An imputed predisposition could not be sloughed off so easily. Even Nina's father, Captain Maximov, the head of the Russian monarchist organisation in Brisbane, felt compelled to resign the post after holding it for twenty-eight years. People would cross the road rather than speak with him, something for which he never forgave his daughter.

'Editor clashes with Q.C. at Petrov Inquiry', screamed the Sydney *Daily Telegraph* the day after the Christesens' appearance. In its report the royal commission found there had been no Russian penetration of Australian security or the External Affairs department, and could make no recommendations for prosecutions. Murray-Smith, a Communist cultural activist and correspondent for a Czech international news service, had not been called before the commission—but Clem, and unlikely people such as Clive Turnbull (who worked for the *Herald*) had been. Holding the ring 'to provide a genuinely liberal forum, to help achieve mutual understanding', as Clem explained *Meanjin*'s role to Ian Milner, was easily construed as fellow-travelling. The royal commission took on the aspect of a show trial, the parade of witnesses serving to inhibit progressive opinion. More, the fact that three of Dr Evatt's staff were mentioned in the Petrov documents conveniently ensnared the leader of the Opposition—who made matters worse by appearing as advocate for his staff, naively then telling parliament he had written to the Russian foreign minister, Molotov, for an assurance that there had been no Soviet espionage in Australia. Hostile pressure within the ALP from the Catholic right had been building up, and would soon come to boiling point: 'Can't you understand the significance of the struggle now raging?' Nina had asked Susan. 'The aim is to wreck the ALP. The Petrov affair has a direct bearing on this struggle.' It succeeded: the split Labor vote delivered Menzies an easy victory in the early election of 1955, and would continue to boost the conservative parties until the Whitlam victory of 1972.[36]

Quadrant and mobilisation of the right

Clem made little direct reference to the Petrov case in *Meanjin,* or to the royal commission. Reluctantly he followed advice and found it expedient to step sideways, publishing Brian Fitzpatrick's analysis of the commission as a separate pamphlet. The piece Fitzpatrick did write for *Meanjin* was altogether more elevated (while pointed), 'The Importance of Being Earnest about Liberty'. Pieces on McCarthyism were cautious or deflected. They included Arthur Miller's 'A Modest Proposal for Pacification of the Public Temper'. In a neo-Swiftian satire, Miller postulated a situation where every male, on turning eighteen, should present at the police station—for classification or clearance on security grounds. Jail was the default position. The context was changed to Australia (without any convict resonance). The young were susceptible to distempers, Miller pointed out, and 'If an Australian boy is good enough to fight, he is good enough to go to jail for the peace of his Country.' Clem considered publishing the piece to be 'an important national service … during this period of "clear and present danger"'.[37]

The souring political climate was resisted in other ways. First there was the threat to academic freedom. When the American social democrat Sidney Hook attacked card-carrying Communists, asserting that they should be dismissed from their university posts, Clem invited two other philosophers to take prominence in *Meanjin* with a discussion of Hook's new book.

Another attack was in the offing. Frederick Macartney, a notable critic if a lesser poet, had been known to Clem for quite some time—he had frequently published him, visited his house, and sent him manuscripts for comment. Years earlier Macartney regretted that *Meanjin* seemed to have 'gone in for sectional politics', and now vigorously returned to the fray. Challenging an editorial Comment, Macartney would claim that *Meanjin* was leftist to the point where writers 'often indirectly or even unconsciously' became 'useful instruments of communism'. A controversy followed, and when Clem later agreed to publish an extensive piece, though not immediately, Macartney withdrew it and published the article as a pamphlet.

There he repeated the argument he had made more fully to Clem in correspondence, that since *Meanjin* was in receipt of public money, it was obliged to publish his article. More to the point, the journal had no business, while thus subsidised, to be so political, so leftist, 'with a bias repugnant to most Australians'. Springing to Clem's defence was Ian Maxwell, with a piece written as chairman of the board; meanwhile Stephen, in the infant *Overland*, got AD Hope to review the pamphlet. Hope, opening by declaring Communism 'a form of mental derangement', was all the more effectively able to do the job. But that did not satisfy Macartney, nor Clem, and the controversy dragged on.[38]

Meanwhile there were threats closer to home. One was the emergence of *Overland*, from the *Realist Writer*: Clem warily extended a welcoming hand. His own views about Communism had been formulated during the war, when he stated that 'the absolutes of Marx have been too drastic'. In another broadcast he showed that he was well aware of the 'seductive power … of crude materialism'. As for socialist realism, he felt that too often 'What oils the proletarian novelist … in addition to his generally bad writing, is his almost unanimous belief that misery has no dreams'.[39]

A more potent threat to *Meanjin* came from the right. Clem had been tracking the Congress for Cultural Freedom since its foundation in 1950: from 1953 it had sponsored the compelling and intellectually brilliant monthly *Encounter*. This drew together the best of the New York intelligentsia with English names (when not rising stars) already known to Australians. One of the editors was the English poet Stephen Spender; by decidedly not enquiring too closely, he was able to share in the illusion that much of the funding came from American philanthropists. In fact it came from the CIA—bent on creating an intellectual front that, while advocating the highest expression of liberty, would not only counter Communism but also attack neutralism. It was undoubtedly the best money the CIA ever spent. (*Encounter*'s other founding editor was Irving Kristol, who would later become known as 'the godfather of neoconservatism'.) Despite himself, Clem admired it. But now the congress proposed to extend its tentacles to Australia, which Spender would visit. And it would start a magazine.

Rumours surrounded the activities of the Australian Committee (later Association) for Cultural Freedom: a persistent one was that PR Stephensen was said to be 'hysterically excited' about its activities. Clem must have wondered: could not people see the nature of the new organisation? At the time of the Petrov affair, its cyclostyled newsletter reported approvingly that 300 intellectuals in America had sent a congratulatory telegram to Menzies for his 'humanitarian action'. Later, when someone close to the prime minister was said to be seeking an editor for the new magazine, the names Christesen and Hope came up, to be dismissed immediately. The editor finally selected was Catholic convert James McAuley, a man strident in his political views. One writer saw 'little hope for the Australian *Encounter*': 'It will bore everyone to death.' But *Quadrant* thrived, and McAuley with it. Despite his articulated anti-*Meanjin* stance, he continued to submit poems to the established journal, and Clem to publish them. Clem was well aware that this would blot his copybook with the left, but he believed that, in addition to high technical competence, McAuley was capable of producing 'long (and to my mind brilliant)' poems. Quality counted most, and he was happy to accept the back-handed compliment.[40]

Clem's anxieties were manifest in the last issue for 1954. First he ran a symposium, 'Culture, Congress and Freedom'. JG Latham (a rare conservative anti-McCarthyist) provided a brief for the congress, for he was chairman of the Australian committee. But the other contributors—who included the English historian Hugh Trevor-Roper—wrote of how the congress had been essentially political from the very beginning, and that fundamentally the 'cultural freedom' advocated 'turns out on close inspection to be no more than the arid freedom to denounce communism'.

Clem also wrote a long editorial, 'Culture, Congress and Freedom', an urgent plea for *Meanjin*'s continued importance as an 'open' journal, providing space 'for opposing or conflicting viewpoints'—all the more important given the move towards political conformism, the erosion of civil liberties and even the emergence—'entirely new to this country—of a large force of secret police and police agents'. Clem was prepared to state that, when it came to the published aims of the congress, he found himself almost entirely in agreement. However—after listing the members, and noting that some were undoubtedly men held in high esteem—he also noted that there was a disconcerting number who had been 'notorious' for their 'downright illiberal statements', and few distinguished writers and artists. Indeed, given McCarthyism at home, it seemed an odd time for an American-sponsored organisation to be promoting 'cultural freedom' in foreign countries. The real threat to the free mind '*in this country and at this time*' came mainly 'from the political Right, and not from the political Left'. And there was a cultural component to the question: the chief threat to 'decent cultural development' came not from the USSR, 'but from the United States, which is flooding this and other countries with debased forms of "culture" on almost every level'.

The pressing question was whether this new organisation came from 'an Australian need, or is it part of an overseas drive'? It was the latter. A chain of magazines was created, girdling the world, financed, as Clem noted, by respectable US foundations, but also from 'other sources not officially disclosed'. Long before most people, Clem smelt a rat. In 1967 the disclosure of CIA funding impelled Stephen Spender to resign from *Encounter*, but McAuley, still an editor of *Quadrant*, had no such qualms.[41]

This mobilisation on the right made Clem feel very much exposed. The *Meanjin* committee did not meet, as such: consultation had come to be conducted with members by correspondence. An utterly absurd situation, Clem grumbled. Unsure of himself, he felt that 'One slip, and it could mean the end of the journal'. It was, Clem maintained, one of the very few literary journals in the West that would now 'dare to publish even moderately "Leftist" material'. Having experienced university censorship before—and printed a blank page—Clem considered it wiser this time to send the draft of his editorial about the ACCF to the vice-chancellor, only to be told that it was 'arrogant and unsophisticated', indeed exaggerated. (Paton was mollified in the end.) Ian Maxwell, and others, believed the ACCF should be given a chance to prove itself, 'until it quite clearly shows the cloven hoof'; perhaps it would be best, Maxwell believed, to liberalise it by giving support, rather than advocating a 'purge'.[42]

Meanwhile Clem had been advised by a friendly bureaucrat that members of the Commonwealth Literary Fund advisory board considered *Meanjin* 'politically biased'. In his editorials Clem's tone could be shrill, but it would be true to say that most of the charge of political bias arose from his ferocious commitment to civil liberties—in particular freedom of speech, of debate, access to information and freedom to read. If those people who made assaults on civil liberties, he told Ian Maxwell, 'smear *Meanjin* with Communist tags, then those tactics should be resisted with all the strength genuine liberals can muster'. True, he was a democratic socialist himself, but it was 'a new union between our political ideas and our imaginations' that Clem sought. He deplored the 'fatal division' of ideologies.

Of immediate concern was the attitude of writers. Vincent Buckley saw any genuine competition from a new magazine only as a positive good—and, announcing that he would contribute to *Quadrant* (since he approved of its anti-communism) urged Clem to see the challenge as 'a blessing, as I think it is'. He would not be a party to 'any attempt to drive you out of business', and had corresponded with Alec Hope on the matter, who said the same. But Hope would go further than contribute to *Quadrant*, and joined its board. Clem, who had been friendly with him—to the point of having Hope's daughter stay at Eltham—felt it a betrayal.[43]

Meanjin's very own cold war: the university dimension

AR Chisholm had been a stalwart on the *Meanjin* advisory board, and indeed a contributor to the magazine since its Brisbane days. His attachment to literature was not to English, but to Australian literature as well as French; he had been directed by his friend Christopher Brennan to the poet Stéphane Mallarmé—and had then happened upon the poetry of John Shaw Neilson, in which he saw real similarities with the work of the French Symbolist. In 1956, Chisholm was on the point of retirement. Clem was at the end of his tether—needed a respite, and might be off to Europe with his wife—so tossed around the idea that Chisholm might take over the journal. Other conservatives, and Chisholm himself, saw the prospect of him taking it over permanently. *Meanjin*, he believed, was 'on its last legs': the time had come for it to become a proper university journal.

As a younger man Chisholm had flirted with the ideas of (and had met) the French proto-fascist Charles Maurras, and just before the war had written privately that, should he have been a German, he would have found it difficult not to become a Nazi. But with the fall of France he had turned decisively against the Germans, becoming president of the Free French organisation in Melbourne. His earlier inclinations had become tempered into regular conservatism. As someone strongly anti-communist and decidedly anti-egalitarian, Chisholm had quarrelled with Clem about his politics: he could be relied upon to steer the journal into calmer waters. But Chisholm would need to be remunerated as befitted his academic station, which the university itself was not prepared to do. At the same time, vice-chancellor Paton told Maxwell there was little hope of *Meanjin* receiving any further grants while Christesen remained editor.

While efforts were being made by the university to secure external funding for Chisholm's appointment, and *Meanjin*, Clem was paralysed. He was crippled by his sense of academic inadequacy, and transfixed by Chisholm's extra authority as one of the trio constituting the powerful advisory board of the Commonwealth Literary Fund. For a long time they did not meet; Clem was hesitant to approach him. Moreover, Clem was feeling increasingly unhappy about surrendering the journal for two years, as now stipulated (not one). Chisholm would neuter it—the plans were to make it concerned with literature and art only, relegating (if not shedding) its creative component. Chisholm might be reluctant to hand it back, and a university committee might be more controlling. In addition, one of the scenarios was that, should the journal remain financially unsatisfactory, then it would be returned to Clem, the connection with the university severed.

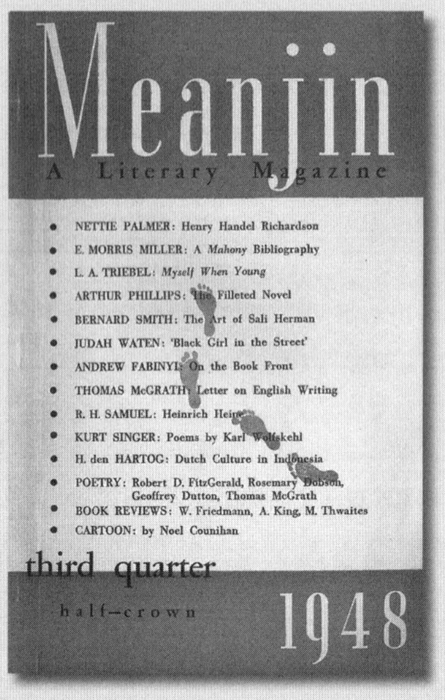

Meanjin 3/1948

This is the issue Stephen, then living in London, wrote about to Clem, expressing admiration: it leads with the only short story, by Judah Waten, but there is a strong showing of poetry, from Rosemary Dobson, RD FitzGerald and Geoffrey Dutton. Nettie Palmer writes on Henry Handel Richardson (she was moving towards a book), while AA Phillips castigates contemporary Australian writers for flat, boring prose. An insert contains four black-and-white illustrations of Australian paintings (rare, then), all by Sali Herman, the subject of an article by Bernard Smith. The number then becomes more international, with a piece dismissing contemporary English writing, another on Dutch culture in Indonesia, and one on the German-Jewish poet Karl Wolfskehl. Melbourne's professor of German, RH Samuel, offers a lively assessment of Heinrich Heine. And, in view of the decline in the number of Australian books published, there is a call by Andrew Fabinyi for government subsidy. Book reviews range from poetry to the conduct of relations with Japan.

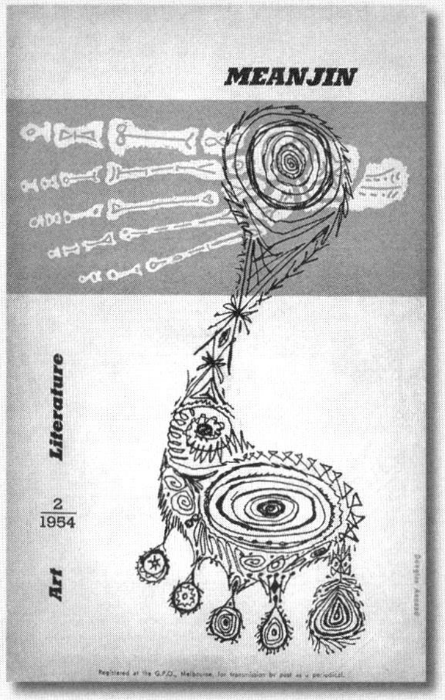

Meanjin 2/1954

A particularly 'composed' issue, which sold out rapidly. It opens with AD Hope on Australian literature and the universities, and—to show the depth of field—publishes some Australian letters by Dickens' associate RH Horne; includes two articles on television (imminent), plus two on film. There are also two on science fiction, one giving it the academic nod; articles on creative writing in Canada, and the arts in South Africa. There are 'Letters' from Paris and Lahore, and a piece on literary Hungary, paired with the eminent Marxist critic Lukács writing on 'Literary Standards and Writing for the People'. Ian Milner and Stephen Murray-Smith reverse the flow by commenting on British and Australian literature in Czechoslovakia. Articles appear on the Australian Elizabethan Theatre Trust, UNESCO and Australia, together with a suave response to an English assessment of the Australian classical music scene. Editorial concern is expressed about censorship—and comics. With the stories, Clem ventures one of his own—upholding the Australian social realist tradition—together with one by David Martin. Poems come from Judith Wright, RD FitzGerald, Ray Mathew and Louis Johnson, among others. Book reviews include AR Chisholm on Christopher Brennan's just-published *The Burden of Tyre*, with Frederick Macartney reviewing a selection of Aboriginal legends.

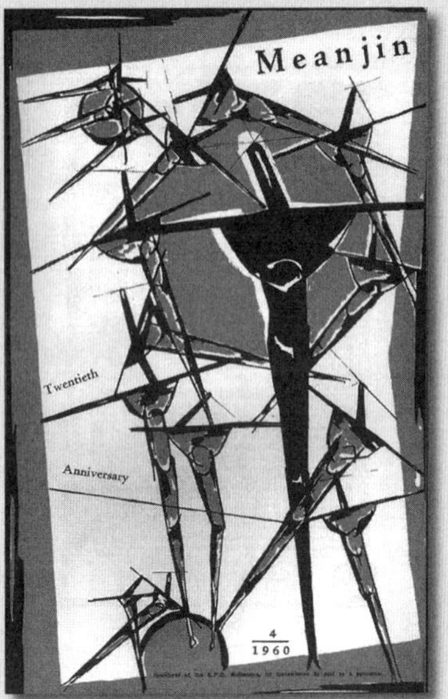

Meanjin 4/1960

Picking up the issue—cover designed by Roger Kemp—a Kahan pen-and-ink sketch of Dame Mary Gilmore prefaces an appreciation of her by RD FitzGerald; one of her poems follows (only one, for she was now ninety-six). Further poetry appears from AD Hope, Gwen Harwood and Geoffrey Dutton, among others. Next comes an article on Christopher Brennan, followed by a neglected poem; later, pieces on E Morris Miller and Alexander Harris (two very diverse Australian literary figures). Contemporary writing—top-dressing the canon—is dealt with in Fiction and Poetry Chronicles. The world beyond is present in a second nexus, an article on Indonesian writing accompanying a story by Achdiat Karta Mihardja. In a characteristic touch, Clem placed immediately after this an article on Zen and the West—as if to bring Asia home. But Paris has not lost its magnetism: Catherine Duncan reports on the intimidation of intellectuals in the turmoil surrounding the Algerian war. The visual arts—and Nina responding to Manning Clark's *Meeting Soviet Man*—are among the book reviews. Finally, since it was the twentieth anniversary of the journal, Clem writes a reflective editorial—more gloomy than celebratory.

Meanwhile AD Hope, a veteran of academic politics, helped to guide him over the points as well as he could from Canberra. Clem, in habitual fashion, began to hesitate, even prevaricate. He began discussing matters with the young historian Geoffrey Serle: in his calm, understated way Serle had a gritty commitment to *Meanjin*. He had returned six years earlier from Oxford, and, coming from a cultivated Melbourne background, had a concern for its high culture—he was writing a history of the gold-rush period, and would become involved in the preservation of old buildings through the National Trust in Victoria. Thoughtful, considered, taking a pipe from his mouth when he decided to speak, Serle might be the solution. Clem was prompted to play a masterstroke. *Meanjin*, after all, was still his. He announced that Serle, assisted from time to time by Brian Fitzpatrick and Vance Palmer, would mind the shop as acting editor.

For Clem, recent years had taken their toll. Since 1954, there had been the Petrov royal commission, the appearance of *Quadrant* (and *Overland*) and the rejection by the CLF of additional funding for an impressive suite of issues, featuring leading international writers, to mark the Olympic year. (It would have been a crowning achievement.) The uncertainty surrounding the continuing connection with the university did not help either: 'For years, it seems,' Clem told Ian Maxwell, 'my stomach has felt like a swarm of crawling maggots.' His morale was low: his own creative writing was suffering, there were no openings in publishing, while he felt he had been a failure at newspaper work because he had 'no liking for it, no "faith" in it'. Clem was well aware his personal relationships were fraught. He told AD Hope that 'I've been finished for some years …' Beaten, perhaps, but 'not quite defeated. Perhaps Serle and the others can achieve what I've failed to do.'

Clem would be anxious about the journal while away—he had toyed with the idea of editing it from Europe. But a holding operation was now in place, and as the prospect of his first trip overseas for nearly twenty years came closer, Clem's spirit lightened. Instead of the feared 'crack-up', his creative juices might start to flow again. Two years earlier he had returned from Queensland with 50,000 words written towards a novel, several short stories, the beginnings of a radio play, plus 'Five paintings also; sold two'. Now Nina would be finishing her research for a higher degree and meeting other Slavists at Oxford. He would be there alongside, Clem fancifully told Hugh McCrae, looking 'for flibbertigibbets, kobolds, spandulae, bogles, nixies, and expatriated disenfranchised bunyips'.[44]

In fact Clem would make a number of overseas visits, to conferences, with longer ones coinciding with Nina's study leave. He attended—as an observer—an Asian Writers Conference in New Delhi, and in the account he wrote of it (for Stephen) was alert to 'the new spirit of emergent Asia'. In Russia, he once attended the Bolshoi for the ballet, and had been given a very good seat in the Grand Tier. People in the audience turned round, some nodding to him; after a while, he thought he had better respond, so raised his hand, nodding his head from time to time. With some horror he suddenly realised they were acknowledging the dignitary in the next box. (Clem could tell a good story against himself.) Nonetheless he did make a good impression overseas.

He was repeatedly offered enticing jobs—'English editor' for UNESCO publications, with London publishers, or heading a new literary monthly in Warsaw among them. But as he once told Tom Inglis Moore, '*Meanjin* is my bloody misshapen infant and I'll keep it alive somehow.' There was also Nina's career to consider: however romantic the alternatives, he could not simply resign and tear off somewhere without considering her. For the same reason, flirtations with the idea of taking *Meanjin* elsewhere also came to naught. Unlike the 1945 removal to Melbourne, when a job had been found for Nina, she was now too senior to be accommodated so easily.[45]

Meanjin's outlook

For all the challenges—editorial and otherwise—*Meanjin* ploughed on. Clem had always felt there was a need for national quality commentary—a weekly, and yes (a persistent ambition of his) a monthly. Failing that, he felt obliged to comment on various subjects editorially. So there was a wide range of topics discussed, from publishing and the book trade to censorship issues, the need for an independent cultural body to replace the Commonwealth Literary Fund, and violent comics;

together with broader, compelling issues such as Australia's relations with Asia, McCarthyism in America (with its application here), and the international peace movement.

Clem had written editorials in his Brisbane days; he could coast along on a lofty plane and, when he chose to, even display a fine wit—something generally absent from *Meanjin*'s pages. But occasionally the irritation frequently expressed in his letters would show through—particularly in matters close to home. One editorial, while acknowledging the help and goodwill of the university, also spoke of his being 'subject to humbug [empty talk] on a monumental scale'. Combined with political and other pressures, Clem complained, this meant that 'we have been caught by the genitals'. *Meanjin* might be 'completely emasculated'. He had already had to suppress an editorial in 1950, given the 'prevailing mental climate—the most deplorable in Australia's history'. Being under most pressure then, Clem had taken to calling his column—with a nod to Shakespeare—'The Uneasy Chair'.[46]

The item *Meanjin* carried that would have most raised the eyebrows of the right was an article by the newly knighted (but onetime anarchist) critic Herbert Read, written in collaboration with regular English contributor Alex Comfort. 'No Annihilation' was a vigorous statement in favour of neutralism, given the hovering nuclear threat. 'We are not simpletons, sentimentalists, or fellow-travellers', wrote Read and Comfort, as they drew attention to the perils of being allies to an 'irresponsible Power'. But in the end, survival under Communist rule—if needs be—was a better option than extinction. (They had a touching faith in the power of British civilisation to come through and gradually ameliorate the worst effects of any occupation.)

Comfort was joint secretary of the Authors' World Peace Appeal, and Clem became caught up in the movement. He would speak at peace conferences, and more immediately wrote about peace activities in his editorials. In 1953 he reported that more than 800 English writers had signed the appeal, adding the names of many Australian authors who had—but then rushing on to list the names of those who had not. Clem's ally on the CLF advisory board, Tom Inglis Moore, was aghast to find himself appearing among '*Meanjin*'s list of fascists': he had explained to Clem, privately in his office, why he wouldn't sign. So it is not surprising that Alan McCulloch would write some years later that *Meanjin*'s greatest handicap—even deterring some writers—'is still that ancient red/pink tag'.[47]

As a counterpoint to Cold War issues, Clem, and those advising him, pointed to what should be the enduring nature of Australia's interest in the region. These were not 'tinpot' countries. Engagement with them should be real, given Asian poverty, and should be aimed at narrowing the gap rather than 'carry[ing] on a crusade against a political doctrine [Communism].' Reluctantly, after considering a number of options—including neutralism—*Meanjin* saw the American alliance as 'probably the only practical one at the moment'. In the meantime, the region's increasing reliance on the English language provided new opportunities for extending influence, albeit carefully.[48]

Despite fluctuations in physical size and format, in number of pages—and number of subscribers—*Meanjin* had, by the beginning of the 1960s, acquired the shape that would see Clem through to the end of his editorship. He had always, so far as he could, composed an issue, taking care to place an article next to a poem if he saw an unexpected affinity. But now this principle was elevated to becoming the cornerstone of the magazine: led off by a Louis Kahan sketch, the chosen writer would be represented by a piece, followed by an academic analysis of his work, and occasionally by an additional autobiographical piece as well. Sometimes the fictional piece would be an extract from a forthcoming novel—a come-on for readers.

Somewhat surprisingly—perhaps in an attempt to mollify him—the suspicious Xavier Herbert was the first to receive the treatment. But an Art Chronicle did not last the distance: the idea was transferred to effective round-ups of literary forms—first in a Poetry Chronicle, then extending to a Short Story Chronicle and a Fiction Chronicle. The idea was not only to note new work, but also to monitor shifts and developments, particularly towards urban sophistication and experimentalism. (In practice the chronicles were difficult to sustain: they came in two waves.) A section called Variety, lively in the first Melbourne issues—as people would sometimes contest reviews of their work—faded away. But the diversity of the journal remained, combined with a growing projection of its authority in an increasingly promising cultural context.[49]

For all Clem's reluctance to embrace things English, a London Letter periodically appeared in the journal—until AA Phillips' denunciation of the cultural cringe seems to have jolted him out of it. There remained, though, a sensitivity about Australians who still practised it in England. A radio program was described as 'misrepresent[ing] ourselves to the point of annihilation'; there was also mild exhilaration that Ray Lawler's play *Summer of the Seventeenth Doll* should be a success in London. An imaginative stroke was to get the rising Marxist critic John Berger to review an English exhibition of Australian art: gratifyingly he endorsed it as demonstrating 'the birth of a national tradition'. Meanwhile a New York Letter, despite Clem's sense of affinity with America, appeared only once; seven years were to pass before another such American article appeared in *Meanjin*. McCarthyism, and the threats to academic and other freedoms it presented, came to eclipse all else.[50]

European coverage—recognising that the magazine should bring the world to Australia as well as projecting a construct of Australia to the world—was strong. For a time, under the heading 'Intertraffic', articles on classic writers were provided by Melbourne academics (as the university intended when issuing its invitation in 1945). The focus was mostly French and German. The tilt towards eastern Europe began late, not becoming a continuing presence until 1954.

National cultural institutions—and *Meanjin* was on the way to becoming one—have a double role, not always appreciated. While they may aim to encourage the best—or the most significant—expression of cultural concerns in a national community, they should also provide exposure to the best the world has to offer. Hence *Meanjin* not only published what it saw as 'quality' Australian writing, but also sought to include leading writers from overseas.

In the period 1945–60—when the magazine was acquiring definition—Clem published single poems by Pablo Neruda, Paul Éluard, Sean O'Casey and a number of British writers. The American Karl Shapiro exited from *Meanjin* with a long poem envying this country its isolation from the rest of the world and its problems; Roskolenko trailed away too. Poems appeared soon after from Randall Jarrell and Kenneth Rexroth, but the only sustained American presence (from 1957, and for almost twenty years) was that of a writer Clem was particularly partial to, Charles Edward Eaton.

Sometimes *Meanjin* took work already known to overseas audiences, but a notable coup was the first publication of Ezra Pound's *Canto 90*, arranged by Melburnian Noel Stock. ('You are getting', Stock wrote, 'World Premiere of a poem that a literary magazine almost anywhere in the world would be jubilant to have.' Moreover, Pound subscribed to the journal for a time.) There were also poems from the Turkish Communist romantic Nazim Hikmet, and a whole segment of Chinese verse in translation. From nearer to hand there were poems from CK Stead and Allen Curnow, but a notable presence in the magazine was James K Baxter, who provided stories as well; indeed a New Zealand presence in the magazine was pretty much sustained by Baxter alone.

Short stories—or segments from work in progress—came from Anaïs Nin, Dylan Thomas, Henry Miller, Arnold Zweig, the Filipino writer NVM Gonzalez, CP Snow, Lu Hsün, and Jiří Weil (a Czech writer, said to be the first to set a novel in a gulag.). Articles and essays from overseas were no less distinguished. Energised by the postwar Labour government, British writers were well to the fore—but beyond that, the higher the Australian culture, the more it was still effectively predicated on England. (Labor leader HV Evatt had said, at a private function in Washington during the war, that if he had to choose between England and Australia going down, he would choose Australia—'For England is the bastion of us all.')

British writers included Arthur Koestler, William Plomer, John Berger, Frank Kermode and Alex Comfort. (Comfort, a scientist and activist, wrote widely until 1975, when—adding joy to comfort—he produced a famous sex manual.) In addition the versatile Victor Purcell, East Asian specialist and historian, contributed a number of pieces, including a playful one on satire and the establishment. From continental Europe came pieces by Jean-Paul Sartre and Louis Aragon, from Bertolt Brecht (recently deceased), and—timed as a defensive manoeuvre against the emergent *Overland*—a piece from the eminent Marxist critic György Lukács, pointing out the sterility of much contemporary writing, owing to the isolating individualism of the bourgeois writer.[51]

Towards the close of the war, *Meanjin* had placed itself squarely on the Pacific rim. It was not only the American material included, but also the sense of discovery of the world at Australia's doorstep. 'Asia ... on whose nipples we hang', as David Martin put it in his 1951 guest editorial. Over the next fifteen years interest in Asia remained a presence in the magazine. For CP Fitzgerald it was 'A New World Arising';

a theme followed by others, urging an engagement well beyond strategic considerations. But it was a question of knowing where to start. Interest in Japan tended to fall away as the war receded; India was negotiated mainly through its art, ancient and modern; Pakistan scarcely at all. China, Communist since 1949, occasioned some direct comment (in one case by a pair of visitors, one a Labor politician to the mainland, balanced by JG Latham writing on Taiwan, 'The Problem Island').

In 1953—just as the Korean War ended—*Meanjin* produced a special segment on Chinese literature, curated by Rewi Alley, a New Zealander who had been a member of the Chinese Communist Party since well before the war. Alley wrote of the 'cultural renaissance' China was experiencing. ('Generally speaking, in mission and Kuomintang circles, Western culture was lauded, Chinese neglected.') And while *Meanjin* gave the South-East Asian mainland scant attention, Indonesia was the object of several well-focused articles—whether on nationalism, Dutch culture there, or modern literature—with the featured writer being Archdiat Karta Mihardja, who would shortly take up a chair at the Australian National University. More importantly, Clem perceived the importance of the Bandung conference of 1955—the first assemblage of Afro-Asian nations—publishing two articles on it and compounding them with an editorial.[52]

Closer to home, *Meanjin* had marked off from the Indigenous people with those footprints on its first cover: the urge to understand and accommodate them remained strong. But such was the general assumption of their inevitably 'dying out' that a contributor found it necessary to strongly assert the contrary. In the meantime, there was anthropology—with its detached respect—and Clem published pieces by the Berndts, AP Elkin and Leonhard Adam (a regular visitor at the office). With 'primitive' art increasingly in vogue across the world, Aboriginal art excited particular attention—'the oldest art in existence', Alan McCulloch pointed out when the Art Gallery of New South Wales mounted a major exhibition. It was the first to identify individual Aboriginal artists. Clem's own bent was towards convergence, and in 1950 he revealed his synthesising vision: a *Meanjin* insert reproduced not only bark paintings and other Aboriginal art, but placed alongside were images of Sidney Nolan's Central Australian paintings. Plus a photograph, positing it all on place—the Jindyworobaks' environmental values. Elsewhere the anthropologist WEH Stanner commented on Donald Stuart's *Yandy*—a novel about the 1946 Pilbara strike—and Brian Fitzpatrick excoriated racist legislation, notably in Western Australia. But it was too early for there to be sociological articles, particularly any addressing the challenges facing urban Indigenous people.[53]

Book reviews were an irregular feature of the magazine. They were problematic: publishers supplied books spasmodically, or disregarded deadlines, so reviews appeared late. Often Clem had to buy the books himself, particularly if from overseas. So his policy varied. He often talked of abolishing the section altogether, but he also tried the other tack, of expanding the review section, making it more significant. Poetry books, which had preponderated, were eventually hived off into separate, recurrent review articles; fiction too.

The reviews, while still often engaging in tone, became less bold. 'Mr Arthur Koestler is not an important writer,' began *Meanjin*'s review of *The Yogi and the Commissar*. 'He is a self-important writer. He is not a creative artist. He is an actor. He is not a critic. He is an opinion-monger.' (No further contributions came from Mr Koestler.) Similarly Bernard Smith had taken a hefty side swipe at the art of Sidney Nolan: 'I prefer this kind of art from children: they invariably do it better than their imitators.' While Brian Fitzpatrick could be gently dismissive of the elegant shallowness of JD Pringle when reviewing his *Australian Accent*, by the end of the 1950s *Meanjin* reviews were generally more earnest. Academics were brought in more frequently, drawing the attention of the readership to specialist books of broader interest than usual. More imaginatively, overseas reviewers were sometimes lined up for Australian subjects, bringing a fresh perspective.

And sometimes Clem pulled off a coup: just as people were becoming aware of the iniquities of apartheid, a 1957 issue of the magazine led with a telling review of Trevor Huddlestone's *Naught for Your Comfort*, by the internationally famous South African writer Alan Paton.[54]

Popular culture and elitism

At this time there was much concern across the Anglosphere about the influence of comics. Their production had increased enormously: in Australia, seven times as many titles were available in 1954 than at the end of the war. Alarm was surprisingly general, ranging across the community from the Catholic Church (moral) to the Communist Party (most comic books were local printings of American titles). *Meanjin* was on the case quite early, and in 1954 produced an issue that was framed by it. The Australian Journalists Association had urged measures to protect Australian writers and artists from what was 'cheap and foreign'; Clem warmed to the theme. 'Surely any country has a right to protect its own culture from being perverted and corrupted by debased forms of a foreign culture,' he wrote. Otherwise 'indigenous art forms will in time disappear'. He was describing white cultural production—but went on to draw the analogy with Aboriginal culture, withering under the battery of European impact.

As Clem was writing, a number of states were introducing heavy-handed censorship. For there were cases known like the one *Meanjin* reported, of an English boy influenced by comics who murdered a policeman … and was hanged. The assertion of a direct connection between comics and 'juvenile delinquents' seemed self-evident; it took some time to wane. That was because other arguments were also powerful. Boys in particular were exposed to brute power, violence and (in the words of one *Meanjin* contributor, Norman Bartlett) were imprinted with 'cheap responses to the problems of everyday life'. Popeye, Captain Marvel, Dick Tracy, Hopalong Cassidy … none were exempt. 'Comic and sex books are now a definite evil influence in Australia,' Bartlett wrote. Children were 'wast[ing] time that should be devoted to more worthwhile hobbies'. In fact they were emerging as a new consumer group, the 'teenager'. Meanwhile the large adult readership among the poorly educated was acknowledged, but seen as too embarrassing to dwell on.[55]

Another threat to children was television, and on the eve of its introduction in Australia *Meanjin* was apprehensive. Clem's concern soon became that again it might see Australia becoming a 'dumping ground' for syndicated foreign product. Reports 'reaching this office' told of 'an enormous quantity of sub-normal trash' bound for Australia from America once transmission started. *Meanjin* also carried a number of articles on film during this period, as it edged towards becoming accepted as an art form; Clem was not moved to express his own opinion. It was quite otherwise with another category of popular culture, science fiction: he had been vaguely aware of a growing interest in it, and was surprised to find the English writers Angus Wilson and Arthur Koestler among those disposed to take it seriously. When FB Bryning offered a sci-fi story that was well written, 'but too "magaziny" for this journal', Clem asked him to write instead an article on the genre. In an editorial comment Clem backed it up with a somewhat wide-eyed run-down of Australian sci-fi networks, including 'fanzines'.[56]

For Clem's understanding of a literary magazine was that it should function as a cultural one: literature, among other things, was the cockpit where ideas were expressed as the whole culture took flight. Solid literary articles might give the magazine heft, but the whole landscape must always be kept in view. *Meanjin*'s mission was to advance an Australian (high) culture—while the general public was still immersed in the popular culture of the Anglosphere, as well as its local variants. At the time, it must be remembered, Australia was still overwhelmingly Anglo-Celtic: in the 1961 census, 95 per cent of the population could still be categorised as 'British subjects', whether born in Australia or overseas. Moreover, tertiary education was still rare. While today some 35 per cent of school leavers go on to attend university, in the early 1960s the figure would have been around 5 per cent. Melbourne had just ceased being the only university in the city.

The charge has been made that *Meanjin* was elitist, most tellingly by John Docker. But Clem was fundamentally opposed to class-based ideas of exclusivity, attacking public (today's private) schools—'they prepare the minds of their pupils for Fascism rather than Democracy', he wrote. Clem saw *Meanjin* as a kind of vanguard, a forum where ideas and issues could be discussed. The only hard edge of exclusion (a primary characteristic of elites), was—as far as Clem was concerned—the measure of 'quality' he applied to submissions. Similarly, in calling for the establishment of an arts-funding body like the Canada Council or a national theatre, *Meanjin* was addressing a profound lack in Australia's institutions, rather than seeking to exert undue influence; today similar appeals would be made in the name of the arts 'industry'—probably by people keener to control them.

In the postwar period and well after, when social democratic values were most widely held, the belief was prevalent among intellectuals—even economists—that art and (high) culture provided a core of values that should inform the whole society. Clem quoted with approval Jack Lindsay's formulation that culture sets about 'to integrate the various elements of new experience in a whole which combines tradition and the new possibilities'. Later, AA Phillips would enunciate what many felt to be a commonplace: 'I believe … that Australians have not yet achieved a firm sense of their identity, and that we need the help of our artists in this task.'

Clem's belief was that high culture could be appreciated by all, if 'given suitable direction'. He believed in 'the common man', and his right to realise what the poet Bernard O'Dowd called 'the Just City'. But Chifley's rejection of the proposal in 1949 for a grant for *Meanjin*, on the basis that it did not appeal to 'the common man', seemed to Clem a kind of tautology: the 'ordinary working man' didn't read '"quality" literature'. Clem therefore redefined the 'common man' as 'the school teachers, writers and would-be writers', plus 'a section of middle class people', who comprised the *Meanjin* readership. Given their loosely shared politics, the common reader was superimposed over the common man.

Much of this, looking beyond perceived national needs, increasingly takes on the aspect of being a post-Christian transposition of high spiritual values—even more apparent in the countervailing Leavisite universalism. Hence Clem's concern about 'the lolly-water … splashed in the newspapers', and the way 'the public's ability to receive better quality work and to form value-judgments is being slowly sapped'.[57]

As is the nature of progressive editors, Clem was disposed to aim for the highest plane, articulate the broadest trend. Even the loyal Harry Heseltine detected a regular cycle, apparent in the editorial columns once every five years or so, of optimism and talk of cultural breakthroughs alternating with 'the blackest prognostications of gloom'. Clem's sense of apartness ran deep, and came to be ratified by *Meanjin*'s mission. ('I'm an anachronism,' he would grumble.) As Alan McCulloch wrote in 1959, putting it bluntly, 'The climate and the time is wrong for *Meanjin*. You're on your own with it, necessarily so, and you mustn't expect too much from anyone.' Clem snorted in response that

> our *values*, and the values of the overwhelming majority, are poles apart. For myself, there is scarcely anything right in this society.

> Every day (in every way) I find I am disgusted with the values of the majority! I am alienated from this socio-political system.

After what he had been put through, this was scarcely to be wondered at. But 'the alienated Australian intellectual' would become a haunting presence in *Meanjin*'s pages.[58]

Clem, Nina and the Palmers

Before leaving the 1950s, we must return to Vance and Nettie Palmer. Clem's relations with the Palmers were never easy. One thing he did not realise was that Vance had, in a sense, been waiting for Nina. Years before he had twice used the name for women in his fiction—once even adding the surname Byrne, one of Clem's family names. Moreover, he had felt a strong affinity with Russia, through the revolution, and more particularly through its literature. Nina pressed the right button when she remarked of his novel *Daybreak* that it had a 'Tolstoyan stream of consciousness'. Old Russia was personified in this dainty, beautiful woman, striking in her simple goodness: Vance became smitten. He was persistent, though somewhat coy. He 'simply didn't know how to make love to women', Nina said later.

For her part, she was much taken with Vance—'I think you know', she told him, 'I believe [your work] to be one of those few things that make life worth living.' But the time came when she had to put him off. She let him down gently, while delivering the brutal message: 'Sorry if I'm too "detached" … I'm deeply sorry, but I don't love you.' So she wrote—in a letter that she may not have sent. It goes on to list the complications and betrayals any such commitment would entail. Melbourne was not Bloomsbury, nor the 1950s the 1970s. Instead Nina offered a deep, admiring friendship—extending to Nettie, who thought her a 'grand, constructive person', and the two daughters, whom she would have over to Eltham to stay.[59]

Clem had suspected Vance's interest long before Nina showed any awareness, but having implicit trust in her, chose to ignore it. 'I am jealous—pleased, but still jealous!' he told her. Instead of showing this—apart from a few hints—he constantly sought from Vance support and reassurance regarding *Meanjin*. This was readily given, extending to

Clem's short stories. Such praise was music to Clem's ears, for there was an element of hero-worship in his regard for Vance. 'The corpus of your work means more to me personally than that of any other Australian writer,' he told him. Indeed Vance wrote the kind of fiction that Clem would like to write. Part of the reason why he never produced his novel may well have been that he could not quite see how to do it distinctively.

Despite the considerable demands he made on Vance for time and advice, Clem could never be satisfied. When Vance went to England in 1955, he wrote him first one querulous letter, then another. Need was alchemised into accusation—the unacknowledged love triangle providing an edge. Vance's support, while great, should have been much greater: he should have responded to this, to that, and especially when Clem had recently said to him: 'You can make this journal, you know. It's in your hands.' (Vance probably didn't know what to say.) Clem also expressed the view that his novels 'lack *passion*'. Even so, Vance managed to write a conciliatory reply, including praise for *Meanjin*'s 'gallant showing' over the years. Even as he attacked it, Clem relied on Vance's detachment: it gave him a margin of safety. Vance could always be counted upon to take an exalted, Olympian view of affairs, seeing beyond human entanglements to the broader cause.[60]

Apart from half a dozen of Vance's stories, the Palmers published a steady stream of articles and book reviews in *Meanjin*. Then, when Clem went overseas in 1957, he asked Vance to help Geoff Serle when he was acting editor—particularly in suggesting ideas for articles and the people who might write them. Clem relied on Vance rather more as a sounding board once he returned, but various suggestions he made for short pieces Vance quietly resisted. Nevertheless Vance's magnificent short story 'The Afghan'—demonstrating that the English realised that racist assumptions about Asians would no longer wash, whereas Australians didn't—duly appeared in *Meanjin*. It would have confirmed Clem's feeling that Vance (and Nettie) should be commemorated—if only to help the young appreciate what had been written here already. Almost a year before it appeared, Clem drew up a list of likely contributors for a special Palmer issue. In the event, *Meanjin* 2/1959 carried a strikingly different range of articles and authors, buttressed by a set of appreciations. Vance was ambivalent about the venture. Once, as they were travelling by car, he said, 'Oh Clem, I feel as if I'm being buried before I'm dead.' Clem was silent for a moment, and then said, 'Oh, when that happens, we'll really put on a show.'[61]

Clem and Nina were visiting the Palmers one wintry afternoon in July 1959. Vance, talking about the autobiography he was writing, and a play, paused and got up to refuel the slow combustion stove. That done he turned round, and suddenly collapsed. Nina was at hand and tried to steady him, some say in her arms. But death was instantaneous. Lined up were the forthcoming special issue, a big dinner to mark the impending publication of *The Big Fellow*, and the University of Melbourne awarding him a Doctor of Letters. Only the special issue eventuated, now suddenly a memorial. The praise that Vance had been meant to see, along with Nettie, had become a series of eulogies, culminating in Arthur Phillips', spoken at the funeral. Clem felt the loss keenly. One of his prime markers in the world was no longer there.

4

STEPHEN

TEMPER DEMOCRATIC, BIAS AUSTRALIAN

1954–1959

Edging towards *Overland*

STEPHEN CHOSE THE moment to launch *Overland* well. Clearly there was no shortage of good Australian writers, but outlets were, if anything, diminishing. Book publishing was particularly poorly served. Stephen had pointed out that by 1952 the number of Australian books appearing was, at 616, almost exactly half of what it had been six years earlier, 1228.

But the marked scarcity of literary magazines might also present an opportunity. At this stage, in addition to *Meanjin*, there was the more esoteric *Southerly* in Sydney and two other less important ventures—*Ern Malley's Journal* (a more broadly conceived and now faltering version of *Angry Penguins*) and a short-lived Melbourne magazine aimed at new writers.[1]

To strengthen the venture, Stephen stressed continuity: 'incorporating the *Realist Writer*', the new magazine proclaimed on its masthead. *Overland* could simply be represented as a broader version of the old. In fact the editorial board was essentially an enlarged and national one—with no resignations or absences. Even Jack Coffey, the man who laid down the Party line to writers in a fairly humane fashion, was a key figure, advancing from issue number five to become associate editor with

Ian Turner. A broader magazine—aimed at readers, rather than writers—had been on the Realist Writers Group agenda, so Coffey and Frank Hardy could subsequently claim that it was the group, not Stephen, who set up *Overland.* But at the beginning it seems that Stephen's commitment, drive and organisational capacities engendered a number of tacit understandings: sharp political differences would emerge soon enough to disturb them.[2]

The decisive factor in the emergence of *Overland* appears to have been the intervention of Judah Waten. Waten was a force in the Australasian Book Society (ABS) and elsewhere, a powerful presence. Large, with bushy eyebrows, he could display an exacting scrutiny. But he could also project great affability: 'I wish I could have taken down all his good voluble talk,' noted Nettie Palmer. 'His consciousness of people's problems, differing from his own, is so acute and humorous.' In his sociability Waten was perfectly prepared to sup with the Devil—as personified by Mr Menzies—if need be. He could do so because at the same time he had a will of iron. On essentials, no-one could be more uncompromising.

Believing—to the end of his days—that the Soviet Union was the one great revolutionary power, Waten also believed that in Australia—given the struggle against the established order 'from the earliest days of convictism ... the democratic spirit is essentially revolutionary'. These were romantic views, but they enlarged his commitment to the cause. Waten had been resisting authority since, at the age of sixteen, he had been before the courts on a charge of handing out subversive leaflets at the Anzac Day march. When he graduated to founding a magazine (with Brian Fitzpatrick and others), it would provocatively be called *Strife*, for his style was a brash nihilism. Later he would be expelled from the Party—twice—and then, in a spirit of affirmation that amazed everyone, decide to rejoin it immediately after the Soviet invasion of Hungary.

Waten's strong sense of self had arisen from circumstance as much as character. Brought to Western Australia as an infant, he was nurtured in a family very proud of their Jewish and Russian culture, cast away though they were on the outskirts of Perth. But he became acutely aware of the dangers inherent in his mother's resolute backward glance, and from an early age had been committing large chunks of Australian poetry to memory. The struggles of his family to make a life here—his father as a hawker and bottle-o—would provide him with the materials that made his name, most notably in the collection of stories *Alien Son*, which appeared in 1952. The first notable literary treatment of the problems confronting non-English-speaking migrants, it was already on its way to becoming an Australian classic.

Waten had just published a novel, *The Unbending*. It revisits the same family material used in *Alien Son*, only this time the mother figure is not mute in English, but all the more vigorous for the blunt way she uses it. This mother is one of the strongest women in Australian literature, and the novel a fine study of the shifting weights in an enduring marriage. The complexities of neighbourhood relations are also deftly sketched, particularly as affected by men going off to war. Suddenly there is a strong presence of the IWW—the socialist Industrial Workers of the World—and the amplification of a union leader into the other 'unbending' main character. Waten had originally thought of placing the novel in the interwar period, but decided to move it to the earlier time—so that the rounding up, trial and jailings of IWW members would present an allegory with the increasingly McCarthyist climate, stiffening resistance. By June 1954 (as indicated in chapter 3) there was a strong counterattack.

It would be as well to broaden support. At the time, Waten was working part-time at the Jewish Council to Combat Fascism and Anti-Semitism. He had access to a fund and, he told Stephen, could come up with £15 to turn the *Realist Writer* into a printed magazine. The money was welcome, and vital. It was such a turn-up that Stephen had to ditch the advertisement for the *Realist Writer* he had just placed with *Meanjin*, substituting one for the new magazine.[3]

Waten's intervention was effective because Stephen's turn towards the literary life had been steadily strengthening. He was active in the peace movement, dutifully wrote pamphlets and in the Party press on subjects ranging from Indo-China to Melanesia, but remained marginalised in the Party. An ASIO assessment, that the view was held that he was unsuitable for executive positions because of his bourgeois background (and lordly style), may not have been so wide of the mark. Party functionaries may also have suspected that behind that flurry of activity they had a romantic on their hands. Not least was this evident in the way Stephen toyed with writing a novel—and produced a short story—based on the liberation struggle then underway in Malaya.[4]

Gradually that interest faded, for it was a product of his London years. Increasingly Stephen turned—returned—to Australian literature. Although as a child he had taken some years to open his set of Henry Lawson, he made up for it now. (An appreciative booklet would come later.) Lawson he saw as primal: at a time when Australian literature was largely written 'by expatriates on expatriate themes', Lawson had, in the bush ballad, been 'the first of our writers to evolve a specific national form'. It was being taken further, 'to a more serious social end', by poets such as John Manifold. But it was the short story where he shone, laying the foundation for the Australian realist tradition. The stoic bush types, with their capacity for nobility despite the harsh, madness-inducing conditions of their lives, would have appealed to Stephen. So too would the blunt descriptions of the bush by a man who had grown up in it—not as something hostile, but as an environment that was indifferent and testing. Lawson was our Chaucer, said Stephen, our Gorki. The second comparison was also one that the visiting British actor Peter Ustinov came to make, after being tossed a volume of the short stories by a passing stockman. And yet Lawson was out of print in Australia—though not in the Soviet Union.[5]

Since Stephen regarded Lawson as head and shoulders above them all (an old-fashioned view, he realised), it is not surprising that his work should have prompted Stephen's first project for a short-story anthology, in Prague. Now his concern was broader and, cheerfully disregarding academic prognostication, he took a challenging line from Lawson, *The Tracks We Travel*, as the title for this new collection. (It appeared in time for Christmas 1953.) The introduction asserted the need to resist the continued campaign of the 'vested powers' to 'undermine man's faith in himself, and in the betterment of society'. Around the time of Federation, the battle for the recognition of Australian cultural nationhood was won by Lawson, Tom Roberts 'and other giants of the period'. But now it needed to be fought anew.

Appealing to a still largely reading public, Stephen denounced 'foreign decadence', manifested in comics, movies, 'music', in syndicated journalism, in pornography, sadism, sex and violence. All this, he maintained, worked for hatred between people and nations, 'thus conditioning our people to the thought of war'. Given the wave of amerikitsch, it was timely to assert—in a spirit of cultural independence—the 'enduring qualities of our inheritance'. Stephen did not name socialist realism either; but he believed that as in no other English-speaking country, Australian writing 'has remained true to the people it deals with'. For *Tracks* he had sought stories 'close to life', consciously following the Lawson tradition, rejecting 'high writing' and any displaying an excessive psychological preoccupation. On the other hand, he gladly included a couple of stories from New Zealand—the anthology was published by the Australasian Book Society, after all. Everyday life and working conditions were felt to be much the same in the two countries.

Tracks indicates how much Stephen's predilection was moving beyond the narrow focus of the *Realist Writer*. Vance Palmer, Flexmore Hudson, Alan Marshall and Frank Dalby Davison spoke for a broader left-centred humanism rather than any Party rigidity. A number of social realist writers—distinctly lesser names—were bundled towards the back: some were to re-emerge in the early pages of *Overland*. Stephen had cast the net wide, so he thought—with stories set across the nation, in country and city, in various workplaces, and among the Indigenous; the writing varied from the comic to the tragic. Ian Turner, while heartened by the way the anthology demonstrated that there *was* an Australian tradition, felt that there should have been more stories about industrial workers—since they would shape the Australia of the future. But Stephen's own taste could incline towards the classical, particularly in verse. With a burst of editorial brio he closed the collection not with a short story but a long poem, John Manifold's 'Lawson's Birthday'. Set in Heaven, it has many droll touches, as when a bored Henry Lawson—plucking a quill from the wing of a passing angel—decides to complete his fragment on Eureka. Its conclusion ended the book with a ringing peroration:

> So to earth the verse descends …
> Someone here may catch a couplet of it, someone there a rhyme,
> Someone else a single image—just a fragment at a time!
> All dispersed, that mighty ballad! You can glean it grain by grain
> From your workmates, from your comrades, from a stranger in the
> train …[6]

For Stephen there was another great figure in Australian literature, a figure normally relegated for an anthologist or magazine editor by the fact he was not a short-story writer. This was Joseph Furphy, whose *Such Is Life* he saw as a 'rambling picaresque novel of intricate construction written by an outback worker'. Stephen praised its humour, and the ferocity of Furphy's opposition to inequality and social injustice. 'If not the greatest work produced in our country,' he told an overseas correspondent, 'I think it is the most important.' It had been little known until a new edition was published just before the end of the war. Furphy's formulation for describing his novel, 'temper, democratic; bias, offensively Australian', lodged in Stephen's consciousness.[7]

It would emerge, with the word 'offensively' dropped, as the slogan for *Overland*: Stephen had too much of a sense of the rest of the world to retain it. England had produced radicals too, people who had influenced Australia. One of these was Francis Adams, who spent six years here in the 1880s: novelist, shrewd observer of Australian life, an opponent of racism and imperialism, and a passionate egalitarian. As a well-spoken middle-class firebrand, he functioned as a kind of examplar for Stephen, who was repeatedly drawn back to him.[8]

Early issues

The first issue of *Overland*, appearing in spring 1954, was a delicate balancing act. The aspirations of the magazine were evident on the cover, in the names that book-ended the list of authors: Nettie Palmer and AD Hope. Above it, to reassure readers of the *Realist Writer*, was a vigorous sketch by Noel Counihan of a pair of diggers off to the goldfields. Over the page, a short editorial. The new magazine, it was promised, would aim high, 'but has no exclusive or academic standards of any kind'. *Overland* believed in 'developing writing talent in people of diverse background', and asked readers, 'however inexpert', to write for it, so long as they shared 'our belief in the traditional dream of a better Australia'. Endorsements from literary figures followed—from Dame Mary Gilmore, Vance Palmer, Alan Marshall, and a guarded one from RG Howarth of *Southerly*. Clem endorsed it too, welcoming the way the magazine promised to stand 'four-square behind genuinely Australian democratic values. Providing it honestly adheres to its progressive editorial policy', he added—aware that many of the writers appearing in it were likely to be members of the Party—he was happy to support it.

Given its aims, the new magazine would not challenge *Meanjin* directly: its eyes were too close to the ground. Moreover, it provided another platform to defend dissident writers such as Judah Waten, whose novel *The Unbending* had recently drawn fierce attacks from the daily press, and on the Commonwealth Literary Fund for subsidising it. Brian Fitzpatrick, who appeared regularly in *Meanjin*, wrote a vigorous account of the affair for *Overland*—which Stephen placed at the front of the magazine.

Also in that first issue was a long first half of a piece by John Manifold on 'Banjo' Paterson (an anarchist by temperament, he decided), a poetical spat between AD Hope and David Martin, and pieces by Nettie Palmer and Katharine Susannah Prichard on Henry Handel Richardson. Again, as with Furphy, her work had been slow to gain traction; but Prichard believed—and there is a case—that Richardson's sensibility was formed in musical Leipzig, and that her writing revealed her to be rather remote from Australia. To offset this cultural infill, Stephen made sure that the longest piece in this opening issue was a John Morrison story about wharfies. And almost unwittingly, the short poem that led off the issue did provide a keynote for much that was to come, particularly later: called 'Swans in Footscray', it used the birds, and a loose environmental consciousness, to link the industrial suburb to the vanquished Indigenous people.

Anniversaries can be useful things. *Overland* number 2 highlighted the Eureka Stockade, since it was prepared in time for its centenary. Stephen's old mate Tim Burstall groaned when told about it in the pub, and a number of people would have had that reaction. Momentarily Stephen was carried away with the idea for yet another book—a Eureka anthology—but when it came to *Overland* he was much more measured. Also in that issue was a perceptive piece by David Martin on Miles Franklin, who had just died; the main piece on Eureka was a rather ponderous essay by HV Evatt. It was not even new. But it was by the leader of the Opposition, and usefully drew attention to an older benchmark of radical revolt. Indeed a casual reader could have picked up these first two issues of the magazine and not connected it with the Party at all: a pronounced interest in the literary world of eastern Europe in 'Swag'—Stephen's rag-bag of editorial observations—was the main give-away. 'We ask our readers to espouse no particular political philosophy', Stephen would shortly say, while being alert to the broader implications of cultural issues.

Stephen wanted to include a prominent workers element. Another event helped here, too: the mining disaster in October 1954 at Collinsville, in Queensland, when seven men died as the coalface exploded. They were tough, these miners, working underground bare-chested, using only picks and shovels. That second issue of *Overland* led with poems about the disaster; Stephen was moved to appoint a coalfields representative to the board. Meanwhile the debate with Vic Williams in Perth continued. Stephen was determined to show goodwill, and put Williams' wife on the board. This helped to keep exchanges polite, but Williams was appalled by the overwhelmingly middle-class nature of the board. The worker, he believed, instinctively understood the laggardly gradualism of reform, so made the better socialist; the intellectual, on the other hand, came to it 'from book understanding, from personal frustrations. The intellectual starts at the roof, and has to build his foundations.'

Apart from ideological considerations, Williams felt that the magazine would become something that he could no longer sell to his workmates. He was dogmatic in his insistence that everything must ultimately be based on the economic struggle of the people, and written 'in such a way as to give them political direction'. This made him an easy target: Len Fox wrote to Stephen that Williams seemed to rate 'a bad poem about a strike [as] better than a good poem about a man's thoughts ...' Nonetheless, even though he derided the middle class as being out of touch with reality, he did put his finger on the problem: 'the ever-present danger is for *Overland* to drift with the tide away from the working class, the trade unions'.[9]

In order to ease *Overland*'s passage to acceptance, Stephen decided to sell the magazine at one shilling rather than two, which meant that subscribers to the *Realist Writer* now got two copies of the new magazine in place of a single one of the old. Printing it on high-grade newsprint helped. He had hopes—sustained—that its reach would be wider. The first issue rapidly sold out its 1000 copies. By February 1955 he was able to boast 'an *immediate* sale of 1500 copies'—three times that of *Southerly* 'and nearly as great as *Meanjin*'.[10]

Stephen was always aware, as was everybody else, of *Overland*'s positioning in relation to the older magazine. There was real concern that Clem's venture should not be imperilled: a Sydney correspondent hoped that the new magazine might even 'help' *Meanjin*. Stephen, who on returning to university had become 'quite friendly' with the senior editor, was always quite deferential to him—and would publish tributes and other material by or about Clem. He went so far as to say to his editorial board early on that '*Overland* is not seeking to replace *Meanjin*, nor to outshine it.' Their roles were quite different, even as *Overland* moved outwards from its working-class concerns. Through its literary content, *Overland* would hope to 'wage a vigorous battle on the middle class intellectual front'. *Meanjin*, for all its fine qualities, could not do this. It had its 'cosmopolitan tendencies', and beyond that should operate as 'the forum & organ for *all* the writers in Australia'.

Overland's mission, as Stephen came to see it, was to explore traditional popular culture in Australia while encouraging new literature, and, following the example of the *Bulletin*, draw 'the two streams together … and hence strengthen both'. On the one hand, Stephen believed, no serious author now could write without paying attention to working people and their speech. And on the other, the magazine could not be aimed only at the working class. Bill Wannan, his predecessor as editor of the *Realist Writer*, was in complete agreement: 'It has to try and reach all sections, based on its "aggressive Australianism" as opposed to the rubbish coming in from overseas.' But the two aims were at variance. One reader, on renewing her subscription, chided that there were a lot of people 'besides waterside workers, railway workers, mechanics and farm workers, and a lot of these others might appreciate [*Overland*] if it were not overloaded with stories about workers at work'. The radical journalist Clive Turnbull had similarly excoriated 'the current bucolic cult', causing much offence.

Overland, Stephen believed, was 'reaching an audience with a new and awakening interest in books and literature', a progressive audience. It was important, said Bill Wannan, 'to give this movement leadership and direction'. Thus Stephen editorialised, aligning the future with the past, giving radicalism some ballast. 'Tradition and Today', he headed one piece: 'A distinctively Australian literature', Stephen asserted, 'was born among the native-born and nationally-minded men and women of the "lower classes"', who rejected 'instinctively and impatiently' the Anglophile culture of 'their social and economic betters.' But the backward glance would only take you so far. It was more important to produce 'a rather more radical magazine which would encourage ... younger writers, writers particularly with a working class background who ... have something important to say'.[11]

Short stories and poetry

This, alas, was easier said than done. Looking at the short stories published in the first dozen issues of *Overland*, freshness and vibrancy are not their most striking characteristics. The name writers include Waten, Hardy and, shortly after, David Martin, together with lesser lights of the Realist Writers Group. Hardy spins a couple of Billy Borker yarns—with engaging drawings by Vane Lindesay. But first came his 'Death of a Unionist', a heroic tale of working-class struggle appalling in its sexist assumptions—the wife is called 'Shorty' (as if a working mate), and unconvincingly, following Bill's death, gratifies a whim of his to give their new baby to a childless couple. Fiction by women was published later, but with the exception of a story by Gwen Kelly—about a promising boy shunted into tech school—they were generally on 'feminine' subjects.

Occasionally the men produced what read like working-class fairytales—an early one by Rex Mortimer drew negative comment, and highlighted the problem. Responding, Stephen referred to 'the greatest defect ... of our writers, to capture that *human* quality, that link with life, without which even the most militant story is dead and useless'. John Manifold picked up on the way there seemed to be more of a sense of the people, more vividness and humour, among the 'moleskins' in the country than among 'the industrials'. With them, writers who were not 'born' proletarians seemed to be overdoing it. But from the other direction, genuine workers with a patchy, bourgeois education often found themselves paralysed when writing. Maybe, thought Stephen; but the paralysis was partly induced by 'progressive writers ... being hagridden by fear of not having the right "content"'. (The column 'Smoko', drawing on incidents from working life, collapsed in a belly laugh after half a dozen issues.) The real problem was that while there was much demand for more stories, the quality was lacking.[12]

The one great exception was John Morrison, who provided two short stories in this period. One story is set on the waterfront, as are a number of his (for he had been a wharfie), exploring the human situation behind industrial politics: 'He stands not merely on the side of his proletarians,' wrote AA Phillips, 'but among them.' The other, with its careful construction of life among the hands on a sheep station, draws on Morrison's early experience in the new country. It is a rite-of-passage story, the youth inducted into Australia and as a recognised working man by getting his first union ticket. Both stories involve bosses unsuccessfully trying to put one over workers: almost tailor-made for *Overland.*

But Morrison's writing is far more accomplished than that. (Interestingly, when Stephen wrote an introduction for a book of his short stories much later, neither of these two appeared in it.) Although he also wrote a couple of novels, it is Morrison's short stories that have an enduring if limited reputation. Many are centred on small incidents or chance encounters among ordinary folk, told with deft characterisation and actualisation of place. Stephen became an enthusiast, and thought one of Morrison's stories a candidate for the best written in Australia since Lawson.

Reclusive, hard-working, and modest in his needs, Morrison was content so long as he had enough money to write. He was a member of the Party, but would not party. He would, if need be, 'refrain from saying certain things I know to be true, but I'm not prepared to say things I know are not true'. Harmony was what he sought, and he was delighted that Stephen had managed in *Overland* 'to have kept clear of anything smacking of sectarianism'.[13]

Compared with the short stories, the poetry in the early issues of *Overland* was rather better. Around half a dozen pieces (the length varied) appeared each time. New poets such as Rodney Hall and Chris Wallace-Crabbe were published, along with Dorothy Hewett, whose 'Atomic Lullaby' was exemplary: bitterly it drew on an intimate traditional form to take a tough political stance.

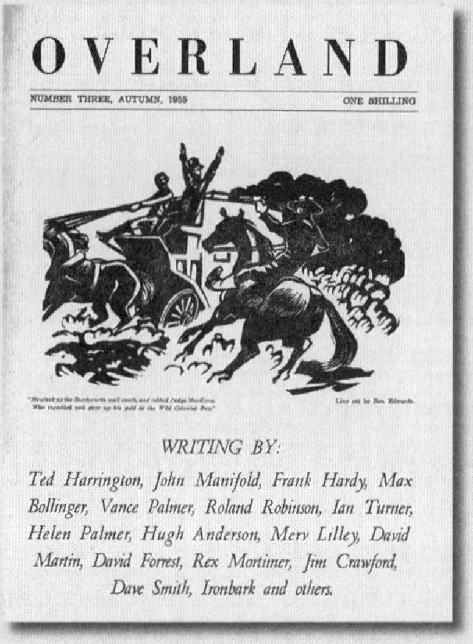
OVERLAND

NUMBER THREE, AUTUMN, 1955 ONE SHILLING

WRITING BY:

Ted Harrington, John Manifold, Frank Hardy, Max Bollinger, Vance Palmer, Roland Robinson, Ian Turner, Helen Palmer, Hugh Anderson, Merv Lilley, David Martin, David Forrest, Rex Mortimer, Jim Crawford, Dave Smith, Ironbark and others.

***Overland* 3, Autumn 1955**

This issue—only twenty-four pages—begins with an editorial referring to McCarthyism: 'Culture? That's Red!' It features Frank Hardy writing on Ted Harrington—the last of the bush balladists—with examples of his work and a sketch by Noel Counihan. The four stories include an effective piece by David Forrest (David Denholm), with an ageing Indigenous man empathetically described—and shafted by white-man one-liners. Hugh Anderson contributes the second part of his article on the colonial minstrel Charles Thatcher. Vance Palmer and his daughter Helen review books, along with Ian Turner. Poetry by John Manifold, David Martin and Merv Lilley.

Overland 12, Winter 1958

Katharine Susannah Prichard issue. There is a short story by her, a credo, and a tribute to the late poet Hugh McCrae. Appreciative pieces come from Aileen Palmer, Gavin Casey and Dame Mary Gilmore. But there is also a strong contemporary component: Elizabeth Vassilieff counters the right-wing warrior Frank Knopfelmacher, while Laurence Collinson writes on the Hiroshima Panels, then touring Australia. (Dorothy Hewett's blistering 'Atomic Lullaby' opens the issue.) There is an interview with Richard Beynon, author of the highly successful new play *The Shifting Heart*. David Martin writes on Thailand. Two Henry Lawson poems, buried in newspapers in New Zealand, provide historical infill. Book reviews include Judah Waten on Vance Palmer's latest novel, Vincent Buckley on Kenneth Slessor, Bill Harney on Ted Harrington, and two reviews of Nino Culotta's *They're a Weird Mob*. Ian Turner is uncomfortable about *Voss*.

Prominent among contributors was the well-known John Manifold, the energising force in the Brisbane Realist Writers Group. Manifold was a patrician—he came from a Western District pastoral family, had taught at Geelong Grammar, still spoke with a Cambridge accent. One young writer found him patronising, with a 'knack … of pinpricking in exactly the right spot'. For all that, Manifold thought of himself as an anarchist who—to achieve results—had compromised to become a Communist. He was indeed the manifestation of his name, a man of diverse talents. The house at Wynnum was full of musical instruments; Manifold was also a scholar, working at the time on his *The Music in English Drama, from Shakespeare to Purcell.* Capable of translating Molière into Queenslandese—and reciting it humorously over the dinner table—Manifold was also a keen advocate of Australian folk music: his group the Bandicoots was one of the longest-running bush bands. Ballads were a particular enthusiasm, as was the sonnet: traditional forms appealed to him.

Stephen had met Manifold in London, and had looked him up when in Queensland. Their relationship became warmly professional. Manifold sent many poems—some, such as 'Bellerophon' (about a wild horse), among his best. There were urbane translations from French poets, and also the suite 'A Red Rosary', described by Rodney Hall as 'a kind of revolutionary's calendar of saints'. Although uneven, it was a major offering, the fruit of ten years' thought.[14]

People picking up *Overland* in its first six years would have been struck by the regular appearance of two new Melbourne poets, David Martin and Laurence Collinson. Stephen had published David Martin in the *Realist Writer*: he would become a stalwart of *Overland*. Martin appeared in eight of the first ten issues, occasionally turning his hand to functional prose, but primarily as a poet. He had already published poetry extensively, in German and in English. Indeed, Martin once had the extraordinary experience of hearing a Russian choir on the radio singing a lyric that he recognised as one of his own.

Martin was born in Budapest as Ludwig Detsinyi, of a Jewish family who participated in the old cosmopolitanism of *Mittel Europa*. In fact he wore his Judaism lightly; he was not even circumcised. Brought up in Berlin, as an eighteen-year-old Martin fled to Holland after Hitler came to power, for he was also a Communist. Then followed a spell in Hungary, on a kibbutz in Palestine, and next a period in Spain as a member of the International Brigade. Because of his short-sightedness, he could not fight in the front line, but was wounded twice; he acted as an interpreter and medical orderly. Rejoining his family in England, Martin married soon after, and worked as a journalist, and then when war broke out translated for the European Service of the BBC. It was as a journalist he left for India in 1948, arriving the night Gandhi was shot. After having gathered material for a novel, he decided to move on with his wife and small boy to Australia. There was no particular intention to settle when they went to live in Sydney. But, with the prompting and help of Judah Waten, they decided to move to Melbourne—and stayed.

Far from being a rootless cosmopolitan, Martin had a rare capacity for serial affinity with new countries and people. His poem 'Bagpipes in Hobart' may be unequalled in the way it captures the atmosphere of that city, through the prism of a Scots band on a rainy day. Truthfully he could claim, as he did when interviewed, to have been 'excited by the Australianism of Australia … I've always tried to find what Australia has that other countries have not.' The old British-derived Australia was not, he came to believe, 'a simple country, [and] Australians not a simple people; rather, a complex country and a subtle people'. The surface was often deceptively placid, but there were tensions beneath; Martin did not feel ready for a long time to draw them out in prose, addressing conflict. But poetry was another matter.

Martin had discovered an 'elective affinity' with English almost as soon as he got to England. So much would English eventually become his working and thinking language, that towards the end of his life he found he could no longer write a literate German letter. His English could be rich and resonant, his good ear enabling him to assume a naturalness in it with surprising mastery. Early *Overland* poems included a sparely written ballad of mourning for those lost in a mining disaster; a highly satirical response to white Australia's appropriation of Indigenous names; and others that compound sharp observation with a combative conclusion.

Stephen told Martin that he considered it one of his 'peace duties' to ensure that the writer received private financial support to write a novel. But having taken him on board, Stephen made the mistake of issuing orders. When still running the *Realist Writer*, he dashed off a note requesting a poem 'by Monday, please'. Back came a response saying you can't have a poem by Monday, *Obersturmbannführer* Murray-Smith! The spat quickly subsided, as there was much drawing the two men together. Apart from his impeccable left-wing credentials (he joined the Communist Party of Australia in 1951), David Martin would have appealed to Stephen as an enlargement of the Jewish ambience Nita had brought with her—even though Martin was inclined to castigate the notion of the Chosen People, since it had helped to bring upon the Jews so much persecution. In the end, for him Jewishness was just another form of tribalism, which he detested. Martin had married a Quaker; Stephen was impressed by the fact that Richenda was the great-granddaughter of the prison reformer Elizabeth Fry. Despite Martin's reclusiveness, their friendship deepened as the years rolled on.[15]

Another poet, also Jewish, was taken under his wing and promoted by Stephen. This was Laurence Collinson, English-born but a leading light in *Barjai*, the Brisbane-based magazine put out by schoolboys that—with Clem's encouragement—had grown into a national youth one. He was also a notable painter, and a prominent activist in Brisbane's art politics. Collinson had since moved to Melbourne, where he began with odd jobs such as mail-sorting before training to become a teacher. His talent was strikingly multifaceted: Collinson wrote for the theatre (acting in his own plays), while his painting came to express a rare note of gaiety and social satire. But poetry remained his forte.

Stephen was intrigued by Collinson's poetry—despite the occasional flat lines—and published a good deal of it in the magazine. Perhaps he saw him, as an *Overland* reviewer did, as 'one of those poets who may help us to find an Australian synthesis of the personal and social moods of poetry'. Certainly few poems have spoken as 'Warning'—as elegantly as a parable—of individual failure to respond to creeping fascism. But generally, running through Collinson's poetry, is a strong sense of everybody's essential isolation: this can give a sudden stab often when it has been most accomplished. 'Love' he saw as including all spontaneous sympathy, even affinity. Collinson stated an interest in what he termed the 'marginalised', in particular women, children and old maids—although strikingly his poem 'Old Maid in a Late Tram' begins with a sympathetic scrutiny of the woman sitting opposite, then moves across a bridge of frustration to focus on himself as an ageing gay man.

Collinson, a member of the Party, was surprised when Stephen told him he would like to publish a book of his poetry: he did not think it political enough. Moreover, it would be *Overland*'s first published book; a gamble. The sums were done on paper, and it was thought the venture would just about break even: 'We hope', a large hand pencilled in.

The Moods of Love drew widely divergent responses: RA Simpson thought 'Old Maid' one of the best poems written in Australia. People from Dame Mary Gilmore to Ray Mathew to Douglas Stewart on the *Bulletin*'s Red Page thought highly of the book. But the readers for the Commonwealth Literary Fund and Vincent Buckley, who deemed the central set of sonnets 'a depressing failure', disliked it. The *Age* disapproved of its 'embarrassing emotionalism', code perhaps for its hint of gay sexuality. Stephen, aware of the value of controversy, put out a sheet highlighting this range of opinion. *The Moods of Love* turned out to be one of the most successful books of Australian poetry for a long time, selling out both hard and paperback versions. Nonetheless the whole edition ran to only 600 copies.

Collinson himself, despite a brisk way with words that could be humorous, was generally lugubrious. When visiting the Murray-Smiths at Mount Eliza, he would stay overnight; Nita thought him a *schlemiel*, a bumbling, unfortunate person. But Collinson could socialise effectively, and in 1960 was president of the Fellowship of Australian Writers. He joined a group of poets, associated with the anthology *Eight by Eight* (1963), and also had success with play scripts. Encouraged, he decided to seek his fortune in London. David Martin, encountering him in Collins Street with a furled umbrella hooked over one arm and his mother guided by the other, already thought him a displaced Englishman.[16]

Ian Turner and radical nationalism

Once back from Czechoslovakia, Stephen caught up with his friend Ian Turner. Turner had worked in the railways union, as a cleaner—sent there by the Party. Intellectual though he was, his sturdiness, good humour and engaging capacity to listen soon won the confidence of the men. For a time he had been secretary of the Peace Council, the job Stephen now held; Turner had become secretary of the Australasian Book Society (ABS). The two resumed their friendship: once Turner's wife Amirah wrote to Stephen in exasperation about 'your dear mate Turner ... I could never get either of you two to admit to any faults about each other'. With Turner an associate editor of *Overland*, for a time the magazine and the book society were run in double harness. ASIO, on the money for a change, reported that the 'liaison' between Turner and Murray-Smith functioned with Stephen as the driving force, while Turner 'was the man who was supplying the ideas and tactics'.

However tight-lipped Stephen may have been before others about Turner, he was certainly prepared to let fly at the man himself. Turner was good at handling people and building up confidence, but his romantic persona extended to a lackadaisical attitude towards solid commitments. When in 1954 Stephen went interstate, he was appalled to find on returning that Turner had seemingly disappeared for a month. Yet the ABS was short-staffed and in a perilous position, while there were various pressing tasks connected with *Overland*: Stephen had assumed that Turner, having hung on to manuscripts and correspondence, would have been around to deal with them. 'I feel your well-known weakness of not being able to say no', he remonstrated, 'has got you in again'.

Meanwhile Turner began writing more for *Overland*. Emboldened by being an associate editor, he began to assemble the ingredients of a historically based radical nationalism: essential 'if we are to arrive at a full understanding of our democratic tradition, and its literary expression'. While attending to historical materialism, the romantic kept coming through: 'in our time an old society is dying and a new society is being born', Turner wrote in connection with the novelist James Aldridge. 'To destroy inevitability—that's the aim of all liberty.' But individualism must be tempered: 'Man cannot tear himself apart from society.' It was the context for all freedom, even as man took 'to himself all that human history has created for him ... to shape it to his own conscious purpose'. Turner also wrote on cultural matters, including a review of Patrick White's novel *Voss*, which he initially dismissed as a signpost pointing 'towards no land of experience that we can recognise as our own'.[17]

It was a richly suggestive piece by AA Phillips on 'The Australian Tradition', published in the fifth issue, that first got Turner going. He returned to the fray four years later, discussing Russel Ward's *The Australian Legend*. For Australian radicals, socialists and Communists, Turner wrote, traditionally oriented towards overseas and borne along by what they supposed to be the tide of history, it had come as a surprise to learn that aggressive, militant democracy was not only characteristic of the international labour movement; it was also 'deep-rooted in Australian popular history … fraternity existed not only in the Popular Front, but in the Australian tradition', so '"comrade" had much in common with "mate".' This, Turner believed, added 'another dimension' to postwar leftist thinking, giving rise to what he termed 'radical nationalism'.

It was often apparent in the new interest in the broadsheets and the bush balladists, and in particular the 1890s, which, with the rise of organised labour, many Australians felt 'to be the birth-years of the Australian spirit'. As Turner pointed out, 'Australia is unusual, if not unique, in that the qualities which are valued had their origins very definitely among the "lower orders".' But with the growth of material prosperity, and the rise of consumerism, egalitarianism had become 'a passive acceptance rather than an active assertion'. Indeed traditional Australian values ran the risk of being smothered by 'the T-bones and television of the welfare state'. It was to be hoped they would survive, even if they had gone underground. In writing, though, ideally they should remain 'dominant'. 'The attitudes of a writer', Turner maintained, should be 'independent rather than subservient, radical rather than conforming, egalitarian rather than aristocratic, brotherly rather than individualistic'.[18]

Turner's more marshalled arguments helped Stephen to clarify his views on the innate working-class orientation of Australian culture, and to strengthen his view that this was a country 'whose social dynamic is plebeian in origin and is, or should be, egalitarian in operation'. *Overland* was thereby provided with a cutting edge as it moved forward, advancing cultural nationalism. 'We Australians are unable to shelter behind a deep-rooted cultural stability,' wrote Stephen. 'We are still trying to establish it. We have no great population … nor a national language of our own', which in many countries would act as a shield. Australian culture needed 'legislative protection, and nurture, just as our industrial and agricultural life does'.[19]

At the beginning people told Stephen that the journal should be more contemporary: it could lay itself open to the charge of advocating 'romantic nationalism'. Gradually *Overland*'s interest in folksong slackened, apart from book reviews. Now there were articles on theatre—it was the time of *Summer of the Seventeenth Doll*—the Sydney Opera House, the Melbourne Olympics, the perceived need for an Australian film industry. Broader contemporary issues were present too, such as two contrasting views of Pasternak's *Doctor Zhivago*, and articles on the film *Blackboard Jungle* (juvenile delinquency) and television (approached warily). A particularly vigorous attack was made on Charles and Elsa Chauvel's film about an Indigenous girl. '*Jedda* is a thoroughly bad film,' it began. 'It peddles the worst kind of racist nonsense.' Stephen published pieces on Albert Namatjira, whose portrait (by Counihan) was put on an *Overland* cover. Elsewhere a poem about him was placed under a newspaper cutting, reporting the arrest in Swanston Street of an Indigenous war veteran, for being a vagrant.

Stephen's particular contemporary concern, indeed professional one as state organising secretary of the Australian Peace Council, was the tour in 1958 of the Hiroshima Panels. These were graphic depictions by a Japanese artist of the effects of the first atomic bomb: the exhibition, which Stephen organised, became a mainstream event. There was a general anxiety about nuclear war, so three-quarters of a million Australians saw the panels as they toured the major galleries. 'Although', Laurence Collinson wrote in a major spread in *Overland*, 'the figures were Japanese, the method alien, the events historic and in a different country, the spectator realised that he himself was the subject.' The following issue carried a major essay by Marcus Oliphant, pointing to the threat of nuclear annihilation.[20]

As comic relief, Stephen picked up on another contemporary phenomenon, Barry Humphries. At a time when Party members (and others) were squirming in their seats at the New Theatre, he noted the element of pathos in Humphries' work, declaring that he might be 'the first great new comic to develop in Australia since the hey-day of Mo'. Stephen was quick off the mark in recognising Humphries partly because of his indulgence towards yarn-spinners: 'They are the modern epitomes of the minstrels and Vogelsangers of old: poets in speech, who can weave an enchanted ribbon of anecdote, reminiscence, narrative around any audience they speak to.' And foremost among them was Bill Harney in central Australia, with his Indigenous and bush lore. 'Bill Harney's War' had gone to air on the ABC, and Stephen snaffled the transcript for *Overland*. Exuberant, bouncy, with elements of naivety, it also traces the transformation of an intelligent bushman into a soldier. A hatred of war is palpable, because of all its dashed hopes—including those of defeated Germans marching back to their ruined country.

The Harney piece appeared just after *Overland* noted that the comic yarn *They're a Weird Mob* had sold 100,000 copies. Purportedly by an Italian migrant, Nino Culotta ('big arse'—a rear view of the author was featured on the dust jacket), Australians revelled in the way their speech and habits were gently ridiculed by supposedly being found incomprehensible. A satirical device, 'Nino' turned out to be an Australian, John O'Grady. It was, in one sense, the literature of ultimate assimilation: totally lacking from the public response was any realisation that Nino, in his comic way, was a portent. The newcomers would come to change Australia radically—and in an entirely different sense from how *Overland* understood the term.[21]

The tug of London

By the time *Overland* was founded, as well as the 'Ten-pound Poms' coming here, there was a host of people setting out in the opposite direction. Writers and artists (and apprentice academics) had traditionally left to seek their fortune in London, usually in a spirit of cheerful renunciation; they were often ambiguous about returning. The long boom made travel of this kind a real possibility—so long as one was prepared to save. Meanwhile material conditions in England, while still tough, at least no longer included food rationing. The question of whether to leave or stay, at a time when there were no British immigration restrictions for Australians whatsoever, was a real one—at least among the politically uncommitted. Stephen and Nita, having lived in Europe themselves, were sympathetic to expatriates: Clem—having merely visited England—was not. Later he would refer to the 'venomous crap' of 'disaffected expatriates', as they wrote disparaging articles on Australia. He owned to 'a strong anti-English bias, tinged with sadness—and respect'. That would sometimes trail off into his quoting a French remark: 'There is something sad in the dying of empires …'[22]

What was undeniable were two factors that limited Australian life. One was censorship: that the novelist Robert Close had been jailed for obscene libel in *Love Me, Sailor* (1948) still resonated strongly. The *Bulletin*, in a far from enthusiastic review of the novel, nevertheless pointed to the significance of such prosecution: it placed 'literature in handcuffs', and could only encourage self-censorship and sentimentality in writing. But many conservatives did not believe in the necessity of an Australian literature: what existed already seemed overwhelmingly left-wing. Even when it wasn't, there was a feeling that 'culture itself became a fellow traveller of Communism': ASIO even opened files on centre-right figures such as Kenneth Slessor and Christopher Koch. For respectable conservatives, there was always the cultural repository of Britain—whose more modern effusions could be blocked, if necessary. Over the forty-year period from 1933, the Department of Customs considered nearly 16,000 titles for banning. It is not surprising then, that when they got there, many Australians were bowled over not so much by the depth of London's cultural life as by its breadth, vigour and diversity.[23]

The second element they would have noticed was the lack of much awareness of the activities of the security services. In contrast, since its establishment in 1949, the Australian Security Intelligence Organisation (ASIO) had gradually become an intrusive presence in left-wing circles. 'We have a source ... who has been targeted on to Murray-Smith,' one ASIO official noted. Sometimes conversations were reported that had taken place in Stephen's home. Meeting places—even the *Meanjin–Overland* cricket match—were watched. Too often ASIO informants—'sparrows'—were poorly educated volunteers who frequently got things wrong.

Frank Dalby Davison's identity was merged with a Davidson who was secretary of the Australian Journalists Association; repeatedly the magazine was called 'The Overlander' (confusing it with the train to Adelaide). Nothing was too trivial to report, such as Stephen attending the children's Christmas party (in red?) of the Victorian Peace Council. Prime minister John Gorton would later dismiss ASIO operatives as 'stumblebums', but people's careers were halted, and jobs lost. A migrant friend of Rodney Hall's in Brisbane lost his, since he refused to act as an informer on the local Realist Writers Group. And then a strategic conversation with the Education Department had ended Stephen's prospect of re-employment there.[24]

Stephen leaves the Party

The foundation years of *Overland* also saw Stephen gradually detach himself and then resign from the Communist Party. The death of Joseph Stalin, when it occurred in March 1953, proved to be momentous. This was because unlike most strongmen, he had given little attention to the matter of the succession: his penchant for total control extended to the horizon and beyond. For a short time it seemed that Beria, his secret police chief, might run the Soviet Union; but so determined were the members of the Politburo to avoid a continuing possibility of arrest and liquidation that they quickly turned on Beria and executed him. In his place—and Stalin's—there was a new doctrine, one of 'collective leadership'.

The grip of Stalin had been so tight that even Beria had felt it necessary to relax it a little. Some prisoners were released from the Gulag, and satellite states in eastern Europe given a slightly freer rein. But, as de Tocqueville warns, a repressive regime is in greatest danger when it embarks on reform. Revolts broke out in the Gulag on such a scale they had to be put down with tanks and planes; in East Berlin, an uprising in June demonstrated the East German government's unpopularity, drawing the wry comment from Bertolt Brecht that the regime would have to dissolve the people (its supposed source of authority) and elect another.

The Communist world was clearly challenged by the post-Stalin vacuum. Riots in Poland, and reconfiguration of the leadership there along more liberal lines, were followed by more complicated manoeuvres in Hungary. These led to a return to power of the liberal Communist Imre Nagy in October 1956. Soon radical groups and workers councils, some of them broadly Communist, were active in a revolution. In response, Nagy declared Hungary would become a neutral country, and that the Communist Party would take moves to share power. The Soviet Union faced the prospect of an unbuffered central European frontier; at the same time, abnegation of the idea of dictatorship of the proletariat struck at the root of Communist legitimacy. Russian troops rolled in, and bitter street-fighting followed; Nagy, enticed by promised negotiations, found himself a captive.

Hungary became a symbol, and for many Communists was the last straw. Across the West, people left the Party in droves. But more significant had been the secret speech made by Nikita Khrushchev, as Communist Party First Secretary, to the Twentieth Party Congress a few months before, in February. The speech attacked the crimes of Stalin, and the 'cult of personality' he had created. It referred to the liquidation of loyal Party members, the mass deportations, and questioned Stalin's military leadership. (Many of those present—including Khrushchev—had been willing accomplices.)

There was no apology for atrocities in Ukraine and elsewhere at the time of collectivisation, for this was a speech to Party functionaries. What the congress was given was a vision of Communism as a system purified of its recent excesses, drawing more directly on Leninist doctrine. Given its nature, the speech would not be published in the Soviet Union until 1988. But Western intelligence agencies had copies within a matter of days, and three weeks after being given it appeared in the *New York Times*. Once it was printed in the Melbourne *Herald*, Stephen eagerly distributed copies of the speech among Communist friends and acquaintances—some of whom would have been chary about reading the capitalist press. A number of people recalled how they went off to read and re-read it, numbed by a sad recognition. Much now became plainer.[25]

Stephen had never been comfortable in the Party: as a student he had bridled when, at a national Labor Club conference in Tasmania, he had learned of the Zhdanov decrees, laying down a Party line in cultural and scientific matters ranging from music and literature to botany. In Prague he had persistently marginalised any doubts—easier to do when the detritus of the war against fascism was everywhere evident—developing a 'humorous cynicism'. Back in Australia he was absorbed in the work of the Peace Council and the ABS—interacting with the public, raising consciousness of both the major international issue of the day and a developing Australian culture. 'As idealistic individuals', he said of himself and Turner, 'we were not interested in the inner-party power struggle.'

Then, on joining the Realist Writers Group, he often clashed with Frank Hardy, whom he saw as self-serving. He strongly opposed the ABS publication of Hardy's account of a recent journey to Russia, and disliked his promotion of reductive Communist literary theory. 'I began to question the whole political base from which these theories emerged,' he later reflected. Turner, Martin and Eric Lambert took a similar line;

Lambert left the country and, visiting Hungary during the revolution, wrote newspaper articles attacking the Party—which would trouble Stephen further. As it happened, Stephen had already reached the crisis point: he gave a discussion paper on socialism and literature to the Realist Writers Group on the same day Soviet tanks were crushing Hungarian resistance. No-one, not even hardliners, had the confidence to challenge his remarks, 'and from that time on the RWG [in Melbourne] was … largely a broken reed'.

What had concerned Stephen was the way the Australian Party had sought to brush these difficulties under the carpet. It was partly that the CPA had 'never been interested in the "battle of ideas"'. The state secretary, Ted Hill, a lawyer by training, was a man of uncompromising forcefulness and remorseless logic: the Party must be a well-tuned, disciplined machine. (Years later he was capable of having a good lunch with three journalists and telling them they were very fine fellows, but come the revolution they would be lined up against the wall and shot.) An unswerving 'Party-mindedness' was necessary, many felt, because Communists had so many enemies. In addition to that of the government, and the police ('I haven't forgotten my twisted arms and breasts and body, black and blue with their manhandling', Jean Devanny told Stephen), people now often encountered hostility in public and in the workplace. Stephen, underpaid for his peace work and forced to work at night, lost his part-time job as a copy reader for the *Age*.

And so it was that, while Hill had been present in Moscow when Khrushchev made his famous speech, to everybody—except those in a private meeting—he denied that it had been made. It was said to be a forgery, by the US State Department: the fact that the Soviets had not released the speech effectively withheld any stamp of authenticity. There was less printed discussion of it in Australia than in most other Western countries. Stephen took the line that it was not even necessary for the Australian Party to admit its 'essential truth'. But people should be able to read it and appraise it themselves, 'on the basis of our own background as Marxists'.

The attitude seemed to be to 'Stop your bloody whinging, and get on with the job', or, 'What's done, is done'. Stephen found himself out of sympathy with Ralph Gibson, the well-born committed Communist from a family of academic philosophers; they shared a public-school background, and a taste for literature and music. But Gibson would not be deflected from the primary purpose of working for the dictatorship of the proletariat: ultimately, what advanced it was good, what impeded it was bad. Stephen, too, saw that the crimes of Stalin were themselves less important than the bigger issues, which he increasingly came to discern in an entirely opposite way to Gibson.

What if Stalin's crimes were not an aberration, but almost inseparable from the Communist system? That they were the inevitable consequence of the idea that 'the truth exists to be handed down from on high', instead of being hammered out in debate between 'men of goodwill'? It was a conclusion Stephen was reluctant to draw, but increasingly felt in his bones. Apart from anything else, there was the appalling treatment of Jews—evident in the manufacture of the 'doctors' plot', and the murder (among others) of forty Jewish writers. Stephen made a public speech about the dark ages of socialism. He was hauled over the coals at the Victorian state conference of the CPA: 'there were no dark ages of Communism', he was told. Meanwhile the leadership took the view that the Party would be strengthened by the exodus of all those who did not unswervingly follow the Party line.[26]

Still, Stephen was not 'overtly disloyal', and as an effective peace activist was sent overseas, to India in 1958, but more importantly to the World Council of Peace in Berlin in 1957. His return home took him across the Communist world, where he was intent on gathering further evidence for the 'revisionist' cause. Years later he reflected that he was probably kept under surveillance by two organisations, ASIO and the KGB. In Moscow he talked to survivors from the concentration camps, expressed dissenting views and argued against Soviet policy on the Jews. In China he met Mao, and also Wilfred Burchett, who told him to tell the Australian Party that a well-advanced plot existed in North Viet Nam to liquidate Ho Chi Minh and General Giap. Once back in Melbourne, Stephen addressed a special state committee meeting: he told of the reign of terror imposed by secret police, of imprisonment without trial, unjust executions, unfair trials, massive deportations. 'His was the first detailed account,' recalled John Sendy, 'based on internal Party sources, to reach us.' But it had little impact. One senior Party official said it had been a waste of time. If people wanted that sort of thing, they could read it in the daily papers.[27]

Stephen, post-Communist

On his return, Stephen discovered that a man had been placed in the ABS office to straighten out its affairs and keep an eye on Turner. Before, Turner had been contrite, attending a one-month CPA school, which he said had taught him to see his own faults more clearly. But now he was chafing under the system, dissatisfied by the Party's rock-solid refusal to discuss the implications of recent events. He maintained that democratic centralism itself should be examined, along with the idea of the inevitability of capitalist crises, relations with the labour movement and so forth; in short, there should be careful examination of all the Party's policies. Outraged by the Soviet execution of Nagy, Turner decided to write a letter of protest to *Pravda*. Stephen, who was in the habit of having lunch with Turner every day, may have been present when he was verbally provoked into denouncing the execution as 'bloody murder'. Immediately the new ABS manager ran to Hill with the story. It was what he had been waiting for, since he suspected Turner and Murray-Smith were intent on taking over the Victorian leadership. The state secretary moved to have Turner expelled from the Party. The next morning, Stephen slipped his resignation under the door of Hill's office. Dorothy Hewett heard it as an item on the ABC News.

While decided on the necessity of severance, Stephen went out of his way to show that he was still a Marxist: he advised his friends, in a statement, that while the Turner expulsion was the immediate cause of his leaving the Party—along with his repulsion at the Nagy execution and the '"imperialist agent" bunkum' used to justify it—he made it plain that 'I *do* consider the Soviet Union a workers' state, and a socialist one; I *do* consider Soviet foreign policy is for peace; I *do* consider that the essential historical phenomenon of communism is progressive.' The 'division' would not affect his work in the peace movement and cultural affairs, 'but make me want to do it better'. So Stephen had no intention of harming the Party (Nita remained a member, for a time): it remained a cause both he and his antagonists believed in.

It was soon clear to Stephen that Hill would have preferred them to have taken an anti-communist position. To Hill's surprise, Stephen turned up with Turner to discuss how they would handle the matter, now that the daily press seemed to have got wind of it. Stephen suggested frankness. But Hill was intractable, telling them to solve the problem themselves, since they had got themselves into this mess; then told the Party press of the conversation, with the implication that it was they who had informed the capitalist press. The *Herald* soon lost interest in the story. (ASIO, which had bugged Hill's office for some time, did not.)[28]

Stephen seemed to have got off lightly. For many these years, which (for those who lasted the distance) were to culminate in the splits of the 1960s, were traumatic. The Khrushchev speech had been truly shocking, cutting the ground from under their feet; then came Hungary. Many of the things that capitalist enemies had said turned out to be true. 'There was', Ken Gott recalled, 'at least one suicide and several spectacular psychotic breakdowns directly attributable to these troubled times.' Marriages broke up; one man, who had laboured for the Party for a pittance, went off on a spending spree. Slanders were put about by the Party. 'Those who prided themselves on their lofty motives, including myself,' recalled Rex Mortimer, 'stooped to acts of devious malice which in normal circumstances most would have regarded as unthinkable.' People were described as police spies, embezzlers, moral degenerates. Later it was whispered that Ian Turner was a homosexual, at a time when such activities were illegal and particularly suspect—so that the charge could not be dismissed, as it should have been, as ridiculous. Jenny Love remembered going to her front gate to pick up the *Age*: Russian tanks in Budapest were all over the front page. 'None of my friends will ever speak to me again,' she thought, 'because I've got to leave the Communist party.' Others followed her out: the Party lost a quarter of its members in the year 1956. More would follow. ASIO recorded Stephen asking whether someone was still a member of the Party: 'his wife replied that she did not know. Murray-Smith then said to their friend, "It is like that these days."'[29]

Early in 1959, Turner left Melbourne for the ANU, to take up the PhD scholarship that would launch his academic career. Meanwhile Stephen had become increasingly uneasy about his position in the peace movement, and had been there for six years; but, concerned about his growing family, he was anxious that he 'had no particular skills or trade'. Suddenly an advertisement appeared, and shortly after he took up a position with the Victorian Teachers Union, as research officer and editor of their journal. He was ready for a new start.

Jean Devanny had written advising Stephen not to do anything further to widen the breach with the Party, and he had snorted in response. His own impulse, nonetheless, was always towards affability—even if a smile had to be plastered on. He consciously sought not to publish anything in *Overland* directly opposed to Party policy. Pasternak's novel *Doctor Zhivago*, though, had become a worldwide cause célèbre, and Stephen decided to run a brace of articles about it. One was an open, liberal response from the New Zealander Maurice Shadbolt. For the other, he had taken on board the suggestion from Party cadres that he should approach Katharine Susannah Prichard for a hard-line piece—even though he felt David Martin (whom they distrusted) would have written a better one.

The appearance of the Prichard piece in double harness was not appreciated. Stephen soon found himself the subject of an attack in the Sydney Communist paper *Tribune*, where Rex Chiplin criticised that whole number (14). Stephen was castigated for pointing to 'the hostility of the labor movement to the intellectual'—it was 'incorrect theorising' by a 'revisionist', while the dual response to Pasternak showed that *Overland* was 'obviously not partisan'. It should be. For good measure, Chiplin smeared Laurence Collinson and attacked David Martin—leading Stephen privately to refute the charges by saying (just as wildly) 'Mr Chiplin blasts an anti-religious story for being religious and an attack on pornography for being pornographic.'

That the backbone of the offending issue had been a concern about the future of the arts entirely passed Rex Chiplin by. For him intellectuals could play their part, 'but they are subordinate to the main force, the will of the people'—i.e. the Party. *Overland* had become 'a shackle on the Labor Movement'. The point was taken up by Frank Hardy: Murray-Smith was acting 'under the strange delusion that he could grow more branches on the *Overland* tree by severing its trunk'. Stephen was a man, chimed in Ralph de Boissière, who 'assists the cold war while talking of peace'. But Stephen had been right in saying that more people would come to his defence than *Tribune* had bargained for. Prichard herself penned a considered defence of *Overland*, pointing out that it broke the ice beyond Party circles, reaching people 'who may be influenced to a better understanding of the labor movement'.

Since *Overland* was not a Marxist magazine—but the only non-communist journal in Australia where Party members were welcome to have their say—there was no point in using it to respond in Marxist terms to the *Tribune* attack. Rather, Stephen decided to distribute a circularised response, and gathered names. Ken Gott supplied some who needed to have 'it brought home to them that a pretty sharp situation has developed around *Overland*'. In a draft for the circular, Stephen stated that the objection seemed to be to the very existence of an independent journal of the left, with discussion based on evidence rather than handed-down truths: the intent was to destroy it. The even greater hostility shown by the Party to Helen Palmer's *Outlook*—for which *Overland* carried advertisements and Stephen wrote occasionally—was a further instance.[30]

In April 1959, battle intensified for control of the magazine. But Stephen was well prepared: on the morning of his resignation from the Party, he had gone with Turner to the ABS office and made off with the *Overland* subscription cards (and hidden them). Already he had registered the name when creating the new magazine out of the *Realist Writer*; now he had captured the sustaining network. As far as Stephen was concerned, he ran the magazine since he took responsibility for its finances and production. He had also established primacy in (or indeed over) the board, which was essentially consultative. When objections had been raised earlier to Eric Lambert's continued presence on it, given the nature of his articles on Hungary, Stephen declared that *Overland* had no particular line on those events; therefore a board member's attitude to them was irrelevant. Since then Stephen had left the Party—which meant that he could not be controlled. At the same time, though, Stephen did not want to sever the connection, if at all possible. Repeatedly denied support from the Commonwealth Literary Fund, *Overland* needed support from wherever it could get it. The aim for the moment would be 'to give CP members enough incentive to remain with *Overland*, without giving the power to take it over'.

On the board there had been increasing opposition from Jack Coffey, public servant and sportswriter, who, although well read, exhausted even the patience of John Morrison with his dogmatism. Beyond, in addition to Hardy and Chiplin, there was now Judah Waten, who threatened, 'We'll pick up every ounce of shit we can and throw it all over you.' Some of it would stick. While David Martin urged a fight, Stephen was keen to broaden out, to continue working with others in 'the kind of popular front we believe in'. He (very briefly) contemplated resignation—as one or two correspondents suggested he should, since the magazine appeared to have drifted so far from its working-class roots. Instead, he considered transferring the ownership to a diverse group, who would also double as an editorial board. In the cultural sphere, Stephen had always wanted 'to *unite*' the left in defence of peace, democratic rights and national independence.

There was a showdown. Coffey attempted to stack a board meeting, which ended in a fiasco; the cracks were temporarily plastered over with a formal truce. A more serious attempt to unseat Stephen came a month later. Charged up, Coffey made the tactical mistake of advising him by phone the night before a meeting that he had invited along 'other members of the board'—staunch Party members who had rarely attended in the past. Stephen was inclined to ignore the meeting—he had to steel himself for confrontations, and this would be another 'screaming match'—but Collinson and Elizabeth Vassilieff persuaded him to call up his supporters. The 'beautifully stacked meeting', as one of them described it, had its wild moments. But 'the Stalinists were dealing with people who knew exactly how to interpret their fine phrases, and moreover, were as well organised'. Coffey had to retreat, and the board meeting proceeded along normal lines. Later there was a private meeting. Hardy and Coffey insisted that the magazine remain in the hands of the Realist Writers, but without much enthusiasm. The point had already been conceded in public that *Overland*'s orientation was pluralist left. The battle had been won.[31]

Both Turner 'and I were very happy we left the CP', Stephen told Jean Devanny. It was not the only way forward; 'it could have been, but the dogmatists have the upper hand'. He doubted that 'the CP will ever be in tune with the dynamic of the Australian working class'. The thought may have crossed his mind that, cleaving as it did to Stalinist practices, the Party exhibited a kind of cultural cringe of its own. Stephen decided to join the ALP, although well aware that obstacles would no doubt be found there to 'a decent socialist way forward … no fewer frustrations, bastardry and foolishness'. As that comment suggests, he was deeply browned off with party politics, and would eventually drift away.

For now, in a romantic way, he still considered himself something of a Marxist. 'Ian and I didn't lose our faith,' he told Keith McEwan: 'we lost the vehicle for its expression.' Eight years later he could still write that to some extent he and others still thought of themselves 'as better Marxists than the party people ever were or ever can be'. The Party had taught him much, even if it had scarred him: he was 'intensely grateful' for the way it had saved him 'from becoming another middle-aged, middle-class ex-public schoolboy'. But gradually that feeling ebbed away. Stephen had been attracted to Communism by its progressivism, its promotion of culture, its identification with the march of history (particularly across the third world) and by its professed anti-racism. For Stephen the class struggle was a romantic ideal to which he was prepared to subscribe, but he was now released from any need to concede its primacy.[32]

All through his Party troubles, *Overland* had functioned for Stephen as a kind of refuge, particularly 'from the somewhat arid nature of the peace council work'. It functioned as a vehicle for the broader, Australian radical tradition to which Stephen saw himself and others contributing, something that 'not even the Party' could stop them doing. But it would take a while to clear the magazine of its Party entanglements. In an interview with Hazel de Berg in 1969, Stephen said that 'up till now we have been fighting for a clearer vision of our own perspectives'. *Overland* was now reaching out to something 'broader'. Perhaps it was at this juncture that the magazine's typical reader began to crystallise for him, postulated as the matron of the Port Hedland hospital. Whatever the case, he was confident about *Overland*'s function. This Stephen saw—even as he apologised for the terminology—as exploring the relationship between 'the low culture and the high culture' in Australia: more positively, 'how literature emerges from the experiences and feelings of the ordinary people in ordinary situations'. But real financial security was, alas, 'as far away as ever'. Even so, he was quietly confident. Judah Waten (who had his own network of spies) was tipped off by an MP that this time *Overland*'s application to the Commonwealth Literary Fund would be successful. It was not. The CLF was suspicious of the magazine's connections, unsympathetic to its inclusive nature. Cold War tensions had been rising. Shortly after, the Berlin Wall went up.[33]

5

CLEM AND STEPHEN

'ALL THOSE WONDERFUL CULTURAL RENAISSANCES WE'RE HAVING NOWADAYS'

Meanjin and *Overland* in the 1960s and after

COLD WAR POLITICS, the prime contextual factor for the magazines in the 1950s, gave way in the following decade to a strong sense of cultural development in Australia, and optimism. The mood was caught in the title of Peter Coleman's symposium, *Australian Civilization*—whatever was felt about the slant of its contents, people recognised the aspiration. As the country's leading historian, Sir Keith Hancock, remarked at a seminar in 1969, 'I sometimes feel I'm watching the birth of a new civilisation.' Australia was felt to be 'coming of age', as the phrase went—so commonly that Dame Edna was sending it up in the year of Coleman's book, noting 'All those wonderful cultural renaissances we're having nowadays!'

Important validation had come from overseas. Stephen picked up on the way the novelist CP Snow had described Australia as 'the only hope of the world'. Then had come the astonishing success of the Whitechapel Gallery exhibition in London of recent Australian art. Australian cultural production was receiving international recognition in the places where it counted.

Beginning with the first Adelaide Festival of the Arts (modelled on Edinburgh's), the decade seemed to gain cultural velocity as it progressed. Menzies, while noting with interest a South Australian inquiry into the arts, had deemed a federal one 'inopportune'; on succeeding him,

Harold Holt broadened government subsidies beyond literature almost immediately. Another Liberal prime minister, John Gorton, would found a national film and television school; for a time the aspiration remained well ahead of achievement. An early film projecting tanks rolling down the streets of Sydney had rock music as a soundtrack, but no dialogue: revolutionary, but also a way round the fact that Australians were not used to their accent and idiom being used as material for 'art'. (Paul Hogan had only just clambered down from the Harbour Bridge.) Change was coming with the emergence of the new playwrights and independent theatres La Mama in Melbourne and Nimrod in Sydney. Meanwhile book publishing of local titles began to boom, and preservation battles were often won—sometimes by an unlikely alliance between trade unions and the National Trust. The up-beat mood was symbolised by that extraordinary week in October 1973, when the Sydney Opera House was opened and Patrick White won the Nobel Prize.[1]

Credos

In January 1966 Clem journeyed to Armidale to give a paper at a seminar entitled 'Functions of the Literary Magazine'. It was an impressive performance, displaying confidence and clear purpose—almost coinciding, as it turned out, with the retirement of Sir Robert Menzies as prime minister.

While acknowledging there were many shared characteristics—and there were many slippages in the exposition—Clem drew a sharp distinction between the 'little' magazine and the 'literary review'. 'We ignore the "little magazines" at our peril', Clem conceded; they had energy, commitment, were often radical, and could be 'exploratory and stimulating'. But they were usually small, published few writers, and lacked *continuity* (his italics). On the other hand, the 'seriously purposed literary review'—as *Meanjin* clearly was—'provides a forum for vital discussion not only on questions of art and literary interest, but on the whole field of intellectual enquiry and activity'. Writers thus acquire 'a meeting point … the results of which are a formalising … of the various underlying tendencies of the time'. If the little magazine could be most readily identified with the intellectual 'protest' of the first half of the twentieth century, then the literary review 'should strive for the spaciousness, the cosmopolitanism, the full play of mind, the easy and confident dignity of the great European reviews of the 19th century'—even as they were 'responsive to contemporary modes and trends'.

There were many motherhood statements in the paper. One was that Clem believed such a magazine should be 'urbane in its editorial policy, tolerant of differences, maintain a strong belief in freedom of expression, in the supreme importance of the arts, [and] in the viability of excellence, from whatever period and whatever direction and whatever source'. It followed that 'the ideal editor of such a magazine should accordingly be a liberal, independent, adventurous, ardent spirit, yet of fine discrimination and firm judgement'. It was a recipe for enlightened despotism—partly stemming from the assumption that Australia was still developing into full cultural and political independence, and hence there was a common national project. On each issue, one sought to gather the best minds, 'always in the dream that they might finally unite in agreement', Clem noted ruefully, 'always in the realisation that they never will and never should'.

Clem vigorously rejected the idea of a 'purely literary' magazine. Instead, he delivered a paradox: 'A magazine completely devoted to literature cannot be completely literary.' What was needed was one that would not only carefully examine 'our whole cultural situation', but would also provide 'a platform for sober, searching, comprehensive political inquiry'. This should be done while remaining independent of political parties and programs. Helping to bring about 'more community of interest', Clem believed, could become as much the guiding principle of a literary review as creative partnership so often was with little magazines. Moreover, appreciation of our heritage was as important as any response to the immediate situation, and so should appear alongside 'the free exchange of new ideas and techniques'. This would help the creative artist not to feel he was working in a vacuum. 'Such a magazine', Clem maintained, 'is in a sense the writer's laboratory … his weapon against society.'

Clem was well aware of the usual difficulties of such a venture: the small proportion of people interested, even in France, the brusque indifference artists had been subject to in most societies. But there were also peculiarly Australian challenges: the small population and its geographical spread, so that, as Clem put it,

> an Australian literary editor is confronted by a sort of vast cultural Simpson Desert. A few literate natives huddle beneath ragged

> ghost-gums or brigalows near brackish billabongs and soak-holes. For the most part they live solitary lives, mumble to themselves, go on random walkabout; but certainly there is little *communication* in any recognisably civilised sense between them.

There wasn't even any sense of the need for the 'educated Australian' to be familiar with the literature of his own country; the cultural cringe still lingered. But politicians and bureaucrats should understand that we needed to have, 'and do in fact have, a worthwhile culture of our own'. It needed careful nourishment and intelligent support, for it provided the seedbed of national values. From Raymond Williams Clem took the idea that the common culture brings together an understanding of natural growth in a community, acting as a major 'incentive to its necessary extensions'. And from Lionel Trilling, a call to a 'new union between our political ideas and our imagination'. 'Art is important to the life of people,' Clem added, 'and without it the political community falls short of its ideal potentialities.'

While thankful, as a citizen, for the 'comparative tranquillity' of Australian life, Clem felt that 'our material advantages may be said to have been gained at destructive cost to the spirit'. There was, he felt, 'No imperative note sound[ing] above the general dullness and flatness, the suffocating blandness, of Australian life ...' The literary magazine thus assumed importance, as a place where a sense of debate could be kept alive—through imaginative, expository and critical writing. Ideas would be 'shot like arrows into the body politic quarter by quarter', prodding the nation's elites into cultural and reformist activity. But Clem spoke on the very eve of the government announcing that conscripted national servicemen would go to Vietnam. New divisions would appear, the word 'committed' would come to be applied more widely to writing from a political stance, and *Meanjin*'s context would be changed irrevocably.

Clem was very conscious of how much things had improved culturally—the difference from the Australia of 1940, he remarked a number of times, was extraordinary. 'It has been rewarding that through this journal', he wrote in 1960, 'one has shared in the "renaissance"; perhaps contributed a little towards its realisation.' Two years later, addressing an overseas audience in the *Texas Quarterly*, he claimed that literary magazines had been 'potent agencies' in bringing this about.

More, he prophesied that Australian writers and artists 'are on the verge of making a major breakthrough'.[2]

A few months before Clem's Armidale address, Stephen produced an anthology, *An Overland Muster*, to celebrate *Overland*'s first ten years. Unlike Clem, who kept circulating his paper as a kind of manifesto, Stephen does not appear to have issued a comparable lengthy statement. Nevertheless he was always ready to express ideas about his magazine. *Overland*, he reflected in a lecture, worked on the assumption that there was no reason why 'ordinary people' should not enjoy books and writing, and participate in them. ('Art and literature is their right too, and reflects their lives as much as anyone else's.') In stating this, Stephen made a double assertion:

> firstly, that writing was *not* confined simply to the best that had been said, written or thought in the world, [but] that there were all sorts of traditions, and not just a 'great' one; secondly, that other things being equal, writing dealing with our local reality, Australia and our jobs and our politics and our history and, if you like, our beaches, would be meaningful in a way that 'better' writing more removed from us was not meaningful.

If that meant adopting the 'dreaded "double standard"' in literature, then so be it. Some years earlier Stephen had offered 'a distinction between "high" and "low" (or folk) culture', saying that *Overland* was trying to do precisely what the early *Bulletin* did: draw the two streams of 'literature' together, and hence strengthen both. His view at this time was that

> culture by definition is a majority affair. We believe that no country can have a true culture unless all writing, art, music, journalism is based firmly on this premise. We agree that the road to a democratic culture is not easy … The work for a genuine Australian culture is not an intellectual struggle in the narrow sense. It is a political struggle in the broadest sense … We in this country are fantastically isolated, geographically and socially … in fact, there is every danger of most of

> the world's people by-passing us with hardly a glance in our direction ... 'Commonwealth' is a proud title for our nation, but we have yet to earn the honor. In earning it those who care for culture, in the broadest sense of that term, have a vital role to play.

Elsewhere in that same number, Stephen remarked that a magazine could only be successful when 'nearly every reader can get something from say sixty per cent of each issue'.

While this issue (number 19) was still on sale, Stephen revealed his cultural and political assumptions in a letter to Dorothy Hewett's husband, Merv Lilley. Influenced by the recent work of English culture critics Raymond Williams and Richard Hoggart, Stephen spoke more assertively of a 'common culture'—not imposed from above, but something that would 'genuinely arise from the people and will be a real major culture of the kind that ... bourgeois intellectuals of today say cannot exist.' The way forward would, of necessity, involve complexities and complications; but there were a number of encouraging factors. 'The bourgeoisie, unlike in the nineteenth century', he wrote, 'are not today united in an effective campaign against the people.' Stephen felt—with all due vigilance re civil liberties—'we are winning'. Indeed it was plain that, for all its 'tragedies', Australia was 'still a much better society to live in than the USSR', with its purges, attacks on intellectuals and Jews, and 'byzantine ... monolithic and bureaucratic' character. Here he was much safer attacking the establishment than he would be in the Soviet Union; and, 'I like my head on my shoulders.'

For the *Muster* (five years later), Stephen elaborated on what his credo had meant in practice for *Overland*: implicit was a clear differentiation from *Meanjin*. The present selection would be as 'friendly and fresh' as he hoped his magazine had been. Literary quality was not the only principle working for inclusion; a 'living literature is not self-conscious about assessing its own quality', he asserted. (One in the eye for Clem.) Stephen relished *Overland*'s occasional note of 'good-natured larrikinism', and the way his magazine had published material that was 'effective but unsophisticated'. He realised this was an unfashionable attitude—for there was too much of a premium placed on writing offering little more than 'the graces of a refined technique.' In art generally, form and content were rarely perfectly matched: the important thing was to give space to those with something to say, even if they were struggling to express it. Later Stephen would concede that, with the break from the Party, 'We lost many mass contacts, something of our populism and to some extent our political edge.' Indeed a concern with the role of culture in a fully democratic and socialist society had gradually become occluded.

Nonetheless the journal had evolved, and *An Overland Muster* was arranged chronologically to emphasise this. 'Australia has changed, the composition and education of the population have changed, the political issues have changed.' And while the political *position* of the journal had changed with the rupture of 1958, Stephen felt there had been no change in *Overland*'s role. It had always sought to 'make the voice of humanism, radicalism and social protest' more effective, through being 'broader, more humorous, more conscious of literary standards, and less dogmatic in every way'. It was, in consequence—the dust jacket claimed—'Australia's most vigorous literary magazine.'[3]

The basic problem *Overland* faced in the 1960s was to avoid becoming, as Frank Hardy had put it bluntly, 'a kind of poor man's *Meanjin*'. For as an *Age* reviewer noted in 1963, commenting on the newest issue, some authors were unique to *Overland*, 'but, for the rest, it is sufficient recommendation that most of them also contribute to *Meanjin*'. Moreover, some features of the senior magazine migrated to *Overland*. One or two of its early Queensland contributors found sanctuary in its hospitable pages, while the *Meanjin* feature 'Letter to Tom Collins', deferentially modulated to Joseph Furphy directly, made a brief appearance. For *Meanjin*, the commemorative Palmer issue of 1959 (a flop) turned out to be Vance's tombstone; Clem seemed to lose interest in him after that. But Stephen too felt for the Palmers 'a compound of affection and respect'.

It was in *Overland* that a series of recollections Vance wrote continued for some time after his death. Stephen was also close to the Palmer daughters: to Helen, whose journal *Outlook* provided a platform for those disillusioned with the Party, and to the more troubled Aileen, whose poetry he often published in the magazine, and with conspicuous success as an Overland book. He became a kind of mentor to her, whereas Clem, she felt, had become 'rather prejudiced against both Palmer daughters'. As Aileen descended into breakdown, and wrote more demanding letters, Stephen too began to distance himself from her.[4]

Overland 18 / August 1960

The scientific element announced by the cover is Sir Mark Oliphant's lecture 'Science and ethics'—broken up by a characteristically complex cartoon, on social mobility, by Bruce Petty. Elizabeth Wolf Vassilieff vigorously attacks a review of three recent Australian books on China, written by an American in *Quadrant*. In a rare explicit editorial, Stephen welcomes an official visit by two Soviet writers—and looks forward to vigorous discussion. Meanwhile Ian Turner writes on the sociology of CP Snow, with interest in Britain taken further with an article by English political scientist Norman MacKenzie, on the importance of the broader program of the New Left as an alternative to apathy.

In a special section, headed 'From Abroad', there is an appreciation of Boris Pasternak by Jack Lindsay; a review of an Australian art exhibition in Moscow by Noel Counihan; and Kenneth Tynan declaring that Western bourgeois culture is in trouble. Among the short stories there is one by John Morrison, with poetry coming from Judith Wright, David Martin, John Manifold, Aileen Palmer and Laurence Collinson. Reviews include Randolph Stow on Mary Durack's *Kings in Grass Castles*, AA Phillips on the second volume of Jack Lindsay's autobiography, and pieces on recent novels by Thea Astley and Colin MacInnes.

Overland 46 / Summer 1970–71

The centrepiece of this issue—brilliantly captured by Vane Lindesay's cover—is RW Connell's 'The Manipulators', a scathing but elegant attack on a recent pamphlet by Peter Coleman, which pointed to a conspiracy by left-wing activists to infiltrate the schools and 'destroy our way of life'. Alongside it is placed an article, 'How I got radicalized' (reprinted from *Harper's Magazine*), in which the writer states the compelling urgency of environmental issues. *Overland*'s long struggle against censorship is given a new twist with a first-person account by the author of a novel recently taken off the banned list, where it was placed in 1934. There is a tribute to Alexandr Solzhenitsyn, Nobel Prize winner, and a review of Patrick White's *The Vivisector* (both by John McLaren). Nancy Keesing reflects on her Jewishness. Poetry is reviewed, but new poems are thin on the ground.

Overland, priding itself on its accessibility to would-be authors as to readers, effectively placed itself in the tradition of the *Bulletin* in its heyday, and beyond that, of antique miscellanies like the *Gentleman's Magazine*. It was impelled by Stephen's enthusiasm, and for a long time read and looked like a step up from amateurism: articles would awkwardly extend to a corner of the following page, visuals would sometimes clash in style. Usually it was printed on newsprint, with only a slightly stiffer cover, and was (until the 1970s) simply stapled together. But it spoke of urgency and engagement, and looked at now propels the reader straight into the issues of the day. Occasionally it carried transcripts of long discussions, predictably beginning with the Australian Myth, but advancing to discuss contemporary American art. The magazine's short articles and book reviews tended to merge; responses were encouraged and sometimes, like that arising from historian Jim Griffin's review of Ronald Conway's *The Great Australian Stupor*, went on for too long. There was little of *Meanjin*'s sense of distillation: instead, a capacity to surprise. In the midst of a yellow insert of a paper on science and ethics by Sir Mark Oliphant, placed in centrefold position was a large, diagrammatic cartoon by Bruce Petty, then returning to Australia. *Overland* could look like Stephen's scrapbook—and in a way, it was.[5]

The heartbeat of the magazine was Stephen's column 'Swag'. The title jarred with some because of its self-conscious Australianism, but it was accurate. There Stephen would range across the scene—commenting on public affairs, literary matters, publicising a short-story competition here, a new publication there. Stephen would draw the reader's attention to particular articles in the current issue, and the continuing pinpricks of censorship. The tone was generally relaxed, but because it was genial, it could easily switch to seriousness. Casually he could drop the most pertinent observations—seeing, for example, Melbourne's Student Action of 1961 as an underestimated incubator of 'liberal-radical attitudes' that would endure. Beyond issues of state patronage—and the implacable stance taken by the Commonwealth Literary Fund in withholding funding to his magazine—Stephen repeatedly pointed to the nexus between politics and literature.

In 1960, for example, a paragraph on attacks on the Commonwealth Literary Fund was followed by another on a letter he had organised signed by writers and sent to the prime minister, expressing anxiety about the sweeping provisions of the Crimes Act. As shall be seen, there were often comments on developments in the Soviet Union. But when in 1967 the scandal burst of the CIA having funded *Quadrant* and *Encounter*, Stephen resisted the temptation to gloat. Ultimately the magazines, he wrote, should not be judged by the scandal 'but essentially by the kind of magazine they are, the things they say'. Shortly after, 'Swag' disappeared for five years. But people asked for it to be restored. 'I'm not particularly keen,' said Stephen as he revived it. It was difficult to be up-to-date in a quarterly commentary; the whole thing became a chore. 'Editors should disguise themselves, not display themselves,' he believed. 'As AG Stephens used to say, justifying his Olympian detachment, "Only the unknown is terrible".'[6]

Overland articles, and issues

'I expect that people like us', Stephen wrote to the Turners,

> are among the tiny but growing fraction of people, desperately in love with our country and its people, but watching it roaring towards misery and upheaval like a train towards a wrecked bridge. Perhaps though we tend to be too apocalyptic about all this; perhaps by the time we die this country will be a bit like Finland, sturdily independent of its overtowering neighbours, united in a progressive program of social reform, and preserving its independence because of the political morality of those neighbours and because its own traditions, coupled with policies of cooperation and neighbourliness, have engendered for it a healthy respect.[7]

There was a tempered optimism about this vision, and it kept Stephen going.

The broad front of articles on politics continued in the magazine, with civil liberties well to the fore. There was also some discussion of the ALP and its problems, by Race Mathews, Anthony Clunies-Ross and Jim Cairns, and forays into the world of work. The trade union leader Pat Mackie gave a first-person account of the Mt Isa strike of 1964–65. Shortly after, Stephen started a 'Men at Work' series, but it died after two instalments. This was not owing to lack of interest on his part: in

1966 he turned up at an Arbitration Court hearing as a witness, arguing that the tilemakers deserved a larger margin for their skilled work: 'the Australian tradesman has suffered because of the "handyman" tradition', he believed, 'and has never been rewarded for his skills to the degree found in other societies.'[8]

Looked at with 2020s vision, *Overland* in the 1960s reveals how far back the progressive battlelines then were. There was little on women—unsurprising, when it is remembered that Germaine Greer's *The Female Eunuch* did not appear till 1970. But despite its sturdy male origins, *Overland* had always been more receptive to female contributions than *Meanjin*: feminism would burst upon its readership with a lengthy discussion between Germaine Greer and Ian Turner. A year later appeared a companion piece, an interview with Dennis Altman, in which he placed gay liberation within a broader context of social reform. (He had great faith, as we all then did, in the way technology 'has an enormous potential for liberation'.)

While *Overland* carried incisive travel pieces about Asia, the prospect of ethnic diversity within Australia was disregarded. It was still early days for multiculturalism—a concept then just being formulated in Canada. But from 1969 on, environmentalism was an intermittent presence in the magazine, consciousness heightened by the consequences of the mining boom. ('Officially there is yet no Minister for National Destruction', wrote George Farwell.) Also to the fore was Judith Wright, beginning to become well known as a conservationist in addition to her being a poet. Urgency was conveyed by the title of her article: 'Survival of Our Species'.[9]

Partly because he had married a Jewish woman from a family decimated by the Holocaust, Stephen was unusually sensitive to racism and colonialism. Papua New Guinea became very much Stephen's beat—one of the functional concessions Clem made to *Overland*. After the pace of political change there began to quicken, *Meanjin* did carry a couple of high-quality, reflective articles, but Stephen, ever mindful of his experience of New Guinea during the war, had been attuned to developments there for quite some time. In 1961 his crusading instinct was roused when Brian Cooper, a former field officer with the New Guinea cooperative movement, was convicted of sedition and jailed for two months.

His offence was to advocate independence—to secure a conviction, dubious statements about wished-for Russian intervention were reported at his trial. (It proceeded without a jury.) 'Black Men—and a White Conscience', Stephen headed an editorial comment in *Overland*: Cooper's was, in effect, a show trial, designed to discourage all talk of independence. The Labor Party, even the Communists, withheld support from this passionate, scholarly looking young man. Stephen sought him out and gave him space in *Overland* to tell his story, whereupon he pointed to increasing unrest in Papua New Guinea and drew the conclusion: 'Let us retire with dignity before we are forced out.'

A trickle of articles on PNG kept up through the decade—culminating in a special issue in 1971 that included pieces from leading indigenous politicians such as Michael Somare, Albert Maori Kiki and Leo Hannett. There was also a significant creative-writing component; the appearance of further PNG material in the following issue, in a large green supplement, may have tested the patience of some readers. But rather than being an exotic place, New Guinea directly presented Australians with issues of race and decolonisation. Few saw any urgency. *Overland* had already reproduced a statement from the minister for territories, the sophisticated Paul Hasluck, who declared: 'We must not educate the people out of the ground that nourished them.' Sometime before, Stephen had told readers of the Melbourne *Herald* that New Guinea 'will soon need its own doctors, labour leaders, lawyers, economists and administrators'. And the people were keen to advance. He was glad then to publish an account by Ken Inglis (UPNG's future vice-chancellor), 'University in a Hurry'. Indeed it was, and in challenging conditions. History students had no usable textbook dealing with their past—did not want to be told their country was 'discovered'—so oral history was encouraged. One of them returned from his village, where he interviewed the elders, and presented a paper entitled, 'How my ancestors ate Mr Green'.[10]

Being more politically engaged and less concerned with high culture than *Meanjin*, *Overland* was also more responsive to the early Indigenous rights movement. Stephen saw that notice was being served on the white established order by cooperatives not only in Papua New Guinea, but also by those set up among Indigenous people in Western Australia. Stephen had been in contact with Don McLeod, a union activist and one-time member of the Party, right from the time he was involved in the

Pilbara strike beginning in 1946, when there had been a massive walk-out of Indigenous workers from white-run stations.

McLeod is glimpsed in number 17 (1960), where he is described amid a cluster of articles on Indigenous matters. (Among the contributors was Mary Durack.) Later, *Overland* would have nothing to say about the successful 1967 referendum—Indigenous people were now to be included in the census, and the Commonwealth enabled to legislate for them—perhaps because in these matters there was no cause for self-congratulation. Instead, the magazine had earlier carried a lively article on the student Freedom Ride in New South Wales, exposing segregation in outback towns. Their bus had been run off the road by a truckie ('We didn't like to admit', wrote Beth Hauser, 'that he may have been sober.') Stephen would not have been surprised. In 1960, mindful of the South African police shootings at Sharpeville, he suggested that white Australian attitudes were not so very different:

> Australian racialism is mean and ugly. It hides in the corridors of Parliament and in the fastnesses of the Melbourne Club, and in the ignorant and frightened minds of many who know nothing of these retreats. Its weapons are not Sten guns and armoured cars, but complacency, institutionalised selfishness and icy callousness.[11]

It is not to be wondered at, then, that *Overland* took a decided stand against the Vietnam War. As a poem Stephen published put it, 'It's too much like helping the big boy batter the small.' A related issue was the conscription of twenty-year-olds to fight the war: in 1966, just before the first intake, a statement against conscription signed by some sixty literary figures appeared in the magazine. The usual suspects were joined by people such as Martin Boyd, AD Hope, Walter Murdoch and Mary Durack. Further on—the issue being edited in Stephen's absence—came a piece from CP Fitzgerald on America and Vietnam, together with a Letter from Saigon from 'A young Vietnamese intellectual'. ('Can you imagine a city with the troops in the war time? They always want to have a last fling.') By 1971, led by a cover that showed a self-immolating monk, an issue was 'respectfully dedicated' to the 'true heroes … the people of Vietnam'. A statement from the editorial board conceded that a Communist regime might not be ideal, 'might [even] betray the people of Vietnam', but the American claim that they were helping South Vietnam to resist foreign aggression was specious. As for the Australian involvement, it was 'if anything, even more disgraceful than the American.' Moreover, its military effectiveness had been 'negligible'.

The following year, Stephen commissioned RH Morrison to produce an anthology of poetry—it took up a whole issue, and was styled 'Vietnam Voices: A Retrospect'. 'Vietnam', Stephen wrote in his introduction, was a 'cause not for pride but for shame—shame not because we came away defeated but because we went'. Its purpose had not been to protect Vietnam; 'it was to preserve Australian conservatism'. Indeed no poets could be found, wrote Morrison, who, inspired by patriotic motives, wrote in favour of the war. (He had even approached 'a leading ex-service organisation'.) Even so, the range was wide—including a poem from James McAuley, written for a charity for Vietnamese children.[12]

When it came to looking beyond Vietnam to America, in *Overland* as in *Meanjin* there was rare engagement. The high watermark was a 1968 issue that included Peter Mathers' alienated response to Pittsburgh, and a reprinting of Hans Magnus Enzensberger's letter resigning an American fellowship. It was not merely that the Vietnam War eclipsed the invading power. England—where Stephen spent his first eighteen months abroad, in his mid-twenties—would always exercise more influence upon him than it seemed.[13]

Stephen could occasionally slip into describing things as happening 'out here', but he would never refer to England as 'home', as a few elderly people still did (including his Australian-born mother—to annoy him). Nonetheless, he saw it as a resource: *Overland* published writers such as Raymond Williams, CP Snow (then a household name, after his identification of the 'Two Cultures'); also men of the theatre such as Arnold Wesker and Kenneth Tynan. In a metropolitan society, issues could be more readily articulated and clarified. So Stephen republished Wesker on the poor support the arts received from the trade union movement, then later published half a dozen Australian responses. The most engaged was from Merv Lilley, who—while upholding the integrity of working-class culture—nonetheless pointed to a number of ways in which the Australian labour movement supported the arts.

Once the Wilson Labour government came to power, there was a shift. Instead of Laurence Collinson's inventories—comparisons made usually to Australia's disadvantage—there was a more appraising tone: in 1968 David Martin noted that England had quite suddenly drifted into crisis, 'with a universal sense of stagnation and lack of purpose and direction.' All the more opportunity, then, for the brash: Martin's article was followed by Richard Neville, advising 'How to Bluff Your Way through Britain'. ('Suddenly ... Australians have crawled out from behind their inferiority complexes and are thrashing out in all directions ...') *Overland* continued to monitor—sometimes with astonishment—the exuberance of England in the Sixties. (The implicit question would be formulated elsewhere, by the French philosopher Raymond Aron: How was it that the English had changed from being Romans to becoming Italians, in one generation?)[14]

There was also, of course, Stephen's personal tar-baby, Communism, and a nagging need to square off with the Soviet Union. *Overland* had always stood for 'dialogue and friendship' with Russia—so Stephen felt all the more entitled to criticise 'our disgust at the continuing persecution of ideas in the Soviet Union'. More broadly, he agreed with Edward Crankshaw, who had written, 'We shall feel like stopping talking about the atrocities of Stalinism, when the Russians start talking about them.' The persecution of writers was a particular concern. *Overland* had published a speech by Khrushchev on art, in which, while referring to the relative openness of recent years, he had maintained the standard Party position. Carlos Fuentes was placed alongside to say that to have such an instrumentalist view—seeing literature and art 'purely as weapons of socialist transformation' was in fact 'explicitly rejected by marxist thought'. A tough interview with Yevgeny Yevtushenko completed the trio, the poet insisting on individualism and high standards in art, but cleverly placing them within the constraints imposed by the Party.[15]

The limitations of the Khrushchev thaw became more apparent under his successor Brezhnev. *Overland* republished Solzhenitsyn's letter to the Union of Soviet Writers, in which he protested about the suppression of recent work. In the same issue appeared another reprinted letter, from Graham Greene, about the jailing of the dissident writers Sinyavsky and Daniel. Sinyavsky, who was Russian, had taken a Jewish pseudonym; Daniel, who was Jewish, took a Russian one. The accusation was made that they were Zionist agents. Further arrests followed, of those who had smuggled out reports of the Daniel–Sinyavsky trial; these were described in the pages of *Overland*, while Ian Turner organised a letter of protest from left-wing magazine editors, Clem being one of the signatories. (Nina had already published in *Overland* an appreciation of Anna Akhmatova.)

The whiff of antisemitism in the Daniel–Sinyavsky trial would not have surprised Stephen, who had every reason to be alert to the issue. 'At one and the same time Soviet citizens can be objectively lending their support to anti-semitism', he had written, 'and yet [be] sincerely revolted at the idea that they are anti-semitic.' In his Moscow visit of 1957 (when still a Communist), Stephen had been taken to task by a Party functionary for his detection of anti-Semitism. I am a Jew, said the apparatchik.

> He also explained to me at great length why there was no Yiddish press or publishing in the Soviet Union: 'There's no demand for it.' I remember how furious he was when I said, on our parting, 'Well, when you come round to reinstating Yiddish again, please remember to write and tell me just how the demand suddenly re-developed.'[16]

The Soviet invasion of Czechoslovakia—prompted by the 'Prague spring' of 1968—was the last straw. *Overland* had already been going to lead its August issue with a letter from Prague by David Martin; an editorial statement now had to be inserted instead, signed by the whole panel. The invasion was 'a tragedy for us all', particularly those associated with the magazine, 'a great many of whom have always felt at least a residual sympathy' for the achievements and aspirations of the Soviet Union. There may, Stephen conceded, have been 'the shadow of a case' for intervention in Hungary. 'But Czechoslovakia was trying to make socialism work … It was too imaginative for the Russians', a sad indicator of 'the central social tragedy of the twentieth century: the perversion of socialism … The invasion and occupation of Czechoslovakia is probably the end of the possibility of socialism in our time.'[17]

Creative writing

Clem always claimed that his main interest was in finding and publishing first-rate poems and short stories. He had a knack for it; but it is also true that his own tastes seemed increasingly old-fashioned. For the *Texas Quarterly* in 1962 he described Australia as 'still predominantly a pastoral and mercantile community', a trope of his that completely overlooked urbanisation and recent industrialisation. So it is not entirely surprising that the list of ten significant Australian works he compiled for UNESCO three years earlier was conventional to the point of being passé. Richardson's *The Fortunes of Richard Mahony* was there, along with Boldrewood's *Robbery Under Arms*, Lawson and Furphy; also Stewart and Keesing's *Australian Bush Ballads*. First listed—as a kind of cornerstone—was Vance Palmer's *National Portraits*; later Prichard's *Coonardoo*, Davison's *Man-Shy*, and Slessor's poems. Patrick White's *Voss* was included, one suspects partly because of its theme.

There is no Xavier Herbert, let alone Christina Stead, Miles Franklin or Martin Boyd. Judith Wright had been considered for inclusion, Christopher Brennan wondered about. But the range of Clem's final list is strikingly narrow. To some extent his tastes broadened with the 'breakthrough', and the editorial net would always be cast wider than his personal predilections might suggest. Within a year, a whole segment of the magazine would be devoted to Herbert. Critical appreciation often came first, but by the end of the decade Clem had published work from both Stead and Boyd, and—following reviews of his work for some years—admitted Hal Porter.[18]

Clem would, in the eight years from 1957, three times publish extracts from forthcoming novels by Patrick White: although the author had told him he could not 'convey what I want to convey within the bounds of a short story'—a feeling shared by a number of writers—he did manage to place two in *Meanjin* in the early 1960s. One was set in Greece; the other, 'Down at the Dump'—extending across a quarter of the number—not only revealed the compulsions of people living ordinary lives, but caught the halts and the cadences of Australian speech with extraordinary accuracy. But one story—which White thought his best—was rejected. White thought that might have been because it depicted 'a certain kind of dated left-wing intellectual'—and had a lesbian tinge. 'I had hoped it would jazz things up a bit at *Meanjin*,' he wrote to a friend. 'Australian literature is inclined to become unbearably solemn.'[19]

It is striking that the short-story writer Clem published most in the 1960s was Peter Cowan. Cowan—who came to look like Kipling—Clem saw as a new Vance Palmer: his first story in *Meanjin* was given pride of place in an issue not long after Palmer's death. In these stories it is a sense of isolation that comes through most strongly: of people on the rim of the continent in Western Australia, people often avoiding others, people in fractured relationships, others reaching out flailingly. While the stories are expansively written, authorial reticence goes with a pointillist precision. The underlying sombre tone is often kept at bay by convincing dialogue.

Clem's sense of Australianness may have been essentialised and rendered static partly by its juxtaposition with writing brought in from the rest of the world. With little innovative writing appearing at home, it was easy, by default, to identify innovation with overseas—leading him to enact a very personal cultural cringe. With Professor Chisholm close to hand, and the writer-actor Catherine Duncan on the ground in Paris, Clem was well placed to be advised about bringing French material into the magazine. Apart from stories by Raymond Roussel and Eugène Ionesco (a first English translation), in 1963 there appeared a whole French number, featuring practitioners of the *nouveau roman*. Some of the pieces had not yet appeared in French. The East German writer Stefan Heym appeared in 1966 and, in the early seventies work from the German writer Rolf Hochhuth and the Austrian Peter Handke.

There were writers from the eastern bloc, culminating in an extract from the forthcoming translation of Solzhenitsyn's *August 1914*. Asian writers included the Indian RK Narayan and the Indonesian Pramoedya Ananta Toer. From Africa came stories by Chinua Achebe and Ngũgĩ wa Thiong'o. Clem was hopeful of having something from the South African Nadine Gordimer, but could net nothing suitable; major international writers would occasionally fob him off with inferior work. (Others included Joyce Cary and Doris Lessing.) Moreover, since Clem had long been out of joint with America—he had refused an invitation to go there as a protest against the recent execution of the Rosenbergs—in his last dozen years an American fictional presence in the magazine was both slight and oblique: an extract from Norman Mailer's play *The Deer Park*, and an interview with Kurt Vonnegut Jr.[20]

'Short stories are a recurring misery', Ian Mair grumbled in the *Age*, and it was Clem's constant plaint—to some extent Stephen's too—that it was difficult to get good short stories. For *Overland*, the need to include stories about the struggles of working-class life, and a more general attitude of encouragement than that of *Meanjin*, resulted in porpoise-like appearances: authors who would never appear in its pages again. The most published writer was John Morrison: five of his stories led the issues in which they appeared. Thus Stephen could be seen paying his social realist dues up-front. But a sixth story, which didn't have pride of place, was 'Pioneers': later he would describe it as 'the best story we have ever published'.

Meanwhile *Overland*'s fiction—while rarely including contributions from overseas, beyond the region—was broadening. A coup, given the magazine's less than rapturous reception of *Voss*, 'was the publication of Patrick White's short story 'Clay' in 1963. Out of the everyday, the surreal. A few years earlier Stephen began publishing fiction by Peter Mathers, which appealed for its variety in style and the way it proceeded from different (unsettling) assumptions. *Overland* must always have a place, Stephen told uneasy advisory editors, for 'experimental writing of this socially-relevant kind.' At the same time, he exhorted *Overland*'s readership to try harder, and persevere with 'difficult' stories. They were important, for 'trying to heighten our sensibility and understanding of the interactions of mind, personality and environment'. So other new writers began to appear in the magazine: Frank Moorhouse and Michael Wilding had each published a couple of stories there by 1973.[21]

Turning to poetry, *Meanjin* had always prided itself on its international component. Clem published the Italian Salvatore Quasimodo and contemporary French poetry in what he genteelly termed 'a Little Anthology'. Major figures continued to appear in the journal, with a tilt towards Russia becoming more evident. Work appeared from Anna Akhmatova, Andrei Voznesensky and the international celebrity Yevgeny Yevtushenko (who visited Australia twice). Nina and members of the Russian Department were a prompt here, but also important was the enthusiasm of the Australian diplomat-poet, JR Rowland, who sometimes provided translations. The American Kenneth Rexroth sent Clem a poem at the time of his abrasive visit (famously fictionalised by Frank Moorhouse), and later *Meanjin* published WS Merwin and Robert Bly. From across the Tasman came poems from Charles Brasch and Ian Wedde. With his eye cocked to Canada—from an Australian perspective, always half a beat ahead—Clem again published Earle Birney. So too did Stephen. But in the period from 1960 to 1973, with the exception of Papua New Guinea (whose poets were featured in two spreads in 1971, as part of Stephen's great interest in the territory), barely half a dozen foreign poets appeared in *Overland.* Essentially Australia was its bailiwick.

Looking at number 17 (the first *Overland* for 1960), of the thirteen poets published there, ten also appeared in *Meanjin* between that date and 1974. This should come as no surprise: poets were anxious to be published—generally they did not care much about the political stance of any of the magazines. (Indeed they would increasingly become caught up in politics of their own, some later writing about *Meanjin* and *Overland* as if they existed only to publish poetry.) Rodney Hall, writing to Clem, assured him that he always saw his poems first—before Stephen did, despite Hall's formal association with *Overland.* Clem had already been trying to lure Hall to Melbourne for direct involvement in *Meanjin.* Requesting that Clem keep this in confidence, he added 'I don't pretend to send ones to him first.' Had he heard, Stephen would have probably shrugged his broad shoulders. Once in a while the editors would pass on poems they thought more suitable for the rival magazine.[22]

Nonetheless Stephen's commitment to poetry was real, extending to *Overland* continuing to publish books. In the 1960s these included John Manifold, *Nightmares & Sunhorses* (1961); Aileen Palmer, *World Without Strangers* (1964); a second volume from Laurence Collinson, *Who's Wheeling Grandma?* (1967); and Dorothy Hewett's *Windmill Country* (1968). Meanwhile the magazine itself gave a platform to people who had broken with Clem, such as Max Harris and, in particular, Judith Wright.

Even so, *Meanjin* was seen, until the end of the 1960s, as the place to appear: for a poet—for authors—this signified arrival. A number in effect graduated from *Overland* to the senior magazine. RA Simpson and, more gradually, Thomas Shapcott moved across; academic poets such as Chris Wallace-Crabbe and Andrew Taylor switched allegiance early, partly because *Meanjin* also offered a place for serious criticism. Meanwhile David Martin and Dorothy Hewett, broader in their creative writing, favoured each editor as it pleased them, as we shall see.

Other poets chose to appear in both journals regularly. Among them were Bruce Dawe (with poems that were taut, confident and vernacular),

Noel Macainsh, Judith Green (later Rodriguez), and Laurence Collinson (always fearful that he might offend Clem). But then, from the inner *Meanjin* circle, Dorothy Green—demonstrating her independence—placed as Dorothy Auchterlonie a poem in *Overland*, while Arthur Phillips gave Stephen a surprisingly well-turned love poem. Even Clem himself—in addition to publishing his own poetry—placed a poem in the rival journal. 'At Rest'—complete with spaced-out lines—is a rare venture into the contemporary. The persona is a man lying on the beach, exhausted after lovemaking—a demonstration that the old guy (and editor) was still 'with it'.

Meanjin's regulars included Gwen Harwood—it was pleased to publish female poets—though Harwood also appeared there under a male pseudonym, Francis Geyer. The magazine was also the preferred outlet for intermittent appearances by AD Hope, his elegant verse adding a welcome classical ingredient, universal rather than Australian. The Canberra region also provided other poets, including JR Rowland and David Campbell, a pastoralist who was finding a regular place in the magazine just as Geoffrey Dutton, another one from an old South Australian family, was increasingly discomfited by Clem's rejections. (Dutton slid across to *Overland*, where Stephen—in Geelong Grammar rather than Communist Party mode—made a feature of his poetry.). *Meanjin* also carried a late surge of poems from the much admired RD FitzGerald.

Clem was predictably partial to the lyrical verse of Vivian Smith, but also liked the way JM Couper, a Scot living in Australia, chose to write on historical themes. In his poetry, Couper was striving for the synthesis in miniscule that Clem sought for the whole magazine. Closer to hand was the poet Lynne Duncan, later Strahan (and later again *Meanjin*'s historian). But the most notable contributor who chose *Meanjin* was Francis Webb.

The poet Francis Webb, by nature a solitary and a wanderer, had three fixed points: Sydney, Canada and England. But mental illness ran in the family, and he was troubled with paranoid schizophrenia. There had been early attacks, but from 1960 until his death in 1973 Webb was mostly confined in various mental hospitals. His earlier poetry is characterised by landscapes ranged as if for action, and monologues of essentially solitary figures, mostly known to history because of their audacity. A man in existential pain, Webb desperately tried 'to throw off the tyrannical self which rode him like an incubus'. He became preoccupied with death, and with religion. It was always there: in the radio play [Hitler's] *Birthday* (1953) Goebbels tells his leader, in a metaphor extending to blasphemy, that getting his family to take cyanide constitutes a sacrament to the Führer. By the time Webb was confined at the Rydalmere psychiatric hospital, the books by his bedside were nearly all devotional. 'He was, in fact', said AD Hope, 'always and only talking to God.' Spasmodically, Webb kept writing. The poems are impacted, dense, allusive. Some of them, confessed the critic HP Heseltine, 'defied me'; he could not make sense of them, or like them. But 'in the end they defied me to leave them alone'.

Webb was an early subscriber to *Meanjin*. He told Clem that 'Meanjin under your editorship is become the ideal literary magazine, sophisticated as anyone could want but wide open to what is in process of becoming.' Clem returned the compliment, telling Webb 'you are by far the best poet of your generation in Australia', asking him to send poems from time to time. And so he did, while appealing to Clem to help him, for 'In this hospital I take daily the most wicked succession of bloodless little needle-jabs of hate, as well as the filthy outspoken abuse and insult.' Couldn't he get the Commonwealth Literary Fund to intervene in some way? Clem did what he could, but the correspondence eventually spluttered out. 'If you write at all to me', ran Webb's last letter, 'remember that all mental hospitals in Australia are now Communistic and vile institutions. No mail addressed to me will reach me.'

In the meantime Clem published Webb poems, which included some of his best. The poet's material was right in front of him, in the hospital, accurately described but shot through with an infusion of pity: 'To see in ugliness and agony a way to God', Webb wrote. Notable is 'Harry', a portrait of a man with Down syndrome seriously setting about 'writing' a letter nobody will ever receive. Later came the splendid 'Incident', a light, derisory account of the brutally functional hospital, giving way to shards of contact and implicit meditation on a life's meaning. The diction varies from the elevated to the idiomatic: the phrase 'McMurtrie's dead' returns at the end of each verse like a liturgical response. Indeed Webb had an intense love of music, and he was pursued by the pounding rhythms of Bruckner's scherzos ('greater than Beethoven'). But it was the brisk, driven, almost hysterical character of the 'Rondo Burleske: Mahler's Ninth' that led to a poem with Webb's characteristic slippages and a sardonic note well to the fore. Also placed in *Meanjin* was his finest musical poem—uniting a number of his preoccupations—'Nessun Dorma', a tribute to Jussi Björling.

The famous English writer on art, Sir Herbert Read, visiting Australia in 1961, was so impressed with Webb's *Socrates*, given him by the poet David Campbell, that he searched out earlier volumes. Some years later he wrote a preface to Webb's *Collected Poems*, and concluded that the Australian's achievement should be placed on the same level as Rilke, Eliot or Pasternak. He was, Read had already asserted in the *London Magazine*, '*the most unjustly neglected poet of this century*' (his italics). Equally tellingly, Webb commanded enormous respect among fellow Australian poets such as Vincent Buckley, AD Hope, Judith Wright and Les A Murray. And for all his Catholicism, Webb's condition as an ultimate outsider also attracted the countercultural young. A particular admirer was the poet Robert Adamson.[23]

Playing the field: Dorothy Hewett and David Martin

Dorothy Hewett won a *Meanjin* poetry competition when just a first-year student at the University of Western Australia, submitting a number of poems under the pseudonym Jael Paris. 'These are extraordinary poems for an eighteen-year-old', wrote Clem, exhibiting 'a distinctive poetic talent'. He even toyed with the idea, given that he was then publishing books of poetry, of producing one devoted to hers. But he was less comfortable with later poems submitted: they all needed further work. Dorothy wasn't interested; that was the way she wrote poetry. Their both joining in a delegation of writers to the Soviet Union, in 1965, brought them closer together. Shortly afterwards, Clem accepted a story. Thereafter he would air his grievances quasi-confidentially, but Hewett's increasing preoccupation with play-writing took her further from *Meanjin*'s ambience. She sent a scene from *Bon-bons and Roses for*

Dolly, but it was sniffily received by Clem's readers. 'This relies entirely on coarseness for laughs,' advised one. 'I see nothing in it.'[24]

Dorothy's relations with Stephen were deeper and fuller. A year younger than Stephen—and after a much more tempestuous youth—she drifted into the Communist Party, dropped out and joined it again about the same time as he did. Leaving her husband and child in Perth to run away with her lover, a boilermaker, she shed all literary ambitions as bourgeois (at the Party's direction), and became the leading cadre in South Sydney. Looking back, she saw herself as having been incarcerated in a 'proletarian gulag'. It was worse than that: her partner proved to be a paranoid schizophrenic, who accused her of trying to poison him and their children—and burnt her manuscripts.

Dorothy fled, back to Perth. She had begun to write seriously again, after nearly twenty years. 'I am now making my second run,' she told Clem. Stephen wrote her encouraging letters, particularly about her novel, *Bobbin Up* (1959), which was centred on a group of women textile workers as they organised a strike. It would do well, selling out in six weeks. But there was puritanical criticism from the original typist (who called in the Vice Squad), from the Party, and even from the publishers, the Australasian Book Society. Stephen was well aware that a writer's confidence needed bolstering; it could be easily sapped. But not for long, in the case of Hewett. When he asked for her support, in the row with *Tribune*, she made it plain she could not give it.[25]

Hewett fiercely contested Stephen's view, expressed in a recent editorial, that the intellectual in Australia was 'generally despised and rejected', even 'mistrusted' by the labour movement, given its singular contempt for ideas. 'It is precisely among the working class that I and many other intellectuals', she wrote, 'have found the bulk, if not all, of their audience and support.' Then she continued, resisting any idea of a 'trickle-down' effect of the arts:

> Culture in a country is something far deeper than the written word, the paint on canvas, the note of music … The creative urge in the labour movement is, I feel, so much more than application and understanding of accepted art forms … It is the life, the idiom, the attitudes, the peculiar brave and bitterly sardonic and salty humour [of the people] … in short the attitudes to life itself.

Stephen had, in his editorial, 'reduced culture to only one of its denominators and in so doing ha[s] perpetrated a gross injustice'.

Unsympathetic to Stephen's concern with building cultural infrastructure, Hewett did not stop there. She wondered where he was taking *Overland.* It was all very well saying it could survive, cut off from the Communist Party—but 'there is no substitute for them ... they are the most advanced thinkers and the most active members of the working class'. There was a real risk *Overland* would lose its trade union support. 'It may gain readers among the vaguely left or non-left intellectuals, probably will, but is that the role you wish it to play?'[26]

Stephen's response was to ask Dorothy to join the *Overland* board. No, she said; living in Perth, I am too far away, would have insufficient influence on content. But in 1965 she agreed, even though she thought *Overland*'s editorial policy 'often timid', and that Stephen was 'inclined to equivocate too much, feeling the academic and the intellectual breathing down your neck'. It was their 'bland assumption of being always so cynically right' that got to her. Nonetheless she taught for nine years as a tutor in the English Department at the University of Western Australia, while putting in for academic jobs elsewhere. This was, she wrote, becoming 'embarrassingly perpetual, like entering a beauty contest one never wins'.[27]

The 1960s were to see Dorothy Hewett moving from writing Lawsonian short stories towards becoming a successful playwright—in a uniquely expressive, non-naturalist mode. She was, writes Susan Sheridan, 'a brilliant self-mythologiser', and nowhere more so than in her poetry, which remained her prime activity all through her life. Sometimes the readers for *Overland* (filtering manuscripts) felt they had seen it all before, and rejected it. Stephen could be sharp: Hewett could be 'very moving' in her 'frank, simple ballad-rolling way', he told her, but she was also capable of 'a pastiche of your own style'.

Shortly afterwards RD FitzGerald praised a Hewett poem as one of the best new poems he had seen in years; Stephen immediately sent the letter on. He continued to comment on the way he felt her verse should be going, but on meeting a riposte, would backtrack. 'Please don't be cross,' he said. 'This is what I'm here for. Even if I don't know what I'm talking about.' By 1968 he was so impressed with her corpus that he decided to publish her book of poems *Windmill Country*, which sold its

500 copies quite quickly. Barrie Reid, at Stephen's right hand, said on the ABC that there had been no book like it by an Australian woman since Judith Wright's *The Moving Image*.[28]

Although Stephen had left the Party, Communism still yoked Hewett and him together. 'I still believe in the *idea*,' she had told Clem, 'and my Party membership, although often bitter and difficult, is important to me.' She likened it to persevering with 'a rather unsuccessful marriage'; felt she needed the discipline. (With Stephen she would despair about their shared weight problem, and inability to work properly.) But Hewett was troubled about the treatment of writers in the eastern bloc, and organised petitions about them: 'If this is not solved in the next decade', she wrote, 'there can be no freedom under socialism.' A magnificent long poem published by Stephen, 'The Hidden Journey', offered impressions of the Soviet Union—a sequence spun around things Hewett had noticed, but done her best to suppress. He suggested subtitling it 'For the Fiftieth Anniversary of the Soviet Revolution'. She was not yet ready for that. But a few years later, when Soviet tanks rolled into Czechoslovakia, Hewett resigned from the Party.[29]

Shortly afterwards Hewett trained her guns on someone she had much admired—had named one of her girls after—Katharine Susannah Prichard. KSP had remained inflexible, doctrinaire to the end (she had recently died). In a fine essay drawing on her academic skills, Hewett showed how the senior writer had already withered within—relying on idealised stereotypes, tending to fuse them with the landscape. Stephen (and Nita) were ecstatic about the piece. 'It is the kind of thing that comes along every few issues,' he wrote, 'to persuade one that editing *Overland* has some point, after all ... I admire you for doing [it]. In a way it is a breakthrough expression of belief for us.'[30]

Unlike Hewett, David Martin played his hand carefully right from the moment the *Realist Writer* graduated as *Overland*. He'd had a satirical exchange with AD Hope, in verse, and suggested to Clem that he publish it. 'I don't see how I could use this kind of thing in *Meanjin*', Clem advised, although he would like to. The journal had become a little too grand for its own good: Clem would not have been pleased to open the first issue of Stephen's new magazine and find the poems printed there. He was well aware of the close friendship between the Murray-Smiths and the Martins, but knew he could offer Martin higher standing as a writer; something Martin respectfully acknowledged. For his part, Clem craved Martin's approval for his own attempts at writing a novel. But crucially, he regarded Martin as 'one of the very few people in the country capable of turning out the kind of work I am looking for'. *Meanjin* was 'not too bad' as it stands, Clem wrote, but 'it still lacks a hard muscular intellectual core' compared with its European counterparts. 'That's where blokes like you come in,' he urged, 'coming from outside, you take a "long clear look" at us in a way we cannot do.' Martin could help materially

> to make articulate a national condition with universal applications. We need to abandon whatever is still conducive to a distorted, or even false view of life in this country—a calculated rejection, therefore, of certain attitudes or 'traditions' that have too long been part of our intellectual and emotional baggage.

By 1960 Martin was being lined up to write a major article for each issue of *Meanjin*: bravely, and aware of the antagonism it might draw, he had already written an incisive article on the Socialist Realists—a school that he saw as having 'more or less petered out'. (Indeed: the contraction from socialist realism to social realism was becoming more common.) 'Not a single Communist writer in Australia has written a good love story,' he pointed out. Martin dawdled over further pieces, but saw the broader context more clearly than Clem. *Meanjin* had to go 'with the New Left that is slowly developing, and developing outside narrow party confines'. There had to be a middle way between *Doctor Zhivago* (referring to Pasternak's novel) and Khrushchev. 'Yes to History,' Martin wrote, 'but not a slavish yes. But never No to History. That's ridiculous.'[31]

Twice Martin discussed with Clem publishing books of his at the Meanjin Press, and twice failed to follow through: material for a grievance. But, seeing him as a cornerstone of the journal, Clem did not press the point. Instead, he responded favourably when Martin suggested he should be given the treatment: a 'full dress' critical essay. They agreed AA Phillips should write it, and he did, dubbing Martin 'the most improbable Australian writer who ever existed'—plus a segment from Martin's new novel, and (at Clem's suggestion) an autobiographical piece. Instead of the last there appeared, as a response to Phillips, a convincing credo. Martin's ego expanded with the project: he referred to it as '"my" *Meanjin* issue', pressed for a beard to be added to the Kahan etching (it was), then basked in the glory of thirty-two consecutive pages of Martiniana. 'The best way to repay such generosity is to continue faithful to *Meanjin*,' he wrote, 'and through this, faithful to oneself.'

Speaking of the annual cricket match between the two magazines, Martin declared he would bowl for one team and bat for the other. And so metaphorically he did, spreading his poetry across both magazines: a tilt towards *Overland* was not checked by his being awarded a *Meanjin* poetry prize. A couple of short stories also appeared in *Overland*, none in *Meanjin*, but now Martin was intent on writing full-length novels. He had promised Clem that should he write anything in the article line, he would write it only for *Meanjin*. But his disinclination ran deep, even though he felt guilty about it. As he would later explain, 'I lack the energy. My other work absorbs it all … Rightly or wrongly, novels are closest to my heart. I also feel … that criticism is almost too thin-iced a pond for me to skate on.'

His was the empathy of the writer, not the systematic analysis of the academic. Clem would have to take him as he found him, not impose a set of expectations. So it was only when Martin was stirred by the events of 1968, and the strivings of the radical young, that a varied group of Martin articles appeared in *Meanjin* again—on topics such as the capitalist media, Noam Chomsky and the Soviet invasion of Czechoslovakia, which he witnessed.[32]

The fact was—despite a bumpy beginning—Martin's affinities with Stephen and *Overland* ran deeper. For a start, with their wives they formed a quartet, for both marriages united Jew and Gentile. Stephen—the one now receiving the critiques of each issue—spoke of 'a rare empathy between us', even if at times he found Martin, peering at the world through bottle-thick spectacles, rather voluble and thin-skinned. Stephen was a keen supporter of Martin, and helped to steer him through creative blocks. He had also come to depend on him. Both saw themselves essentially as revolutionary humanists, who, despite persistent attack, had weathered their break with the Party. 'We have been hit so far into the ground', Stephen told Martin, 'by different kinds of hammers wielded by different kinds of people.'

Even so, Martin was impatient with Stephen and Turner's reformism, their limited, specific objectives, the way it blunted the drive towards their professed socialism. *Overland* seemed full of 'piddling reformist pieces'. 'I do not hanker after the title "communist" [note the small c]', replied Stephen,

> though this is a semantic matter. To use another loaded and inaccurate word, I would *not* deny that I am a 'reformist'. How the transition to socialism in this country will take place I don't know. Perhaps by external force. Perhaps by internal revolution. Perhaps by other processes ... I'm a political agnostic when these questions of social change are raised. I'm pretty sure that, while we've got to aim straight, that it is at any given period the act of *firing* more than that of *aiming* which matters. Perhaps few of the explicit aims of the Bulletin republicans came true in the way they fought and thought they would: but the Bulletin republicans have had a mighty and beneficent effect on the kind of Australia you and I live in today. So may it be with us and the future.

Stephen, while hailing Martin as a citizen of the world—before the world was quite ready for it—was a little ambivalent about Martin's intrinsic cosmopolitanism. He knew he could leave Australia relatively easily—that for him, he once wrote dismissively—'it is much more of pied-à-terre than it is for us'. But, Stephen had warned, 'I'll close *Overland* down if you do.'[33]

Martin duly appeared in almost every issue in the 1960s; often twice. First there was the poetry, which could vary enormously in quality, from a poignant treatment of respectful recognition between Soviet sailors and a tsarist naval officer (Nina Christesen's father), to comic verse and brisk rhymes. But most markedly—since he was also a journalist—Stephen got him to write a kind of column, 'Hinterland', where Martin could be incisive and speculative, rather than scholarly; offering talking points, take a broad perspective, or deal with a couple of issues at the same time. It suited him—so he switched and took up this offer rather than Clem's series of serious articles. Much of 'Hinterland' was taken up with international affairs, and working through the implications of the recent crisis in the Communist world. Martin also attacked the sclerosis he saw in the Labor Party, yearned for an Australian writer who would turn to the towns and cities for subject matter, and wrote, of a Vance Palmer play, 'However [much] you stir it with the national spoon it remains cold porridge.' Martin's novel *The Hero of Too* would, with a gay bushranger, turn Palmistry on its head. And it contained a schoolteacher character compositely called Stephen Turner.[34]

Aust. Lit.

While Clem always sought to publish good short stories or poetry, literary criticism of the highest kind was central to his purpose. In the 1950s—perhaps prompted by the total omission of local context from some reflections on poetry he published by James McAuley, he had thought of running a series, 'The use of myth in Australian poetry', but only Vincent Buckley came to the party (to some extent). Clem was too far ahead of the pack. So he modulated that into a discussion of the place of Australian Literature, ('Aust. Lit.') in universities.

Nonetheless there was a quest for myth to deepen the white Australian experience, and seemingly earth it in this land. So Sidney Nolan had turned to Ned Kelly and the stranded Eliza Fraser, and Patrick White had alchemised Leichhardt into Voss. But the basic problem in developing a deeper Australian culture, as AA Phillips had discerned, was that although a process of national 'solidification' was now underway, it had been made more

> difficult because the character of our life has been built on the values of the Frontier. If we lose that character, we forfeit our individuality and all the staying tradition we possess; but frontier-values do not easily mature, and they are difficult to carry into a predominantly urban society.

Not unsurprisingly, the *Overland* review of *Voss* had been somewhat dismissive. Geoff Serle advised Clem, 'If England and America think he is a master and we don't, it's vital to our whole critical situation to see why.' John Barnes, writing from Western Australia, thought that Australian literature had been set on a new course with the advent of Patrick White. 'He's the most potent force in our literature today. He's redrawing the map of Australia, as all literary explorers do.' For his part Clem welcomed this; in his quest for spiritual values—and despite being a rationalist himself—he had tried for some years to get articles on religion. But 'the subject seems to scare people'.[35]

Believing primarily in the need to develop a sense of cultural integration among Australians—and that literary and sociopolitical affairs were enmeshed—Clem looked to rising academics as the explicators. There was a need, he felt, to construct a canon of Australian works. That was self-evident: fibre for a national culture. So Clem wrote to people such as Barnes, saying that he wanted 'full-dress critical essays' (skirted by footnotes) on a number of people, including Stead, Elizabeth Harrower, Marshall, Porter, Morrison, Waten, Stow, Douglas Stewart, 'Brent of Bin Bin' ... Half of these did not come to fruition: apart from the fact that sometimes submissions were not up to scratch, there was now a competitor. The journal *Australian Literary Studies* began in 1963, and while more technical in its approach, it did draw away some academic energies.[36]

Some writers might have felt that was a good thing. Geoffrey Dutton once sent a young man's article on symbolism in Patrick White's work to the author, who noted the claim, carefully elaborated, that it was all based on TS Eliot's *Four Quartets*. 'I found this a fascinating academic study,' White responded. 'I have not, however, read the *Four Quartets*.' Similarly AD Hope, although an academic himself, expressed scepticism about an article *Meanjin* was publishing by SL Goldberg, of the Melbourne English Department. 'Pity you devote so much space to feelthy poet from Canberra,' he wrote, 'but no doubt I shall be able to read Sam and find out all about myself at last.' Clem tended to be dazzled by academic discourse, like a rabbit caught in a car's headlights.[37]

Given his own chequered university career, Clem must have drawn additional satisfaction from being able to offer encouragement to bright young men as he marshalled a team of contributors. 'For the first time, really, we now have a team of academic critics of our native literature', he told John Barnes, reeling off the names of the rising generation. But the critics he published most, from 1960, were a mix: Barnes, HP Heseltine, Dorothy Green, Chris Wallace-Crabbe, and those old stagers AR Chisholm and Tom Inglis Moore. RF Brissenden continued strongly at first, but relations broke down. Thematic essays figured among those Clem published—he wished for more—but studies of particular authors predominated.

Patrick White led the field, as did *Meanjin* with him, publishing the first Australian appreciation. More than a dozen further articles about him would appear in the magazine; not far behind was Christopher Brennan, and increasingly, as the 1960s turned into the 1970s, Dorothy Green on Henry Handel Richardson. Essays on Henry Lawson and AD Hope recurred, and among younger writers Randolph Stow and Peter Mathers occasioned two or three articles each. Somewhat surprisingly, the Palmers over this period warranted no more than an occasional paragraph. The caravan had moved on.[38]

Clem's most enduring ally among literature academics was Harry Heseltine. While they had met earlier, it was after a meeting at the University of New South Wales that things gathered pace. Heseltine was a young Western Australian, whose upbringing had taken place in a 'mix of Anglocentric but Australian-grounded attitudes'. These would tug his elder brother to England, where he would become private secretary to the Queen; Harry, more curious about Australia's divergence and its literary manifestations, went first to the United States to study American literature. To Clem he described himself as a man with a range of interests, including Aust. Lit.—these 'interests strong & developing but still incompletely formed'. It was a come-on to any editor. Heseltine's first appearance in *Meanjin* was as a compiler of the Fiction Chronicle: 'I suspect I've been too kind to too many people, but—that's my fatal flaw as a critic.'

He showed his mettle shortly afterwards in an article assessing Australia's literary heritage. It was sweeping, and incisive: Heseltine argued that if our literature really was centred on 'the simple virtues appropriate to a frontier society', then we would be right to reject it, as a husk. Instead, he proposed that literature in Australia was essentially a Romantic and post-Romantic phenomenon, and in some ways came to deal *earlier* than the Europeans with the idea of nothingness, and of ultimate solitariness shading into madness. Lurking behind the facade of mateship, egalitarianism and democracy—marked out by convict origins and geographical necessity—writers here 'acknowledge[d] the terror at the basis of being', and built 'defences against its dangers'. This was the true distinction of Australian literature, guaranteeing 'its continuing modernity'. Clem had encouraged Heseltine to be bold, and his argument was perhaps overstated. But it struck a new note.

Clem developed close ties with Heseltine early, putting him up at his home in Eltham, and holding a party so that he could meet Melbourne notables. Believing in his academic potential, Clem told Ian Maxwell that if ever he had to 'relinquish control' of *Meanjin*, then this 'is the one man I'd like to see as editor'. Heseltine provided a stream of critical articles, and—with RF Brissenden—compiled a theatre and drama issue. It had a difficult birth: the new dramatists who would give Australian theatre its force had not quite emerged. Later, Heseltine would provide, at Clem's request, a temperate and generous assessment of the magazine for its one hundredth issue. 'The cover's a beauty', he told Clem when it eventuated; 'that fierce & enigmatic bird stares out at you defying you to ignore the magazine if you can.'[39]

In contrast to the mildness of Heseltine, Clem drew on the moral intensity of Dorothy Green. In 1961 Green took up a lectureship at Monash, at a time when there were very few women career academics. She came closer to the Christesens again—but then her husband HM Green died, and Dorothy had an emotional crisis followed by a breakdown. She then went to the ANU, but was uncomfortable in a department where she felt marginalised. Contact with Clem and Nina slackened for a time: once (when Clem was away) Dorothy penned the immortal line, 'In haste, in exhaustion, in extremis, in Melbourne'. But, for all her grumbling about the dishonesty of the academic critical scene, her own standing quietly grew: as a lecturer, as a published poet, and particularly with her masterly metaphysical study of Henry Handel Richardson, *Ulysses Bound* (1973). She also developed a reputation for being intimidating. 'Her integrity,' recalled David Headon, 'her keen mind, and her need to assess people before deciding to befriend them, was unsettling.'

Clem's relationship with Dorothy Green was a teasing, contradictory one. Her moral certainties were a fixed point in his tempestuous life; yet repeatedly she stepped aside from his suggestions to involve her more fully in the magazine. At the same time, she constantly reaffirmed her commitment to the Christesens, saying that once she loved somebody, she would always do so: it was part of her formidable consistency. Moreover, Dorothy was grateful to Clem for his faith in her as a writer: if it hadn't been for him, she told him, she would have given up years ago. She 'was not as independent as I seem to be', and given a personal life riddled with untimely deaths, feared further reverses. 'Use me as a wailing wall', she wrote—somewhat rashly. But Clem also gave her worldly advice, on occasion sent her flowers, wrote flirtatiously to her; sometimes she would respond. But in a way she acted as an authority figure, the kind of mother he would like to have had. She even had a word on that vexed subject: 'P.S. Are Your Parents Really Necessary?'

Writing lectures, books, and bringing up two young children, Dorothy—anxious about competition—was loath to take on commissions from Clem. For his part Clem was 'insanely jealous' when she appeared in print elsewhere; she'd been 'badgered', she said. And it was also the case that 'Like a lot of people, I am frightened of doing articles for *Meanjin* because they *have* to be good.' She would not contribute to his Temperament of Generations series—believing herself to not quite fit; and when it came to a projected Notes from the Underground, she remarked that 'underground is where a female in Australia usually lives, and I'd write with more conviction from that standpoint'. She didn't.

'I often think the journal should be written by you entirely,' Clem declared in 1971. In his final issues he came to call on Green more and more, and, realising that he and *Meanjin* were in distress, she obliged—not least with blasts of advice. Among many notable essays she wrote—on Henry Handel Richardson (and her father), Patrick White and Christina Stead—was one on the forgotten figure Grant Watson, a scientist and anthropologist described as 'the earliest writer of fiction to deal with the Aboriginal culture without ethnic prejudice'. Martin Boyd—along with Watson—was another favourite: on each she hoped one day to write full-length studies. Meanwhile, as Dorothy Auchterlonie, she also contributed poetry. Notable here was 'The Second Coming', an excoriation in classic metre (à la Hope) of LBJ's visit to Australia in 1966:

> Caesar's majesty is here scaled down
> To fit the image of a Texas clown.

It had been intended for the *Australian*, but—given the increasing polarisation over the Vietnam War—the newspaper's editorial conference had deemed it too hot to handle.[40]

Overland trod carefully in its literary coverage: offering ideas, generally without footnotes. The master expositor was AA Phillips, his acute judgements always delivered in an accessible style. Phillips' analysis of Patrick White's play *The Season at Sarsaparilla* was measured and appreciative even as it was critical—and implicitly accepted by the author, since he published a story in the following number. White was seen as a phenomenon, perhaps a game-changer—'We continue our Patrick White debate', wrote Stephen, introducing a pair of articles on him. 'At last', wrote Russel Ward, 'we have a great Australian novelist precisely because he is first a novelist and only incidentally an Australian.'

Gradually the chatty pieces on individual writers faded away, although accounts of meetings with them still appeared. Memoirs also featured strongly—most notably half a dozen pieces about or by the popular Labor politician Frank Anstey, an orator and writer; Stephen, (in response to demand) published them over three issues. Among other notable pieces was Christina Stead's recollection of her father, the original for *The Man who Loved Children*. Recollections of the recently dead also appeared—less frequently and less formally than in *Meanjin*. But Stephen probably got a stronger reaction than he bargained for when he published Dorothy Hewett's assessment of Katharine Susannah Prichard. (That *Overland*, of all journals, would publish such an attack!)

An undoubted coup was the publication of a correspondence between Bernard O'Dowd and Walt Whitman (a useful boost to Aust. Lit.—greatness by association). Indeed much less appeared now on Lawson and Furphy; more striking was the way *Overland* was reaching across the board. Stephen twice published Leonie Kramer, since it was not as a cultural conservative that she wrote for *Overland*, but as the only designated professor of Australian Literature. The magazine also carried material on Martin Boyd—one piece being his rejoinder to those critics who dismissed him as an Anglophile. Stephen also drew attention to the expatriate Peter Porter (neglected by *Meanjin*). Book reviews extended the range of material covered. They could be more lively, useful in sounding a clarion call: Peter Mathers, said Owen Webster of the antic comedy of *The Wort Papers*, 'has no peer in Australian letters, unless one goes back to Furphy'.[41]

Right-hand men: Brian Fitzpatrick and Ian Turner

'You are my most dependable contributor', Clem told Brian Fitzpatrick, whom he would summon to the office. 'More than a leading contributor: my main backstop and adviser.' Fitzpatrick's advice could be frank and fearless, but also playful. 'Come, come', he wrote when Clem sent on a draft statement: 'What makes you think that a 3,000 word memo addressed to persons whom you have found wanting will either (a) be read, or (b) induce them to attend a meeting?' Indeed so persuasive could Fitzpatrick be that when he wrote disapprovingly of a recent editorial, Clem became capable of writing in reply, 'No hard feelings—why in God's name should there be?' Fitzpatrick wrote some editorials, and drafted a difficult letter to Vincent Buckley for him. In 1961 two pieces by Fitzpatrick—on very different subjects—appeared in the same issue. But not everything he wrote was accepted: Clem 'was not too happy' with a segment of autobiography he submitted, although it was difficult to be precise about the 'fault'.

Nevertheless he fell in with the suggestion that Fitzpatrick should write an article attacking the idea that there was a 'Counter-revolution in Australian Historiography'—the phrase was Peter Coleman's, but well to the fore was Manning Clark, accusing Fitzpatrick (and Gordon Childe) of being 'disappointed radicals' who 'thought of the past as a vast manure heap for some future harmony'. Fitzpatrick rebutted that claim, defended his work, surveyed the whole field and demonstrated that the 'Counter-revolution' was a beat up; there was little connection between the writers cited. It was all done with his characteristic lightness of touch. Writing to

Clem shortly afterwards, he said of Manning Clark, 'May all the muses except Clio bless him!'

Fitzpatrick had failed to get a university post, even when invited to apply, as he was three times: at one point, in desperation, he applied for a job on the Hamilton *Spectator*—also unsuccessfully. He was politically active and too unconventional, while there were too many stories about his drinking. At Melbourne University, there was the implacable hostility of his first wife Associate Professor Kathleen Fitzpatrick, as well as rumours circulating about his current unhappy family life. 'My own situation is that I see no future', he wrote to Clem in 1957. 'Brian's drinking self', his daughter Sheila later recalled, 'seemed to be taking over from his sober one'; arch pedantry emerged in his conversation, along with grandiosity, sentimentality and a compensatory self-regard.

To cheer him up, Clem became active in organising a testimonial dinner. It was attended by some 300 people, drawn from across the political spectrum. Harold Holt (soon to be a Liberal prime minister) spoke warmly of Fitzpatrick's integrity, and of the courteous, persuasive manner in which he would point out the errors committed by Holt's own department (Immigration). Another speaker, Jim Cairns (later a Labor treasurer), spoke of how it was Brian who 'changed' him, the ex-policeman, 'in my view that unconventional people are outcasts'. Clem was in Romania, and found that he could not get away. So his message was read by Ian Maxwell (chairman of the *Meanjin* advisory committee). 'He taught me, perhaps unwittingly, at least the meaning of urbanity, tolerance, compassion', Clem wrote. 'And I feel confident that most of you will acknowledge that, directly or indirectly, Brian was *your* teacher too.' A little over a year later, Clem would sadly deliver these words himself: Brian Fitzpatrick died suddenly in September 1965. At least—unlike Vance Palmer—he had lived long enough to see the general esteem in which he was held.[42]

Stephen's right-hand man—indeed ally—was Ian Turner. At the beginning of 1959 Turner had moved to Canberra, where he was doing a PhD at the Australian National University. He was struck by the sumptuous conditions—the ANU provided a house as well as an office, and assistance with typing as well as various other benefits. It was the era of the *acastocracy*: the university sector was expanding, and some academics still thought of themselves as being 'gentlemen'. At first Turner found the adjustment difficult, but eased by his own gregariousness and fondness for a beer, he adapted quickly. Before long, as he applied himself to his work, he declared to a friend that there was 'nothing like this academic life for sheer drudgery'.[43]

Turner needed the isolation: he was discovering that 'a closed intellectual system [Communism] cannot survive the destruction of any one of its interlocking elements'. Years before, Tim Burstall had felt that Turner had sacrificed much of his intelligence and integrity in turning himself into a Party functionary. Now Turner was no longer sure exactly what he thought, but was reconnecting with an earlier self. Perhaps the old Communists who said that those who resigned after Hungary were really fellow-travellers who had joined the Party by mistake, were right. Whatever, Turner was reluctant to go back to Melbourne. People would expect him to make pronouncements, drawing on 'a self-confidence and an arrogance I no longer have'. History-writing was good for him, since 'it enabled me, in the guise of writing about the militants in World War I, to work out a new assessment of my own position'.[44]

Turner's thesis (later published as *Industrial Labour and Politics*) took from WK Hancock the contention that 'in Australia the labour movement has been the principal initiator of social change'. Opposed to it were the conservatives, with an eye turned back to England, whereas democrats (many Australian-born), were invigorated by the prospects of advancement. In Australia, unlike overseas (where originally they had been banned), the trade unions have been the radical force. The first form of workers organisation, they facilitated the movement of labour into politics, initially as a pressure group and then as an independent working-class party. But because of this evolution, the movement—and the party—tended to be reformist and empirical in character, wedded to parliamentary politics, rather than aiming at radical social reconstruction. Union leaders would generally set the pace, whereas the politicians in the movement 'have characteristically tried to make their party look as much like their opponents as possible'. The result was a struggle between unionists and politicians for control of the party machine.

Turner began his academic work focusing on the Syndicalists. While he rejected their 'anarchist abnegation' of politics, he valued their insight that if there were to be a socialist democracy, then 'the processes of production must be controlled and administered by the producers themselves'. Disillusioned with Communism, Turner nonetheless remained convinced that 'the present social order is corrupt and unjust and ought to be done away with'. Change would have to come from somewhere in the labour movement, led by someone controlling a union. But the prospects were not good. Goals in Australia always tended to be immediate, of direct interest to trade unions, 'whereas in Britain there has always been a stronger element of theory, a clearer socialist aspiration'. Here an intellectual would always be on the outer.[45]

Turner knew his capacities, and felt impelled to make a contribution. He was a fine orator; historical breadth and legal training had developed in him an unusual power to sustain a convincing argument. Once, uncharacteristically, he introduced himself to a visiting Sydneysider as 'Melbourne's leading left-wing intellectual'. But increasingly he realised that he had little capacity for theory. His deepest impulse, arising from a critical reading of the present, was to identify the crucial elements of a situation and trace their historical genesis before offering a diagnosis and a strategy. Turner's ultimate aim was not only to achieve progress, but, wherever possible, a greater harmony. If there could not be reconciliation, at least there would be rightness—vigorous but courteous. Implicitly Turner was still battling his parents, who disapproved of him to the point of disinheritance. 'What follows the revolution is ashes,' Turner once wrote to Stephen. But 'the revolution is fine', he added, commenting on the libertarians revealingly. 'The politics of permanent protest.'

With the collapse of his commitment to Communism, Turner discovered his inner meliorism. Usually it was laced with some radical common sense. He soon came to see, for all its faults, that it was best to work with or within the Labor Party, for in Australia 'The class war has been muted by economic well-being.'[46] Capitalism was not just going to collapse. Similarly, even while working on his whitefella thesis, he did the groundwork for a history of white–Indigenous relations: while impelled towards reconciliation, Turner unusually at that time questioned assimilation, stating the need for whites to 'create the conditions within our society for the continued existence of [Indigenous] culture'.

Turner's respect for Indigenous people arose partly from a recognition of their deep sense of belonging to the land. By comparison, whites were rootless, rattling around in ignorance. Growing up in Nhill in western Victoria, Turner had not known that the poet John Shaw Neilson had lived and written there, that the artist Percy Leason came from a nearby town, or that the prime minister, RG Menzies, had been born up the road at Jeparit. High culture did not really help: there was a howling disjunction between it and ordinary life. It was elitist, essentially imported.[47]

Turner was therefore attracted to the *Overland* project, quite apart from his deep friendship with Murray-Smith. He believed the essential values of Australian literature lay in its being 'democratic in temper, human in approach, national in spirit, plebeian in orientation, and above all faithful to the realities of Australian life'. He recognised that high culture was concerned (particularly in Leavisite criticism) with 'the great moral issues'; it would always aspire, through experiment and innovation, to a greater subtlety of style. But he was suspicious of it, and its sense of embattlement, evident in the editorial pages of *Quadrant*. This was particularly so as it went with talk of a now 'classless Australia' (a view endorsed by Menzies). The ideal, Turner noted, seemed to be a literature 'cut off from its traditional roots in Australia', one more influenced by current 'western' literary fashions of sex, sadism and despair than by the Australian environment in which it was created.

Yet the Australian legend had never been enunciated so comprehensively as in Russel Ward's exploration of it a few years before—or by Vance Palmer's account of the generative influence of *The Legend of the Nineties*. So initially Turner was wary of creative figures such as Patrick White and Sidney Nolan. Although informed by the Australian tradition, he saw them as incorporating elements of it into their personal visions as artists steeped in European culture. They might be effecting 'the transformation of tradition or legend into myth'; but it was an interesting phenomenon, ultimately irrelevant. Patrick White was 'exploring … a mind, a way of thinking, that is foreign territory to most Australians', Turner believed. 'Our tragedies', he wrote dismissively of *Voss*, 'have been forced on us by our surroundings, rather than our natures.' But he would soon change his opinion, coming to see White and Nolan as stressing the universal element within the local.[48]

For Turner, as he explained to the Catholic readers of *Prospect*, the important thing about *Overland* was the way it successfully provided a bridge enabling intellectuals and artists 'to cross the widening crevasses which separate them from ordinary Australians'. Moreover, it was important to encourage workers to write stories and poems arising from their own experience, although he was well aware of the danger of 'the lowering of standards'. The Australian folk-culture of earlier times might be found to have something to offer, he believed, although he was aware that such a quest could become 'romantic antiquarianism'. Writers in the 'democratic tradition' clearly found more general acceptance than most others.

Turner did not use the term 'radical nationalism' immediately, but that was what impelled him, as it did Stephen (more inclined to its cultural aspects). For Turner the break with the Communist Party firmed up for him personally the nexus between radical politics and national sentiment that had been quietly gathering. He had then noted how, in the postwar years, people across the left had made the discovery 'that aggressive, militant democracy was not only a function of the international labour movement, but was deep-rooted in Australian popular history ... that "comrade" had much in common with "mate"'.

The left need not neglect its traditional internationalism; the new concern with national origins—and particularly popular culture—served to add another dimension to its trajectory. But Turner was increasingly aware that there was a dissonance between the traditional values of the bush and those of contemporary society. 'Traditional Australian values', such as egalitarianism, mateship, the fair go, the stoicism underlying laconic humour, all were now 'being subtly modified by modern industrial society'. Class structures were hardening, and egalitarianism was tending to become 'a passive acceptance rather than an active assertion'. Moreover, Turner was uncomfortable with the bedrock assumptions of White Australia, and would later take on board feminist and New Left critiques.[49]

Turner, the strategist, realised when he and Stephen left the Party that it would be some time before the pair of them found their way politically. For a while Turner hoped for a Socialist League–type organisation, Marxist but revisionist, embedded in the trade unions: 'We need an organisation', he told Stephen, and 'they've got the apparatus'. But they were mindful of aiming at the broadest possible unity of the labour movement, so could settle for working through the Labor Party—even though Turner stated it was not a socialist party. (He believed it would be more realistic, and a tactical advantage, if the party were to drop this plank from its platform.) Meanwhile a distinct position needed to be articulated, as other ex-Communists were doing in Helen Palmer's *Outlook*. This should address not only economic issues but also increasingly urgent questions of social justice.

But Turner was exhausted by his struggle with the Party, and increasingly aware of the difficulties of mobilisation. Meanwhile rumours flew around about his and Stephen's activities: Vin Buckley asked him whether Stephen had rejoined the Communists. In fact each was more inclined to pluralism. 'No group on the left has a monopoly of concern for socialism or for economic and cultural democracy', Turner wrote, and no real advance would be made until that was recognised and acted upon. It followed that *Overland* should reflect this. In the end, although Turner thought romantically of 'a community of protesters, from Melbourne to Moscow', 'the left' came down to a collective term for 'the opponents of Menzies'. Stephen concurred, seeing *Overland* as a magazine of discussion and disagreement 'within limits'.[50]

To some degree they were rightly seen as a pair. 'I lean on you to some extent,' Stephen told Turner, 'and this is one of the crosses you have to bear.' That sometimes involved badgering. Stephen was inclined to send lists of things that needed attention; Turner tended to follow them dutifully, or else ignored them altogether. But Stephen also provided strong moral support when it was needed in Turner's personal crises—frank advice, gently given. Stephen regarded Turner as his best friend, the embodiment of a bohemianism he himself had lost. But for Turner—detached, even hard—Stephen was one of a number. Stephen could live with that, since their friendship was regularly refreshed during group bushwalks in the Victorian High Country, and later on Erith Island.

Turner's contribution to *Overland* was vital. He served to sharpen Stephen's commitment to radical nationalism, and his desire for a greater Australian involvement in the region, from a stance of neutrality. Moreover, Stephen shared Turner's dislike of consumerist culture, effectively American cultural imperialism. So he put up with Turner's reluctance to come to important meetings, though at times felt that

Turner should 'be taking a more active role in shaping the way forward'. But from Canberra, and later Adelaide, Turner did comment regularly on the contents of the magazine. He was—as so many people were, right across the board—disappointed in the quality of short stories generally, and—when it came to poetry—dismissed most of it with a shrug, as if to say: 'live and let live'. Turner constantly urged the need for good, popular sociology, so that Stephen drew attention to the poor showing of sociology in Australia. Meanwhile he found that he could delegate specific tasks to Turner, but made sure he was part of a consortium to run the magazine when he went abroad in 1971.[51]

Most important of all, Turner functioned as a utility player. Stephen appreciated the common sense that went with his intellectuality, resulting in 'a capacity for intelligent generalisation', plus his courage; moreover, Turner had 'the kind of personality which makes these gifts … doubly useful'. A regular stream of articles appeared from him, their style rather like the one just then coming into fashion with the *New York Review of Books*: spinning a thoughtful, probing essay around new books. He was the best person on hand to attack Peter Coleman's argument, advanced in *Australian Civilization*, that there was a counter-revolution underway against the 'the prison of radical interpretation' in Australian history.

But Manning Clark, far from leading this charge, wasn't really of it, Turner wrote: he was too individual, too concerned with matters of the spirit. His history was thicker, richer, more fatalistic, almost single-handedly challenging the 'easy optimism' of the traditional Whiggish view of continual material progress—and its Marxian offshoot, the idea that progress was embodied in the advance of the working class. But beyond these concerns, Turner's range was impressive—although less so in two taped discussions for *Overland*. In one on contemporary American painting, he had difficulty in moving beyond consideration of the social context, while in another with Germaine Greer, a professed 'anarchist communist', he was soon outpaced by her intelligence and trenchancy.[52]

Meanjin articles

While literary criticism of one form and another (some loose) was a major feature of *Meanjin*—sometimes introducing, or discussing, international writers—Clem always believed that the magazine should advance on a broad, integrative front. Nevertheless there were some shifts in the shape of the journal, as it had now unequivocally become. In the early 1960s, business was much the same as usual: the new appellation *Meanjin Quarterly* was more a ratification, a statement of having finally shed the chrysalis of being a 'little' magazine, rather than an indication of greater earnestness. Editorial ambition would take another form. Clem had published a couple of series earlier, but after 1966–67, when *Meanjin* ran the 'Godzone' series, he sought to run another half-dozen sets of articles. Clem was adding reiteration to continuity, partly in the hope of repeating Godzone's considerable impact. Then, towards the end of the editorship, as the 1960s curled into the 1970s, *Meanjin* would sometimes lunge uneasily into radicalism—while remaining generally conservative artistically (particularly in poetry).

There remained an eagerness to connect with the rest of the world. (Travel pieces, as such, were rare.) Indeed, in the quest for a more effective role, Clem would toy with the idea of making the journal more international. Apart from anything else, constraints imposed by the Commonwealth Literary Fund and the university rendered this impracticable. But Australia's relations—political and cultural—with countries in the region and beyond were repeatedly assessed.[53]

The American alliance in particular came under scrutiny once the Vietnam War accelerated. The Winter issue for 1968 (in an article by Macmahon Ball) opened with the statement, 'It is high time for us to make a searching re-examination of our relations with the United States.' A protesting letter from Clem had been featured in the *New York Times*, timed to coincide with Harold Holt visiting America. The issue was brought home with pieces in *Meanjin* on president Johnson's visit and the Vietnam moratoriums, while two articles by Alex Carey subjected American policy there to searing analysis. The Vietnamese were unpersonned, subject to 'redemptive' bombing, their rural society often destroyed as they were herded into urban areas. Australians were complicit in this; in 1965 prime minister Menzies described the American intervention as 'the greatest act of moral courage since Dunkirk'. And who—Carey concluded, directly addressing *Meanjin* readers—'if not the most articulate custodians of our humanist traditions, will keep guard against the abuses of language, power and technology that can lead to ends like Vietnam'?[54]

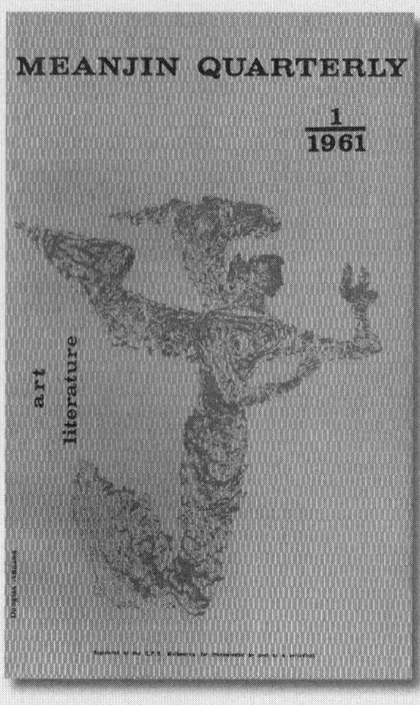

Meanjin 1/1961

Beyond the cover design—an etherealised angel, bearing a cup with laurel wreath—this issue features David Martin. The now standard Kahan etching prefaces a story, a poem and a critical essay by AA Phillips, with a rejoinder by Martin—who later again appears as a book reviewer. Next comes an extract from a novel about to be published, Patrick White's *Riders in the Chariot*. There is poetry from AD Hope and Gwen Harwood, among others. AR Chisholm contributes the first 'Remembrance of Things Past'. A South African segment consists of an article on censorship there, plus a story by Jack Cope. There is a piece on three Hungarian memoirs of Communist oppression, notes on Soviet theatre. Recent American novels are also briefly surveyed. Local focus is provided by Brian Fitzpatrick, in two articles: one on the rise of the professional/technical/managerial class, the other on the Orr case. Plans for the new Melbourne cultural centre are also discussed. Book reviews include Daniel Thomas on Robin Boyd's *The Australian Ugliness*, RF Brissenden on Bernard Smith's *European Vision and the South Pacific*.

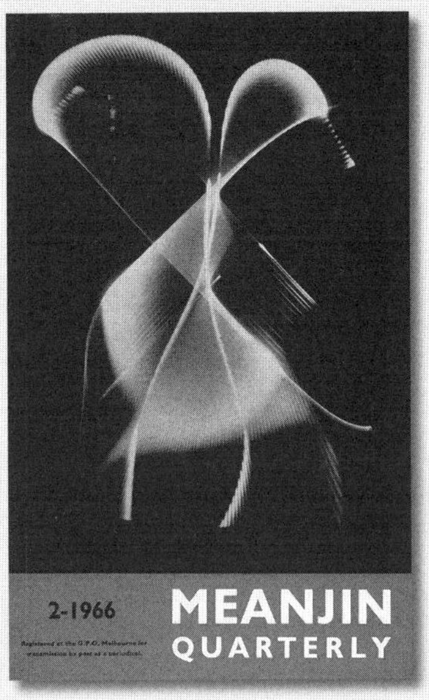

Meanjin 2/1966

This issue appeared with *Meanjin*'s most modernist cover—one of a series of electronic images by Stan Ostoja-Kotkowski. It opens with the first 'Godzone' article, Ian Turner's 'The Retreat from Reason', capped by Christesen's closing editorial, 'Godzone's Coolie Culture'. There is a strong fictional component, with stories from the East German dissident Stefan Heym, the Nigerian writer Chinua Achebe, and Australians Dal Stivens and Murray Bail (an early appearance). There is poetry from overseas, from DM Thomas and Jules Supervielle, plus verse from AD Hope, Chris Wallace-Crabbe, Rodney Hall and Dorothy Auchterlonie. Catherine Duncan reports on a French production of Alan Seymour's play *The One Day of the Year*. Criticism by John Barnes addresses the stories of White, Porter and Cowan, while AR Chisholm writes on Christopher Brennan. Book reviews include a piece on Caribbean literature, La Nauze's *Alfred Deakin* and AD Hope's *Collected Poems* (by English poet Roy Fuller).

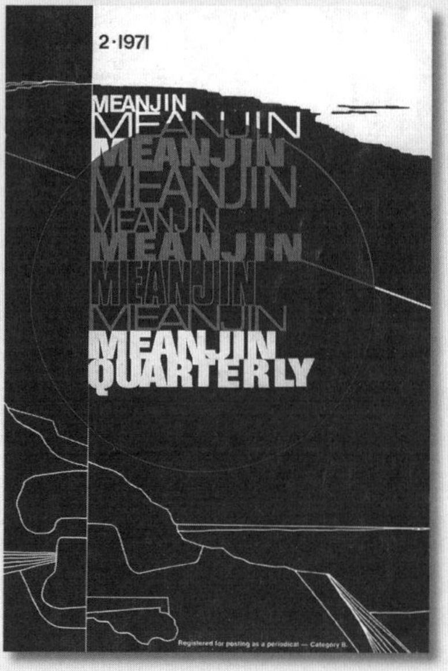

Meanjin 2/1971

Stan Ostoja-Kotkowski again provided a contemporary cover design, in post-1968 garishness. The contents, too, were unusually radical. The issue leads with Russel Ward's 'Home Thoughts from Abroad: Australia's Racist Image', followed by Humphrey McQueen with 'The Sustenance of Silence: Racism in 20th Century Australia'. Environmental issues in Australia—and a more general threat of world overpopulation—are discussed by Geoffrey Leeper. Striking is the inclusion of a play script, part of the second act of Rolf Hochhuth's *Guerillas*—postulating (in blank verse) a takeover of the American government from the inside, by a group who would act for the common good. Over the page Craig McGregor, from New York, announces 'The Revolution will not be Televised', while LJ Clancy contributes 'Revolution Without Guns: Thoughts on the Counter-Culture'. Meanwhile 'Australia's China Problem' is seen by Stephen FitzGerald as 'Self-Imposed Isolation'. A surprise is François Truffaut writing on 'How I Filmed *L'Enfant Sauvage*'. But familiar elements remain. The Short Story Chronicle reappears, while Clem slips in one of his favourite story writers, Esme Gollschewsky, and one of his own poems.

Meanjin's interest in domestic American matters was slight, and did not emerge strongly till 1971, by which stage Australians visiting such as Craig McGregor and LJ Clancy sent back reports on the emergence of the counterculture. Contact with American writers was also made by them. Clem's own American contacts had withered away, and not been replaced. For him, the United States was the Great Satan: in publishing Jean-Paul Sartre's 'Why I Will Not Go to the United States'—occasioned by Vietnam—he was implicitly adding to his own log of claims. Clem disliked American popular culture and its penetration of Australia, and was highly suspicious of American foreign policy—and (despite himself) could still be transfixed by Britain.

Meanjin's concern with peace issues in general almost disappeared, mutating in 1961–62 into a concern about the ever-bigger nuclear bombs that were being tested. At the same time, the gradual if bumpy normalisation of relations with the Soviet Union legitimated a continuing Russian presence in the journal. When in 1968 the Christesens travelled to Europe (first stop Prague, three weeks before the Soviet invasion), Nina went on alone from Prague to Russia, and in addition to pursuing her academic interests, moved in dissident circles, meeting the recently released Yuli Daniel and also Alexandr Solzhenitsyn. This would eventually lead to *Meanjin*'s coup in securing first English-language publication rights for a portion of *August 1914*. But the Soviet invasion of Czechoslovakia, coming hot on the heels of their own visit, harrowed Clem. 'The Czech invasion really did knock the stuffing out of me,' he wrote to Nina. 'It's obvious that something must be fundamentally wrong with socialism/communism, as we have known it to date—and as you yourself have always told me.'[55]

Unlike the 1950s, direct comment on public affairs at home was rare. There might be an article on an issue such as the hanging of Ronald Ryan, because of the moral issues it raised; sometimes social and political shifts could be dealt with tellingly in book reviews. Some space was given to universities—given their boom in the 1960s—with Clem publishing a stricture by Max Charlesworth: 'If the university is doing its job and fulfilling its social role of creative dissent within the community, then it *ought* to be unpopular. My fear about Australian universities is that they are not unpopular enough.' *Meanjin* was actually more exercised about the poor state of libraries, returning to the theme frequently.

This was part of a general concern with building cultural infrastructure. The work of the Canada Council, noted in *Meanjin* shortly after it was established, continued to be followed, for Clem saw it as an appropriate precedent for Australia, as it turned out to be; but first the government had to be prodded into holding an inquiry into the arts. *Meanjin* did this repeatedly, Clem railing against what he saw as 'the long divorce between intellect and political power', with resultant 'intellectual torpor'—clichés from politicians, and discouragement for artists and intellectuals. Moreover, such an agency could project a cultural image of Australia overseas. Once moves were made towards establishing an Australian Council for the Arts, Clem delegated commentary on the matter to the astringent AA Phillips.[56]

The journal continued to hold a brief for the arts in general. Visual-arts coverage became more spasmodic ('Clem seemed to take a sudden dislike to them,' Bernard Smith later reflected.) Alan McCulloch remained a stalwart—though less concerned with exhibitions—while Elwyn Lynn also contributed a number of pieces. Architecture did not normally receive much attention in *Meanjin*, but a pair of articles appeared on the Sydney Opera House, sometime after Utzon's sacking. Philip Parsons ably summed it up: 'Utzon, undoubtedly one of the world's great radicals, entered upon the conservative, rather small-scale scene of Australian architectural bureaucracy.' Opera itself scored one article, by Robin Grove, on the woes of the national company; he also contributed a number of articles on ballet (a visual spin for Clem on music, otherwise not much covered).[57]

Clem's early experience of theatre and radio meant that he was not averse to circling the footlights, but publishing is a dicey business: the Theatre and Drama issue (3/1964) turned out to be a case of *Meanjin* peaking too soon. Certainly, a wider audience for theatre was emerging, and Patrick White busy writing and producing plays; but the Pram Factory and Nimrod, with their new generation of activist playwrights, were still just over the horizon. The original plan, submitted by Harry Heseltine, was for a study of the ecology of theatre, extending to criticism and education; there was no mention of any playscript.

No satisfactory one appeared—to the embarrassment of Bob Brissenden, who had come in on the project and provisionally accepted one. Clem was apprehensive about their plans: 'I didn't feel particularly *excited*', he told them, wondering whether he really could publish such a specialised issue. His gut feeling was right: judged by sales, the Theatre and Drama issue was 'the biggest flop ever'. Had it been a book in hard covers, he lamented, it would probably have been widely reviewed, and sold. Later, Clem would run a number of articles by Margaret Williams on the new theatre.[58]

Television (feared as theatre and film's supplanter) would also occasionally be discussed, AA Phillips having the last word when he wrote, 'The reason we get vulgar nonsense is that most of us want vulgar nonsense.' Concern was expressed about the declining amount of Australian drama appearing on TV, particularly given the way the local film industry was struggling to be reborn. Clem had been made aware that Norway, with a population less than half of Australia's, produced twenty-six feature films a year. But while one of his short stories ('The Albatross') would be made into a film by Tim Burstall, *Meanjin*'s articles on film in this period were more concerned with demonstrating how 'cinema' had become a legitimate art form.[59]

Meanjin's greatest value lay in providing broader, contextual evaluations of Australian culture and the national experience. A notable example was KS Inglis's article 'The Anzac Tradition', which appeared in 1965, and drew additional pieces in response. Inglis was puzzled by the way historians then were inclined to avoid military history (although shortly they began to nibble at conscription). In a richly speculative article, he showed how the official historian, CW Bean, saw the digger as bringing into alignment existing elements of the national character. Inglis then turned to CJ Dennis, as a popularising rhymster, concluding by noting—in a prefiguration of his later work—the secular stoicism of the great monuments to the First World War. 'A study of the ceremonies of life and death performed on Anzac Day', he concluded, 'should tell us much about our society; and a national history which does not explore the meaning of these ceremonies is too thin.' The editors of *Historical Studies*—neither of them pedants—rejected the article in its original form. When offered to Clem, he leapt at it. But no-one was quite prepared for the amount of interest it engendered. It was written up in the

Age and the *Sydney Morning Herald*, for it was the first sign, after Alan Seymour's controversial play *The One Day of the Year*, of the reappraisal that would eventually turn Anzac Day into a national obsession.[60]

Clem was concerned to have historians speculate on our past, bringing out its resonances and implications for contemporary Australia. Following the Inglis article, he had Geoff Serle writing on the Digger tradition, with insightful remarks on the First AIF arising directly from its character as a volunteer army. And, with characteristically deft editing, he placed in the same issue an article showing how far DH Lawrence was responding to contemporary currents when he wrote of right-wing activism among returned soldiers in *Kangaroo*. More literary articles on mateship and Henry Lawson added to this examination of what was seen as Australia's cultural core—with Noel McLachlan later pointing out that the Digger tradition had, in fact, been divisive: the RSL badge was 'a formidable instrument of social intimidation'.

The Russel Ward thesis of an 'Australian Legend' being formed by a chain extending from convicts to bushmen to the Diggers—newly stated then—now seems, as a national ethos, markedly inadequate. Clem gave Michael Roe space to question it, drawing Ward to make the response that while 'the semi-literate bushman' was not the prime agent in Australian history, he was (and here he was right) the model for a 'highly romanticised' national image.[61]

Apart from anything else, it was too masculinist and reductive—and loosely hegemonic, sidelining women. A rare push-back to the recent male musings—'men have always shown a remarkable facility for believing the very best of themselves'—came from Coral Lansbury. But it was still too early for a feminist assault: Lansbury based her rebuttal on English pastoral utopianism, and the impact of miners—as each was necessarily reliant on a 'mate', they were the real pioneers of unionism in Australia. Meanwhile Kathleen Fitzpatrick, in a book review, described the '"woman problem"' as 'an exhausting and exasperating one because there is no end to it and no solution'. Lansbury, in a later article, wrote that for women truly to gain equal status with men, there would need to be equal responsibility for the raising of children—so that factories would need to be equipped with crèches and kindergartens. 'Sexual feminists' like Greer, Lansbury believed, were 'essentially frivolous' in the way they evaded this essential challenge.[62]

Multiculturalism, of course, was scarcely evident in *Meanjin*'s pages either—even the antecedent term 'ethnic' was yet to be widely used here, the assimilationist (if well-meaning) designation 'New Australian' being commonly used till the end of the 1960s: it carried the implication that ultimately difference could be disregarded. A hope Clem had of publishing 'cultural sociology' was not able to be realised, let alone extend so far.[63]

Similarly, after Alan McCulloch wrote on Indigenous art, reviewing what he saw as 'One of the most remarkable exhibitions ever circulated in Australia', *Meanjin*'s interest in Indigenous people almost lapsed in the 1960s. But at the very end of Clem's editorship it was reactivated, most notably with an early article by Henry Reynolds that foreshadowed his continuing interest in frontier violence.[64]

The self-engrossment of Anglo-Celtic Australia was directly linked with an anxiety, among intellectuals, about how the place was perceived. There was a standing joke that international celebrities, arriving by boat, would be asked by journalists—even before they had landed—'What do you think of Australia?' *Meanjin* in a sense practised its own version of that, almost in reverse, publishing a string of articles by Australians overseas on 'The View from London Bridge', or the highly favourable British responses to the 1961 Whitechapel Galleries exhibition of Australian art. The implicit claim was that distance and immersion in the parent society enabled one to see, as one of these articles proclaimed, 'The Object as it Really Is'. For Russel Ward, also contributing to the 'Home Thoughts from Abroad' series, 'Australia's Racist Image' was now perceived as a primary characteristic. It was the one thing he agreed on with Humphrey McQueen, whose *A New Britannia* he otherwise thought 'a bad book'.[65]

Something of that book's vigour was carried across to the pages of *Meanjin,* where McQueen pointed out that while Australia was not necessarily the most racist country in the world, it was 'primarily different because it has avoided the necessity for an articulation of its racism'. Just over the horizon, Alan Healy noted that in Papua New Guinea, in truth a colony (a word generally avoided), Australian officials imperturbably executed their duties in ignorance of developments elsewhere in the world, fortified by a sense of racial superiority.[66]

'Is Australia Still an Outpost?' Nicholas Tarling had asked exhaustively in 1962, addressing the country's high culture and its international connections. Among other things, he pointed to a compensatory impulse to regard 'the label Australian as a sufficient guarantee of quality'. A few years later, AA Phillips shrewdly put a different spin on the old problem: 'Provincialism has its own positive qualities', he asserted, including a resistance to modishness. 'We have only recently acquired a sense of rootedness in our land,' he wrote. Literature, helping to shape and clarify communal attitudes, might show the way forward. But 'The only sure way to achieve an eventual metropolitanism is to work out the existing phase of one's cultural development … frankly, unashamedly, and even proudly.'[67]

Censorship

The great impediment to cultural maturity was Australia's heavy censorship. This was a prime concern for both editors: censorship was exercised not only by the Customs Department, as publications entered the country, but also by the postmaster-general and by state governments. In Victoria, the chief secretary in 1964 banned Mary McCarthy's bestselling novel *The Group*—on the grounds that its sexual frankness made it unsuitable reading matter for his teenage daughter. After that incident, Ian Turner helped set up the Freedom to Read Association: indeed his collaborative effort *Cinderella Dressed in Yella*—the first study of Australian children's play rhymes—would be seriously considered for banning by the Post Office five years later.

By then the battle was looming over Philip Roth's *Portnoy's Complaint*: one enterprising Australian postgraduate, studying in America, mailed the book separately, chapter by chapter, to a group of friends back home. Clem sometimes had a special courier: Catherine Duncan's husband, a ship's captain, could occasionally hand-deliver dubious material when in port. But at the end of the decade he found his copies of the *Evergreen Review* were still being confiscated. When, as a senior literary magazine editor, Clem asked the minister (Senator Henty) whether he could be allowed to import copies of particular works by Nabokov, Baldwin and Burroughs, he was told the university librarian should make application: if permission were granted, Mr Christesen could then read them in the library.

Trouble began closer to home. Occasionally contributors were aware of the difficulties: AD Hope submitted a promised poem, adding, 'Not too forthright, I hope, for the chaste pages of *Meanjin* … If it is, send it back and I shall send you one with its pants on.' In addition, fear of prosecution would worry the magazines' printers. *Meanjin*'s printer was reported by Clem as saying, 'Jeez, mate, I can't fucken print that fucken story by Patrick fucken White—it contains two "fucks"!' And sometimes there was resistance in the office. One secretary flatly refused to proofread a night-cart story. Taking that response as an indicator, Clem sent the story back to the author. 'So what can an editor do?' he shrugged.[68]

Fighting back, Stephen and Ken Gott in 1962 put out—originally in a duplicated, stapled typescript—a collection called *Snatches & Lays: Songs Miss Lillywhite should never have taught us*, edited by Sebastian Hogbotel and Simon Ffuckes. 'Fucking made all of us', they gently reminded the reader, introducing a collection ranging from Stuart times to the day before yesterday. Their aim was two-fold: the lyrics chosen were to be *sung*, loudly, in company: they were 'inseparable from the grape and the grain which inspired them no less than the cock and the cunt'. (Stephen was offering himself as a Falstaffian figure.) More significantly, the pair hoped to help transform the attitudes generating censorship. How was it that society had come to adopt the position where hanging—a true obscenity—could be blithely referred to, while such centrally human activities as fucking, shitting and pissing were taboo?[69]

Meanwhile the struggle continued in the magazines. 'A good dose of filth', thundered Stephen, 'might help to break down the walls of our insularity and help us live in the world as it is.' Clem pointed out in an editorial that the worst thing about censorship was the way it had come to seem 'normal'; people accepted it as part of the landscape. At least things had improved to the point where the titles of some of the banned books were published, but repression still ensured that not only was DH Lawrence's *Lady Chatterley's Lover* banned, but so too was the book about the celebrated obscenity trial surrounding it in England. Later, Clem would run a series on censorship: a mixed batch of articles came from a psychiatrist, a philosopher, a historian and the schoolmaster AA Phillips, who had gone against his personal inclinations to act as a censor. The psychiatrist hit the nail on the head when he wrote that 'book censorship in Australia betrays a very insecure view of Australian society'. The overall problem would only worsen, noted Dennis Altman, for 'the use of obscenity as a political weapon has increased'.[70]

Stephen truly declared to David Martin that 'This journal is hot on censorship.' In 1959, just before the ban was lifted, he published an extract from Brendan Behan's *Borstal Boy*. A large part of an issue was given over to censorship matters four years later, Max Harris leading with 'The Decaying World of Senator Henty': 'sooner or later Australia must feel the need to share in [the] new European adulthood'. The segment also included reviews of banned books, and a scathing satirical poem by AD Hope. Aware of the absurdity of the Australian government maintaining stricter controls than were evident in Britain—the source of most books then—Stephen followed developments in England closely. *Overland* reported a number of obscenity trials there: the *Lady Chatterley* trial was covered and presented on six yellow pages. It was an unusually important issue, Stephen explained to Turner, 'a turning point in the fight against philistinism—but … unfortunately, a turning point *against* us rather than for us'. Meanwhile the assiduity of customs—Stephen noted with some glee—extended to scrutinising books such *Bedtime Stories* (Enid Blyton), *Between Man and Man* (by theologian Martin Buber) and *Fun in Bed* (games for sick children).[71]

Although Laurence Collinson reviewed *Portnoy's Complaint* with heavy-handed satire, its banning in 1969 went beyond a joke. Penguin Books decided to get round Customs by publishing it locally—but knew this would be provocative. The police duly raided bookshops and confiscated copies, and there were prosecutions or trials in every state but South Australia. In Melbourne, Stephen (and ex-censor Arthur Phillips) testified as to the book's worth—as did Patrick White, who flew down specially from Sydney. In the end Penguin was found guilty under Victorian law, but fined a nominal amount. *Portnoy* was the last work of fiction to face an Australian court. Three years later *Snatches & Lays* would find a respectable publisher. Years later, Stephen would say that it was his only publication which earned him any money.[72]

Expats and Godzone

Expatriatism continued to be a major undertow in these years. For most that still meant England, top-dressed (even undressed) by the image of 'Swinging London', which swept in with the Beatles, Mary Quant and the Wilson Labour government. Symbolically, the editors of *Oz* magazine, wearying of battles with Australian censorship, relocated the magazine and themselves to London. On the broader stage, the Empire was subsiding into the Commonwealth, like a huge melting candle. But Britain was still seen to have some moral leadership. The philosopher Bertrand Russell had intervened effectively in the Cuban missile crisis, and even at the end of the decade, in the Melbourne University Bookroom, pride of place was held by a stack of copies of the *New Statesman* (just flown in).

In 1962 the expatriate Charles Osborne, as assistant editor of the *London Magazine*, put out an Australian issue. His was the first English literary magazine to do so. Publicly, Clem saw it as an opportunity wasted, noting the 'thoroughly odious tone of much of the content'. Privately, he conceded that much of what was said was 'true enough, but the tone is all wrong'. He would have agreed with Alan Seymour that what 'so many "educated" Australians take to be the frills of existence are what genuinely "cultured" people regard as absolutely central to a satisfying life'. But the editorial belief that Australia had produced some of 'the most exciting talents of this century', many of whom had successfully managed to shake off a 'stultifyingly conformist' country, Clem found infuriating. (It reminded him of the condescension towards Australia he had experienced from the *New Statesman*'s editor Kingsley Martin.) As a response, Clem commissioned Jack Lindsay—himself an expatriate—to write on 'The Alienated Australian Intellectual'. In a wide-ranging piece Lindsay traced the Hegelian-Marxist origins of the term, urged Australian writers to ground themselves in Australian realities, and wrote that 'alienation' of intellectuals was a universal condition.[73]

Even so, there *was* a problem. Ken Inglis and Noel McLachlan wrote of their 'love-hate' relationship with England, while Geoff Serle—and no-one was more rooted in Melbourne culture—confessed that despite the social injustices of English society, 'one feels part of it, whereas at home one is an outsider'. If the Liberals won at the polls yet again, some people said—as, a little later, they added their names to open letters in the paper—they would consider emigrating. Few did. Geographical divorce, real or contemplated, was just another indication of the deeper problem. Clem—who had been applying the term 'alienation' to intellectuals' (and his own) relations with Australian society for some years—eventually decided to pass over a series on the expatriates he had been contemplating. Taking his cue from Lindsay, Clem decided to explore 'the strange love-hate relationship of so many of our writers and artists to their native land'. That Senator Henty in a television interview could dismiss objections to oppressive censorship as being of no interest to 'ordinary, healthy Australians'—but only to 'a small minority'—was indicative of a pervasive anti-intellectualism.[74]

Three years later, writing to Rohan Rivett, Clem proposed that he should open what could be 'a very important series', Godzone—a good hard look at God's Own Country. 'I feel in my bones', Clem said, 'that some pretty big changes are pending': Menzies would shortly retire. The idea seems to have come from a recent article in the *Times Literary Supplement*, on 'Sounding the Sixties', looking at the Kennedy era. But there were also a number of intensely self-scrutinising books emanating from England at the time, including Anthony Sampson's bestseller *Anatomy of Britain* (1962). 'An anatomy of Australia' had been used by Donald Horne as his working title for *The Lucky Country*, almost to the end. For his part Clem believed 'The Australian Dream of the Good Society is today almost as dead as the dodo. It's time we cut the bull,' he told Tom Inglis Moore, 'had a frank look at ourselves, where we're heading, and sized up our possible ends and means.'[75]

The series had a lumbering start. One of the contenders to begin it, Rohan Rivett, pulled out when he realised that the articles would not appear in one issue, but sequentially; he was uncomfortable with the idea of later contributors picking over his piece. Clem's idea was that there should be four long general essays of up to 10,000 words each. But Noel McLachlan, now delegated to organise the series—and anxious to avoid duplication—came up with an articulated scheme involving shorter articles centred on nine discrete topics. Clem was having trouble enough turning promises into usable scripts, so shied at the suggestion. He also declined to take up another of McLachlan's ideas, that he should write a concluding piece. Perhaps he wished to keep the option open of continuing the series spasmodically.[76]

In the end seven pieces appeared, in successive issues in 1966–67. With Rivett gone, McLachlan's Monash colleague Ian Turner launched the series. *Overland*'s resident intellectual now made his first appearance in the senior magazine: the tone he adopted was rather grand, a thousand miles away from the prince of popular culture he would become. Addressing the 'machino-facture' of politics—in part a consequence of mass industrialisation—Turner lamented the 'retreat from reason' he discerned there. Turning then to cultural matters, the blues and jazz aficionado railed against the Beatles, asserting that 'the fascination with pop is a denial of the claim of reason'. Sensation was being asserted over rationality everywhere, and was seeping into literature. At this stage Turner was even disapproving of 'the cult of sport', more a cross-class phenomenon in Australia than anywhere else.

But the most famous article, beginning with an excoriating invocation of suburban life ('Behold … the Australian man of today—on Sunday morning in the suburbs, when the high-decibel drone of the motor-mower is calling the faithful to worship …') was Allan Ashbolt's. Rugged individualism was effectively only a folk memory, he believed; in its place were suburban ciphers. Ashbolt despaired of conformity, and the way the country was not only isolated, but the people insulated from each other—not least by the easy egalitarian manner that worked to smother real inequalities. There was a tendency towards authoritarianism and a pervasive 'anti-Communist vigilantism', which Ashbolt described as 'a permanent New Guard'. Writing just after president Johnson's visit, he saw that Vietnam would polarise opinion in a way that could be a crucial experience in Australia's evolution. 'Otherwise', he wrote, 'we can only retreat into the cynicism which, from our beginnings as a colony of jailed and jailers, has always been our special curse.'

Among the other pieces included were an incisive article on Australian intellectuals (something Clem had wanted all along) from Noel McLachlan. As a recent returnee from London, McLachlan was struck by their preoccupation with themselves and their 'dislike of, or even contempt for, many of the habits and attitudes of most of their countrymen'. Unexpectedly, given *Meanjin*'s general line, JBD Miller next argued the positive benefits of American influence, and implicitly of the alliance; but Geoff Serle, picking up Robin Boyd's derisive term, had his doubts, twirling the title of his piece to 'Austerica Unlimited?' The country, he believed, seemed to have exchanged one neo-colonial situation for another. 'Australia has abandoned the prospect of independent nationhood', Serle wrote; 'we are going to become just slightly different sorts of Americans … What is there which might stop us going all the way?' The final piece, by Geoffrey Blainey, generally commented on the previous contributions. He asserted that Australia was, in fact, more independent than it had ever been before—reliant on foreign investment as it was on immigrants, it was true, but for its proper development. The Australian Legend was all very well, but no-one could have foreseen that technological innovation would do more to raise the living standards of working families than any political protest. Things change; in the end, even the American alliance was 'largely an alliance of convenience'.[77]

A few months after Ashbolt's piece appeared, Craig McGregor responded to Clem's invitation to contribute to the series. 'For all their disparity', he wrote,

> the three articles published so far display a common contempt for the ordinary Australian and the life he leads; the common assumption among intellectuals is that Godzone life is awful and their real task is to discuss, analyse and (if possible) change the formal super-structure of Australian society: politics, literature, power, culture … I'd like to argue against that point of view, and maintain that the starting point for any discussion … should be the Common Man himself.

As he read McGregor's outline, Clem was encouraging. But he reasserted—as if he had not read McLachlan, then in the pipeline—that 'Godzone *is* pretty awful, isn't it, for those concerned about things of the mind and spirit? The *quality* of life here is simply not good enough; our values are all ass-up.' When McGregor's article arrived, Clem found the overall argument weak, and—revealingly—said it had more to do with the attitude of a younger generation than other Godzone articles. 'The alleged contempt of Turner and Ashbolt for the common man simply will not do.' Clem suggested that McGregor make some changes, but would publish the article as it stood, if he insisted. Perhaps it could be slipped into another series he was contemplating … McGregor, publishing the piece himself in a book of essays, quietly withdrew it, hoping not to offend the editor. 'The fault, I feel, is mine, in not writing an absolute KNOCKOUT which you would have rushed into print.'[78]

Right from the beginning, Clem hoped that the series would ultimately appear in book form. But he was turned down by a number of publishers—until Macmillan showed interest in 1970. Too late, replied Allan Ashbolt, who said that the pieces would need considerable revision to be made to work now; besides, he was about to use his essay in a book of his own, and would not be happy to see the original republished. The letter confirmed Clem's own misgivings; he dropped the idea. Even so, the series became well known, appearing on university reading lists and in schools. Craig McGregor, despite his rejection, thought it the 'most illuminating series I have read for years'. He was right; for while Asia was discounted, Indigenous people and migrants more or less ignored, and none of the pieces written by women—it nonetheless caught a moment. That was of an isolated Anglo-Celtic nation at the end of the 'Menzies torpor', trying to face its challenges and come to terms with its place in the world.[79]

'Godzone' may have been the most well known, but Clem ran a number of series in *Meanjin*. Advancing a theme by the shifts in perspective each contributor brought to it validated the 'continuity' he so prized. The first and most exhaustive series was 'Remembrance of Things Past', a miscellany of snatches of autobiography and recollections of encounters with the great, both in Australia and overseas. The stand-outs were Leslie Rees's account of a meeting with James Joyce, FC Green's glimpse of growing up in rural Tasmania, and Oscar Mendelsohn's memoir of Max Meldrum. Catherine Duncan provided a swirling piece capturing the temperament of the notable left-wing composer Hanns Eisler.

In 1968 came 'The Temperament of Generations', occasioned by student unrest. This time the pieces were shorter, almost a dozen, and ran three to an issue. Responses ranged from the novelist Thea Astley's 'Monstrous Accent on Youth' to Alan Seymour's excoriating 'To the Gutless Wonders'. Generally the articles were in sympathy with student unrest—even AR Chisholm disapproved strongly of conscription—and seeking to explicate it. The best of them was LJ Clancy's 'The temperaments are the same'—in which he managed to slip in a lengthy quotation from his friend Craig McGregor's essay originally written for 'Godzone'.

A contribution also came from Ian Turner. 'I believe in Reason', Turner had written in Godzone, 'as some men believe in God, for the acceptance of reason is finally an act of faith.' But by 1968, when Turner wrote for Clem again in 'The Temperament of Generations' series, he was hailing the counterculture, and stating that he didn't blame the students for rejecting the values and ideas of their elders. Turner was impressed by the way the best of them, in the movement against the Vietnam War, combined 'moral absolutism with personal witness and even an acceptance of martyrdom'. Perhaps there need not have to be a fundamental choice between sensation and reason after all. Two years later, in a piece for *Meanjin* on the first Melbourne moratorium, Turner spoke of 'a culture and sensibility ... being transformed before our eyes'. In a sense it was a desperate throw: by 1972 Turner had virtually given up on socialism. Its realisation had become too theoretical in a society given over to consumerism.

Other series were to appear in *Meanjin*—including 'Pacific Signposts', which systematically addressed the international context. But none would have Godzone's impact. The 'Temperament' series, with its divided opinions, was lost in the churn as a program of radical change was being elaborated by Gough Whitlam. In May 1970, 70,000 people marched in the streets of Melbourne in the first Vietnam moratorium. As a friend remarked to Ian Turner, Melbourne was no longer a place the adventurous and talented left to go overseas, where the action was. The country had come alive; 'the action was happening here, too'.[80]

The backward glance

A few years earlier *Meanjin* had enjoyed a special year: 1965 was book-ended by its hundredth issue and then its twenty-fifth anniversary. Appreciative notices acknowledging Clem's achievement appeared in the press, extending overseas to Geoffrey Moorhouse writing in the *Guardian*, and the *Times Literary Supplement* running a leading article on the journal. 'Catholicity of taste,' it ran, 'relentlessly high standards, and the deliberate juxtaposition of the best of Australian writing and the best from overseas, the two meeting on even terms, have been continuing characteristics ... *Meanjin* has become progressively more sophisticated.' (It was placed there by Noel McLachlan, who had worked for *The Times*.) Two separate reviewers in the *Australian* ranked Clem as an editor up with the greats of the *Bulletin*, JF Archibald and AG Stephens, as Bernard Smith had already done. Across the Tasman, AD Hope told the readers of the literary magazine *Landfall* that the tone of *Meanjin* was 'national without jingoism, and international without pretentiousness'. Unusually, *Meanjin* took unsolicited contributions seriously, and at one stage had held workshops to help young writers. Now it was an intellectual journal in the best sense, transcending academic or scholarly approaches.

Regrettably 'its prestige, and consequently aura, was higher beyond the seas than in our own country'. It may have 'the status of a national institution', Hope concluded, but was 'operating on a shoestring'.[81]

Recognition had already been given to Clem personally. In 1962 he was awarded an OBE; he was aware that it was an honour rarely given to writers. Clem claimed he was talked into accepting it by AA Calwell, the Labor leader. 'But it means damn all,' he wrote to Dorothy Hewett four years later, 'and now I regret having fallen for it.' Of greater tangible benefit—as well as an honour—was the Encyclopaedia Britannica Award for 1970. It was worth $10,000, then almost twice a young lecturer's annual salary.[82]

Since *Meanjin* had at best a precarious permanence, it was important to draw attention to the magazine itself. Increasingly this combined with the impulse to retrospectivity, always strong in Clem, seen most positively in his desire to help provide Australia with a usable cultural past. For some time he had been considering publishing what he originally termed 'A Meanjin Miscellany'. Then he recalled a book by an American critic, *On Native Grounds*, and it was under that title that a massive anthology of nearly 500 pages appeared in 1968. It presented a wide range of material from the magazine up to 1965, foregrounding literary assessments, omitting social and political pieces. International contributions went too. There had been difficulties, not only of compression and proportion. So much material had already been 'pinched' for other anthologies that Clem had to keep substituting new material. 'The truth is', he told Chisholm, 'one can't successfully carry over to book form the spirit of a "continuing" magazine—the sense of "continuous dialogue" to which I refer.'

Nevertheless, the result was a success: Stephen saw it as 'a kind of apotheosis of *Meanjin*, for it splendidly carries out the editor's intention of giving us a feel for the changes that have taken place in Australia's intellectual and emotional life over this quarter-century'. Heartfelt congratulations came from unexpected quarters, such as from the somewhat-estranged Bob Brissenden: 'The book wonderfully solid... *Meanjin*, like all journals, has always been something of a group effort, but you have really kept it going and given it purpose and direction: it is very much your magazine and you have every right to be proud of it.' The impressive result of Clem's grit and endurance was there for all to see.[83]

Closer to Clem's heart was *The Hand of Memory*. 'This book has been made for my wife NINA', the dedication proclaimed; apart from anything else—given Clem's addiction to anniversaries—he thought twenty-five years of her running the Russian Department worth celebrating. Indeed it was; against considerable odds—and without promotion to the professorship she deserved—Nina had created the most notable Russian Department in the country, and was famously a beloved teacher. Clem's book was a personal selection of his poems and short stories, pieces that she had liked, or of significance to them both. Many of them, he would remark, 'are in a sense autobiographical'. (Clem had recently been approached for a collection by a commercial publisher, which would have entailed a different selection.)

Handsomely bound in buckram and canvas, the book contained drawings by Douglas Annand, and was presented in a slipcase. It generally fared well at the hands of reviewers, but Clem was aware that 'for most people it is like one of Jane Austen's plain but virtuous girls—they are compelled to admire, but reluctantly find themselves a good deal less than captivated!' In fact, while a number of these pieces had seeped into the pages of *Meanjin*, well over a dozen had been anthologised or published in other periodicals. But sluggish sales led Clem to conclude, ruefully, 'I am in fact a minor lyric writer.'[84]

A corollary of *On Native Grounds* was the issue, the following year, of a complete index to *Meanjin* for the same period. The Commonwealth Literary Fund committee, evidently impressed by the anthology, gave Clem a special grant. But his ambitions extended further. He had hoped that *Meanjin*'s story might be written, and first approached Geoffrey Blainey. Blainey politely declined. Then the thirtieth anniversary was to be crowned by a long piece by Frank Strahan, which would act as a pilot for a book. But relations with the Strahans were tempestuous, and the proposal was dropped. Clem never lost sight of it, and eventually it was Lynne Strahan, rather than Frank, who years later would write a history of *Meanjin*. Clem and Nina would be so challenged by it that they went to see the publishers to try to suppress it.[85]

Once Clem complained to Ray Marginson that 'I'm *drowning* in a quagmire of archival material'. But Marginson knew that he relished it—and told him his letters were consciously written 'for posterity'. (Clem was shocked by the imputation.) Increasingly his vision was clouded by the past. A few months before the election that brought Whitlam to power, Noel McLachlan suggested lining up a series of articles: 'What Labor must do first'. And, should they not win, 'Is this the end of the ALP?' Neither suggestion was acted upon.[86]

And the young …

'I myself am greatly troubled by the "generational problem"', Clem wrote to Chisholm in connection with his 'Temperament of Generations' series—'it's quite a struggle to retain flexibility of mind, critical response, etc.' His own tastes were quite narrow, and as the years rolled on appeared like cataracts obstructing Clem's vision for the magazine. Even in the 1950s he had had some difficulty in accepting the new wave of English novelists, such as Kingsley Amis and Iris Murdoch, and owned to liking very little of the poetry he published. There was too much 'endless contemplation of the poet's own tortured soul.' Now it was worse. 'These so-called "Underground" poets are being allowed to get away with murder,' Clem wrote of Tim Thorne. 'His verse certainly has a "contemporary feel" about it, but technically it's pretty inept. I'm damned if I believe this sort of thing is poetry.' The work of another—which his advisers liked—he thought to be all 'on the surface, with no real content or bite'. Urgency was no substitute for quality.

To young literary editors and their followers, the existing literary magazines just went on 'producing facsimiles of themselves'. They understood the issues that were generating the new writing, and the protests that were powering them: the Vietnam War, the beginning of second wave feminism, young males being at the pointy end of conscription. Beyond that, there were the lifestyle changes prompted by the counterculture, with its thrust to communalism, drugs, open relationships and sexual experimentation. The cry was beginning to be heard that the personal is political, and people were beginning to see the political in everything. Poetry, reformulated, could act as a lance for these causes; it was no longer, as Clem still termed it, *verse*.[87]

Clem did go some way to meet the young. He responded well to Peter Carey, publishing early work and declaring him 'the most original talent in the story field I've come across for some years'. He also published four pieces by Barry Oakley. But the surrealism of one and the streamlined larrikinism of the other were easier to accommodate than writing that proceeded from countercultural assumptions. Clem invited a poetry manifesto from Kris Hemensley—and published it, with a note explaining that he had not edited it in the least (since he would not know where to start). Effectively this made it an exhibit; the rejoinders came later.[88]

This confrontation arose directly from two different conceptions of the small-circulation magazine: that of the little magazine and that of the 'seriously-purposed literary review', as Clem termed it. Cyril Connolly, the editor of *Horizon*, would shortly identify their different nature, labelling the first 'dynamic', the second 'eclectic'. The eclectic magazine, Connolly maintained, 'cannot ignore the past nor resist good writing from opposing camps'.

On the other hand, a truly dynamic editor of a little magazine would completely ignore the past, despising Clem's prized continuity and regularity of appearance: these were oppressive, perhaps bourgeois levelling devices. The dynamic editor's magazine would be 'short-lived, his authors violent and obscure'. (Connolly quoted an editorial from *transition*, 1929: 'The writer expresses. He does not communicate. The plain reader be damned.') But while the eclectic magazine generally lasted longer and paid better, it was 'in constant danger of becoming complacent and middlebrow'. Shortly afterwards Ian Hamilton, in his influential study of six editors, wrote that ten years seemed to be 'the ideal life-span for a little magazine'. After that, they slipped into 'faceless survival'. They might survive, as *Meanjin* had, by becoming broad in girth, 'but could never quite manage to recapture the excitements of their youth'.[89]

So Clem rarely failed to be encouraging, even as he was rejecting work. 'I have a strange regard for you,' Hemensley conceded. Clem did publish an early Frank Moorhouse story, but didn't care for his writing, or Michael Wilding's. His constant refrain was that much contemporary short fiction was brittle and lacked full characterisation. As is often the case, a longed-for quickening or cultural revolution—since it can take on new forms—may not have its manifestations recognised for what they are. Clem was convinced—as the Australian short story was entering its most fruitful period since the glory days of the *Bulletin*—that 'the genre … seems to be pretty well buggered'. And told Wilding so. He pinned his hopes on expository prose renovated by drawing on fictional techniques, as evident in the work of James Baldwin, Truman Capote and Norman Mailer. It could be 'the new voice of the seventies', he declared, but *Meanjin* 'can't find the writers'.[90]

The tide was moving against the magazine more than it seemed. The move of the new radical *Nation Review*, from Melbourne to Sydney, was a portent. The emerging Australia Council was based there too, and would soon withdraw the Literature Board office from its outpost in Melbourne. The *Australian* had also made the move, from Canberra. Cultural power was building in Sydney, where the ABC was long established. The tone was young, confident and well to the left of the Labor leader and now prime minister, Gough Whitlam. Hemensley had warned Clem that 'there exists feeling ranging from reluctance to outright hatred of established literature in which category *Meanjin* so easily falls'. Characteristically, when the editors of the radical *Tabloid Story* were launching their magazine (Moorhouse and Wilding to the fore) they at once symbolically reversed all the requirements *Meanjin* made for contributors submitting manuscripts. There was no need, they felt, for haughtiness and disrespect.[91]

Increasingly *Meanjin* appeared fustian. The format leading with the Kahan etching of the featured writer, together with an appraising article, reeked of an establishment cosiness. The publication—in the incandescent year 1968—of *five* articles in sequence, celebrating the geographer and man of letters Marcel Aurousseau (unknown to the general reader), emphasised *Meanjin*'s remoteness. There were jeers about 'the old men of *Meanjin*'—not unjustified, as Clem's most regular readers of manuscripts, AA Phillips and Geoffrey Leeper, both hovered around the age of seventy. (Meanwhile Clem had fallen into the habit of writing of 'young *x*', and 'young *y*') Nor was the magazine helped by misfirings: the holding over of an article marking the centenary of three influential books from Victorian England to the year after, or the sheer bad luck of a major British postal strike severing the publication of an interview with Rolf Hochhuth from that of an extract from his play *Guerrillas*. 'I don't wish to renew my sub, thank you,' Godzone contributor Owen Webster had written a few years before. 'I'm afraid I find *Meanjin* too square and passé, and I can see no prospect of an improvement.'[92]

In 1970 the appearance of *A New Britannia*, a radical recasting of the history of Australia by the 28-year-old Humphrey McQueen, set a further cat among the pigeons. It was an attack on the Australian Legend and its old Left historian interpreters—McQueen spoke of the 'sterility of the marxism of [that] generation': his was a New Left 'revolutionary history', challenging their assumptions. ('History is not on our side. The past belongs to the enemy. We must understand it in order to end it.') In *Meanjin*, Noel McLachlan found the book unusually 'stimulating and provocative … highly chastening'; AA Phillips was alarmed by its looseness, and thought the book crossed over into becoming 'propaganda'.

Russel Ward, in *Overland*, defended the legend, pointing out that Australia and New Zealand did, after all, 'create the most egalitarian democratic societies that had existed anywhere up to that time.' He shared Phillips' misgivings about the representation of Henry Lawson as a fascist. Readers of the two magazines were then treated to McQueen replying as if in stereo, engaging in acrid debate with the reviewers. Clem decided to bring him in to write on Australian racism, which he did with telling restraint—pointing out that it was the twentieth-century variety that had 'slipped by unremarked … It was no accident that Australia was the last of the colonial powers.' Ward found this article both 'timely and penetrating'. Indeed, it appeared at the time of the massive anti-apartheid demonstrations against the 1971 Springbok rugby tour.[93]

McQueen's article was published in what would be Clem's most radical issue. At that very moment he told Ray Marginson: 'I have a most unhappy and quite demoralizing feeling that the journal is slipping away from me. I don't feel that it is any longer within my grasp. Something has happened during the past few years, but what it is I can't quite put my finger on.' Matters were not helped by Clem's reluctant acknowledgement of the need for change, and a striking incapacity to effect it.[94]

'Do you want to take over the whole box and dice—as secretary, manager, editor? I'm ready to walk out.' Thus Clem to Catherine Duncan, safely in Paris. Closer to home, Clem had flirted with the idea of taking the magazine to La Trobe University, where he had found a number of academics who were prepared to help. He spoke loosely to one of them about his possibly editing an issue. Then, consciously buttressing the 'three old men at the helm', he took on the poet Lynne Strahan, long in *Meanjin*'s orbit, as an editorial assistant (for a time) together with LJ Clancy.[95]

Meanjin Quarterly

A Review of Arts and Letters in Australia

25th Anniversary

4
1965

Registered at the G.P.O., Melbourne, for transmission by post as a periodical.

Clem and Nina, not long married, in their Brisbane garden

Clem as editor, about the time of *Meanjin*'s move to Melbourne in 1945

Judith Wright, shortly after being *Meanjin*'s first secretary

Brian Vrepont, dressed for the concert platform

James Picot: Clem spoke of his friend's 'Norman countenance'

Paul Grano, dressed for the Brisbane climate

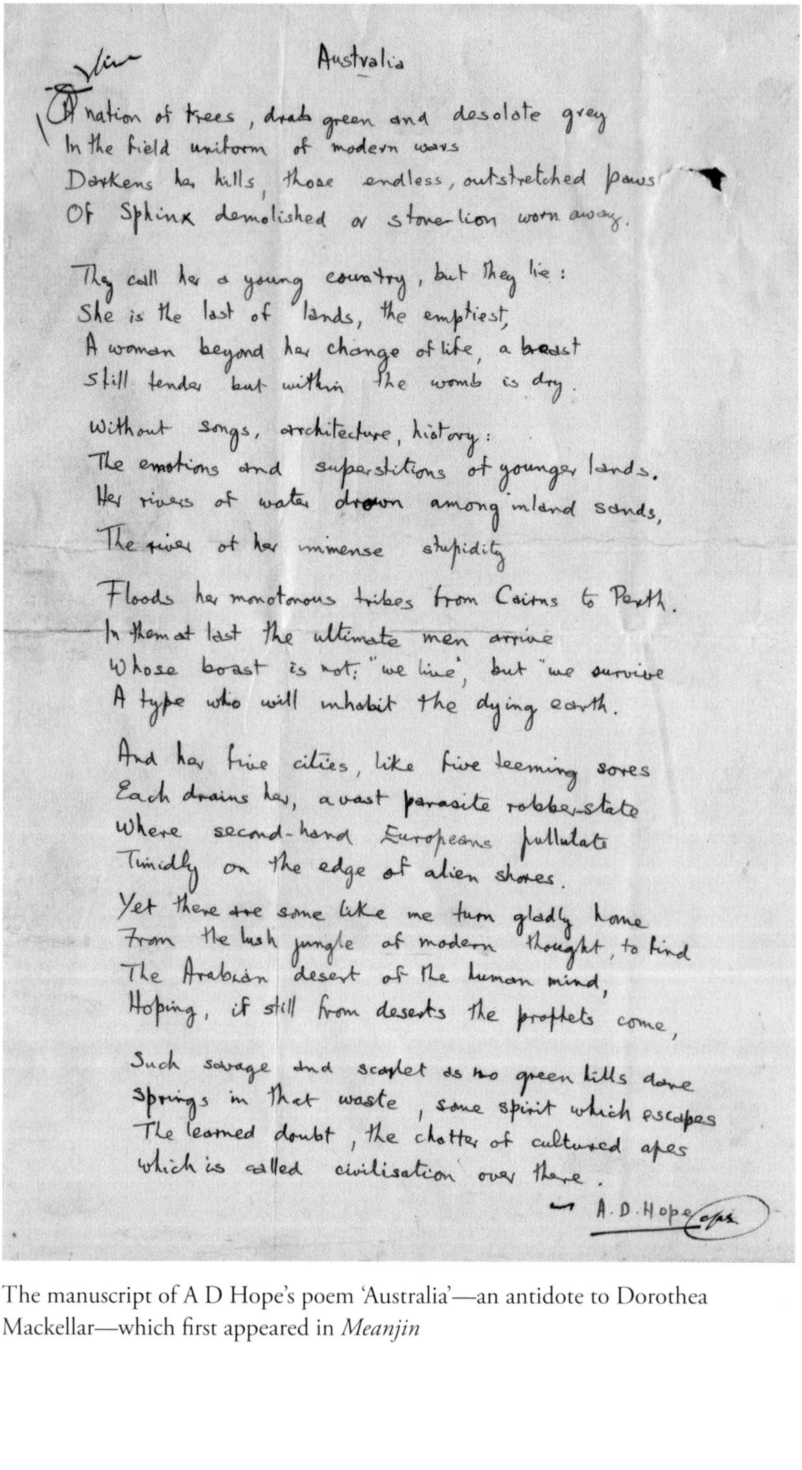
Australia

A nation of trees, drab green and desolate grey
In the field uniform of modern wars
Darkens her hills, those endless, outstretched paws
Of Sphinx demolished or stone-lion worn away.

They call her a young country, but they lie:
She is the last of lands, the emptiest,
A woman beyond her change of life, a breast
Still tender but within the womb is dry.

Without songs, architecture, history:
The emotions and superstitions of younger lands.
Her rivers of water drown among inland sands,
The river of her immense stupidity

Floods her monotonous tribes from Cairns to Perth.
In them at last the ultimate men arrive
Whose boast is not: "we live", but "we survive"
A type who will inhabit the dying earth.

And her five cities, like five teeming sores
Each drains her, a vast parasite robber-state
Where second-hand Europeans pullulate
Timidly on the edge of alien shores.
Yet there are some like me turn gladly home
From the lush jungle of modern thought, to find
The Arabian desert of the human mind,
Hoping, if still from deserts the prophets come,

Such savage and scarlet as no green hills dare
Springs in that waste, some spirit which escapes
The learned doubt, the chatter of cultured apes
Which is called civilisation over there.

— A.D. Hope

The manuscript of A D Hope's poem 'Australia'—an antidote to Dorothea Mackellar—which first appeared in *Meanjin*

Meanjin cover by Douglas Annand, 4/1950

Stephen looks out from 'The Loft'

An overland trail in the Alps: Stephen with Ian Turner at Dibbins Hut, 1961

Australian Communists participating in the Budapest Youth Festival, 1949. Stephen and Nita are in the second row, centre; the artist Noel Counihan behind the banner pole on the right

Czech street scene, 1951: Nita, Stephen, and their life-long friend the translator Zorka Wolfovà

A A Phillips, not long after he coined the term 'the cultural cringe'

David Martin, the amended sketch by Louis Kahan

Brian Fitzpatrick, 'managing to look sensitive and brutal at the same time' (Burstall)

The persistence of the vernacular: *Overland* covers, issue no 1 and issue no 84

OVERLAND

Incorporating The Realist Writer

NUMBER ONE, SPRING 1954 — ONE SHILLING

Off to the diggings, 1854. — Drawing by N.C.

WRITING BY:

Nettie Palmer, John Morrison, Katharine Susannah Prichard, John Manifold, David Martin, Brian Fitzpatrick, Senator Donald Cameron, Elizabeth Vassilieff, Eric Lambert, Professor A. D. Hope and others.

NED KELLY ANNIVERSARY ISSUE

84

overland

Registered for posting as a periodical, Category B

stories

features

poetry

$3

Ardent supporters of Clem and Meanjin: Geoffrey Serle (Kahan's second go), and the poet and critic Dorothy Green

Vance and Nettie Palmer, their attention caught in the 'Stanhope' garden, New Year 1953

Clem and Stephen with Kylie Tennant, at Monash University after the conferral of Clem's D.Litt., 1975

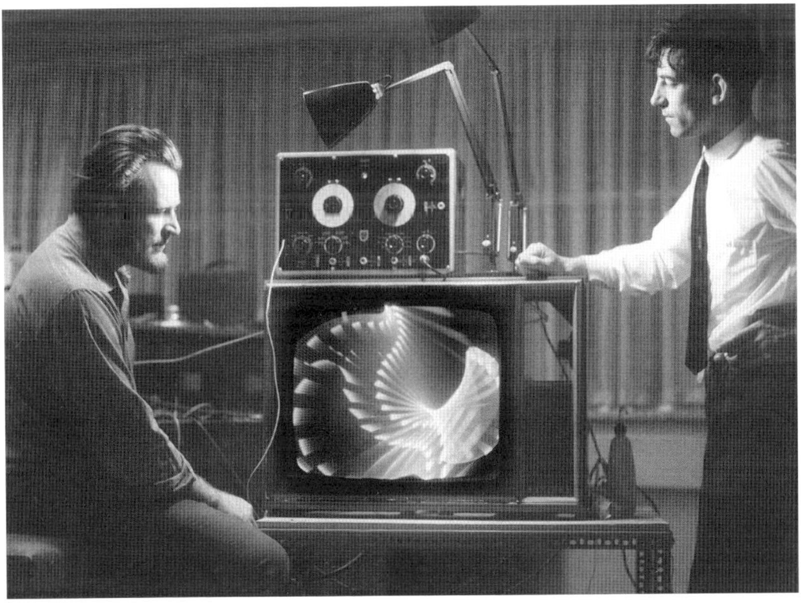

Stanislaw Ostoja-Kotkowski (left) won recognition both in Australia and internationally for his pioneering work in laser technology. He produced more *Meanjin* covers than any other artist.

Dorothy Hewett, feminist, playwright and poet, c. 1980

Clem happy to receive the emu egg trophy, presented by Gordon Bryant MHR after a *Meanjin-Overland* cricket match

Clem Christesen found peace in painting. His subject here is a country road near Eltham, the treatment influenced by his companion the artist 'Jock' Frater.

The two sides of Erith Island: tin-foil emperor, and being given the rounds of the kitchen

Stephen Murray-Smith as painted in 1980 by his good friend Fred Williams

Clem and Nina in the garden at 'Stanhope', late 1970s

Laurie Clancy was now lined up to edit an issue of the magazine, but it failed to appear. Clem had been close to the young man, a favourite contributor, occasionally offering fatherly advice; Clancy reciprocated with loyalty and respect. He wrote regularly from America, where he was on a Harkness fellowship, patiently accepting repeated rejection of a favourite story he had written. Meanwhile Clem had a gathering feeling that he must do something to meet a rising hostility—again apparent in an attack by Morris Lurie (who took issuc with his intrusive editorship, and arbitrary relocation of a story's setting from Europe to Australia). So Clem proposed to Clancy (recently returned) that he edit the Spring issue of 1972. He would be given complete responsibility for it—though naturally he would show Clem what he was lining up for the magazine.

Simultaneously Clancy was writing a new set of lectures; he was not able to give *Meanjin* his undivided attention. Clem picked holes in his proposals, pointed out where they duplicated his, doubted whether some proposed contributors would deliver. He warned that there could be no overmatter, material which could be used later, for this issue was 'in a sense an experiment'. And he wasn't happy with an issue that had less literary criticism, more stories, and—despite an earlier nudge to include rapportage—more political-sociological material. Nor was he comfortable with the idea that regular features of the format should go. Clem grumbled that Clancy wanted to make the magazine entirely contemporary. At the same time, he found the planned contents less radical than might have been expected. The day came—so the word went round—when Clem reached for the drawer and produced an issue of his own he had been quietly preparing.[96]

Stephen too had his difficulties with the young. In conversation one day over lunch he remarked, of Humphrey McQueen and the New Left generally, 'Why do they want to kill their fathers?' But he was aware of the energies that they were releasing, and he was being urged to respond to them by David Martin and Barrie Reid in particular. 'After all', Reid wrote, 'you wear little stickers saying "me left" and even "me left long time"'. Stephen was also prodded by Ian Turner, particularly once he returned from sabbatical leave spent in England, where he met the historian EP Thompson and attended a cultural studies conference convened by Stuart Hall in Birmingham. Stephen had also long thought the expansion of high school and tertiary education would add to public awareness. The result was that the feature articles in *Overland* had recently shown an increasingly radical tilt. Pride of place was given in one issue to RW Connell, attacking Peter Coleman's booklet *School Power in Australia*, with its allegations of a far-left conspiracy to subvert the young. The piece was elegant, trenchant and fair-minded; Stephen might have thought he had found another Brian Fitzpatrick.

Overland would be saved by its relative accessibility and multiplicity of styles (symbolised by its artwork): it was not trapped in its own aura, as *Meanjin* tended to be. In practice, it could be segmented. When it came to fiction, Stephen's preferences if anything lagged behind Clem's: sometimes literally, when he published a Peter Carey story six months after *Meanjin* did so in 1972. He would not espouse social realism as such, but spoke of favouring 'readable, non-mannerist stories', given what Stephen saw as the magazine's diverse (and traditionally inclined) audience. He too felt the short story had seen better days.

Poetry, however, presented a real challenge. A host of poets had suddenly emerged with the rise of the counterculture, assuming high visibility, and a crop of new magazines (many short-lived) appeared with them. These could be roneoed—sometimes only a single sheet—use silk-screen, or increasingly the cheaper offset printing, rather than the traditional letter press. Stephen saw these magazines, correctly, as largely catering to a coterie; in one bad-tempered moment he told the poet and editor of one of them that the 'younger editors are looking up their own arse-holes'. Nevertheless there was energy there, and the editor of an eclectic magazine had to find a way of harnessing it. Stephen decided to appoint Barrie Reid, useful in his prodding, as his poetry editor. From 1968 Reid would guide *Overland* over the points, enabling the magazine to assume, at least in part, a convincingly contemporary aspect.[97]

6

CLEM AND STEPHEN

THE LITTLE MAGAZINE NEXUS

Early days

WHEREAS *OVERLAND* HAD begun by transforming an existing magazine, *Meanjin* had to start from scratch. In a way it began almost as a local collective: all four poets were equally represented in the first issue. But Clem was the first among equals: later he would talk of having 'demanded' manuscripts from three other poets. As the well-known dynamic secretary of the Queensland Authors and Artists Association, the editor managed to get some support from the society. But this meant Clem was also subject to the poetic effusions of its members. These included the white-haired Emily Bulcock, a leading light in the organisation and Vance Palmer's sister: it did not help that she perpetrated 'dreadful little poems'. Partly to ensure that the promising young would be pointed in the right direction, Brian Vrepont made the suggestion that there really should be a *Meanjin* school—i.e. workshops for aspiring poets. But even a year after the magazine first appeared, Clem felt the need to tread warily. He hesitated to invite contributions, since this often implied acceptance—and should he feel obliged to reject them, that caused resentment.[1]

By the end of 1941 Clem had raised his sights higher; 'the crisis' had created a new perspective. Since there was an inchoate Australian national consciousness, it could be articulated from Brisbane just as well as from anywhere else. Assiduously he set about building up networks. People such as Percival Serle and Nettie Palmer in particular suggested possible subscribers; another keen supporter was the poet Harry Hooton, who despite his anarchic/humorous style of writing, was a man of serious intent. A considerable number of those suggested would eventually become names in their own right.

Initially Clem had so little confidence in *Meanjin* continuing that he would refer to it as 'bi-monthly booklets'. There was no provision made for subscriptions. People were sent a copy with the request to buy it for two shillings, or return the magazine. Postage was provided, so it was scarcely a hard sell. Even so, copies were sometimes returned irately, as from the future *Meanjin* stalwart AA Phillips. Distribution was the problem, and always would be. Subscriptions were the best solution: regularity of supply was exchanged for guaranteed sale. Moreover, there was no bookseller's commission.

By June 1942 Clem was gratified that every major public library and every university library subscribed. 'Gradually, you see,' he told Percival Serle, 'we are becoming better known, and our audience is increasing month by month, as we capture the interest of other groups.' Increasingly, *Meanjin* claimed, it was being used in classrooms and study groups. British and American libraries were subscribing, and there was a pleasing number of copies going to individuals overseas.[2]

Financing the journal was always a problem. At the beginning of 1943, Clem claimed that *Meanjin* had cost him £60 to date; as late as 1970, even after the University of Melbourne had given him some support and there were government subsidies, he stated that *Meanjin* still cost him $2000 a year out of his own pocket. Relief had come for a time with James Duhig, but Clem never acknowledged the real sums the doctor had paid, seeing his financial assistance simply as a guarantee against loss.

Initially Clem did not pay contributors; no Australian literary magazine did. Writers were given a number of extra copies, with the hope that this would extend readership. To sharpen interest, Clem held poetry competitions, with prizes; this was later extended to contributions from people on active service. Financial support from a number of people, including Duhig and Judith Wright, meant that from autumn 1943 he was able to pay a flat rate of ten shillings per item.[3]

Shortly after *Overland* began, the historian John Tregenza warned that since the appearance of *Vision* in 1923, there had been thirty-seven little magazines in Australia. But of that number, only five lasted more than ten issues, and eight produced one issue only. Stephen reproduced those figures in an early issue: it would be a challenge. But with *Overland* having arisen out of the *Realist Writer*, and beyond that from the Party, at the beginning Stephen was inclined to assume it was essentially a matter of mobilising support. Once people saw the product, and its quality, they would buy copies and many would subscribe.

Indeed there was heady growth at the beginning. The 750 copies of the first issue soon had to be augmented by an extra 250, and by the appearance of the fourth issue in July 1955 the 2500 copies—the most printed so far—were also supplemented, until 4300 copies had been produced in all. That was largely owing to a deal done with the Waterside Workers Federation: there was great interest in Frank Hardy's story 'Death of a Unionist', based on a real-life incident. But for the first two dozen issues—stretching to 1962—that figure was matched only once. Effectively it indicated the outer limits of aspiration.[4]

The view could be taken that *Overland*'s evolution from the *Realist Writer* was much more gradual in content than in administrative structure. Indeed the reconfiguration of a magazine always entails the risk of losing existing supporters or subscribers before gaining new ones. Vic Williams had simply been the most persistent critic of many, feeling that in pursuing broader objectives the magazine had become more writerly, more intellectual, and had abandoned the working class. Not everybody shared—or could see—Stephen's vision of high and popular culture proceeding in tandem, to the benefit of each.

Thus the distribution of *Overland* followed the seismograph of enthusiasm. That surge for number 4 was almost entirely due to Frank Hardy, spruiking his story at meetings on the wharves. Similarly, Brisbane was a hotspot: in mid-1955—owing much to the influence of John Manifold—it accounted for thirty-five subscriptions, which was more than the total in Sydney. 'Sydney', snorted Stephen in a circular to his board, 'have shown so little interest in and support for the magazine that they need hardly exist for our purposes.' Flying visits to Brisbane and Perth helped shore up support there, but for a long time Sydney was a problem. Perhaps it was as Vincent Buckley diagnosed: in Melbourne if you have something to say, you start a magazine, whereas in Sydney you throw a party.[5]

Stephen recognised early that subscriptions were the ideal way of selling the magazine. By mid-1955 there were a total of 365—just under half in Victoria. Stephen believed he needed a thousand for safety, as indeed he did. Although he remarked in a letter to Judah Waten that (after two issues) *Overland* was selling nearly as many copies as *Meanjin*, the costs were alarming. The poor writers were the least of it, their total payments amounting to £12, compared with the printer's £73. One way and another, with commission and concessions, complimentary copies and wastage, only £45 in cash was made by each issue. The remaining £40 had to be found somehow. Judah Waten's mysterious patron helped with a regular £15, but there was still a £25 shortfall.

Apart from robbing the till—using the money that came in from subscriptions, intended for future issues—Stephen began asking for donations from the very first issue. Companies have a 'sinking' fund, he wrote; *Overland* would have a Floating Fund, the donors acknowledged each issue. The need was urgent: from the second issue on there were intermittent crises at the printers', who would be unwilling to start typesetting the coming issue when the bill from the last had not been fully paid.[6]

When Stephen made his first application to the Commonwealth Literary Fund, in 1955, he rather cockily told his board members that he was not particularly concerned if the CLF rejected it. Mindful of the core of left-wingers sustaining *Overland*—distributing copies, holding fund-raising parties, making donations—Stephen claimed, 'We are in a stronger position than any cultural magazine in the history of this country has ever been in.' Rising costs would change his tune. The continued unresponsiveness of the Commonwealth Literary Fund meant that other expedients had to be found.

One was to increase advertising. The net was cast extraordinarily wide, including not only other left-wing causes but also sympathetic businesses. On one occasion there was even an ad from the World Record Club, the best-known way of getting classical music at regular cheaper prices. Advertising the journal was expensive and difficult—because of its perceived politics, the *Bulletin* would neither carry an advertisement nor review *Overland*. Some newspaper advertisements did appear: 'The new literary magazine everyone is talking about'. But the best method of promoting the magazine was by circulars, distributed in a favourable social context.

Otherwise, apart from sending the hat round to supporters—'Overland is succeeding fast in its aim of becoming a mass magazine of the Australian people', ran one such appeal—there was the drastic measure of putting up the price. Stephen was loath to do this: it was his boast that '*Overland* is one of the cheapest literary magazines in the world.' The parallel claim that it also had one of the largest circulations of such magazines in the English-speaking world was clearly related. Crucial here were bulk sales, particularly through unions and writers groups. But no opportunity was missed: the address of one intending subscriber was scrawled on a paper serviette and filed away. However keen, it always seemed to be a case of squaring the circle. Subscriptions would tend to slacken, but printing costs in particular would go up steadily. And so the price of the magazine had to go up, too: to one shilling and sixpence from number 7, to two and six from number 10.[7]

For a time it looked as though there might be another way to reach the market. The Australasian Book Society (ABS) had been conceived as an exercise in literary consciousness-raising, in full awareness that this country comprised the largest export market for British books. Surely it would be possible to redirect some of that purchasing power to local publishing? Indeed, by July 1955, Stephen was referring to the ABS as the fourth-largest publisher in Australia. Perhaps a wedge could be created, Stephen and Ian Turner began to think, if an ABS subscription included one to the magazine. Certainly it would help *Overland*. The plan was announced in number 6—as a decision of the ABS. *Overland* would remain completely distinct (although it would carry more ABS news); it stood to gain some 2000 extra subscribers.

Immediately things began to go wrong. Number 5, which was well received, was poorly distributed among its members by the ABS. Although Turner was an inspirational secretary—building up that list of 2000—office nitty-gritty was another matter entirely. There were regular complaints about neglected correspondence, or no receipts being issued; that when delivery was promised, the wrong number of copies might be sent, or someone might go to the station only to find the parcels had not been put on the train. By September 1958, half of all moneys owed the magazine were debts from the ABS. While some of this was paid soon after, it was too late to get the printers to lift their embargo. A special election issue had to be scrapped, the next reshaped. Stephen was not happy. Although he hesitated to send a formal letter, matters reached the point where he had to threaten to withhold the ABS copies until payment was made. A manager had now been imposed upon the ABS, but the arrangement with *Overland* broke down just as Turner was leaving Melbourne for the ANU.[8]

Despite the existential threat, *Overland* kept growing physically in its first five years: life meant growth. The pages were never reduced, even if the number stalled: it was a steady progression from the sixteen of the first issue to forty-eight in 1959. A truer measure of its difficulties was its uneven rate of appearance: later Stephen would place, under the masthead, the humorous apologetic that '*Overland* is a literary magazine that tries to appear quarterly.' Generally it appeared three times a year (mostly): when it was able. It was not till Stephen's last decade that four issues appeared with some regularity. As late as 1984 it could still miss a beat.

Meanjin's reluctant patron

Meanjin had less apparent struggles over basics, but was beset with problems nonetheless. For (Sir) George Paton, vice-chancellor of the University of Melbourne from 1951 to 1968, the journal was essentially a Medley inheritance. Paton was notionally enthusiastic: he seems to have promised Clem the possibility of a lectureship, and, recognising that conditions in the office needed improvement, the services of a junior. (Neither happened.) In temperament as by training, Paton was a jurisprude—he always preferred the middle ground, which in practice meant a conservative solution. He was alarmed by *Meanjin*'s political dimension, given the Cold War context. It suited him, therefore, to keep *Meanjin* at a distance from the university: the last thing he wanted was to comment professionally, as Clem invited him to do in 1950, on the proposed Communist Party Dissolution Bill.

When the magazine began to receive money from the Lockie Bequest, an Advisory Committee was set up, vetting the page proofs—a particular interest being taken in the editorials. Cuts were imposed. 'I do not want to give the impression of setting up a censorship,' Paton had written to Clem, 'but I think you will agree that so long as the University provides trust moneys, it cannot evade all responsibility.' So the journal, while unintegrated with the university, was ultimately controlled by it. Moreover, alone among literary magazine editors, Clem had no direct dealings with the Commonwealth Literary Fund: the CLF insisted that all submissions should be made through the vice-chancellor, since the university was the magazine's sponsor. Clem could not rely on Paton to meet deadlines. Repeatedly he complained that he was kept out of the loop.[9]

The university regarded *Meanjin* as a financial liability, and constantly nibbled at the grant—which it regarded as an extra, given that the journal had been given premises, gratis, for what was still technically a private venture. By 1953 the original university grant of £400 had twice been reduced, before being abolished. Some money had since come in to assist with the publication of articles from the Modern Languages Department, and then, most notably, from the Lockie Bequest; but once the Commonwealth Literary Fund regularised its grant, as it did in 1950, there was a feeling in the administration that the magazine should, after all, be able to stand on its own two feet. Gwyn James at MUP had foreseen that *Meanjin* would need 'perpetual subsidy'. The university's response, whenever financial problems seemed to worsen, was to look to other agencies for support—whether Victoria's State Cultural Fund, other universities, or the Australian Humanities Research Council (which for a time made a small grant). Clem cooperatively lobbied people associated with these bodies where he could.

The main source of university subsidy became, after 1950, the Lockie Bequest for the encouragement of Australian literature. There were other claims upon it, not least from the English Department. 'Its machinery of priorities and ear-markings and legal technicalities', remarked Chisholm, made it hard for *Meanjin* to access the Lockie funds. Only council could make a change to the financial position, and in Chisholm's view, it didn't care enough; Clem was inclined to see darker forces at work. Whatever the case, the university would not fund *Meanjin* properly. The solutions were always temporary.

> It was like giving a patient shots of adrenalin [Clem told Ian Maxwell]; periodically he would scream out in agony, and would be

> given another and slightly larger shot; but the bastard remained pretty sick. Perhaps the prescription and treatment were wrong, the illness incorrectly diagnosed?

Clem claimed, with some justice, that he hadn't been set up properly to do the job he had been brought down from Brisbane to do. The journal really needed a grant of £5000 a year—to ensure a quality product, to pay contributors adequately, to run an office efficiently, spend some money on publicity and advertising, and to pay him at least the basic wage. 'And why not. We are doing a job of national value'.

In the meantime, the university accounts department would fob Clem off when he asked for financial statements. The day came when it was revealed that the journal's accumulated deficit amounted to £2440. The university argued that, since the council had never authorised the removal of the magazine from Brisbane and its attachment to Melbourne, in no sense was the university obliged to pick up the tab. 'We make a grant and there our liability ends', Paton declared, instructing the accountant to pay no further sums without his special authorisation. Later, when this ban was relaxed, Paton insisted that the deficit must be reduced by annual payments from current revenue. Eventually a compromise was reached, since Clem justly pointed out that the deficit had risen when the university itself handled *Meanjin* finances (an arrangement that was then ended).[10]

Part of Clem's problem was that the university was still part of the late British (academic) world. It was understood that sabbatical leave would be granted only to go abroad, and in the mid-1970s Lloyd Robson caused a stir when he took overseas to mean Tasmania—since he was writing a history of it. The cultural cringe was well in evidence: overseas journals might require subsidies of the kind sought, 'but', opined the registrar, 'it is absurd for an Australian literary magazine.' The Arts faculty took two years to agree to sponsor the journal. The English Department, apart from a few more creative spirits, generally held itself aloof. *Meanjin*'s strong commitment to culture in the broadest sense, and as a living thing, resulted in its being regarded as 'a hybrid'. Failing to see *Meanjin*'s necessity—particularly as the humanities became more research-oriented—academics could be patronising. The view reached Clem that some thought it a nice hobby. No-one saw it as a full-time job.[11]

Clem felt isolated. At a remove from the university's structures, he felt an 'intruder' when he went to University House (the staff club) for a meal. He wanted consultation, encouragement, ideas—but on his own terms. If a particular person did not turn out to be the solution—or even if he did, such as the former bank clerk John Anwyl (a committed socialist who sorted out the dog's breakfast in the office), he could become suspicious. The editorial committees—there were a number of attempts to set them up—were to some extent at cross purposes with the editor. From Paton's point of view, the *Meanjin* advisory committee members were there to keep an eye on Christesen; yet the magazine was Clem's—so general advice as to content was in no sense mandatory. (Clem also periodically appointed panels of associate editors, or consultants. Unlike a number of specialist academic journals, *Meanjin* was not *edited* by a committee, so there was some frustration.) The advisory committee might meet only once or twice a year, and Clem was not authorised to convene it. When subjected to his grievances—many of them justified, but some of them inaccurate—busy professors tended to melt away. At one stage Chisholm had been the only active member—and censor—and did not relish the 'hopelessly autocratic' position he had been placed in, determining whether *Meanjin* could go to press unaltered.

Clem found a champion in Ian Maxwell, the professor of English, who, although he declared *Meanjin* 'not my cup of tea', was aware both of the university's obligation and of the value of the work the journal was doing—particularly once English professors elsewhere made their support known. Maxwell had a better grasp of *Meanjin*'s difficulties than Clem gave him credit for, and recognised that the university had taken the journal 'at least half-way under its wing'. Better than anybody else, he would brandish the sword of old-fashioned decency with a moral force.

But Maxwell, too, would tire of Clem's correspondence—he rarely met with him, since pressed for time—and often he quietly put the latest letter aside. 'I might as well live in Wyndham,' Clem muttered. When Clem complained that he had no direct access to council, Maxwell would reply that he didn't either. But there was also the problem of Clem's contradictory behaviour, the 'stubborn streak' he was aware of in himself. Once he wrote to Vance Palmer that 'lit. mags. can grow too old—and editors too!' as he contemplated closing *Meanjin*; but no sooner was that written than there came the correcting surge: 'God knows I'm just beginning—if I could get support, proper support.'

Ian Maxwell conceded that it was in the nature of editors to be always seeking to expand their ventures, and influence. But it was hard to support Clem's case when he might recklessly extend the journal's pages. 'What really stuck in the committee's gizzard', Maxwell told him, leading to the decision that 'the University would have to limit its liabilities, was the 3rd big issue [of 1955]'. Eventually a separate finance committee—which included businessmen—was set up to patrol the journal's parameters. It was some years, though, before it began to function effectively.[12]

While the trajectory was always thrusting upwards and onwards—Clem had material that had been accepted as long as three years before—*Meanjin*'s size tended to fluctuate. In the crisis years of 1955–56 it became a squeezebox: 1955 saw three issues of 160 pages, one dropping back to 128; 1956 saw two issues of only 96 pages, with 128 pages now the optimum for the others. Page numbers were still bumpy in the 1960s, though generally more than 100 pages each issue, sometimes nearly 150. Clem argued, correctly, that a quarterly had to maintain a critical mass in order to function properly: the breadth and range of *Meanjin*—its size—had been a major factor in establishing the high reputation of the journal. Thus, when subscriptions increased substantially in 1955, he had quickly reverted to 160-page issues, not yet being aware that production and distribution costs had cancelled out 'spectacular' gains. Even when faced with a financial crisis the following year, he would talk occasionally of a monthly—the aggregate number of pages significantly exceeding those of four quarterly issues.[13]

This time impetus towards a larger *Meanjin* came partly from the inclusion of more academic material. That was done partly to gain standing in the university, and increase viability; as Australian academics 'began to exert themselves' (as Clem put it), and the number of non-academic writers decreased (not least from old age) the balance was bound to shift—and at the risk of alienating non-specialist readers. Lists were produced—showing that by the beginning of 1956 some 200 academics had written for the journal, some of them a number of times. Many of these articles were general in nature, addressed to a broader audience, but in a desperate moment Clem had been prepared to consider publication of material to fit in with university courses.[14]

Yet his primary impulse was always for a broader, wide-ranging cultural journal. He wanted to build on the Princeton ranking of *Meanjin* as standing seventh among the best literary journals in the English-speaking world. Indications were that in England there was a perceived gap that *Meanjin* might fill: it was reviewed enthusiastically in the *Times Literary Supplement*, while the rising critic John Berger admired its vigour and the way it demonstrated that it was in Australia that the best (English-language) poetry was now being written. Occasionally its pieces were picked up and republished abroad. 'We have the opportunity', Clem told Ian Maxwell, 'of producing a first-class literary journal, of world range but orientated mainly towards the Pacific basin … an exciting prospect.'[15]

In Australia itself, Clem believed, because of a small and dispersed population, there was not the critical mass of people interested in cultural matters as existed in Europe: the 'protection' of a university was therefore all the more essential. Indeed it was: Clem wrote to a Brisbane poet advising in 1950 that twenty-three journals had folded in the last three years. At that moment there was not a single experimental little magazine in the country. Only *Meanjin* and *Southerly* remained, and 'seem to exist on borrowed time'. No wonder he did seem, to a literary outsider, 'to like living up there among the Fossils'. But it wasn't really like that. Clem 'shuddered' at the perceived need to be 'responsible'. As he told Dorothy Green, 'The more I have to do with academics, the more I love my dog Rob Roy.'[16]

The problem with *Meanjin*, he told FR Leavis, was that 'no one at this University has yet begun to understand the role or function of such an organ in the cultural life of the country'. Positively, the university connection might enable the magazine to be developed as had, in concert with their institutions, the *Sewanee*, *Hudson*, *Yale* or *Kenyon Review*(s). 'I don't think the term "little magazine" any longer applies' to *Meanjin*, Clem wrote, '… regrettably in some ways'. It had become 'more of a literary quarterly'. When, at the time of the Chisholm candidacy, Clem had spoken of a 'reconstructed' and narrower *Meanjin*, he proposed it should be christened 'The Australian Journal of Literature & Art (Incorporating Meanjin)', occasionally saying that he had never really liked the present name. Eventually he would settle for *Meanjin Quarterly*, the title the magazine bore from 1961 until the end of his editorship, and beyond. If it became a more conventional university publication,

Clem fervently hoped, at least the journal might be funded to pay contributors properly.[17]

This was not to be. It is no exaggeration to say that during its first twenty years association with the University of Melbourne, *Meanjin* stumbled along from one crisis to the next. Apart from early problems when associated with MUP, the situation was particularly bad in 1953, 1960 and again in 1961–62. In 1963 resources had become so stretched that Clem had to destroy twenty-three galleys of overmatter—articles already set up to print.

Perhaps worst of all was the crisis of 1955–56. Finances were by then desperate. In addition to the newly discovered deficit of more than £2000, costs continued to rise: the printing bills had risen by 200 per cent since 1940. Clem threatened—as he could, not being a university employee—to produce only two issues the following year (1956). The office was at a standstill: no bills were being paid, and no moves were being made to appoint a new secretary. Ian Maxwell thought it a case of whether 'we should try to carry on or close up now'. It might be prudent for Clem to consider some sort of career elsewhere.

In a statement prepared for the vice-chancellors' committee a few days later, with a view to obtaining a joint commitment, Maxwell recognised that 'help has never been nearly enough'. Mr Christesen would be willing to hand over the magazine, he told the vice-chancellors, either to Melbourne or to an editorial committee representing all Australian universities. Academically, at least, its range could be broadened. 'The important thing is simply that *Meanjin* should go on.' Concern was very general. Dr Evatt offered to address a public meeting to rally support. The Students Representative Council at Melbourne was so apprehensive that there was talk of it making the journal a grant.

Clem recognised that, as the position now stood, he was 'merely the owner in theory'. The day of the editor-publisher-owner, retaining some degree of independence, was over: 'I am the last of the Mohicans,' he declared. Since Petrov he'd become 'doomed. But *Meanjin* need not be doomed,' he averred. Part of his argument—the old argument—was that the university should take over the journal, '*With or without me as editor*'. He wrote that in italics, for that *was* new, or nearly.

Bernard Smith had told Clem in 1948 that 'I admire the way you stick to *Meanjin*, and the way it sticks to you.' In fact he was incapable of relinquishment. When Chisholm's candidacy was being discussed, Clem nevertheless saw himself coming in from time to time as a consultant. Nor would he let go unless fully convinced the university would publish the journal and support it properly—in which case, why the need to hand it over? But by September 1956 the situation was desperate. If *Meanjin* were to continue, a compromise would have to be reached. Ian Maxwell advised that either the journal should be handed over to a 'university editor'—an academic—or else become fully independent. Reluctantly, Clem told Maxwell to go ahead and do what he could—at the same time dicing the second part of an editorial which Chisholm and Maxwell thought might 'impair any good will' the university brought to the negotiations.

As often the case, when it came to the crunch, Clem would equivocate or say things he did not really mean. Again—as he had done before—he suggested a limitation to art and literature, this time to satisfy the university. He went so far as to say he could then conscientiously refuse contributions he now felt morally bound to print. Maxwell had repeated this argument, 'hoping that you meant it'. Perhaps Clem recalled Dorothy Green's injunction, 'For God's sake, don't do anything to prejudice the existence of *Meanjin*, even if it means eating large quantities of dirt.' Clem's ultimate manoeuvre—in the space created by university dithering—was when he slipped Serle into the (temporarily vacant) editorial chair.[18]

The thing Clem most wanted was to be contracted by the university, as a non-academic person, employed to carry out a specific task, that is, the editorship of *Meanjin*, with a properly set up editorial board to guide and assist him. It should not have been so difficult: while these conversations were going on, a salaried manager was appointed to run the Union Theatre. Clem similarly wanted to run *Meanjin* with security and independence; but he could not have both, and in practice did not quite have either. Chisholm had thought that once Clem left Heinemann, a salary of some sort might be possible, but moves to give him the equivalent of a tutorship—whatever the department—came to naught. The central question of paying him a salary was either ignored or deferred. Clem had, at one point, threatened to have nothing more to do with the journal, effectively withdrawing his services and letting Patricia Excell carry on as best she could. Repeatedly he spoke of closing it down; in practice he could not do it. Referring to Clem's 'sweated labour', Ian Maxwell was sympathetic, but nothing was done. Perhaps one reason why Clem took up Hope's suggestion that Chisholm should be (temporary) editor was that on return his own prospects for payment might become brighter.

The journal's success, with its standing never higher, meant that it needed more attention, not less: to ensure that, Clem could not take on another full-time job (the new one paying, the old one not). And if he *were* forced to turn to some other occupation, 'then we can write "finish" to *Meanjin*'. It had burst the bounds of the three days a week originally envisaged in Melbourne. In the meantime, Clem paid himself modestly from the magazine's account (£80 a month in 1956)—but was well aware, then as later, that he might have to pay back a large portion of it to liquidate any deficit.[19]

Not least among the people puzzled by the University of Melbourne's approach to *Meanjin* was RG Menzies, who as prime minister oversaw the meetings of the Commonwealth Literary Fund. 'The whole set-up for *Meanjin* is wrong,' he declared. 'Either it is a University magazine, or it isn't.' He was surprised to find that the magazine had no capital reserve, and that in 1961 the university made a direct grant of only £50. After a direct approach from Clem, there was prime ministerial correspondence with Paton, but no change for the moment. Paton explained, as one grandee to another, 'the very qualities which make Christesen an excellent editor make it difficult to work with him on the financial and administrative side'. (He was not a 'sound' man.) Besides, Paton added, 'the success of the magazine is its freedom'—as if the university exercised no control over its contents at all. Clem may have been right when he said that the university did not really want *Meanjin*. They 'will not take really effective steps to establish it on a firm business-like basis,' he told Maxwell, 'hoping that I'll finally pack up and so solve this awkward problem in a "gentlemanly" manner.'[20]

Indeed the university's sense of financial liability was so limited that it was reluctant to finance campaigns to attract donations. Paton was prepared to sign a begging letter (which did not do so well, as people felt the university should be supporting the journal); but when Ian Maxwell pointed out that the money remitted for the publicity campaign was only half that voted by the Lockie Committee, and that Clem himself had to make up the difference, the vice-chancellor advised that since *Meanjin* expected to make a profit from the campaign, it should bear the cost from the proceeds. Apart from that, Clem was despondent about fund-raising efforts, even general support. When thinking of increasing the visual arts component in *Meanjin* he had seen something of Keith Murdoch, who professed interest; but it became clear that Clem 'would have to play ball under his terms', so he withdrew. He expressed his disappointment with fund-raising to Ted Harris of Georgian House: the publisher told him to grin and bear it. 'The people in this country that have the money', he wrote, 'are not interested, and the people who are interested haven't the money.'[21]

Clem had often had a fantasy about a benefactor, or more particularly a benefactress—and wrote a story about one. In Brisbane Mrs Hamlyn-Harris had to some extent assumed the role of Lady Bountiful, and in 1959 he had hopes that 'a female friend' might have given *Meanjin* financial aid on a regular basis: to his chagrin, she passed 'all that money' over to the Stanford creative writing fellowship. This would have been Neilma Gantner, whose interest in literature was so pronounced that she would go on to write nine books. Four years earlier she had been determined to help *Meanjin* in one of its many hours of need.

Gantner worked in the office regularly, taking her pay as gift subscriptions for friends. She organised publicity, and arranged dinners and other functions at which Clem said he felt uncomfortable, because he didn't know many of those present—and put in a great deal of time and effort in promoting *Meanjin*. But she was not really the person to do it, he thought, being 'totally inexperienced in this kind of work'. Worse, when it came to the magazine, 'people now think the "Myer millions" are behind it'. To which Clem added an extra grievance, to the effect that when Neilma had seen some paintings in his studio and decided to buy some, she must have misread the prices: she sent him a cheque for half the agreed-upon amount. 'If I say that her efforts mainly resulted in further "humbug",' he concluded, 'it is kindly meant.' Clem had a way of projecting onto people an entire adverse situation, and because that could not be resolved, then they could not be absolved either. And so the Stanford won out over *Meanjin*. (*Overland* would, too.)[22]

Pressed for funds, Clem battled to make ends meet. In the mid-1950s he was gardening at Eaglemont, toyed with buying a tip-truck (he'd get paid more, carting dirt from one place to another), but found a recurrent spine injury limited his capacity for manual work. Clem thought of the public service—had some grounds for hope there—but may have been blocked by ASIO. Newspaper work no longer appealed—*Meanjin* had spoilt him for that. He drew heavily on existing resources.

Clem sold some land at Heidelberg, and began to peel away slices of property from his Eltham home. He also sold off his library of Australiana. He was surprised to learn from his accountant, in 1956, that all in all he had sunk into *Meanjin* about £7000 of his own money [about $70,000 today]. By 1972, it had become £40,000 ($400,000+). There were long stretches where Nina had to pay most of the household bills. He simply could not have done it without her: in addition to her bringing in the salary they could both draw on, she showed her loving support in other ways—such as contributing (anonymously) £250 to the *Meanjin* Sustaining Fund.[23]

Not surprisingly, when Clem went on leave for the year 1957, things fell to bits. Geoff Serle, a busy man, was an effective steward, bringing together the issues and putting them out. But otherwise the office slowly seized up, despite the best efforts of the secretary—whose salary had fallen behind. The correspondence necessary to keep the operation in working order was not maintained. Manuscripts piled up, stationery was depleted. Regular statements of accounts were not sent out, and renewal notices went out irregularly. Clem claimed some 800 subscribers were lost—and that the 1958 selection files were empty. Since then he had never dared, he told AD Hope, to go away for so long again.[24]

There was worse to come. The nadir occurred in 1959—not long after the Commonwealth Literary Fund had required *Meanjin* to be fully 'sponsored' by the university. Ever since arriving in Melbourne, *Meanjin* had been located in cramped conditions in the Social Studies building, originally a professorial residence. Fine Arts occupied the ground floor, Social Studies that above, while Clem's office was located in what had been the maid's room, on the landing. Later there were shifts and accommodations in the building, so that *Meanjin*'s bookcases ranged along a corridor to the loo. Clem was warned that accommodation in the university was now particularly tight—we are eight rooms short, said Paton.

He might have to take *Meanjin* off campus. But with the Micawberish streak that had usually carried him through, Clem's concern had stopped well short of high anxiety. None of the alternative accommodation offered was satisfactory.

One day in the winter of 1959, some men came to inspect the building. The next thing Clem knew he was told that demolition would begin the next morning, a Saturday; light and water would be cut off. A reprieve was won until the following Monday, with the promise of men and a truck to help *Meanjin* make the move. But on the Saturday morning the vice-chancellor rang Clem at home to say that the wreckers had already moved in, and had started work. Clem was advised to come in immediately and start packing. Nina, who took the call, said, 'But he has nowhere to go!' Paton replied that '*Meanjin* must be out … by Monday morning. The building has been sold to the wreckers, and is no longer ours.' So in Clem went with a friend, working all day, packing by candlelight, and then transporting boxes to a cottage owned by Nina's father (fortunately) in nearby Macarthur Place. On the Monday, there was still work to be done—even as a gang of workmen turned up. Clem's defiance was nothing short of magnificent. Years later Stephen recalled how

> with bulldozers roaring around him, dust falling from the cracking ceilings and men pulling up his floorboards—Clem [stood] behind his desk, a fistful of galley proofs brandished in his hand, declaiming 'By Jesus, the bloody bastards, they will have to carry me out of here unless they give me somewhere else decent to work. Yes, I know some people want to drive me out of the University, but I'll see them in Hell first'—and so on, to the great admiration and edification of his stream of visitors.

Some helpers arrived, along with the promised team and their truck, but there was chaos, light rain and a dispersal of *Meanjin* files and books around the university. Spaces could not be found for all of them, so in desperation more were crammed into the little cottage. Much was damaged—probably half the back numbers, Clem thought, and many of his beloved files. That weekend, he told Vance Palmer, 'was one of the most miserable in my whole experience'.[25]

Shortly after, Bernard Smith spoke at an Arts Faculty meeting, attacking the opinion expressed earlier that *Meanjin* was not an academic journal:

> The thing I want to stress, Mr Dean, is this: If *Meanjin* folds up at the end of the year it will be a victory for those tendencies in our society which are fragmenting the humanities into specialised compartments and making it increasingly impossible for us to talk in published writing to one another. Whatever you may think of *Meanjin*, it has provided for twenty years a place where the best writers of original prose and verse could publish, and were pleased to publish in the company of academic and at times, thank God, not so academic critics, and where representatives of the different academic disciplines of this Faculty might meet on common ground and discuss issues of more than departmental interest. A whole generation of Australian letters has grown up with *Meanjin* and in the closest possible contact with it ... *Meanjin* has without doubt been the most successful literary journal ever published in this country.

Smith's intervention helped to sway university opinion, together with the emergence of real support from an unlikely quarter, the medical faculty, as professors RD Wright and Sydney Rubbo exerted influence. And so the tortured relationship went on. 'I am getting old', Clem sighed, 'and it's been a very long haul.' In 1962 another attempt to make *Meanjin* an official university magazine foundered. In 1964 a grant from the Myer Foundation cut out, while the following year the small AHRC grant was discontinued, and the money from the Lockie Bequest almost halved. Chisholm calmly spoke of *Meanjin*'s 'fate', which only made Clem fight on all the more doggedly.[26]

Then in 1966 Ray Marginson was appointed vice-principal of the university. On his second day in office, Marginson rang Clem. Recently a finance committee had been set up, but Marginson asked whether he could join the advisory board—'if I'd have him'. Soon after he was able to have Clem appointed a Lockie Fellow, in other words pay him the elusive salary. (Marginson even managed to get it indexed.) Meanwhile *Meanjin*, which had come to be housed satisfactorily in a university-owned terrace house in Royal Parade, was later in 1966 moved to

34 Story Street, Parkville, where it would remain in solid occupation for fourteen years. But as a quid pro quo of the kind the university was practised in, any direct financial support for the magazine was nominal. Clem had his salary, his premises, and could make local phone calls free; but everything else had to be paid for. University stores charged *Meanjin* for everything it provided, right down to blotting paper and pins.[27]

The state and mendicant editors

Meanjin's other main sponsor, in counterpoint to the university, was the Commonwealth Literary Fund. Set up in 1908 for the purpose of providing pensions, it was not till 1939 that it began to award fellowships to writers pursuing their careers; not till after the war did it begin to give grants to literary magazines. *Meanjin* was the first recipient, with an emergency grant of £100 for 1946–47. The CLF was most reluctant to fund the magazines, partly because the view was held that government subsidy might imperil the independence of these publications, or imply government support of their views. More importantly, it (rightly) feared that grants would become subsidies, acquiring a de facto permanence.

The *Meanjin* subsidy was slow to start. The cause had not been helped by a Trailer in the Summer issue of 1946, which was both too political for the fund's taste and seemed condescending: while asserting the importance of building community cultural values, it had managed to excoriate both the Labor government and capitalist assumptions. At the same time, *Meanjin*'s concern about the status of the writer in society—'There have been repeated witch-hunting outbursts in the Federal Parliament which have amounted to calculated intimidation'—could be construed as being primarily political.

For all Clem's expectations of the Labor government, prime minister Chifley maintained that the magazine was not good enough to deserve subsidy; it needed to be 'of outstanding merit'. There was also some reluctance on his part to spend public money beyond the prescribed federal sphere of responsibility. Beyond that, as Tom Inglis Moore confided, 'Chif feels that the literary magazines cater only for a small minority of intellectuals, that they offer nothing to the great mass of horny-handed workers … therefore he is out of sympathy with them.' For his part Opposition leader RG Menzies—while having some respect for literature—felt that magazines should fight to survive, 'as examples of free and private enterprise'. Clem had to pull in his horns, deal with an unsympathetic printer, and talked of closing *Meanjin* down.[28]

For much of the 1950s things did not improve. Some months after the Christesens' appearance before the Petrov commissioners, Clem received word that while his proposed Olympic issues featuring famous international writers impressed the Advisory Board, no additional funding would be made available. The CLF was still mindful of the parliamentary attack three years before. Then late in 1955 Dr Evatt, as leader of the Opposition a member of the CLF proper, rang Clem to say that a recent meeting had been 'the stormiest ever; the atmosphere was electric ... If he hadn't attended the meeting', Clem told Dymphna Cusack, '*Meanjin* would have lost its grant.'[29]

Even so, Clem was fortunate in that from the beginning there were always—among the three members of the Advisory Board (advising the politicians' Committee) usually at least one 'friend of *Meanjin*'. These included Vance Palmer, Tom Inglis Moore (who served for twenty-six years) and AR Chisholm. Often they had to calm Clem down. 'Your idea of a "concerted effort" to deny a CLF grant to *Meanjin* is purely subjective, frankly', advised Professor Chisholm. More, it was 'dangerous: it can easily lead you to state things in print that you can't substantiate'. Chisholm nonetheless took the view that his university, Melbourne, should have been doing more for *Meanjin*; and that if it had, it might have been a little easier to get the fund to allocate the magazine more money.

With some justice—although with poor judgement and scant temperance—Clem would repeatedly claim *Meanjin*'s exceptionalism. It was 'not in the same category' as other magazines aided by the CLF: larger, more comprehensive, influential abroad as well as at home. (The way both the university and the CLF 'opposed' his policy of publishing non-Australian writings was perplexing.) *Meanjin* was the one literary journal of 'national' importance—comparable, Clem told Tom Inglis Moore, 'to a national art gallery, orchestra, ballet'. When *Southerly* failed to appear in 1960, he proposed to the CLF that it should be merged with *Meanjin*. For a CLF struggling to make ends meet, this preposterous suggestion might have almost seemed a solution.

Advisory Board members were also troubled by how a literary magazine could be defined. In the late 1950s, *Meanjin* had become dormant: its 'political' material, Clem believed, was less of a problem because the political climate was now 'less torrid'. It was the new magazine *Quadrant* that presented a difficulty: while its politics in the Menzies years was more than acceptable, its relatively low literary content made funding problematic. For a time the CLF elegantly sidestepped the problem, determining that only one magazine per state could be funded; and New South Wales already had *Southerly*. This policy would also provide a part-solution to the CLF's own financial problems: in 1957, fully one-third of the money allocated for literature (as distinct from literary pensions) went to the magazines. As board member and poet Kenneth Slessor observed, 'Literary magazines permit the quickest publication of work of merit.'[30]

There were, however, two deeper problems that repeatedly became apparent. First, just as the university was itching to retreat from its commitment to *Meanjin*, the CLF was unhappy about the way subsidy had drifted into permanence. 'We do not make grants', resolved the Advisory Board; 'we make guarantees against loss.' The idea was to put the magazines on their feet. But subsidy would always be necessary, given their limited appeal and small circulation—and the difficulty they had in expanding it.

Second, there was often a cleavage on the board, between those such as Inglis Moore, Chisholm and Hope who, as university people, were sympathetic to *Meanjin*'s aims, and those from the broader literary world, who increasingly were not. *Meanjin*'s expenditure on travel, entertainment, books and periodicals came to be questioned more and more, while some thought its production values extravagant. Any idea of a paid editorial assistant was generally discounted. The CLF, Clem complained to Inglis Moore, doesn't want *Meanjin* to develop into a 'really first-rate literary quarterly … I should be content with the magazine as it is; but I'm not. And therein lies the rub.' Once he submitted to the board a long list of topics for projected articles, impressive in its range: Clem was brimming with ideas. *That* he might own up to. But the word 'intellectual' (as distinct from 'academic') is conspicuous by its absence in the correspondence. This was Australia, after all, not France, where all sorts of people were happy to claim the designation. Instead, board member Kylie Tennant would mutter 'Napoleonic grandeur delusions'.[31]

As Tom Inglis Moore warned, 'You can't run a champagne mag on a beer income.' The board was annoyed—as others had been—about the way any increase to help *Meanjin* in its difficulties was likely to result in bigger issues and greater debt. 'Literary people in general', Inglis Moore added, were 'fed up to the teeth with your moaning about *Meanjin*'. But Clem was understandably frustrated, and as he had written to the CLF secretary, 'If I hadn't made a damned nuisance of myself, there would not be any *Meanjin* today.' Supported by Chisholm and Inglis Moore, Clem believed that if the CLF and the university would each put in £1500, *Meanjin* could more or less balance its books. But no progress was made. There was nothing for it but to continue to draw on money paid by subscribers in advance, and dig into his own pockets. As John Anwyl observed in 1958, 'insecurity has embarrassed the magazine, limited its expansion, devitalised its editor and forced even devoted secretarial help to go elsewhere for employment'.[32]

Beyond this stalemate, there was a change in context. More and more magazines were demanding and receiving subsidy: *Southerly* and *Meanjin* alone were subsidised for ten years, from 1950–51; then four magazines, until by 1965 there were nine. At the point where the CLF was dissolved in 1973, the number subsidised had crept up to twelve. New, younger publications had taken their place beside the older established ones. What was to be the relationship between them? 'No-one reads *Meanjin* any more,' Geoffrey Dutton had said at a CLF meeting in Adelaide.

The newly formed Literature Board (part of a broader Australia Council) held a four-hour meeting to discuss whether 'ossified magazines should be allowed to die gracefully, or should be kept alive by injections of State semen'. (One new member, Richard Walsh, made his feelings plain when, as managing director of Angus & Robertson, he cancelled the book chain's standing order for *Meanjin.*) There was talk of 'concocting a scheme of euthanasia for magazines which had lost their liveliness', of increased support for new magazines, even of the board 'nationalising' literary magazines. It might set up or select one or two 'grand monthlies' to publish poetry, short stories and serialise new novels. There was talk, too, of subsidising a monthly magazine of literary content and debate, the format perhaps following the *New York Review of Books*.

Meanjin still led in the grant stakes, at $10,020; *Southerly* and *Overland* were next, with each awarded more than $8000. (*Quadrant* was then well down the list.) But Clem was disconcerted by the signals he was picking up. He was aware that he was out of joint with the times, and with recent shifts in the attitudes of the young. AD Hope, believing at this time that *Meanjin* was still generally less partisan than any other literary magazine, fought a rear-guard action for him on the Literature Board's magazine committee—so much so that sometimes members referred to him as 'The Friend of Clem'. But Hope wrote to Arthur Phillips saying that Clem's last letter to him had abused the poet David Campbell and the academic Bob Brissenden—'two genuine well-wishers'. Cranky behaviour; but he knew that Clem 'is old and sick and beset'.[33]

Meanwhile, at a time when the Literature Board was increasingly concerned with encouraging (new) fiction, Clem published only five short stories for the whole year 1973. (His own inclinations led him back to Alan Marshall, whose stories had appeared frequently in recent years.) Clem also took a stag-at-bay objection to the board's insistence that subsidised magazines publish their rates of payment to contributors. But then he had also sent telegrams to Gough Whitlam, who doubled as minister for the arts, complaining that 'your inordinate delays' in paying the subsidy 'almost killed this journal'.

In the meantime he had a row with Nancy Keesing, who did not wish to take up his invitation to write a piece on Marjorie Barnard, in case Clem deemed it not up to scratch. Intimately associated with *Overland* as she was, Keesing was careful to draw a distinction between *Meanjin*'s right to reject submissions—if mistakenly—and 'a friendly relationship' with Clem. But this was not good enough. Adopting a headmasterly tone, Clem asked her 'what would be the situation if all … writers had a similar attitude'. Sensibly Keesing wrote back saying, let us draw a line under all this. But that did not stop Clem from writing a letter six months later, beginning 'That was a very silly comment of yours in a book review last Saturday …' She ignored it—and could afford to. In 1974 Keesing was appointed chair of the Literature Board.[34]

Overland's problem with the CLF was to get to first base. At first Stephen was told the magazine had not been around long enough to prove itself. Then the Advisory Board believed it to be 'not … of sufficiently high literary quality'. But in 1961 a report by Tom Inglis Moore noted real improvement: no longer was the magazine 'too gossipy and too biased politically', it now enjoyed good standing as a literary magazine. While stating the journal 'remains on the popular left', Inglis Moore noted the breach with the Communist Party. The Advisory Board therefore recommended limited subsidy. However Menzies, at the full meeting of the board and the committee, pulled out ASIO reports and breezily said he wouldn't agree to a grant for *Overland*—although *Quadrant* should be given one. Yet Inglis Moore's report had shown that over the last four issues, *Overland* had averaged 30 per cent 'political' matter and 70 per cent 'literary'. For *Quadrant*, the proportions were reversed. Inglis Moore wrote to Clem, 'The CLF preferred the ugly, reactionary *Quadrant*' to the well-earthed decencies of *Overland*. Another correspondent wrote to Stephen, 'You must remember that the Right is firmly in power, and is now calling the tune more and more.'[35]

In *Overland*, Stephen viewed the decision as part of the same onslaught that saw recently ramped-up censorship, and published the reaction of more than a dozen writers. Katharine Susannah Prichard: 'What does the Prime Minister object to in *Overland*? Its democratic temper, or Australian bias?' 'An injury has been done', declared Chris Wallace-Crabbe, 'which involves a wide misinterpretation of *Overland*'s nature and purpose.' Frank Dalby Davison could see no rational basis for objection: the magazine was economical in format, 'good quality', sold at a low price, and had a comparatively wide circulation. But Kylie Tennant (soon to be on the board herself) believed it was not 'dignified' for a left literary paper to apply for a hand-out from a right-wing government. Beyond the magazine, Stephen did not keep his cool. In a circular letter he owned to being 'very, very angry', describing the decision as 'One of the most scandalous and mean-spirited pieces of outright discrimination and provocation that this country has seen for many a day'. He then proceeded to mount a campaign to overturn it the following year.[36]

In 1962 came another rejection: Menzies' task was easier this time, as the opinion of the Advisory Board was not unanimous: one member (the chair, Grenfell Price) bitterly attacked *Overland* on 'literary grounds'. How come 'the gutless wonders' of the Board, Stephen asked, 'allowed themselves to be ridden down and trampled by one opposing voice, however fanatical'. To the *Overland* inner circle, he wrote of deliberate, subtle tactics this time—and of the matter being a civil liberties issue, an indicator of things to come. But in the magazine he adopted the persona of taking the rejection more calmly, sagaciously observing 'Our comment is hardly necessary'. Although much of it was prompted, support had come from articles in the press, questions in parliament, protests, donations, together with an unsolicited letter of support from Patrick White.

Even Leonie Kramer, on the ABC, pointed to the current issue of *Southerly* as 'possibly the worst to have appeared', while the current *Overland* 'is certainly one of the best'. Shortly afterwards, Stephen attended a seminar on literary magazines convened by the Australian Association for Cultural Freedom, taking the view that it was rather like attending a peace conference, 'knowing that manipulators are at work but determined to do a bit of manipulating oneself'. There he pointed to the irony that 'as the editor of the only Australian quarterly operating on the market principle ... it gives me pleasure to think that Australia's only "capitalist" magazine is *Overland*'. That won over his largely conservative audience. He succeeded in getting all the editors present to sign a statement saying they 'feel uneasy' about the CLF's refusal of funding for *Overland*, urging it to reconsider the matter.[37]

Limited success came the following year, when a special grant of £361 was made to meet *Overland*'s accumulated loss. But Stephen did not let up. In an editorial he pointed to a supportive statement elsewhere in the issue signed by a dozen professors of English, and concluded, 'While the CLF continues to demonstrate its crass bias against any kind of non-conformity, the demands must grow for it to cease being a tool of the narrow Establishment.' Responding to pressure, Grenfell Price came round, and *Overland* received its first regular grant in 1964.[38]

Subsequently *Overland* came under pressure from the fund from time to time, concerned as it was to stress literary content in the magazines and to minimise political commentary. There *Overland* could be seen occasionally sailing too close to the wind. A 1968 issue (number 32) contained a segment of pieces on the Labor luminary Frank Anstey, smuggled in the Marxist Guido Baracchi paying tribute to Nettie Palmer, and capped it with a cover story in which union leader Pat Mackie wrote forcefully on the recent Mt Isa strike.

By 1975—under the Whitlam government—the Commonwealth Literary Fund had been complemented by other boards, and the Australia

Council was up and running. Relatively speaking, it was awash with money: the new Literature Board was able to support as many full-time writers in its first year as the CLF had done from 1940 to 1970. But seeing a danger in the way distinguished members of the Literature Board—not least of them Geoffrey Blainey as chair—had been dropped as a bloc in the manoeuvres leading to its foundation, Stephen would fulminate against the powerful new body: much more power was being wielded by the bureaucracy. Stephen did not care for the emergence of the career arts administrator, and bridled at what he saw as arbitrary impositions thoughtlessly imposed. Twice he was driven to write 'Swag' as an Open Letter to the Australia Council. Timothy Pascoe, the first full-time chairman was told, rather firmly, that his 'Challenge' scheme—whereby the magazines would receive a segment of their grants proportionate to moneys they raised themselves—was not only time-consuming, but would throw arts practitioners into the arms of corporate donors:

> Has it occurred to you, Dr Pascoe, that the whole point of the arts in society is that they should not, repeat not, appeal to your 'corporate donors'? Have you reflected that once paintings and writings become board-room cosy (or for that matter politbureau cosy) they become a veneer around an empty box? Do you not understand that a perfectly proper definition of 'the arts' would be: 'that section of the imaginative work of a community which challenges the received, the proper, the respectable and the familiar'? Do you not understand that the attempt to create a forced marriage between your Australia Council and the wealthy will end up depriving your own work of its significance?

Stephen kept up the fight almost to his death. A second open letter was addressed to Donald Horne and Di Yerbury, in 1985 its chairman and general manager. In public appearances they seemed dedicated to avoiding the issues people in the arts wanted discussed, snowing them with generalities; there was increasing reliance on 'a self-nourishing bureaucracy'. So much was this the case that first the special project officers attached to each board were removed, then restored (partly as a result of Stephen's prompting), only later to see the art-form boards themselves abolished. The idea was the managerial fantasy of pooling expertise, that is, reorganising the council staff along the lines of administrative function. So Stephen attacked that too, in the *Australian.* Meanwhile the director and members of the Literature Board didn't seem to know quite what their bureaucracy was doing—Stephen wrote of 'harassment', in particular the requirement that two separate sets of audited accounts, with different time frames, must now be supplied.

Stephen felt there was no understanding of the important work *Overland* was doing, helping to sustain writers and also offer criticism of their work. Nor of its practical requirements. 'You people on the Literature Board never think that the magazines have to spend $2500 on envelopes,' he told Tom Shapcott. Things were not helped by the fact that the board was, in the mid-1980s, heavily lopsided towards Sydney. Moreover, *Overland* was increasingly regarded as unfashionable, old hat: its funding was reduced. Both *Meanjin* and *Scripsi*, a newcomer, would henceforth receive more—in *Scripsi*'s case, a lot more. Given that *Overland* had, in the past two or three years, almost doubled its circulation, Stephen declared that such malapportionment called into question the competence of the board and the Australia Council itself. Then, after having written a 'rude' letter to the minister about Sydney's overrepresentation on the board, he found himself 'turfed off' the Archives Council by arts minister Barry Cohen in retaliation. For better or for worse, Stephen was beginning to develop a reputation like Clem's.[39]

Magazine mechanics and the need for subsidy

The question arises, what was the case for subsidy—either directly from the government, or from the university? One answer was (and remains) that the literary magazines functioned as a vital—if largely unacknowledged—part of the publishing industry, for which they acted as talent scouts. For aspiring writers, submission to a little magazine was often their first real test, and a number of important writers made their debut in them. Beyond that, they were a vital part of the cultural ecology. While not always read by arts practitioners, they did have some influence among academics, journalists and teachers. They got into libraries and into schools, where articles were sometimes taken up in classrooms, as in university courses. Moreover, they provided a vital supplementation to daily newspapers and overseas journals. Only towards the end of the period under consideration were there the first signs of local quality weeklies or monthlies emerging.

Thus Australian literary journals were, generally speaking, as Peter Craven wrote in 1986, 'broadly-based journals of socio-political commentary'. They earned their name because 'the articles they print, as well as poetry and fiction, aspire to a condition of quality which we associate with literature'. This gave them 'an authority and importance out of all proportion to their modest circulation and meagre resources'. Indeed, the magazines provided a forum where specialists—of all kinds—could address (at greater length than usual) a wider audience within the same set of covers. If to journalists they appeared academic, and academics thought them journalistic, then they were doing their job.[40]

But circulation was small. *Meanjin*'s peak wartime sales of 4000 copies would never be neared again. A series of blows fell, one after the other. The Army Education Service, winding down, took a large standing order with it. Big city bookshops cancelled or dramatically cut back their orders, while the British Board of Trade, applying the terms of the American Loan Agreement, banned bulk imports of Australian books and publications altogether. Not long after, following the change of government in Canberra, the Department of Information was disbanded: *Meanjin* lost a further 1000 copies that had been placed overseas. In addition, further subscriptions had been lost at the time of the embroilment with MUP. Sales were badly dented, and while in the early 1960s they recovered to just over 3000, they had tapered off to less than 2000 at the end of Clem's editorship.

There were occasional upswings: Clem boasted to Dymphna Cusack in 1955 that subscriptions were at an all-time high, and in 1962 was sufficiently confident to print 3500 copies of the Summer issue. But it was easy to misread the signs. Sales had been unusually good of the Autumn issue for 1965, the first for the twenty-fifth anniversary year. Heartened by this seeming endorsement of the magazine, Clem printed a great many more of the following issue. Unfortunately (in those pre-photocopying days) an awakening interest meant that people were after Ken Inglis's article on Anzac. The second issue did not sell well: cartons of them continued to clutter the *Meanjin* office.[41]

Overland, founded in 1954, had no wartime boom to launch it. Instead there was the increasingly problematic relationship with the Communist Party. While the number of copies printed quickly reached 4300 within a year—a figure not matched again until 1958—any further increase was stopped in its tracks by Stephen's leaving the Party, and, shortly after, its deep hostility to the two-bob-each-way approach the magazine took to Pasternak's *Doctor Zhivago*. Circulation fell immediately—the Party cancelled the ABS bulk order of 600 copies. It would never be as large again. In the 1960s circulation generally hovered in the high 2000s, and by 1976 Stephen described it as 'a very poor' 2000. It was less than that. A few years later, he wrote that 'I can personally identify quite a high proportion of our subscribers, which is both a good and a bad thing.' He was more or less resigned to the fact that the magazine seemed to have reached a plateau, its readership extending to 5000–6000 when additional readers through institutional subscriptions were taken into account. So Stephen was gratified by the way *Overland*, in the mid-1980s, picked up new readers to the point where he could claim that it had 'risen towards 3000, almost doubling its circulation'.[42]

Meanjin sent out a questionnaire in 1947, but a much fuller, 'professional' one was commissioned from a university psychologist in 1960. Basically the highly technical report endorsed Clem's approach: '*Meanjin*', it concluded, 'could almost congratulate itself on being *the* review of arts and letters in Australia.' A high number of readers responded—two-thirds of them graduates. But only 28 per cent regarded *Meanjin*'s political line as 'desirable'. The demand, Lynne Strahan commented, seemed to be 'for a broadly-based, non-specialist, non-contentious product that appealed to the educated'.

Marginalisation of the idea of the magazine forming values, helping to bring about social change, would have disappointed Clem. Indeed he was prompted towards a glossier product, and the name *Meanjin Quarterly*—taking refuge in elevation. For his part, Stephen was rather sceptical about questionnaires: they produced 'a bewildering variety of love and hates'. But he held to his notion that each reader must be satisfied with 60 per cent of the magazine's contents. While taking note of readers' responses—particularly if they wrote letters—his report on *Overland*'s one questionnaire indicated his masterful approach; 'a magazine must strive to lead rather than to follow. Even if it often makes mistakes'.[43]

Advertising campaigns were costly, the results usually disappointing: some advertisers complained that the standards of *Meanjin* were too high. More important as a way of recruiting new readers were newspaper reviews. But these had become less frequent. In the late 1940s, *Meanjin* had not only received notices in the urban press, but even in the country; ten years later, the fall-off was sharp. Nor were they always satisfactory: while some were upbeat—and could lead to a 'rush' on the magazine—others provided uninspiring summaries. And then there were the attacks, such as a wounding one by Max Teichmann in the *Review* in 1972. Clem got as far as drafting a reply to that, but then thought better of it—leaving it to his lieutenants to spring to his defence. Once again he had maintained a sound policy of refusing to be drawn by hostile reviewers.[44]

For both magazines, distribution was always a problem. Newsagents were generally not interested, and bookshops often unsatisfactory. For much of the time, Clem did quite well with them, but sales there could suddenly be discontinued by caprice. Stephen complained of how parcels of three or half a dozen copies would come bouncing back months later, as returns. Only when he kept a strict eye on display and the size of the pile, such as at the Melbourne University Bookroom, did shop sales become effective. There was also another problem, identified by Gwyn James: casual buyers tended to prefer the lighter material in the magazines, subscribers the heavier.

In addition, there was a loss of 35 per cent of the cover price in commission to the bookshop. Subscriptions therefore were best—and a way of reaching readers in remote locations. In Queensland, *Meanjin*'s Palmer issue had made only a dozen over-the-counter sales. In Perth, Clem complained in 1959, the journal was taken by no bookshop—and there were few subscribers. As might be expected, both magazines did best in Melbourne, and *Meanjin* better in Sydney than *Overland* (where Frank Hardy had helped establish a new *Realist Writer*). But *Overland* did well in Brisbane, where *Meanjin*'s links had gradually become frayed. A source of satisfaction was that both magazines steadily increased their international subscriptions—*Meanjin* going to more than fifty institutions in North America in the early 1970s.[45]

Meanwhile there was a constant battle against inflation, in particular rising printing costs. Clem would be clipped by the Whitlam-era inflation just as he was leaving *Meanjin*, but sometime before he noted that by 1960 printing costs in Australia (twice as expensive as those in Britain) had already risen by 600 per cent since publication began. An apparent solution would be to raise the price of the magazine, and this both editors did from time to time. But only with the greatest reluctance: *Meanjin* was aware that every time the price was put up, there was a risk of a fall in subscriptions. For its part *Overland* was aware of the limited means of its working-class readers, and prided itself on its cheapness. There was a 'deliberate policy of publishing under cost, in order to keep our price to a popular level'. The magazine preferred to rely on the donations to its Floating Fund: in mid-1961, between issues, as many as 213 people made a donation. In the 1980s, modest ones of two or five dollars would still float in from pensioners.

While funding bodies pointed to Clem's bills for books, journals, travel and entertainment, the real problem was that he had to run an office, and pay for the secretary out of *Meanjin* revenue. There was also the bugbear of mailing costs being raised by an increasingly unsympathetic post office. In 1962 Clem complained that almost half of the CLF grant to *Meanjin* was clawed back by the post office; by 1976 Stephen was at war with the new agency Australia Post, not least for its justification, as it abolished concessions for printed matter, that books and magazines had 'lost relevance'.

Approximately half the magazines' income in the 1960s came from subscriptions and bookshop sales. *Meanjin* in particular drew some revenue from selling back issues, and also from advertising. In 1969, this brought in more than the CLF grant. A group of public relations officers of big Melbourne corporations, meeting regularly over Friday lunch, were happy to place expensive full-page advertisements in the journal. But Clem felt something of a hostage to them. Had he stayed on, he needn't have worried: these advertisements withered away as the 1970s advanced. Apart from any post-Dismissal discomfiture, big business came to see that there was far more kudos in sponsoring the performing arts.

And so the magazines struggled: Stephen was particularly annoyed when on one occasion an accountant's trick gave *Overland* a surplus, when in fact there was constant financial improvisation. The ideal outcome was a small deficit, seemingly ratifying the existing financial structure, including subsidies. Years before, Cyril Connolly had spoken of 'the genteel deficit expected of literary magazines'.[46]

Stephen, with fewer overheads, was at one stage—following a surge in subscriptions—able to boast that he passed on 70 per cent of the Literature Board grant to *Overland*'s contributors. For *Meanjin*—flaunting its university connection on its letterhead—payments to contributors could be a contentious issue. Clem was driven to reduce them at times, even suspend them. Ideally, they were pitched to fall on the lower slopes of acceptability. One expedient was to pay academics—who held salaried positions—a reduced amount, or sometimes nothing at all. But Clem knew that low payments were self-defeating: major critical essays on leading Australian authors remained unwritten, partly for want of financial inducement. As for overseas contributions, the journal could scarcely afford them. Yet including these would help the magazine to sell, internationally, perhaps drawing people into Australia and its concerns. Moreover, while Clem dug deep to pay Patrick White £25 for a story, he was well aware that White would have got £100 for it in England, and five times that in America. The expatriate Alan Seymour said not only was work more plentiful in England, but payment rates were regularly up to five times as much as those on offer in Australia.

Even so, Arthur Phillips, speaking at *Meanjin*'s twenty-fifth-anniversary dinner, said how it always gave him greater satisfaction to write for the journal (and for *Overland*) than for any of the newspapers, which paid more. He was more 'confident' in his audience, and had 'far greater freedom to try to write as I would wish'. Similarly, David Martin told Clem it would be a sad day for poets if *Meanjin* went out of existence. 'There's nobody who has done anywhere near as much for us poor bastards than you have.' Knowing how stretched Clem was financially, some of *Meanjin*'s closest supporters, like Vance Palmer and Brian Fitzpatrick, would return their payment cheques. But with the upsurge of writing from the mid-1960s, and the replacement of the CLF by the larger Literature Board (with its greater representation of writers), pressure to raise payments became more insistent. At such moments Clem would mutter that few of them subscribed.[47]

Given that nobody worked on it full-time (and himself at the equivalent of six or seven weeks an issue) Stephen liked to think of *Overland* as a collective—in the early days, at least. Tasks were delegated, particularly with regard to discrete activities, such as artwork, advertising and distribution. For a time short stories were bundled off to John McLaren in Toowoomba and Gary Engwerda in Kyabram. Although consultative,

Stephen's preferences in selection and claims to leadership generally were validated by his superior organising abilities. He even used the train as his temporary office as he attended to correspondence. No time was ever wasted. At home, Nita would attend to secretarial tasks, and in the early days send handwritten letters asking lapsed subscribers to renew. (Hilary Newton would later take over the job, then Shirley McLaren.) *Overland* was a volunteer, fugitive venture of high purpose, rather like a government on the run—or a commando operation.

Its national orientation was reflected in its committee: Stephen, ever Australasian in outlook, for a time included a New Zealand representative. But it was impractical: it also proved to be too difficult to have a coalfields representative. The activism of the Brisbane Realist Writers Group presented problems of its own. John Manifold would have liked to have had greater editorial involvement, and to that end Stephen made over virtually a whole issue (number 15) when the Queensland centenary happened along in 1959. Stephen conceded that it would be good if all board members could have a greater say in the final editing. But he relied on circulars, effectively newsletters: indeed fuller participation was unlikely to have been wanted by him. The Brisbane RWG was particularly wedded to short stories about workers, and rather bruised by one or two rejections. Generally they didn't like the way *Overland* seemed to be heading, away from the working class. For his part Stephen gleefully printed a comment made to him some years before, that Queensland was 'the only banana republic west of Nicaragua'.

It should be pointed out that it was hard—in the days long before video conferencing—to run a little magazine *nationally*: in practice, it devolved back to Melbourne. Communication generally was difficult: until the 1960s, not everyone was in easy reach of a phone. Access to a car could not be assumed either. So when Stephen invited David Martin to come to Mt Eliza for the first time, he spelled it out:

> Come and see me! … Bus to Frankston from Dandenong [which he had to get to first]. Mt Eliza buses from Frankston station quite frequently, get off at Williams Rd. Ti-tree Lane (where we live) is 1st on left after you get off bus. If stuck in Frankston ring [from a public phone] Mt Eliza 221 (twopence) & ask my parents if they can give me a message to come & pick you up.

The early *Overland* boards' Melbourne members consisted of people who had been associated with the Realist Writers Group—Eric Lambert, Ian Turner, Jack Coffey, Ralph de Boissière—plus interstate representatives. But with the rupture following Hungary and his leaving the Party, Stephen had to improvise, and for three years no list of board members was published. When one reappeared with number 18 in 1960, reconstruction was drastic. It was still conceived geographically: antennae. There were no Melbourne names. Apart from Ian Turner (in Canberra, then Adelaide), members included Kylie Tennant in Sydney and, a little later, Rodney Hall in Brisbane. Laurence Collinson in London and later again Don Maynard in Papua New Guinea would be overseas additions. Dorothy Hewett, in Perth, joined in 1964 and notably stuck with Stephen to the end. By then she was a contributing editor, a second tier Stephen introduced in 1980, differentiating the 'contributing editors' from the associate editors mostly in Melbourne. These were more intimately involved with the production of the magazine, particularly as Stephen took on more writing projects of his own.[48]

Important here was Vane Lindesay, right from the second issue, when Stephen appointed him art editor. Growing up poor in South Melbourne, Lindesay had found his feet during the war when working on *Salt*, an army journal that at one stage appeared weekly. Publishing poetry, stories, nonfiction articles and drawings, its tone was radical: also working there was Frank Hardy. Stephen would have seen the magazine as a precursor to *Overland*. He was appreciative of Lindesay's decency and friendliness, saw him as an original and encouraged him to become an author. For his part Lindesay—having been amazed when first encountering Stephen that he had never been inside a factory—would come to consider him (much, much later) as the most missed of dead friends.

A quick and efficient worker, Lindesay showed his admiration by always doing the paste-up of the magazine promptly, ready for Stephen to collect and take straight to the printers. Primarily a cartoonist, Lindesay occasionally brought people such as Petty, Tandberg, Barry Dickins and Leunig to *Overland*'s pages. (Stephen was also partial to the literary cartoons of Michael Sharkey.) But while his reputation as a book designer rose, Lindesay's black-and-white drawings were attacked on the board as being old-fashioned. At a time when *Overland* needed to reach the young, they sent out the wrong vibes. Privately Stephen was inclined to agree, and on one occasion felt he had given in 'weakly … but on the other hand people who work most loyally for *Overland* and me have to be humoured'. Vane could always be relied upon to knock up a cover should other plans collapse.[49]

Once Ian Turner returned to Melbourne, as he did in 1964, he would help in dealing with the printer. More importantly, *Overland* now had a resident political tactician, his advice soon augmented by the high liberalism of John McLaren. Barrie Reid brought to the table his experience as a professional librarian as well as contacts with the new wave of poets. In 1979, aware that a distant Dorothy Hewett could not provide what had become the essential input from women, Stephen invited Nancy Keesing to join the board, along with the rising academic Leonie Sandercock.

Another notable appointment was Martin Duwell in Brisbane, who joined when his poetry magazine *Makar* folded. Board members would remain solid for Stephen's last decade. They had been augmented by two returnees to Melbourne, Stuart Macintyre, former Communist and formidable scholar, and Ken Gott. But Stephen's one-time CPA university branch associate—and roistering mate—would remain somewhat detached from the magazine. Perhaps that was because—improbably—he had made his name in international business journalism, and was now working for CRA (Rio Tinto). Gott was witty and urbane, but Stephen would feel let down by him in various ways; towards the end he felt he could not quite trust him. 'He's shrewd, though', he noted, 'and has an unsentimental and unromantic view of the world, good correctives for me.'

Stephen's experience of the Party made him hostile to the idea of *Overland* being run 'as a tight bureaucratic ship', with frequent editorial meetings and decisions taken by vote. 'But I do expect to be influenced by my friends. And, when they want to, by board members.' Meetings might be called only two or three times a year, to discuss ideas for coming issues, criticise past issues, and discuss 'material questions' concerning the magazine. Held in people's houses, and gravitating more and more to John McLaren's, often these turned out be 'a merry, argumentative, affectionate evening, sometimes with three of four conversations going on in corners of the room at one time.' (Later they would be disrupted by serious antagonisms.) Stephen professed to be not much concerned by the fact that his board was ageing, or that it was overwhelmingly male; but then he 'had never been particularly concerned with arguments stressing the need to provide for the indefinite survival of *Overland*'.

He was more aware of what it could never be—bigger, indeed better, since this would require an office and staff. 'If *Overland* were to do all that those who believe in *Overland* want it to do, then it would not be *Overland*, and it would be necessary to establish another kind of periodical for these purposes.' As John McLaren saw it, *Overland* was 'the expression of a community which includes its editors, its subscribers and its contributors'. Even so, much of the burden fell upon Stephen; this was not so much a board as a sounding board. Often in reporting mode, he would tell of the tasks he had been doing. 'Sometimes with a sigh', Stuart Macintyre recalled, 'but he never complained'.[50]

Delegation was nonetheless evident in a fresh bid to increase *Overland*'s presence in Sydney, when Stephen asked Nancy Keesing to join the board. He saw her as being a 'kind of alternative editor' of the magazine, speaking with authority as the head of a Sydney committee, authorised to spend *Overland* money in promotional ventures. But these hopes were not realised. Keesing did edit one issue (number 81), centred on the centenary of the *Bulletin*, but she seemed to 'tire' of real editing. The content was stiffened by Stephen including *Overland*'s first contribution from Hugh Stretton.[51]

Good relations with printers were essential for a little magazine editor, and Clem had notoriously bad relations with his. He was peppery in asserting things must be faultless: none of *Overland*'s sloppy proofreading here. One firm got their own back. An article commemorating Brian Fitzpatrick, until the last possible moment, rendered the name repeatedly as 'Brian Fitzprick'—and enjoyed Clem's indignation. Stephen, though, remained constant with his printers, although relations with the *Richmond Chronicle* broke down after their refusal to print the mildest of swear words. He then took *Overland* to Bob Cugley at National Press, installed in a 'magnificent' former brothel.

Styling himself 'the printer of last resort', Cugley was an amiable, forthright idealist who put his money where his mouth was. He had expedited Nettie Palmer's *Fourteen Years*, carried Brian Fitzpatrick's *Newsletter* for three years free of charge, while he alone took the risk (given censorship) of publishing Frank Dalby Davison's *The White Thorntree*. Now Cugley would help out *Overland*—to the point where Stephen owed him $6000 in 1980. Stephen admired him. 'He was the archetypal, felt-hatted working-class Australian of the northern suburbs', he recalled at his death, 'the man who never turned his back on his origins, and for this very reason, was never ill-at-ease in any company.' Notable for his personal generosity, Cugley's conversation was peppered with wisecracks: 'Old professors never die,' he'd say, 'they lose their faculties.' His staff were of a similar cast: one typesetter complained that an issue had been so interesting that it took him twice as long to set it. But Cugley didn't care for computers or for photo-setting, and the acceptance of what he saw as inferior standards. The day came when, customers having drifted away, he sighed, 'It's technology!' and closed his business.[52]

Editing

Clem once described the challenge of editing to the CLF as 'the unity conferred on diversity by intelligence and imagination'. There was the clustering of articles, in particular the beachhead of pieces focused on a chosen writer, capped by a Kahan. 'If I may be immodest,' Clem told Tom Inglis Moore, 'this is … creative editing at its best.' In consequence, *Meanjin* could hold its own against the best overseas journals, 'which certainly don't plan to the extent that I do'. He planned up to a year ahead of publication, and the overwhelming majority of articles and reviews were commissioned, perhaps 90 per cent. Clem was constantly on the look-out for contributors. Once at a social occasion Arthur Phillips, holding forth on some matter, was immediately asked to put his views on paper, for *Meanjin*. Later Phillips would be fed ideas he hadn't thought about—but felt he should have. Phillips would remain impressed by the way Clem had created a literary review virtually out of nothing.[53]

Clem had many talents, but he was not an original thinker. What he did have, and what made him a great editor, was a rare capacity to sustain a broad vision of Australian culture and society—for him the two were inseparable—plus an unusual ability to recognise distinctive new voices. Clem had a strong sense of where Australia should be headed, and of its place in the world—on which he held a firm geocentric grip. But he was well aware *Meanjin* appealed to a minority audience, even among 'the so-called educated classes'. He could not go too far left, or he would lose them, since they were middle class. And he would not readily find another. And so, he told David Martin in 1951, 'I'm trying to take my audience with me, slowly, gently—almost without them realising it.' Accelerating Cold War tensions and the rise in anti-communism would soon put paid to that: *Meanjin* was seen less as a 'meeting ground' than identified with the suspect Left. Given the context of increased polarisation, Clem was inclined to see himself as an anachronism. But by the time he gave his Armidale paper in 1966, he had found a strong holding position: 'By sticking to its proper business', he said of the ideal literary magazine, 'it should be independent of political parties and programmes, but keep concerned about political ideas and movements.'

Vital to Clem's project was his wide and extensive reading, notably of overseas journals. Noel Stock—associated with Ezra Pound—was struck by the way Clem was always 'better informed than … the Left intelligentzia' [*sic*]. As Nina explained to Clem's sceptical mother, he was 'constantly reading, absorbing, digesting, as alertly concerned with national and international problems as with literature and the arts'. Clem was acutely aware that he was 'sensitive' about his lack of formal education—and that he had to work twice as hard to avoid making serious mistakes. He told Dorothy Green that he and Nina 'put in about 16 hours a day', seldom in bed before one or two in the morning, and that their social life was virtually nil, except at weekends.

As he read, and read, Clem's continuing questions were: How could our understanding of Australia be deepened? And how could broader issues be given an Australian slant? In 1958 Clem sent to the Commonwealth Literary Fund a list of some 150 suggestions for *Meanjin* articles or symposia. Grounded in literature, it is nonetheless notable for its extraordinary range. The elitist assumptions of the day are evident—'Is the Common Man too Common?'—but the challenges facing Australia are there, balanced by an exploration of the past. Indeed Australian views of the past is one of the topics listed, with its prehistory fingered; an alternative scenario, 'If Australia Were French', also appears. Broader issues are there, too: literature in an age of science, the relationship between biography and poetry, and … do economists know anything?[54]

Many of these articles did not materialise. John Anwyl, acutely observing the *Meanjin* office as he sorted out the accounts, remarked to Ian Maxwell that 'Christesen finds difficulty in obtaining quality writing in Australia unless it is commissioned'. He constantly had to write to contributors to keep them to their word, and deadline. Sometimes Clem sailed close to the wind, wondering where the next batch of articles would come from. So he kept up a voluminous correspondence—writing fifty to sixty, sometimes ninety letters a week, a good many of them lengthy. (Some memorialised complaints: the offender would be told a letter had not been posted, but put in the file: sometimes they would be invited to come in and inspect it.) A good number went to overseas destinations, sometimes answering general queries addressed to the *Meanjin* office.

A number of people complained that they couldn't keep up with Clem as a correspondent, and that *Meanjin*'s high standards were (truly) awesome: as Hugh Stretton explained, perhaps humouring Clem, 'What other editors have got that you haven't got is lower standards and more trivial concerns. That's why we work for them instead of you.' Even Dorothy Green said as much. And there were others who, not prepared to revise and resubmit, withdrew their pieces and successfully placed them elsewhere, as they stood.

At the same time, a regular tide of submissions came to the magazine—the figures vary, but Geoffrey Serle as acting editor in 1957 reported as many as 1000 poems and 250 stories, which (throwing in some nonfiction) roughly correspond to the incoming mail when I took over in 1974. *Overland*'s numbers at this time amounted to some 200 poems and about 100 stories a year. To *Meanjin* a persistent trickle came from overseas, occasionally from surprising places. In one instance, having probably got the address from an old *Writers' & Artists' Handbook*, a man in Ghana sent a story. Unfortunately the 'N.2.' of the old postcode was read as NZ, and off it went to New Zealand. But the manuscript was eventually delivered, someone there helpfully adding, 'Try Australia.'

Clem told AD Hope that up to 95 per cent of manuscripts were rejected. First they were read by consultants, who would comment. Usually these remarks were confidential; Lynne Strahan, commenting on the tone of some of them years later, found them decidedly sexist. (Harold Stewart: 'It is harder for a woman to be mentally creative than a man.') For his part Clem would occasionally write a letter—sometimes appropriating consultants' observations holus-bolus—but usually the author received a comment or two on a rejection slip. This could be a tricky business: an editor could be damned if he did, damned if he didn't. Once a rejection slip came back to the *Meanjin* office with a sheet of toilet paper attached. Few were the editors who could match the suavity of Stephen Spender at *Encounter*: 'Your piece was good enough to accept, but not good enough to publish.'

It would not have been amiss to approach the mailbag with a little functional paranoia. There was always the possibility that some piece—particularly a poem—might not be quite what it seemed. The memory of *Angry Penguins* still hovered, and in 1961 Gwen Harwood published a pair of poems in the *Bulletin*. Purporting to be an exchange between the famous medieval lovers Héloïse and Abelard, the first letter of each line (highlighted in bold) comprised a pair of acrostics. It read: 'Fuck all Editors, So long Bulletin'. The issue had to be suppressed.

Barrie Reid once remarked to Stephen, 'Sad, isn't it—we have to publish bastards who write well, and disappoint our friends.' For his part Clem assumed, and maintained, the position that 'quality' was all-important—a literary value that informed the whole magazine. 'I've published all kinds of writing', he told Nancy Keesing, 'by authors whom I've personally disliked, even perhaps detested.' Deftly Clem would pick his way. He said of Dymphna Cusack, 'I admire her tremendously as a person, though frankly I don't much admire her fiction.' So he published none, while continually taking her articles.[55]

Clem developed a knack, if someone showed any talent, of turning down a manuscript in such a way that any prospective author might not feel discouraged. With those such writers he met, his tone was usually quiet, confidential, friendly. For the rest, there was the word or two on the rejection slip. But he could be tough on an established writer. 'In my opinion', he told Laurence Collinson:

> the whole thing is off-key—like a lot of your writing these days. I shouldn't be surprised if one day some critic tears right into you. There is a sneery, whiney, off-colour note creeping into some of

your recent work, which must be jettisoned before you can reach the heights you are capable of reaching.

'Very few contributors to this magazine seem to know how to submit a decently written script,' Clem would mutter, deploring the lack of professionalism. Then, after circulation to his consultants, he would set to work editing, in consultation with the author. A few writers were alarmed by the liberties taken, which increased as Clem went on; but others, such as Frank Moorhouse, would later say that resubmission always resulted in a better story. Once the piece had been accepted, Clem found people often slack about the return of proofs—so he had the proof sheet headed in red, with Douglas Annand's intimidating emu (alert, ready to peck any miscreant) placed alongside.[56]

Clem understood that the prime obligation was to use whatever material was at hand to produce the best possible issue at that moment: some scripts might have to wait for up to five years before publication. Sometimes key articles would fail to materialise; no matter, the issue must always appear as though planned that way. At the same time, while each issue stood alone, the consecutive pagination made it plain that the volume ran for a year: what was missing in one particular issue might be made up for in the next. This became particularly important when—owing to financial problems—variations in the number of pages could turn *Meanjin* into a squeezebox. Quarterly appearance was itself constricting. Publishing correspondence was not an effective option, although fuller rejoinders could be encouraged and taken. The editorials too suffered from the quarterly's stately rhythm: that could be got round, to some extent, by inclusion in the last of the five sections of the magazine to be sent to the printer. Hence Clem's recurrent fantasy about more frequent issues.

Instead, as we have seen, he was beset with problems. Clem's conversation, as the loyalist Harry Heseltine was driven to remark in the pages of *Meanjin*, could seemingly consist of 'only two topics … the magazine, and its finances'. Obsessed with his task as he was, Clem saw it as self-evident, and couldn't understand why other people didn't see it. He would duck and weave to preserve the magazine—at times seemingly prepared to shed its sociopolitical content, if necessary. Beleaguered, he could be unjustifiably suspicious. Privately he conceded that he was impatient, and 'irritable by temperament'. But it has to be said there were some spectacular provocations. Xavier Herbert, after his star billing in the first issue of 1960, was paid well, subsequently came to Melbourne, where he was wined and dined and stayed with the Christesens, but—an adept at biting the hand that fed him—soon after made an attack on *Meanjin* in the *Bulletin*.

Increasingly—since there was always work underlying all the distractions—Clem would resign from committees and attend fewer functions. There were occasional supportive *Meanjin* dinners, but usually he was not relaxed at them. Although the transcripts of speeches made at a special twenty-fifth-anniversary dinner duly appeared in the magazine, he remarked to Ian Maxwell, 'If my assumptions are even partly true, the comments made by speakers at the anniversary dinner were akin to a mockery.' Prompting these remarks was the feeling that he was constantly being deflected from his true creative purpose. Clem would point to 'three half-written novels', baulking at the idea of remaining just 'a kind of untutored literary midwife'. 'Perhaps it is all an illusion,' he would periodically reflect, 'and I have been wasting the past [twelve, or] twenty years of my life.' But he had his own way of dealing with that. 'When you feel a bit "down",' he told Dorothy Green,

> just yell 'Up Australia, Long Live Freedom', and do a crazy jig around the room. It does you wonders if you can laugh like a maniac and poke ugly faces at photographs of your friends. Of course, a working knowledge of extra-choice obscene language is also a help.[57]

There were, of course, compensating satisfactions. Clem often exhibited a boundless enthusiasm. He wrote to Hugh McCrae describing how he had read his new book, '& have now missed two trains, a pint of beer & my dinner. No matter. My feet on the desk, room full of smoke, the window dark with night, a cricket drilling the silence—I must read on.' And then there was the way he made friends of contributors, carrying on a mildly flirtatious correspondence with a number of women. One of them was the highly creative Catherine Duncan, in Paris. 'To be taken by you to Arles,' he mused, 'and in turn to be taken in an olive grove—what bliss!' But then Catherine had already included in a letter a limerick she had devised, spun on her address:

There was an old girl of the Rue Lacépède
Who'd not had a man for at least a decade
She went to Bermuda
Where somebody screwed her
And now just her ghost remains to be laid.

Duncan was married, and Clem's hopes of meeting up when he was abroad were not realised. With him she always remained 'Catherine', instead of the Catie she used with her friends.[58]

Sometimes it was also necessary to exercise a duty of care. So it was, Clem found, with Francis Webb. When Webb was in a mental hospital, Clem took an active interest in him, sending (rival) literary magazines, and visiting and talking with the medical officer. So Webb appealed to him—as the only person who had understood his need for 'freedom and peace in which to write'—'Clem, I'm begging you to help me into freedom.' He asked Clem to approach the CLF to arrange his examination as to health, intelligence and stability. Immediately Clem wrote to the secretary of the CLF: 'All I can do is to beg you or your colleagues to make a thorough investigation and do everything humanly possible to bring peace and happiness to this suffering man.' He hoped some Catholic order or institution could provide suitable accommodation, but—he was told after Webb's further incarceration—the poet's fluctuating condition of paranoid schizophrenia involved violent episodes. These necessitated Webb's remaining in a mental hospital. Indeed, a lot of the things he complained about were not the case. 'Thank you,' Clem told the medical officer. 'It seems all I can do is to continue taking an interest in his poetry.'[59]

Stephen, rather more than Clem, saw *Overland* as a secondary source of patronage. One of his arguments for more sympathetic consideration by the Literature Board was that the magazine recycled part of the grant to help support writers. On occasion he would help people out financially. As did Clem; but *Overland*, particularly with its cohort of young poets, was more involved in directly helping its contributors. Barrie Reid was struck by the poverty of poets, some of whom didn't have the money for the train fare to come and see him. One of them started a fund to fix the teeth of a mate, once and for all; Reid made a significant donation. Others had lost their teeth altogether.[60]

By nature Stephen too was a great encourager—an important attribute of editing. 'You've got no idea how hard it is to knock contributions back', he wrote, 'when you could give pleasure to many people by accepting them.' The sympathy was genuine. Stephen said of himself, 'If you haven't got the talents to be a writer, a novelist, or something of the kind yourself', there was 'a genuine measure of creative satisfaction in editing a magazine'. Here his organisational abilities came into their own. Moreover, since his days as a working journalist in Prague, he could nearly always write straight on the typewriter.

A politically conscious worker-writer, Stephen maintained, had to accept a duty to become better at it, reading widely. 'Why should he not', he asked of a mutual acquaintance, 'like tradesmen—do apprentice work as a writer?' But if a work stood at the threshold, he was always prepared to help. When the sailor and cane-cutter Merv Lilley emerged as a writer, Stephen used his musical ear and sharper imagery to tune a line. A poem about a horse, speeding forever away from a man, had been written as 'and she reached the seaside foam': under Stephen's blue pencil it became, 'and she sniffed the salty foam'. With experienced writers, intervention was sparing, and telling: Frank Hardy's short story lost the definite article to become 'Death of a Unionist'.

There were, though, difficult customers. The knockabout Donald Stuart, who had spent most of his life wandering around north-western Australia, sent *Overland* a short story. It did the round of readers, none of whom cared for it. But Stephen saw promise in it, and wrote a reasoned critique. 'What a mountain of patience and industry you are in your endeavour to encourage possible contributors', commented Jack Coffey. But Stuart returned the manuscript, refusing to alter a word. Stephen found two further readers to report, saying that if Stuart remained adamant, there was nothing he could do. Stuart's response was to publish the story in the *Maritime Worker*. Stephen, uniquely, had seen the story as 'quite one of the finest, potentially, we have ever yet received at *Overland*'. He had recognised the talent that would eventually produce eleven novels. Sometime later, Stephen tipped off Stuart that the Advisory Board of the CLF had recommended him for a full fellowship, but Menzies had stymied it. Nonetheless, the grant had been 'postponed' rather than turned down flat. Literature was long, and so too, hopefully, would be the life of *Overland*: it was as well to practise the gentle editorial art of recycling enemies.[61]

Not quite cricket

A notable gathering of Melbourne's literary clans occurred with the annual *Meanjin–Overland* cricket match. At the first one I attended, in 1975, Stephen could be seen rollicking along in creams, summoning his men in stentorian tones through a loudhailer. *Meanjin* had opted for results over authenticity sometime before, and since its leading figures were not necessarily good cricketers, had sublet the management of the team to the Clancy brothers. Clem had abandoned the match two years earlier, writing a ten-page Clemmiad to Max Marginson giving all the reasons, many and various, for his absence. It struck me on that leaden Melbourne Sunday morning, that the two editors had been rather like a pair of feudal barons, visiting each other with their retinues in their country seats.

Late in 1958 Clem had written to Brian Fitzpatrick saying that 'we hope to stage a cricket match between *Meanjin* and *Overland*, at Eltham'. Asking whether he would play for *Meanjin*, Clem cautioned that nothing might come of it. 'By the way,' he added, 'you don't need to be able to play cricket! … it is likely to be a riot.' The 1st of the following February turned out to be a blazing hot day: some Mittel European people had ventured out for a civilised picnic. An ample flow of grog was insufficient to ease the hardship experienced by the players. So 'the opportunities for refreshment provided by the luncheon break', Stephen reported, 'were at least partly responsible for a disastrous *Overland* rout immediately following'. Some serious cricket was played, but the match was noted for its more exotic elements. Each side had employed an extra 'honorary batsman'—Vance Palmer for *Meanjin* and David Martin for *Overland*—and since it was not clear whether their scores should be included in the final tallies, it 'concluded as a *draw*—with both scores approximately equal'. The *Age* reported that David Martin had achieved a rare cricketing trifecta, going out on one ball 'in three ways at once—he stepped on his wicket, was run out and, for good measure, was stumped.'

The following year, on the principle of alternation, the match was played at Mt Eliza for the first time. The emu egg perpetual trophy made its appearance: Stephen had found this nineteenth-century relic in a second-hand shop a few years before. It was presented to the winning team by Gordon Bryant, MHR, as it would be for many years. The match became a major event in Melbourne's literary calendar: occasionally there would be a jazz band—later, Graeme Bell recordings. All manner of people turned up: John McLaren, a regular attendee, among them recalled novelists, poets, artists and musicians, academics and reviewers, activists, Fabians, Stalinists, Trotskyites, plus the odd eccentric. 'This is a grudge match', Stephen wrote on one year's invitation; 'bring your bicycle chains.' More seriously, Clem was never really happy about it. Nita felt that he envied *Overland* its relatively youthful team, and 'would have liked to control both sides'. It was Stephen who gradually came to exert control: the match was increasingly played at Moorooduc or Mt Eliza, often concluding with a barbecue and party at the Murray-Smith home.

There had been serious cricket played from the beginning. Geoff Serle played with an added edge since he was resentful, given that he had been a notable cricketer in his youth, about not being chosen to play for *Meanjin* in the first match. There were other stars, too, so that gradually the match became more 'professional'—once including the well-known sportsman Brent Crosswell. In later years Robert Newton was the *Overland* wicketkeeper, a role he also played in the Artists and Writers cricket match, which began in the 1970s as an offshoot of *Meanjin–Overland*: eventually it would overshadow it. By that stage insistence that editorial staff should be allowed to play once extended to the inclusion of a *woman*, Finola Moorhead (an experiment that would turn out to be a forerunner). In 2009, to celebrate the fiftieth anniversary, Chris Wallace-Crabbe sought a commemorative game, 'but the young editors preferred soccer'.[62]

Eltham and Mt Eliza

One might have thought that, when they came to Melbourne, the Christesens would have settled somewhere on the coast, given Clem's yen for the sea. But as it turned out, the settlement of Eltham, tucked away in hilly country on the outskirts of Melbourne, suited them perfectly.

(Clem found that there even his asthma attacks dwindled away.) The place had long been favoured by the occasional artist, and now middle-class bohemians were beginning to move in, building fashionable mud-brick houses. Clem and Nina were a bit removed from that, as indeed from an earlier group, those involved in Justus Jorgensen's artists colony at Montsalvat. From nearby hilltops these two cultural figures—both of Scandinavian descent—respectfully acknowledged each other.

Surrounded by pines, 'Stanhope' was designed by Desbrowe Annear for the artist (Sir) John Longstaff. Once in full possession—he rented the property at first—Clem was mindful of the cultural continuity, even to the allotment having first been owned by a distant relative of Virginia Woolf. The house itself had no distinctive appearance, but did possess a large living room with redwood panelling. From the windows, through the bush, no other house could be seen. (A bushfire once came within a kilometre of the property.) Until Clem was compelled to sell it, there was an orchard complementing an increasingly attractive garden, with blossoming trees in spring and an active bird life. Here Clem found peace. 'It really makes my heart turn over', he told Dorothy Green, 'when I catch a glimpse of Nina pottering about the garden, with the two dogs in tow and damn-near a halo of blackbirds around her head!' Stephen loved the place, finding it 'timeless … very Chekhovian … slightly at a tangent to the rest of life'. Meanwhile the house was filling up with books and paintings—by Ian Fairweather, Arthur Boyd, Lina Bryans and William Frater among others, with some by Clem himself.

By 1955 Clem was saying that he didn't move about much: 'if people didn't call on me at this office, or at my Eltham home, there was little chance of meeting socially'. There Clem and Nina would hold gatherings to entertain diverse people, ranging from regulars such as Frank Dalby Davison and Lina Bryans (almost locals), *Meanjin* consultants, writers visiting from overseas, and various people from interstate, some of whom would stay. These included AD Hope, Dorothy Green, Harry Heseltine and, later, Christina Stead. Melbourne house guests included John Morrison and Vance and Nettie Palmer's troubled daughter Aileen (AD Hope's daughter Emily was also welcomed). Here Clem showed himself to be open and friendly, and a born raconteur; Nina, by his side, dignified, charming, her conversation pointed. The Christesens would also hold elaborate children's parties ('parents with or without kinder welcome'); Clem knew how to entertain them with entrancing stories. He was a dutiful godfather or guardian to half a dozen, maintaining friendship into their adulthood. Clem said that he had never wanted children himself; but as 'the ashes of disappointment' piled up, increasingly he felt the lack.

The gala event in the Stanhope calendar was Russian Easter. Nina's parents and an aunt had moved down from Brisbane shortly after Clem and Nina had, and lived in a cottage in the grounds. Clem once told Nettie Palmer how he had driven them all to church at 11 pm, then on to a meal with friends, and that they got back home at 5 am. Later on there were big parties, the house thrown open for the day to lecturers, students, literati and locals. There was Russian food and Russian songs; among the flags flying was the imperial double-headed eagle. (It was a reminder, too, that Stanhope was a dual monarchy.) Clem was an ambient host, if not quite comfortable in his secondary, non-Russian role. 'Can I give you a *pivo* (beer)?' he'd ask, ironically.[63]

Sometime after Clem established himself in Eltham, Stephen and Nita returned from Czechoslovakia and shortly after—on being given a block of land by the Murray-Smith parents—built a house not far from them at Mt Eliza. Lying just beyond the railway line to Frankston, Mt Eliza had an unusually picturesque coastline for Port Phillip Bay, and had been sought out by Melbourne's well-to-do. It ran to a polo ground, while the girls school Toorak College (where Nita would teach) had relocated there in the 1920s. Stephen and Nita's house, in unmade Ti-Tree Lane, was by contrast small and functional—people were impressed by its plate-glass windows, labour-saving devices and *two* toilets—'a pretty polished modern-looking sort of place'.

Financed by a war service loan, it began as a standard architects' Small Homes design, modified by the architect Kevin Borland (a friend), later noted for his brutalism. As the house expanded from two bedrooms to four, supplemented by a sun-deck, its domestic front slid into clean-line elegance. A later book-lined study abutted into the garden, which contained some rare remnant orchids. Eventually the bush gave way to a lawn, at the far end of which were a treehouse and a cubby house: Stephen, relaxing, was quite the handyman, and he loved the chirpiness of his children.

For many years there was little of the implicit formality of the Eltham gatherings. Stephen had long been involved in organising meetings and fundraising activities, so barbecues for that purpose were second nature. The house and garden provided the perfect setting. 'Grand Annual Overland Barbecue', ran an early flyer, with specifics. Then, 'Some press comments on our last party: "A model of decorum and sober enjoyment of the good things of life" (*Methodist Times*). "A saturnalian orgy of Neronian proportions. Lust and licence played their full part" (*Truth*).' At least there was a barrel of beer rolled onto the deck, Stephen usually being found playing the host. People circulated selling tickets, which could be traded in for a beer or for the sausages and steaks that were sizzling over the fire. Such parties were long remembered: twenty-five years later John Morrison reminded Stephen of one held in 1954, with

> Vance Palmer sitting on the floor reciting 'The Man from Snowy River' in that exaggerated bush nasal drawl … John Manifold playing his guitar and singing his songs; Frank Hardy and Ian Turner jointly reciting Something that made [friend] John wonder if he should intervene to save the ladies' blushes … Every literary person in Melbourne was there.

The soundtrack, especially in the 1950s, was folk: a few years later, the American singer Pete Seeger celebrated his birthday here. Then there were romances that began on a balmy summer's night among the tea-tree: Nita used to tell of a party given for the Czech athletes visiting for the Melbourne Olympics, when their gold medallist discus-thrower flirted with an American hammer-thrower. It wasn't quite hammer and sickle, so Czech secret service men watched with alarm from the sun-deck, 'fearing a defection might take place among the wattles and the fairy lights'.

Since Mt Eliza was difficult to reach—and return from (particularly in days when cars were scarcer) a dinner invitation to Ti-Tree Lane often entailed an overnight stay. It was made to seem easy. Interstate *Overland* advisers, such as Dorothy Hewett or the Turners, were among those who would stay longer. But among the regulars were Amirah, now with

Ken Inglis, David and Richenda Martin, occasionally Clem and Nina, Arthur Phillips, Fred and Lyn Williams, Hal Porter, Christina Stead and many others. From Prague came their lifelong friend the translator Zorka Wolfová. Among foreign writers, the Englishman William Golding made a particular impression. But the Murray-Smiths were also well connected to the Mt Eliza community. While Nita looked after the more social side—an extension of her school activities—Stephen cultivated scientists who lived locally, including a marine biologist, meteorologists, and an industrial technician; he also befriended not only environmentalists but also a town planner. Many of them at some stage went on the annual expedition to Erith Island. Otherwise, this local nexus served to earth Stephen's encyclopaedic curiosity. Indeed he could find surprising connections in the neighbourhood. In the late 1950s he was delighted to find that one of his children's primary school teachers was the now elderly son of Bernard O'Dowd. Later, he was thrilled to meet and interview Herbert Dyce Murphy, sometime Antarctic dog-handler for Mawson, transvestite, and reputed spy—who would provide the inspiration for Patrick White to write *The Twyborn Affair*.[64]

Office work and secretaries

Overland had no office: until the Murray-Smiths retired, it didn't even have a photocopier. The large post office box at the GPO was the physical expression of its corporate identity, emptied every few days by Stephen on his way home. There Nita (in the beginning) attended to subscriptions and accounts. Stephen relied a great deal on Nita's support and judgement: she 'unofficially co-edited' the magazine, says her daughter Joanna. The kids would hear them talking long after they went to bed. Nita's advice was mostly general, and political, occasionally extending to whether a story should be taken or cut. Her own tastes had developed far beyond working-class and rural short stories: to George Eliot, Thomas Mann, Jane Austen, Trollope, PG Wodehouse and Christina Stead. ('Her catastrophic loss may have been the source of her great enthusiasm,' says Joanna Murray-Smith.) But Nita remained grateful to ordinary Australians for the way they had been open and helpful to her when she had arrived in this country without a word of English—and now she taught it. So Nita seemed to accept such writing as part of the deal. The fact that she tended to be more consistent in her leftist politics also inclined her to this position.[65]

Meanjin did have an office, and for a long time it was centrally located and a place where people dropped in. But as space became tight, the university shunted it across the road to Parkville. Visitors, who in the 1950s extended to Jindyworobaks and bush balladists, shrank to academics and a core of writers, then became fewer. Most of the time it was just Clem and his secretary. It was a demanding job: when Clem spelt it out, the duty statement ran to a full page. He would arrive in the morning with letters to be typed, pacing up and down puffing his cigarette as he threw his arms about, turning anxiety into urgency. One secretary, Neilma Gantner, recalled how she would customarily listen to his troubles for half an hour, and then settle down to work.

Part of it was that Clem saw himself as a man with a mission—to help create and define an Australian high culture. So he would proselytise, want to be inclusive, share his obsessions—and his complaints about all the unjustifiable obstacles. When Hilary McPhee turned up to help with subscriptions for a few hours each week, that was what she got—no details about tasks, pay or even the customary question about typing skills. But she learned a great deal, having arrived at the *Meanjin* office with scant knowledge of Australian literature, and leaving with a sense—as she came to reflect on it—that 'editors should be active not passive, that grammar and punctuation and spelling meant much … but that what was being *said* meant more'. Clem's punctiliousness in these matters meant that he could exclaim that 'Christina Stead is a dreadful writer!'—and simply mean that she needed a lot of editing.

The first full-time secretary, from 1950 to 1955, was Patricia Excell. She had sought Clem out when feeling discouraged about an MA on Yeats, and always said how much he helped her. In the office Excell found him sometimes overbearing, a hard taskmaster, capable of pushing her into situations—like collecting debts—beyond her capabilities. 'He was two people', she recalled, for he was a marvellous teacher. She was taught the rudiments of putting the magazine together—including a literal paste-up of the galleys, into pages—as well as being consulted on poems and short stories. Clem soon styled her assistant editor: they became close. She was 'a strange lass', he told Harry Heseltine, 'shy, tiny, with beautiful eyes'. And, while he thought its range was narrow, Clem believed in her poetry.

For people interested in some kind of career in the arts (vaguely put, as there were not many openings), working at *Meanjin* seemed to provide a rare gateway. At one stage even Frank Moorhouse was interested in working in the *Meanjin* office—although he had never met Clem. For a number of women it was a vital first step. The skills Excell learned she would take into publishing, as more notably did Hilary McPhee, when she founded (with Diana Gribble) the pace-setting firm McPhee Gribble in the 1970s. Other notable *Meanjin* alumni were the poet and academic Fay Zwicky, Sandra Forbes, who would become head of the Literature Unit of the Australia Council, and Jean Griffiths, who as Jean Melzer became the first female Labor senator from Victoria.

Few were to last as long as Patricia Excell did, and even she found that despite her best efforts the backlog of work kept rising. It literally made her weep. Another fine secretary, at a time of crisis would go off to work somewhere else in the afternoons (insurance, in case the magazine closed), returning to the office at night and on weekends to work, unpaid—until she became ill. It was a lonely job—at times there were also unwanted attentions, but Clem took any rebuffs like 'a gentleman'. He was kind to the very young: Fay Zwicky described hers as a 'daughterly' relationship. But for most it was often thankless. Mistakes were pounced upon.

Once a secretary duly typed a letter Clem had written in which he complained about her, but felt constrained to add: 'Dear Mrs Green/ Although I feel that Mr Christesen's comments regarding office staff are totally unjustified, I am signing this letter on his behalf only to keep the office routine running as smoothly as possible.' Unsurprisingly, turnover was high. But these were highly principled, capable women, able to see the *Meanjin* project as something bigger than Clem himself. Gradually they began to hold annual dinners, construed by some men as a kind of Clem fan club. Clem, in an autobituary he wrote for Stephen, put his own spin on this, fantasising about there being a guard of honour of ex-secretaries lined up at his graveside. He was onto something: at the dinners they would reminisce about an extraordinary episode in their lives, with high idealism offset by trying conditions. The dinner was also a kind of trade union—ladies only—offering support to the present incumbent.[66]

CBC and SMS

Clem and Stephen were rivals—aware that each might be scooped by the other. 'We have trailed *Meanjin* too often lately', Stephen wrote to Ian Turner in 1960, 'and I hear from my spies that *Meanjin* is doing an article on [CP] Snow in September.' Despite their common interest in fending off McCarthyist attacks, and intermittent discussion extending to showing each other letters from difficult contributors, or even occasionally passing on short stories, there was a certain wariness about their relations. Largely thanks to Stephen, they operated on an implicit Treaty of Tordesillas, dividing up the literary world.

Clem must have had a sense of *Overland* snapping at his heels. He would have found a number of irritants on picking up the magazine: a few of his old Brisbane contributors, perhaps, or the way the *Meanjin* feature 'Letter to Tom Collins' had been given a new lease of life in *Overland*. Or the way that since the death of Vance Palmer, Clem had shed articles about him from *Meanjin*, but there they were, with some by Vance himself, plus additional contributions from his daughters, in *Overland*. Perhaps in turning its pages he even felt some nostalgia for the perky little magazine *Meanjin* used to be. For the existence of *Overland* pushed *Meanjin* further into high ground: with academic articles (*Overland* was uncomfortable about footnotes), the great series, publishing overseas writers. Towards the end, given his difficulties with emerging Australian writers, Clem spoke wildly of running stories from them alone. But he knew that both the CLF and the university had reservations about *Meanjin*'s international aspirations. And now there was *Overland*, 'often naïve but decent'.

For his part, Stephen was publicly deferential. *Meanjin*'s purpose was higher: when Clem had David Martin as a featured writer, Stephen wrote as if it were an *Overland* contributor's elevation. He never forgot the pioneering work Clem had done, the beacon *Meanjin* had been for him when living in London. When, after the Petrov affair, *Meanjin* experienced one of its worst financial crises, Stephen and Judah Waten rallied round, organising a function that raised £85 in support of Clem's magazine. Again, when the CLF increased subsidies to magazines in 1967, Stephen noted in 'Swag' that *Meanjin* had done particularly well—'it needs and deserves it more than most'. And a few years later, he honoured *Meanjin*'s thirtieth anniversary with three articles appearing in *Overland* on Clem and his magazine, one of them Clem's own 'Autobituary'.

Privately, the path was rockier. Clem was a hard man to please. Stephen was the prime mover for the *Meanjin* twenty-first celebratory dinner, and performed other acts of kindness. One of them was to induce a *Meanjin* secretary who had walked out on the job to go back, since he had somehow persuaded Clem to apologise to her. 'God help me for [being] a professional meddler,' he told Ian Turner. But it was not good enough. Clem told David Martin that he would much rather have dealings with him, and people like John Morrison, than with 'the Gotts and the Murray-Smiths'. Writers, rather than political heavies. Then Stephen had tried to tell Clem 'not to overdo the "gloom"—a different psychological approach would get better results'. He offered to set up a supportive meeting with Ian Turner and Rex Mortimer in the pub, might come along himself; but this was declined. Clem was reluctant to meet them, he said, because it would result in 'the usual let-down'. It had happened so many times before.

Overborne by a sense of 'failure', a seeming futility, Clem was well aware that he had 'almost degenerated into a psychotic state'. That was why, he told Stephen, 'I have warned you several times not to get into a similar one.' (And yes, Stephen did come to write of 'creeping paranoia, the occupational disease of editors'.) Stephen tried to reassure him, ridiculing his declared '"sense of failure on the personal relationship level" … How can I convince you in what love and regard you are held by so many.' True: universally referred to simply as 'Clem', the older man was a kind of mascot, drawing affection tinged with amusement at his constant intractability.

All Stephen was asking for was a bit more light and shade in Clem's continuing plaint. But Clem would not cease. At the time when the right was mustering to produce *Quadrant*, he claimed that 'the Left, and not the Right, could be responsible for the death of this journal'—as had happened (he believed) elsewhere. Stephen, exasperated, told him not to be 'a stupid maudlin idiot'. Alive to Clem's paranoia about *Overland*, Stephen said it could never do *Meanjin*'s job, and none of those associated with the magazine imagined that it could. There is a gap it can fill, and that's what it does. 'That's all.'

Three months later, Clem said that he and Nina were thinking of buying land next door to Stephen at Mt Eliza, to become neighbours. Stephen professed delight—perhaps the best way of smothering the idea. Indeed it would be Clem's non-appearance at Mt Eliza, for the *Overland–Meanjin* cricket match in 1973, that would be the low point in their relationship: the long explanatory letter to Max Marginson was clearly intended for Stephen's eyes. There Clem said that he had tried 'to keep alive the illusion that there was a sort of *rapport* between the two journals and their editors … but I've never been able to get close to him, and I can't recall having one really decent talk, in a relaxed and productive atmosphere. Perhaps a marked difference in our temperaments is responsible …'[67]

A marked difference there certainly was. Clem always felt himself the outsider, never completely at home in Melbourne. Whenever possible, he would always return to his Queensland roots. He would have been conscious of Stephen's protean past: on the one hand, the Toorak and Geelong Grammar connections, so that he could move easily among the right in Melbourne and beyond. On the other, given the years spent in the Communist Party, and as a union activist, he could also be seen as having been a more complete man of the left. Moreover, whereas Stephen had secured control of his magazine, Clem never felt secure with his. *Overland*'s failure to secure a subsidy 'was not entirely a bad thing', he told David Martin. For Clem had a constant struggle with his reluctant patron the university, and to a lesser degree with the Commonwealth Literary Fund, where he needed the support of both political parties. And until the late 1960s, the fact that he had a Russian wife would always make him vulnerable to attack.

Nina, in fact, generally kept clear of *Meanjin*, certainly with regard to content, except for Russian literature; she had her own challenges in running the Russian Department. As Clem acknowledged, her moral and intellectual support—to say nothing of her independent income—was vital. Her loving support reaffirmed his natural tenacity. Nita, while occupied with her own teaching career, was more fully engaged in the *Overland* project. She handled subscriptions, gently kept Stephen from straying too far away from the left, and helped determine which stories got published in the magazine.

While the situation of the two editors was very different, so too were their personalities and general approach. Clem's upbringing was difficult. His mother was manipulative and demanding, his father indifferent to him and feckless. They were constantly shifting house, so that Clem formed very few attachments in his youth, and would always have trouble with the middle ground in relationships: there was himself, and then the high aspirations. At the same time, unlike Stephen's robust health, he was subject to a procession of ailments and accidents. As early as the 1950s he wrote of being in constant pain, owing to an early spinal injury; by the end of his time at *Meanjin* he had effective sight in one eye only. Boldly, and bravely—and possessing both an athlete's build and what Paul Keating calls 'the mad gene'—Clem battled on, projecting upwards and outwards. There was about him something of the blind visionary, compensating for the deep insecurities that not even his steady, reciprocated love for Nina could completely alleviate.

There was always a hint of the inconsolable child about Clem. He could never forget a slight, and constantly nursed grievances—such as Stephen's 'betrayal' by having attended the Australian Association for Cultural Freedom little magazine seminar in 1962. It is telling that whereas Stephen was someone people would turn to in domestic crises, on occasion leading him to intervene directly, Clem was rarely called upon to give personal advice, but to discuss projects or write references. Although Stephen was the active public intellectual, Clem had the reputation of being a public figure.

With Stephen, more securely grounded as he was, any sense of hollowness came to be confidently ascribed to the society he lived in: for most people, he decided, being Australian was 'an existential way of life', just a lifestyle. Stephen's childhood was late imperial, with a Scots father and strong connections with British India. The home was virtually bookless; in compensation, Stephen would become an assiduous book collector. As a young man, on reading Henry Handel Richardson's *The Fortunes of Richard Mahony*—and being moved by it to the point of tears—he had an epiphany: the realisation that imaginative literature was the key, the thing that could clinch white Australia to this land.[68]

So Stephen's project—emerging in concert with commitment to the Communist Party, and then with greater clarity as he moved beyond it—became one of striving to articulate a national culture. This was done mainly through *Overland*, but also with the *Dictionary of Australian Quotations*, *Right Words*, his commitment to broadening technical education, and to writing its history; also work on various committees. Clem, on the other hand, had one big idea—to create a journal that would be national, articulating the general will in cultural matters. But it would also be international—or at least internationally respected. For him *Meanjin*, like all leading cultural institutions, should be a double-header: presenting the best Australian product and placing alongside it the best (when he could get it) international writing or perspectives.

Both editors, to some degree, faced the same two problems. One was how to raise standards—in Australian life generally, as well as in literary matters; and how (what we would now see as monocultural) Australians could become more fully themselves. But these two aims could be at variance. With Stephen, there was less concern about standards, more with authenticity. Both editors held the hope that Anglo-Celtic Australia could create something new, and distinctive: through their magazines they would help to achieve its realisation.

Stephen was more of a *literary* man than Clem, a Dr Johnson figure. His knowledge was encyclopaedic, rather than based on familiarity with texts. He loved connections, resonances, the possibilities of accretion and depth: for this reason he was drawn to Tasmania, the place in Australia where they were most likely to be encountered. His own favourite reading centred on travel accounts and biography, much of it English. Clem—as a short-story writer and poet (his editorial work did not obviate this work, as it could have done, though it did impede it)—was more alive to 'quality' (his catchword). For thirty years Clem exercised flair in finding and encouraging writers. Stephen's own literary tastes were relatively pedestrian, although when it came to editing manuscripts he was no less a dab hand than Clem.

Clem's editorial style was that of an embattled autocracy, Stephen's one of leadership, *Overland* functioning (in Sukarno's formulation) as a 'guided democracy'. This arose partly from the history of the magazines—and from their continuing structures. *Overland* had its origins in the Realist Writers Group, a Communist front but a collective enterprise.

It never lost this sense of community. Stephen would remark on the intimate relationship the magazine had with its readership, borne out by the continuing donations to *Overland*'s Floating Fund. Occasionally Clem would describe some notable as a 'friend of *Meanjin*'; *Overland* had 'supporters'.

Overland was informal, improvisatory; *Meanjin* august, an institution. Whereas *Overland* occasionally held parties, *Meanjin* was inclined to the formal dinner—particularly when there was an anniversary coming up. Stephen became inclined to dismiss such occasions, remarking of *Overland*'s upcoming thirtieth anniversary that there were no great celebrations planned, 'not even a mutual-admiration drink for the editors'. Later, he would institute an annual *Overland* dinner, in the Victoria Room at University House, with its 'silver and polished wood and flickering candles—marvellously effective for the kind of night we want'. There were no speeches; the only attendees were his Melbourne associates and their wives, plus a guest of honour. (Once that was Patrick White, more tight-lipped than usual, for at that very moment Sidney Nolan was in Stockholm collecting the Nobel Prize for him.)[69]

In a sense *Overland* graduated into grandeur: Stephen's last issues were almost plush, printed on fine paper, but the magazine appeared on newsprint for many years. Clem's greater visual sense, combined with his high purpose, meant that the pleasing appearance of *Meanjin* was an integral part of the product. It announced the considered nature of its content. Occasionally even loyal supporters were critical: Did *Meanjin* have to be quite 'such a nice-looking job', asked Dorothy Green. It's the content that counts. Clem countered by saying that he chose his printers carefully. Small ones were less efficient, and in practice '"excellent" printing does not cost any more than "bad" printing'.[70]

Visual attractiveness was for Clem a ratification of the importance of continuity, of cultural accretion: regularity of appearance was in itself a cultural statement. *Overland*'s aims were more modest. Its shortcomings were admitted under the masthead, warning the reader that publication—despite the best intentions—was intermittent. In Stephen's time it remained a struggle, so it is not surprising that the magazine would have gaps in advancing the causes it particularly cared about. No-one was more aware of this than Stephen. 'I always feel sick, nervous and depressed', he told David Martin, after putting out '*any* issue of

Overland'. Clem similarly felt the gap between vision and realisation. 'Every time an issue appears I feel like howling like a dog,' he wrote. 'However, I do the best I can.'[71]

Clem was desperate to have the apparent security of association with the university (as well as intellectual respectability). He had an office, and a secretary, so could be prolix (particularly in correspondence): Stephen had none, was terse, regarded the phone essentially as an instrument of interruption. In practice, there was tension between Clem and the university at a number of levels, apart from funding. He was the founder-editor of the journal, a one-man band; therefore others—except on the finance committee—could only advise. They might have that advice ignored, getting doses of complaint instead, so tended to withdraw. The formulation was eventually hit upon (since there were few meetings), of dubbing these and others 'Consultants', as accurate as it was vague.

Clem's cantankerousness was legendary—and not helped by his propensity, as Marie Davison put it, 'of always stirring hornets' nests and then complaining about the prevalence of hornets'. He was not a committee man, was a poor interviewee, and generally lacked social skills. (Barry Jones tells a story of how Clem, at a dinner given in 1959 for the visiting Robert Graves, proceeded to recite *Meanjin*'s woes—to the increasing boredom of the guest of honour and the suppressed annoyance of everybody else.) Stephen, on the other hand, was urbane—if he struck many as pompous, he usefully projected an utter self-confidence. In fact he could be kindly and friendly. It is not surprising then that he should have good relations with his printer, Bob Cugley of National Press, who almost became family. Clem's dealings with printers—and there was a succession of them—were invariably fraught.

When it came to succession, Clem could not really conceive his journal being controlled by anyone else. It was his baby, another wife. He did paint, and write, but his commitment to *Meanjin* was total: despite persistent ill-health, he stuck doggedly to his vision, his one big idea. Stephen, on the other hand, always had other major projects on the boil—apart from enjoying a fuller domestic life. Moreover, it was as if Stephen was on a lifelong quest. Clem's editorial column was styled (since he felt assailed) 'The Uneasy Chair', whereas Stephen's (indicating the journey) tellingly 'Swag'. Stephen kept evolving, despite the emergence of more conservative instincts as he aged. Clem's voluminous correspondence is remarkably uniform in tone, whether from 1950 or 1970; Stephen's was much more focused on the recipient. And at the end, Stephen graduated from editor to author; he was reaching out not only to Antarctica, but also to the remote islands Pitcairn, St Kilda and Tristan da Cunha.

Nonetheless it was Clem who, so far as the magazines were concerned, put the runs on the board. Apart from one hiccough in its first year in Melbourne, *Meanjin* made its quarterly appearance, without missing a beat, for twenty-eight years. Clem could be forgiven for being imperious; the achievement—against all odds—was magnificent. For much of his editorship, one splendid issue succeeded another. He was the right man for his place and time. 'Only someone with Clem's temperament and lack of dogma', Catherine Duncan wrote to Laurence Collinson years later:

> could have survived and made the journal as good as it was. No doubt the brave days cannot be prolonged indefinitely, and the burning brand usually gutters into a staid and academic reflection, but I feel that if *Meanjin* hadn't fought as it did during the cold war period, the situation, culturally and politically, might be a good deal worse in Australia than it is today.[72]

7

CLEM (AND JIM)

POWER STRUGGLE IN THE CLEMLIN

1974–75

Here the narrative changes modes. The following account, of how I became Clem's successor at Meanjin, *is written in the first person. That way leakage from recently gained perspectives could be prevented from seeping in to distort perceptions acted upon at the time. The reader who has traversed the previous chapters will know more about Clem than I did, on turning up at the* Meanjin *office in 1974.*

IT WAS A temporary existence, marking time between intensities past—South Africa—and intensities anticipated—London. I had a job as acting lecturer at the University of Melbourne, in the History Department, retailing a simplified form of medieval history to first years. It was 1969; the time of Australia's commitment to the Vietnam War, made even less credible by prime minister Gorton's gangling sentences. There was a stirring, and a hope of change—but as the *Don's Party* election later that year would demonstrate, a considerable way to go before any of it was realised.

One day, having had a short piece on South Africa published in a respected fortnightly, I was passing the terrace house that contained *Meanjin*, hesitated, and decided to go in. Directed to the presence of the editor, I found at the desk a big man looking like a rough draft for the recent governor-general, Lord Casey (I thought then); he spoke with the same imperial stresses, if with a more Australian accent. He received me well, but was not much interested in any writing about South Africa. He asked about other ideas for articles. For a man at the centre of Australian cultural life, he seemed surprisingly halting and inconclusive. I suggested music, and how interesting the composer Peter Sculthorpe had been in a recent prefatory talk: he might write a very good article.

The editor responded warmly, but seemed out of touch with the whole area, generally a bit remote. Politely he asked how Sculthorpe could be found. I suggested he contact a music critic and well-known bookdealer. 'Ah, Kenneth Hince. Of course he'd know. I published some of his early stuff years ago.' Wistfully he then spoke of the 1940s, and of the idealism that a subsequent generation could not possibly understand. 'We had hoped', he said, with weary emphasis, 'to reshape Australian society, to make it a truly just one ... But if you speak like that today, you're regarded as a nut.' What did I know about the defeat of Chifley? he suddenly asked, as if it were still a puzzle to him. Perhaps I could help him draft a letter to Chifley's biographer, raising the right issues. But (I did not tell him) I was seven when the Liberals had been voted in; could scarcely remember it. I pointed to a particular historian on his board. 'Ah, yes', he said, repeating the name as his voice trailed away.

Meanjin turned up when I went to London the following year, and I read it with great interest. Not so much because of any particular articles or writers one would look forward to, but because its very existence pointed to a distinct critical mass. It was, after all, still the time of the great expatriation, partly for political reasons, but even more for cultural ones. In 1970 there was still no Australian film industry, just the beginnings of Australian drama, a hit-and-miss opera company, and barely twenty novels published a year. Most people with cultural aspirations felt they had to go to London, if only to 'check it out'. Some, of course, stayed—and played dirty. In 1971, when judge Argyle jailed the editors of *Oz* for obscenity, a bunch of sensitives wrote a letter to *The Times* expressing shock and horror, because such legal repression—said they, appealing to the snobbery of the Brits—was precisely the reason they had left that distant, abrasive place Australia. *Meanjin*, by its very existence, indicated another view, of something that, still in the process of articulation, might yet be born.

Donald Horne's book *The Next Australia* was a blueprint of what that might be like. Somehow I got hold of a copy quite early in the piece, and thought highly of it: less cynical than *The Lucky Country*, it was positively idealistic. Strange that it should come from a professed Liberal; it seemed so Whitlamite. In an article I said so, and sent the piece to *Meanjin*. Clem took it enthusiastically, and paid well.

At the end of 1972 I made a return visit. With a change of government in the air, who could stay away? I duly paid my respects to Clem, and was soon included in a number of his activities. There was lunch with Geoff Serle, who spoke seriously about many things but with a certain buoyancy: he had just finished his 'primer' on Australian cultural history, and he was hopeful about a Labor victory at the polls. Clem was not: his tagline was 'In a sense my Australia died with the fall of the Chifley government'. He even spouted it at the *Meanjin* Christmas party, which I was surprised to find a small affair, attended by little more than twenty people.

I was invited out to Stanhope and wined, dined and photographed, with Clem and Nina on either side. (They had a collection of photographs of various authors, with themselves invariably placed as bookends.) Perhaps I might like to stay there when I returned. Perhaps I could help look after Nina's mother, Mrs Maximov … I was being enlisted. Otherwise it seemed too easy, as if too much was being conceded—for while there was affability, there was not the warmth of pronounced affinity. Meanwhile Clem had decided to have me write a 'Home Thoughts from Abroad' piece, and also drawn and quarterlied—i.e. sit for a sketch by Louis Kahan, which would then be published in the magazine. It was the *Meanjin* equivalent of a commemorative stamp. Then, a week or two before I went back to London, he offered me the position of assistant editor, with the prospect of succession.

There were no details; presumably they would be worked out after an in-principle acceptance. The offer was attractive; I wanted to come back, and felt increasingly uncomfortable both with British imperial history and as an academic—as lecturers were habitually called then. But I also felt I had been drawn in too quickly, almost as if being sucked into a vacuum. Then there were stories of how difficult a man Clem was: working in the same office could be disastrous. I was also beginning to realise that, more often than not, for important positions a deputy might be passed over for a more glamorous candidate. So shortly after I went back to London I wrote a letter, declining with thanks. That was that.

One day six months or so later, the phone rang. Geoff Serle. He was in London, and said—with grave purpose—that he would like to see me. So what was this about? *Meanjin.* I don't think there's anything to discuss, I said; I declined the assistant editorship. This is the editorship, said Serle. Oh; I suppose that's different.

While this second approach was distinctly flattering, I was puzzled as to why I was being favoured. Serle (whom I scarcely knew) seemed to think I was the one who could do the job. (He had seen a statement of my world view a year or two before, and as it had been shaped by England and South Africa as well as Australia, he might have been struck by its breadth in one still relatively young—certainly among historians, as we both were.) An academic, perhaps a historian with cultural sensitivity, seemed to be what was wanted. Perhaps the recent favourable reviews of my scholarly edition of Trollope's *South Africa* suggested I could deliver the goods, even the editorial nitty-gritty. Moreover, a number of more eligible candidates might not be prepared to take it on. The pay was poor: until quite recently, fixed at two-thirds of the fifth point of the lecturer scale. As I was (to say the least of it) unmarried, without family responsibilities, on this salary I could get by. And I was keen to return home.

But the operation would be a delicate one, Serle warned. Clem had reached the point where he wanted to retire, but divesting himself of the journal would be an intricate business. Although it operated from university premises, and he was in receipt of a salary from the Lockie Bequest (supplemented by the university), he was not an employee of the university but the proprietor of an independent journal. An instrumentality would have to be created—a company limited by guarantee—to take over the proprietary rights. As part of the overall deal, and to provide a form of superannuation, Clem was to be paid $70,000 for the *Meanjin* archive. (No-one questioned this valuation, since he had been offered a higher amount by an American university. The sum would then have come close to buying two large terrace houses in Carlton.) But there was always the possibility, warned Serle, that the whole thing could come unstuck.

I assented, and Serle told me I would hear from Clem in due course. But I did not. Suddenly his wife Nina appeared on the scene, and suggested we meet. We attended a meeting together: one of the speakers was Jack Lindsay. As I was sitting next to her, Nina produced a document, a statement of appreciation and support for Clem. Why don't you go round and get people to sign it? she asked. Looking at the rangey lot of scattered expatriates, I knew this would be quite a challenge; I also thought that, if I really were to take over *Meanjin*, it would immediately cast me as handmaiden. Word would get about. So I said no. Not that I had tabs on myself: asked by Jack Lindsay that evening what I did, I said I was 'a minor academic from Australia' (which immediately got him interested).

In the meantime, still hearing nothing, I thought I had better substantiate that claim by becoming a minor academic *in* Australia. So I applied for a senior tutorship at the University of New England; a long way from Melbourne, where I needed to be located because of my ageing mother. It was a start. Besides, it would be good to get to know another part of the country intimately; except for my long sojourns overseas, I had never lived outside Melbourne.

Eventually a crisis point was reached. There was still no letter when I heard from the University of New England, offering me the position. What was I to do? I would have to ring: still a rarity in those days, when it cost £1 a minute (equal to three Penguin books or three packets of cigarettes). But perhaps not ring Serle. I did call Melbourne, and was surprised that a heavily accented female voice should answer, since I had placed a person-to-person call. Nina. She was reluctant to bring Clem to the phone, but eventually he came. He was so lapsed into passivity that, through the wires, I could almost hear the heat of a Melbourne summer's day. After a minute or two, when I told him I had to decide what to do, he said to come to *Meanjin*. 'Russel Ward's a friend … He'll fix you up if it doesn't work out' … Not very encouraging, but at least there had been some form of commitment.

Clem now seems to have suffered from anxiety as to whether he had done the right thing. He asked me to see various people in London, hoping for some assessment, some confirmation from them—or possibly the complete opposite, which would furnish grounds for repudiation. I went to see Dorothy Green, in the University Women's Club;

Bernard and Kate Smith, who were kindly and open; John Burton, who gave me a clenched ten minutes between lectures at the London School of Economics; and Jack Lindsay, who made over the better part of a day at home in Castle Hedingham—where he was an excellent guide to the intricacies of the local church.

All this was a long way from Australia. It was only when I got back that I came to realise that the streets of Melbourne were littered with the corpses of putative *Meanjin* editors. An exaggeration, but not for the people concerned. (There was also a candidate in Brisbane.) As noted earlier, Laurie Clancy had started preparing an issue, but at the last minute Clem jibbed and placed on the desk advanced plans for an issue of his own. In truth he was at his wits' end. 'I simply can't cope, mate,' he wrote to Humphrey McQueen. 'Wish you were here in Melbourne, or that I was in Canberra.' McQueen was one of the few of the rising generation of writers with whom he established fruitful contact, indeed relied on for moral support. He was mortified when McQueen suggested he should close the journal down. Clem would have preferred to hand it over to near-contemporaries like Dorothy Green, Dennis Pryor or Guy Manton, seeing it as an energy problem rather than one of outlook. It was all too much. Exhausted, sometimes ill, in 1973 Clem stayed away from the office for weeks at a time.

Finally, four or five weeks or so after our phone conversation, I received a letter fairly up-beat in tone. Clem said he had been preoccupied with the question of changing *Meanjin*'s printing to offset (not undertaken). He then explained how the office was organised, stating that 'When you arrive you might want to make other office arrangements.' While he would keep me afloat financially until things were reorganised—he was keen that I should do some teaching when I returned—or even better, write a history of *Meanjin Quarterly* on a Literature Board grant. As for the editorship, 'For my part I'll do all in my power to "ease" you into the job,' he wrote. 'I'm sure we both realize that the entire operation is not without its dangers … The die is caste [*sic*].' Puzzlingly, the letter ended, 'Up Australia! Long live freedom!' Only much later I saw in this the tone of a captain prepared to go down with his ship.

The day came, late in March 1974, when I turned up at the *Meanjin* office. The building was a double-storeyed Victorian terrace in Parkville; downstairs were musicians. *Meanjin* occupied the top floor. One little room was given over to periodicals received; cartons of back issues were relegated to the rear of the ground floor, near the kitchen. You could trip over them every time you went to make the coffee. Returning up the stairs, a hush was induced by the lines of Kahan etchings of Australian authors, leading past the editor's room to the front office. More Kahans, though fewer—this time of women, a gesture to the secretarial staff. With its steel filing cabinets, housing the extensive archive, the office seemed quite contemporary. It had a golf-ball typewriter, and was about to get a photocopier. But it was still the days of carbon paper, white-out and razor blades; there was no answering machine or fax machine. There wasn't anywhere. It would be ten years before word processors made an appearance, and another ten till the internet. A secretary of 1910 could have walked into that office and within a day or two feel quite at home.

'*Meanjin Quarterly*. Office of the Editor'. So it was proclaimed on the letterhead, under the banner of the University of Melbourne. All very grand. But no-one worked at *Meanjin* full-time, except Clem, who spent a considerable time away from it. Having worked at Eltham well into the night, he would turn up before eleven with a heap of material to be typed. His script looked like old barbed-wire: red biro on white paper. There would be another surge, often just before the secretary was supposed to leave at four. Margaret O'Connell was efficient, typing away like a woodpecker; she had to be, as she was there only three days a week. Dedication gave her a detachment that seemed to suit her, and she had a well-developed sense of the absurdity of things. Two days a week Nancy Kellock came in to do the bookkeeping: a level-headed, cultivated Old Leftie who seemed to know everybody. Most afternoons two others appeared: Italian Angela, who filed away the press cuttings Clem habitually amassed, and Win McAlpin, who was helping sort out the files before they went off to the Baillieu Library—and she to social work in Vietnam.

Then there were the readers. Foremost was AA Phillips of 'The Cultural Cringe': he would come in twice a week wearing an old sports jacket, from time to time inserting a hand in one of its pockets in time-honoured schoolmasterly fashion. But despite the shaky hand and the quavery voice, he was as sharp as a tack. He was also keen to be humorous, wearing authority lightly. Rather more serious was the emerging feminist writer Finola Moorhead; she also looked at submissions, and Clem saw her as a Girl Friday. He didn't approve of what he saw as her broad speech, and thought she should take elocution lessons. In addition there was a poetry editor, Paul Fahey, who would come to collect the poetry sent in, make his selection and return to discuss it with Clem. Other manuscripts were sent out to academic experts.

I was ushered into the small room at the end of the passage, a view over Parkville backyards extending from my desk. I began commenting on manuscripts, and editing them. Clem would issue instructions, and I would carry them out. If I raised an objection, forward would go his hands in a stately, resigned gesture: an excellent technique for exacting compliance from a younger man. But he took it badly that I had not agreed to have my name on the issue just coming out—I had no hand in its preparation. Clem also could not comprehend why I should think a review of my edition of Trollope's *South Africa* would be out of place in the journal.

There were outbursts of anger, and I soon realised that whereas for most people losing your temper served as a discharge, Clem had the unusual capacity to work himself up into a lather again within ten minutes. Nonetheless we got on well, enjoying a glass or two of Black Label Johnnie Walker in the evenings with whoever happened to be about. Often he would rail against somebody or other, looking anxious and moving his hand up to stroke his beard, comfortingly; at other times he could be quite jolly, recounting a past episode. But there was something sealed off about him, a touch of the grandee. It was hard to work out how to relate to him best.

Gradually it dawned on me that I was being pushed back into the position I had explicitly rejected: an assistant editorship. The puzzling references in his February letter to my arrival bringing 'exciting' possibilities—'for me, anyway', now took on an unwelcome aspect. I was being cast as cabin boy to Clem, on his tempestuous voyage. Apart from having offered me the editorship the moment I stepped inside the door—a feint, since I was clearly unprepared—there was no talk of a date of transfer. Since Serle had convincingly cast himself as the architect of

Meanjin's transformation, it seemed best to raise the matter with him. His replies were gnomic.

In the meantime Clem steamed ahead, thinking up more articles that tied the journal irretrievably to the past. Nina meanwhile was exultant about having got 'a scoop for *Meanjin*', a speech by Patrick White at the Sydney Opera House that was just an adumbration of the obvious. When asked to organise for the next issue a second 'Tribute' to the recent literary dead, I thought it inadvisable, as people were beginning to talk of 'the *Meanjin* morgue'. I ignored the request. But Clem was getting bossier. Shortly after, when I came into the office after a particularly hard morning, there was the request for the tribute again; underlined, with the original date ringed in red. This couldn't go on. Even as I flew off the handle I made a split-second calculation: if I got away with charging into his office, and whatever came after, I would come through. If not, at least—after fifteen months—there would be resolution. Clem, seated, looked at me with wary composure. I said some hard things, peppered with a swearword or two, and rushed out.

It was not my finest hour, nor the sequel his. I apologised quickly, and within an hour or two was talking with him as though nothing had happened. It was important to re-establish a sense of normality; the drawbridge had gone up once before. Suddenly Clem's brother Paul arrived; out came the Black Label. 'You two look as though you're getting on like a house on fire,' he said, evidently pleased. Clem semi-spluttered, I smiled and nodded, and nothing further was said. Merrily conversation proceeded.

But he didn't come in the next day. Or the next. Rather than sacking me, which would have been his right, Clem had decided to withdraw and apply sanctions. *Meanjin*'s secretary was instructed to communicate via the Russian Department, soon dubbed the Soviet Embassy. But I remained in the office, and, since deals regarding the archive and the formation of the company were in the offing, and I had the support of the university vice-principal, Ray Marginson, as well as Geoff Serle, I would soldier on.

What I did not then know was that Clem did appreciate, intellectually, that it was time for him to go. He told Humphrey McQueen that 'Jim Davidson is taking over *Meanjin* responsibilities, and I'm confident that he'll make a success of the magazine.' But as in Brisbane thirty years before, the trouble was he could not bring himself to let go. Then he had talked of resigning as editor, but in the same breath spoke of doing 'the routine work, if required, and assist[ing] financially … and just stay[ing] on, being helpful'. In other words, he would resign, but not abdicate. The same impulse was at work now. 'The more he had to face getting out', recalled Jessie Serle, 'the more fraught he became … All those trips Geoff made up and down to Eltham were about getting Clem to be sane.'[1]

Meanwhile I went about an editor's business, making myself known. The climate was not favourable to *Meanjin*. In Sydney, where the Australia Council was based, there was a strong feeling that the existing grants to magazines should be revised, or held down, so as to enable funding to be extended more broadly, in particular to new magazines. There were also manoeuvrings to put money into one big literary magazine, which the board would sponsor. More immediately I was shocked when, during a student arts festival in May, not one writer bothered to walk down the road to the *Meanjin* office. So Mohammed went to the mountain.

I wanted to meet Frank Moorhouse, who had been involved in setting up *Tabloid Story*. This was a perky supplement that migrated from publication to publication, assuming the form of its host as it promoted fiction in unlikely places. Moorhouse had quite a lot to say, none of it of comfort to *Meanjin*, which he attacked strongly. At the end of the talk I went up to him as he came off the stage. 'Hey, mister … Want a dirty magazine?' He looked at me quizzically. 'I have reason to believe', I said introducing myself, 'I will be the next editor of *Meanjin*.' We began talking. After ten minutes I asked whether he would consider writing for *Meanjin* again. Yes, he would.

But the crisis continued. Apart from any personal sense of woundedness, Clem was still smarting from my reply when asked what I thought of the magazine: 'moribund', I said, believing it to be a bit of in-house candour. But Clem told others—as though it was more revealing of me than of him. Then occasionally I would walk into the office and find loads of typing for the secretary, plus a flutter of notes and instructions. Meanwhile, I was moving about, testing opinion. I heard lots of complaints from hurt contributors, who had received readers' candid comments on scraps of paper. An academic asked whether I thought I had 'suffered enough' to edit *Meanjin*. Vin Buckley—who habitually looked at the world across acres of self-regard—thought my attitude that of 'a dutiful daughter'. Then there were visits from Geoff Serle, who, when feeling upbeat, would allow his voice to louden and his grin to broaden; he might also limber up with stretching exercises. Meanwhile I was learning the mechanics of the job, and building up good relations with the printers. It was difficult, trying to rebuild the magazine while fighting a cold war with the outgoing editor. One day, when he did come in, Clem had a long conversation with his confidant Geoffrey Leeper. As I was walking from the back room to the front office, through the door I heard Leeper remark, 'But Clem, you're being fiercely inconsistent!'

Shortly afterwards Geoff Serle managed to secure an interim agreement. Clem delegated the signing of *Meanjin* cheques to Serle and Leeper. I was obliged to use as much accepted material as possible, and to show proofs to Leeper (a pedant). Clem would remain editor to the end of the year, for the sake of completion, although I would be given full editorial control from the third issue. Until the new arrangements were in place, Clem would retain ultimate control; but he would go on leave from early June to the end of the year.

Sometime afterwards, walking down the corridor from the back room to the front office, I thought it time to cross the Rubicon. I would move into Clem's office; no-one said I shouldn't. Otherwise the situation would remain in abeyance. About this time Arthur Phillips, aware that there was a fight going on in which he wished to play no part, decided it was safe to reappear. On the mornings he came in he now occupied the back room: I would go and talk to him, and for want of anything else, sit on the rubbish bin. One day I tentatively asked him about Clem. 'Oh, he's mad!' he said dismissively. His eyes then shot straight back to the manuscript he was reading.

The archive agreement was signed, but then there was another demand: $5000 for what was laughingly called the 'goodwill' of the business. At the time an Andy Warhol movie was showing, *Flesh for Frankenstein*: the sequel seemed to me to be 'Cash for Clemenstein'. Nonetheless, by the end of July Clem had been persuaded to transfer the Lockie Bequest salary to me, as acting editor. But I was still in leading strings, and while various university people had been lined up for the Meanjin Company, there was not yet talk of a date for its assuming control. 'Pazienza', Nina had said to me; the need for unusual patience I assumed is what she meant. Whatever the case, we were soon in crisis again. The letters I wrote Clem, explaining what I was doing, were provocative by their very existence—and were not entirely innocent. My growing confidence in the job (a necessary demonstration of competence) could easily have struck Clem as impertinent. Certainly the small but symbolic changes in the office would have seemed so.

A sixth sense told me something was stirring, and that I should be on the alert. There had just been another one of Clem's raids—clandestine Clemenstein—despite his being 'on leave'. It might be necessary to remain in the office all the time, particularly over weekends. I would have to sleep there. Sure enough, breaking the calm of a Parkville Saturday afternoon, I was aware of people entering the building. There was a creak outside my open door, then a female voice, 'Somebody's there': Nina, with Clem. I got up from the desk to greet them, showed them into the main office, and excused myself as there was work to do. They stayed for five minutes, then left. Only later, much later, did I realise what the visit had been about.

As with the row with Duhig in 1944, Clem had decided to make off with the subscription list. (He was defeated not only by my presence, but by its bulkiness, as it consisted of trays of carbon cards for an addressograph.) A few months earlier, he had reverted to a Douglas Annand drawing of a brolga as the cover design for the year—the bird brought to its knees by being tilted to fit into the available space. He was exhibiting a tottering merry-go-round of mind, replaying his greatest hits.

Not long afterwards I received a phone call from Geoffrey Leeper, who wanted to see me. 'I've come as Clem's ambassador', he announced in his high-toned, declaratory manner. 'Oh,' I said. 'You realise that makes you the ambassador at the Court of St James?' There was a characteristic quick smile. A rather repressed man who habitually dressed in schoolboy greys, Leeper was a distinguished soil scientist who prided himself on his rationality, indeed rationalism—a reaction to the Anglicanism of his father, the unpleasant Alexander Leeper, first warden of Trinity College. Leeper proceeded to put Clem's case vigorously. Even so, he listened carefully when I explained it was more of a succession dispute than a question of insubordination. I spoke in an unbuttoned fashion about this and the wider difficulties facing the magazine.

But Leeper stuck to his brief. Clem was unhappy about the present secretary, since the material he sent down was not being typed quickly enough. He thought her inefficient, and that I was probably intervening to delay his material receiving attention. He had forgotten that he had appointed her, unlike previous secretaries, part-time: *Meanjin*'s needs must come first. Then Leeper said that Clem wanted to come into the office, but that I must absent myself when he did. This, I said, would be very difficult: I had to be on the job. Apart from that, I did not see the necessity. I then said how unhappy I was about the whole situation, how I had hoped for better relations. Most reluctantly, I agreed to Clem coming in on Mondays; that way, taxes paid, the rest of the week would form a block.

Leeper would have left that meeting thinking I might crack. I thought I might, too. When, at a recent artists lunch, Roger Kemp asked couldn't I be nicer to Clem, I let out an involuntary sob. And there was something else. Just as I was unwillingly being cast as assistant a second time, so I was being asked to leave the building on a regular basis. There had already been an earlier row with Clem, a withdrawal to Eltham, and mediation. I recognised the pattern, from experience of my father: row, agreement-cum-resolution, and then the reliance on your desire to keep the peace to quietly but steadily push you back to where you were in the first place. The night of the Leeper meeting I visited some friends, and said I might chuck it in. No! said Sarie, emboldening me. Next morning I phoned Clem's ambassador, and said to tell him that he can come into the office any time he likes. But, sorry, I can give no guarantee I won't be here.

Nothing happened for a week or so, and then the news came that Clem intended to close the journal down. It was, after all, his prerogative; exactly what some people had urged him to do. Meanwhile rumours also reached us that he had taken soundings from members of the Literature Board to ascertain whether he could close the magazine down temporarily, and then, after a decent interval, start it up again—without me. Another story was circulating to the effect that he would take *Meanjin* to Eltham, and from Stanhope put out a 'handsel', as he originally had done in Brisbane: in the end was its beginning. But that could eliminate all he had achieved in between.

I decided to take soundings of my own. Clem could not evict me from the office, for it was university property. What if there were a complete severance—and I were to produce a Son of Meanjin, say? Ray Marginson, as committed a university hierarch to cultural causes as one could hope to find, said no. *Meanjin* had enough difficulty securing university funding—and indeed was still subject (after thirty years) to an annual grant. Its enemies (many and diverse) would take the opportunity of ending the association. I should have known. The university had paid that large sum for the archive; built a special place for it in the Baillieu (complete with pissoir, which made Clem very proud); and paid the *Meanjin* archivist a higher salary than the *Meanjin* editor. It seemed the University of Melbourne believed that the only good *Meanjin* was a dead *Meanjin*.

Meanwhile there was a magazine to produce: the turbulence had delayed it dreadfully, as we were constantly reminded by phone calls from subscribers, in particular librarians, asking where it was. (It was a month late.) Margaret the secretary suggested, half-humorously, we should all go on strike; Nancy Kellock concurred. No-one would notice, I said; all that would do would be to justify appointing new people. We should just settle down to *Meanjin*'s new address: 'Between Story Street and Melodrama Lane'.

At this juncture I was visited by a publisher friend of Clem's, who was also friendly to me. Clem was railing against everybody, he reported, saying 'All the bastards have deserted me!' And I was waging 'a personal vendetta' against him. He felt persecuted. The only solution, Jeff Prentice said, was for me to allow him back into the office for one month. That idea was as welcome to me as the restoration of Governor Bligh to office for one day would have been to the colonists of New South Wales. If I didn't, said Prentice, people would say I pushed him out. That was a risk I was prepared to take. In the event Clem's character was so well known that I only once heard the accusation.

That was in the context of an hour, two days running, spent with Nina. Unlike Leeper, she presented herself as not being some kind of emissary at all: rather, she assumed a mantle of impartiality. When I showed no enthusiasm for her idea of me being editor while Clem became publisher (which would only give new form to the existing situation), she came straight to the point. 'Why don't you go? … You're young, you can easily find another job.' I didn't feel I should do that; the magazine would not survive. Well, she reminded me, it was Clem, ultimately, whom I had to satisfy. Fine, I said, but why does he always have to deal with me through intermediaries? I would like to see him, perhaps go to Stanhope. Nina didn't think that a good idea, since an Englishman's home was his castle. In Australia, expressed in a Russian accent, the proverb sounded even odder. But such a visit would probably achieve little anyway. Nina had a log of claims about my misconduct, completely discounting any consideration I had shown in this difficult situation. When I raised a few gripes of my own, she changed tack.

'You're as bad as Clem.'

'No,' I laughed. 'Not yet.'

'You're worse.'

'Worse, maybe. But not as bad.'

We were getting nowhere. The meeting ended in impasse.

Immediately afterwards I spoke to Ray Marginson, who said that the trust to take over the magazine would be set up in three weeks. He said, to my surprise, that he and the trust members generally had tried to keep Clem and me apart. Clem's charges as to my incompetence were ridiculous; 'He's nearly technically incompetent to run it himself, in law.' Marginson said he could not recommend him to be in receipt of the Lockie Bequest again. But it would be as well to write Clem a letter, he said. Butter him up. Shortly afterwards a suggested draft arrived from Serle. I followed most of it, protesting against the prospect of closure. But I added elements of my own. I pointed out that my general approach had been to keep the old order wherever possible, that I had established good relations with the other *Meanjin* senior men; and that I would like him to be 'a kind of patriarch to *Meanjin*', whom, once our position had been regularised, I would gladly consult from time to time.

Eventually, on 18 August, Serle announced that Clem had decided that the magazine should continue, and that he would not oppose my appointment by the trust—shortly to be the Meanjin Company—initially for twelve months. I was to remain in leading strings until the end of the year, which was neither a surprise nor particularly irksome. What was surprising in Serle's memorandum was Clem's insistence that I should not write anything about him in the journal. Clem also wished to see 'all this year's correspondence' when he came in; a request that contained the seed of further difficulty, since later he would insist on all subsequent files for the year being transferred as well.

The filing cabinets holding the archive were just sitting there, waiting to go to the Baillieu Library. I found a way of triggering action; Serle, aghast, went into a huddle with Clem. A time was set for when he would come to the office, but an additional requirement of the recent agreement was that I should absent myself (with the secretary, also now suspect). Clem would oversee the removal of the files, and simultaneously take away his books—I was to designate the current review copies. So I placed them on the couch, with a note saying the rest were his for the taking. I did not expect to be taken literally. When I returned to the editor's office, all of them had been swept away—including the best books for review, and even the editorial chair. The usurper would pollute it no more.

It did not take me long to see that this scorched earth policy might not be so terrible a thing. While designed to cripple, symbolically it liberated *Meanjin* from the dead, Clemmy hand of the past. Perhaps *Meanjin* needed to scale down a bit, become a little magazine again, in order to open itself to the new. More immediately, I decided to show people what Clem had done. There was an issue to launch, so I held a party in the office—among the empty shelves.

Clem had started calling me 'the lemming', as he imagined me hurtling towards self-destruction. Well, if there was going to be a propaganda war, I was determined to win it. A little flyer I had prepared (extremely restricted circulation) proffered forthcoming titles from the Meanjin Press: 'Meanjin, from Clemlin to Clothes Horse (The Story Street Years)'; 'Christ-Satan: A theological exposition of the problem' etc. Later, when Lynne Strahan was installed in the *Meanjin* archive in the Baillieu Library, I rang one day and enquired, 'Is that the Clematorium?' Irreverent, yes. But I was young. And there was a touch of bravado in all this: to make a success of *Meanjin* would take all I had, and perhaps then some.

The Meanjin Company held its first meeting in December 1974, and confirmed my appointment. I could now travel. I went for a holiday to the Blue Mountains, and Sydney. On this trip, or the next, I visited the critic DR Burns. At the other end of the couch sat a dachshund, which kept eyeing me balefully. 'Be careful,' said Ailsa Burns, 'he bites people.' Oh. 'What's his name?' 'Clem.' I was clearly a right candidate for the incisors, but somehow survived unscathed.

Not so in Melbourne. The remaining segment of the year's correspondence had to be delivered in due course to Nina, who received it icily. When it was suggested there be a public function to celebrate him, Clem declined. Occasionally we met, and he would slide into affability, even shaking hands; but two or three days later, there would always be a kick or a pinprick, as if to restore his integrity. I became disinclined to put into effect what I had proffered, that *Meanjin* under my editorship would bear the legend 'Founded by CB Christesen in 1940'. Meanwhile Leeper seemed to have washed his hands of the whole business: seeing me in University House, he came over, shook me by the hand, and wished me well.

The first issue over my name appeared in April 1975. Clem, I have recently learned, didn't think much of it, but was assured by Serle that the next would be better. It did contain an article on Clem's poetry, by an effusive Italian; I softened its asperities. As is often the case, a quarterly contains sleepers, in this instance the first published story by 'a new writer', Alex Miller. I was interviewed by the *Age*, presenting a doleful image to the world as I had gone there on crutches. There would be some radical shifts … A week later there was a response from Dorothy Green. She took umbrage at much of what I'd said, not least for the suggestion of a *Meanjin* tram. I sketched a reply. One of the lines ran, 'As for the *Meanjin* tram, 'twas a joke. I never expected to see it, least of all with Mrs Green conducting it up and down the columns of the newspapers.' But Clem held the ace: he still had not signed the deed of transfer. I screwed up my response and chucked it in the bin.

Eventually, in June 1975—fifteen months after I had first stepped into the *Meanjin* office—ownership of the magazine passed to the company. Meanwhile circulation increased dramatically, at one point reaching 3000 copies. The name of the game had been to make haste slowly, so that old subscribers wouldn't be frightened off before new ones were found. But Clem's dog-in-the manger attitude continued. He rose from the grave to oppose—alone among the directors—my change in format, even though it was a restoration of an earlier one of his own.

Nothing would satisfy him. When I ran across him a few days before *Meanjin* celebrated its fortieth anniversary with a big conference, I asked him to appear, saying I would do anything short of not being present myself to make that possible. But no. The feud continued even after

I resigned in 1982, since he claimed the right to read the total correspondence of my editorship. This I resisted, on the grounds that I had not held the position of editor in suzerainty to him; it was the company that had appointed me. He had already taken all correspondence from the period when he could claim that I was his employee. But Clem was insistent. When Judith Brett, my successor, told me that she had been out to 'Sans Hope', and that the only thing Clem wanted to talk about was me, I became even more wary. 'I think he wants to go through your correspondence to find a basis for legal action,' she said. Poor Geoff Serle found himself in the midst of another fight, this time an utterly sterile one.

Returning to these events forty years later—I am now a good bit older than Clem was at the time—I see them with greater clarity, if with some loss of detail. I also now know, as a result of working on this book, where Clem was coming from. (To be succeeded by a Jim—but the wrong one!) It seemed tragic that he must part from *Meanjin*, which he had founded and built up; but there comes a time when everybody must accept generational relegation, and appreciate that one can no longer claim a central position by right. This does not, of course, preclude surges of influence and effectiveness—but they will be on a more restricted scale.

There was another problem. By personality, Clem always preferred dominance to definition. When it came to choosing options, he was always too conscious of what he might be relinquishing; he was never fully convinced that any decision meant that certain options were now closed, and that a particular path could no longer be taken. In his personality, an itch to authority held together elements that were inchoate and centrifugal, and important wellsprings of his multi-talentedness. But this diversity brought fresh frustrations, since none of his skills could ever quite be advanced to excellence. He needed others to do that for him—which is why he was such a good editor.

Nina had partly coped with Clem by retreating into her own Russian world, and although she had been more active in securing eastern European writers for *Meanjin* in recent years, she does not seem to have exerted herself to clarify the issues. On the contrary, as one or two contemporaries remember, she stiffened his resistance.

Clem's predicament was worsened by a number of factors. One was that people had forgotten—and I scarcely knew—how much of his own money he had put into the magazine, on top of everything else. Another was that on the face of it, while he held the proprietary rights of the magazine, this did not fully correspond with workaday reality. No-one thought of *Meanjin* operating as a private venture; it continued as the result of extensive subsidy from the university, from the Literature Board and, as Clem was leaving, from the Victorian Ministry for the Arts. These agencies had become stakeholders too, and university notables had wearied of Clem. It would be Monash, not Melbourne, that gave him an honorary degree.

Beyond that, there were the many people who felt *Meanjin* must continue. Later, both the Marxist political scientist Alastair Davidson and the conservative critic John Carroll would, for a time, attend meetings of my group of consultants. But more immediately there was Geoff Serle, acutely aware through his own work (and that of his father) of Australian cultural traditions. He had been Clem's lieutenant, was a trusted friend, and was recognised as such by others involved with the magazine. Discussions with Marginson were in the direct line from those they used to have as student politicians. Holding his cards close to his chest, Serle had, in addition to sobriety of purpose, the coldness of temperament necessary to trudge determinedly on. Necessity demanded transfer, and he had found a successor.

And myself? I did not think it inappropriate to be asked to be assistant or associate editor; I was unsure of my ground when Serle returned and offered the editorship. But a second chance was not to be knocked back and, since I had specifically turned down the assistant position it seemed plain to me that editor I should be. Clem knew that—and, since I had no other base, had to give me a room in the building, something not given to any other aspirant. He wavered, and could be contradictory; the long-awaited letter he sent in February 1974 spoke of me rearranging the office, but also had me 'joining' *Meanjin*. Given the sale of the *Meanjin* archives, and the quid pro quo implicit in that, I thought I could trust to things being sorted out when I arrived.

Given the situation I found myself in, it seemed that the mandate of heaven would have to pass rather bumpily from Clem to me. (Would that it had been otherwise.) *Meanjin* must be rescued and revitalised: failure to do this would haunt me for the rest of my days. The magazine had become a community resource. Should it go, a whole nexus of funding and a subscription list would go with it. And so took place the *Meanjin* civil war. Out of it came conditions that have extended the magazine's life by some fifty years, sustaining a further ten editorships.

Just before I went to *Meanjin* Peter Handke produced a play, *The Ride across Lake Constance*. It referred to a German tale about a man who was lost in a blizzard, and just kept riding, all the more desperately because he could see no lights. He kept going, and eventually reached a small village. He went inside the inn, and, having ordered a drink, asked a man at the bar where he was. Once told, he turned pale and fell to the floor. Dead. Unwittingly, he had ridden across the large Lake Constance; that he had been on thin ice for so long hit him like a thunderclap.

The year 1974 was my ride across Lake Constance. For a long time I could not bear to look at Clem's issues of *Meanjin* with any thoroughness; they were still radioactive. That has now passed. This book is my delayed response to that wild ride. I now wonder (in both senses) how I had the nerve.

8

STEPHEN

LATE BLOOMING

1974–88

The changing context

STEPHEN SAW CLEM'S going as inevitable. He tried to counsel him, and regularly spoke with his old mate Geoff Serle, the architect of the changes at *Meanjin*. Instinctively he understood that the disappearance of that journal would create a vacuum that *Overland* could not hope to fill; on the contrary, its demise might accelerate changes in the cultural climate that could weaken his own magazine. But there were no immediate fears on that score, so he was conspicuously kind to the incoming *Meanjin* editor. I was invited along to an *Overland* lunch (and meeting); when it was over, Stephen walked with me part of the way. On parting, he suddenly said, 'I may be a bit of a prick, but I do my best'. A disarmingly humble thing to say to a novice.

Stephen at this stage had come to tag himself 'the senior literary magazine editor'. For Writers Week in Adelaide, 1976, he produced a photo of himself standing, in a lordly fashion, with a copy of the magazine firmly in hand. But a generation gap was apparent at the little magazine editors' conference that was held there. When Stephen spoke disparagingly of Ringwood, as a metaphor for suburbia, Michael Wilding gleefully retorted 'Penguin Books!'—for that was where they were then located. Jokes went the rounds about Stephen being the editor of *Overweight*. And that when he had flown to Perth he had demanded *two* seats.

But Stephen had never been so much on the inside running. In 1976 Ian Turner was deputy chair of the Australia Council, Barrett (Barrie) Reid on its Literature Board, while his old friend Nancy Keesing was appointed chair. It was an *Overland*-tilting board, not a *Meanjin* one. Stephen began to feel that he had tamed Sydney—a place where he never felt at home—symbolically conquering it with a large reception held at the Opera House. Seemingly he was in command. The moment did not last long.

In 1977 Stephen began keeping a diary: he felt that there had not been enough 'recording' in Australia, but it was also an indulgence. Seated in his newly completed library, with a fire roaring, he felt 'quite the gentleman'. Ever the Johnsonian figure, he even tried writing with a quill. He would pepper its pages with foreign phrases, for it was written with an eye to posterity: 'the diary is the most complex and the rarest of literary skills', Stephen maintained. Certainly he had a talent for it: in the early volumes there are extensive pen portraits of major literary figures, but also sharply caught impressions, such as these on board a naval vessel:

> the young sailors strangely touching with their combination of King's Cross tattoos, and simple kindnesses ('this is my mother's cake') and half-formed curiosities and awarenesses—one has artistic inclinations, another wanted to read up on [Erith] island; the young cook in his diffident way a combination of brashness and honesty.[1]

The diary also became a rampart, leading away from the world; refuge lay behind its battlements. There Stephen could express a growing uneasiness.

Part of this was physical: increasingly Stephen was aware of his own mortality. First there were spells of dizziness: he began to feel the need to slow down, to restrict the broad front of his activities. He gave up smoking—for a time—and then took up his pipe again. 'Am annoyed', he complained to his diary, 'with the way my stomach gets in the way when I do up my shoe-laces.' Dieting was essential—losing weight was a constant battle. There were also problems with an irregular heartbeat. Then, shortly after starting the diary, Stephen had the most serious depression he had ever known. Such episodes would recur: a little later, although a keen traveller, the thought of going overseas with a sore foot was enough to trigger 'the wicked & foolish thought of wishing for a mild heart attack, to keep me home or send me home'.[2]

But part of his 'dis-eased' condition, as he termed it, arose from the fracas surrounding the public lecture at the University of Melbourne given in September 1977 by the visiting psychologists Hans Eysenck and Arthur Jensen, who had propounded theories of variations in intelligence based on race and genetics rather than environmental factors. Stephen explained, in a letter to the *Age*, that he did not know whether such propositions were true or false, indeed he hoped they were false; but these high-standing researchers deserved a hearing, as a preliminary to analysing and discussing their views.

Stephen had nothing to do with the invitation, but had been put in charge of security for the lecture, which at the last moment was transferred to the exposed Wilson Hall. It was a melee: protesters, applying early, had managed to obtain a huge block of tickets, and turned up with drums and whistles. To these they added jeers and Nazi salutes, so that the meeting was disrupted. There were too many for the police to try to remove; Stephen ill-advisedly lunged at an Indigenous female demonstrator, trying to grab her whistle. A friend manoeuvred him away. 'I must have been very white', he recalled, as he walked back to his car and drove home. Tension now was overlaid with sadness: this was 'not really my scene any more'.

It was worse than that. Stephen's world view had been badly shaken. Liberal openness could no longer be presumed; instead he despaired at the 'increasing hold of "Left" totalitarianism'. He believed the protesters were Maoists, who had also taken over community radio station 3CR and were present in the ABC; and he was wary now of someone he saw as one of their leading spokespeople, Humphrey McQueen—for all his (conceded) charm. Stephen's depression returned: 'it's almost like walking in darkness all the time'. It deepened to the point of his becoming suicidal, perhaps partly because he had come to an unwelcome conclusion. He had begun to speculate that it might be necessary—in the long run—to 'go into alliance with the authoritarian right to guarantee the order without which we cannot function—confirming the prejudice of the fascist left.' Later he would moderate that, reflecting that 'the only place for *Overland* conservative left to go is to the progressive right. In a way it's the same place.'[3]

Old comrades: Ian Turner and Dorothy Hewett

Stephen nonetheless drew considerable sustenance from old associates, particularly those who had followed him out of the Party and continued to make waves in political and cultural life. Foremost among these was his closest friend, Ian Turner.

By 1975 the intensity of Turner's gaze shone through his passport photo; garbed in black, he looked like an Orthodox priest. Later, with his beard more florid and grizzled, he developed a surprising resemblance to Karl Marx. His politics though remained moderate—Marx he now styled as 'a moral philosopher before a political philosopher'. Turner had been sustained by the prospect of a Whitlam victory, and had worked hard for the Labor Party, using all his skills in argument and persuasion, as well as a tactician, to prevent a split at the time of the 1970 federal intervention in Victoria. His particular contribution was to draw up a new constitution for the party, formalising the factions. But the infighting he had often found 'degrading', so withdrew from active politics. He was sorely missed. Turner had little inclination to return, despite having remarked that he was 'an addict. There should be a Politics Anonymous for people like me.'[4]

As a public debater on the Vietnam War, with his terse, evidence-based, steadying way of speaking, Turner had become so well known that the ABC produced a television program on him as *The Making of a Radical*. Meanwhile, having sought out in England Stuart Hall and academics associated with the new cultural studies, Turner was sympathetic to the counterculture. He had been struck by the way it seemed some 90 per cent of the demonstrators in the first Melbourne Vietnam moratorium (1970) had been young. It was possible, Turner thought, that society might be seeing the first signs of a transformation of values as significant as that of the Renaissance and Reformation.

So he was indulgent towards student radicalism. He identified with it at Monash, seeing himself as its major explicator to the university authorities and the public. Then there was Turner's Ron Barassi memorial lecture—begun as he cast aside his coat, blew the whistle he wore around his neck, and opened a can of Carlton Draught. It had become an annual fixture, hailed by an audience of up to 500 beer-can popping students, who whistled, threw streamers and showered ticker-tape.[5] King of the kids, perhaps, but Turner was also a prince among men—strong, articulate, tactical. But his domestic life had never been so turbulent.

It went back a long way. In 1961 Stephen and Nita had been shocked when Turner left his first wife, Amirah. They thought of them both individually and as a couple, matching themselves; long before, Stephen may have had a rare fling with Amirah. From the great distance of Melbourne, Stephen had become Turner's counsellor, unobtrusive, and—so far as he could be—confirming. He told Turner in Canberra to cast away intellectual self-doubts, and realise that they were directly linked with his domestic crisis. Yet he knew there was more to them than that. More deeply, Turner was one of those people with 'a psychochemical predisposition to mordant humors', he wrote, and an incapacity for the simple happiness enjoyed by 'more simple and superficial people like myself'. At one point he urged Turner not to abandon the marriage, for the sake of the children.

But Turner had been determined to take up with his new love, Ann: her marriage with Edgar Waters had broken down. For Amirah, the crisis was compounded by the fact that Ann worked alongside her at Lyneham High School, a situation relieved when Ann went off to England. Some months later Ann joined Turner in Adelaide, where he had taken up a lectureship. For her part, Amirah lost little time in floundering. Instead of acting in an aggrieved fashion, she adopted a high tone, and managed to continue to show Ian love ('in the broadest sense'), accepting—up to a point—Turner's fecklessness. (He was exasperatingly casual about money matters.) But she drew the line at his repeated backsliding when it came to parental responsibilities. Her letters were characteristically good-humoured, although sometimes with an edge—once she signed off as 'A. Turner (the original)'.[6]

Turner had written to Stephen that, obsessed as he was with 'various deficiencies, failures and psychoses', he wasn't 'any good with any sort of relationships'. In the early 1970s that was an understatement. Not long after his first heart attack, Turner had gone to England on sabbatical leave and there became involved with a woman who was a potter. It ended once he returned to Australia, he told Ann. Then it emerged that they had remained in touch, and had—once Turner was in England again—resumed their relationship. Ann returned home, leaving him to it. (Later she went back to Edgar.) Meanwhile the English lover decided it was not working, and ended the relationship. Turner was suicidal: if only he could break through 'the wall of withholding which surrounds the centre of my being … to that innocent giving and accepting of intimacy that my childhood lacked'. In a way, he realised, he had been looking for a mother/lover. Women found that disconcerting.[7]

Stephen, whom Turner felt was the only person he could communicate with, once more was at hand (though again distant) with steadying advice. While telling Turner that he lacked a talent for pragmatism and improvisation, constantly seeking to insert things into patterns or theories, Turner nonetheless—paradoxically, wrote Stephen—had 'a genius for inspiring affection … You are, as you must know and as I have told you, the most loved man [in our circle] of our generation.' But in matters of love, it seemed, he was hopeless: too cerebral and too romantic at the same time. Although fully aware of a clash in expectations, Stephen told Turner that he thought it quite possible that Ann and he could come together again—despite his womanising. 'The unnerving thing about you, Turner,' he wrote, 'is that these women you discard, Gust and Waters, keep on loving you in their own masochistic way.'[8]

But events were to take another turn. Turner had drifted back into an affair with Leonie Sandercock, recently an ANU doctoral student who was now in London. He had misgivings, for she was much younger—playfully she referred to him as her 'Ancient Lover'. Leonie wanted to live with him; Turner was resistant at first, aware that she was yet to reach her peak—in most respects—while he was well past his. But there was little pressure, no expectation of it lasting forever: 'I have a fair idea', she told him, 'that most of Turner's relationships end when the lady decides she wants more of you than you're prepared to give.' Soon they returned, with Leonie moving into the Richmond house. Her acceptance in the *Overland* circle was immediate.[9]

The house—a high red-brick Victorian in Lennox Street, Richmond—was already the scene of great and varied parties, attracting writers, artists, musicians, academics and students, Richmond supporters and footballers, as well as political heavies, even before Turner became deputy chair of the Australia Council. It was a kind of open house, John McLaren recalled, 'the virtual centre of a free university, arts workshop and political think-tank'. For his part Stephen was capable of requisitioning it, announcing to Turner that an *Overland* meeting would be held there. Although they might meet formally only a dozen times a year, the annual boot camp on Erith Island served to prime the relationship and to refresh it.

In the mid-1970s Turner contributed solidly to the magazine, in particular his essay in autobiography, 'My Long March'. His pieces extended to a poem, written while in London. He could still be a laggard—'*I mean it too*', Stephen had to italicise, prodding him about a deadline. But Turner's contributions remained invaluable, providing, when needed, a necessary element of rigour. He wrote an important piece after the Dismissal of 1975 and the following election (which broke half a nation's heart). Cast in the style of a *New York Review of Books* article, it became a searching analysis of the difficulties of Labor in government, as well as a discussion of the Dismissal itself. Turner was cautious about collusion between Kerr and Fraser, which he said could not (yet) be proven. Beyond that, he offered a magisterial statement of Labor's prospects and challenges, offering the broadest sociological perspectives. But as if aware he hadn't much time left—the contributions tapered off as Turner focused on his short history of unionism and what was intended to be the keystone of his work in popular culture. He had always had an interest in adult bawdry, children's games and graffiti—as the last survivors of a popular culture in the old, orally transmitted sense; now he was focusing on writing a history of the (then) VFL, the Victorian Football League. As *Up Where, Cazaly?* it was completed by Leonie.[10]

Stephen also remained strongly attached to Dorothy Hewett, now living with Merv Lilley, whom he saw as a '*Summer of the Seventeenth Doll* man … a cane cutter fallen among eggheads'—with their two daughters, in what he saw as a squalid Victorian den in Jersey Road, Woollahra. The ambience was one of criminal chic, 'where people just walk in off the street and take whatever of Merv's tools and Dorothy's books they want'. But she was always 'the same dear old Dorothy, with whom we share so much of our pasts and we talk a special language to each other'.

In the wider world, censorship had ceased to be an issue in the 1970s, but as Australia drifted towards a more litigious culture, defamation emerged as a serious threat to writers. Dorothy Hewett would be in the front line. Ever lightly transmuting her own experience in her work, she had written a poem called 'Uninvited Guest'. It is strong stuff: despite a smothering in lyricism as the poem progresses, allusions to rotten genes, an autistic child and the present wife's hysterectomy altogether makes it a savage attack. Lloyd Davies, Dorothy's abandoned husband, didn't react to it strongly at first, probably regarding it as going with the territory. Indeed, he had always been indulgent towards Hewett, and on her return to Perth even gave her free legal advice. But—urged by his wife (more insulted than he) and perhaps by the reaction of others, once the poem appeared in a collection he decided to sue. Later, when Currency Press published Dorothy's play *The Tatty Hollow Story*, he demanded they withdraw it—along with *The Chapel Perilous*—or he would sue them too.

Given the loose nature of the libel laws, writers generally felt threatened by this turn of events. Stephen, with Turner, was at the centre of a Literary Defence Committee: David Williamson was active on it, while Patrick White and Manning Clark lent their names. In the midst of it all sat Hewett, roly-poly with her head on her hands, making mordant remarks. So scabrous, yet also showing a terrible vulnerability. 'My dearest ogress', Stephen began one letter to her.

When the battle was still centred on the poem, Stephen visited the Davies' home in Perth. (Indeed while there Stephen was told by Nita that the impending *Overland* contained a serious libel, which resulted in a recall of all issues and the insertion of a new page.) He had been moved to intervene as one of the few people who had 'open lines' to both parties. (Twice he had published stories by Davies.) Stephen saw the difficulties, and the pain, the Davies sustained with their eighteen-year-old autistic child, but found the mother a termagant: Hewett was 'Your fucking psychopathic no-hoper friend …' 'Just a moment, Jo,' Stephen interrupted. 'Dorothy's a friend of ours. May I remind you that your husband married her.' 'There was a very pleasing silence for a few moments', Stephen told Turner, 'until the fusillade started again.' The outcome was that Stephen managed to persuade Davies to settle out of court, and to reduce his claim for damages substantially.

Turner, abroad when the poem was the issue, now acted as Hewett's champion. (There had been a time when they had been spasmodic lovers—she had found him crippled by an incapacity to trust, whereas for Turner, Dorothy was 'more knowing, more vulnerable and more articulate than the others'.) In a broadcast Turner pointed out that, when it came to art, invasion of privacy was an unusually difficult matter. Any law, or possible fear of the legal process, should respect 'the right of the creative artist to rework imaginatively their life experience'.

The general (legal) opinion was that Davies had, in the new battle with Currency, overreached himself. But Hewett found considerable damage had been done: for a while publishers and booksellers were wary of handling her work. And for 'quite some time it stopped me from writing'. Around this time, since we got on, I asked her to write a couple of nonfiction pieces for *Meanjin*—the journal she always remembered as having first taken her up. Stephen, understandably after all his efforts (most of which I was unaware), was annoyed—Dorothy was an *Overland* person, and I had poached her. But ultimately the choice was hers. She admired Stephen's loyalty, and the way he had fought for her. But as a writer she was on the lookout for opportunities, and did not feel obliged to practise reciprocity.[11]

Faculty and university

People lunching at University House—the former professorial residence now the University of Melbourne staff club—did not do so unobserved. For across the lounge, with his back to the bay window, Stephen watched people as they signed in guests. For the one-time commando and signals man, a vantage point was second nature … gathering intelligence.

Stephen's career as an educationist—or rather, a historian of education—reads impressively. After the Nuffield fellowship, which enabled him to write his PhD, he joined the School of Education staff in 1966, and was appointed reader nine years later. Even by the standards of the day, his duties were light—a couple of dozen lectures a year, seminars, some postgraduate supervision, and the editing of *Melbourne Studies in Education*. Already latitudinarian, that annual series was tweaked to include AA Phillips' superb memoir of three schoolmasters, more material on Papua New Guinea, and the texts of the lectures by Eysenck and Jensen—which had no overt reference to race.[12]

In the faculty Stephen, while capable of kindness, was a fractious presence: he would turn up at staff meetings with a pile of letters and papers he would (ostentatiously) read, stand over the photocopier for long periods attending to *Overland* business, and was rarely seen in the tea-room. This caused resentment—at least among some colleagues—whom Stephen dismissed as being less productive than he (true). The imperturbable, lordly behaviour extended—so Stephen recorded in his diary—to coping with heatwave conditions by sitting at his desk in the nude.

Like an eighteenth-century clergyman, Stephen regarded the university as providing him with a living—enabling him to pursue his intellectual interests. It was a time when one well-known philosopher could submit, as his research report, 'I spent my time at Oxford thinking.' For his part, Stephen was appreciative of the way sabbatical leave (or study leave, as it was now styled) enabled him to travel abroad for up to six months at a time, carrying out various pursuits (including book-collecting) in England. (An earlier trip to Canada was, however, specifically focused on technical education.)

It was not only on return that Stephen found himself chained to uncongenial colleagues—he 'despise[d] their narrowness and conformity', and particularly the empire-building sociologists. For them, apart from lacking expertise, he was too quirky. Stephen (of all people) had shocked a notable educationist when he told him, 'Schools have to be structured for rebellion, not message.' His belief that 'we are interested in the past because it is part of the present' also had a radical edge; together these two statements point to an underlying progressivist narrative. Hence the importance, Stephen believed, of the historian—not overly specialised, but a supreme generalist—acting as an integrative agent, drawing these elements together. When a professorial colleague retired, Stephen had hopes of a chair. But he was soon made aware that being 'too much of a generalist' told against him, as did his 'insubordination'. 'Too sceptical,' Stephen noted. 'Not enough of a machine man.'

Stephen's consolation lay in his 'delightful, decent but pretty rough students from the western suburbs, struggling up into the middle classes, with their unruly technical school pupils and their families and houses on the basalt plains!' Loyally they came to all his classes, and he was more appreciative of them than this language might suggest: his years as Party functionary and peace activist had taught Stephen to recognise working-class decencies. When—before a group of these students were invited to Ti-Tree Lane—Nita asked, 'Shall we watch out for our books?' Stephen replied, 'No. They're not middle-class.'[13]

Towards the end, particularly when he (correctly) believed he was being pushed into retirement when most productive, Stephen was quite outspoken. 'He has taken care', Kevin Childs reported in the *Age*, 'to see the university as no more than the place where he works, and that, to a large extent, his real life exists outside it, fond as he is of his students.' In 1971 Stephen had noted the potential for a drift towards managerialism in Canadian universities, a portent for developments in universities here. For this reason—although originally he thought it would be ineffective—he came to support the University Assembly, drawn from across the staff and student body: 'the very fact that a powerful group among the academic mafia want to get rid of it suggests it has some nuisance value'. He had never been asked to sit on an appointments committee—despite being perhaps the only staff member working on Indigenous history and sociology, and with experience of publishing. A spell as deputy chair of his department did little to change his perspective. Increasingly (given he had the customary tenure) Stephen felt a free agent.[14]

The issue that really inflamed him was the university's proposed ultimate demolition of the Percy Grainger Museum. (The building was commonly held to look more like a public lavatory than anything else.) Elected secretary of a Grainger Museum Protection Committee, Stephen worked with Barry Jones, who elicited statements of support from such musical luminaries as Benjamin Britten, Michael Tippett and André Previn. This came as a bit of a shock to many: Grainger's rising international standing had in Melbourne been eclipsed by the continuing buzz about his sexual proclivities.

Meanwhile Stephen had written to the *Age*, pointing to the over-mighty medical-science lobby, who wanted the site: 'To destroy the

Grainger Museum', he concluded, 'would be to demonstrate the intellectual vandalism of the university, not only to this generation but … to the future.' 'The more I think of the bloody university,' he told his diary, 'and its determination to destroy that building the more I grind my teeth and am determined to prevent them.' His tactics varied: writing to the chancellor to point out the university would be in legal contempt of Grainger's will, to suddenly getting up and ostentatiously walking out of a special meeting on the matter. Ray Marginson, who was propounding the plans, looked on with distress at this antic of his old friend. Perhaps there came a flashback from their student days: Stephen had then once been even more emphatic, when, after some dispute, he was helped by a Labor Club colleague to hold Ray by the feet as they dangled him upside-down from a window. Or perhaps not. Later in the day, they were seen at a university function, chatting to each other amiably over drinks.[15]

Overland: poetry

If, in the university context, Stephen played the part of a Tory radical, in the wider world it was his (liberal) conservatism that people found most characteristic. Stephen knew he needed a countervailing influence, and poetry—where there was now more heat than light—might provide the locus for it. Radicalism here could offset the more traditional tone of the articles and stories elsewhere in the magazine.

Right from the time he was appointed *Overland*'s poetry editor in 1968, Barrie Reid was not so much a breath of fresh air as a wind of change. He advised Stephen on many matters, including how to engage with the New Left; despite his own classic tastes, Reid was a keen reader of *Rolling Stone*. A poet himself, he had been something of a protégé of Clem's when starting out in Brisbane as an editor of *Barjai*, and was on the verge of having a book published with the Meanjin Press: it had advanced to proof stage when it was pulled. Thereafter Reid had no further business with *Meanjin*—but did with *Ern Malley's Journal* and other literary ventures. Meanwhile his chosen career as a librarian put him in charge of establishing and maintaining standards of library service throughout the state, so that he travelled frequently. Capable, deft and controlling, Reid dismissed his library colleagues as 'mainly dull bureaucrats, public servants of the dreariest kind'. He went to considerable pains to keep his literary life altogether separate.

For a time that was centred on a house at St Andrews, to the north-east of Melbourne, which he shared with his partner, the bookseller Philip Jones. It became a magnet for young poets: for the Greek anarchist Pi O, it was the first place he got to know outside Fitzroy. 'I long ago thought that the best I could do,' Reid noted in his dairy, 'given my limitations, was to write poetry, passionately build libraries, plant as many trees as possible, feed my friends when I could …' There was a kindness behind his waspish humour. But in a short space of time Greenhill burnt down, Reid developed Hodgkin's disease, and had to end his career in librarianship. Following a long association with John and Sunday Reed, in 1983 he moved into Heide (splitting up with Jones in the process). There, as custodian of the legend, he became rather grand: after serving tea and cucumber sandwiches, he would sit imperiously—oblivious of the house smell of dogs and cats—'a lean old man with long legs and radiant blue eyes'. Perhaps he would reminisce, of the journey he had made to Fraser Island, with the young Sid Nolan when he first explored the Eliza Fraser myth.

Drawn more and more towards Barrett Reid (as he now styled himself) was the tearaway poet Shelton Lea. 'Being a poet is the living of it,' Lea told his biographer. He was a riveting performer of his verse. Barrett was struck by Shelton's good looks, his presence and his raw intelligence—this orphan boy, adopted and brought up in a severely disapproving Toorak household, this veteran of jails … in need of mentoring. For his part, Lea recognised the rebel in Barrie—'It is you who are the dangerous one', he declared; smoothed down by culture, a preference for a formal style, and a native talent for intrigue. Acknowledging Barrett as the most important influence in his life, the bisexual Shelton became Barrett's lover.[16]

While he favoured the young—every issue brought a clutch of new names, some of which would never be sighted again—Reid was capable of layered editing. He had praised—and criticised—people on both sides of 'this nasty gang war' the poets were waging, and had no personal friendships (or enmities) with leaders on either side (the perfect public servant). He expected, though, he would find 'more good poems, by my lights', on the *Poetry Australia* side of Murray, Gray, Hart et al. than on the *New Poetry* side of Adamson, Tranter and Forbes. Having been an isolate himself—still writing poetry—his response was 'Give me … the great isolates … every time.'

Indeed, his choices could not be anticipated. In the period under consideration (1974–88) Shelton Lea made nine appearances in *Overland*, but another in the circle, the performance poet Eric Beach, appeared twenty-two times, complete with interview and songs. (Plus a book of poems, once Stephen ventured into poetry publishing again.) Similarly, women were well represented, the poet JS Harry being second in the listings; others included Fay Zwicky and Judith Rodriguez. Moreover, Reid was always glad to publish a number of 'names', particularly for special issues. Robert D FitzGerald, AD Hope and Judith Wright were sighted in the magazine, while more regular contributions came from poets such as Thomas Shapcott, Dorothy Hewett and Vincent Buckley.

'Barry has virtually a blank cheque with the poetry,' Stephen explained to his advisers. Poets were strange beasts, best walled up in a kind of national park: Stephen lumped them together, italicised, on the contents page of the magazine, without benefit of the poems' titles, sometimes without page numbers. He appreciated that poetry was the workshop of the language, even if he did not always appreciate the poetry. Indeed he likened it to dentistry (implicitly placing himself in the dental chair), for 'serious poetry has become professionalised', poets writing for each other. He told of one poetry editor he met who was happy with his magazine's circulation of 200, 'because that was the limit of those who understand'. The problem was that in the wider world more poetry was being written—and published—than ever. 'It is a phenomenon of our time', Barrie Reid told Graham Rowlands, anxious about covering the ground when reviewing poetry books.

Stephen, ever the realist, realised *Overland*'s readers felt 'more cut off from the poetry than from any other part of the magazine', but understood that beyond the 'professional stream' there was little good poetry being written. The problem for *Overland,* as Barrie Reid formulated it, was that of 'a "democratic" magazine going for a mass readership and believing in poetry at a time when the poets do not believe in a mass readership'. Nonetheless he made concessions. While the concrete poetry of Richard Tipping made for a vigorous presence, Reid also published the work of John Blight—direct, committed, environmentally alarmed and edging towards contemporary techniques. Blight was the perfect crossover for *Overland* readers: tactically, his poems appeared repeatedly. Also to the fore were Frank Kellaway, gently meditative and reassuring in his rhyming, and Bruce Dawe, his work as mordant as it was accessible. Stephen declared Barrie Reid 'the best poetry editor in Australia'.[17]

But Reid was seen as a schemester, arousing intense dislike from a number of the members of *Overland*'s board. Stephen handled him with kid gloves: when a stand-in during Reid's three-month absence usurped the title of poetry editor and began to act accordingly, Stephen made a handsome apology. Later he made Reid assistant editor. He accepted the way Reid preferred to work behind the scenes—he had been the initiator of the Victorian Premier's Literary Awards, and had characteristically ducked being interviewed on *Overland*'s poetry policy. Stephen put up with being prodded into greater contemporaneity, but resisted 'the insatiable quest for modernity and youth that Barrie thinks *de rigueur*'.

What he found harder to take was the tone of Reid's remarks, with 'that irritatingly *de haut en bas* [condescending] way he gratuitously affects'. In public, all was praise; the grumbling went into Stephen's diaries. There he complained of Reid's dilatoriness in handling manuscripts, the last-minute pulling of material already set—involving, he wrote, the 'kind of scene' that had to be accepted 'in return for the many benefits when one works with homosexuals'. (That was a flickering prejudice he never quite shook off.) In practice he and Nita regarded Barrie as 'a dear friend and support, who has taught us much and shares our outlook'.

Part of the problem was that Reid's suggestions always entailed more work for Stephen—at a time when his interests were diverging away from *Overland*. So Reid took every opportunity to press for more space: at times the poetry section could take up to a quarter of the magazine. 'Here are the singers', he wrote in submitting one batch for publication: 'let them sing, you prosy old bastard.'[18]

Overland: short stories and Swag

Apart from the poetry, Stephen explained to his advisers, 'I feel that the main responsibility for the feel and tone of the magazine is mine.' This extended to the short stories. Generally, like *Meanjin*, *Overland* published eight or nine a year. Although Stephen's own taste was centred on John Morrison (author of 'the best Australian short story in this century'), the writer to score highest was Morris Lurie, from whom eight stories appeared in the magazine between 1974 and 1988. Their comic exuberance is invariably centred on a young male character always slightly at odds with the world, wherever he may be, for some of the stories—foregrounding their sophistication—were written about being an expatriate. Lurie is also more preoccupied with Jewish fathers than Jewish mothers.

Second-most appearing was James McQueen, whose carefully written stories, often based on a particular incident, owed something to the yarn: there was life in social realism yet. In contrast, almost as many stories came from Jonathan Dawson: short roller-coasters, switching subjects and levels of seriousness (a kind of splicing—he went into film), witty and urbane. Stephen was indulgent towards the expatriate writer Desmond O'Grady, but three times published stories by the emerging writers Garry Disher and Barry Hill. Among the double scorers were Elizabeth Jolley and DM Foster; Stephen quickly got behind Tim Winton. As before, overseas writers rarely appeared: a notable exception was two stories from Naomi Mitchison, who had become a personal friend and whom Stephen visited in Scotland. Otherwise, among the un- and scarcely knowns, an impressive number of 'name' writers made a single appearance.[19]

The tent pole of the *Overland* print circus remained 'Swag'. Stephen found it a challenge to write: he could be garrulous enough when he wanted to be, but—underestimating his own combativeness—declared himself 'ridiculously diffident' when it came to pontificating editorially. Part of it was that, as he grew older, there 'was less I want to convince others about … burning spears become sparklers'. The editorial tone was muted: the word was specially added for 'An Editorial Swag' in the twenty-fifth anniversary issue.

Overland was so 'closely linked' with its readers, he believed, that it did not feel it should tell them what to think, indeed was not always sure itself of what it thought. It remained open—'There is no single way forward', Stephen declared. While always on the Left/liberal/Labor/socialist side of the political spectrum, the magazine must always remain accessible to the 'intelligent general reader'. That remained the hypothetical matron of the Port Hedland hospital: Stephen joked that she deserved a free subscription.

Because it eschewed outright editorialising, 'Swag' could assume a genial tone as Stephen presented his patchwork quilt—announcements of prizes, reflections on his own reading, news of new and local ventures that needed encouragement, and comments on the literary scene in general. There were too many academics on committees awarding prizes; many increasingly wrote in a jargon all of their own; similarly, as editors emerged more confidently as a profession, they tended to behave more and more arbitrarily. Then there was his concern about the 'extremely restrictive and dangerous' libel laws, and a beef about rising postal charges. They could tip the balance: magazines, with their hand-to-mouth existence, could be forced to close.[20]

But most of all he was concerned about the Australia Council. Stephen had not been happy about the old Council for the Arts, and the dominance of advisers (even with the Whitlam government), like the formidable bureaucrat Jean Battersby; he was appalled by the way Geoffrey Blainey had been rolled as chair of the Literature Board. Mollified to some degree by Ian Turner's appointment as deputy chair of the new Australia Council, Stephen—endeavouring to be fair—handed 'Swag' over to Turner to expound the council's policies. But his general line remained unchanged, and clear. When it came to the arts, government agencies were clunky. As his ally John McLaren pointed out (also in 'Swag'), the Industries Assistance Commission had, when investigating the performing arts, simply applied the 'demonstrably false assumptions' of the free market economy 'to what was essentially an issue of values'. And the Australia Council, instead of being lean and decentralised, had become, in Stephen's words, 'a monstrous enterprise … bureaucracy for bureaucracy's sake'. The battle to win government subsidy had been bad enough, but now there was an ongoing struggle with a bureaucratic tar-baby. 'Swag' provided readers of *Overland* with the latest instalments.[21]

Once, separate from 'Swag', there was an editorial account of a visitation made by officials. They seized a manuscript on Menzies' overruling a government committee in order to permit British atomic testing, in adverse weather conditions, at Maralinga in 1956—despite the threat to local Indigenous people, and ultimately to cities on the eastern seaboard. The typist was compelled to hand it over: there was no official communication with *Overland*. Twenty-one years later the article was scarcely radioactive: the weapons were obsolete, while British 'delusions of imperial grandeur … are now fortunately laid to rest'. But the article had been destroyed, and sources intimidated.

Overland: other articles

Generally, Stephen had relied on Ian Turner to provide an *Overland* commentary on politics. A year after Turner died he went for broke and, prompted by one of Max Harris's newspaper columns, decided to set down his own thoughts about the political scene. 'I do believe we have constructed,' he wrote, 'partly by luck, a better society than exists anywhere else', but there were those—mostly the 'socialist Left' of the Victorian ALP—who would undermine it. Effectively they were totalitarian in their aims, speaking of the Australian people's 'false consciousness'—a concept, Stephen believed, 'used by the Left to excuse themselves when they had failed to move the people'. China was no 'white hope', just as Russia had proved itself not to have been. And the Whitlam government was 'more disastrous than most of us on the Left are willing to admit.' What Labor could get done in power was actually quite limited, even in the unlikely event of his comrades allowing Hawke to become leader and then prime minister.

Stephen's remark that Malcolm Fraser was, for all he knew, 'personally, a nice enough fellow', caused some offence among readers, and the piece as a whole drew more letters or comment than he had received in the previous twenty-five years of running the magazine. His closest friends did not dissent, although two said, 'We may think these things, but we don't tell people.' He subsequently explained that, given his past—having fought in an anti-fascist war, spending thirteen years in the Communist Party (half of them as a functionary), living in Communist societies, and with a wife whose family was wiped out by the Nazis—he was skewed against any prospect of totalitarianism. 'Far more than my younger colleagues, my thoughts are in the concentration camps.' And this could take very practical forms. Once, driving to the airport to catch a plane, the Murray-Smiths noticed some anti-Semitic graffiti. On the way back, Nita was surprised when Stephen stopped the car there, got out, went over to the shop window, and applied a paint scraper he had specially bought in Adelaide.[22]

But now Stephen gladly handed over 'Swag' to Leonie Sandercock, who wrote a vigorous rebuttal of his column. Much of what Stephen had written, she declared, could be run as an editorial in *Quadrant*. What had happened to equality, social justice, redistribution? Socialism had become 'such a dirty word'. Capitalism throughout the world was in crisis—given rising unemployment—just when the right had seized the ideological initiative. 'It's indicative of the ground *gained* by the Right that ordinary workers ... are in favour of tax cuts that would contribute to the dismantling of that very welfare state for which a previous generation of Lefties in Australia fought so hard.' It was not true for Stephen to say that politics is not as important as we sometimes think. The Left must fight back. Particularly now, when we were on the cusp of great changes brought about by technology. Shortly afterwards Sandercock returned to the theme, with a review article as resonant now as the day it was written:

> the new technologies, combined with limited sources of energy in a laissez-faire society confronting diminishing resources, could produce a future dominated by a technological elite, with a permanent caste of unemployed ... incorporating [new] methods of social control with perhaps a bit of genetic engineering thrown in too. The new miniaturized technology [the silicon chip] increases the likelihood of these dystopian futures.

Sandercock had hoped that other contributors would explore the various challenges she had highlighted, but practically no-one continued the debate. Even so, Stephen recognised the importance of her views and the value of her name on the masthead: he urged her not to resign from the editorial board when she moved to America. Her feminist perspective was sorely needed—and largely absent—despite Stephen's reflection that 'all females should be given a handgun at birth, to counter male physical superiority'.[23]

A debate did occur over multiculturalism. It was temperate at first, cautionary, occasioned by Geoffrey Blainey's assault on immigration policy, argued in his *All for Australia* (1984). Immigration historian AT Yarwood was to some degree persuaded by the book—particularly as, in a time of rising unemployment, it was the *scale* of Asian migration that was being attacked. Appearing alongside was Robert Birrell's comparison with the Canadian experience, identifying a number of factors that worked for greater liberality there, despite higher unemployment.

A couple of years later, given the greater sense of possible white backlash, *Overland* returned to the subject. Sean Regan, having lived in Suva, drew comparisons with Fiji: its divisions persisted, but it had successfully moulded institutions around them. Australia was muddling through. 'We have undermined the nation,' he wrote, 'but do not have the disposition to build a healthy republic. We will therefore go half-way ... and then call a halt, degenerate before the fact ... The civic culture ... will soon become irretrievably sterile ... A multicultural society has, by definition, no cultural heart.' John McLaren vigorously responded in the next issue. There was no inevitable creation of 'mutually exclusive and warring tribes': the United States was a shining example of one nation having arisen out of the elements of many. 'Multiculturalism', McLaren wrote, 'is neither a movement nor a doctrine, but an approach to Australian history and society based on recognition of the fact of our diverse origins.'[24]

As ever, Stephen was alive to Indigenous issues. He agreed with Regan's summation of white Australians: 'They took the land on credit. Now they must pay the interest.' Although he thought land rights to be largely a symbolic issue, he gradually drifted into supporting them. Stephen was alive to the enormity of the dispossession—he took Nita's pupils to the site of middens, telling them they were standing on 249 centuries of history, whereas they represented only one. He was always saddened when he came across these remnants: in the end he came to see the eradication of the Indigenous as Australia's equivalent of the Holocaust.

It was 'the collective memory hole of white Australia', something for which all whites in this country—whether the descendants of those who came 150 years ago, or only recently arrived themselves—had 'to bear moral responsibility'. He rejoiced that the Tasmanians in particular, far from being extinct, now had a stronger presence than at any time since the 1820s. Indeed what turned out to be Stephen's very last *Overland* contained a segment of articles about the fate of their nineteenth-century ancestors. And to drive the point home, a piece of rapportage from northern Australia packed a real punch: the author comes to realise that the laconic, slightly hostile treatment he'd been receiving is because he's a little dark-skinned himself. The old mindset is still there.[25]

Overland also began to include material that Clem had been desperately looking for: cultural criticism, with a sociological dimension. Looking at popular culture was becoming fashionable—it seemed to be the key to understanding broad social shifts—and Stephen Alomes provided a useful conspectus of the development of cultural studies. But first came an insightful article by Glen Lewis, concerned about the rightward shift in politics after the Dismissal. It was, he pointed out, part of a worldwide phenomenon; conservatives had succeeded in creating a more dynamic image for themselves. Here this had proceeded hand-in-hand with a resurgence of the old ocker values—indeed the new conservatism and the new ockerism were related developments. There was a tacit alliance between Joh Bjelke-Petersen and the advertising man John Singleton.

Alomes carried this further in a piece called 'The Patriot Game', looking at the Bicentennial Authority and a number of advertising campaigns including 'Advance Australia'—which he saw as clearly aiming 'to change Australian social attitudes and nurture a compliant work force'. The ultimate aim was 'the end of the Australian weekend and penalty rates … replaced by unlimited shopping hours and American business practices in white or blue collar workplaces'. Picking up from Ian Turner, Alomes wrote of consumer capitalism. The transition from a general moralism to hedonism was not simply tactical: it was matched by the transition from production-oriented capitalism to consumer capitalism. Things were more shallow now: visual images and consumer goods were at the heart of it. Writing of the Bicentennial Authority, Alomes predicted, 'Whatever the budget, whatever the disputes, patriotism will be as common as beer in Australia by 1988.'[26]

Much of *Overland* was like a conversation. This could be seen in the tone of David Martin's random perceptions after the Dismissal; and in the continuing discussion (until semiologists joined in) on popular culture. A politician like Neville Wran was caught thinking aloud—for so reads a graduation address Stephen published. But the political sinews could always be tightened. Stuart Macintyre, in 'Righteousness and the Right', conceded that there was a place for a conservative journal in Australia, only *Quadrant*—whose twenty-fifth anniversary was celebrated with the book he was reviewing—wasn't it. In fact, it had run off the rails at the very beginning, since James McAuley concentrated 'on ideas rather than historical processes, on values rather than social relationships'. The journal had always been 'ideologically compulsive'. An acrid exchange concerning CIA involvement followed—until Stephen closed it, agreeing with Macintyre that 'This *Quadrant* business is becoming silly.'[27]

International affairs were not much present in the pages of *Overland*, but Stephen's own affair with Papua New Guinea continued. Articles appeared on a number of subjects, ranging from the Russian anthropologist Nikolai Miklouho-Maclay (known to Tolstoy) to descriptive accounts and an important review article, entitled 'A Nation in the Womb', on Paul Hasluck's account of PNG when he was minister for Territories. It was written by John Gunther, a leading official in the territory for much of the time. On another tack, an article by WR Stent picked up the case of the activist schoolteacher Brian Cooper, whom Stephen had championed years before. It traced the whole, sad story, through to his trials, subsequent imprisonment—and suicide. A cultural activist, Ulli Beier, reviewed a Papua New Guinean autobiography, a glimpse into another world. Stephen also provided the obverse: an appreciative review by the poet Russell Soaba of Randolph Stow's novel set there, *Visitants*. Papua New Guinean poetry also trickled through the magazine.

In May 1974 Stephen (and Nita) went back to the territory, invited to attend a major seminar at the new university. They stayed with Amirah and Ken Inglis (now the vice-chancellor); Stephen, in the 'New Guinea Notes' he wrote for *Overland*, was struck by the contrasts with the New Guinea he had known, and by the goodwill of ordinary folk; it could not hide an edginess from some of the local elite, as they nudged the whites forward to relinquishing power. Moving about, they met the famous white pioneers Jim Taylor and Mick Leahy, who had brought the Wahgi Valley into contact with the rest of the world: with its 1 million people, it was the most significant 'discovery' of the twentieth century. Meeting these men, he reflected, was like meeting Hume and Hovell.

In the Highlands, Stephen was overcome by the spectacle of the Goroka Show—with its mud-men, moss-men, and the rest of the males decked out in bird of paradise feathers, pulsating and ululating as they beat their drums and danced, mobs of them, their mock fights threatening to spill over into real violence. Stephen declared it 'the last great spectacle of its kind the world can mount'. At times in Papua New Guinea Stephen felt like a ghost, a voyeur; but there was something very appealing about it.

Both Stephen and Nita were reminded of Prague in 1949: something revolutionary was in the air. 'To move from the Australian beer-guts society to this', he felt, 'was like a triple shot of adrenalin. I would like to have the courage to take a job there for a while.'[28]

One of the ways Stephen held the readership of *Overland* was by ensuring that the material it carried varied so widely. There was something in it for everyone. '*Overland* manages to do', David Martin told him, 'what is very hard: it somehow never changes—at core—but yet it reflects change.' Part of the trick—apart from a breadth of opinion—was to have some personalised pieces. So while there were few articles on international affairs, there were a string of 'Letters from …' with people giving their personal impressions of a place. Eventually this would extend to a series on Australia, with Peter Goldsworthy notably inverting the usual image of Adelaide to write about 'The Detroit of the South'. Among the overseas letters, Irish ones were prominent—Ian Turner perhaps providing the explanation when he said, 'There is nothing of Ireland in my blood, but … something of her in my heart.' The 'Letter from Moscow' was, unusually, written by a local, the dissident Roy Medvedev, who reported in 1986 of hopeful signs of a cultural thaw in the Soviet Union. Later came a 'Letter from China', written under the pseudonym Victor Ye. Stephen was rather proud to have made an arrangement to take regular contributions from him on daily life in China, believing it to be the first such arrangement to be made by an Australian publication.[29]

A second stream of easy reads were the pieces of memoir and autobiography that *Overland* published. Having written himself on colonial childhoods, Stephen was unusually keen to have others recall their earliest years. A winner here was Rupert Lockwood's remarkably layered account of a Wimmera boyhood. That was an extract from an autobiography, not completed. Others were major stand-alone pieces, such as Ian Turner's 'My Long March', an account of his journey with, and through, the Communist Party; and the historian WK Hancock's 'Testimony'—more reflective on reading and observing, and ending with an assault on the American alliance. Another elderly gent, Sir Walter Crocker, turned in a number of elegant, realistic assessments of people he had known—Evatt, Hasluck and Casey; Elizabeth Riddell chimed in with a sprightly account of her late friendship with Maie Casey.

A refreshing counterpoint to these retrospectives was John Herouvim's buoyant, detached and humorous account of his Greek mother joining in an anti–Sir John Kerr demonstration. Often there were short pieces, such as Manning Clark pondering the battlefields of France, or the vignette Iris Milutonivic wrote, correctly seeing the appearance at her front door of a pair of vacuum-cleaner salesmen as the moment (1935) the Depression was ending. Among the others—too numerous to mention—were pieces on recently deceased writers. Alan Seymour's long article on Laurence Collinson was a case of *Overland* burying its dead, but others were recalled, Brian Fitzpatrick a number of times. As time went on, there were more and more of these, the price of the magazine's increasing longevity. Essays, rather than *Meanjin*'s shorter, funerary 'tributes'; the felt obligation to run them was among the barnacles literary magazines acquire as they sail on.[30]

At the same time, *Overland* was the site of a continuing discussion on the nature of the Australian poetry scene. 'This is a good time to embark on a career as a poet in Australia', remarked Peter Porter, who volunteered that if he had been a generation younger, he would have stayed, not gone to England. But Stephen's anxieties expressed in 'Swag' about the contradictions evident in the writing, marketing and reading of poetry were argued back and forth, until Mark O'Connor struck a new note in 'The Graying of the Underground'—'they over-promoted themselves'. Even so, the new small presses had become 'central to our new poetry publishing'. Among many pieces on individual authors (Lawson and Furphy still a presence), *Overland* ran a couple of articles on Bruce Dawe. His sardonic, ear-to-the-ground poems were both authentically Oz and contemporary, suggesting a way forward.

A sardonic note administered like a Chinese burn was also present in an important article by John Docker, 'Leonie Kramer in the Prison House of Criticism', playfully likening her to a prison governor as he pointed out the severe limitations of the *Oxford History of Australian Literature*. Indeed, he wondered 'how much Professor Kramer enjoys Australian literature, or literature as such'. Similar remarks were made by others in the pages of *Overland*. There was 'a growing tendency', wrote Christopher Koch, 'towards hostility instead of nurture' among academics who 'do not love literature at all. They see it as a tool: a tool for messages; a tool to advance their careers.' Peter Porter was milder, but no less dismissive: 'Critical articles smother poetry under heaps of prose.'

But increasingly footnotes—the foot soldiers of academic articles—invaded *Overland*. Forty years later, few of these pieces warrant particular attention; a highly contestational interview by Christina Stead is of greater interest, as is David Malouf's searching article on John Manifold. But Stephen had discerned a change in the overall situation—and not one to his liking. 'I dislike lit. crit. exercises more & more as I get older,' he declared, 'see more clearly their parasitical nature.' But the Association for the Study of Australian Literature had been founded in 1977 (and at its conferences academics and writers would dance with each other), while *Meanjin* was seen to have become less hospitable to academic criticism and more sociological. An opportunity had presented itself, which an alert editor must act upon.[31]

Space does not permit attention being paid to other notable articles, or indeed to other areas covered by the magazine. *Overland* was indulgent towards contributions on science fiction, and spasmodically the primary literary interest broadened out to include matters such as writers' incomes, publishing, and the Australia Council. Beyond that, music (of all kinds) was rarely covered. Television—although Stephen had come to watch a great deal of it—still seemed to be regarded as not worthy of serious consideration. But—padded out with stills—most of one issue showed how Tim Burstall turned a Hal Porter storyline into a film.

Cinema ran second to theatre—the art form closest to literature—the articles on the whole less historicist than concerned with contemporary challenges. ('When will the great Australian play appear,' asked Geoffrey Hutton, 'sharply observed without being brittle, topical without being trendy, truthful without being turgid?') It was the visual arts that fared best—most notably with a round dozen of articles by Eric Westbrook, the director of the Victorian Ministry of the Arts. Diplomatic, on Stephen's part; but each earned their place, appearing with a caricature by Rick Amor. Westbrook's mandarin prose was pointillist and perceptive. He wrote of Albert Tucker: 'At its most superficial the face is the mock-sinister poster portrait of the stage magician, but at its most truthful it is a powerful and almost threatening mask, in which narrow eyes rarely smile in parallel with the lips.' Tucker seemed to take this in his stride, for later his 'Faces I Have Met', a series of portraits, was reproduced in a colour supplement in the special *Overland* 101.[32]

There remains the important element of book reviews. Stephen's policy here was that when it came to reviewing—since there was no hope of being comprehensive—*Overland* should choose to review books by an expert readily to hand, or not at all. He might suggest, but would not set word limits; if a review was extensive, and good, it was bled into the rest of the magazine by becoming a feature article. This added to the liveliness of *Overland*, and, with the poetry, increased the sense of its being up to date. And Stephen could be quite ingenious in finding reviewers.

To have the former Labor treasurer Jim Cairns (also a former cop) review a history of the Victorian police force was a master stroke. Later he would turn to the famous police commissioner in Bjelke-Petersen's Queensland, Ray Whitrod, to review Richard Hall's *Disorganized Crime*. For *The Whitlam Government*, by Gough, he chose Sir Paul Hasluck (governor-general for most of the period), who turned in a shrewd but fair assessment. (For two books on Kipling, Stephen deftly chose himself.) Poetry and novels were almost invariably reviewed by locals, but a telling exception was Chris Wallace-Crabbe's and Peter Pierce's anthology of Australian war poems, given to the well-known British poet Gavin Ewart (himself a war veteran) to review. Moreover, dangling a book for review might act as a bait: the historian and social reformer Hugh Stretton was thereby induced to appear in *Overland*'s pages.

As would be expected, creative writing was well covered, and the reviews usually temperate. But not always: a mid-1970s reviewer, having all but demolished Xavier Herbert's *Poor Fellow My Country* (an unexceptional response—a later reviewer of another book mentioned, in passing, that he deserved the *Poor Fellow My Country* award for perseverance) then swept on to denounce David Malouf's *Johnno* as 'a total disaster … pretentious, uninventive, unoriginal, and dull, dull, dull'. Foremost among a number of poetry reviewers was Graham Rowlands, who, while dismissive of some of the pretensions of 'the Generation of '68', managed to maintain critical standards while being encouraging to young poets.

More generally, reviews were a way of extending the range of the magazine, indicating a breadth of interest wider than might be evident in the articles. Indonesia, for example, occasioned only one article, on political prisoners, but this was supplemented by four reviews of diverse books about the country. Similarly, the one piece about the nuclear threat and the option of armed neutrality for Australia—so pressing a cause in the early 1980s—was covered by a review article prompted by the appearance of three books on the subject. As the rise of publications such as the *New York Review of Books* demonstrated, discussion focused on new books at once demonstrated connectedness and contemporaneity.[33]

Stephen understood, when putting *Overland* together, that pieces should be sequenced by affinity (or contrast): from Clem he had learned the trick of clustering—so that, for example, an article on 'The People's Poetry' in China was followed by a critique of a big Chinese exhibition in Melbourne. While it was no part of the duty of an editor to be a critic, he believed, every magazine has a personality, and an editor *moulds* as much as any writer. Fiction, poetry and nonfiction must be balanced; and, aware as Stephen was of his ageing peer group, the magazine must strive to be as intergenerational as possible. There must be serious pieces, but addressed to the general reader. These precepts were not always achievable, even after urgent invitations to particular writers. Pressure of time—and the poetry editor—meant they might not shape a coming issue, but they should be evident over the course of a year. Running debates, and comments, also helped to thread the magazine together. Occasionally, *Overland* had special issues, such as those on Jack Lindsay and Ian Turner, but Stephen understood that these were impositions on subscribers who did not share that particular interest, so always managed to include some pieces on entirely different subjects.

There was, importantly, often an element of surprise as one turned the pages. This was achieved partly by the variety of the artwork, ranging from old-style cartoons by Vane Lindesay to high-quality work from Noel Counihan, Rick Amor and Jiri Tibor Novak. (Stephen's neat italic hand would also be in evidence from time to time.) In one issue the reader turned the page to find a cartoon of a voluptuous nude, sprawled in front of a fire, chucking in lumps of coal; she was blotto, and as she was a housemaid, it's likely Toorak made short work of her. Readers were invited to speculate, Whatever happened to Rosie? It was the first of a number of competitions. For unlike Clem's *Meanjin*, *Overland* could easily change registers. Stephen, who had early seen his significance, proposed to have a Barry Humphries issue—only the book of scripts on which he would centre it appeared much sooner than expected.

Again, *Overland* could more readily have a clutch of articles on Ned Kelly to mark the centenary of his death; *Meanjin* had only one.

Glen Lewis, a regular contributor, summed up the situation thus: '*Meanjin* [is] fundamentally too elitist, *Arena* too ideological, and *Overland* … too ocker. But of those magazines only the last one seems to have any reasonable chance of making contact with the ordinary Australian people.'[34]

Portrait of Stephen

You saw the worst first. A lumbering figure, habitually wearing a houndstooth jacket and corduroy trousers, his glasses hanging from his neck; silver-haired, the expression on the jowly face usually abstracted, until his attention was caught, sometimes registered by a quick smile. The patrician tones could be stentorian, the style pompous. Stephen had a way of making impromptu pronouncements—instant editorialising—and sometimes getting the tone wrong, particularly if they involved personal relations: a legacy of days in the Party, of having to say things you might not really believe in, just churning them out. But sometimes, in his provocative fashion, he could hit the nail on the head. At the fiftieth anniversary of the International Bookshop, he remarked that the foundation of the Communist Party was the biggest tragedy in Australian politics. People had missed that, being preoccupied with the DLP; Turner would have made an excellent prime minister. Back in Lilliput, his immediate response on hearing of my resignation was to say that the next editor of *Meanjin* should be a woman.

He could be easily ridiculed. 'The lordly Stalinist' sneered one contemporary, 'followed by a train of gutter poets', chimed in Don Watson. Alex Miller referred to him as 'Steamroller' (affectionately abbreviated in the *Meanjin* office to 'Steamies'). But his sense of presence was undeniable. At Erith Island, he was capable of going out in a dinghy to a naval vessel, sheltering from a storm and bellowing, 'Can I be of any assistance?' He would turn up at the door of the lighthouse keeper's house, dressed in a sarong with a knife thrust inside it. This self-confidence was not without naivety: Vane Lindesay recalled that once, when they were camping on the Bogong High Plains, some louts were playing up nearby. Stephen went up to them, declaring 'I am Dr Stephen Murray-Smith'. Yet he could also vary the tone. While he was a puzzle to many in the establishment, to their ladies he was a charmer, a man who would draw out chairs for them to sit down. But then he also claimed to be the first person to use the F word from the stage of the Melbourne Town Hall. When uttered by Stephen, there was always an unusually clear 'G' in 'fucking'.

It was as though now, in his mature phase, he was combining elements of all he had ever been—from school, the army and the Communist Party (the three institutional oppressors that had shaped him)—with a long career as a man of letters. He had become a man of the world, sought out as a committee man—but his opinions, while shrewd, could be eccentric and disconcerting, so sometimes it did not end well. Stephen thought he was thrown off the Advisory Council of the Australian Archives by the minister because he was displeased by a letter he wrote, on Sydney dominance of the Literature Board; but he was already an isolate on the committee for raising fundamental questions, questions other members did not want to hear. He was also on the literature committee of the Victorian Ministry of the Arts ('pleasant and useful'), involved in setting up the National Book Council—for a time its national president—and, as a result of two particular enthusiasms—president of the Australian Lighthouse Association and vice-president of the Anti-Metric Association. He was also on two Tasmanian committees. (The functions associated with these organisations were often a useful hunting ground for *Overland* articles.) But, by temperament, he was not a committee man.[35]

It was leadership that came naturally to Stephen. (At school he struck a contemporary as being like a Roman emperor looking round for his toga.) He had the necessary magnetism, authority and personal skills. Barrie Reid noticed, at a hastily improvised dinner for Peter Carey, how accomplished he and Nita were in talking to include the whole table, at getting people to open up. Or even to assemble: Stephen's 'old gang' of friends increasingly didn't bother to get together for a University House lunch unless he was coming in. It went further than that. Bass Strait identities, including lighthouse keepers, turned up for the launch of his bibliography of the region; his half-dozen best friends specially went to Flinders Island for that of his edition of Canon Brownrigg's journals; 'virtually the whole Erith mob' attended the funeral of his mother. For Stephen delivered the goods.

'What I liked about him', wrote Vincent Buckley—from the other side of the political fence—'was his central honesty, a generous decency and sense of justice … He was a manager and tactician, as honest brokers so often are.' He would readily help people by writing supportive letters and, when he returned from overseas, came bearing gifts. But there was a downside: even when at home, working, there were people constantly dropping in, sometimes with manuscripts, or seeking advice, and sometimes with requests he felt not competent to meet.[36]

It was the price of so much outward projection. There were the team quizzes he appeared on, television discussions, and the radio book reviews—his emphatic tones calling us to intellectual attention on a Sunday morning. One way and another, Stephen seemed intent on editing the neighbourhood. He was less involved in protests, now, than in being publicly outspoken—his remark that developers should be banned from holding any municipal office, for example, made at a planning seminar, hit the news. There was also his long campaign against metrication. 'Metric madness' was 'the most astonishing bullying of a dumbfounded citizenry that our country has ever seen … a declaration of war on traditional, accepted and useful standards'. Privately he would write to those holding power, and publicly to the Letters columns. Once, annoyed about being charged for a stamp of patriality in his passport (allowing free movement to and from the United Kingdom) he wrote a letter to *The Times* about it—and was gratified that the charge was repealed. Some, not altogether wrongly, saw him as a congenital interferer. 'Something will have to be done about that man', grumbled a director of education some years before. Nothing ever was.[37]

Even so, he was far less confident than he seemed. There were the ongoing health issues, the constant battle to lose weight. And there were the depressive episodes, more frequent now: once he confided to his diary that he laid down on his bed and 'and shed a few tears of self-pity'. Stephen was much more self-aware than he let on. 'My appetites are more romantic than my moral fibre, and always have been,' he reflected. Generally, he thought he had been 'fairly cowardly in matters of the body, fairly brave in matters of the spirit'. After Eysenck and Jensen he felt there was an increasing risk of physical injury from political opponents, and was inclined to withdraw from public involvements. 'Go on, Stephen,' said Geoffrey Blainey, 'you are a public meeting all in yourself.' Indeed he was. He may have shared his birthday (9 September) with Captain Bligh, of the *Bounty*, but as Lyn Williams remarked, 'The trouble with you, Stephen, is that you never know if you're leading the mutiny or opposing it.'[38]

When, in Scotland in 1978, his cousin said he couldn't understand how a nice bloke like him could be a Marxist, Stephen replied: 'I'm not really.' (Nita was on hand to assert, 'He is!' somewhat desperately.) In fact he was tending more and more to the position of 'a small-l liberal bourgeois'. He had even allowed his membership of the ALP to lapse—when he tried to reactivate it, factional manoeuvres led to its being blocked. Subsequently he did rejoin, went along to a branch meeting, and was distinctly unimpressed. As Stephen saw it, the fact that the introduction of an Australia Card had greater support among Labor voters than Liberal ones indicated the way the chief danger to traditional civil liberties now came from the Left. The ghost still walked of the Left tradition of 'physical intervention' to bring about change. From there, he wrote in 'Swag', it was 'an easy slide … to the belief, secretly or subliminally held … that people aren't ready to be trusted with the vote'. Behind the concept of 'hegemony', Stephen asserted, was the belief that 'the attitudes of ordinary people have been so twisted and distorted by various cultural and ideological interests' that they simply 'don't really understand what is good for them … "Nuts"!' he declared.

Stephen was well aware of the aphorism that people become caricatures of themselves after turning fifty, 'and I don't want to become a choleric Evelyn Waugh figure without the talent to sustain it—or even with it.' He claimed to have 'obliterated' all memory of the 1950s; and had come to recognise himself as a natural conservative—with an anti-authoritarian overlay. Indeed, he could slip into describing people as 'servants' if they were working for an institution, such as the university's residential Graduate House—where, indignant in his red nightshirt, he clamoured for one as he stood with the doorknob to his room uselessly in his hand. On specific issues Stephen could be surprisingly right-wing: the British should stay in Northern Ireland, the Americans were right in 1983 to invade Grenada—while he was disinclined to visit Japan, because of memories of the war. And, as an educationist, at a time when a 'core curriculum' was being proposed, his prescription was: Latin, typing, tree recognition, the Bible. Perhaps car mechanics.[39]

Stephen simply didn't like the way the world was heading. He would stir up his intellectual friends with his social pessimism in after-dinner discussions at the Twenty Club. What worried him about technological progress was that 'the government has suddenly found the means to put itself so far ahead of the people—with "experts" and "advisers" and "policy teams" and "planners"—that the people can no longer exercise an influence on the government'. That was why asking writers and readers to oppose the technological imperative was not to ask them to become Luddites; 'it is to ask them to carry out one of the classic functions of literature, to help people see themselves as people'.[40]

Perhaps the rising generation would address these issues—but Stephen's attitude towards the young was ambivalent. As far back as 1959, Stephen picked up on the first signs of the New Left, saw that the young were proceeding on different assumptions, and was aware that these people 'were looking for leads in finding a pattern'. Moreover, he appreciated that the surge of baby boomers would present educational challenges. But as time went on, while fully realising that *Overland* needed a regular inclusion of new names, Stephen became resistant to the tide—not least because of Barrie Reid's constant exhortations about changing the format to something more contemporary, together with his general preference for the young and the new.

Stephen was dismissive of 'the new breed of PhD illiterates', who knew nothing beyond their chosen fields. And he was alarmed by the rise of 'theory', the adoption, as he saw it, of trendy ideas from Europe by 'yearning cosmopolitans, high-level "cultural cringers" … with only a minimal interest in the roots and props of our own literary and intellectual life'. But he realised there was something defensive about this attitude: perhaps they were 'on to something important … beyond my capacity to recognize'. He liked his daughter Joanna's friends—'fun-loving, witty and extrovert in a way my generation never was'. With Jo and husband Ray's advice, in 1986 he arranged a highly successful meeting with a group of young people—'a brilliant evening', Reid declared. Stephen hoped that much would flow from it—and indeed *Overland* did come to take in a number of promising new writers, such as John Herouvim and Robert Darby, in the years before his death.[41]

Meanwhile Stephen maintained friendships with his own generation, or those half a beat behind. He remained indulgent towards

Denison Deasey, a bohemian who had a strong influence on him in his first unhappy year at the university. There was the 'Erith mob', and assorted university colleagues. Among the latter was Geoffrey Blainey, summed up by Stephen as 'a democrat, but not a man of the Left'. But friendship with Judah Waten (who was) was more problematic. They would gossip together; Stephen admitted they shared literary tastes, but on the whole he didn't think much of his writing, since—for all the affability—Judah lacked a basic humanism. Waten remained a Stalinist. 'We can become a prey to vultures clad as canaries', Stephen reflected. 'That's what Judah is; he even makes a play of his hard-linedness, knowing that [some] people ...will regard it as part of his chic.' The ambivalence was deep: when Judah died, Stephen wrote an appreciative entry in his diary, but returned to write a much less favourable one the next day. 'My old friend and enemy', he had publicly described Judah years before. But Stephen remained unequivocal in his hostility to Ted Hill, the former CPA state secretary—still a quietly spoken, deadly manipulator.

The great compensation was the new friendship with Fred Williams. Fred had, with Clifton Pugh, gone with Stephen and Ian Turner to Erith in an 'artists' camp'; a resulting discussion—and particularly the coloured reproductions of their paintings—had graced a special issue of *Overland* in 1975. 'Good art is a quest for generalisation and simplification', Stephen later observed: that was 'Fred's great triumph'. It was on Erith that they got to know each other; Stephen, in his fifties, had not expected to make 'another profound friend'. Nor had he imagined he would lose him so soon—to cancer, at the age of fifty-five. Gone with him was 'honesty bleached like a bone, an honesty tempered by a wicked wit and love of human inconsistency'.[42]

In every sense, though, the primal relationship was with Nita. Stephen would quote Disraeli to her: 'My dear, you are more like a mistress than a wife.' To the children Nita would say, 'You'd be surprised what we get up to!' Theirs was a deep love, but it could be rocky. At one point Stephen seriously thought of leaving—but then the desire for reconciliation stole upon them suddenly, and they made up—conscious, apart from anything else, that to part would be a disaster for each of them. 'Let's stick together', said Nita, 'it's just not worth it.' An occasional row would serve to clear the air.

Nita supported Stephen and encouraged him—even in his prodigious book-buying. More importantly, she complemented him, seeing herself as a kind of necessary corrective. Hers was the keener political instinct, sometimes curbing Stephen's impulse towards an optimistic reading of human behaviour. For all that she was diffident, didn't want to draw attention to herself. With her style, elegance and social skills, on occasion Nita would ease his directness: Stephen would characteristically begin a conversation, 'Which school did you go to? Where are your people from?' Nita had, moreover, built up a reputation as one of the best teachers at adjacent Toorak College. When the time came for her to retire, she told the assembled company: 'I will miss the girls: they have broadened my knowledge of a world that is to be', adding, and 'broadened mine at least as much as I hope I have broadened theirs about the world we have grown out of'.

Nita did feel valued—Stephen thought her 'by far the most intelligent person I know'. Each was grateful for the way the other provided a gateway to a different culture: Stephen keenly took part in Jewish family occasions. Nita also knew that—unlike many women married to Stephen's contemporaries—she was listened to; her views were sought on *Overland* as on other things, and sometimes she could hold Stephen back from his drift to the right. And, unlike Turner (whom she adored), he did not have a roving eye. For his part, Stephen was aware that Nita might find him 'refractory in ways I can't or won't recognise'.

There were three children: Cleeve (born 1952), David (1953) and Joanna (the playwright, 1962). Parenting brought its problems, but Stephen was invariably supportive as his children matured, a benign father who gave them room to move. When they had all left home, Stephen and Nita found themselves living just as a couple for the first time in thirty years—and enjoying it. The house, especially on Sunday mornings, was filled with the sound of music: Beethoven, Haydn, Mozart. (Stephen also delighted in Gilbert and Sullivan, but his light baritone was more in evidence when he was at the centre of group singing.) Later there would be the chirping voice of his grandson Joseph. The marriage was getting better all the time, Stephen felt, and increasingly he recognised his good fortune. 'Nita waiting for me', he wrote in his diary, 'and as always a renewal of my whole existence to see her.'[43]

Stephen had become a home body, leaving the house reluctantly: it was a place where the university did not impinge. Friends did, sometimes inviting themselves down to stay overnight—a variation in the fare offered by what Nita sometimes exasperatingly called 'the Mt Eliza commune'. But Stephen liked nothing better than to settle down to work in his 'semi-subterranean' library (against the backdrop of some 30,000 books), the log fire providing comfort as rain pattered on the roof. He felt secure in his fortress—having taken defensive steps. When, after the death of both parents, the children prepared the house for sale, three pistols were found hidden in a wall. Metaphorically the drawbridge was also being raised: travel had lost much of its allure for Stephen. With the annual expedition to Erith Island becoming more and more of a fixture, it was now a case of 'my loyalty divided between two loved homes'. Gradually Stephen would come to talk of being 'on the Island' or 'off the Island'—like a lighthouse keeper.[44]

Mt Eliza and Erith were not Stephen's only bifurcation. He was, as Keith Hancock put it, 'British, with a small b'. He was not displeased that Patrick White should exclaim, on meeting him in Sydney, 'Good heavens! You're more John Bull than ever.' For among his greatest heroes was the Duke of Wellington (the victor at Waterloo)—and Dr Samuel Johnson. He was an Anglophile in cultural formation and affinity, if much less so in basic values. Stephen still had relatives in England, and in Scotland, where he made a pilgrimage to the ancestral island of Gigha. But London was the real magnet, placing him 'in the middle of the world's greatest support system for people like me'—with its libraries, second-hand bookshops, splendid newspapers, urbane conversation, specialists and experts readily contactable. The large scale of it all sharpened people up, and it was 'as though the end of Empire brought out all sorts of hidden fires and skills and insights and interests … It's not my culture the whole way through', he recognised, 'but by Jesus would life be worth living without it?'

He deplored the poverty and ugly slums, recognising that much of what he admired was 'so often the end products of centuries of privilege'. Stephen had access to what was termed 'good society', but often encountered an alienating style—'that invariable upper-crust mixture of kindness, reserve and condescension'. In the literary world, so far as he moved in it, he found incestuousness, superficiality and triviality; the class system was so strong that many writers didn't ask for each other's company, 'but long for and seek that of lords and ladies'. After spending a couple of months there in 1982, Stephen declared, 'I leave with pleasure; the seductiveness of England has run out for me.' Australia might be relatively thin, culturally, 'but we have the compensating honor of having to master two cultures, instead of one'.[45]

Sustaining Stephen, and impelling *Overland*, was a firm belief that ordinary people would share high culture if it were extended to them without condescension. He was, in his way, a *narodnik:* 'how I admire the solid humanity and common-sense of many of the working class or non-middle-class people I know.' A fisherman who daily battled with the elements and also read exploratively was for him an enviably complete human being.

He loved meeting people like a Ballarat rate-collector, who collected avant-garde literature; or a steamroller driver in Brisbane, and a Melbourne boiler attendant, who were also serious book collectors. Stephen lamented 'the self-taught men of intellect and culture, now vanished'—disappearing even as Furphy (who was one of them) was writing. So he was heartened that a woman who had bought a copy of *Overland* on impulse in Horsham had read it, began to study, and had become a university lecturer. He could do something appreciably after all, to help reverse the general trend. Similarly, he hailed the appearance of good bookshops in the country. For Stephen envied the quality of English civilised life, the pervasive resonances of the past, the patina of age: even his own circle at times felt thin. Perhaps the depth would come.[46]

And then there was Clem. In 1972, when on a university 'working group', Stephen described himself as 'the only radical on the bloody thing, with no help even from the bloody students. Dear me, I do sound more and more like Clem.' Respectful and solicitous of his elder contemporary, he had nonetheless begun to tire of the litany of complaint. In 1971 Stephen had asked Clem to write an 'Auto-obituary' for *Overland*, and Clem agreed. (He was the one person to take up the offer.) It was a strange piece: half of it was taken up with Australia having become the dumping place for the world's human waste—a sour comment on his own imagined demise. The problem, he wrote in a letter, was to know when to bump himself off. In truth Clem could not let go—of the past, or of anything. He stewed over the loss of *Meanjin.* For a time, after a trip to North Queensland, his spirits seemed restored. Perhaps he would pull out of it. But *Meanjin*'s fortieth anniversary—anniversaries were always of prime importance to Clem—reactivated his deep sense of grievance.

Clem was invited to take part in the celebrations, but, after consulting various friends, declined. Instead, he decided to organise a twenty-fifth anniversary dinner for *Overland* and Stephen (a year after the event) a few weeks before. *Meanjin*'s own celebration was more contemporary than retrospective, being centred on a landmark seminar, 'St Petersburg or Tinsel Town? Sydney and Melbourne: Their Differing Styles and Changing Relation'. An impressive line-up of speakers explored the subject right across the board of what was then a hot topic, the way Melbourne seemed to be losing ground to Sydney. It was even reported on the front page of the *Sydney Morning Herald*.[47]

Dorothy Green, fiercely loyal and loving, had become somewhat exasperated with Clem. Dorothy was now very much a political activist, campaigning against uranium mining, nuclear weapons and American bases. But Clem showed no curiosity about these issues: his outlook had become frozen. Stephen now thought of him as 'an old fellow-travelling Stalinist', while to the very end Clem remained a staunch member of the Rationalist Society. Clem should 'waste no more time on the past', Dorothy was driven to write (in the pages of *Meanjin*). Repeatedly she had urged him some years earlier to give *Meanjin* away, and allow his own creative juices to flow—returning to short-story writing, painting, his stalled autobiography. He did manage to revisit his stories and verse, adding some more, and published them in books and booklets. But Clem continued to mutter about the 'lost years' since the trauma of 1974–75. There were troubles with Lynne Strahan over her history of *Meanjin*, *Just City and the Mirrors*—at one point she was deemed to be as bad, if not worse, than me. Judith Armstrong, author of *The Christesen Romance*, would similarly come to displease him. If only Dorothy Green had written the history of *Meanjin*. Or Harry Heseltine.

Matters were not improved when he finally learned that during the war his dear friend James Picot had been savagely beaten to death by the Japanese. And then there was a fire at Stanhope: it did not destroy the house, but water from the hoses swamped books and documents—among them Clem's draft autobiography. He seemed as much relieved as saddened by the loss. By this stage even Jenny Lee, the most accommodating of subsequent *Meanjin* editors, had fallen out of favour. When Nina died, in 2001, Clem followed Russian Orthodox practice and sat next to the open coffin, exclaiming, 'This is the worst day of my life!' Soon after he found himself in a nursing home.[48]

Stephen, witnessing a good deal of this, was kind and hospitable. So, too, was Clem in return, inviting the Murray-Smiths to Stanhope. It was 'an unchanging and magnificent haven,' Stephen thought, 'the garden and house a unity of peace and civilisation, a unity within the higher unity of Clem and Nina's life there together, among their books and pictures'. Clem gave them presents, and with Nina was particularly kind to Joanna: Stephen felt they seemed to regard her as a kind of god-daughter. He responded by giving them a large joint party—but Clem was still unpredictably curmudgeonly. 'Had a few words with Clem Christesen', Stephen noted, 'boorish and abrupt as he always is these days. I keep on writing him nice letters, partly to annoy him.' There was little he could do. In fact Clem would outlast him by fifteen years. After a long, sad physical deterioration—charming the ladies as he faded—Clem passed away in 2003.[49]

Editor becomes author

Apart from his thesis, Stephen would never write a tightly argued, book-length text. Indeed he could be said to have sidled into authorship. Early on, there were edited collections of songs and later bawdy lyrics (*Snatches & Lays*, reissued 1973). There was an early bestselling booklet on Henry Lawson, but even his perceptive venture into autobiography, *Indirections* (1981), was essentially three lectures he had given in Townsville. Stephen's life was a campaign extending to many fronts. If not distracted from the project in hand by some immediate task, or the need to write a letter to the paper, he was just as likely to be distracted by another major venture. Then, apart from continuing work on *Overland* and *Melbourne Studies in Education*, there were occasional chapters in books and also the editing of historic texts.

Important here was Stephen's new edition of Marcus Clarke's novel *His Natural Life*: the title was deceptively shorter than the common one (*For the Term of His Natural Life*), which he undertook to edit for Penguin. Published in Britain in 1970 as part of the Penguin English Library, it proved to be some 80,000 words longer than the then standard version: Stephen decided that the text must be that as originally serialised in the *Australian Journal.* It had not been published since: the ending of the revised version might be cleaner, but important material of documentary, historic and even literary interest had been lost. The work still spoke to us, eloquently: the convict system it described, Stephen believed, was not so aberrational as the people who came immediately after liked to think: Auschwitz showed us that.[50]

Earlier, when casting around for a major subject, Stephen had intended to write on industrial movements. But ASIO got to his intended collaborator, and so he turned his attention to another field, education in its more sociological aspects, finding 'it's really got me in'. The result was a massive PhD thesis, 'A History of Technical Education in Australia: with special reference to the period before 1914' (1966). This would long remain the key work on the subject: even ten years later there were weekly requests to have the whole work photocopied. But Stephen could not get it published without drastic revision. Nonetheless it gave him academic standing—together with a tour of technological tertiary institutions in Canada in 1971—so that he had toyed with applying for high-powered academic jobs at Monash and in Hobart. But in the end he was too wedded to the patterns of his existing lifestyle.[51]

An unexpected opportunity to recycle much of the thesis occurred in 1977, when RMIT approached him to write its history. He wasn't keen, unless he had a collaborator: to hand was his student and friend Anthony Dare. RMIT acceded to the request, but Stephen was not happy. While the fee would provide financial relief (he was always rather money-conscious) the book would effectively end all hopes of the thesis ever being published; it would also put paid to a volume of selected prose of Francis Adams, which he had hoped to bring out with University of Queensland Press. But Stephen could write the section of the book roughly corresponding with his thesis, the golden period of Australian technical education; and there was some point in focusing on what was then Victoria's biggest and most successful technical institution. He soon saw that he was lucky to have Dare: 'gifted, humorous, with a nice literary sense'. The younger man would simultaneously do a PhD, covering the later years of the institution, under Stephen's supervision.

The Tech, as the book came to be called, is a lively and detailed account of the institution, and appeared just in time for RMIT's centenary in 1987. A number of themes emerged: the first was how the place had moved away from ideas of a broad, liberal education not only for workers—it began as the Working Men's College—but for other people too. Gradually the technological imperative narrowed the range of subjects taught, at the same time as the working class became more politicised and came to reject 'bourgeois' education and culture. While the motto lingered on—'The skilled hand, the civilised mind'—the essence had gone. 'It was the victory of the twentieth century over the nineteenth', Stephen ruefully noted, along with the cost: a correlative decline in institutional self-esteem.

There came to be a voluntary acceptance of a subordinate place in its social standing and economic position. This mindset was in part British-derived, strengthened by the lack of industrial innovation in Australia—wool and wheat being exchanged for printing presses and pianos. And there was also the sense of the techs helping to maintain the social order, keeping the unruly off the streets. RMIT, for most of its history, had little esprit de corps: by the 1920s repeated attempts to found a college journal had foundered. Stephen felt, on the eve of massive tertiary education reforms and the impact of computerisation, that it was only in recent years that some sort of theoretical or philosophical basis for the colleges had begun to emerge. 'As long as we remained, in general economic terms, near the top of the tree', Stephen wrote with Tony Dare, 'there wasn't much to worry about.' But now that Australia, like Britain, was 'in industrial, economic and social decline', it was another matter altogether.[52]

Stephen had scarcely squared up to the task of writing *The Tech* when the first major distraction came along. Nick Hudson of Heinemann rang to propose a *Dictionary of Australian Quotations*. Stephen jumped at it—he loved the apt reference, was set up to do it, and could see the book becoming a standard reference, part of Australia's cultural infrastructure. It might even make some money. He soon set it up with six consultants (one of them Joanna), and more than fifty specialist contributors. Stephen also appealed to the general public, wrote to poets and friends, and asked some people to put things down in writing so he could quote them. But he found much of the best material himself, 'the most rewarding task I've ever undertaken'. 'The dictionary', he reflected, 'will express my own outlook on life, I think: ironic, somewhat detached, yet … committed and humane.'

With its 4000 entries, *DAQ* was a kind of encyclopaedia, aiming to make people more aware of their own country. Following the model of the *Australian Dictionary of Biography* (to which Stephen was a steady contributor), his compilation would not follow English elitist precepts, but rather be as inclusive as possible. Stephen was particularly pleased when he could find a colourful, earthy phrase in an unexpected place, such as 'Pull out digger, the dogs are pissing on your swag'—written by a Liberal parliamentary whip to a flailing speaker on his own side. He did not, though, stoop to the national fascination with the dunny—not even to Bazza McKenzie's memorable curse, 'May all your chickens turn into emus, and kick your dunny down!' It was a rich loam all the same, extending from Péron the French naturalist urging the Mauritius garrison to wipe out the English settlement at Port Jackson while they still could, to Henry Miller's reference to the kangaroo having a double penis—'one for weekdays, and one for holidays'. There are great slabs of poetry, much of it scarcely working its passage. And there is less humour than might have been expected—although few could beat Alan Marshall describing a wowser [killjoy] as 'a gentleman who uses a contraceptive as a bookmark in his Bible'.

Inevitably, with any reference book nearly forty years old, the approach seems dated. (Stephen was reluctant to include the youngest writers, since their contributions had not 'settled.') Given the deeply ahistorical nature of the contemporary world, the desire to trace Australian antecedents, thickly, now seems simply backward-looking; the preoccupation with visitors' responses a little cringe-making. Moreover, the concern with an Anglo-Celtic Australian national character has become outmoded. Stephen was well aware that the *DAQ* was weak on migrant (ethnic) responses, but rightly said that they were 'rather thin on the ground'. 'Aborigines', so designated, take the first four entries in the book, but in fact there is a sprinkling of quotes from them throughout. The bushranger Musquito's legendary description of hanging as 'very good for white fellow, for *he* used to it', is there, and more importantly, a number of chilling references to systematic extermination ('dispersal') of Indigenous Australians. Mum Shirl of Redfern is quoted recalling the taunt she had to endure as a schoolgirl: 'Nigger, nigger, pull the trigger!' Otherwise women are not greatly in evidence, although Germaine Greer and Anne Summers are powerful presences.

The *Dictionary* was well received, following a lyrical review by Geoffrey Blainey and the 'hard yakka' of appearing on 'dozens' of radio and TV shows. Even though it sold at a stiff price, booksellers moved some 10,000 copies—leading to a paperback and preparations for a second edition. But perhaps it was more an ikon as it sat on people's bookshelves rather than a well-thumbed favourite. 'Australians simply do not quote poetry,' Judith Wright told Stephen. Rather cheekily, I remarked to him that it was a combination of scout-mastering, stamp-collecting and gumnutry. Stephen replied (putting on a fixed smile), 'Jim, that's the nicest thing anyone has said about it.' He was a past master at smothering criticism.[53]

Stephen's only sibling, Barbara, became best known as a columnist in the *Toorak Times*. Shallow, conservative, and long-dominated by her mother, she took a long time to fully emerge. Now she relied on her older brother to straighten and strengthen her prose as she struggled to write a second book on etiquette. He did so, then decided to write one of his own—a guide to English usage in Australia. He was tired of hearing people whinge about the ABC and other organisations using or pronouncing words incorrectly, he said. Penguin jumped at the idea when he proposed the book and—drawing on long observation—*Right Words: A Guide to English Usage in Australia* was written in a few months.

'The way words are used depends on some kind of agreement between the present and the past', Stephen stated in the introduction, offering the book as an attempt to draft such agreements: it would shave off the excrescences while it noted legitimate mutations. It was ridiculous that English speakers in Australia had to remain dependent on British language guides, books that did 'not approach [the] language through two hundred years of cultural adaptation'. Stephen was aware of his bias towards 'traditional English form', and in pronunciation towards what could then be styled Cultivated Australian. But he also saw that, with lexicographers, language strained like a dog at the leash: 'The dictionaries will have to change', he says at one point; at its best, slang was 'the yeast in the dough of words'.

Again the book takes the form of alphabetical entries—generally rather like editorial slips, occasionally little essays. AA Phillips, kind as well as being common-sensical and incisive, helped him find the right tone, muting the impulse to be prescriptive. Stephen was well aware that while class might seem relatively absent in Australia, certain pronunciations might invite a negative snap judgement from those considering themselves socially superior. (Following the British historian EP Thompson, Stephen preferred to see class as a *process* rather than a *structure*.) He therefore lists 'indicator words' and 'bully words'—those technical terms that often function as 'a means of social control'.

The book reveals the contradictory elements in Stephen's personality. Among the side-swipes taken is the description of academic English as a 'horrible corrupt dialect', while later he deplores 'the barbaric cult of the backyard barbecue'. Stephen also beats his drum against metrication, and for the loss of real and metaphorical language. But while he condemns, as succumbing to 'cultural imperialism', the wholesale adoption of American practice ('offensive intruders'), he concedes that America can be the source of useful words and phrases as much as anywhere else. As might be expected, he misses some of the newer usages of the young, such as 'hoon', or the frivolous meaning of 'rage'. But in many respects *Right Words* is quite progressive. Stephen is open to modest spelling reform. And he is well aware of how language has been made by men to the point where the 'normal' is implicitly masculinised.

Right Words may be the product of a grandee (Australia's Dr Johnson) but it attracted considerable interest—on radio, and even television. The Melbourne *Herald* placed it Number 3 on its bestseller list. It sold 8000 copies in a few months, and was reprinted. The book, Stephen noted with satisfaction in his diary, 'continues to draw almost daily praise'.[54]

Erith Island

Stephen had gone to Flinders Island in his student days, and had trained on Wilsons Promontory as a commando; Bass Strait had long occupied a corner of his imagination. In his wide reading—extending to *Sailing Directions for Bass Strait*—he had come across a passing reference to Erith Island in the Kent Group, and began to think of one day going there. He wrote to the Tasmanian government, who directed him to the lessee, a grazier on Flinders Island. Stephen learned of a serviceable hut on the island, only recently abandoned. In 1962 he decided to organise a party, inviting another three families to join the Murray-Smiths.

The Kent Group had been 'found' by Matthew Flinders and named after a friend of his. The highest of the three islands, Deal, had a lighthouse; standing at just over 300 metres above sea level (only one in Greece was higher), it was often covered by low cloud. A low window gave 'an illusion of perspective, as each island curved around to connect with the next'. Deal Island was separated from Erith and Dover by Murray Pass: on days that were still it became a 'flat expanse of shimmering colour, enclosed by the rugged cliff and pale honey sand of three islands masquerading as one'. The sense of something special about the place was enhanced by a swashway between Dover and Erith—at low tide it was possible to walk on the stones across the narrow passage between them. On Erith there was a long, curving beach, ideal for landing.

The island was difficult to reach, and once there life was tough. That first time, no-one had understood what they were signing up for. There were, whatever the official handbook might say, no wallabies, no rabbits; just lots of flies. There was no fresh water, either, except in a tank adjacent to the hut, which Stephen and Nita occupied with the permission of the man who built it. With everyone else in tents, Stephen's occupancy underlined the authority he effortlessly exerted, and which in the case of the first expedition probably saved the day. He was hooked. As their craft sailed away, he looked back at the West Cove beach with tears in his eyes. 'Island, I shall come back to you', he declared. Shortly afterwards he told Nettie Palmer, 'Some day I'd like to write a book on the Bass Strait islands.' Immediately he had recognised (as he would put it later) that 'Bass Strait is a collection of all sorts of ideas for me … It fits in with a lot of my romantic and intellectual impulses.'

Generally the group consisted of around twenty people, though could shoot up to nearly thirty; sometimes there were a few additionals staying on a yacht in the bay. What is striking is that, while the group were sympatico and loosely of the left, *Overland* was scarcely a consideration. Its nexus, too, was part of the world they were all escaping from. So Barrie Reid and Vane Lindesay never went, and John McLaren not till quite late in the piece. Even Ian Turner was slow to join, although once he came he took to Erith like a duck to water; his was a calming presence.

Australians of that generation and earlier always fancied themselves as being able to handle a pioneering life in the Bush, and people returned to the challenge of Erith again and again. For Stephen, December–January became another season: 'We had a good Erith', he would write. Each year from 1966 he would return heading the customary group. The kids of course loved it, and Stephen felt that Erith in a way was for them, since it was a child's paradise. It was secure, offering a whole world to explore—snakes, while present, were not dangerous; the notorious Bass Strait black tiger snake was fortunately absent, while there were no human dangers. On the contrary, Erith functioned as a village, with adults teaching their own and other people's kids various skills. One of these was crayfishing, preparing the pots.

Another adult activity was putting out the nets, producing rich pickings; a haul would usually yield at least twenty edible fish. Then there was swimming; when over fifty, Stephen experienced water-skiing for the first time. (Characteristically, he was less thrilled by the sensation of speed than by 'gliding over wrecks, peering down at mysterious kelp reefs and trying to catch up with a shoal of trout'.) Beach cricket was another pastime, with eccentric rules, the topsy-turvydom of adults playing in kids' teams, and the umpire, Max Marginson, strolling about with a pot of beer in hand while officiating with nothing on. Stephen too would frequently walk about in the nude, aiming at the Erith ideal of becoming 'brown all over'. Other activities included card games and reading, although Stephen found it hard to get as much reading done as he'd have liked.

There was a general expectation that people should participate in the various activities, but they were always free to go off and do something else. On special evenings all would assemble for drinks and to eat cray at the hut or at 'Kampong', where most people pitched their tents. After going off to prepare their meals—unless Nita was turning it on for the whole band down at the hut, as she would from time to time—they would turn up there later, for a night of storytelling, perhaps discussion, and a sing-along. It was a generation that still liked to make its own music, running the whole gamut from choice *Snatches & Lays* and Australian folksong to 'Rule, Britannia!' (Their Australia, after all, was not particularly anti-British, but in some ways saw itself as 'England—with improvements'.)

Stephen was the leader partly because, in the words of Robert Newton, 'he was a superb quartermaster'. The loading up at Port Albert became legendary, and people came to watch. Apart from tents, bedding and personal effects, there was fishing gear, small boats, emergency equipment, a gas refrigerator, stoves, food, fuel, beer, and other supplies. Provisions had to be on an ample scale, Stephen felt—too lavish, grumbled some of the party, for when Erith was reached they had to land them by forming a human chain. Stephen's organisational capacities extended further. He detailed how the camp would operate, and was particularly conscious of communications and recording functions. There was a daily 'sked', or radio contact, with Deal Island, and later an improvised telephone between the hut and Kampong.

Meanwhile a thermohygrograph ('the hermaphrodite') recorded temperatures and humidity, while records were kept of wind velocities, visiting ships and the daily catch. In addition, Stephen had, with Max Marginson (among others), explored the botany, bird life and geology of the Kent Group, publishing joint articles in specialist journals. Stephen had found a small but defined realm; exploring it thoroughly was a way of taking possession. It became his anchor, finally vanquishing any residual sense of absence or hollowness about white life in Australia.

It also gradually fed a fantasy. On the island Stephen became known as 'the Emperor', and took to flying a flag above the hut—a red flag with an 'E' emblazoned on it. He and Nita would hold an annual garden party (with printed invitations). People would come in all kinds of clothing, some of it impressively improvised, while Nita put on white gloves (actually long socks) and perfected a royal wave. Stephen wore a crown made of tin foil. Awards would be made, to all and sundry: one year Max Marginson was 'decorated' for his 'long and distinguished service as Imperial Sycophant'. In 1974, they were at it again a week or so later, with a dinner for the Erith Island Yacht Squadron organised by Don Anderson (the Commodore). There was even a Ladies Auxiliary. It was a game they all enjoyed, a make-believe realm far from the apprehension felt on returning to the island, where vandals might have wreaked havoc. Authority took tangible form when in 1981 Stephen's friend Andrew Lohrey, the Tasmanian national parks minister, appointed Stephen a Crown Lands Bailiff.

On First Hearing That A Friend Had Become "Emperor" Of A Beautiful Bass Strait Island
I somehow feel it in my bones
That there was once an Emperor Jones
But he grew old and lost his pith
And now makes way for Emperor Smith
Who puffs his pipe and smiles with glee
A ruler OVERLAND and sea!

Thus Ken Gott. Certainly, Stephen came to relish the role. On a visit to England, the Murray-Smiths had contacted the mayor of Erith (now in the borough of Bexley) as one equal to another. A successful meeting occurred, although conversation at a luncheon paused when Nita was asked about the population of the Australian Erith; apart from ourselves, visiting, she replied, just a few penguins. Nonetheless the Murray-Smiths returned with a score of the English borough's medals to confer at the next garden party. Inclined to regard the management of the island's affairs as 'his' government, Stephen wrote in his journal of a subcommittee (Max and himself) rejecting one 'application' concerning works, and passing another.

While he was deferred to, Stephen's leadership was sometimes resented. Once mutterings were dealt with by putting his diary on open display. He was aware of continuing tensions, particularly with Robert Newton, who was resistant to assumptions of majesty, seeing the whole project as a democratic, cooperative exercise. Tensions were greatest on the boats, where the men instinctively became competitive in displaying their prowess, and were usually most assertive. 'I am astonished at the ability of good mates like us to be utterly jealous and vindictive if we don't get our own way. In more ways than one Erith is a return to childhood.' So Stephen wrote in what he termed 'An Epistle of Stephen to the Erythreans'.

Generally his response to difficulties was a certain world-weariness, arising from their familiarity and recurrence. On Erith there were always 'second week blues'; bickering could become a problem. As far as Stephen was concerned, Erith was not an encounter group: rather, it displayed 'a form of modified anarchy'. The difficulty was in finding the right proportion between individual autonomy and the collective project. There were also territorial issues. People were happy to stick to their tents, even in the wildest weather, but there was the matter of the hut. It was the nerve centre of the island, where the water tanks were placed: how much was it Stephen and Nita's, and to what extent everybody's? On the whole people regarded it as private (as Nita did), so long as there was ample hospitality. As John McLaren observed, Erith was probably saved by the fact that it was an intermittent encampment: otherwise antipathies might have become entrenched.

But there was a lot to like. The elemental way that, on a small island, the sea and the sky seemed to become *all* sea, and *all* sky; and then the occasional 'still, even-tempered' evenings, with 'just the gulls in the distance squabbling …The gentle wash of the waves below, a susurrus, gives a constant background to our quietness. We wake and sleep to it.' But once they woke up to the sound of a yacht 'chug-chugging under a rather tired old motor into the cove'. It turned out to be two possums copulating just outside the door. Nature was not always benign: wild weather could suddenly swoop upon them.

> Of course we always realise that if the weather were better we wouldn't be on Erith—someone or some company would have snaffled it long ago. But, as the house shakes around me, the door rattles, the salt cakes on the windows, the curtains in the hut swing, the buffeting and moaning persist, the boobyalla swing madly outside the back window and quite big rollers cross the cove, I reflect that we must be a hardy lot at least to take all this not only without complaining but even with a sense of pleasure.

That pleasure arose from being isolated with a group of friends in a community built on interdependence. Stephen believed Erith was 'analogous' to a good marriage, where the mutual support in struggles against adversity 'make many marriages deeper and perhaps more spiritual experiences'. This, together with shared attitudes and experiences, led to a certain disdainful attitude to the outside world. 'We see ourselves,' Stephen wrote, 'with some rough justice, as some sort of elect, and have a kind of "queer affection" … for each other'. When Jim Hammerton, as a passing yachtsman, happened upon Erith and was shown around, it struck him—with bread being baked in buried ovens—as being surprisingly like a hippie commune in Melbourne. The Erythreans found it hard to pack up. 'As Max and I often say,' Stephen told his diary, 'we are leaving home for ten months' exile, and we ought to be paid a living-away-from-home allowance by the university.'

But the island was not immune to disaster. Two sudden deaths took place there in the seventies: the first that of Dick Love, a popular GP, and the second that of Ian Turner, in December 1978. He was playing in a game of beach cricket, ran the length of the 'pitch', then suddenly dropped on the sand. People thought he was mucking about, for a moment, but the stillness was too complete. Stephen took command: attempts to revive him were to no avail. A massive heart attack had carried him off, twelve years after the first. Contact was made with the lighthouse keepers on Deal: a helicopter was called, and landed with policemen—armed, as they were taking nothing for granted. The body was covered with a tartan rug, and for want of anything better, placed on an old hatch-cover; then airlifted to Melbourne. A couple of other accidents followed in quick succession, one of them requiring Robert Newton to be flown out. Max Marginson 'pronounced the end of Erith', recalls a participant, 'but of course it wasn't'. For Stephen it was the end of much else: 'A whole part of me is wrenched bodily away', he said at Turner's cremation. 'Only scar tissue will remain.'

While Stephen had occasionally fantasised about spending six months there, one year he did manage to go back a second time. At Ian Turner's suggestion—and to opposition from one or two regulars, who felt it an incursion—Stephen and Ian returned in March 1974 with Fred Williams and Clifton Pugh. It would be a kind of artists' camp: the pair would paint during the day, and at night there would be discussion, some of it recorded and published. Turner was keen to see what they would make of the landscape, which he likened to the Hebrides; a different light, perhaps, but nonetheless one of greater clarity than seen on the Mainland. He was a bit put out when they did not share his rhapsodic response to the sublime: the artists were too busy working out how they would relate themselves to the landscape, and get the most telling results.

The taped conversations were interesting, but not a complete success. Murray-Smith and Turner wanted to talk about expatriatism, the market, arts politics and the role of the artist in the necessary dissemination of his images. Pugh was the more articulate, but resisted some of these lines of questioning. Williams was blunter: 'if you want to be a painter, you have to cut your tongue out'. So he thought at thirteen, and so he thought now. The work should speak for itself. He gave sincere, but curt and pointed answers. Unlike Pugh, he did not love the bush. 'I simply want to paint pictures from it.'

Although less extrovert by nature, with his paintings less 'framed' but more formalist, it was Williams who worked with 'a frantic bravura'. Turner, writing the introduction to the transcript of the taped conversation early in 1975, thought that Erith had not been quite caught by either painter. But in Williams' case, the real work was back in his studio. There, a year later, he finished his *Erith Landscape II*. 'One of my better achievements,' he declared. Patrick McCaughey later described the Erith seascapes as initiating Williams' new palette 'into a grander, more generalised style'.

Stephen enjoyed unusually good relations with the working people of the Strait. He had felt an affinity with lighthouse keepers and their families ever since he and Nita had been befriended, when just out of university, by the keeper at Wilsons Promontory: letters were exchanged when the Murray-Smiths went to England. In 1970 he collaborated with Robert Newton in making an ABC television documentary on them. Stephen admired the necessary work lighthouse people did in isolation, and for the support they could provide in emergencies. He was livid when, in 1971, the Commonwealth automated the lighthouse on Cliffy Island and blew up the staff quarters, buildings well over a hundred years old. The same must not be allowed to happen on adjacent Deal. He therefore decided to establish a maritime museum in the original head keeper's house—using his influence at the university to acquire the necessary display cases.

Stephen fiercely opposed gathering government plans to replace the lighthouse keepers with automatic beacons, and in 1980 formed the Australian Lighthouse Association. The committee included scientists, engineers, seamen and former keepers; Ken Gott was Stephen's lieutenant, doing the necessary research. In 1983 the House of Representatives Standing Committee on Expenditure invited submissions to its inquiry into lighthouses, and Stephen spoke at the committee's public meetings. He was provoked by the narrow base of bureaucratic intent, concerned only with a more favourable economic outcome. His argument, and that of the association, was that lighthouses and their keepers contributed to the whole of Australian society. They provided coastal surveillance, weather observations, and helped protect the environment and built heritage. By contrast, the policies of the Department of Transport were 'capricious, sectional, and against the interests of most users of the sea'. The committee was won over by these and other arguments, but the department was not to be deterred. The lighthouses were eventually unmanned and automated.

The lighthouses had been made a network by the supply craft and visiting seamen. Stephen developed the greatest admiration for them: they were romantic figures, commendable for their physicality, their open-minded practicality, their deep attachment to the sea and detailed local knowledge. They responded to his directness, respected his intense interest in the Strait, and laughed off the lordly style. Some of them became friends and turned up not only at his funeral but also at Nita's commemoration twenty-five years later. They had 'an unforced humanity', Stephen said; if he were on trial for a crime, he would prefer to have them as the jurors rather than high-flying urban professionals.[55]

Islands

By the time Erith had been a fixture for ten years or so, Stephen had begun to ponder its meaning. Social dynamics were much more visible in small groups. He asked a participating sociologist to make a formal analysis, but he was not keen, not wishing to intrude professionally upon something dear to him. The prehistorian Rhys Jones was more forthcoming: comparing them with the Gidjingali, the Erith people were like 'an outstation mob'. And there were parallels, Stephen came to see, between 'primitive' camp layouts and personality dispositions, and the ones that had 'instinctively' evolved on Erith. Meanwhile he had been looking outwards.[56]

Following his participation as a student in an archaeological expedition to Flinders Island in the 1940s, Stephen continued to be fascinated by its distinctive Indigenous history. This led to him spearheading a successful campaign in the late 1960s for the preservation of the chapel at Wybalenna, the last surviving building of the ill-fated settlement established by George Augustus Robinson to 'protect' the remaining Tasmanian Indigenous population. The chapel had been used as a barn and a shearing shed: no-one recognised its importance.

On the other side of Flinders Island lay Cape Barren Island, the traditional home of a population descended largely from sealers and Tasmanian Indigenous women. Stephen became fascinated with the place: he made a television documentary about it with Robert Newton, then wrote an extensive account of its nineteenth-century history. What struck him was that the early 'eradication' of the Tasmanian Indigenous people was now being doubled by 'a second extinction, more subtle and more protracted than the first'. The distinctive islander community and culture, a product of isolation, was being whittled away by a 'majority culture which eventually has engulfed and almost destroyed it'.

He noted that the taint that the sealers were largely escaped convicts (never true) still lingered, and fed into a disdain for the islanders, who once they lost their original leaders, were relatively unsophisticated in dealing with the world. Although quite settled by the 1830s, they were eventually driven by white encroachment from the smaller islands to Cape Barren, where a reserve was proclaimed. There visiting Anglican high clergy tried to turn them into a God-fearing, regular, orderly community. But institutionalisation, Stephen noted, had virtually killed off the Tasmanians on Flinders Island; and the Cape Barren Islanders were wedded to a slower, independent life built around the seasonal muttonbirding. They resisted the pressure coming from Hobart, while whites resented the way they seemed to be 'taking it easy'. Bishop Montgomery ended up dismissing them as needing to be 'strictly governed as an inferior race', reforms being introduced gradually.

Stephen was ready for an epiphany. It came one winter's day in 1977. 'Today I have been in paradise', he wrote in his diary '—almost that.' He had been invited, in one afternoon, into three of the Islanders' homes. He felt privileged, hearing them talking and arguing among themselves. Particularly striking was the matriarch Madge Mansell, with her

> marvellously tumbledown house—decayed, rough-cut weatherboards on the walls, uneven & often unnailed; a widdershins stick-picket fence outside; a sagging doorway only about 4½ feet high; papered walls … and bits & pieces; a poor fire again, in an open grate. A remarkable period piece, this house. Madge, rheumy-eyed & dirty & ill-clad at her great age, & with no family to look after her, was still dignified & quick on the uptake.

It was the culmination of Stephen's Bass Strait quest; what he had been circling round for years. In these islands, so early 'settled', lay clues to earliest white Australia: something of the physical conditions endured then lingered yet, in a windswept and rocky landscape. But it was also a step through the looking glass: the people of this community were also Tasmanians and, in maintaining some of the customs and phrases of their ancestors, were directly connected with a culture of the ancient peoples who had inhabited the whole region. At last Stephen had found the kind of resonance in Australian culture he had been looking for.

His long interest in Indigenous Australia and strong feelings against racism in general now had a particular focus, in this exotic community in what could almost pass as his own back yard. Moreover, his own instinctive antipathy to institutional interference made him naturally sympathetic to the Islanders. They fascinated him for the way they had 'developed a nuclear strength and identity that even a hundred and fifty years of material and psychological pressures from outside have not been able completely to wash away'. As the world began moving towards conscious globalisation, there was a lesson in that.

Soon Stephen was editing the sympathetic accounts of the missions to the Islanders by Canon Brownrigg in the late nineteenth century. 'It would be nice if people of colored origin one day write their own history,' he reflected. 'All I can do is put historical evidence at their disposal.' He returned to Flinders Island often (owning a block of land there), and came to know its identities. So well known had he become that when he turned up with the governor-general, Sir Paul Hasluck—who he had persuaded to come and open the restored chapel at the old Tasmanian Indigenous detention centre, Wybalenna—the locals asked, 'Who's that man with Stephen?' He planned to edit more early accounts, and to write 'a proper book, historical and sociological and geological' on Bass Strait. But he had already begun to think of other comparable islands, and his imagination flew outwards. The idea of embarking on an Island project began to take hold. Eventually—picking up the word from *Mastermind*—he found a word to dazzle academic sceptics—'ekistics', the science of human settlements.[57]

Even in his first piece on Cape Barren, Stephen alluded to Pitcairn Island and Tristan da Cunha. Later—perhaps prompted by the appearance of Tom Steel's famous book—he added the Outer Hebridean island of St Kilda to the list. All that we are left with, apart from the Cape Barren material and some diary entries, is a fascinating essay on the three islands. It is so rich and suggestive that there can only be regret that Stephen wasn't spared to write the book.

Nonetheless he did manage to reach two islands of the additional three. St Kilda was the first: 'it arose out of the dull, grey evening sky like—I'm sorry to say!—another Kent Group [Erith]'. He explored the small island, but came back to its long, curved, single street, 'representing the fundamental commonality ... the old black houses interspersed with the later homes, representing a traditional past from which the islanders were being weaned'. On Tristan da Cunha—perhaps the remotest island in the world—he found the people rather like Cape Barren Islanders, 'very strong individualists within an anarchistic but (against outsiders) closed community. Not sophisticated; like the Cape Barreners, don't understand the motivations of those from outside who are interested in them.' He nonetheless managed to enter one house—the only double-storeyed one—and found a traditional spinning wheel and a subnormal daughter. Beyond lay The Patches—strips of land, as in medieval times—handed down the family line. And over all hovered the Peak, as high as Kosciuszko, the eruption of 1961 lingering in its wisp of sulphur fumes.

Stephen was intrigued by what his three original islands had in common. All were extremely isolated; were peopled by basically working-class settlers who intermarried with the local 'native' communities; had a common language base in English, although functionally illiterate; were settled in the Napoleonic period, though experienced little imperial interference; and maintained a subsistence economy centred on a few crops, fowling, or fishing. Small was not always beautiful, he was well aware. Pitcairn had suffered a murderous episode, while on Cape Barren misdemeanours within the community had begun by the 1890s, accelerating its fragmentation.

Nonetheless, there was a central question: 'How do small groups of people live, for close to two hundred years, without violence and without ostensible leadership, to create against all odds small societies far more successful in commonality than larger ones?' Indeed, they might point the way 'for people to live with one another without aggression or resentment'.

Tristan was particularly fascinating, in that the three men who remained on the island after the garrison withdrew in 1817 made a compact, stating their absolute equality and recognising their right to a third of the island's resources. Similarly, Stephen found on Cape Barren ('quite recently') an insistence on equality, that 'no-one is better than anyone else', and that 'we each make our decisions for ourselves'. Given this loose communalism, it was plain that the 'establishment of a moral code' became a vital element of survival for such communities; while they did not explicitly elect a leader, they usually deferred to a strong personality who upheld it. John Adams on Pitcairn was merely the archetype; the Bass Strait Islanders had Lucy Beeton. With Erith, the appellation and trappings of 'Emperor' might have been a humorous absurdity, but embedded in it was a recognition of the island's efficient secret.[58]

Had Stephen's project on islands been realised, as a thorough-going book it would have crowned his life's work. It would also have united, as nothing else would have done, the deeply intellectual strand of his life with his outdoor adventuring, his love of remote places, and his intrinsic sense of community. But it was not to be. Instead, there would be another diversion—itself producing a book that was as unexpected as it was remarkable.

Antarctica

Shortly after the Hawke government came to power, Stephen's old quiz partner Barry Jones asked him, What job would you like? Stephen gave no immediate answer; but years earlier, when recently returned from active service in New Guinea, he had written to the polar explorer Mawson, enquiring about joining an Antarctic expedition. Later in life he still admitted a fantasy goal of being a polar explorer like Amundsen. (When in Hobart, he would always try for the room the Norwegian explorer had taken when staying at Hadley's Hotel.) Meanwhile, in his avid book-collecting, Stephen sought out explorers' and travellers' accounts. It was Jones who alerted Stephen to the existence of Herbert Dyce Murphy, Mawson's dog-handler and the prompt for Patrick White's *The Twyborn Affair*. The details of this fascinating life Stephen took pains to record.

Now Jones was keen to get an independent assessment of the issues raised by the continuing Australian presence in Antarctica. Taking up the offer to go there, Stephen saw an opportunity to write a travel account of his own—indeed *Sitting on Penguins* was originally subtitled 'A Voyage of Discovery in Antarctica'. He would formally advise the minister for science (together they concocted the title 'Ministerial Observer'), in a private and confidential report. But he would also—with Jones' consent—go as a journalist, thinking through the implications of his observations in a set of articles for the *Australian*. And subsequently produce his book.[59]

In December 1985 Stephen joined those engaged in 'the changeover': the change of personnel, with replenishment, in the window of opportunity lasting only two months, when the Sun does not set. Even so, while they visited the bases Casey and Davis—and made a brief inspectorial visit to the French base—'fast ice' would prevent their visiting the other Australian base, Mawson.

Stephen sailed from Hobart on a custom-built German ship, the *Icebird*, chartered by the Antarctic Division of the Department of Science. The voyage leader was pleasant, but a worrier and a ditherer, and did not discuss matters with the Ministerial Observer. 'I just had to use my native wit and pick up what I could', Stephen noted.

He was aware he was not a good mixer, did not play bridge or other games. But he had curiosity, and a real way of engaging with people: a good handyman himself, Stephen had a respect for practical tasks and for those doing them. (He traced his empathy with the diesel mechanics, 'the diesos', to having been a private in the army.) Meanwhile he was already closely observing people: the 'delightfully kind and good-natured and rather sad cook—I can picture him crying into a stew as he stirs it.' Quickly Stephen picked up a variety of tensions on the ship: 'between the professionals, scientists and the like, with their toffy accents, degrees, and eccentric senses of humour, and the diesos and tradesmen; between the "round-trippers" and those going down for the rest of the summer; and between those going down for the rest of the summer and those going down for the winter as well'—who saw themselves as the genuine article. All were 'pleasant decent, ebullient, uncomplicated, timid Australians ... I'm not picking up any resonances from the "heroic" age'. At least there was no tension between the passengers and the German officers and crew. They were always obliging and, Stephen thought, ran a ship that, more than an Australian one would be, was surprisingly democratic in mood—despite the captain's penchant for playing German marches over the loudspeakers.[60]

There was an ever-present sense of vulnerability. Other ships then sailing were beset by ice; the captain himself—although exculpated—had been involved in the sinking of another ship, while recently a German ship in the Arctic Sea had hit an iceberg and gone down with all hands. Icebergs Stephen saw as 'glistening ice castles ... so remote from us, so contemptuous, so serene, outliers of a world which doesn't need to know us'. On one occasion a small party cruised around islands and inlets and right under the great cliffs of the Astrolabe Glacier. '"No-one is to talk", said Ewald as we passed under the overhangs. The resonance could have brought down a hundred tons of ice on us.' But there were also moments of exaltation. 'The last three hours', Stephen wrote in his diary at midnight as 20 January began,

> have been, in a visual sense, the most ravishing, the most transcendental in my experience. As I went to the bridge we were coming up to the great iceberg and pack-ice barrier that is the rampart of Davis. Soon we were pushing and breaking through. Then we were threading the iceberg needle, insolently thrusting our bow, and then the whole ship, between great bergs that towered above us, so close that the ship's shadow, its *Doppelgänger*, accompanied us through the gaps on the ice-walls beside us. The whole sea covered with pack-floes and stranded bergs, beautifully set off by the low sun to our west.

> How magnificently fortunate to have this fine weather, this sunshine, this hour of the day to see this wonderland at its best. A crowd on the bridge, and cameras running hot, but hardly a word: people seemed overawed, silent as in a great cathedral.

Stephen felt 'a wonderfully liberating feeling' once in the Antarctic '"wilderness"'—the word put in questioning quotation marks—with the vast expanses of snow and ice on either side. Once he saw a solitary Emperor penguin—a mirroring of himself—'standing in a dignified way on an ice floe'. It was, he declared, 'one of the reasons I came to Antarctica.'

Stephen found, despite himself, that he was impressed by the scale and efficient organisation of the unloading: the annual Erith event on a larger scale, 2300 tons of it. Launches, a variety of land vehicles, thousands of bags of cement, fuel and other provisions were lifted overboard by the ship's great cranes—and, noting the risks that were quietly taken as a matter of course, Stephen felt a surge of pride in his countrymen. Generally he threw himself into activities as much as he could. But he was appreciative of a friendly photographer helping him with his gear: 'I don't like being treated as an ancient, but excitement, struggling with cameras, scrambling up and down snow slopes and rubble, and trying to cope with ill-fitting and … largely inappropriate Antarctic clothing. Made me grateful for help.'[61]

Stephen warned in his preface to the book that there would be some contradiction in his views, and he was tugged by two alternatives. One arose from the scale of the new Australian base at Casey, then under construction: 'These cavernous buildings we are putting up', he wrote, whatever their amenities, are for 'aggression-display, not accommodation for scientists.' While the building program proceeded, it would chew up 90 per cent of the Antarctic Division's budget. Stephen was well aware that, under the recent Antarctic Treaty, territorial claims in Antarctica 'rest in suspended animation'.

But, with the growing belief that the continent was moving towards a resources boom (oil—and the first stirrings of tourism), international pressure on the Australian claim could be expected to increase. Massive infrastructure indicated Australia's determination 'to put down roots in Antarctica'. Earlier on Stephen had referred to a 'Maginot line' mentality, but appreciated that if the treaty were to collapse—the front line—then 'the second will hold. It is not magnificent, but it is a form of war.'

Sometimes he oscillated to a second approach, developing a suggestion made to him by a research scientist on the *Icebird*. Perhaps all that was needed was a 'spectacular' polar research vessel, which could be moored securely all the year round in the cove at Casey. From there a series of 'commando raids' could be made on the continent—small, highly trained teams being placed at selected sites by chopper to carry out intensive work. Given that there were to be only eight Australian scientists during that coming winter, at enormous cost ($42 million), this was less reductive than it seemed.

But the bases were there, the massive expenditure continuing (to the detriment of science), since Australia *did* need to maintain a presence. Australians, Stephen declared, were beginning to see Antarctica as 'an extension of their homeland'. As 'intimidatingly permanent as Ayers Rock', the bases had to be made more human: with women and families. Another article in the *Australian* spoke of the strong possibility of eventually there being 'not stations, but Australian townships in Antarctica, distinguishable from Shepparton or Hay mainly because the children have to be taken to and from school in blizzard-proof buses'. (It was a pale echo of Stephen's young man's dream of extensive white settlement in New Guinea.) A country that could not provide a decent taxi service in its capital, he noted, 'now has an empire'.[62]

It was being treated like a rubbish dump. 'We've gone a long way towards buggering up one continent,' Stephen wrote. 'There's no reason why we shouldn't start on another.' He was appalled by the ugliness of the old base at Casey, and horrified by the mess being created at the construction site of the new. But if Old Casey was 'a slum', the abandoned base of Wilkes was worse. Early warnings on approach were the wrecked vehicles, and the vast pile of fuel drums; the buildings lay under deep ice and snow. 'A dismal place, a junkyard', Stephen declared, indicative of 'the mutual contempt between man and this continent'. All purpose was immediate.

Stephen, though, sought history where others saw none. Approaching the explorer Mawson's hut, he thought, 'Above all I want the past to foreclose on me. I want to be precipitated back those seventy-five years and come into physical contact with Mawson and his men.'

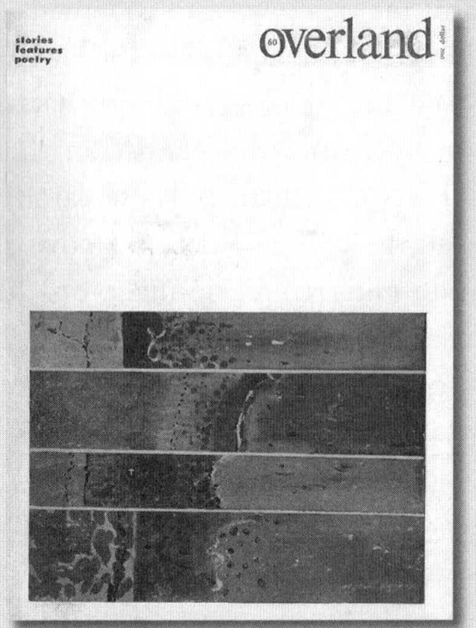

Overland 60 / Autumn 1975

The stories in this issue are by Morris Lurie and Peter Mathers, with the poetry unusually varied and strong, coming from Vincent Buckley, the Papua New Guinean Jack Lahui, Vivian Smith, Thomas Shapcott, Vicki Viidikas, Malcolm Brodie, Katherine Gallagher, Stefanie Bennett, Laurence Collinson, Peter Porter and Geoffrey Dutton. The main feature of the issue is an account—and discussion—from the artists camp on Erith Island, complete with an eight-page colour supplement of paintings by Fred Williams and Clifton Pugh. Alongside those bright colours John McLaren elaborates Solzhenitsyn's moral vision, and Cyril Pearl writes from Dublin. Judah Waten writes in praise of AA Phillips, for his 75th birthday. Books reviewed include the First Annual Report of the Australia Council for the Arts (Geoffrey Blainey, John Timlin), John Docker's *Australian Cultural Elites* (Geoffrey Serle), and recent poetry anthologies (Thomas Shapcott).

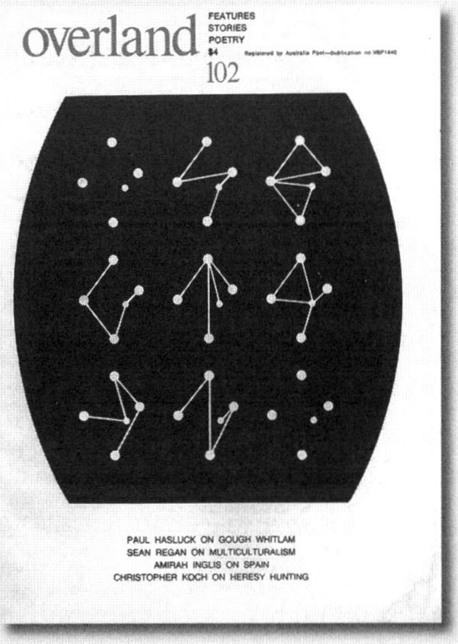

Overland 102 / April 1986

This issue contains only one story, 'Pick-and-Shovel Hero', by Peter Skrzynecki. But some of Lily Brett's Auschwitz poems are a main feature, with striking illustrations by David Rankin. Robert Harris, Elizabeth Riddell, Bruce Dawe, Eric Beach and Barney Roberts are among other poets represented. There are a number of high-powered articles. Sean Regan, in 'The Prison House of Cultures', raises questions about multiculturalism, considering the situation in Australia compared with Fiji; Paul Hasluck reviews Gough Whitlam's account of his government; and Robert Darby attacks the australophobe 'new critics' in 'The Fall of Fortress Criticism'. There is a Letter from Spain by Amirah Inglis, coloured by her work on the Spanish Civil War, and a Peloponnesian Diary by an Australian resident there, Gillian Bouras. John Sendy appraises early issues of *Overland*, and Don Charlwood pays tribute to the recently deceased AA Phillips. There is also a piece on the South Melbourne Football Club, recently turned into the Sydney Swans. Among the book reviews are Barry Hill on John Bryson's *Evil Angels*, Roger Millis on recent novels, and Boris Schedvin on a pessimistic collection of essays on Australia's economic future.

Crawling through a ten-metre ice tunnel into the heart of the hut, he found Mawson's small room, complete with his pillow on the bunk and his super-strength peppermints on a nearby shelf. 'In a way', mused Stephen, 'it's a bit like finding Ulysses' camp sites intact.' He was alarmed by talk of dismantling the hut to put it on permanent display in Melbourne. That would destroy continuity: something already evident in the way the officers-in-charge (OICs) had been told that the station log books would no longer be officially necessary.

There was, he reported to Barry Jones, no information at hand—it was all centralised at headquarters in Hobart—so there was no readily available guide even to such things as seasonal ice conditions or previous field expeditions. 'Every year in Australian Antarctica begins anew.' This came as no great surprise. It was just a heightened version, Stephen believed, of a general Australian lack of consciousness that we live in a continuum of past, present and future—as apparent in 'the supposedly "educated"' as much as in others. 'History', Stephen insisted, 'is not a luxury', something surplus to requirements.

Part of the problem was that operations were over-directed from headquarters. Scientists were not permitted to attend vital meetings. 'The old Antarctic spirit is dead', Stephen wrote, 'and that unfortunate continent is now firmly in the hands of soulless bureaucracies.' Decisions were taken regarding the ship's progress without consultation—and chopping and changing occurred to the point where the catch-word 'flexibility' became a joke. Even snow vehicles could not go out on the pack ice without specific authorisation. At the outset of their journey, Stephen and the other pressmen found that the officials on board the *Icebird* were contacting Hobart (or Canberra) to get a clearance for their 'inoffensive' articles.[63]

Shortly after becoming minister for science, Barry Jones had indicated his dissatisfaction with Australian activities in Antarctica, saying, 'We do face a massive credibility gap ... claiming so much (42% of the whole) and performing so little.' Stephen in his report made many suggestions, telling his friend how it was. Some of his recommendations were organisational, and stemmed from the great, 'serious' lack: 'the absence of any *experiential basis* to our work in Antarctica'. He was struck, he said, by the genuine, even selfless, dedication of most people to the task at hand. (Risks were taken to such an extent at the unloading that 'you are going to have a serious accident … before long'.) Scientists must cease to be marginalised. Something must also be done for the voyage leaders and officers-in-charge of bases, who 'are now ciphers, because Hobart Thinks It Knows'.

Then there were problems on the bases themselves—there had been a virtual insurrection at Casey, where in addition the OIC had lost the respect of the men. He was replaced, but the unruly element remained in control—until the arrival of the *Icebird*, which they were ordered to board. Clearly there were problems with recruitment—extending to the latest Casey OICs both having been ex-Rhodesians. People should only be appointed, Stephen cautioned, if they are 'through and through Australians, to run the mixed mobs you get at our stations'. Tensions could run high between young scientists—'who think they have their discipline *and* the whole world sewn up'—and the diesos.

Indeed the remark of one of the diesos, 'Antarctica is a people problem', kept reverberating for Stephen. Morale was low. 'The real problem', he wrote in the *Australian*, 'is that, as presently constituted, life at our base is a monastic life. As such, it is psychologically demanding. Violent tendencies have to be suppressed by self-control, for otherwise there is no knowing where they may lead.' The bases 'have got to be humanised and culturised', Stephen wrote, 'whether or not they turn into townships as I believe they should'. Many more women, and families, would help. And they should be less isolated: an airfield, with the possibility of short visits of all kinds being made, was absolutely necessary.

The report Stephen wrote revealed many of his idiosyncrasies: tellingly the book would come to be subtitled *People and Politics in Australian Antarctica*. He emphasised the need for the minister to have more personal involvement in Antarctic ventures: if he could not go there himself, then he should make sure that he farewelled each voyage, congratulated people on particular achievements, and saw to it that winterers got birthday greetings. Stephen's humanist concern then segued—in a move up from the make-believe of Erith—to recommending the inauguration of an Antarctic medal. ('No opportunities should be lost to impress on those going south that they are "special" people.')

But what concerned him particularly was the lack of cultural facilities. Young men went out as moderate drinkers, but returned as alcoholics. 'Crudities, the lack of inner resources, hostility to the different, resentment of the reflective, do rise to the surface here', Stephen noted. The libraries—such as they were—were 'a disgrace'. He recommended that the best new books be sent down each year, that there should be many more videos and films, together with a program of visiting Australian writers (including poets) and artists. It was *Overland*'s mission to the Antarctic: '*People will react to the image you demonstrate you have of them.*' Later he persuaded the authorities to send down classic accounts of Antarctica—and was mortified to learn that these were passed over by the men for *Playboy* and girlie magazines.[64]

Stephen's metaphor, *Sitting on Penguins* (to which some people unkindly added the rider, 'and squashing them!') nonetheless implicitly asked the question, Is that all we're doing? The book ran a stethoscope over Australia's involvement in Antarctica, and was progressive in outlook. Stephen noted the plastic being found elsewhere in the stomachs of petrels, and urged that something be done about this 'before someone denounces us for not doing it'. And while he did not discuss global warming as such, he was aware of the importance of research in glaciology, and that melting icecaps would drown all coastal cities.

The book, together with the articles in the *Australian*, helped to increase public awareness of Antarctica and its challenges. There was also some official response, including the resumption of station log books, and a program for removing long-standing rubbish. Antarctic medals were also awarded. Barry Jones praised Stephen for his work. Indeed *Sitting on Penguins* played a significant part in the 'dramatic shift from a resources view to an environmental view' of Antarctica. It helped to create the climate for the Hawke government—in one of Australia's most successful international ventures—to stand alone and take an important environmental initiative. Other nations followed, with the result that in 1991 a Protocol on Environmental Protection (banning mining) was added to the Antarctic Treaty.[65]

After Antarctica

Antarctica had been, for Stephen, 'a Dante-esque voyage to unimagined regions', but also one that, punctuated by long stretches of shipboard boredom, had tested him in unpredictable ways. He thought of the First AIF, coming back from France, and their folk wanting to share something of a transformative experience they could not really fathom. Nonetheless Stephen was determined to spread as much of the word as he could. Apart from *Sitting on Penguins*, he speculated on writing a history of Australia in Antarctica (if paid enough), and also spoke of an ambitious television series, with himself as front man. In his report to Barry Jones, he even said that he could improve 'behaviour and morale 500 per cent in two months if I were given the job' as director of the Antarctic Division. But the reality was that the bronchitis he brought back with him would never completely go away, and his chest pains were symptoms of an enlarged heart. Towards the end, as he lay in bed at night, excess fluid in the lung manifested itself as 'feeling that you're drowning, and not being able to do anything about it'. Increasingly life would become a physical struggle.[66]

Sometimes he wondered if it was worth it. Behind the bluster—for so it increasingly seemed to him, when he spoke in public—Stephen suffered panic attacks. But he surged on with his work, and was happiest when doing it. In 1980 he confessed that he had not made a sufficient mark upon the world, and was weighed down with 'subtle accumulative frustrations'. So with some pride he recorded, shortly after returning from Antarctica, that no less than six publications were pending. He was completing *Right Words*, editing a book for the ABC on Bass Strait, writing *Sitting on Penguins*, preparing a second edition of the *Dictionary of Australian Quotations*, while *Mission to the Islands* was being reprinted and *The Tech* was in production. This had been his response to the looming prospect of compulsory retirement—apart from joking about a 'Life Begins at 65' campaign in 'Swag'. 'My fucking pride', he wrote in his diary, 'was deeply hurt by retirement and [later] the heart trouble, perhaps interconnected.'[67]

It was hard not to have gloomy thoughts—the phrase 'failed radicals like me' insinuated itself into what would be his last 'Swag'. He missed Ian Turner, thinking of him still as his *wantok*—applying the Pidgin term for someone who speaks the same language, in a world of strangers. And Fred Williams, who had been close so briefly. There had been the pleasant surprise, when being invested with his AM, of being approached by a stranger, for it turned out to be his old school friend Rob Hamilton; but the friendship proved incapable of resuscitation. There were other disappointments: a serious one, in the case of Pitcairn. Stephen, with

Joanna, prepared to sail there on a schooner from Tahiti. But it was a jinxed trip right from the start, with harassment from customs officials. The vessel turned out to be unfit for a transoceanic crossing—it had been designed for lagoon work—and its fitting out had been slack. The five passengers were not fed for 36 hours, all were dehydrated, the weather was worsening, and a number were seriously ill: Stephen called a meeting (mutiny?), and the boat turned back.[68]

Ruefully Stephen remarked to David Martin that 'An important book like *The Tech* vanishes without trace.' John McLaren knew about this disappointment, so arranged for him to give the annual commemorative lecture at Footscray Institute of Technology. Stephen had only a few months left as a salaried academic; he decided on a blistering valedictory performance. Denouncing 'rogue technology'—evident in Antarctica as much as anywhere—again he yearned for wholeness. The failure to recognise technical education in Australia as part of its intellectual life was at the heart of most of our problems. No institution, no rising scholar, was investigating its relationship with society.

Yet 'Thoughtless technology, thoughtlessly applied ... is ruining us,' he declared. Stephen embroidered this assault with a quote from the Duchess of Marlborough one minute, the next aggressively stating that 'people in technical education have cut their balls off'. His audience would never have heard of Sir John Vanbrugh, equally famous as a dramatist and as an architect, and certainly never considered him as a possible exemplar. In front of them stood a tweed-coated, overweight man with a posh accent, crossing all boundaries, raising all kinds of questions, erudite and quirky—with hints of bad temper. Stephen's performance must have been a puzzle to them.[69]

It was entirely consistent with his own persona. In 1969 he had said, in an interview, 'I am something of an eighteenth-century, rather shop-soiled man of letters translated into the middle of the twentieth century, no longer particularly concerned at being somewhat out of alignment with his times.' Laurence Collinson, meeting him again nine years later, told him he looked well, but was too fat, hadn't his old equanimity, and was 'more crotchety'—which shocked Stephen, 'for I thought I had been affability incarnate'. The older he got, the more curmudgeonly he became. In a 1986 letter to Leonie Sandercock in America, he reported that he was currently fighting four battles: with La Trobe University over

PhD examination procedure, and with the Literature Board both over its Sydney-heavy composition and 'the persistent bias against *Overland*'.

Then there was the plan of ASAL (Association for the Study of Australian Literature) to sponsor a rival dictionary of quotations to Stephen's. He thought it a betrayal, given that he was a member, from people he had regarded as 'genuine comrades' in the campaign to advance Aust. Lit. His *DAQ* had aimed at bringing together, in an Arnoldian fashion, 'the best that has been thought and written about Australia … and expressed memorably'. For the young academics, it was not literary enough, 'too eccentric'. Fiery letters were exchanged; attempts by Brian Matthews to arrange a meeting were unsuccessful. Then one day they were both present at a book launch at the MCG. They nodded, and later Stephen came to stand alongside Matthews as he stood gazing out the plate glass window at the pitch. He began by saying he thought he owed him an apology. 'I haven't been that well', he added, flashing his quick smile. 'And my wife has been ill.' Then, in another key, as if it were a general statement, 'I haven't behaved … all that well.' The hatchet was buried. A few months later, Stephen was dead.[70]

As for *Overland*, it seemed to be more or less self-regulating, which suited Stephen. He did not want it radically changed, or to lose it. But now that he was involved in so many other projects, he understood how 'editors come to hate their magazines', given that their 'life's energies' were 'drained away in the service of writers and readers'. *Overland* was given little space in Stephen's diaries. He was even inclined to see something in a point of view that once would have shocked him: editing the magazine was, to a large extent, a job. There appeared in his diary, in quotes: 'I just work here.'

There was always ambivalence. 'I'd really love to dazzle people with *Overland* over the next twelve months,' Stephen wrote, 'show them that we're just starting our run!' If so, the fireworks were seen as Queen's Birthday rather than Guy Fawkes. 'Tradition is the keynote of *Overland*', wrote Peter Craven, approving its lack of 'strident ideology', with 'not a whiff of jargon'. In the two issues celebrating a centenary of numbers, 'the theme of personal memory and the mutating variations of history sounds over and over, as distinguished contributor after distinguished contributor takes part in a kind of collective elegy for "times past"'. The critic Don Anderson commented on those issues appreciatively—but then added: as a literary magazine, '*Overland* may be said to speak for the past.' As Barrie Reid noted, literary committees now saw Stephen as 'establishment' and 'past it', despite his own publications and the evidence in *Overland* generally. 'It's an image that the reputation-setting mid-career trendies have settled on *Overland*, and, despite its falsity, it is going to stick I'm afraid.'[71]

Was *Overland* reaching out to the young, more than was noticed? The answer is yes—quite apart from new poetry. In one late issue, Number 107, all three short stories could be seen as coming from young (or recently young) modish authors: Frank Moorhouse, Kevin Brophy and Beth Yahp. In Stephen's last years, a number of new names were recurring among the article writers: John Docker, Don Watson, Robert Darby, and John Herouvim. To make the point, once or twice their ages appeared in their by-lines.

Moreover, two of these contributors savaged the *Oxford History of Australian Literature*, edited by Leonie Kramer. Its authors were too concerned with establishing a canon, emphasising 'literary values' as they closely read texts and excoriated social or historical contextualisation. Kramer had written for *Overland*, and Stephen had been on good terms with her; even so, he had little hesitation in publishing the piece. Soon David Malouf, having put the Sydney English Department behind him, joined the fray. 'Professional handlers of literature', he reminded everybody, 'have no special authority in the making or breaking of canons—they are readers like the rest of us.' At the same time, he asserted, 'We won't become Australians by a deliberate act of will, and we won't have a national literature by declaring one.' We are just at the beginning.[72]

The balance Stephen aimed for persisted, and had been broadened: as well as the young, there were veterans like Sir Walter Crocker, with his elegant memoirs of contemporaries supplemented by writings on foreign policy. Book reviews were as much by writers as by academics. And as a historian himself, Stephen could still call on people such as Ken Inglis, Geoffrey Blainey or John Mulvaney when he needed to. Or even HP Heseltine, who felt more comfortable in *Overland* these days than in *Meanjin*. Indeed, *Overland* had moved into ground seemingly vacated by the senior journal. Christopher Koch chose it as the place to make a rejoinder to one of its articles (which *Meanjin* took well). There were also a few think-pieces in the old Clem style, such as John Herouvim's rousing 'Civilising Australia' (which appeared in Stephen's last issue). 'The whole tone of this country is becoming dangerously uncivilised,' he asserted. Amid the rise of ideologies of greed, the New Left has undermined the Australian Legend, which was a deep source of decency, while the ALP, Herouvim declared, 'is a mental condom on the penis of socialist strategy'. 'A civilised nation looks after its people', he asserted, which is no longer happening; 'but there is a population not yet ready to listen to socialism.'

Despite changes in context—such as the rise of the internationalist, decidedly literary journal *Scripsi*—Stephen displayed his wares with even more assurance than in the past. (*Scripsi* helped define his ground.) Rubbing shoulders in one issue were Crocker and Docker—aged Adelaide mandarin next to Sydney cultural tearaway. Or Crocker again, in another, with the Literature Board's Michael Costigan, running a metaphorical stethoscope over the memoirs of Charles Osborne, the Brisbane boy who became England's arts czar. There was continuing engagement in the magazine, along with a capacity to come up with the unexpected. Repeatedly Stephen received plaudits from older readers, and others. Ken Inglis summed it up: 'So many of us readers think it's been getting better and better. Span? Tone? A ripeness in the editor?' The proof was in the pudding, in the notable rise in subscriptions. What might be done, Stephen was tempted to think, were there an office and a secretary …[73]

Stephen had always felt himself under constant pressure from Barrett Reid, who would just turn up: once he brought along the poet Robert Harris, who, straight and with a religious bent, was a kind of antidote to Shelton Lea. Stephen therefore detected an ominous note when Reid stated his desire to come down and discuss the future of the magazine. 'He doesn't want to take over *Overland* from me', he wrote with relief in his diary, 'well, not all of it.' There was 'definitely a power drive, but I think I can manage it'—so he agreed to name him assistant editor. Reid had a stream of ideas, some of which Stephen needed to hear. Reid believed the magazine was 'too historical', and had 'no appeal for young people'. He wanted format change, and constantly feuded with Vane Lindesay over design issues. *Overland* needed to include 'something positive, something new, something trendy.' The magazine's critics depicted Stephen as 'an old fossil'. 'I know you're not', Reid reassured him in 1987, but they must not be given ammunition.[74]

A countervailing figure to Barrie Reid was John McLaren. McLaren, while a product of Scotch and Ormond Colleges, had grown up partly in the country and returned there as a teacher. He stood for parliament: Stephen noticed the name of a recent contributor, and wrote to ask if he were the same person. Yes, he replied. *Overland* turned out to be McLaren's consolation prize for having lost the contest for Indi. Appointed to the Secondary Teachers' College, and later to Footscray Institute of Technology, he quickly moved to the centre of the *Overland* circle. A big, shambling man with a resonant if rasping voice, McLaren had solid literary tastes and thorough knowledge; his best students were devoted to him. But his was a flat majesty; charisma was not in the mix. When he wrote 'Swag' in Stephen's absence, it read like a school notice board.[75]

There was much bitterness between McLaren and Reid, who had suggested McLaren become involved in the new *Australian Book Review*, which he came to edit. Others found McLaren somewhat inflexible; Reid, resigning from the new journal's management committee, declared him 'too pedagogical and too politically sectarian', muttering about 'abnormal psychology'. Reid, McLaren felt, was always intent on advancing his own interests, and had not supported him sufficiently as chair of the National Book Council (which owned the journal).

Later McLaren would be removed from the *ABR* editorship, but before then, when fired up by drink, he was a danger when in one of his 'roaring moods', as Stephen called them. At an *Overland* board meeting held in McLaren's house, both Reid and McLaren were 'utterly intransigent … spoke unpleasantly to each other … stormed out of the room and were brought back, both …white with passion and rage'. Nonetheless Stephen decided Reid should edit *Overland* while he was away—McLaren had done it before, and after all still then edited *Australian Book Review*. Although he won that battle, Reid was surprised by what Stephen termed the 'vicious hatred' of his opponent. He also had issues with McLaren's intrusive wife Shirley, opening his mail and answering letters on her own initiative. He resolved never to attend a board meeting in the McLaren household again.

But McLaren was a serious contender. Contrasting himself directly with Reid's inefficiencies, McLaren earlier had, in Stephen's absence, bulldozed out five issues in little more than a year. Moreover, his letter from Cambridge published in *Overland* years before had cleverly linked an academic row over structuralism with the onrush of Thatcher and monetarism; displaying a cogent liberal argument against the doctrinaire, it was an implicit advance towards eventual editorship. But Reid, although gravely ill, was not done yet. In 1986 he proposed that Stephen hand over to a younger editor, perhaps in a year's time, so that, as Stephen recognised, 'I should just become "publisher and general editor" (i.e. nothing)'. Among other things, the existing board should be dispensed with entirely. Stephen was not surprised by Reid's 'byzantine intrigue', but was rather shocked to discern 'his real purpose—to sacrifice me in order to defeat John McLaren'.

The person Stephen would most have liked to succeed him—when the time came—was Stuart Macintyre. But the rising historian had his eyes very firmly on an academic career: there his contribution would be exceptional, his list of publications prodigious. Stephen also cast an eye over friends of Joanna's when they came down to Mt Eliza, looking for a prospective editor there. He thought of John Herouvim; towards the end he was impressed with the Canberra-based Robert Darby, who as a former Maoist (and public schoolboy) had followed a similar trajectory to his own. Moreover Darby was in addition an Aust. Lit. scholar with a trenchant pen and a developing taste for book collecting. Stephen gave him some. He asked him to become a corresponding editor.[76]

The day following Darby's visit to Mt Eliza, Stephen spent some time vigorously polishing his shoes. Not feeling particularly well, he played on the bed with his little grandson, Joseph. He then got up to go to the library. Short-breathed, he sat on the steps leading down to his desk, and the comforting fire. He never got up. In his typewriter, ready for sending to the premier, was a letter pleading the cause of a prisoner.[77]

Stephen wrote his last diary entry on 30 July 1988, the day before he died. Then come two lines in a different hand: Nita's. 'My great and only love—the grief and sorrow is too much to bear.' The funeral took place at the Springvale crematorium: there was an impressive turnout, as expected. But some were puzzled that there should be, among all the public figures—writers, cabinet ministers and academics—a number of fishermen and lighthouse keepers. Unfortunately I was in England; but I returned soon after, in time for a tribute to Stephen in the Public Lecture Theatre at the University of Melbourne. Presiding was John McLaren; it was his finest hour. His deep grief and sense of loss was transforming—the onetime Christian socialist assumed the calm, deliberative manner of a Presbyterian minister.

Among the speakers were Manning Clark, Geoffrey Blainey, Barry Jones and Geoff Serle. Dorothy Hewett sent a piece read out by John McLaren: 'Until the day he died', she wrote, 'this Geelong Grammar School boy, born with a silver spoon in his mouth, was always a radical, even when, or maybe especially when, the cause was unpopular and the friend or colleague was in disfavour.' Interspersed with the tributes was some of Stephen's favourite music. One piece was the engaging rondo from Mozart's first horn concerto: a glimpse of Stephen as dancing bear. But behind the lectern, like a series of handbills on a protest wall, were ranged the covers of Stephen's *Overland*, all 111 issues. The last few jaggedly began a new line. As Barrie Reid, grief-stricken, duly noted, 'It is as if a young man had died.'[78]

The two-year-old grandson: 'My magic man is gone.'

Stephen's ashes were taken to Erith—as Ian Turner's had been—and buried under a cairn. It was a more elemental, and only slightly less imperial, equivalent of Cecil Rhodes purloining an African hilltop for his grave. But Erith more than the Matopo Hills crystallised a 'World's View'. It was, Stephen felt, perhaps the most successful of all his projects. Indeed it united a number of basic aspects of the man. First it expressed that yen for the primitive, for a testing hardship, that had been part of him since the end of his schooldays; a counterweight to a more urbane and sybaritic self. It was also an expression of communal living, a primitive do-it-yourself socialism that gestured towards an ideal for organised society. Hence Stephen had reached out to other small communities, permanent ones, with questions as to how they survived and how they ran themselves, on islands scattered across the globe. He deserved his place overlooking the sea.

Both Clem and Stephen held tightly in their minds the image of islands. Clem's was in childhood, something distant, almost unattainable; Stephen's became not one island, but many, though always centred on Erith—and the nearby lighthouse. Sometimes, at his death, people likened the man himself to a lighthouse; high on a headland, the enabling beam raking the landscape to warn of the hazards ahead. Clem, on the other hand, was the fiery ship's captain far out to sea, railing at the elements like the Flying Dutchman, without rest or respite, determined to overcome all obstacles, his eye always on the horizon. Stephen, as he aged, became mellower; at times he could look seraphic. So one can see him now, a gigantic *putto* gambolling above Erith, reducing chaos to order—with a loudhailer in his hand.

Afterword

After Stephen died, *Overland* was set up as a company limited by guarantee (as *Meanjin* had been). The first chair of the Overland Society was Geoff Serle. Twice he had rescued *Meanjin*, ensuring its continuity; now he would do what he could to advance the legacy of his old mate Stephen. There's no real surprise in this double allegiance: it seems that one of the ideas Clem floated at the time of his retirement was that the two magazines should merge, under the editorship of Stephen.

Immediately after Stephen's death, the editorship passed to Barrett Reid. John McLaren deferred his claim in view of Reid's mortal illness, becoming editor in 1993. Since then there have been seven editors of *Overland*, successively Ian Syson, Nathan Hollier and Katherine Wilson, Jeff Sparrow, Jacinta Woodhead, and now Evelyn Araluen and Jonathan Dunk. John McLaren worked to establish links with Victoria University, and for a time that institution's support was considerable. But in 2019 it was withdrawn.

Overland today is conscious of Stephen's legacy, and prides itself on being 'Australia's only radical literary magazine'. While its outlook is more global, it has found distinctiveness in seeking to publish 'under-represented perspectives on issues rarely given space in traditional media'. *Meanjin* similarly aligns itself with the vision of its first editor, aiming to display 'the breadth of contemporary thinking, be it on literature, or other art forms, or the broad issues of the times'. Recognising the surge in local complexities, it now chooses to do this from Australian contributions alone.

Meanjin was first to be set up as a company limited by guarantee, once Clem signed the papers in 1975. I then formally succeeded him (having run the magazine for six months already), and in turn was succeeded by Judith Brett. Since then there have been eight more *Meanjin* editors: Jenny Lee, Christina Thompson, Stephanie Holt, Ian Britain, Sophie Cunningham, Sally Heath, Zora Sanders, and now Jonathan Green. The Meanjin Company was dissolved in 2008, when the magazine became an imprint of Melbourne University Publishing. In 2019 a new dispensation ensured fuller university support than there had ever been. The part-time editor is well paid, and there is now—as Clem had always wished—a more or less full-time assistant editor.

Meanwhile Clem's name, and something of his reputation, still lingers. As Michael Heyward explained years ago:

> Christesen was obsessed with his journal and had a maniac's tenacity. He badgered and hectored and bullied and flattered everyone within range about the importance of the University maintaining a journal that was politically independent and internationally agile. It is our great debt to him that he did this so persistently and so well, however many people he rubbed up the wrong way in the process. The image of the editor that Christesen presents is an heroic one: a man being buffeted about and buffeting others under the shifting pressures of making good a form of cultural exchange that was not otherwise available.

It was a handsome tribute from one of the editors of *Scripsi*, a consciously international magazine.[1]

Although it was never articulated as such, Clem Christesen had a three-point plan. First was to publish new Australian writing, which, while usually occupying only a segment of his magazine, was always felt by him to be *Meanjin*'s most important single ingredient. Second was the creation of a context for it, involving the creation of a canon and the advancement of Australian Literature, especially in the universities. As was remarked at the time (by an expatriate) this was not simple historicism. It was a matter of necessity: in Australia new work alone did not appear in sufficient quantity or quality to sustain intense critical involvement. (Nor was there the body of high-flying critics and commentators that existed elsewhere in the Anglosphere.) For most of the period of Clem's editorship, creative writers were appreciative of this creation of context: too often they had a sense of working in a vacuum. Finally, the emergence of Australia on the world stage had to be matched by a fuller international engagement. *Meanjin* always cocked one eye towards the horizon, including material from or about other countries, in particular new writing. To his credit, Clem had no compunction about rejecting inferior work despatched Down Under by well-known names, to what they saw as a literary Botany Bay.

Stephen's project was quite different. While his Communism sharply fell away, an element of radical nationalism long remained, and eventually became expressed in a concern with building Australian cultural infrastructure. In *Overland* he strove to bring together popular culture and the emergent Australian high culture: the magazine was open to all comers, a collective enterprise. 'Personally,' he wrote to his readers, appealing for support, 'we think it a good idea to have a magazine where professors and slaughtermen, wharfies and politicians and professional writers can all have a go …' But *Overland*, while the flagship, was only part of Stephen's activities. He became the doyen of Australian historians of technical education, produced a gloss on standard English for Australia (*Right Words*) plus a *Dictionary of Australian Quotations*. And he patrolled the frontiers. As a young man he had been exposed—in wartime—to the heat of New Guinea; when elderly he undertook a mission that took him to the ice and snow of Antarctica. While Clem's magazine was the greater achievement, Stephen was the more interesting man.

Both men, and their magazines, were often dismissed by much of the reading public as too self-consciously Australian, exercises in gumnutry—a charge which, in the case of *Overland*, had some point. But their projects were national(ist), seeking to subvert a prevailing English cultural hegemony. It was the necessary first step towards a fuller cultural self-realisation. Moreover, both editors daily negotiated the Other: at a time when it was most unusual, both men had decided to marry 'out'. Nina was Russian, Nita Polish and Jewish.[2]

Clem and Stephen's thirty-four-year editorships are almost inconceivable today. It is not only a question of gender; the style in such ventures is more consultative, procedures often more bureaucratic. Then there is the pace of change: Ian Hamilton's contention that a literary magazine should only run for ten years or so has never seemed more plausible. The greater segmentation of society has led to a drop in public support for state funding of the arts. Meanwhile the replacement of the idea of 'the public' by the concept of 'consumers' has undercut the very notion of 'the general reader'. Indeed, the tide began to draw away from literature quite some time ago: since the 1970s, the term 'the arts' has increasingly come to mean only the performing arts. Literature itself has become performative. These days the common reader goes to writers festivals.

More broadly, digitisation and ever-advancing technology have led to an increasing belief that precision exists only in numbers. Constant measurement—flattening out nuance and variation—has risen with what could be termed (to update Eisenhower) the technoid-managerial complex. Lawyers, of course, continue to gerrymander the language—twisting, contorting and cluttering it—all in the pursuit of a more evasive precision. But once competence in it was such that a bright Victorian schoolchild could make a good fist of describing a pair of scissors in a sentence. Not now. There is a general impatience with complexity. 'Four-minute read', 'five-minute read' state tags on the internet; on social media people read for affirmation as much as for discovery. Ours is becoming a glance culture.

While all this makes the position of literary magazines particularly perilous, Stefan Collini pointed out some years ago that the talk has *always* been of decline. ('The golden age that never was', he called his article.) As Stephen Murray-Smith would wearily remark, the old battles always have to be re-fought. Indeed the Australian Association for Cultural Freedom 1962 seminar he attended had one session asking, 'Are Literary Journals Obsolescent?'

The short answer is, no. 'The point of little magazines', wrote Mark Lilla, 'is to think big in them.' Jonathan Green points to there being 'many speeds in public conversation, but there's a deeper current to which the big ideas are held, and they slowly sort of tumble along the bottom of the river.' And tumble they do. Many important issues in Australian public life were first raised in literary magazines, not least in response to the Indigenous people or the consequences of economic rationalism and globalism. As WH Auden put it, 'our intellectual marines / Landing in little magazines / Capture a trend.' Meanwhile they have continued to provide entry points to the print culture for a variety of writers.[2]

The appeal of literary magazines has always been a minority one. (Collini notes in passing that *The Times* carried more authority when its circulation was a mere 50,000, rather than the 700,000 it enjoyed when he wrote at the turn of the century.) The basic problems associated with them today remain the same as ever. There's the difficulty of paying contributors—and editors—adequately, of extensive publicity, and the costs and challenge of effective distribution (if still printing). As Emmett Stinson put it, 'Because no viable market-based model exists for literary magazines, dependence on a mix of subsidy, institutional support, patronage and especially volunteerism remains a necessity.'

There should always be a place for lengthier discussion. Given the screen's in-built resistance to longer pieces, in one sense the new technology adds an extra argument for the continuation of the literary review-type magazine. Yes, people can get their reading more directly from particular sources. But synergy will come from placing articles and creative work within the same set of covers, offering different perspectives as the magazine probes culture and society. The contemporary editor becomes a kind of curator. In the end, whether her offerings are made on the internet or in print (or both) is relatively secondary.[3]

Certainly there are enough questions to address. Australia today faces probably the greatest concatenation of crises since this land mass became known by that name. It goes beyond COVID-19 (bad enough) to climate change, to the need for full recognition of Indigenous participation in our national life, and to following through the implications of multiculturalism. Rather than advancing towards a republic, recent events have shown that the federation itself might need some reconfiguration. Meanwhile, there has been a continuing corrosion of public confidence in our politicians. Of particular relevance here has been the Morrison government's assault on science, the universities and the arts—intellect and the imagination. But no nation (for that's what we are—not an 'economy') can survive on lifestyle and business alone. We are a small country, in an exposed situation, now feeling the breath of the dragon. We need all the new ideas we can get.

We also need a more perceptive understanding of ourselves. Globalism has had a punishing effect on localism (which was one of the prompts in writing this book). Concerned with laterality as it is, globalism tends to ignore the historical dimension. Literary-review-type magazines, on the other hand, have thriven not only on amplitude but often on depth—verticality. Less concerned now with building up a national culture, among other things they can still provide much needed fibre for national debates. Instead, funding is being withdrawn from literary magazines as from many arts activities. Publishing itself has been attacked by the Productivity Commission, for diverting capital and skilled labour from other industries.[4] The designated chairs in Australian literature, which Clem fought so hard for, are now disappearing. The universities themselves are in dire straits; the national archives needed a public campaign to rescue them. The country is in danger of losing its memory, if not its mind.

That is how it seems, as we hurtle on to we know not what.

Notes

Abbreviations

CBC	CB (Clem) Christesen
DMS	David Murray-Smith
FLUQ	Fryer Library, University of Queensland
HoM	CBC, *The Hand of Memory*
Ind	Stephen Murray-Smith, *Indirections*
LaT	La Trobe Collection, State Library of Victoria
M, MP, MQ	*Meanjin/Meanjin Papers/Meanjin Quarterly*
NAA	National Archives of Australia
NLA	National Library of Australia, Canberra
O	*Overland*
RW	*Realist Writer*
SLV	State Library of Victoria
SMS	Stephen Murray-Smith
SMSD	Stephen Murray-Smith, Diaries
SMS Box	Stephen Murray-Smith Papers, MS 8272, La Trobe Collection, SLV
UMA	Meanjin–Christesen, CB, 2005.0004, University of Melbourne Archives

Issues of *Meanjin* are listed according to Clem's house style, by number and year

Introduction

1 Fintan O'Toole, eulogy in 'Robert B. Silvers (1929–2017)', *New York Review of Books*, vol LXIV no 8, 11–24 May 2017, p 35.

Chapter 1 Transcending the Prison House of Self

1 Townsville: CBC, 'The Island', in Petersen and Torre, *North of Capricorn*, esp. pp 71, 79; CBC, 'A Young Man is Impressed', UMA Box 72. Clem's full name was Clement Byrne Christesen.

2 Susan Christesen: CBC, NLA interview (1969), 2; CBC to SMS, 4 Oct 1975, SMS LaT Box 166; Armstrong, *Romance*, pp 20, 22; brothers, McLachlan, "*M* and Australia in the Fifties', p 94.

3 Patrick, and CBC relations with parents: Armstrong, *Romance*, pp 20–6; CBC interview (1969), NLA, 1.

4 Schooling and wool classing: Armstrong, *Romance*, pp 28–30; *Brisbane State High School Magazine*, (1927), pp 31, 32, 49; CBC interview (1969) NLA, 3.

5 CBC becomes a journalist: Armstrong, *Romance*, p 31.

6 CBC at UQ: student record card, CB Christesen, UQA 5157; athletics, McLachlan, '*M* and Australia', p 94; 'uninspired', CBC to SMS, 5 May 1975, SMS Box 166; *Galmahra*, Armstrong, *Romance*, p 32; Morrow Prize, Board of Faculties 3rd Report (1933), in Minutes of Meetings of Professorial Board, 1932–34, UQA; mother's letter, Armstrong, *Romance*, p 33; King's, Faragher, *Men and Masters*, pp 37–42; King's listed in CBC *Who's Who* entry (1980), p 187; radicalism, McLachlan, above.

7 CBC as government publicist: Armstrong, *Romance*, pp 32–3; CBC, *Queensland Journey*, p 45.
8 'Chris Byrne'—news cuttings, UMA Box 72.
9 CBC abroad, 1939: Travel diaries (2 vols), esp. I, pp 34, 40, and II, pp 5, 9, 11, UMA Box 76; Armstrong, *Romance*, pp 33–7.
10 Brisbane, 1939–40: 'The long sweep', from Barrie Reid, 'Brisbane', in MS book in UMA Box 284; Mee-an-jin, Vrepont, CBC, *Queensland Journey*, pp 13, 31; 'cultural aspect', CBC, 'A Playhouse', Scripts, UMA Box 72; earlier poets, CBC, Yearly Survey of Literature and Art in Queensland 1940, Appendix to QAAA Annual Report 1940; orchestras, Green, 'Three Editors', p 207; Armstrong, *Romance*, p 4; also Wright, 'Brisbane in Wartime' and Strahan, *Just City*, pp 9–10.
11 CBC, Notes on Excell paper, 'Flying Without Plumes', Patricia Excell.
12 Devaney: listener, Rodney Hall, 8 Dec 2011; Devaney to CBC, 21 June 1936; CBC, statement of appreciation, UMA Box 110; CBC interview by P Excell, 2 May 1988.
13 Vrepont: 'Vrepo', EM Anders to CBC, 2 Jan 1945, and CBC to Carol Cooper, 24 Oct 1962, both UMA Box 342; Clem on Vrepont, 'Poetry in Q in 1940', in Appendix to QAAA Annual Report 1940; Grano, 'Memories of Early *Meanjin*' (1970), pp 4–6, Grano Scripts UMA Box 148, also Comments on CBC's '21 Lives of *MQ*', Hayes Papers, UQFL 2/380.
14 Clem meets Picot: Buckridge, *ADB*, vol 19, p 609; 'enthusiasm', CBC Notes P Excell (1990), and elsewhere.
15 Picot personality: Grano, 'Memories', p 9; 'Norman', CBC, Intro to *With a Hawk's Quill*, p vi; Russell N Hill, MS on Picot, UMA Box 268; Devaney's and other tributes, *M*, XIII/1 (1954), pp 88–105.
16 Picot's poetry: 'Romantics', Picot to CBC, 6 Jan 1941, UMA Box 268; Grano, 'Memories', pp 9–10; nightingale, Martin Haley, 'A Queensland Poet, JP', *Advocate*, 3 Mar 1955, UMA Box 268; 'surest application', CBC, Yearly Survey of Art and Literature 1940.
17 Grano: 'Memories', pp 1–2; Grano Comments on CBC broadcast, pp 1–2, UQFL 2/380; instinctive dislike, Grano to Father Hayes, 20 Mar 1964, UQFL 2/3240.
18 *Meanjin* appears: CBC, Notes on Excell paper; CBC, 'Twenty-One Lives', pp 85–7.
19 Queensland poetry: Macartney, Picot to Nettie Palmer, 1941 [*sic*], UMA Box 268; 'disappointed', HM Green to CBC, 27 Feb 1942, Box 245; tradition, Strahan, *Just City*, pp 12–13.
20 *MP* 1, and response: CBC, 'Twenty-one Lives', pp 85–6; *Bulletin*, 'Red Page' extract and Devaney in *Catholic Leader* in letter book, pp 1–3, UMA Box 244.
21 Clem's poetry: 'Lantern Light', Picot to Nettie Palmer, 1941 [*sic*], UMA Box 257; 'pretty awful', Notes on Excell paper; 'Milhaud', cut from 'Paul Pentecost and the Mocking-Bird', *North Coast*, pp 12–13, cf. *HoM*, pp 74–5; Grano, 'Twenty-one Lives', p 87; one poem, 'Regent-Bird and Girl', *HoM*, p 49.
22 Nina Maximov: 'dashing Best Man', CBC to Ingamells, 5 Dec 1941, LaT MS 6244/1/69; Nina Christesen, 'A Russian Migrant', pp 56–73; Armstrong, *Romance*, pp 1–19, 39–40; 'good hair', Jane Sullivan, 'From Russia with a love of language', *Age*, 11 Aug 2011.
23 Nina and Clem: 'adaptation', Nina Christesen, 'Russian Migrant', p 76; 'idealism', Armstrong, *Romance*, p 42; 'second wife', CBC to Palmers, 11 Jan 1945, NLA MS 1174/1/6693-4; conversation, McPhee, *Memoirs of a Young Bastard*, p 206; bleeding, Armstrong, *Romance*, pp 50–1; 'bough', 'My Love is a Golden Bower', *HoM*, p 151.
24 Tommerup: Nazism, see *Courier-Mail*, 21 Nov 1934; 'father', CBC to P Serle, 27 May 1943, UMA Box 300; Armstrong, *Romance*, pp 14–17, 40, 110–11.
25 CBC political attitudes: 'herd', McLachlan, '*M* and Australia', p 94; organic/eugenic, see CBC to JV Duhig, 28 May 1941, UMA Box 112; 'Great Dynamic', CBC to Rex Ingamells, 5 Dec 1941, LaT MS 6244/1/69; 'Monstrosities of people', 2nd diary 'English Autumn—1939', p 3, and multicultural, 1st diary, 29 July, p 25, UMA Box 76; 'very Fascist-minded', CBC to Ingamells, 9 Aug 1942, LaT MS 6224/1/87-93.
26 PR Stephensen and CBC: Lenin, Munro, *Wild Man of Letters*, p 39; place, *Foundations*, p 15; on Qld poetry, *Publicist*, April 1941, *Meanjin* l. bk, p 11, UMA Box 244; mother, WJ Miles to CBC, 21 April 1941, above, p 85; CBC as supporter, SB Hooper to CBC, 27 July 1941, p 129, and for *Hamlet*, Stephensen to CBC, 22 Dec 1941, adamant, 16 Sep 1941, both l. bk, p 155, UMA Box 244; Stephensen, 'Queensland Culture', *MP* 1/6, pp 7–8; 'A Mopoke attacks Ian Mudie', *Publicist*, Dec 1941, l. bk, p 178, and 'Sydney Führer', Herbert to CBC, 19 Oct 1941, l. bk, p 165, both UMA Box 244; sue, JK Ewers to Rex Ingamells, 8 Dec 1941, LaT MS 6244/1/198; 'poeticals', CBC to Ingamells, 11 Nov 1941, LaT MS 6244/1/64.

27 *Conditional Culture*: text in Barnes, *The Writer in Australia*, pp 245–65; McQueen, 'Rex Ingamells and the Quest for Environmental Values', *Meanjin* 1/1978, p 29.
28 CBC and Ingamells: CBC to Ingamells, 8 Oct and 23 Oct 1941, LaT MS 6244/1/61, 1/63; uniquely, Ingamells, 'Australianism', *MP* I/6, p 3; space between, CBC to Ingamells, 25 Mar 1942, LaT MS 6224/1/80; 'meanjeering' (T Inglis Moore), 8 Oct 1941, LaT MS 6244/1/62; re Stephensen, CBC to Ingamells, 5 Dec 1941, LaT MS 6224/1/70-71; anguish, Ingamells to CBC, 2 Mar 1942, LaT MS 6244/1/75; nexus, not straight, Ingamells to JK Ewers, 19 Feb 1945, LaT MS 6224/1/278; 'whispering gallery', Ingamells to CBC, 15 Apr 1942, l. bk, p 16, UMA Box 245; young man, CBC to Gifford, 26 June 1944, Box 143.
29 Harris and *Angry Penguins*: Jindy, Ingamells to CBC, 21 Sep 1942, UMA Box 245 and Heyward, *Ern Malley*, p 14; Harris, 'Directions in Australian Poetry: Dance Little Wombat', *MP* II/2, pp 33–5; 'so important', CBC to Harris, undated memo, Barr-Smith 92 H315P/SR/Ser 1.5; 'alive', *Angry Penguins* 2 (1941), p 7; review of *AP* by 'Mopoke', *MP* 6, 27–8; 'keep the peace', CBC to Harris, Thursday [1943], UMA Box 162.
30 Ern Malley: Hughes, quoted in Heyward, *Ern Malley*, p 16.
31 AD Hope and *Meanjin*: mischief, Hayward, *Ern Malley*, p 114; 'Maxie's head', Hope to CBC, 6 and 27 Mar 1944, UMA Box 179; 'utter injustice', Heyward, *Malley*, p 167.
32 *Meanjin* and Malley: 'more forcefully', Brian Elliott in *Angry Penguins*, 7 (1945), p 10; *Meanjin* coverage, review, 'Penguin Pot-Pourri', *MP* III/2, p 113, editorial, pp 121–2, and 'decent burial', p 116; editorial III/3, pp 134–5, and Elliott, 'Taboo—or not To Boo', II, pp 180–2; Green, in *AP*, 7 (1945), p 16; Murray, quoted Heyward, *Malley*, p 231.
33 Poetry: canon, Nettie Palmer on T. Inglis Moore, *Six Australian Poets*, *MP* I/10, p 17; 'intuitive understanding', editorial, I/5, p 2; Vrepont, 'Letter to Tom Collins', I/5, p 15; 'singing quality', editorial, I/3, p 3.
34 The shape of *Meanjin*: Miles Franklin to CBC,17 Aug 1944, UMA Box 134; CBC, 'The Meanjin "School"', *MP* II/2, pp 49–53; CBC, 'Should Australian literature be national in outlook?", ABC talk 30 June 1942, UMA Box 7; 'religiosity', CBC to HS Temby, Sec CLF, 13 Feb 1948, NAA A463/1963/2565/I; 'virile Australian culture', Notes to Contributors, *MP* I/7; 'bacon', AD Hope in *Honi Soit*, 7 Oct 1943, l. bk, p 104, UMA Box 245.
35 Notes to Contributors: 'writers-at-arms', *MP* I/9, insert; 'second rate', II/2, p 64; 'genuineness', II/2, p 50; 'Australia and abroad', II/2, inside back cover (IBC); 'social consciousness', III/2, IBC; 'chauvinistic', I/7, IBC; 'Political pressure', II/1, p 57; *Pacific Review*, CBC to Nettie Palmer, 11 April 1944, NLA 1174/1/6256-33.
36 Negative responses: Bedford, *MP* I/3, p 12; McKinnon, CBC to Nettie Palmer, 7 Nov 1942, UMA Box 257; 'the *left*', Olive Stevens to CBC, Feb 1942, l. bk, p 60 Box 245.
37 Positive responses: Macartney to CBC, 30 Dec 1940, l. bk, p 21 UMA Box 244; Amiet, in *Daily Mercury*, Mackay, 23 May 1942, l. bk, p 24 Box 245; 'established', Ingamells to CBC, 3 Mar and 14 April 1942, CBC to Ingamells, 25 Mar 1942, LaT MS 6224/1/80; Chisholm, *Argus* cutting in l. bk, p 82 UMA Box 245; insufficient direction, e.g. *Bulletin*, cited *Advocate*, 21 Nov 1945, l. bk, p 121 Box 245.
38 Turning point: O'Dowd letters, Nettie Palmer to CBC, 23 Jan 1942, l. bk, p 9; *Pygmalion*, [June 1941], two contradictory reviews in l. bk, p 128, both UMA Box 245.
39 Crisis and Nationality Numbers: Max Harris, 'Dance Little Wombat', *MP* II/2, p 33; Vance Palmer, 'Battle', II/8, pp 5–6; 'rubbish', 'War on the Intellectual Front', I/8, p 4.
40 The debate: 'name only', JK Ewers, 'Towards an Adult Literature', *MP* I/12, p 25; 'colony', Vance Palmer, review of Penton, *Advance Australia, Where?*, III/1, p 42; mateship, H Drake-Brockman, 'Australia Phoenix?', I/12, pp 9 and 11; 'un-Australian', CBC, 'War on the Intellectual Front', I/8, p 4; Manning Clark, 'Letter to Tom Collins: Mateship', II/3, p 40.
41 Jindyworobaks: disjunction, HD Brasch, '-Isms in Poetry', *MP* I/9, p 23; appropriation, Gina Ballantyne, '"Forbidden" Song', I/11, p 11; 'silly', Ingamells to CBC, 23 Nov 1941, l. bk, p 189, UMA Box 244.
42 Contra soul-searching: 'uneducated masses', Editorial, *MP* I/5, p 2; 'class consciousness', Neil Smith, 'A Reply from the Herd', I/12, p 38; 'hearse', AD Hope to CBC, 18 Aug 1944, UMA Box 179; Donald Horne, 'Some Cultural Elites in Australia', *Angry Penguins* 7 (1945), pp 133–4.
43 Cultural crisis: 'War on the Intellectual Front', *MP* I/8, pp 3-4, religious values, Peter Bennie, 'For What Do We Struggle?', I/8, pp 19–21; 'This Unimagined Australia', II/4, p 63.
44 Born editor: 'liaison officer', Nettie Palmer to CBC, 29 Oct 1942, and CBC to Nettie Palmer, 7 Nov 1942, UMA Box 257; 'mixtures', unidentified cutting, l. bk, p 142 Box 244; puzzled,

Ewers to CBC, 8 Oct 1941, l. bk, p 164 Box 244; subversive, Nettie Palmer to CBC, 9 Jan 1943, NLA 1174/1/6379-87; 'apple', AD Hope in *Southerly*, l. bk, p 177, Box 244.

45 CBC as encourager: page, Reid to CBC, 4 June 1943; his poems appeared in *MP* III/1 and 3.

46 Difficult relations: puzzlement, CBC to Ingamells, 25 Mar 1942, LaT MS 6244/1/79; 'name', Kate Baker to CBC, 22 Nov 1941, l. bk, p 180, UMA Box 244; short notice, CBC to Max Harris, [1942], Max Harris Series 1.5; 'disappointing', CBC to Nettie Palmer, 7 Nov 1942, UMA Box 257; 'both true', Grano, Comment on '21 Lives', FLUQ 2/3/380; CBC to Kennedy, 29 July and 11 Aug 1941; Kennedy to CBC, 6 and 17 Aug 1941, l. bk, p 125, UMA Boxes 244/5.

47 Throwing it in: prioritise, Devaney to CBC, 27 Feb 1941, UMA Box 110; writer, CBC to AD Hope, 1 Jan 1944, Box 179; 'Nothing doing', CBC to Nettie Palmer, 7 Nov 1942, Box 257; not vacate, CBC to P Serle, 27 May 1943, Box 300; 'Appeasement' Number, editorial, *MP* I/3, p 3.

48 Pressure: CBC in street, Grano, 'Memories of early *Meanjin*', Grano Scripts UMA Box 148; in office, *Bulletin*, 17 Jan 1945, l. bk p 112 UMA Box 245; rejected, CBC to P Serle, 8 June 1942, Box 300, but see also Green, 'Three Editors', p 307; 'Want to say', CBC to Ingamells, LaT MS 6244/1/87.

49 CBC, archivist: bound sets, *MP* II/1, p 56; 'documentation', editorial, II/4, p 63. The second index was prepared by Judith Wright; Wright to CBC, 11 Feb 1945, UMA Box 356.

50 Aboriginality: anthropology, 'Trailer', *MP* II/2, p 64; rough sketch, P Excell interview with CBC, 2 May 1988; AP Elkin, 'Steps into the Dream-time', II/2, pp 14–17.

51 Aboriginality and regionalism: Willkie, *MP* II/2, p 64; 'axis', Kate Baker to CBC, 19 Oct 1941, l. bk p 166, UMA Box 244; CBC to the Palmers [1944], NLA 1174/1/6471-72.

52 *MP* and America: 'fiery warmth', Shapiro to CBC, 25 June 1943, UMA Box 301; screed, l. bk, p 84, and *Christian Science Monitor*, l. bk, p 93 both Box 245; correspondence, CBC to P Serle, 27 May 1943, Box 300; subscribe, Editorial Notes, *MP* I/12, p 3.

53 JV Duhig: harmful, Duhig, 'Letter to Tom Collins: Contemporary "Culture"', *MP*, I/12, pp 27–8.

54 Duhig arrangements: CBC reluctance, Vrepont to CBC, nd [c 1942], UMA Box 342; came to hand, CBC to P Serle, 8 June 1942, Box 300; poetry, Duhig to CBC, 6 Sep 1941, l. bk, p 132 Box 244; self-supporting, Duhig to CBC, 23 Dec 1943, Box 112.

55 Rupture: 'arrogant', CBC to Grano, 1 Sep 1970, UMA Box 148; 'self-opinionated', Grano, Comments on CBC, 'The Twenty-One Lives of *MQ*', FLUQ 2/380, p 4, excised, CBC, 'Lives'; see also Duhig to CBC, 4 Feb 1963, UMA Box 112; 'wish', Duhig to Mrs Balding, 21 Apr 1959, Box 112.

56 Dorothy Green: McDonald, *Warrior for Peace*, esp. pp 3, 18–20; Sheridan, *Nine Lives*, pp 136–52.

57 Judith Wright: *Half a Lifetime*, pp 142, 168; 'your staff', Wright to CBC, 29 July 1942, UMA Box 356; Wright, 'Brisbane in Wartime', esp. p 66.

58 Wright and McKinney: McKinney, 'Memoir of Jack and Judith', in Clarke and McKinney, *The Equal Heart and Mind*, esp. pp 5–12; 'language and culture', extract from draft autobiography quoted in Brady, *South of My Days*, p 121; 'translate ideas', Wright, *Half a Lifetime*, p 210.

59 CBC, McKinney, and Wright: Wright, *Half A Lifetime*, pp 202, 206, 217, 221, 224; Clarke and McKinney, *The Equal Heart and Mind*, pp 35, 140; Wright, 'Brisbane in Wartime', p 68; CBC to Wright, Friday [1945] and undated letter (Aug 1945), NLA MS 5781/7/505; *Bulletin* on McKinney's death, 17 Dec 1966, p 27.

60 Frayed associations: Vrepont to CBC [Apr 1941], l. bk, p 84 UMA Box 244; Grano to CBC, 19 June 1965, Box 148; 'so excited', CBC to Nettie Palmer, 7 Nov 1942, and re Nina, Nettie Palmer to CBC, 7 Sep 1942, both Box 257; 'resentful', Devaney to Grano, 13 Feb 1944 and 'clash badly', 21 June 1944, both UQFL 2/Hayes.

61 Printers: Excell, i/v with CBC, 2 May 1988, also CBC, Notes for Excell 'Borrowed Plumes', pp 2–3, 'threatened', CBC to SMS, 5 May 1975, SMS LaT Box 166; censorship, CBC to Ingamells, 20 Apr 1942, LaT MS 6224/1/83; Grano, comments on '21 Lives' [1964], FLUQ2/380, p 3.

62 Brisbane, 1944: a year, Editorial, *MP* III/3, 135; dignitaries' indifference: Duhig, 'Letter to Tom Collins', I/12, p 28; *Angry Turtle*, CBC, review of *Galmahra*, I/12, p 32.

63 QAAA: 'boots', Wright, 'Brisbane in Wartime', pp 66–7; 'established', Haley to CBC, 21 Aug 1942, UMA Box 158; move, CBC to K Murdoch, 2 Mar 1944, UMA Box 241; tram, Grano to CBC, 16 Aug 1944, UMA Box 148.

64 National stance: 'sapling', Editorial, *MP*, I/6, p 2; 'renaissance', Wright, 'Brisbane in Wartime', p 67.
65 Sydney and other options: difficulties inferred from Howarth to CBC, 13 Feb [1944], 'big way', Howarth to CBC, 26 Aug 1944, UMA Box 181; Stewart, Vrepont to CBC, 21 Mar 1944; 'delays', *MP* III/3, p 207.

Chapter 2 Casting off the Chrysalis of Conservatism

1 SMS, antecedents and upbringing: *Ind*, pp 2–6, 8, 9, 13; WD Murray-Smith, family information; Yarwood, *Walers*, esp. pp 96, 112; Alice Margrett, Nita Murray-Smith, 23 Mar 2011, obituary, [*Toorak Times*], SMSD (18 Mar 1980) vol 14 p 223; 'darling son', Alice to SMS, 23 May 1943, LaT SMS Box 259/66; Hindustani, SMSD (3 Mar 1978) vol 7, p 77.
2 Geelong Grammar School: Glamorgan School reports, SMS LaT Box 258; run away, EWH Pinner to M-Smiths, 14 May 1942, SMS Box 263/2; reading, *Ind*, pp 13, 20.
3 JR Darling, Bate, *Light Blue Down Under*, pp 180–213: mass plays, Persse, *Well-Ordered Liberty*, p 21; 'best employer', Ward, *A Radical Life*, p 93.
4 Stephen's progress: Pinner, Bate, *Light Blue*, p 188; 'in class', school reports, esp. for 1939–40, SMS LaT Box 258; SMS on Manning Clark, *Corian*, (Dec 1940), p 255; *Henry V*, *Corian* (Dec 1940), p 256; speech problems, school reports 1937, 1939, 1940, SMS Box 258; 'any British university', Darling to SMS, 28 Feb 1941, SMS Box 260/4; against the herd, David Murray-Smith, 30 May 2012, 'premature rebel', SMS de Berg interview, NLA (1969), p 6.
5 Transition to university: 'troubled', Clark, *Quest for Grace*, p 123; company secretary, RK Whately to Darling, 18 Aug 1937, SMS LaT Box 258; traditional education, Bate, *Light Blue Down Under*, pp 209–10; student union, De Berg interview, NLA (1969), p 11; Darling's 'national service', SMS 'Recollections' in *1988*, p 422.
6 Stephen's values, 1941: 'world crumble', Rob Hamilton to SMS, 2 Aug 1941, SMS LaT Box 263/7; reading, *Ind*, pp 7, 12–17, 19; schooner, SMSD (27 Jun 1984) vol 24, p 216; joining up, SMS to Rob Hamilton (26 May 1941), SMS Box 259.
7 Stephen in New Guinea: Pirie, *Commando Double Black* (SMS drawing on diaries) pp 26, 31, 90, 99, 143, 262, 299, 304; further extracts from diaries, 3 June 1942, p 6; 3–11 July, 1942, p 17; 2 Sep 1942, p 124; 31 Jan 1943, pp 48, 76–7, all SMS Box 262/1-2; 1943 journal, p 38, Box 262/1-3. Also SMS, 'Men of the Bush', radio script LaT Box 264/2-1(1); two important lessons, *Ind*, p 23; Ryan, *Fear Drive My Feet*, p 7.
8 Stephen on New Guinea: 'New Guinea Now & When', two papers, Box 264/21-1(1).
9 University, and ex-servicemen: numbers, Poynter and Rasmussen, *A Place Apart*, p 77; conservative students, Buckley, *Cutting Green Hay*, p 58.
10 The left-ward shift: Medley, Poynter and Rasmussen, p 72; 'unprecedented fervour', Gott, lord mayor, autobiographical piece for 'Dear Bill' [in America], p 2, Gott LaT Box 3802/4; Frankston, SMS in Dow, *Memories of Melbourne University*, p 122; Flinders, SMS to Rob Hamilton, 1 July 1945, SMS LaT Box 260/6; 'unawakened', SMS in Dow, *Memories*, p 130; Murdoch, Munster, *A Paper Prince*, p 34; theological student, Manning Clark, 'On first seeing Ian Turner', *O* 76/77, p 21.
11 Labor Club dynamics: numbers, *Ind*, p 23; victimisation, '[Communist Policy] in the University', MU Branch, ACP, SMS LaT Box 265/1-3; underplayed, Marginson, in Dow, *More Memories*, p 108; Free Thought Society, and convergence, Gott, 'Forties', p 10, LaT Box 3802/4; 'The facts', Geoffrey Serle, 'Left Front, Right About Turn', *Shop*, vol 1 no 4.
12 Labor Club as way of life: could not remember, Marginson, in Dow, *More Memories*, p 107; 'borrowed radicalism', SMS *Ind*, p 24; conference, *The Shop*, vol 1, no 3 [1945], 'Presbyterian free love', Ray Marginson, 2 Dec 2012.
13 SMS broader activities: Pinchas Goldhar, 'A Tribute', 'The old school tie', in 'Left Turns', SMS LaT, Box 268/1-21; 'anarchy and romanticism', handwritten document purporting to be a [comic] *Farrago* interview [1947], SMS Box 268/1-21.
14 Peter Ryan and Geoffrey Serle: Ryan, intelligence report, 27 Aug 1947, NAA119/68/1-3; Serle: 'bloody Yank', GS, 'A Tribute to the Editor', *O* 50/51 (1972), p 3; see John Thompson, *The Patrician and the Bloke*, esp. for 'incurious', p 74, and Percival Serle on Geoffrey's socialism, p 125; mateship, SMS, 'On Your Feet, Men', *Shop*, vol 1 no 1 [1945]; 'tough and open-eyed', Serle, 'Left Front, Right About Turn', *Shop*, vol 1 no 4 [1945].
15 The Loft and the Party: SMS in Dow, *Memories*, pp 122–5, 133–6; Turner, 'My Long March', 31–4; Moscow map, report, 27 Aug 1947, 1-3, NAA A6119/68; 'future leaders', 'Swag', *O* 67

(1977), p 38; 'People's Art', Max Marginson, Dow, *More Memories*, p 105; Gott chair, *O* 76/77 (1979) p 9; SMS joining Party, NAA ASIO A6119/68/123, Ken Inglis, *ADB* vol 14, p 203; SMS to Keith McEwen, 27 September 1966, DMS. Jenny Love expressed amazement to me that she had ever been cast as the recruiter (Love, 6 Aug 2013). It was most probably Turner, perhaps Gott.

16 Ian Turner: IT, 'My Long March', *O* 59 (1974), pp 3–34; Comments in IT Memorial Number, *O* 76/77 (1979), esp. pp 5, 9, 70, 71; SMS, Intro to *Room for Manoeuvre*; Amirah Inglis, *The Hammer and the Sickle and the Washing-Up*, pp 18–23, 40, 43–5; Nita Murray-Smith, 29 Apr 2012; Knopfelmacher, McLaren, *Free Radicals*, p 246; 'machinery', Turner to SMS, 5 July 1963, SMS LaT Box 197 (2nd parcel); Manning Clark, Serle, speech at SMS commemoration, *O* 112 (1988), p 9.

17 Stephen, Communism, other intellectual interests: 'demented', *Ind*, p 23; 'self-governing unit', Turner, 'My Long March', p 32; 'colonial independence', SMS, Address [1947] to university branch, CPA, SMS LaT Box 265/1-9; professor corrected, Inglis, *Hammer and Sickle*, p 18; 'purpose', SMS, '*Overland*', in Bennett (ed.) *Cross Currents*, p 187; Canby, see SMS Box 264/1-2(2); remains, Martin Flanagan, 'Life's labours learned on an island sojourn', *Age*, 26 Jan 1987; museum, Leonhard Adam to SMS, 13 Aug 1946, Box 264/1-9; CPA branch history [1946], p 7; Labour Club history, Gott to Beth, 18 Jan [1948], Gott LaT 13047/3770/1; Russian lessons, SMS Box 264/1-8; 'ten hard years', SMS, in Dow, *Memories*, p 131.

18 Nita: 'husky-voiced', Inglis, *Hammer and Sickle*, p 14; first meeting, and Nita's family, N Murray-Smith, 24 Mar 2011; Gott parcel, KDG to Beth, 22 June 1948, Gott LaT 3770/1; not confident in English, Nita to SMS, 15 Jan [1946], SMS Box 265/1-1; *Antidote*, intelligence report, NAA A6119/68/5.

19 Nita and Stephen, to wedding: 'assurance', William Murray-Smith to Stephen, 6 Mar 1946, Box 265/1-1; no reference, Gott to Beth, 7 March [1948], Gott LaT 3770/1; family impasse, Beth Gott, 21 Feb 2012; less opposition, Nita to Beth, 14 Jan [1948], Gott LaT 3764/1; forgot ring, KDG to Beth, [Feb 1948], above.

20 For the Jewish ambience, Ray Marginson, 2 Dec 2012; marrying out and 'bigger moral issues', *Ind*, pp 25, 27.

21 London—settling in: Russia, Memo, 17 Mar 1948, NAA A 6119/68/13; not wanted, 'Self-Portrait', p 94; Serle views, SMS to Gott, 22 Apr 1948, SMS Box 269/1-9; Stretton, Serle 'old man', SMS undated fragment, SMS Box 269/1; 'sudden flare-ups', Gott to Beth, 26 Feb 194[8], Gott LaT 3770/1.

22 Teaching: SMS to Prof Browne, 22 Sep 1948, LaT Box 269/1-6; popular, HM reference, 13 Oct 1948, SMS Box 269/1-9.

23 The Party: SMS to Roslyn, 28 Sep 1948, SMS Box 269/1-6; '*colonial* party', SMS to Turners, 12 Nov 1948, SMS Box 269/1-9; SMS to Gott, 7 May 1948, Box 3764/1.

24 Looking for work: Nita, SMS fragment [1948] SMS Box 269/1 and SMS to CBC, 21 Sep 1948, SMS Box 269/1-6; 'hub' and post, to Rob Hamilton, 9 Nov 1948, SMS Box 269/1-9; 'immigrants in a sense'—the sentence then seemed to SMS to have gone too far, so he crossed it out, BBC discussion, 3 Jan 1949, Box 269/1-11; turned down, Policek BBC to SMS, 17 May 1949, Box 270/1-1.

25 *Meanjin* and homesickness: SMS to CBC, 21 Sep 1948, SMS Box 269/1-6; Australian landscapes, SMS to Gott, 24 May 1948, Gott LaT 3764/1.

26 SMS, Account of trip around England and Scotland, August 1948, SMS Box 270/1-2.

27 SMS world view: SMS to Rob Hamilton, 9 Nov 1948, SMS Box 269/1-9; fighting for peace, SMS speech, Paris Peace Congress 1949, SMS Box 270/1-1; 'swimming pool', SMS to CBC, 28 Mar 1950, UMA Box 240.

28 Stephen's journey to Prague: 'everyone raves', Serle to SMS, 26 Oct – 3 Nov 1947, SMS Box 268/1/1-1; Paris peace congress, SMS to Nita, 21 Apr 1949, SMS Box 259/1-3; Nita languages, SMS to DR Steiner, 13 Aug 1948, SMS Box 270/1-2; 'not return', SMS to Gott, 24 Nov 1949, Gott LaT 3764/1; Hamilton warning, to SMS 30 July 1949, SMS Box 269/1-3; first impressions, SMS to Gott, 8 June 1949 LaT 3764/1; the Party and the economy, Judt, *Postwar*, pp 71, 138.

29 IUS and Telepress: no Czech, Ken Marks to SMS, 28 Mar [1948], SMS Box 270/1-1; 'too objective', milieu and Party tactics with affiliates, Gott, essay for Dear Bill, 1964, pp 5, 6, 12b, Gott LaT 3802/4; 'brothel', SMS to Gotts, 25 June 1949, Box 3764/1; Asia and Pacific, Young (England) to ASIO Director, Sydney, 5 May 1950, NAA A6119/68/42; 'spy', Nita Murray-Smith, 29 May 2012; 'first boat home', SMS to Gott, 25 June 1949 Gott LaT 3764/1.

30 Leaving Prague: friends, Bernard Rechter, 13 Aug 2013; Russian propaganda, Gott, 'Dear Bill' 1964, p 13, Gott LaT 802/4; 'arrested', Nita Murray-Smith, 24 Mar 2011.
31 Immediate Australian travels: 'slanders', SMS to Gotts, 8 July 1951, Gott LaT 3770/4; 'educational trip', SMS to Zorka [Wolfová], 14 Aug 1951, SMS Box 271/2-1; Bowen mangoes, *Ind*, p 38; Swan Street bridge, McDonald, *Australia at Stake*, p 132; 'whitewash', *Ind*, p 33.
32 Bumpy return: Sydney, SMS to Gotts, 8 July 1951, Gott LaT 3770/4; 'Future', SMS to the Hamiltons, 13 Nov 1951, McLaren, *Free Radicals*, p 97; Essendon High, former student; ASIO, memo, 4 Aug 1953, NAA A6119/69/7; McLaren, *Free Radicals*, p 110.
33 Settling in and peace activism: own salary, McLaren, *Free Radicals*, p 110; house, 'roots', 'broadening our influence', SMS to Esther and Malcolm, 5 May 1953, SMS LaT Box 275/2-1; Korean Ceasefire Week, *Working for Peace* Newsletter, c. May 1953, Box 275/2-6; Sydney Youth Carnival, SMS to Nita, night 15 [March 1952], Box 274/1-1; *Realist Film News*, Nov–Dec 1952, Box 275/2-6; *R W* 1 (March 1952).
34 Stephen and literature, 1951–52: 'receded', *Ind*, p 28; Malaya, SMS to Zorka [Wolfová], 15 Oct 1953, SMS Box 275/2-4.
35 People's songs, when abroad: 'sing too few', SMS to Ralph [Gibson, 1948], SMS Box 270/1-1; 'thoroughly unpopular', SMS to Gotts, 19 July 1949, Gott LaT 3770/4; more singing, Seeger to SMS [1951], SMS Box 273/1-1.
36 SMS and Australian folksong: Manifold–Stephen exchange, JM to SMS nd, SMS to JM, 9 Feb 1953, SMS Box 276/1-3; idea in exile, SMS to SB Ryerson, Toronto, 10 Mar 1949, SMS Box 276/1-5; Wallaby recordings, McLaren, *Free Radicals*, p 117; Ted Harrington interview, 11 Jan 1955, NLA 2277-12-52, p 2.
37 Politics of folksong: *Reedy River*, Whiteoak and Scott-Maxwell, *Currency Companion to Music and Dance*, p 446; attendance figure, Macintyre, *The Party*, p 295; Davison, 'Rethinking the Australian Legend', p 439, ('Hollywood'), p 445.
38 Frank Hardy: 'weapon', FH in interview with Tony Morphett, 1967, in Adams and Lee, *Frank Hardy and the Literature of Commitment*, p 24; 'concerts', Adams, *The Stranger from Melbourne*, p 21; Muggeridge quoted in Hocking, *Frank Hardy*, p 130.
39 Hardy and Socialist Realism: 'very soul', Radek, quoted in Adams, *Stranger*, p 10; Allan Gardiner, 'Frank Hardy and Communist institutions', in Adams and Lee, *Commitment*, pp 36–8.
40 *Power Without Glory*: Beasley, J McLaren in Adams and Lee, *Commitment*, p 55; Adams, *Stranger*, pp 47, 55, 181.
41 The reading culture: trade union journals, Adams, *Stranger*, p 63; 'transmission belt', Party attitude quoted above, p 45.
42 Australasian Book Society: initial meeting, Adams, *Stranger*, p 62; Seelaf, Beasley, *Red Letter Days*, p 134; subscriptions, and Turner's difficulty, Gardiner in Adams and Lee, *Commitment*, p 43; 'life and spirit', SMS to Zorka [Wolfová], 15 Oct 1953, SMS Box 275/2-4; 'The Organisation of an ABS Group', *RW* 9 (Mar–Apr 1954), p 9; 'something very big', SMS to Lance, 14 Oct 1953, SMS Box 274/3-1.
43 *RW* 1, editorial; SMS, 'In Defence of Australia's Culture and Freedom'; rediscovery of and acclaim for de Boissière, 'Swag', *O* 85 (1981), p 57; alternative to pessimism, 'The Writer and the People' [unsigned article], p 3.
44 Character of *Realist Writer: 'Novy Mir'*, Gardiner, 'Frank Hardy and Communist Institutions', in Adams & Lee, *Commitment*, p 39; 'worker-writers', Hardy, 'My Problems of Writing', *RW* 6, p 12; 'like fists', David Martin, Writer of the Month, *RW* 2, p 12; *Power Without Glory*, *RW* 5, pp 6, 12, 16.
45 Stephen's sense of the past: SMS review, *Settlers and Convicts*, *RW* 8, p 20; SMS, 'Bernard O'Dowd', *RW* 8, p 10.
46 Stephen's views on writers: less recognised, 'The Tasks to Hand', *RW* 7; Phillips' view and 'national in form', 'Looking Backwards—& Forward', *RW* 8, p 2.
47 Socialist Realism and its constrictions: Tennant, McKernan, *Question of Commitment*, p 45; 'positive hero', Ian Turner, MS "Socialist realism', NLA 6206 Box 90/6; Prichard approval, McLaren, *Writing in Hope and Fear*, p 37; Williams, Comment, *RW* 8, p 15; 'not idealise', *RW*, 8, p 2; 'infantile leftism', SMS to Williams [draft, 1954], SMS LaT Box I/2-1; 'review *Such is Life*', draft statement, SMS Box 91/2-3.
48 From *Realist Writer* to *Overland*: quite some time, Wannon to SMS, 21 Oct 1952, and SMS to Zorka, 15 Oct 1953, SMS Box 275/2-2; broader venture, 'Swag', *RW* 8, p 3; cosiness,

Comment, *RW* 8, p 13; '*Communist* journal', SMS to David Martin, NLA MS 6885 Box 19, fol Mc; broadening the front, SMS to Williams [draft, 1954], SMS Box 1/2-1.

Chapter 3 *Meanjin* Finds Form

1 CBC, Inside back cover, *M* vols 2/3; 'The Function of a Literary Magazine', UMA Box 73; esp. p 16.

2 International context: Brooker and Thacker (eds), *Modernist Magazines*, vol I, pp 684, 827, 830, 861; Hamilton, *The Little Magazines*, esp. p 100.

3 New possibilities: Editorial, *MP* 1/1945 pp 1–3, consulted, CBC to Max Marginson, 15 May 1973 UMA Box 224, Coombs, *Trial Balance*, pp 218–22.

4 *Meanjin* and the University of Melbourne, 1944–45: Serle, *Sir John Medley*, esp. p 45; Donovan Clarke correspondence, esp. Clarke to CBC, 17 Apr, 30 June and 31 July, 1944, UMA Box 82; Colin Badger correspondence, esp. Badger to CBC, 31 July, Fri 17 [Nov 1944], 6 Feb 1945, Box 42; Colin Badger statement, Aug 1992, courtesy Patricia Excell; 'sensitive' about education, CBC to Dorothy Green, 17 Oct 1985, NLA 5678 folio 17.

5 CBC and MUP: CBC to Badger, 27 Nov 1944, 'slowly dying' [late 1946], UMA Box 42; CBC to James, 1 Dec 1944, 7 June 1945, 18 Jan 1946, 'six issues' [early 1946], 'yard', James to CBC, 7 June 1945, all Box 242; James, 'Memo concerning MUP policy—1946', p 5, Box 242; 'mustard', CBC to Donovan Clarke, 21 Feb 1945; James 'procrastinating', Fitzpatrick to CBC, 25 Sep 1962, Box 132; 'war', CBC to Harris, 24 June 1948; and cultural monthly, to Harris, 10 May 1946, both Box 156.

6 CBC and Georgian House: to Badger, nd [1946], UMA Box 42. The Georgian House payments related to trade sales only, whereas MUP's also drew on subscriptions.

7 CBC and the university: council grant, Extension Committee Report 1950, Box 246; minute by board alone necessary, Badger to CBC, 30 Nov [1944], Box 42; 'nobody's baby', Chisholm, 'The background to *Meanjin*', UMA Chisholm Papers, Box 1.

8 Vance Palmer: description, Marjorie Tipping, 'Remembrance of Palmers Past', *O* 100 (Sep 1985), pp 10–11; John Barnes, 'Remembering the Palmers', pp 57–8; see also Palmer, 'London Days', *M*, 2/1959, pp 218–24; Turgenev, Nettie P to Allan Edwards, 8 May 1961, in Smith (ed.) *Letters of V and N Palmer*, p 231; guild socialism, Walker, *Dream and Disillusion*, p 5; 'poet', AD Hope, 'VP Reconsidered', *Southerly* 4/1995, p 209; Christina Stead, quoted in Walker, *Not Dark Yet*, pp 284–5; Jack Lindsay, 'The Novels', *M* 2/1959, pp 149, 169; 'smile', AA Phillips, Eulogy, *M* 2/1959, p 270.

9 Vance Palmer, views: *The Passage* (Melbourne: Robertson & Mullens, 1944) pp 274, 276, 280; for 'bush people' and 'local colour', see VP, 'An Australian National Art [1905] in Barnes (ed.), *Writer in Australia*, pp 169–70; 'socialist', David Walker, *Dream and Disillusion*, p 90; 'co-ordinating force', quoted in Ivor Indyk, 'VP and the Social Function of Literature', *Southerly* 3/1990, pp 351, 354.

10 Nettie Palmer: appearance and character, Barnes, 'Remembering the Palmers', p 59 and Tipping, 'Remembrance of Palmers Past', p 10; 'skittish', AA Phillips to NP, 26 Aug 1950, NLA MS 1174/1/7874-76; AD Hope, 'The Prose of NP', *M*, 2/1959, p 225; Spanish, NP to Rex Ingamells, 10 May 1944, Smith, *Letters*, p 177; radio scripts, Ivor Indyk, 'VP and the Social Function', p 351; 'better and greater', quoted Drusilla Modjeska, *Exiles at Home*, p 201.

11 Clem and the Palmers, Brisbane: VP, 'Note on Randolph Bedford' *MP*, I/7, p 7; NP to CBC, 29 Oct 1942, 16 Nov 1942, 20 Jan 1943, 24 Apr 1944, 6 May 1944, 11 July 1946, UMA Box 259; CBC to NP, 7 Nov 1942, UMA, 11 Apr 1944, NLA 1174/1/16526-33; NP to Ingamells, 10 May 1944, Smith, *Letters*, p 178.

12 Leaving Brisbane: 'punk', CBC to NP, 7 Nov 1942, UMA Box 259; 'impotence', CBC to NP, 11 Apr 1944, NLA 1174/1/6526-33; 'material', CBC to NP, Wed [May 1944], NLA MS 1174/1/6546-9.

13 The Palmers, in Melbourne: 'good news', NP to CBC, 21 Jul 1944, UMA Box 257; 'rather philistine', Nettie Palmer, *Fourteen Years* (entry, 6 Mar 1926), p 17; stillborn venture, NP to Coralie Rees, 6 Jul 1936, Smith, *Letters*, p 135; 'dry voice', Barnes, 'Remembering the Palmers', p 57; Phillips, Eulogy, *M* 2/1959, p 270; the Palmers' health: Lucas, 'A fine ruddy mess', pp 70, 73.

14 CBC and the Palmers, Melbourne: NP diary, 22 Feb, 28 Apr and 17 Sep 1945, NLA 1174/16/25; 27 Dec 1946, NLA 1174/16/26; 18 Feb and 29 Sep 1947, NLA 1174/16/27.

15 *Fourteen Years*: Lucas, 'A fine ruddy mess', pp 69–75; 'prestige', CBC to VP, Melb Cup Day 1949, NLA 1174/1/7522-4.

16 AA Phillips: Oxford, Davidson, '"Home" Becomes Away'; Jewish, Davidson, *Sideways from the Page*, p 39; 'cage', AAP, *Australian Tradition*, p 38; Phillips–Christesen correspondence, esp. AAP to CBC, 17 Oct 1945, 3 Feb 194[7], [Sep 1948], 30 May 1952, 10 June 1952, and CBC to AAP, 3 June 1952 [unsent], 20 June 1952, 29 Oct 1956, UMA Box 263; CBC to AAP, 3 Mar 1980, LaT MS 12491/3385/46; Phillips, 'Cultural nationalism in the '40s and '50s' [draft], LaT MS 12491/3386/7d; Phillips, 'The Cultural Cringe', *M* 4/1950, pp 299–302; Phillips, 'Tribute to *Meanjin*', *O* 8 (1956), pp 7–8.

17 Criticism: Phillips, 'Cultural nationalism', p 9; 'body', Waten, '*Meanjin*', *O* 4 (1955) p 21, see also Dorothy Hewett to CBC, 7 Oct 1965, UMA Box 173; CBC quoting Grattan, in letter to HS Canby, [1945] Box 73; 'full-length', CBC to Phillips, 26 Jan 1950, LaT MS 59160/222/3.

18 *Meanjin* and Aust lit: 'The Uneasy Chair', *M* 2/1952, pp 187–9; discussion, see Alan Edwards, 'Australian Literature Courses', *M* 2/1952, pp 173–7, W Milgate, 'Australian Literature and the Universities', *M* 3/1954, pp 429–32, Vance Palmer, *M* 4/1954, pp 591–2, AD Hope, *M* 2/1954, pp 165–9, and on Rudd and Lawson, see *M* 1/1956, pp 24–31; Serle, 'more to say', speech at SMS commemoration, Aug 1988, quoted in Katherine Gallagher, '*Overland* and Australian studies', *Australian Studies* no 4, Dec 1990, p 162; CBC to Dorothy Green, 10 Feb 1981, NLA 5678 fo 16; prompt, see full-page ad in *M* 2/1956, p 185; Bennett, 'Australian Literature and the Universities', p 107.

19 *Meanjin* short stories: whole issue, CBC to John Morrison, 10 July 1952 and 30 Sep 1964, UMA Box 237; AA Phillips reviewing anthologies, *M* 4/1954, p 264, and 'Australian Image: The Literary Tradition Reassessed', *MQ* 2/1962, p 180; Tim Burstall, 'Notes on *Coast to Coast*', *M* 1/1955, pp 141–2; save the day, CBC to Morrison, 2 Sep 1959, above.

20 Morrison: quotes from letter to CBC, 4 Oct 1951, UMA Box 237.

21 CBC and David Martin: 'NOT provincial', Martin to CBC, 20 Nov 1960; 'bursting', Martin to CBC, 9 Aug 1951; 'strong editing', Martin to CBC, 27 Mar 1954; 'Sorry', Martin to CBC, 20 Jan 1960, all UMA Box 227.

22 CBC and neoclassicists: McAuley correspondence, UMA Box 218; and Hope, going to publish, CBC to AA Phillips, 20 Oct 1955, UMA Box 263; 'guts', AD Hope to CBC, Sunday [1946], UMA Box 179.

23 Judith Wright: Clarke and McKinney, *With Love & Fury*, pp 14, 15, 19, 28, 32–3; 'ribbons', Clarke and McKinney, *The Equal Heart and Mind*, p 133; 'strong silence', Wright, *Half a Lifetime*, p 260.

24 Picot: CBC, 'Homage to One Betrayed', *South Coast*, p 17; take over, CBC, 'Twenty-one Lives', p 87; co-edit, CBC to Paul Grano, 1 Sep 1970, UMA Box 148; Picot to Mrs Robinson, 22 May 1941, UMA Box 268; padre, Frank Kellow, Picot Tributes, *M*, 1/1954, pp 104–5; Japanese, (Major) James W Jacobs, Picot Tributes, *M* 1/1947, p 48; RD FitzGerald, 'A romantic in spite of himself', *M* 4/1953, pp 452–7; 'recovered', *M* 1/1951, p 84.

25 Vincent Buckley: VB, *Cutting Green Hay*, pp 84, 146, 194; Martin, *My Strange Friend*, p 264; Irish completion, Davidson, *Sideways from the Page*, p 211; Irish as colonised, McLaren, *Journey without Arrival*, p 322; CBC, To whom it may concern, reference for VB [1955], UMA Box 57; poetry as communion, VB, 'Helicon as Jordan', *M* 4/1954, p 534.

26 Buckley contra *Meanjin*: CBC to Buckley, 5 May 1959, Buckley to CBC 22 June and CBC reply, 15 Sep 1959, UMA Box 132; CBC to Fitzpatrick, 25 June and Fitzpatrick to CBC, 29 June 1959, above; Strahan refutation, *Just City*, p 217; Buckley, *Cutting Green Hay*, p 194.

27 Dorothy Green: 'The Needle's Eye', *M* 3/1950, p 220; 'phoney', Green to CBC, received 3 Aug 1950; 'envied', Green to CBC, 1 July [1954]; children, CBC to Green, 27 Nov 1959, all UMA Box 150.

28 Art: CBC to McCulloch, 15 and 16 Sep 1959, UMA Box 217; Bernard Smith to CBC, 24 May 1953, Box 306.

29 Meanjin Press: Heinemann, CBC to Bernard Smith, 17 May 1949, UMA Box 306; unsatisfactory, CBC to AD Hope, 5 Apr 1955, Box 179; Picot, CBC to Vance Palmer, 1 July 1954, Box 259.

30 *Meanjin* and artists: Fred Williams cover, *MQ* 2/1964; Picasso, *M* 3/1958; Thake, witchetty grub, tenth anniversary issue, *M* 4/1950; Aboriginal women dancers, 2/1951 and the year 1972, design then credited to Anthony Watson; 'chords', Earle Hackett, 'Electronic Painting: The "images" of Ostoja-Kotkowski', *MQ* 4/1966, pp 494–5.

31 Brian Fitzpatrick: This account draws on Don Watson, *Brian Fitzpatrick: A Radical Life*, esp. pp 232, 283; the speeches at the Fitzpatrick testimonial dinner, printed in the *Rationalist*, Nov–Dec 1963, pp 163–9; Geoffrey Blainey, Foreword to Fitzpatrick, *The British Empire in*

Australia, p viii. For 'intimate knowledge', see Fitzpatrick, 'The origins of the people are not in the library', *M* 3/1953, p 350; 'order *things*', Fitzpatrick, *Australian Commonwealth*, p 156, and for Dicey quote p viii of same book; 'intellectual oafs', Fitzpatrick, 'the Importance of Being Earnest about Liberty', *M* 1/1956, p 93; 'sensitive and brutal', Burstall (ed. McPhee), *Memoirs of a Young Bastard*, p 10; Fitzpatrick to CBC, 2 Nov 1954, 1 Oct 1957, 8 and 25 Dec 1957, UMA Box 132.

32 Clem and Heinemann: later claiming, CBC to Aileen Palmer, 8 Mar 1968, UMA Box 256; Heinemann files, Box 166, particularly contract, 25 Mar 1949, 'given notice', H Hall to CBC, 12 Oct 1951, 'publicity officer', CBC to Hall, 8 May 1951; vanilla politics, Hall to CBC, 1 June 1949; largest publisher, CBC to Maxwell, 24 Apr 1953, Box 229; 'resigned', to Bernard Smith, 30 Apr 1952, Box 301; Strahan, *Just City*, pp 124–6, 144–5.

33 Keon assault: 'concerted attempt', clearance, Allan Ashbolt, 'The great literary witch-hunt', pp 153, 155; well-known authors, Strahan, *Just City*, p 151; ANU, 'Uneasy Chair', *M* 3/1952, pp 301, 303; Keon boasting, Strahan, *Just City*, p 146 and CBC to AR Chisholm, 13 July 1954, UMA Box 81.

34 The Russian Department: Armstrong, *Christesen Romance*, pp 85–90.

35 *The Unbending*: attacks, CBC to HS Temby, 25 June 1954, NAA A463/1963/2565 (pt 2); 'Comments on *The Unbending*', *M* 3/1954, pp 456–60.

36 Petrov: Manne, *The Petrov Affair*; Armstrong, *Christesen Romance*, pp 103–15; Petrov case, Correspondence, UMA Box 261, esp. correspondence with James Meagher, 9 Dec 1954 ('absurd'); see also, for 'dissuade him', NLA 4965/1/5764 (17 Jan 1955) and Nina to Susan Christesen, 8 Feb 1955; GW Paton, vice-chancellor, to CBC, 26 Jan 1955, CBC to Milner, 7 May 1954 ('mutual understanding'); *Report of the Royal Commission on Espionage*, p 196; RG Menzies, 'William Queale Memorial Lecture', *M* 4/1954, pp 605–9; *Royal Commission … Official Transcript*, 17 Jan 1955, pp 1754–68; CBC delayed defence, to Ian Maxwell 27 June 1956, UMA Box 229; Ian Milner, 'British and American literature in Czechoslovakia', *M* 2/1954, pp 294–7; expedient to burn, Ray Marginson, 22 Sep 2016; 'cross the road', Jane Sullivan, 'From Russia with a love of language', *Age*, 11 Aug 2001.

37 Brian Fitzpatrick, pamphlet, *The Royal Commission on Espionage: A Commentary* (1955) and 'The Importance of Being Earnest about Liberty', *M* 1/1956, pp 92–6; Arthur Miller, 'A Modest Proposal for Pacification of the Public Temper', *M* 1/1955, p 10; CBC, Comment, *M* 1/1955, p 4.

38 Macartney: Macartney to CBC, 5 Dec 1944, 18 and 30 June 1955, CBC to Macartney, 22 July 1955, UMA Box 214; 'instruments … repugnant', Macartney, *The Increased Price of Liberty*, p 3; AD Hope, 'Red Spots before His Eyes', *O* 5, pp. 32–3; 'Comment', *M* 4/1955, pp 598–603.

39 CBC, 'Social Thought in the Literature of Today', ABC talks, 12 and 26 June 1942, UMA Box 72.

40 ACCF and foundation of *Quadrant*: 'hysterically excited', CBC to Medley, 1 Nov 1954, and to Chisholm 16 Nov 1954, UMA Box 25; 'humanitarian', ACCF newsletter no 21, May 1954, Box 24; names, CBC to Temby, 5 July 1955, NAA A463/1963/12565 (Part 2)/67; 'bore everyone', Muir Holborn, quoted SMS to CBC, 11 Aug 1955, UMA Box 240; 'brilliant' poems, CBC to Milner, 7 May 1954, Box 261.

41 Summer issue, 4/1954: 'arid freedom', Hugh Trevor-Roper, p 616; [CBC], 'Comment: Culture, Congress and Freedom', pp 484, 630–3; 'smelt a rat', CBC to AC Fox, 1 Dec 1954, UMA Box 25.

42 Context and consequences: 'one slip', CBC to Chisholm, 16 Nov 1954, UMA Box 80; before, see 'The Uneasy Chair', *M* 1/1950, p 75 and 2/1949, p 130; 'arrogant', Paton to CBC, 17 Nov 1954; 'cloven hoof', Maxwell to CBC, 19 Nov 1954.

43 Friendly bureaucrat, CBC to Chisholm, 23 Nov 1954, UMA Box 25; 'new union', Meanjin Interim Report 1947–48, Box 246; 'smear', CBC to Ian Maxwell, 27 June 1956, Box 229; 'fatal division', CBC to David Martin, 25 May 1954, Box 227; Buckley to CBC, 28 Feb 1956, Box 57, and *Cutting Green Hay*, p 153.

44 The Chisholm bid: perhaps permanently, see Grenfell Price to Cumming, 3 Sep 1956, NAA AA 463/2563(3), 59; 'on last legs', Chisholm to [Temby], 25 Feb 1956, NAA above, 138; politics, Bird, *Nazi Dreamtime*, pp 178, 185–91; little hope, CBC to Neilma Gantner, 18 Sep 1956, UMA Box 142; remunerated (as Clem was not), Paton to [Temby], 17 Aug 1956; neuter it, Chisholm to Cumming, 15 Oct 1956, NAA above, 62; did not meet, CBC to AD Hope, 20 Aug 1956, Hope to CBC, 24 Aug 1956, UMA Box 179; severed, Maxwell

to Paton, 8 Oct 1956, Box 262; 'maggots', CBC to Maxwell, 1 May 1956, Box 229; 'no liking for it', CBC to AD Hope, 2 Mar 1956 and 'not defeated', to Hope 10 Dec 1956, Box 179; 'sold two', CBC to Derek van Abbé, 22 Oct 1954, Box 340; 'disenfranchised bunyips', CBC to McCrae, 1 Aug 1956, Box 218.

45 Clem overseas: Delhi, CBC, 'Letter from India', *O* 9 (1957) pp 27–9; Bolshoi, Nancy Kellock, c. 1975; enticing, CBC to Inglis Moore, 22 Sep 1958 and 'misshapen infant', to Moore, 25 Mar 1949, both UMA Box 234.

46 CBC Comment: wit, see *M* 2/1956, p 132 and 3/1959, p 276; 'emasculated', *M* 1/1956, p 125; 'most deplorable', *M* 4/1950, p 302.

47 Cold War polarities: Read and Comfort, 'No Annihilation …', *M* 2/1951, pp 185–6; signatory lists, *M*, 3/1953, pp 361, 365; 'list of fascists', Inglis Moore to CBC, 15 Aug 1961, UMA Box 235; 'red/pink tag', Alan McCulloch to CBC, 16 Sep 1959, UMA Box 217.

48 International stance: alliance, *M* 2/1958, pp 221–2; opportunities, *M* 2/1955, pp 164, 286.

49 Fiction Chronicle: CBC to Harry Heseltine, 2 Oct 1961, UMA Box 171.

50 London, and USA: 'annihilation', Florence James, 'The Cultural Cringe Abroad', *M* 1/1951, pp 61–3; Bruce Grant, 'English critics and *The Doll*, *M* 3/57, pp 295–8; John Berger, 'London Exhibition of Australian Art', *M* 3/1953, pp 276–8.

51 International contributions: *Canto 90*, Noel Stock to CBC, 5 July 1955, UMA Box 311; Pound subscription: CBC to AD Hope, 3 May 1955, Box 179; Evatt, quoted in Murphy, *Evatt*, p 192; György Lukács, 'Literary standards and writing for the people', *M* 2/1954, p 272.

52 Asia: Martin, 'Starve the Vanguard', *M* 2/1951, p 207; Rewi Alley, 'Cultural Renaissance in China', *M* 3/1953, p 298; Bandung, Comment, *M* 2/1955, pp 164, 286 and articles by Victor Purcell and Cecily Burton in *M* 3/1955, pp 390–9.

53 The Indigenous: contrary, AP Elkin, 'Aborigine and White', *M* 4/1950, pp 280, 284; regular visitor, Excell, '*Meanjin* in the Fifties', p 6; Alan McCulloch, 'The Aboriginal Art Exhibition', *MQ* 2/1961, p 192; synthesising vision, *M* 3/1950, at p 190; *Yandy*, *M* 3/1960, pp 317–19.

54 Book reviews: Koestler, Eric Bentley, *M* 1/1946, pp 87–8; Nolan, Bernard Smith, review, *M* 4/1947, p 279; Fitzpatrick, review of Pringle, *M* 1/1959, pp 113–14; Paton, review of Huddlestone, *M* 1/1957, pp 5–6.

55 Comics: Norman Bartlett, 'Culture and Comics', *M* 1/1954, esp. pp 6, 12, 13; English boy, Patrick Carpenter, 'London Letter', above, p 109; CBC, 'The Law Grapples with Koka-Kola Kulture', above, esp. pp 154–5.

56 Television and sci-fi: 'sub-normal trash', Comment, 'Television Tremens', *M* 2/1954, p 219; 'dumping ground', Comment, 'Television' *M* 4/1959, p 476; FB Bryning, 'What Has Science Fiction to Say?', and Comment, 'Science Fiction', pp 319–20; both *M* 2/1954.

57 *Meanjin* and elitism: Docker, *Australian Cultural Elites*, esp. pp 85–111; Trailer, 'Those Public Schools', *M* 4/1947, p 336; Lindsay, quoted in 'The Uneasy Chair', *M* 1/1950, p 75; Phillips, 'The Literary Heritage Re-assessed', *M* 2/1962, p 180; 'suitable direction', CBC to LF Giblin, Lynne Strahan, *Just City*, p 94; 'lolly-water', Comment, *M* 2/1958, p 224; 'sapped', Trailer, *M* 1/1960, p 112.

58 Elitism and personality: HP Heseltine, Trailer, 'One Hundred Not Out', *MQ* 1/1965, p 133; 'anachronism', e.g. to AD Hope, 2 May 1955; McCulloch to CBC, 16 Sep, and CBC reply, 22 Sep 1959, UMA Box 217.

59 Vance and Nina: I have drawn here on Judith Armstrong, *The Christesen Romance,* also for 'Tolstoyan', Nina Christesen to Vance Palmer, [1944], NLA MS 1/6470; 'worth living', Nina to Vance [1947], 1/7327; 'grand, constructive', NP to CBC, 12 Nov 1945, UMA Box 257.

60 Clem and Vance: 'corpus', CBC to VP, 28 Nov 1958, NLA MS 1174/1/9069; CBC letters to VP in London, 12 July and 1 Aug 1955, VP to CBC, 20 July 1955, UMA Box 259.

61 The Palmers and *Meanjin*: ideas, CBC to VP, 12 Mar 1957, NLA MS 1174/1/8861; Palmer, 'The Afghan', *M* 4/1958, pp 365–78; commemorated, CBC to Palmers, 28 Nov 1958, NLA MS 1174/1/9068; likely list, CBC to VP, 8 Aug 1958, NLA MS 1174/1/9032; 'being buried', Barnes, 'Remembering the Palmers', p 65.

Chapter 4 Temper Democratic, Bias Australian

1 Context, 1954: book publishing, SMS, *Tracks*, p 9; Tregenza, *Little Magazines*, pp 100–1.

2 *O* and *Realist Writer*: Coffey, Martin, *My Strange Friend*, p 237; McLaren, *Fear*, pp 45–6.

3 Waten: 'voluble', Nettie Palmer diary, 25 Nov 1953, NLA 1174/16/33; Menzies, SMS ASIO file, A463/1963/2565(4)/93 report, 2–5, 1960; 'revolutionary', Waten review of AA Phillips, *Australian Tradition*, *Guardian* 15 May 1958; childhood, Geoffrey Blainey, 'Judah Waten',

O 100 (1985), pp 47–50; interwar period, David Carter, *Career in Writing*, p 77; and foundation of *Overland*, *Ind*, p 30; dish, CBC to SMS, 18 June 1954, SMS LaT Box 2/1; McLaren, *Writing*, pp 46, 216.

4 Stephen and the Party: ASIO assessment, memo for D/G, 6 Mar 1953, A6119/68/112; Malayan story, memo 19 Feb 1953, as above /109 and Report 8 June 1954, A6119/69(2)/27, all NAA.

5 SMS and Lawson: on Australian writing [c 1948], SMS LaT Box 274/2-1; 22; Gorki, SMS to Gotts, 16 Dec 1949, LaT 13047/3764/1; availability in print, *RW* 3 (Sep 1952), p 20 and 4 (Dec 1952), p 4.

6 *Tracks We Travel*: Prague anthology, to have been published by Mlada Fronta, the youth publishing house, *Tribune*, 22 Apr 1950; title [closes] Lawson's 'The Uncultured Rhymer to his Cultured Critics'; Stephen's aims, *Tracks*, introduction; review, Ian Turner, *RW* 8 (Dec 1953/Jan 1954), p 21.

7 Furphy: SMS on Furphy, fragment on Aust literature, SMS LaT Box 274/2-1.

8 Adams: SMS, 'I heard the wild fife's cry', Qld *Tribune*, 10 Oct 1956; SMS, Adams *ADB* entry, vol 3 pp 13–15 (1969), among others.

9 Workers v middle class: 'book understanding', nd, and 'political direction', 'ever-present danger', both 10 Jul [1954], Williams to SMS; 'bad poem', Len Fox to SMS, 22 Oct 1954, all SMS LaT Box1/2-2; 'no particular political philosophy', *O* 7 (1956), p 2.

10 Sales: *O* 2, p 12; 1500 copies, SMS to Waten, 9 Feb 1955, SMS LaT Box 1/2-3.

11 *Overland* and *Meanjin*: 'help', Joan Clark to SMS, 2 June 1954, SMS LaT Box 1/1-1; 'quite friendly', *Ind*, p 28; a 'Tribute to *Meanjin*', by AA Phillips, appeared in *O* 8 (1956), pp 7–8; 'not outshine', SMS to editorial board, 13 Sep 1955, SMS Box 2/1-1; *Bulletin*, *Age*, 13 Dec 1958; 'cosmopolitan', SMS to Williams, nd, handwritten draft, SMS Box 1/2-1; 'aggressive Australianism', Wannan to SMS, 21 June 1955, SMS Box 1/3-2; 'overloaded', Anne Mitchell to SMS, 11 Sep 1958, SMS Box 6/1-4; 'bucolic', Turnbull, *O* 3 (1955), p 18; 'awakening', SMS to Beatrice Davis, A&R, 29 May 1955, SMS Box 1/3-1; instinctive rejection, *O* 9 (1957), p 2; 'younger writers', de Berg interview 1961, p 1.

12 Short-story difficulties: 'dead and useless', SMS to EG Reynolds, 24 Apr 1955; Manifold to SMS, nd [1954], SMS Box 1/2-3; 'hagridden', SMS, 'To all members of the Editorial Board', 6 May 1955, SMS Box 1/3-2.

13 John Morrison: AA Phillips, 'The Stories of John Morrison', *O* 58 (1974) p 32; SMS, Intro to Morrison, *North Wind*, esp. p xii; 'refrain', Morrison to SMS, Friday [1955] and 'kept clear', Morrison to SMS, 20 Aug 1954, both SMS Box 188/3-1.

14 Manifold: Rodney Hall, *John Manifold*, esp. pp 5, 114, 143, 159; 'pinpricking', Collinson to SMS, Thurs midday [1959], SMS Box 10/1-7.

15 David Martin: *My Strange Friend*, esp. pp 98, 122, 135, 229, 236–7; 'Bagpipes in Hobart', *O* 7 (1956), p 23; NLA interview by Hazel de Berg, 6 Dec1969, Tape 443 t/s Side 1-3, Side 2-1; SMS to Martin, 30 Oct 1953, NLA MS 6885/19/fol Mc.

16 Collinson: *The Moods of Love*, SMS Box 168/1-1; sales, *O* 12, p 23; Muir Holborn review, *O* 11 (1958), p 27, and Collinson 'My Poetry', same issue, p 30; not political enough, Collinson to SMS, 20 Feb [1956], SMS Box 2/2-3; Martin, *My Strange Friend*, p 265.

17 Turner: 'faults', Amirah Turner to SMS, nd, SMS Box 3/32-3; 'liaison', ASIO NAA A6119/280/152-3, 17 July 1958; 'well-known weakness', SMS to Turner, 10 Oct 1954, SMS Box 2/1-2; Turner on Aldridge, 'The Necessity of Freedom', *O* 8 (1956), pp 21, 23; towards radical nationalism, *O* 6 (1955–56), p 27; on *Voss*, *O* 12 (1958), p 37.

18 Turner, 'The Life of the Legend', *O* 16 (1959–60), pp 23–30.

19 SMS cultural views: 'social dynamic', *O* 14, (1959), p 19; nurture, 'A Fair Go', *O* 7 (1956), p 2.

20 *O* goes contemporary: Gerry Grant, '*Jedda*', *O* 6 (1955–56), p 7; Namatjira cover, *O* 13 (1958); Swanston Street vagrant, *O* 6 (1956), p 11; Collinson on Hiroshima Panels, *O* 12 (1958), p 18; ML Oliphant, 'Science and the Future of Humanity', *O* 13 (1958), pp 21–7.

21 Humphries, Harney, Culotta: 'A new satirist', *O* 14 (1959) p 39; 'poets in speech', SMS in 'Swag', *O* 14 (1959), p 24; 'Bill Harney's War', *O* (1958), pp 3–12.

22 Expatriates: 'venomous crap', CBC to Brian Fitzpatrick, 27 Sep 1962, NLA 4965/2/767; 'something sad' (unattributed quote in French), CBC to Harry Heseltine, 20 Jan 1955, UMA Box 171.

23 Censorship and its assumptions: 'fellow traveller' and conservative writers' files, Haydn Keenan, film *Persons of Interest*, part 4; Nicole Moore, *The Censor's Library*, esp. pp 180, 200.

24 ASIO: Extensive files were kept on each editor and each magazine, and their wives; 'sparrows', Keenan, part 1; 'stumblebums', Gorton on *This Day Tonight*, 1969; migrant friend, Hall, *John Manifold*, p 29.
25 Khrushchev speech: distributed, SMS to Keith McEwan, 27 Sep 1966, DMS.
26 Stephen, the Party, and the Khrushchev speech: I have drawn here on SMS's apologia to Keith McEwan, 27 Sep 1966; for Zhdanov, Turner, 'My Long March', p 33; Hardy's Russian book was *Journey into the Future*; Lambert troubling, Bruce Grant, 31 May 2012; 'twisted arms', Devanny to SMS, 2 Jan 1958, SMS LaT Box 5/1-6; *Age*, NAA A6119/69 (2) 35 report, 18 Mar 1957; SMS, Some Idle Thoughts on the Twentieth Congress, dissident writers' statement to executive, nd, DMS; 'no dark ages', SMS interview 21 Nov 1969, de Berg tape 426, p 20.
27 SMS abroad: journalists' lunch, Cameron Forbes, 9 Feb 2020; surveillance, SMS Recollections, *Australians from 1939*, p 428; liquidation plans, SMS to Keith McEwan, 27 Sep 1966; 'first detailed account', John Sendy, *Once a Jolly Comrade*, pp 80–1.
28 SMS resignation: contrite, ASIO Report, 8 Dec 1955, NAA A6119/69, and /280/163 for Nita membership; Turner and SMS resignation, SMS to McEwan, 27 Sep 1966, DMS; SMS, A Brief Statement for Some of My Friends [1958], DMS; 'do it better', SMS to Bernie Meyer, 29 July 1958, SMS Box 6/1-1; news, Hewett, *Wild Card*, p 251.
29 Leaving the Party: Gott, life summary, 2–3, and account for Dear Bill, 1964, p 13, autobiographical writings, LaT 3802/4; Rex Mortimer, 'Benefits of a liberal education', p 124; Turner, SMS to McEwan, 27 Sep 1966; Jenny Love, 6 Aug 2013; still a member, Report, 2 May 1958, NAA A6119/280 (3)/107.
30 The *Tribune* attack: Rex Chiplin, 'Overland—Where Is It Being Taken?', *Trib* 11 May 1959, p 7; Martin, SMS to John [Ewers?], 21 May 1959, SMS Box 9/2-2; 'pornographic', George Peterson, 'Tribune and Overland', attachment Lionel Amet to SMS, 5 Jul 1959, Box 9/2-6; Frank Hardy, letter, *Trib* 10 June 1959, p 7; Ralph de Boissière, 'Author Asks Editor Pertinent Questions', *Trib* 3 June 1959, p 6; KS Prichard, letter, *Trib* 10 June 1959; 'sharp situation', Gott to SMS, 6 June 1959, SMS Box 9/2-3; *Outlook*, Box 9/2-2.
31 Battle for *Overland*: I am indebted here to John McLaren's accounts in *Free Radicals*, pp 174–7, and *Writing in Hope and Fear*, pp 45–50; 'incentive', SMS to Turner, 17 May 1959, NLA 6206 Box 38 *O* file; 'shit', SMS circular, draft, 29 May 1959, SMS Box 9/2-2; 'screaming matches', SMS to Keith McEwan, 27 Sep 1966 DMS; 'to *unite*', SMS, Note for Barry, NAA A6122/2156 (1), 1; for participants' observations, Jo Josefs to SMS, 5 June 1959, SMS Box 9/2-5.
32 SMS reflects: 'very happy', SMS to Devanny, 4 Mar 1959 SMS Box 169/10-1; 'better Marxists', SMS to McEwan, 27 Sep 1966 DMS.
33 *Overland* prospects: 'arid … work', SMS to McEwan, 27 Sep 1966 DMS; de Berg SMS i/v 1961 Oral TRC 1/65; Waten, NAA A463/1963/2565 (4) /121, 16–19 June 1961.

Chapter 5 'All Those Wonderful Cultural Renaissances We're Having Nowadays'

1 1960s context: 'only hope', SMS to Rod Shaw, 18 June 1960, SMS LaT Box 196/1-1; 'inopportune', Brian Elliott to CBC, 31 July [1962], UMA Box 117.
2 Armidale and after: CBC, 'Functions of the Literary Magazine', UMA Box 73; quotes have been drawn from throughout this 20-page paper. 'Potent agencies' and 'major breakthrough', CBC, 'Twenty-One Lives', esp. pp 85, 91, and Trailer, "Twenty Years After', *M* 4/1960, pp 459–61.
3 *Overland*'s role: 'anyone else's', SMS to D Mitchell, 23 July 1956, and 'not confined', *Ind*, pp 31–2, both quoted in John Sendy, 'The Story of Overland', *O* 102 (1986), pp 35, 38; 'strengthen both', *Age*, 13 Dec 1958, NAA A6122/2156/68; 'vital role', Editorial, 'A Common Culture', *O* 19 (1960), p 8; sixty per cent, SMS, 'What You Think', *O* 19 (1960–61), p 13; SMS to Lilley, 6 Dec 1960, SMS LaT 176/2-1; SMS, Preface to *An Overland Muster*, pp vi–viii; 'lost', SMS, '*O*' in Bennett (ed.) *Cross Currents*, p 90; occluded, McLaren, *Free Radicals*, p 194.
4 *Overland–Meanjin* congruencies: 'poor man's *Meanjin*', Hardy, relayed by Dorothy Hewett, SMS Box 5/1-1 (1958); reviewer, Ian Mair, 'Overland—John o'Melbourne's Quarterly', *Age* 27 Apr 1963; 'compound', SMS tribute at Nettie Palmer funeral, SMS LaT Box 191/4/1; 'rather prejudiced', Aileen Palmer to CBC, 12 Mar 1968, UMA Box 256; distancing, SMS to Helen Palmer, 19 Mar 1970, LaT Box 191.
5 *Overland*'s mix: Discussions: 'The Legend and the Loneliness', *O* 23 (1962), pp 33–8, 'Two Decades of American Painting', *O* 37 (1967), pp 21–32; 'Greer on Revolution; Germaine

on Love', *O* 50/51 (1972), pp 44–57. Griffin and Conway, Jim Griffin, 'Psycho-Historical Arse-Grass', *O* 52 (1972), pp 2–11; Ronald Conway, 'Retorting to an Improbable Beast', *O* 53 (1972), pp 18–21; Jim Griffin, 'A Reply to a Retort', *O* 56 (1973), pp 45–6. Oliphant and Petty, *O* 18 (1960), pp 25–36.

6 'Swag': Student Action, *O* 22 (1961–62), p 9; CLF and *Crimes Act:* *O* 19 (1960–61), p 13; CIA scandal, *O* 36 (1967), p 17; 'Swag' is absent from *O* 39–55; 'disguise themselves', *O* 56 (1973), p 16.

7 'like Finland': SMS to Amirah and Ian Turner, 2 Mar 1961, SMS LaT, Box 196/6-1.

8 *Overland* and world of work: Pat Mackie, 'The Mount Isa Story', *O* 32 (1965) pp 25–9; Arbitration Court, James Arden, 'Intellectuals and Workers', *O* 37 (1967), p 17.

9 *Overland* measured against today's issues: 'Greer on Revolution; Germaine on Love', *O* 50/51 (1972), pp 43–58; Chris Hector, 'Discussion with Dennis Altman', *O* 55 (1973), pp 35–42; George Farwell, 'Holy Mess', *O* 43 (1969–70), pp 11–14; Judith Wright, 'Survival of Our Species', *O* 43 (1969–70), pp 17–21.

10 *Overland* and PNG: Brian Cooper, 'The Birth-pangs of a Nation', with SMS, 'Black Men—and a White Conscience', *O* 20 (1961), pp 31–6; *O* New Guinea Issue, 47 (1971), with further PNG material in 48 (1971), pp 25–40; [Hasluck], epigraph in *O* 29 (1964), p 21; 'will soon need', letter to *Herald*, 1 July 1960; Inglis, 'University in a Hurry', *O* 36 (1967), pp 25–8; 'ancestors ate', Don Baker to Ian Turner, 7 July 1970, NLA 6206 Box 111, Folio 20. The student was John Waiko, subsequently the first Papua New Guinean to be appointed professor.

11 [Editorial], 'Black Men—and White Conscience', *O* 20 (1961), p 33; McLeod, in Cecil Holmes, 'Experiments in Survival', *O* 17 (1960), p 27; Beth Hauser, 'Our Freedom Ride', *O* 32 (1965), p 38; Australian racism, [Editorial], 'Morality—In Black and White', *O* 17 (1960), p 5.

12 Vietnam: poem, Agnes Millrose, 'Conscript', *O* 35 (1966), p 23; 'Vietnam' issue, *O* 34, esp. pp 23, 29; dedicated issue, *O* 49 (1971), p 4; *Vietnam Voices*, *O* 54 [1972], SMS introduction, RH Morrison Foreword.

13 America: Peter Mathers, 'Pittsburgh: Identity 000000062I', *O* 39 (1968), pp 12–16; Hans Magnus Enzensberger, 'On Leaving America', *O* 39 (1968), pp 41–2.

14 England: 'out here', e.g. 'Swag', *O* 17 (1960), p 26; Arnold Wesker, 'O Mother, Is It Worth It?', *O* 19 (1960), pp 17–18; Merv Lilley and other respondents, *O* 20 (1961), pp 38–41; Laurence Collinson, 'London Surface: Notes from an Alien', *O* 30 (1964), pp 44–6 and 'Notes from a Colonial', *O* 33 (1965–66), pp 38–9; 'Views from the Antipodes': David Martin, 'England Now', and Richard Neville, 'How to Bluff Your Way through Britain', *O* 38 (1968), pp 17–20.

15 Squaring up to the Soviet Union: 'disgust', 'Swag', *O* 56, (1973) p 16, Crankshaw, quoted in 'Swag', *O* 22 (1961), p 10; Khrushchev, Fuentes and Yevtushenko, *O* 27/28 (1963), pp 33–40, Fuentes quote, p 35.

16 Soviet dissidents and anti-Semitism: Solzhenitsyn, 'A Letter to the Union of Soviet Writers', *O* 37 (1967), pp 14–16; Graham Greene (letter to *The Times*), *O* 37 (1967), p 20; protest letter, *O* 38 (1968), p 38, Nina Christesen, 'Anna Akhmatova', *O* 35 (1966–67), pp 47–8; SMS, review of Isi Liebler, *Soviet Jewry and Human Rights*, *O* 32 (1965), p 48; no Yiddish press, 'Swag', *O* 57 (1973–74), p 26.

17 Prague, 1968: *O* 39 (1968), pp 5–6.

18 Clem's Top Ten: 'Twenty-One Lives', p 84; UNESCO list, CBC to Vance Palmer, 19 Jan 1959, UMA Box 257.

19 Patrick White and *Meanjin:* 'convey', White to CBC, 15 June 1956, UMA Box 350; 'unbearably solemn', White to Aurousseau, 5 Oct 1962 quoted in Marr, *Patrick White*, p 401.

20 International: French, interview with CBC, c 1970, p 5, and fob him off, CBC script [nd], both UMA 1999.0014/1966/404; international offerings below par, CBC Editor's Statement, *Aust Lit Studies* vol 10 no 2 (1981), p 244; Rosenbergs: CBC to Catherine Duncan, 7 Jan 1966, UMA Box 112.

21 *Overland* fiction; Ian Mair, 'John o'Melbourne's quarterly', *Age*, 27 Apr 1963; second thoughts on 'Pioneers', *ALS* vol 10 no 2 (1981), p 266; 'experimental writing', SMS to advisory editors, 24 Apr 1963, NLA 6206 Box 38; 'difficult', 'Swag', *O* 26 (1963), p 18.

22 Poetry: Rodney Hall to CBC, 5 June 1963 and CBC to Hall, 5 Jul 1962; poets' arrival, Hall to CBC, 22 July 1962, UMA Box 159.

23 Francis Webb: HP Heseltine, 'defied me', 'The Very Gimbals of Unease: The Poetry of FW', *MQ* 2/1967, p 255, and 'Francis Webb, 1925–1973: A Tribute', *MQ* 1/1974, p 6; blasphemy, Webb, *Birthday*, in *Collected Poems* (ed. T Davidson), p 114; for list of admirers, Davidson

edition, p 1. See also *Poetry Australia, Francis Webb Commemorative Issue*, no 56, Sep 1975 (devotional books, p 8, AD Hope, p 35), and Herbert Read, Preface to Webb, *Collected Poems* (1969), pp v, viii, and in *London Magazine*, Dec 1967 (quoted in *P Aust* Webb issue, p 4). The poems referred to appear in *MQ*, 1/1962, pp 60–1, 1/1964, p 35, 1/1970, pp 34–5, 3/1970 pp 318–19; correspondence Webb to CBC, 13 July and CBC to Webb, 25 July 1961; Webb to CBC 23 Sep 1970, UMA Box 348.

24 Hewett and *Meanjin*: 'talent', quoted in *Wild Card*, p 91; book, implicit in Hewett to CBC, 18 July 1945; 'further work', CBC to Hewett, 22 May 1958, and Hewett to CBC,16 Apr 1963; 'coarseness', GWL comments; all UMA Box 173.

25 Hewett, to *Bobbin Up*: 'proletarian gulag', 'Empty Room', pp 9–10, 'second run', to CBC, 22 May 1958, UMA Box 173; *Bobbin Up* (typist), 'Empty Room', p 7, (reception), *Wild Card*, p 257; sapped, in particular SMS to Hewett, 22 Apr 1959, LaT Box 176/1-1.

26 Dorothy contra SMS: Editorial, 'A General Demand for Art', *O* 14 (1959), pp 19–20; Hewett to SMS, 15 Jul 1959, SMS Box 176/2-1.

27 Hewett and academics: 'cynically right', Hewett to SMS, LaT 176/4-1; 'beauty contest', Hewett to SMS, 19 July 1969, LaT 176/5-1.

28 Hewett in *O*: 'self-mythologiser', Sheridan, *Nine Lives*, p 101; 'pastiche', SMS to Hewett, 3 Nov 1961, NLA 6184 Box 1/3; FitzGerald to SMS, 30 June 1962, above; 'talking about', SMS to Hewett, 30 Oct 1966, NLA 6184 1/3; Reid, Peter Leiden flyer, SMS LaT Box 176/8-1.

29 Hewett and Communism: 'the *idea*', Hewett to CBC, 1 Sep 1965, UMA Box 173; 'unsuccessful marriage', Hewett to SMS, [Aug] 1965, SMS LaT 176/2-1; commiserate, SMS to Hewett, 15 Nov 1965, 176/3-1; 'no freedom', Hewett to CBC, 1 Sep 1965, UMA Box 173; 'The Hidden Journey', *O* 36 (1967), pp 5–8; subtitling, SMS to Hewett, 2 May 1967, LaT 176/5-1.

30 Hewett and KSP: 'Excess of love: The irreconcilable in Katharine Susannah Prichard', *O* 43 (1969–70), pp 27–31; 'breakthrough', SMS to Hewett, 14 Nov 1969, LaT Box 176/5-1.

31 Martin and *Meanjin*, prospects: 'don't see', CBC to Martin, 28 June 1954, UMA Box 227; poems appeared in *O* 1, p 7; acknowledged, Martin to CBC, 24 Nov 1959, craved approval, CBC to Martin, 2 Dec 1959 and 'looking for', CBC to Martin, 23 Nov 1959, all UMA Box 227; 'to make articulate', CBC to Martin, 18 May 1961, NLA 6885/2; 'petered out', Martin to CBC, 31 Mar 1959, and 'ridiculous', Martin to CBC, 24 Nov 1959 both UMA Box 227.

32 Martin and *Meanjin*, rift: AA Phillips, 'The Writings of David Martin', *MQ* 1/20 (1961), p 15; 'faithful', Martin to CBC, 17 May 1961, promised article, Martin to CBC, 20 May 1961, 'thin-iced pond', Martin to CBC, 27 May 1971, and expectations, Martin to CBC, 18 June 1969, all UMA Box 227.

33 Martin and SMS: 'empathy', SMS to Martin, 24 Nov 1961, NLA 6885 Box 19; Martin letter to SMS, 1 May 1961, LaT Box 184; 'been hit', SMS to Martin, 23 July 1957, NLA 6885 Box 19; world citizen, SMS, 'Our Writers, VII: David Martin, *O* 13, p 40; 'do not hanker' and pied-à-terre, SMS to Martin, 2 May 1961, close down, SMS to Martin, 29 Dec 1959, all NLA MS 6885 Box 19.

34 Martin in *Overland*: tsarist naval officer, 'The Captain', *O* 18, pp 9–10; on Vance Palmer, 'Hinterland', *O* 17, p 12.

35 Myth: James McAuley,'Reflections on Poetry', *M* 4/1953, pp 431–41; Vincent Buckley, 'Helicon as Jordan', *M* 4/1954, pp 520–36; AA Phillips, 'The Uneasy Chair', *M* 3/1952, p 196; 'master', Geoff Serle to CBC, 4 May [1958], UMA Box 300; 'potent force', Barnes to CBC, 16 Aug 1962, Box 43; 'scare people', CBC to Harry Hesltine, 4 May [1958], Box 300.

36 Australian canon: Serle, quoted in Katherine Gallagher, 'Overland and Australian Studies', *Australian Studies* 4/1990, p 162; CBC to Barnes, 14 Nov 1966, UMA Box 45.

37 Critics of criticism: Patrick White to Dutton, quoted in Ian Turner to SMS, 2 Mar [1962], LaT Box 196/5-1; AD Hope to Serle, 12 July 1957, UMA Box 179.

38 Academic critics: 'team', CBC to Barnes, 9 Jan 1962, UMA Box 45.

39 Harry Heseltine: 'mix', *In Due Season*, p 7; 'incompletely formed', Heseltine to CBC, 12 Dec 1960 and 'too kind', Heseltine to CBC, Mon 5.45 pm [1961], both UMA Box 171; Heseltine, 'Australian Image (1): The Literary Heritage', *MQ* 1/1962, pp 35–49; 'like to see', CBC to Maxwell, 12 Aug 1965, UMA Box 229; Heseltine, 'One Hundred Not Out', *MQ* 1/1965, pp 132–9; 'beauty', Heseltine to CBC, 16 Dec 1965, UMA Box 171; Heseltine, 7 Sep 2012.

40 Dorothy Green: 'extremis in Melbourne', Green to CBC, 31 Aug 1966; academic dishonesty, e.g. Green to CBC, 27 Oct 1969; 'unsettling', Headon quoted in McDonald, *Warrior for*

Peace, p 172; would have given up, Green to CBC, 23 Apr 1970; 'not independent', Green to CBC, 27 Feb 1973; 'wailing wall', Green to CBC, 8 Feb 1967; Dorothy responds, Green to CBC, 1 July 1954; 'Parents', Green to CBC, nd [1951]; 'insanely jealous', CBC to Green, 26 June [1967], Green reply ('badgered' and 'frightened'), nd; 'Underground', Green to CBC, 26 Sep 1967; 'written entirely', 8 Feb 1971 (all Green–CBC correspondence in UMA Box 150); 'without ethnic prejudice', Wilde, Hooton and Andrews, *Oxford Companion to Australian Literature*, p 731; Auchterlonie, 'The Second Coming, a Video Progress in Five Fyttes', *MQ* 1/1967, pp 24–8; McDonald, *Warrior*, p 78.

41 Literary *Overland*: AA Phillips, 'The Dogs Have Their Day', *O* 25 (1962), pp 33–4; 'We continue', and Russel Ward, 'Colonialism and Culture', *O* 31 (1965), p 15; Anstey articles, in *O* 31 (three), pp 29–40, *O* 32 (three), pp 17–22, and *O* 33 (one), pp 35–7 (all published 1965); Christina Stead, 'A Waker and a Dreamer [David Stead]', *O* 53 (1972), pp 33–7; Dorothy Hewett, 'Excess of Love', *O* 43 (1969–70), pp 27–31; 'Comments', particularly from RP Throssell and Jack Lindsay, *O* 44 (1970), pp 25, 28; 'O'Dowd to Whitman/Whitman to O'Dowd', *O* 23 (1962), pp 8–18; Leonie Kramer, 'Literary Criticism in Australia', *O* 26 (1963), pp 25–7; Martin Boyd, 'De Gustibus', *O* 50/51 (1972), pp 5–9; Dennis Douglas, 'Conversation with Peter Porter', *O* 44 (1970), pp 33–4; Owen Webster, 'Comic Genius', *O* 55 (1973), p 56.

42 Fitzpatrick: CBC to BF, 20 Sep 1962, 11 Feb 1960, UMA Box 130; also 1 Dec 1964, NLA 4965/2/973; BF to CBC, 11 Aug 1963, 28 Sep 1963, UMA Box 132; same issue, *MQ* 1/1961, pp 73–9, 107–111; see also 'Counter-revolution', *MQ* 2/1963, pp 197–213; Sheila Fitzpatrick, *My Father's Daughter*, p 105; testimonial dinner, see the *Rationalist* (Nov–Dec 1963), pp 163–9 and associated papers, UMA Box 130.

43 Turner at the ANU: Hancock, Turner to E and A Waters [1958], and 'drudgery', Turner to Ian Wilson, 14 Dec 1959, both NLA 6206 Box 109.

44 Turner repositions himself: 'cannot survive', Turner to Geoff [Serle], in response to questionnaire, 20 Dec 1970, NLA 6206 Box 20 (drafts); 'sacrificed', Burstall, *Memoirs of a Young Bastard*, entry for 23 Dec 1953, p 43; fellow-travellers, Turner, 'My Long March', *O* 59 (1974), p 31; 'arrogance', Turner to SMS, 4 May 1961, LaT Box 196/6-1; 'new assessment', Turner to David Denholm, 27 Feb 1962, SMS LaT Box 196/5-1.

45 Turner's thesis: Intro, Turner, *Industrial Labour and Politics*, esp. pp xviii–xx; 'Envoi: What Does It Add Up To?', ANU seminar paper, in SMS LaT, 196/5-1, [15 Sep 1961], pp 2–3.

46 Turner: protest and meliorism: 'leading intellectual', Heseltine, *In Due Season*, p 100; 'permanent protest', Turner to SMS, 5 June 1961, LaT Box 196/5; 'class war muted', Turner, 'Reflections on Violence', intro to David Williamson, *The Removalists*, p 5.

47 Turner, Indigenous peoples, white rootlessnes: 'continued existence', book proposal, attached Turner to SMS, 4 Aug 1961, LaT Box 196/5-1; Turner, 'My Long March', p 23.

48 Turner pro-legend: Australian values and high culture, Turner, 'A Comment on Class and Culture' [1976] p 17, NLA 6206 Box 41; 'cut off from traditional roots', handwritten MS beginning 'Fifty years ago now, Henry Lawson wrote …', NLA 6206 Box 77; Turner on *Voss*, *O* 12 (1958), p 37; Turner, 'Legend into Myth', *O* 23 (1962), p 39.

49 Turner on *Overland*'s role, and radicalism: letter to *Prospect*, 27 Apr 1959, SMS LaT Box 196/8-1; Turner, 'The Life of the Legend', *O* 16 (1959), pp 35–6; critiques, Turner, 'Australian Nationalism and Australian History' (1979), reprinted in *Room for Manoeuvre*, esp. pp 13–15.

50 Post-Party political manoeuvres: 'organisation', Turner to SMS, 5 Jun 1961, LaT Box 196/5-1; ALP not socialist, Turner, 'The Nature and Significance of Labor', *Outlook*, vol 2 no 6 (Nov 1958), p 15; SMS rejoining Party, Buckley to Turner, 26 Mar 1959, NLA 6206 Box 38; 'community of protesters', Turner to SMS, 5 June 1961, LaT Box 196/5-1; 'opponents of Menzies', Turner to SMS, 19 Nov 1959, LaT Box 196/7-1; 'within limits', SMS to Turner, 26 May 1960, Box 196/7-1.

51 Turner and *Overland*: 'lean on you', SMS to Turner, 28 Sep 1962, NLA 6206 Box 111; bohemianism, DMS, 6 Aug 2015; 'more active role', SMS to Turner, 26 May 1960, LaT Box 196/7-1; Turner on poetry, to SMS, 21 May 1960, LaT Box 196/7-1; sociology, 'Swag', *O* 23 (1962), p 27.

52 Turner in *Overland*: 'doubly useful', SMS to Turner, 24 May 1961, LaT Box 196/6-1; Turner on Manning Clark, and Coleman: 'Australia: A Beginning and an End', *O* 24 (1962), pp 41–2; also Turner review of Clark's *Short History of Australia*, draft, NLA 6206 Box 20; discussions: 'Two Decades of American Painting', *O* 37, (1967), pp 21–36; 'Greer on Revolution; Germaine on Love: A discussion', *O* 50/51 (1972), pp 44–57.

53 More international: CBC to Chisholm, 16 Apr 1969, UMA Box 80.
54 Vietnam: *New York Times*, CBC to Aileen Palmer, 8 Mar 1968, UMA Box 256; Alex Carey, 'Clockwork Vietnam: Gaining Physical Control', *MQ* 1/1973, pp 45–52, and 'Clockwork Vietnam: 2) The Social Engineers Take Over', *MQ* 4/1973, pp 406–18.
55 International dimension: J-P Sartre, 'Why I Will Not Go to the United States', *MQ* 3/1965, pp 340–4; 'stuffing', CBC to Nina, 17 Dec 1968, Armstrong, *Christesen Romance*, pp 168–9.
56 Public issues, cultural infrastructure: 'Early One Morning: Reflections on the Ryan Case', *MQ* 2/1967, pp 190–8; '*ought* to be unpopular', Max Charlesworth, 'No One Loves the Universities', *MQ* 2/1967, p 231; 'torpor', Trailer: 'Caring about the Arts', *MQ* 1/66, p 127.
57 Art and music: 'sudden dislike', Bernard Smith to Davidson, 13 Mar 1975, UMA 20001 0044 Unit 25; 'Utzon', Philip Parsons, 'Radical versus Conservative Architecture: The Ruin of Utzon's Audacious Vision', *MQ* 3/1967, p 341.
58 Theatre and Drama issue, *MQ* 3/1964: Heseltine to CBC, 3 Jan 1961; not '*excited*', CBC to Heseltine, 2 Mar, 31 July and 13 Nov 1964, all UMA Box 172.
59 Film and television: 'vulgar nonsense', AA Phillips, 'The Pilkington Report on TV', *MQ* 3/1962, p 400; twenty-six films, MS 'That Dirty Word', encl. Alan Seymour to CBC, 5 Mar 1963, UMA Box 298.
60 KS Inglis, 'The Anzac Tradition': *MQ* 1/1965, pp 25–44; further publication history, Di Langmore, paper on his work at the ANU, 'Ken Inglis in History: A Laconic Colloquium', Monash University, 24 Nov 2016; further communication 12 Dec 2016.
61 Diggers and the Australian Legend: see Russel Ward, *The Australian Legend* (Melbourne, OUP, 1958); 'social intimidation', Noel McLachlan, 'Nationalism and the Divisive Digger', *MQ* 3/1968, p 308; Michael Roe, R Ward: 'The Australian Legend: An Exchange', *MQ* 3/1962, esp. p 369.
62 Women: Coral Lansbury, 'The Miner's Right to Mateship', *MQ* 4/1966, pp 435–43; 'exhausting one', Kathleen Fitzpatrick, review of Norman MacKenzie, *Women in Australia*, *MQ* 1/1963, p 31; equal responsibility, Lansbury, 'The Feminine Frontier: Women's Suffrage and Economic Reality', *MQ* 3/1972, p 296.
63 'Cultural sociology': CBC to Noel McLachlan, 27 Sep 1965, UMA Box 221.
64 Indigenous: Alan McCulloch, 'The Aboriginal Art Exhibition', *MQ* 2/1961, p 191; Henry Reynolds, 'Violence, the Aboriginals, and the Australian Historian', *MQ* 4/1972, pp 471–7.
65 Australia viewed from abroad: Noel McLachlan, 'The View from London Bridge', *MQ* 4/1962, pp 469–76; Elwyn Lynn, 'Australia Rediscovered: The Whitechapel Gallery Exhibition', *MQ* 3/1961, pp 337–9; Norman Bartlett, 'Home Thoughts from Abroad: The Object as it Really Is', *MQ*, 1/1972, pp 78–83; Russel Ward, 'Australia's Racist Image', *MQ* 2/1971, on McQueen, p 156.
66 Australian racism and colonialism: Humphrey McQueen, 'The Sustenance of Silence: Racism in 20th Century Australia', *MQ* 2/1971, esp. p 163; Alan Healy, 'The Intercultural Problem: New Guinea', *MQ* 4/1970, pp 483–91. Even Healy does not use the term 'colony' here, but did in 'The Intercultural Problem: Isolated Australians', *MQ* 1/1970, p 63.
67 Provincialism: Nicholas Tarling, 'Is Australia Still an Outpost?', *MQ* 2/1962, esp. p 205; AA Phillips, 'Provincialism and Australian Culture', *MQ* 3/1966, esp. pp. 267, 269, 271, 274.
68 Pervasiveness of censorship: Turner banning, Margaret Corris, 'Child's World', *O* 43 (1969–70), p 52; in port and end of decade, CBC to Catherine Duncan, 27 Mar 1962 and 24 Nov 1969, UMA Box 112; library, CBC to Brissenden, 14 Feb 1964, Box 56; 'pants', AD Hope to CBC, 9 June 1956, Box 179; 'fucken', CBC script in UMA 1999.0014/1966/404; 'an editor do?', CBC to David Martin, 16 July 1953, Box 227.
69 *Snatches & Lays*, introduction; McLaren, *Free Radicals*, pp 178–9.
70 Censorship, mainly *Meanjin*: 'dose of filth', SMS, 'Swag', *O* 49 (1971) p 39; 'normal', 'Censorship and Cant', *MQ* 2/1964, pp 223–4; 'very insecure view', William H Orchard, 'Censorship: A Psychiatrist's View', *MQ* 3/1969, p 387; 'obscenity as weapon', Dennis Altman, 'How I Fought the Censors and (Partly) Won', *MQ* 2/1970, p 238.
71 Censorship and *Overland*: *Borstal Boy*, *O* 15 (1959), pp 41–3; 'hot', David Martin, 'Hinterland', *O* 21 (1961), p 44; Harris, 'Decaying World', *O* 27/28 (1963), p 21; six yellow pages, *O* 19 (1960), pp 31–6; 'turning point', SMS to Turner, 2 Mar 1961, SMS Box 196/6-1; scrutinising, 'Swag', *O* 29 (1964), p 13.
72 *Portnoy's Complaint*: Collinson, 'Matriarchal Death', *O* 42 (1969), pp 38–9; Nicole Moore, *The Censor's Library*, pp 274–8.

73 *London Magazine*: vol 2 no 6 (Sep 1962), 'odious tone', Trailer, *MQ* 4/1962, p 539, 'tone all wrong', CBC to Noel McLachlan, 2 Oct 1962, UMA Box 221; Alan Seymour, 'Four Conversations and a Comment', *LM*, above, p 56; 'stultifyingly conformist', *LM*, p 5; Martin, CBC to McLachlan, 2 July 1962, UMA Box 221; Jack Lindsay, 'The Alienated Australian Intellectual', *MQ* 1/1963, pp 48–59.

74 Alienation: 'love-hate', Inglis to CBC, 2 Oct 1962, UMA Box 186, and McLachlan to CBC [June 1969], Box 221; 'outsider', Serle to CBC, 4 May [1958] Box 300; Column, *Outlook*, vol 7 no 6 (1963), p 2; 'minority', quoted in Column, *Outlook*, vol 7 no 6 (1963), p 2; 'strange love-hate', CBC to McLachlan, 2 Oct 1962.

75 Genesis of Godzone: 'pretty big changes', CBC to Rohan Rivett, 21 Dec 1965, UMA Box 287; Kennedy era, CBC to Noel McLachlan, 6 Dec 1945, Box 221; Horne, Stuart Ward, 'Empire's New Clothes', p 128; 'dead as a dodo', CBC to Inglis Moore, 21 Feb 1966, UMA Box 235.

76 Godzone, organising the series: uncomfortable, Rivett to CBC, 17 Jan 1966, UMA Box 287; four large pieces, CBC to Noel McLachlan, 2 Dec 1965; articulated scheme, McLachlan to CBC, 30 Nov 1965, shied, CBC to McLachlan, 4 Jan 1966; CBC to write, McLachlan to CBC, 28 Oct 1967, all UMA Box 221.

77 Godzone articles: Ian Turner, '1) The Retreat from Reason', *MQ* 2/1966, pp 133–43; Owen Webster, '2) The Need for Intransigence', *MQ* 3/1966, pp 245–64; Allan Ashbolt, '3) Myth and Reality', *MQ* 3/1966, pp 373–88; Noel McLachlan, '4) The Australian Intellectual', *MQ* 1/1967, pp 5–17; JBD Miller, '5) Other Places', *MQ* 2/1967, pp 117–26; AG Serle, '6) Austerica Unlimited?', *MQ* 3/1967, pp 237–50; Geoffrey Blainey, '7) The New Australia: A Legend of the Lake', *MQ* 4/1967, pp 365–80.

78 Godzone, McGregor objects: 'common contempt', CMcG to CBC, 1 Mar 1967, 'pretty awful', CBC to CMcG, 8 Mar 1967; 'alleged contempt', CBC to CMcG, 4 July 1967; 'fault', CMcG to CBC, 19 July 1967, all UMA Box 219.

79 Godzone—fate and estimation: book, Allan Ashbolt to R Cross, Macmillan, 9 June 1970; CBC to Ashbolt, 1 Sep 1970, UMA Box 4; CMcG to CBC, 19 July 1967, Box 219; 'Menzies torpor', a phrase of Paul Keating's.

80 Other *Meanjin* series: 'Remembrance': Leslie Rees, '16. Clongowes, the Tower & a Meeting with James Joyce', *MQ* 3/1968, pp 328–35; FC Green, '9. From King O'Malley to WM Hughes', *MQ* 1/1963, pp 89–98; Oscar Mendelsohn, '14. Max Meldrum and the Science of Appearances', *MQ* 2/1967, pp 204–10; Catherine Duncan, '8. The World of Hanns Eisler', *MQ* 4/1962, pp 477–87; conscription, Chisholm to CBC, 26 Nov 1967, UMA Box 80; Ian Turner, 'The Retreat from Reason', *MQ* 2/1966, pp 133–43; Turner, 'The Politics of Action', *MQ* 1/1968, pp 106–8 and 'The Vietnam Moratorium', *MQ* 2/1970, p 244.

81 Retrospects, *Meanjin* 1965: *Bulletin* comparisons, Grahame Johnston, 'Two magazines: a hundred to one', *Australian*, 12 June 1965, and RF Brissenden, 'Literature of Today, *Meanjin*'s 25th Anniversary', *Australian*, 11 Dec 1965; Noel McLachlan, 'A Hundred *Meanjins*', *TLS*, 16 Sep 1965; AD Hope, '*Meanjin* Comes of Age', *Landfall* (Dec 1962), pp 376–9.

82 Awards: rarely given, CBC to Inglis Moore, 30 Aug 1958, UMA Box 235; 'fallen for it', CBC to Hewett, 14 Jan 1966, Box 173.

83 *On Native Grounds*: 'pinched', CBC to Inglis Moore, 8 July 1969, UMA Box 234; 'continuous dialogue', CBC to Chisholm, 27 Aug 1967, Box 80; 'apotheosis', SMS, Books for Comment, ABC, 16 Feb 1968, Misc Correspondence, Box 246; 'every right', Bob Brissenden to CBC, 4 Mar 1968, Box 56.

84 *Hand of Memory*: CBC to Laurence Collinson, 18 Nov [1971] and 20 Mar 1972, UMA Box 84; 'minor lyric writer', CBC to Harry Heseltine, 4 May 1971, Box 171.

85 Further plans: Marjorie Tipping (compiler), *Meanjin Quarterly Index 1940–1965* (1969); Blainey and Frank Strahan, CBC to Ray Marginson, 18 Mar 1971, UMA Box 224; Lynne Strahan: *Just City and the Mirrors: Meanjin Quarterly and the Intellectual Front 1940–1965*.

86 'drowning' and 'for posterity', CBC to Ray Marginson, 24 Mar and 7 July 1971, UMA Box 224; McLachlan to CBC, 22 Sep 1972, Box 221.

87 Clem and the 'generational problem': CBC to Chisholm, 10 Aug 1967, UMA Box 80; new English novelists, CBC to Derek van Abbé, 6 Jan 1955, Box 340; like very little, CBC to Dorothy Green 30 Oct 1950, Box 149; 'tortured soul', CBC, Comment, *MQ* 1/1958, p 111; on Tim Thorne, CBC to Ian Maxwell, 21 Jan 1971, UMA Box 229; 'all on the surface', CBC to Chisholm, 4 Jan 1967; *Chantacleer*, Dirk den Hartog to author, 1969.

88 Clem and the young: on Carey, CBC memo to AA Phillips, Carey file, UMA Box 69; Hemensley invite, Sonia Garde to KH, 4 July 1969, Box 168; Hemensley, 'First Look at the

New Australian Poetry', *MQ* 1/1970, pp 118–21, plus rejoinders and comments in that issue by Max Richards, and in the following by Carl Harrison-Ford and Anthony Kearney.

89 Cyril Connolly, 'Little Magazines', in *Evening Colonnade*, pp 414, 424; Ian Hamilton, *The Little Magazines*, p 9.

90 Clem and the young, 2: 'strange regard', Hemensley to CBC, 28 Apr 1970, UMA Box 168; 'buggered', CBC to Wilding, 25 Aug 1970, Box 352; 'can't find', CBC to David Martin, 31 May 1971, UMA Box 227.

91 *Meanjin* against the tide: 'outright hatred', Hemensley to CBC, 7 Mar 1970; haughtiness, Wilding, *Tabloid Story*, in Bennett, *Cross-Currents*, pp 230–1.

92 *MQ* fustian: Webster to CBC, 13 Aug 1967, UMA Box 349.

93 Humphrey McQueen: *A New Britannia*, p 12; see Noel McLachlan, 'Tirez sur les pianistes! Humphrey McQueen's "Revolutionary History"', *MQ* 4/1970, pp 547–51; AA Phillips, 'The Cross-Eyed Clio: Humphrey McQueen and the Australian Tradition', *MQ* 1/1971, pp 108–13; Russel Ward, 'Britannia Australia', *O* 47 (1971), pp 47–9; McQueen's 'Reply …', *O* 48 (1971), pp 22–4; Ward's 'Reply …', *O* 50/51 (1972), pp 79–80, whereupon Stephen closed the discussion; McQueen, 'The Sustenance of Silence: Racism in 20th Century Australia', *MQ* 2/1971, pp 157–64; Ward, 'Humphrey McQueen's Article', *MQ* 4/1971, p 477; McQueen, 'Reply to Arthur Phillips', *MQ* 1/1972, p 85.

94 CBC to Ray Marginson, 24 June 1971, UMA Box 224.

95 Clem's manoeuvrings: CBC to Catherine Duncan, 20 Sep 1972, UMA Box 112; 'three old men', CBC to John Barnes, 23 Mar 1972, Box 45; CBC to Alan Frost, 8 and 11 Mar 1971, Box 136.

96 CBC and Laurie Clancy: Lurie, 'On Meanjin, expatriatism and other filthy matters', *Review*, 19–25 Feb, 1972, pp 498–9; LJ Clancy file, UMA Box 83, esp. CBC to Clancy, 17 Feb, 16 Mar, 17 Apr and 15 May 1972.

97 Updating *Overland*: Reid memo, 'The New Left', attached Reid to SMS, 25 July 1972, NLA 6206 Box 38; RW Connell, 'The Manipulators', *O* 44, pp 15–21; diverse audience, statement, *Aust Literary Studies*, vol 10 no 2 (1981), p 266; 'arse-holes', SMS interviewed by Phillip Edmonds, 1976, quoted in his *Tilting at Windmills*, p 70.

Chapter 6 The Little Magazine Nexus

1 *Meanjin* beginnings: 'demanded', CBC, 'Twenty-one Lives', p 85; 'dreadful poems', Patricia Excell, CBC interview, 2 May 1988, p 4; resentment, CBC to Martin Haley, 17 Nov 1941, UQFL48/1/173.

2 *Meanjin* sales, subscriptions: 'bi-monthly booklets', Editorial Notes, *MP* I/9 (June 1942), p 3; no provision, Patricia Excell, 2 May 1988; postage provided, Duhig, Letter to Tom Collins: 'Contemporary "Culture"', *MP* I/12 (1942), p 28; 'better known', CBC to Percival Serle, 8 June 1942, UMA Box 300 and Notice, *MP* II/3 (1943), p 56.

3 *Meanjin*, finance: cost him, CBC to Haley [1943], FLUQ 48/1/172 and to Paul Grano, 17 Sep 1970, UMA Box 148; extended readership, Note to Contributors, *MP* I/7 (1942), inside back cover; active service, News Reel, *MP* II/2 (1943), p 61; flat rate, News Reel, II/1 (1943), p 56.

4 *Overland* circulation: Tregenza, *Little Magazines*, quoted 'Swag', *O* 5 (1955), p 20; circulation figures, DMS.

5 *Overland* and regions: Hardy, SMS, To All Members of the Ed Board, 13 Sep 1955, LaT Box 2/1-1; Sydney party, Buckley, 'Intellectuals', in Peter Coleman (ed.), *Australian Civilization*, p 101.

6 *Overland* economics: a thousand, SMS to Judah Waten, 9 Feb 1955, LaT Box 1/2-3.

7 *O* initiatives: 'stronger position', SMS to Ed Board, 18 Oct 1955, appeal circular, 2/2-2, 'cheapest', circular [1956] 2/22-5, and parallel claim, SMS to Ralph Peterson, 20 June 1956, 3/2-3, all SMS LaT.

8 *O* and ABS: fourth-largest, SMS to Dept Trade & Customs, 17 Jul 1955, SMS LaT Box 2/2-2; plan announced, *O* 6, Summer (1955–56), p 19; poorly distributed, SMS to Ed Board, Feb 1956, LaT Box 2/2-2; ABS subscribers, McLaren, *Free Radicals*, p 120; nitty-gritty, see e.g. Bernie Meyer to SMS, 31 Mar 1957, LaT Box 4/1-7; debts, SMS to Manager ABS, 21 Oct 1958, LaT Box 6/1-8.

9 Paton: comment professionally, CBC to Paton, 30 May 1950, UMA Box 262; 'censorship', Paton to CBC, 16 Sep 1952; deadlines, CBC to Maxwell, 30 May 1962, UMA Box 229.

10 University attitude, financing: halved Lockie, CBC to Maxwell, 6 Mar 1953, UMA Box 229; own two feet, see CBC to Maxwell, 24 July 1950; 'perpetual subsidy', James to CBC,

18 Dec 1946, Box 242; Chisholm on the Lockie, 'The background to Meanjin [1965]', Chisholm Papers, Box 1; didn't care enough, Chisholm to CBC, 31 Oct 1955, Box 80; 'adrenalin', CBC to Maxwell, 17 Feb 1956; 'why not', CBC to Chisholm, 3 Aug 1954; £2440 deficit, CBC to Gantner, 5 June 1956, Box 142; special authorisation, Paton to CBC, 29 Mar 1955.

11 Late British world: CBC to Chisholm, 24 Apr 1963, UMA Box 80; 'absurd', CBC to Inglis Moore, 2 Mar 1961, Box 235; 'hybrid', Bob Brissenden, quoted CBC to Maxwell, 6 Mar 1953, Box 229; nice hobby, CBC quoting C Moorhouse, to Chisholm, 10 Mar 1961.

12 CBC and supporters: 'intruder', to AD Hope, 2 May 1955, UMA Box 179; suspicious, CBC to Anwyl, 8 June 1958, Box 229; 'hopelessly autocratic', Chisholm to Excell, 2 Oct 1952, Box 80; 'cup of tea', quoted CBC to Hope, 29 Sep 1955; 'at least half-way', Maxwell, Open letter to academics [1960], Box 229; 'stubborn streak', CBC to Vance Palmer, fragment [1958], NLA 1174/1/1071; 'just beginning', CBC to Palmer, 8 Aug 1958, 1174/1/9032; 'gizzard', Maxwell to CBC, 27 Feb 1956; finance committee, CBC to Maxwell, 22 Mar 1962, Box 229.

13 *Meanjin* size: and reputation of journal, CBC to Maxwell, 17 Feb 1956; monthly, CBC to Maxwell, 1 Aug 1956.

14 Academic content: 200 academics, *M* 1/1956, p 4; desperate moment, CBC to Maxwell, 6 Mar 1953, UMA Box 229.

15 International dimension: Princeton survey, CBC to HS Temby, CLF, 25 June 1954, NAA A463/1963/2565 Part 1/51; CBC to Chisholm, 3 Aug 1954, UMA Box 80, and CBC to Inglis Moore, 27 June 1956, Box 235; vigour, John Berger to CBC, 23 July [1954], Box 48; republished, e.g. in *New Left Review*, Stuart Hall to CBC, 12 Nov 1960, Box 159; 'world range', CBC to Maxwell, 15 Feb 1954.

16 'Protection', CBC to Maxwell, 2 May 1956; 'borrowed time', CBC to Llewellyn Lucas, 20 June 1950, UMA Box 209; Sylvia Palmer, *Ink in her Veins*, p 231; 'responsible', CBC to Max Harris, 4 July 1960, in SMS LaT Box 166; 'Rob Roy', CBC to Dorothy Green, 3 Jan 1956, UMA Box 151.

17 Role and names: 'no-one at this University', CBC to FR Leavis, 7 May 1956, UMA Box 205; *Review*(s), CBC to Maxwell, 6 July 1960; 'quarterly', CBC to Maxwell, 27 May 1955; christened, CBC to Maxwell, 12 July 1956; never liked, CBC to AD Hope, 25 Aug 1960, Box 179.

18 Recurrent crises: 'borrowed time', CBC to D van Abbé, 22 Oct 1954, UMA Box 340; overmatter, CBC to Maxwell, 30 Apr 1963; 200 per cent, CBC to Chisholm, 22 Aug 1955, Box 80; 'close up', Maxwell to CBC, 21 Feb 1956; Maxwell, *Meanjin* General Statement, 27 Feb 1956; Evatt support, CBC to Hope, 6 Sep 1956; SRC concern, CBC to Hope, 13 Mar 1956; 'owner in theory', CBC to Chisholm, 13 Mar 1956; 'Mohicans', CBC to Maxwell, 22 Feb 1956; University takeover, CBC to Maxwell, 17 Feb 1956; 'the way you stick', Smith to CBC, 31 May 1948, Box 306; consultant, CBC to Maxwell, 22 Feb 1956, compromise, Maxwell to CBC, 5 Sep 1956, and CBC to Maxwell, 6 Sep 1956; 'hoping', Maxwell to CBC, 6 Sep 1956; 'quantities of dirt', Dorothy Green to CBC, 25 June [1954?], Box 150.

19 Salary: contract, CBC to Maxwell, 17 Feb 1956, UMA Box 229; Union Theatre, CBC to Hope, 4 Apr 1956, Box 179; after Heinemann, Chisholm to CBC, 17 Nov 1952, Box 80; tutorship and other possibilities, CBC to Chisholm, 24 Apr 1953, to Maxwell, 6 Mar 1953 and 15 Feb 1956, Box 229; withdrawing, CBC to Chisholm, 24 Nov 1952; 'sweated labour', Maxwell quoted CBC to Hope, 4 Apr 1955; prospects for payment, CBC to Hope, 4 Apr 1956; write "finish", CBC to Chisholm, 22 Aug 1955; liquidate deficit, CBC to Maxwell, 2 May 1956 and 28 Apr 1966.

20 Menzies' view: 'set-up wrong', Chisholm to Maxwell, 25 July 1962, UMA Box 80; no capital reserve, CBC to Chisholm, 6 May 1963, Box 81; direct grant, CBC to Maxwell, 13 Feb 1961; direct approach, CBC to Menzies, 6 May 1955, Box 230; correspondence, Menzies to Paton, 27 Aug 1962, UMA 1999. 0014/1966/404; 'freedom', Paton to Menzies, 11 Sep 1962; 'finally pack up', CBC to Maxwell, 1 Dec 1955.

21 Costs of publicity: Maxwell remonstrates with Paton, 4 Apr 1962, and Paton to Maxwell, 6 Apr 1962, passing on decision of University Council finance committee, UMA Box 262; Murdoch, CBC to Chisholm, 17 Feb 1961; 'not interested', CBC to Harris, 6 Oct and Harris to CBC, 10 Oct 1960, Box 156.

22 Neilma Gantner: 'all that money', CBC to Ted Harris, 17 Dec 1959, Box 156; Rodney Hall, Gantner obituary, *Age*, 4 July 2015; "humbug", CBC to Maxwell, 3 Oct 1955 and 15 Feb 1956, UMA Box 229; *Overland*, DMS, Sep 2021.

23 Financial expedients: tip-up truck, CBC to AD Hope, 13 Mar 1956, Box 179; spine injury, CBC to Hope, 23 Feb 1956; spoilt him, CBC to Hope, 2 May 1955; Australiana, CBC to Collinson, 26 Nov 1964, Box 84; own money, *Meanjin*: Gen Statement, 27 Feb 1956, Box 262, CBC to Chisholm, 10 Mar 1961 and to AD Hope, 26 June 1972; Nina's contribution, CBC to Chisholm, 8 Dec 1955.

24 Office seized up: John Anwyl to Ian Maxwell, 27 June 1958, NAA A463/2565 (Part 3) 212/2; never dared, CBC to AD Hope, [before June 1972], UMA Box 179.

25 1959 accommodation crisis: Social Studies building, Pat Excell, 27 Jan 2015, and CBC to Maxwell, 9 Apr 1958; eight rooms short, Paton to CBC, 18 Nov 1956; alternative accommodation, John Barnes, 2 Apr 2012; 'bulldozers', SMS, 'Clem Christesen: A Tribute', *Gazette* (University of Melbourne), Aug 1975, p 10; 'most miserable', CBC to Vance Palmer, 4 June 1959, NLA 1174/1/9148-9.

26 Difficulties, early 1960s: Bernard Smith, comments at Arts Faculty Meeting 4 Aug 1960, in Lee, Mead and Murnane, *The Temperament of Generations*, pp 98–9; 'getting old', CBC to Maxwell, 15 May 1962; financial cuts, CBC to Maxwell, 2 Apr 1965; doggedly, CBC to Chisholm, 6 May 1963.

27 Marginson intervenes: CBC, speech at *Temperament of Generations* dinner, 10 Dec 1990, UMA Box 22.

28 *Meanjin*, the CLF I: Trailer, *MP* 4/1946, pp 335–6; Chifley's attitude reported by CLF Advisory Board members, LF Giblin (to CBC, 31 May, 1 and 15 Sep 1949, UMA Box 143) and T Inglis Moore (to CBC, 17 Mar 1949, UMA Box 235); 'witch-hunting', Trailer, *MP* 4/1948, p 276; Strahan, *Just City*, p 95.

29 *Meanjin*, the CLF II: CBC to Dymphna Cusack, 12 Sep and 4 Nov 1955, UMA Box 88.

30 CLF Advisory Board: 'dangerous', Chisholm to CBC, 25 Oct 1955, UMA Box 80; doing more, Chisholm to CBC, 5 May 1961; 'category', CBC to RD Marginson, 1 July 1971, Box 224; 'perplexing', CBC to Noel McLachlan, 20 Sep 1963, Box 221; 'art gallery', CBC to Inglis Moore, 15 May 1962, Box 235; 'less torrid', CBC to Inglis Moore, 24 Apr 1958; Slessor, 'Literary magazines', NAA A463/2565 (3)/93, p 3.

31 Deeper problems: 'not grants', Adv Board minutes, 15 Aug 1958, NAA A463/2565/(3); 'the rub', CBC to Inglis Moore, 19 Sep 1961, UMA Box 235; intellectuals, Theodore Zeldin points to 30 per cent of French insurance clerks describing themselves in 1954 as intellectuals, *France 1848–1945* (1977), vol II, p 1121; 'Napoleonic', Kylie Tennant to McCusker, 15 May 1963, NAA A463/1963/2565/part 5.

32 Stalemate: 'beer income', Inglis Moore to CBC, 8 May 1961, UMA; 'nuisance', CBC to HS Temby, CLF, 14 Apr 1955, NAA A463/1963/2565 (Part2) /56; Anwyl to Ian Maxwell, 27 June 1958, NAA A463/2565 (3) /212, p 3.

33 Impact of new magazines: nine, CLF, *Helping Literature in Australia* (1969), p 39; twelve, Shapcott, *Literature Board*, pp 229, 231–2; Dutton, Notes, Second Day, March 1972, NAA A3753/1972/89; Walsh cancellation, CBC to Heseltine, 11 Dec 1973, UMA Box 171; 'sick and beset', AD Hope to AA Phillips, 2 Oct 1973, LaT 12491/3385/46.

34 CBC, stag at bay: telegrams to Gough Whitlam, 23 Oct and 22 Nov 1973, NAA 463/1973/4908; Keesing to CBC, 10 and 30 Sep 1971, CBC to Keesing, 31 Aug and 14 Sep 1971, 8 May 1972, NLA 5378 Box 1/9.

35 CLF, to *O*'s 1961 refusal: 'not … quality', 'Literary Magazines' [1957], NAA A463/2565 (3)/93, pp 8–9; T Inglis Moore, Report on the Literary Magazines, 26 Apr 1961, CLF Combined Meeting, A463 1967/2797, p 5; reversed, SMS to AA Phillips, 23 May 1961, LaT Box 191; 'reactionary', Inglis Moore to CBC, 8 May 1961, UMA Box 235; 'calling the tune', quoted in SMS to Advisory Editors, 24 May 1961, Fitzpatrick Papers, NLA 4965/1/9252.

36 The writers comment: 'Political bias and the CLF', *O* 21 (1961), pp 11–13.

37 The 1962 rejection: SMS to Advisory Editors, 23 July 1962, Kramer statement attached; 'manipulators', 'Swag', *O* 24 (1962), p 24; SMS discussion opening on 'The Voices of Dissent', AACF Seminar on Literary Journals, 25 Aug [1962], UMA Box 24; 'feel uneasy', *Sydney Morning Herald*, 28 Aug 1962.

38 Grant, 1964: 'narrow Establishment', *O* 27–28 (1964), pp 11, 15.

39 SMS and Australia Council: support, Geoffrey Blainey, 'Government Patronage and Literature', *O* 57 (1973), p 43; 'significance', 'Swag', *O* 86 (1981), pp 49–50; 'self-nourishing bureaucracy', 'Swag', *O* 98 (1985), pp 39–41; Stephen's prompting, Michael Costigan to SMS, reported SMSD (5 Apr 1980) vol 14 p 254; Stephen attacks in *Australian*, SMS, 'Change and the Australia Council', 24–25 Apr 1982; 'harassment', SMS Diaries, (14 July 1985) vol 28

p 104; 'envelopes', SMSD (12 July 1986) vol 28 p 91; reduced funding, 'Swag', *O* 101 (1985), pp 21–2; 'turfed off', SMSD (3 Dec 1986) vol 29 p 121.

40 Pro lit mags: Peter Craven in *National Times*, 28 Feb 1986, quoted in Shapcott, *Literature Board*, pp 249–50.

41 *Meanjin*'s difficulties: CBC to AD Hope, 5 Apr 1955, UMA Box 179; Trailer, *Meanjin* 3/1947, pp 210–11; 'Twenty-One Lives', p 90; circulation figures, JD notes, Apr 1974; CBC to Dymphna Cusack, 12 Sep 1955.

42 *Overland*, circulation: *O* record of issues printed, DMS; Sendy, Story of *O*, *O* 102 (1986), p 38; 'very poor', quoted in Edmonds, *Windmills*, p 70; 'identify', SMS, '*O*', in Bennett, *Cross Currents*, p 188; plateau, SMS to Dutton, 1 May 1983, LaT Box 171; circulation, 'Swag', *O* 101 (1985), p 21.

43 Questionnaires: Paul Lafitte, Report on the Meanjin Questionnaire, 1960, Part 1, p 57, Summary, p 2, both SMS LaT Box 166; Strahan, *Just City*, pp 249–51; 'What You Think', *O* 19 (1960), p 13.

44 Reviews: 'too high', CBC to Inglis Moore, 22 Sep 1958, UMA Box 235; Strahan, *Just City*, p 251; 'rush', CBC to Morrison, 29 July 1955, UMA Box 237; Max Teichmann, 'What the hell went wrong anyway?', *Review*, 19–25 Feb 1972, pp 498–9; responses by LJ Clancy, Lynne Strahan and Geoffrey Serle, *Review*, 26 Feb – 3 Mar 1972, p 515.

45 Bookshops: *O* returns, SMS to Dutton, 1 May 1983, LaT Box 171; casual buyers, James to CBC, 18 Jan 1946, UMA Box 187; Palmer issue, CBC to Noel McLachlan, 20 Sep 1967, Box 221; Perth, CBC to Inglis Moore, 6 Jan 1959, Box 235.

46 Financial: 600 per cent, CBC, 'Twenty-one Lives', p 90; 'deliberate policy', *O* 24 (1962), p 25; pensioners, Barrie Reid, 'Swag', *O* 91 (1983), pp 21–2; clawed back, CBC to Ian Maxwell, 14 May 1962, UMA Box 229; 'lost relevance', *O* 65 (1976), p 42; hostage, CBC to David Martin, 22 Aug 1969, UMA Box 227; accountant's trick, SMSD (13 Oct 1983) vol 23 p 155; 'genteel deficit', Hamilton, *Little Magazines*, p 136.

47 Payments to contributors: 70 per cent, 'Swag', *O* 101 (1985), p 21; cost of low payments, CBC to Inglis Moore, 15 May 1962, UMA Box 234; White story, CBC to Ian Maxwell, 14 May 1962, Box 229; English rates, Seymour MS, 'That Dirty Word', p 5, Box 298; AA Phillips, speech published in *MQ* 1/1962, p 106; 'poor bastards', David Martin to CBC, 27 Jun 1955, UMA Box 227.

48 *Overland* board: greater say, SMS to Editorial Board members, 18 Oct 1955 LaT 8272 /2/1-2; 'banana republic', 'Swag', *O* 12 (1958), p 21; difficult communications: SMS to David Martin, 30 Oct 1953, NLA 6885 Box 19, fol Mc.

49 Vane Lindesay: most-missed, Lindesay, *Some Fragments Recalled*, p 100; 'most loyally', SMSD (7 Aug 1981) vol 18 p 119; Vane Lindesay, 20 Dec 2011.

50 Stephen and *Overland* board: on Ken Gott, SMSD (24 Dec 1985) vol 27 pp 33–4; 'bureaucratic ship', SMS to Dorothy Hewett, 15 June 1980, LaT Box 176; 'material questions', SMS to Advisory Eds, 15 Dec 1960, NLA 6206 Box 38; 'merry, argumentative', SMSD (16 Sep 1978) vol 10 p 108 'would not be *O*', 'Some Whys and Wherefores of *Overland*', *O* 75 (1979), pp 20–3; McLaren, same article, p 20; 'sigh', Stuart Macintyre, 20 Oct 2019.

51 *Overland*, Keesing issue: 'Wherefores', p 23; Keesing, SMSD (27 July 1980) vol 15 p 207.

52 Bob Cugley: John McLaren, 22 Aug 2014; 'Swag', *O* 108 (1987), p 20; Watson, *Brian Fitzpatrick*, p 356; SMSD (11 Sep 1980) vol 16 p 26, (6 Oct 1983) vol 23 p 144.

53 Planning: 'imagination', CBC to HS Temby, 13 Feb 1948, NAA A463/1963/2565 (1); 'immodest', CBC to Inglis Moore, 15 May 1961, UMA Box 235; should have, AA Phillips, 'Tribute to *Meanjin*', *O* 8 (Nov 1956), p 7.

54 Its scope: 'without realising it', CBC to David Martin, 11 July 1951 UMA Box 227; 'independent', CBC, 'The Functions of a Literary Magazine', pp 7–8, Box 71; 'better informed', Stock to CBC, 12 July 1959, Box 311; 'constantly reading', Nina to Susan Christesen, 8 Feb 1955, Box 261; mistakes, CBC to Dorothy Green, 7 Oct 1985, NLA 5678, fo 17; '16 hours', to Green, 27 Nov 1959, UMA Box 150; 'MQ: Suggestions for Articles' (1958), NAA 463/2565(3)/157.

55 Correspondence and MSS: 'difficulty', John Anwyl to Ian Maxwell, 27 June 1958, UMA Box 229; queries, CBC to J LeGassick, CLF, 27 July 1971, Box 224; submission figures, Geoffrey Serle, Comment, *M* 3/1957, p 336, and 'Swag', *O* 56 (1973), pp 16–17; sexism, Strahan, *Just City*, pp 66–7; rejected, CBC to AD Hope, 13 Apr 1955, UMA Box 179; 'not good enough', quoted in Morris Dickstein, 'Waving not Drowning', *TLS* 25 Oct 2002, p 15; 'disappoint',

Barrie Reid to SMS, LaT Box 193; 'disliked', CBC to Nancy Keesing, 14 Sep 1971, NLA 5378/1/9; Cusack, CBC to Brian Elliott, 5 Oct 1955, UMA Box 117.

56 Submissions, editing, printing: CBC to Laurence Collinson, 7 May 1958, UMA Box 84; better story, Frank Moorhouse, 29 Apr 2016.

57 Magnificent obsession: 'two topics', Heseltine, 'One Hundred Not Out', *MQ* 1/1965, p 133; 'irritable', CBC to Dorothy Green, 7 Oct 1958, NLA 5678, fo 17; Herbert, CBC to Catherine Duncan, 27 Mar 1962, UMA Box 112. Clem was given the right of reply, but declined. Transcripts, *MQ* 1/1962, pp 99–113; 'mockery', CBC to Ian Maxwell, 14 May 1962, UMA Box 229; 'half-written novels', CBC to Max Harris, 11 July 1960, Box 162; 'illusion', CBC to Bernard Smith, 8 June 1960, Box 306; 'just yell', CBC to Dorothy Green, 22 Dec 1959, Box 150.

58 CBC, relations with contributors: 'must read on', CBC to Hugh McCrae, 24 Feb 1947, UMA Box 218; 'bliss', CBC to Catherine Duncan, 6 June 1974, 'Bermuda', Duncan to CBC, 16 Jan 1974, both Box 112.

59 Francis Webb: Webb to CBC, 16 Jan 1962; CBC to McCusker, secretary CLF, and to Webb, both 21 Jan 1963; I Black, Bloomfield Hospital, Orange, to CBC, 19 Mar 1963; CBC to Black, 21 Mar 1963, all UMA Box 348.

60 *Overland* and poets: Reid Diaries, Easter Friday 1985 and undated 1984 entry, LaT 14854/10/5.

61 Stephen and contributors: 'haven't got talents', SMS, *Self Portrait*, p 97; 'like tradesmen', SMS to Jim [Shea], 22 Oct 1958 LaT 7/1-4; horse, SMS to Lilley, 23 Jan 1955, LaT 1/2-4; SMS–Stuart correspondence, LaT Box 1/3-1; SMS to Stuart, 5 Nov 1955, LaT Box 2/2/1-2.

62 *Meanjin–Overland* cricket match: McLaren, *Free Radicals*, pp 183–4; Clem to Fitzpatrick, 23 Dec 1958, NLA 4965/10/45; ASIO helpfully inserted clippings from the *Age* reports of the 1959 and 1960 matches in its files; 'Swag', *O* 14 (1959), p 24; Nita Murray-Smith, 29 May 2012, Chris Wallace-Crabbe, 3 Dec 2012, and Robert Newton, 12 Dec 2012.

63 Eltham: Virginia Woolf, Patricia Excell, 'Flying without borrowed plumes', p 1; continuity, CBC Notes on same, p 1; 'Nina pottering about', CBC to D Green, 15 Sep 1970, UMA Box 150; 'Chekhovian', SMSD (23 Apr 1979) vol 12, p 32; 'little chance', to Noel Stock, 23 Feb 1955, UMA Box 311; entrancing, Joanna Murray-Smith, 1 Aug 2013; 'ashes of disappointment', CBC to D Green, 27 Nov 1959, UMA Box 150; Russian Easter, CBC to Nettie Palmer, 17 Apr 1958, Box 257, Joan Grant, 19 May 2012, John Besemeres, 29 Sep 2012, Judith Armstrong, *Christesen Romance*, p 153.

64 Mt Eliza: Ti-Tree Lane, Nita Murray-Smith, 9 May 2012, Tim Burstall, *Memoirs of a Young Bastard*, 3 Jan 1954, p 53; Grand Annual Overland Barbecue, 7 Jan 1957; description, John McLaren, *Free Radicals*, pp 95, 127; John Morrison recollection, SMSD (8 Feb 1979) vol 11 p 182; the Czechs, Nita quoted by Joanna Murray-Smith, 'Eulogy for Nita', 28 June 2013, p 7; Mt Eliza circle, Robert Newton, 12 Dec 2012.

65 *Overland* infrastructure: photocopier, SMSD, (9 Sep 1986) vol 28 p 150; Joanna Murray-Smith, 'The Moral Force of Art and the Indifference of our Politicans', *Crikey*, 22 July 2015; and 'Eulogy for Nita', p 2; as business manager, Cleeve Charles, 16 Aug 2017; *O* 46 (1970–71), p 43.

66 *Meanjin* secretaries: Jindyworobaks and balladists, 'daughterly', Fay Zwicky, 22 Apr 2012; Neilma Gantner, Diary, 28 June 2003, courtesy John Thompson; Hilary McPhee, *Other People's Words*, pp 48, 54; 'dreadful writer', Patricia Excell, 27 Jan 2015; CBC on Excell, to Harry Heseltine, 7 Mar 1963, UMA Box 171.

67 CBC and SMS relations: 'trailed too often', SMS to Turner, 5 May 1960, NLA 6206 Box 111, fo 22; 'naïve but decent', CBC to Inglis Moore, 5 May 1961, UMA Box 235; David Martin, 'Swag', *O* 20 (1961), p 10; rallied round, CBC to Waten, 15 Nov 1956, UMA Box 346; deserving *Meanjin*, *O* 36 (1967), p 17; three articles, *O* 48; secretary goes back, SMS to Turner, 27 Oct 1961, LaT Box 196/5-1; CBC's preferred dealings, CBC to Martin, 23 Nov 1959, UMA Box 227; 'creeping paranoia', SMS to David Martin, 2 May 1961, LaT Box 184; SMS tries to talk CBC down, SMS to CBC, 16 and 20 June, 30 Dec 1955, and CBC to SMS, 17 June and 8 Dec 1955, UMA Box 240; Mt Eliza, SMS to CBC, 11 Mar 1956, Box 240; 'marked difference', CBC to Marginson, 15 Mar 1973, Box 224.

68 The two compared: 'not … a bad thing', CBC to David Martin, 18 May 1961, UMA Box 227; 'existential way of life', *Sitting on Penguins*, p 198; Stephen's epiphany: *Ind*, p 32.

69 Parties/dinners: 'mutual-admiration drink', *O* 96 (1984), p 29; 'marvellously effective', SMSD (21 Nov 1981) vol 19 p 41; Patrick White, Nita Murray-Smith, 29 May 2012.

70 The magazines' appearance: Dorothy Green to CBC, 12 Mar 1951, UMA Box 151; 'not cost more', CBC to Harry Heseltine, 29 Jan 1965, Box 171.
71 Editorial postpartum: SMS to David Martin, 22 Sep 1960, NLA 6885; CBC to Dymphna Cusack, 26 July 1950, UMA Box 88.
72 Clem's approach: 'hornets', Marie Davison to SMS, 23 June 1982, SMS LaT Box 169; Graves, Barry Jones, 8 Mar 2017; 'lack of dogma', Catherine Duncan to Collinson, 17 Jan 1985, NLA 6327/2/8.

Chapter 7 Power Struggle in the Clemlin

1 CBC to Humphrey McQueen, 'can't cope', 30 July 1973, and 'success', 24 Apr 1974, UMA Box 220; 'die caste', CBC to Davidson, 6 Feb 1974, Box 105; 'being helpful', CBC to Nettie Palmer, 9 Jan 1943, NLA 1174/1/6279-87; 'all those trips', Jessie Serle, 26 June 2012.

Chapter 8 Late Blooming

1 Stephen's diary: 'gentleman', SMSD (21 Apr 1977) vol 1 p 4; 'literary skills', SMSD (5 Oct 1979) vol 3 p 91; 'young sailors' (27 Dec 1984) vol 25 p 134.
2 Physical condition: 'shoe-laces', SMSD (24 Sep 1978) vol 10 p 126; constant battle (18 Aug 1984) vol 24 p 264; (11 March 1978) vol 7 p 103; 'foolish thought', SMSD (2 Sep 1979) vol 7 p 104.
3 Eysenck & Jensen: SMS to *Age*, SMSD (27 Aug 1977) and (14 Sep 1977) vol 5 pp 228, 246; (16 Sep 1977) vol 5 pp 256–7; (5 Oct 1977) p 280; 'same place', SMSD (31 Aug 1980) vol 16 p 7.
4 Turner and politics, 1: Marx as moral philosopher, SMS notes on Turner at Symposium on Marx, 1967; 'Politics Anonymous', Turner to SMS, 1 Dec 1971, all SMS LaT Box 197.
5 Turner and politics, 2: television program, poster, SMS LaT Box 197; Turner, 'The Vietnam Moratorium', *MQ* 2/1970 p 243; Renaissance and Reformation, 'A Comment on Class and Culture' [1976], p 24, NLA 6206 Box 38; Barassi lecture, *Age*, 18 Sep 1971.
6 Breakdown with Amirah: 'mordant humors', SMS to Turner, 24 May 1961, SMS LaT 197; sake of the children, SMS to Turner, 27 Oct 1961, SMS LaT 196/5-1; love 'in the broadest sense', Amirah to Turner, 3 Oct 1962 and '(the original)', Amirah to Turner, Fri 26th [1963], NLA Box 109.
7 Turner in England, 1976: 'various deficiencies', Turner to SMS, 22 Feb 1961, and 'wall of withholding', Turner to SMS, 3 Feb 1976, both SMS LaT 197.
8 SMS advises Turner: communicate with, Turner to SMS, to Judith, Tuesday [1975/76], then SMS to Turner, 12 Feb and 5 Apr 1976, SMS LaT Box 197.
9 Leonie Sandercock: Turner to SMS and Nita, 21 Sep 1976; Sandercock to Turner, 28 May [1975], SMS LaT Box 197.
10 Turner and *O* in the seventies: 'free university', McLaren, *Free Radicals*, p 265; requisitioned, SMS to Barrie Reid and Turner, 22 May 1972, NLA 6206 Box 38; Turner, 'My Long March', *O* 59 (1974), pp 23–40; 'mean it too', SMS to Turner, 20 Feb 1974, NLA 6206 Box 111; Turner, 'High Noon at Yarralumla', *O* 65 (1976), pp 9–22; popular culture interests, Turner MS, 'A Comment on Class and Culture', NLA 6206 Box 41 p 26.
11 Dorothy Hewett: and Lilley, SMSD (6 Sep 1978) vol 10 pp 95, 97 and (26 Aug 1979) vol 13 p 14 and (4 Mar 1984) vol 24 p 83; 'Uninvited Guest', *Rapunzel* pp 66–7; on Lloyd Davies affair, SMS interview with Bruce Bennett [Mar 1982], NLA 6184/5/37; 'dearest ogress', SMS to Hewett, 24 June 1974, NLA 6184 Box 2/10; Stephen visits the Davies, SMS to Turner, 17 Oct 1976, and Turner on Hewett, to SMS, 3 Feb 1976, both SMS LaT Box 197 (second parcel), also SMS to Hewett, 1 Sep 1976, SMS LaT 176/7-1; libel at home, SMS personal note, 11 Sep 1976, SMS LaT 176/7-1; Turner, 'Private Lives and Public Interest', ABC talk, NLA 6206 Box 110/19.
12 *Melbourne Studies in Education*: AA Phillips: 'Three Schoolmasters', *MSE* 1976, pp 1–10; Arthur R Jensen, 'The Nature of Intelligence in Its Relation to Learning', and HJ Eysenck, 'The Development of Personality and Its Relation to Learning', *MSE* 1978, pp 107–81.
13 SMS in the Faculty: 'Oxford thinking', SMSD (12 Nov 1981) vol 19 p 21; 'rebellion', to WF Connell, SMSD (15 June 1981) vol 18 p 15; 'part of the present', 'Swag', *O* 100, p 30; historian's role, SMSD (10 Apr 1979) vol 12 p 6; no 'machine man', SMSD (16 July 1979) vol 12 p 205; 'basalt plains', SMSD (8 June 1985) vol 26 p 65; our books, SMSD (14 July 1987) vol 30 p 116.

14 SMS in the university: 'taken care', 'The right words from Public Editor No. 1', *Age*, 4 June 1987, SMSD vol 30 p 88; managerialism, second Canadian notebook, impressions; 'nuisance value', SMSD (10 July 1981) vol 18 p 70; never asked, SMSD (8 Oct 1978) vol 10 p 143.
15 The Grainger campaign: musical luminaries, SMSD (20 June 1979) vol 12 p 152; letter to *Age*, 8 June 1979; will, SMSD (15 Nov 1979) vol 13 p 173; window, Ray Marginson, 28 Jan 2015.
16 Barrie Reid, Memo: The New Left, an egotistical excursion, 26 July 1972, NLA 6206 Box 38; as librarian, John Thompson, 8 Apr 2019; colleagues, Reid diary, 12 Oct 1985; 'best I could do', Reid diary, Easter Friday 1985, Reid LaT MS 14854/10/5; receiving at Heide, SMSD (18 Aug 1984) vol 24 pp 205–6 and Diana Georgeff, *Delinquent Angel*, p 190; 'the living of it', Georgeff, p 357; 'dangerous one', Shelton Lea, 'For Barrett Reid' [farewell poem], *O* 142 (1996), p 34.
17 Reid as poetry editor: 'nasty gang war', Reid diaries, undated entry, comment on article in *Age Monthly Review*; 'blank cheque', SMS to friends, 12 Dec 1972, NLA 6206 Box 38; 'professionalised/best poetry editor', 'Swag', *O* 64, pp 54–5; 'phenomenon', Reid to Rowlands, 10 Apr 1986, SMS LaT Box 193; 'poets do not believe', Reid (*O* editorial conference 18 Nov 1978), SMSD (18 Nov 1978) vol 10, p 224.
18 Reid and SMS: apology, SMS to Reid, 30 July 1977, SMS LaT Box 193; 'modernity and youth', SMSD (8 Aug 1987) vol 30 p 142; 'gratuitously affects', SMSD (26 Oct 1977) vol 6 p 20; 'homosexuals', SMSD (7 Oct 1985) vol 27 p 15; 'dear friend', SMSD (3 Dec 1984) vol 25 pp 106–7; 'quarter of an issue', *O* 69 (1978); 'prosy old bastard', Reid to SMS, 13 Aug 1981, SMS LaT Box 193.
19 *O* prose: 'tone mine', SMS to friends, 12 Dec 1972, NLA 6206, Box 38; 'best short story', 'Swag', *O* 107 (1987), p 22.
20 'Swag': 'sparklers', *O* 78 (1978), p 54; 'no single way', *O* 94/95 (1984), p 22; accessible, *O* 100 (1985), p 30, Port Hedland matron, *O* 107 (1987), p 22; libel laws, *O* 93 (1983), p 12; postal charges, *O* 65 (1976), p 42.
21 'Swag', SMS and Australia Council: Turner, *O* 60 (1975), pp 66–70; McLaren, *O* 65 (1976), p 40; 'monstrous enterprise', *O* 96 (1984), p 30.
22 SMS and politics: article confiscated, 'Nuclear Clouding', *O* 67 (1977), pp 2–3; 'more disastrous', 'Swag', *O* 79 (1980), pp 32, 46; 'concentration camps', 'Swag' *O* 80 (1980), p 34; graffiti removal, SMS, 'An Adelaide Festival diary, kind of', *O* 94/95 (1984), p. 58.
23 Leonie Sandercock, and feminism: 'Swag', *O* 80 (1980), pp 34–6, and 'Castes and Outcastes', *O* 84 (1981), p 13; don't resign, SMS to Sandercock, 8 May 1986, SMS LaT Box 193/8-1; 'handgun', SMSD (11 Aug 1979) vol 12 p 258.
24 Multiculturalism: AT Yarwood, 'Ending a Taboo', *O* 97 (1984), pp 48–9; Robert Birrell, 'The Social Origins of Australia's Immigration Debate', *O* 97 (1984), pp 41–7; Sean Regan, 'The Prison House of Cultures', *O* 102 (1986), esp. pp 68–70; John McLaren, Comment, *O* 104 (1986), p 21.
25 Indigenous issues: 'pay the interest', Regan above, p 69; symbolic issue, SMSD (31 Aug 1984) vol 25 p 14; middens, SMSD (25 Feb 1979) vol 11 p 208; 'memory hole', review of Plomley, *Weep in Silence*, *Mercury*, 9 May 1987, SMSD vol 30 p 43; articles on the Tasmanians by Cassandra Pybus, Brian Plomley and David Kerr, *O* 111 (1988), pp 48–63, also Brian Oakman, 'Scraps from a White Man's Notebook', pp 23–6.
26 Popular culture: Glen Lewis, 'The new ockerism and the new conservatism', *O* 78 (1979), pp 33–8; Stephen Alomes, 'The Patriot Game', *O* 90 (1982), pp 34–41.
27 Politics: Stuart Macintyre, 'Righteousness and the Right', *O* 92 (1983), pp 22, 23, and 'silly', *O* 97 (1984), p 40.
28 PNG: James M Holquist, 'Promethean Scientist' (Miklouho-Maclay), *O* 99 (1985), pp 54–8; WR Stent, 'An Individual vs. the State', *O* 79 (1980), pp 60–8; John Gunther, 'A Nation in the Womb', *O* 65 (1976), pp 53–61; Ulli Beier, 'New Guinea Big Man', *O* 76/77 (1979), pp 110–12; Russell Soaba, 'Of Kiaps and Cargo Cults', *O* 80 (1980), pp 64–6; SMS, 'The Hothouse Society: New Guinea Notes', *O* 59 (1974), pp 8–14.
29 Letters from … 'reflects change', SMSD (21 Oct 1985) vol 26 p 237; Peter Goldsworthy, 'The Detroit of the South', *O* 104 (1986), pp 38–40; Ian Turner, 'Letter from Ireland', *O* 66 (1977), p 69; Roy Medvedev, 'Letter from Moscow', *O* 104 (1986), pp 12–14; Victor Ye, 'Letter from China', *O* 98 (1985), p 22.
30 Memoir and autobiography: Rupert Lockwood, 'Wimmera Boyhood', *O* 82 (1980), pp 8–12; Ian Turner, 'My Long March', *O* 59 (1974), pp 23–40; Keith Hancock, 'Testimony', *O* 98

(1985), pp 7–17; Walter Crocker, 'Intellect and Virtue' [Eggleston], *O* 104 (1986), pp 36–9, and 'The Riddle of Herbert Vere Evatt', *O* 94/95 (1984), pp 69–74, and 'Richard Casey', *O* 107 (1987), pp 41–2; Elizabeth Riddell, 'Remembering Maie Casey', *O* 91 (1983), pp 36–7; John Herouvim, 'My mum, Sir John Kerr and other surprises', *O* 101 (1985), pp 64–8; Manning Clark, 'Tramping the Battlefields', *O* 100 (1985), pp 6–9; Iris Militunovic, 'The Day the Depression Ended', *O* 88 (1982), pp 12–13; Alan Seymour, 'Laurence Collinson', *O* 106 (1987), pp 48–54; for Brian Fitzpatrick, see pieces by Manning Clark and Jim O'Connor in *O* 78 (1979) and Manning Clark again in *O* 97 (1984).

31 Literary articles: 'good time', Peter Porter, 'Poets at Large', *O* 64 (1976), pp 45–6; 'over-promoted', Mark O'Connor, 'The Graying of the Underground', *O* 74 (1979), pp 5–9; 'central', Graham Rowlands, 'Small Presses pressing on', *O* 89 (1982), p 63; John Docker, 'Leonie Kramer in the Prison House of Criticism', *O* 85 (1981), p 28; 'hostility', CJ Koch, 'The New Heresy-Hunters', *O* 102 (1986), p 46; 'heaps of prose', Porter (above), p 43; Rodney Wetherell, 'Christina Stead: An Interview', *O* 91 (1983), pp 17–29; David Malouf, 'John Manifold: Life and Work', *O* 73 (1978), pp 47–54; 'parasitical', SMSD (30 September 1981) vol 18 p 230.

32 *Overland*, other articles: film, *O* 71 (1978); 'sharply observed', Geoffrey Hutton, 'Playwrights in Search of Direction', *O* 67 (1977), p 21; Tucker, Eric Westbrook, 'A.T.', *O* 75 (1979), p 41.

33 *Overland* reviewing: Jim Cairns, 'Police for the People?', *O* 103 (1986), pp 5–7; Ray Whitrod, 'Crime and Community', *O* 105 (1986), pp 72–5; Paul Hasluck, 'Gough Whitlam in Office', *O* 102 (1986), pp 16–18; Gavin Ewart, 'Australian War Poetry', *O* 98 (1985), pp 65–8; 'dull', Edward Kynaston, 'Australians in Black and White', *O* 63 (1976), p 59; Graham Rowlands, 'The Wisecrack Manifesto', *O* 79 (1980), pp 74–6; armed neutrality, Kenneth Davidson, 'The Conquering of Australia', *O* 96 (1984), pp 13–17.

34 *Overland*'s character: clustering, see *O* 66 (1977), Joan Grant, 'The People's Poetry', pp 10–18, and GR Lansell, 'The Capitalist Face and Cultural Overkill of the "Chinese Exhibition"', pp 20–4; no critic, SMSD (24 Nov 1979) vol 13 p 198; 'Whatever Happened to Rosie?', *O* 94–5 (1984), pp 66–7; Humphries issue, SMSD (24 June 1981) vol 18 p 43; Glen Lewis, 'Looking for the Great A.P.C. Debate', *O* 74 (1979), p 21.

35 SMS personal style: fiftieth anniversary, Don Watson, 17 Oct 2016; 'assistance', John Poynter, 13 Mar 2018; sarong, Max Lucas, 28 June 2013; louts, Vane Lindesay, 20 Nov 2011; 'G', Ken Inglis, 25 June 2011; thrown off, SMSD (3 Dec 1986) vol 29 p 121; 'pleasant', SMSD (13 Feb 1983) vol 22 p 177.

36 Leadership: toga, Ken Inglis (Jamie Mackie), 26 Nov 2011, accomplished, Reid diaries, 29 Feb/1 Mar 1988; 'old gang', SMSD (29 June 1979) vol 12 p 167; launches, SMSD (16 July 1981) vol 12 p 79 and (27 May 1979) vol 12 pp 108–9; 'Erith mob', SMSD (22 Feb 1980) vol 14 pp 176–8; 'sense of justice', Vincent Buckley, *Cutting Green Hay*, p 193; gifts, Robert Newton, 12 Dec 2012.

37 Editing the neighbourhood: developers, *Herald*, 22 July 1977; SMS, 'Don't yield an inch to metrics', *Herald*, 19 Feb 1975; Joanna Murray-Smith, 'The Moral Force of Art and the Indifference of our Politicians', *Crikey*, 22 July 2015; patriality, SMSD (12 June 1987) vol 30, p 86; SMS to Turner (28 Sep 1962), SMS LaT Box 197.

38 SMS self-questioning: 'tears', SMSD (24 May 1981) vol 17 p 255; 'more romantic', SMSD (14 May 1977) vol 5 p 98; 'cowardly', SMSD (2 May 1978) vol 7 pp 242–3; Blainey, SMSD (17 Sep 1978) vol 10 p 114; 'mutiny', SMSD (17 Sep 1987) vol 30 p 182.

39 SMS's growing conservatism: 'He is!', SMSD (17 June 1978) vol 9 p 116; blocked, McLaren, *Free Radicals*, p 299; unimpressed, SMSD (12 Mar 1981) vol 17 p 115; Australia Card, SMS letter to the *Age*, 24 July 1985; "Nuts!", 'Swag', *O* 100 (1985), p 31; Waugh, SMSD (16 Sep 1977) vol 7 p 268; 'obliterated', SMSD (10 June 1984) vol 24 p 194; natural conservative, SMSD (18 Apr 1978) vol 8 p 11; 'servants', SMSD (13 Sep 1979) vol 13 p 54; Northern Ireland, SMSD (20 Apr 1978) vol 8 p 36; Grenada, SMSD (30 Oct 1983) vol 23 p 177; Japan, SMSD (11 Dec 1981) vol 9 p 64; core curriculum, SMSD (10 June 1983) vol 23 p 20.

40 SMS and modern trends: 'government', SMSD (24 May 1986) vol 28 p 30; 'as people', SMSD (6 June 1980) vol 15 p 119.

41 SMS and the young: 'a pattern', SMS to Alan Barcan, 19 June 1960 SMS LaT Box 191; 'illiterates', SMSD (25 July 1979) vol 12 p 215; 'theory', SMSD (10 Apr 1984) vol 24 p 120; 'recognize', SMSD (11 May 1985) vol 26 p 29; 'never was', SMSD (17 Oct 1983) vol 23 p 168; 'brilliant evening', SMSD (7 Aug 1986) vol 28 p 125.

42 SMS, late friends: Blainey, SMSD (31 May 1988) vol 31 p 182; chic, SMSD (31 July 1981) vol 18 p 108; next day, SMSD (30–31 July 1985) vol 26 pp 20–4; 'and enemy', *Overland Muster*, p vii; Ian Turner, 'Artists' camp: Erith Island', *O* 60 (1975) pp 41–55; 'great triumph', SMSD (18 Jan 1984) vol 24 p 20; 'inconsistency', 'Swag', *O* 87 (1982), p 35.

43 Stephen and Nita: Disraeli, SMSD (4 Mar 1988) vol 31 p 99; 'get up to', DMS, 5 Mar 2014; 'stick together', SMSD (24 Oct 1978) vol 10 p 185; political instinct, Joanna Murray-Smith, 1 Aug 2013; 'Which school?', Cleeve Charles, 16 Aug 2017; 'miss the girls', SMSD (9 Dec 1986) vol 29 p 128; 'most intelligent', SMSD (2 Dec 1979) vol 13 p 231; 'refractory', SMSD (31 July 1981) vol 18 p 111; enjoying it, SMS to Dorothy Hewett, 10 Oct 1980, LaT Box 176/9-1, 'renewal', SMSD (17 Apr 1983) vol 22 p 234.

44 SMS at home: 'commune', SMSD (27 Aug 1977) vol 5 p 232; 'loved homes', SMSD (26 Jan 1984) vol 24 p 37; 'off the Island', Cleeve Charles, 16 Aug 2017.

45 Stephen and England: 'John Bull', SMSD (11 Oct 1980) vol 16 p 86; 'support system', SMSD (1 July 1978) vol 9 pp 148–9; 'not my culture', SMSD (20 March 1981) vol 17 p 123; 'privilege', SMSD (6 Aug 1978) vol 9 p 240; 'condescension', SMSD (24 Mar 1978) vol 7 p 160; 'lords and ladies', SMSD (16 July 1978) vol 9 p 203; 'leave with pleasure', SMSD (21 Dec 1978) vol 22 p 108.

46 Narodnik: 'admire', SMSD (6 May 1977) vol 5 p 96; book collectors, SMSD (11 Nov 1979) vol 13 p 162; 'vanished', SMSD (27 June 1987) vol 30 p 102; lecturer, SMSD (25 July 1981) vol 18 p 95.

47 SMS and CBC: 'like Clem', to Collinson, 15 Aug 1972, NLA 6327; CBC, 'Auto-obituary', *O* 48 (1971), pp 16–19; bump, CBC to D Green, 12 May 1971, UMA Box 150; consulting friends, CBC to Green, 2 Dec 1980, NLA 5678; *SMH*, 1 Dec 1980.

48 CBC, decline: 'Stalinist', SMSD (26 Apr 1980) vol 15 p 20; 'waste no more time', D Green, 'Three Editors', *M* 2/1985, p 205; creative juices, Green to CBC, 18 Aug 1973, UMA Box 150; 'lost years', Harry Heseltine, 7 Sep 2012; trauma, to Green, 9 Sep 1980, and Picot death, CBC to Green, 5 May 1985, both NLA 5678; relieved, Armstrong, *Christesen Romance*, pp 208–9; nursing home, Patricia Excell, 14 Dec 2011.

49 SMS and CBC, late: 'haven', SMSD (9 Dec 1980) vol 16 p 190; god-daughter, SMSD (17 Apr 1981) vol 17 p 175; 'annoy him', SMSD (15 May 1987) vol 30 p 45.

50 SMS, Introduction to *His Natural Life*, pp 7–23.

51 SMS and technical education: ASIO, Minute to BI, 20 Apr 1953, NAA A6119/68/126; 'got me in', SMS to Turner, 23 Oct 1959, SMS LaT Box 196/8-1; requests, SMS to Turner, 17 Oct 1976, Box 197.

52 *The Tech*: characterises Dare, SMSD (1 Feb 1979) vol 11 p 167; RMIT motto, p 38; 'victory of the twentieth century', p 130; 'decline', p 458.

53 *DAQ*: jumped at it, SMSD (25 May 1982) vol 20 p 104; 'most rewarding', SMSD (27 Apr and 20 May 1983) vol 22 pp 239, 274; 'own outlook', SMSD (8 May 1983) vol 22 p 257; youngest writers, SMS to Frank Kellaway, 3 Jan 1983, NLA 7071; 'thin on the ground', Stuart Sayers, 'Writers & Readers', *Age*, 7 Apr 1984; Blainey review, *Age*, 31 March 1984; 'hard yakka', SMS to Kellaway, 23 Apr 1984; 'do not quote poetry', Judith Wright to SMS, 9 Aug 1982, SMS LaT Box 201.

54 *Right Words*: pp vii–viii, 1, 5, 38, 51, 74, 142, 308, 353; 'traditional form', Kevin Childs, 'The right words from Public Editor No. 1', *Age*, 15 June 1987; AA Phillips, SMSD (4 May 1986) vol 28, p 10; Number 3 bestseller, SMSD (24 June 1987) vol 30 p 95; 'daily praise', SMSD (9 Sep 1987) vol 30 p 176.

55 Erith: the major source here has been Stephen's *Many Moods and Many Voices: An Erith Island Journal* (Erith Island Press, 1974: cyclostyled, bound, 20 copies), a record of the Ninth Expedition. See in particular pp 2, 23, 30, 31, 35, 37, 63–5. SMSD have provided supplementations: (5 Jan 1981) vol 16, insert at p 264; (25 May 1981) vol 17 p 269; (3 Jan 1985) vol 25, p 152; (7 Jan 1988) vol 31 p 12. For Stephen's formal publications on Erith and the Kent Group, see McLaren, *Free Radicals*, p 375. 'An epistle of Stephen to the Erythreans', RD Marginson. For first glimmerings of a book, SMS to Nettie Palmer, 5 Feb 1963, NLA 1174/1/9771; McLaren, *Free Radicals*, especially for lighthouses, pp 321–3, also p 342. For description, Joanna Murray-Smith's novel *Judgement Rock*, especially pp 42–6. A revealing interview of SMS by Martin Flanagan appeared in the *Age* on 26 Jan 1987. This segment has also drawn on interviews with Robert Newton 12 Dec 2012, Jenny Love 6 Aug 2012, Jim Hammerton 10 Dec 2012, and Don Anderson 12 Feb 2014; Don Anderson also passed on emails from Dave and Wendy Hughes. For SMS's speech at Turner's funeral, *O* 76/77 (1979),

see p 4. The expedition with Williams and Pugh was written up by Ian Turner as 'Artists' Camp: Erith Island March 1974', *O* 60 (1975), pp 41–55; see also Hart, *Fred Williams: Infinite Horizons*, p 121, and Patrick McCaughey, *Fred Williams*, p 258; also Morrison, *After Fire*, pp 347–9. The quote 'England with improvements' is WS Gilbert's satirical comment on colonial society in *Utopia Limited.*

56 Sociological analysis: SMS, *Many Moods and Voices*, pp 76–8; Don Anderson, 12 Feb 2014; Jones, SMSD (18 May 1980) vol 6 following p 152; parallels, SMSD (27 May 1980) vol 15 p 89.

57 Cape Barren: Television documentary and Hasluck visit, McLaren, *Free Radicals*, p 314, 317; SMS, 'Beyond the Pale', esp. pp 167, 191, 192; epiphany, SMSD (4 June 1977) vol 5 p 151; 'own history', SMSD (18 May 1979) vol 12 pp 95–6; institutionalisation, in SMS (ed.), *Mission to the Islands*, p xvii. Annotated editions of the visitations by bishops Nixon and Montgomery were planned; the projected Bass Strait book mentioned in NLA interview by Hazel de Berg, 1969, NLA t/s p 22; Ekistics, SMSD (25 Apr 1980) vol 15 p 17.

58 Islands: Tom Steel, *The Rise and Fall of St Kilda* (Bungay: Fontana, 1975); SMS on St Kilda, SMSD (15 July 1978) vol 9 p 186; on Tristan da Cunha, SMSD (17 Aug 1982) vol 21 p 56; SMS, 'Three Islands: A Case Study in Survival', esp. pp 209, 222; 'without aggression', 'Life's labors learned on an island sojourn' [interview with SMS], *Age*, 26 Jan 1987.

59 To Antarctica: SMS, 'Herbert Dyce Murphy'; Barry Jones, SMSD (20 March 1985) vol 22 pp 208–9; original subtitle, SMSD (4 March 1988) vol 31 p 90; Mawson to SMS, 22 Jan 1946, SMS LaT Box 265/11.

60 The voyage down, and impressions: 'native wit', SMSD (1 Feb 1986) vol 27 p 188; and ship's cook (1 Jan 1986) p 43; tensions on ship, 'timid Australians', *Sitting on Penguins*, pp 31, 77; German democracy, *SoP*, p 141.

61 Antarctica: vulnerability, and first impressions: other ships, *SoP*, pp 71–2; 'so remote', SMSD (2 Jan 1986) vol 27 p 51; 'No-one talk', *SoP*, p 37; 'great cathedral', SMSD (20 Jan 1986) vol 27 p 132; 'wilderness', *SoP*, p 100; Emperor penguin, SMSD (17 Jan 1986) vol 27 p 119; the unloading, *SoP*, pp 112–13; 'treated as an ancient', SMSD (6 Jan 1986) vol 27 p 68.

62 Antarctica: bases and the alternative, 'aggression-display', *SoP*, p 88, 'Maginot line', SMSD (17 Jan 1986) vol 27 p 119; 'form of war', '*Icebird* spreads her wings for Voyage Home', *Australian*, 30 Jan 1986; moored vessel, *SoP*, p. 87; eight scientists, *SoP*, p 118; 'homeland', *SoP*, p 223; 'empire', *SoP*, p 118.

63 Antarctic problems: 'buggering up', *SoP*, p 86; Old Casey, SMSD (11 Jan 1986) vol 27 p 92; Wilkes, *SoP*, pp 100–1; Mawson's hut, *SoP*, pp 54, 63, 65; station log books, *SoP*, p 228; 'begins anew', SMS, For the information of the Director, Antarctic Division, p 7; 'history', *SoP*, p 230; 'soulless bureaucracies', *SoP*, p 104; contacting Hobart, SMSD (2 Jan 1986) vol 27 p 52.

64 SMS reports to Barry Jones: 'performing so little', Griffiths, *Slicing the Silence*, p 268; '*experiential basis*', Report, p 27; 'serious accident', Report, p 3; 'Thinks It Knows', Report, p 24; Casey and the 'people problem', Report, pp 23–5; 'violent tendencies', quoted *SoP*, p 222; 'townships', Report, p 15; '"special" people', Report, p 12; 'rise to the surface'/ 'disgrace', *SoP*, pp 110, 207–8; 'People will react', Report, p 27; *Playboy*, Stuart Macintyre, 11 March 2011.

65 *Sitting on Penguins*: significance, petrels, SMS, For Director, Antarctic Division, p 9; glaciology, *SoP*, p 145; female involvement, 'Women break the ice at our Antarctic outposts'; Jones' response, SMSD (11 March 1986) vol 27 p 239; *Australian*, 12 Feb 1986, *SoP*, pp 220–3; influence of *SoP*, Griffiths, *Art of Time Travel*, pp 190–3.

66 Antarctic overlay: if paid enough, SMSD (26 July 1987) vol 30, p 131; television series, SMSD (6 Feb 1986) vol 27 p 193; SMS Report, p 29; as director, Report, p 25; 'drowning', SMSD (8 Dec 1987) vol 30 p 253.

67 Publishing: 'frustrations', SMSD (15 May 1980) vol 15 p 64; six publications, SMSD (19 Mar 1986) vol 27 pp 242–3; campaign, 'Swag', *O* 106 (1987), p 37; 'perhaps interconnected', SMSD (23 July 1988) vol 31 p 246.

68 Gloomy thoughts: 'failed radicals', 'Swag', *O* 111 (1988), p 27; Rob Hamilton, Nita Murray-Smith, 23 Mar 2011; Pitcairn: SMSD (24 Oct 1986) vol 29 pp 14–24.

69 Beanland Lecture, FIT: SMS to Martin, SMSD (25 Apr 1988) vol 31 p 143; SMS, *Behind the Mask*, esp. pp 11, 16, 18.

70 SMS, curmudgeon: 'out of alignment', de Berg 1969 interview NLA; 'crotchety', SMSD (14 Apr 1978) vol 7 p 217; four battles, SMS to Sandercock, 19 Jul 1986, SMS LaT Box

193/8-1; 'comrades', SMS letter to DMS, in SMSD (9 Sep 1986) vol 28 p 150; 'the best', 'Swag', *O* 88 (1982), p 45; hatchet buried, Brian Matthews, 16 Oct 2019.

71 *Overland*, and SMS ambivalence: 'drained away', 'Swag', *O* 100 (1985), p 30; 'just work here', SMSD (29 Nov 1978) vol 10 p 240; 'dazzle', SMSD (17 Apr 1984) vol 24 p 131; 'collective elegy', Peter Craven, *National Times*, 28 Feb 1986; Don Anderson, 'Keeping the Literary Magazines Afloat', *National Times*, 7–13 Feb 1986; 'going to stick', Barrie Reid Diaries, 2 Mar 1988, Reid LaT 14854/10/6.

72 The young, Aust. Lit.: 'literary values', Robert Darby, 'The Fall of Fortress Criticism', *O* 102 (1986), p 7; David Malouf, 'The Making of Literature', *O* 106 (1987), pp 5–6.

73 Composing *Overland*: CJ Koch, 'The Heresy Hunters', *O* 102 (1986), pp 43–6, and Judith Brett, Comment, *O* 103 (1986), p 20; John Herouvim, 'Civilizing Australia', *O* 111 (1988), pp 35–44; Crocker and Docker, in *O* 103, Crocker and Costigan, in *O* 107 (1987); Ken Inglis, in 'SMS 1922–1988', *O* 112 (1988), p 16; office, Shapcott, *Literature Board*, p 249.

74 Pressure from Barrie Reid: 'power drive', SMSD (2 Feb 1983) vol 22 p 168; 'too historical', SMSD (24 May 1981) vol 17 p 258; ammunition, SMSD (8 Aug 1987) vol 30, p 142.

75 John McLaren: Stephen wrote, McLaren, *Not in Tranquillity*, p 138.

76 McLaren *v* Reid: Reid's suggestion, *Not in Tranquillity*, p 241; 'too sectarian', SMSD (7 Oct 1981) vol 18 p 240; 'abnormal psychology', B Reid to SMS, circular letter, 16 Jan 1979, NLA 5378 Box 14; 'own interests', SMSD (13 Apr 1979) vol 14 p 70; 'passion and rage', SMSD (8 May 1982) vol 20 p 81; 'vicious hatred', SMSD (8 Mar 1984) vol 21 p 81; five issues, 'Swag', *O* 74 (1979), p 30; McLaren, 'Letter from Cambridge', *O* 83 (1981), pp 57–9; 'defeat McLaren', SMSD (6 July 1986) vol 28 p 86; 'corresponding editor', SMSD (30 July 1988) vol 31, p 254.

77 SMS, last days: Robert Darby, SMSD (30 July 1988) vol 31 p 254; typewriter, David Martin, *My Strange Friend*, p 236.

78 SMS funeral and tribute: Nita, SMSD vol 31 p 259; Tributes published in *O* 112 (1988), Hewett, p 10; Barrett Reid Diaries, 31 July 1988.

Afterword

1 Since CBC and SMS: should merge, CBC to SMS, 5 May 1975, SMS LaT Box 166; Michael Heyward, 'Literary mania: Magazines out of Melbourne', *University of Melbourne Gazette*, Winter 1987.

2 Their projects: expatriate, unsigned review (probably Noel McLachlan), *On Native Grounds*, *Times Literary Supplement*, 8 May 1969; 'professors and slaughtermen', Editorial, 'Please Put in a Penny', *O* 11 (1958), p 2.

3 The little magazines: Stefan Collini, 'The golden age that never was', *TLS*, 18 Jan 2002, pp 17–18; Mark Lilla, 'Two Roads for the New French Right', *New York Review of Books* (20 Dec 2018), vol LXV/20, p 44; Jonathan Green quoted by Beejay Silcox, 'Defying the Moment', *Australian Book Review*, no 400 (2018), p 14; Emmett Stinson, 'Quiet conversations in a very noisy room', *Sydney Review of Books*, 13 Oct 2015, p 3.

4 Productivity Commission, Michael Davis, 'Australian Notes', *Spectator Australia*, 4 June 2016, p x.

Bibliography

Books (and main articles) by CB Christesen and Stephen Murray-Smith

CBC

(ed.), *Australian Heritage* (Melbourne: Longmans, 1967)
(ed.), *Coast to Coast: Australian Stories 1953–1954* (Sydney: Angus & Robertson, 1954)
Dirge and Lyrics (Melbourne: Meanjin Press, 1945)
Ebb-tide: selected verse (Eltham: Stanhope Press, 1997)
(ed.), *The Gallery on Eastern Hill: The Victorian Artists' Centenary* (Melbourne: Victorian Artists' Society, 1970)
The Hand of Memory (Melbourne: Meanjin Press, 1970)
Having Loved (Eltham: Stanhope Press, 1979)
'The Island', in Des Petersen and Stephen Torre (eds), *North of Capricorn: An Anthology of Prose* (Townsville: English Department, James Cook University, 1989) pp 70–82
On Native Grounds: Australian Writing for Meanjin Quarterly (Sydney: Angus & Robertson, 1967)
North Coast (Brisbane: Meanjin Press, 1943)
Queensland Journey [Brisbane: Meehan Publicity Service, 1937]
Six Poems by Anna Akhmatova (Eltham: Stanhope Press, 1980)
South Coast (Brisbane: Meanjin Press, 1944)
The Troubled Eyes of Women (St Lucia: University of Queensland Press, 1990)
'The Twenty-One Lives of *Meanjin Quarterly*', *Texas Quarterly* vol 5/2 (1962) pp 84–93
(ed.) James Picot, *With a Hawk's Quill* (Melbourne: Meanjin Press, 1953)

SMS

(ed.) *Bass Strait: Australia's last frontier* (Sydney: ABC Enterprises, 1987)
(ed., with John Thompson) *Bass Strait Bibliography: A guide to the literature on Bass Strait covering scientific and non-scientific material* (Melbourne: Institute of Marine Science, 1981)
(ed., with JH Horne and FI Norman), *A Bibliography of Bass Strait, 1797–1971* (Melbourne: Royal Society of Victoria, 1973)
(ed., with Judah Waten) *Classic Australian Short Stories* (Cheltenham: Kingfisher, 1974)
(ed.) *Dictionary of Australian Quotations* (Richmond: Heinemann, 1984)
Henry Lawson (Melbourne: Lansdowne, 1962)
(ed.) Marcus Clarke, *His Natural Life* (Harmondsworth, Middlesex: Penguin English Library, 1970)
Indirections: A Literary Biography (Townsville: James Cook University, 1981)
(ed.) *Melbourne Studies in Education* (Carlton: MUP, 1973–1982)
(ed.) *Mission to the Islands: The Missionary Voyages in Bass Strait of Canon Marcus Brownrigg 1872–1885* (Hobart: Cat and Fiddle Press, 1979)
The most famous of Englishmen: an exclusive interview by Stephen Murray-Smith; with an epilogue by John McLaren (Carlton North: Black Jack Press, 2001)
(ed.) *An Overland Muster* (Brisbane: Jacaranda, 1965)
(ed., with Edgar Waters) *Rebel Songs* (Melbourne: Australian Student Labor Federation, 1947)

Right Words: A Guide to English Usage in Australia (Ringwood: Viking/Penguin, 1987)
(ed., with Leonie Sandercock): Ian Turner, *Room for Manoeuvre: Writings on history, politics, ideas and play* (Richmond: Drummond, 1982)
Sitting on Penguins: Australia and the Antarctic (Port Melbourne: Mandarin Australia, 1991 [1988])
(ed. as Sebastian Hogbotel and Simon Ffuckes) *Snatches & Lays: Songs Miss Lilywhite should never have taught us* (Melbourne: Boozy Company, 1962)
(with Anthony John Dare) *The Tech: A Centenary History of the Royal Melbourne Institute of Technology* (South Yarra: Hyland House, 1987)
(ed.) *The Tracks We Travel* (Melbourne: Australasian Book Society, 1953)

Thesis
'A History of Technical Education in Australia, with special reference to the period before 1914' (PhD, University of Melbourne, 1966)

Articles and pamphlets
Behind the Mask: Technical Education Yesterday and Today (Beanland Lecture, Footscray Institute of Technology, 1987)
'"Beyond the Pale": the Islander Community of Bass Strait in the 19th Century', *Papers and Proceedings*, Tasmanian Historical Research Association, vol 20 no 4, pp 167–200 (For details of essentially naturalist articles on Bass Strait, see bibliography in McLaren, *Free Radicals*, p 375)
'Censorship and Literary Studies', in Geoffrey Dutton and Max Harris (eds), *Australia's Censorship Crisis* (Melbourne: Sun Books, 1970), pp 77–95
'Herbert Dyce Murphy', *Australian Dictionary of Biography*, vol 10 (1986), pp 637–8
Indo-China: Intervention and war—or independence and peace? (Melbourne: Australian Peace Council [1954])
'Introduction', John Morrison, *North Wind* (Ringwood: Penguin Books, 1982)
'Memories', in Hume Dow, *Memories of Melbourne University: Undergraduate life in the years since 1917* (Richmond: Hutchinson, 1983) pp 119–36
'Messages from Far Away: Recollections of an Australian Childhood', in Guy Featherstone (ed.), *The Colonial Child* (Melbourne: RHSV, 1981) pp 73–87
'Pinchas Goldhar: A Tribute', *Melbourne University Magazine* (1947) pp 21–2
'Recollections', in McDonagh, Curthoys & Rowse (eds), *Australians from 1939* (Sydney: Fairfax, Syme & Weldon, 1987) pp 422–31
'SMS', in David Foster (ed.), *Self Portraits* (Canberra: NLA, 1991) pp 91–8
'The Novel in Society', in Geoffrey Dutton, *The Literature of Australia* (Ringwood: Penguin, 1964) pp 427–40
There's no 'Iron Curtain': An Australian Journalist in Eastern Europe (Melbourne: International Bookshop [1952])
"Three Islands: A case study in survival', *Melbourne Studies in Education 1986* (Carlton: MUP) pp 209–24

Books
Adams, Paul, *The Stranger from Melbourne. Frank Hardy: A Literary Biography 1944–1975* (Perth: UWAP 1909)
Adams, Paul, and Christopher Lee (eds), *Frank Hardy: The Literature of Commitment* (Carlton North: Vulgar Press, 2003)
Armstrong, Judith, *The Christesen Romance* (Carlton South: MUP, 1996)
Australian Dictionary of Biography (Melbourne: MUP, continuing series since 1966)
Barcan, Alan, *The Socialist Left in Australia, 1949–59* (Sydney: Department of Government, University of Sydney, 1960)
Barnes, John (ed.) *The Writer in Australia 1856–1964* (Melbourne: OUP, 1969)
Bate, Weston, *Light Blue Down Under: The History of Geelong Grammar School* (Melbourne: OUP, 1990)
Beasley, Jack, *Red Letter Days: Notes from inside an era* (Sydney: Australasian Book Society, 1979)
Bennett, Bruce (ed.) *Cross Currents: Magazines and Newspapers in Australian Literature* (Melbourne: Longman Cheshire, 1981)
Bird, David S, *Nazi Dreamtime: Australian Enthusiasts for Hitler's Germany* (North Melbourne: Australian Scholarly Publishing, 2012)

Brady, Veronica, *South of My Days: A biography of Judith Wright* (Pymble: Angus & Robertson, 1998)
Brooker, Peter and Andrew Thacker, *The Oxford Critical and Cultural History of Modernist Magazines, vol 1: Britain and Ireland 1880–1955* (New York: OUP, 2009)
Buckley, Vincent, *Cutting Green Hay* (Ringwood: Penguin Books, 1983)
Carter, David, *A Career in Writing: Judah Waten and the cultural politics of a literary career* (Toowoomba: ASAL, 1997)
Clark, Manning, *The Quest for Grace* (Ringwood: Viking, 1990)
Clarke, Patricia, and Meredith McKinney (eds), *The Equal Heart and Mind: Letters Between Judith Wright and Jack McKinney* (St Lucia: UQP, 2004)
——*With Love & Fury: Selected Letters of Judith Wright* (St Lucia: UQP, 2006)
Coleman, Peter (ed.) *Australian Civilization* (Melbourne: FW Cheshire, 1962)
Coombs, HC, *Trial Balance* (South Melbourne: Macmillan, 1981)
Davidson, Jim, *Sideways from the Page: The Meanjin Interviews* (Melbourne: Fontana, 1983)
Docker, John, *Australian Cultural Elites: Intellectual Elites in Sydney and Melbourne* (Cremorne: Angus & Robertson, 1974)
Edmonds, Phillip, *Tilting at Windmills: The Literary Magazine in Australia 1968–2012* (Adelaide: University of Adelaide Press, 2015)
Elliott, Brian (ed.) *The Jindyworobaks* (St Lucia: UQP, 1979)
Faragher, Trevor, *Men and Masters: A centenary history of King's College within the University of Queensland* (St Lucia: King's College, 2012)
Fitzpatrick, Brian, *The Australian Commonwealth* (Melbourne: Cheshire, 1956)
——(with an introduction by David Fitzpatrick), *The Colonials* (Carlton: MUP, 2013)
Fitzpatrick, Sheila, *My Father's Daughter: Memories of an Australian Childhood* (Carlton: MUP, 2010)
Furet, François, *The Passing of an Illusion* (Chicago: Chicago University Press, 1999)
Georgeff, Diana, *Delinquent Angel* (North Sydney: Random House Australia, 2007)
Griffiths, Tom, *Slicing the Silence: Voyaging to Antarctica* (Sydney: New South, 2007)
——*The Art of Time Travel: Historians and Their Craft* (Carlton: Black Ink, 2016)
Haese, Richard, *Rebels and Precursors: The revolutionary years of Australian art* (Ringwood: Allen Lane, 1981)
Hall, Rodney, *J S Manifold: An Introduction to the Man and His Work* (St Lucia: UQP, 1978)
Hart, Deborah, *Fred Williams: Infinite Horizons* (Canberra: National Gallery of Australia, 2001)
Hamilton, Ian, *The Little Magazines: A Study of Six Editors* (London: Weidenfeld & Nicolson, 1976)
Helping Literature in Australia: The work of the Commonwealth Literary Fund 1908–1956 (Canberra: Commonwealth Government Printer, 1967)
Heseltine, Harry, *In Due Season: Australian Literary Studies, A personal memoir* (North Melbourne: Australian Scholarly Publishing, 2009)
Hewett, Dorothy, *Wild Card: An Autobiography, 1923–1958* (Ringwood: McPhee Gribble, 1990)
Heyward, Michael, *The Ern Malley Affair* (St Lucia: UQP, 1993)
Hocking, Jenny, *Frank Hardy: Politics, Literature, Life* (South Melbourne: Lothian, 2005)
Inglis, Amirah, *The Hammer and the Sickle and the Washing-Up: memories of an Australian woman Communist* (South Melbourne: Hyland House, 1995)
Jones, Philip, *Art and Life* (Crow's Nest: Sue Hines/Allen & Unwin, 2004)
Judd, Tom, *Fifty years will be long enough! A senior porter's story* (Melbourne: National Press, 1971)
Judt, Tony, *Postwar: a history of Europe since 1945* (New York: Penguin Press, 2005)
Kershaw, Alister, *Hey Days: Memories and glimpses of Melbourne's Bohemia 1937–1947* (North Ryde: A& R, 1991)
Lee, Jenny, Philip Mead and Gerald Murnane (eds) *The Temperament of Generations* (Carlton: *Meanjin*/MUP, 1990)
Lindesay, Vane, *Some Fragments Recalled: A Life So Far* (Ripponlea, 2005: privately published/ Trojan Press)
McCaughey, Patrick, *Fred Williams* (Sydney: Bay Books, 1980)
McDonald, Geoff, *Australia at Stake* (North Melbourne: privately printed, 1977)
McDonald, Willa, *Warrior for Peace: Dorothy Auchterlonie Green* (North Melbourne: Australian Scholarly Publishing, 2009)
McEwan, Keith, *Once a Jolly Comrade* (Brisbane: Jacaranda, 1966)
Macintyre, Stuart, *Australia's Boldest Experiment: War and reconstruction in the 1940s* (Sydney: New South, 2015)

——*The Party: Communism in Australia from Heyday to Reckoning* (Crows Nest: Allen & Unwin, 2022)
McKernan, Susan, *A Question of Commitment: Australian Literature in the Twenty Years After the War* (North Sydney: Allen & Unwin, 1989)
McLaren, John, *Free Radicals of the Left in Postwar Melbourne* (Melbourne: Australian Scholarly Publishing, 2003)
——*Journey Without Arrival: The Life and Writing of Vincent Buckley* (North Melbourne: Australian Scholarly Publishing, 2009)
——*Not in Tranquillity: A Memoir* (Melbourne: Australian Scholarly Publishing, 2005)
——*Writing in Hope and Fear: Literature as Politics in Postwar Australia* (Cambridge and Melbourne, CUP, 1996)
McPhee, Hilary (ed.) *Memoirs of a Young Bastard: The Diaries of Tim Burstall, November 1953 to December 1954* (Carlton: MUP 2012)
——*Other People's Words* (Sydney: Picador, 2001)
Manifold, JS, *Who Wrote the Ballads?* (Sydney: Australasian Book Society, 1964)
Manne, Robert, *The Petrov Affair* (Melbourne: Text, 1987)
Marr, David, *Patrick White, A Life* (Milsons Point: Random House Australia, 1991)
Martin, Alan, *Robert Menzies, A Life*, vol 2, 1944–1978 (Carlton: MUP, 1999)
Martin, David, *My Strange Friend* (Chippendale: Picador, 2008)
Martin, Sylvia, *Ink in Her Veins: The Troubled Life of Aileen Palmer* (Crawley: UWAP, 2016)
Modjeska, Drusilla, *Exiles At Home: Australian Women Writers 1925–1945* (Sydney: Angus & Robertson, 1981)
Moore, Nicole, *The Censor's Library: Uncovering the Lost History of Australia's Banned Books* (St Lucia: UQP, 2012)
Morrison, Sally, *After Fire: a biography of Clifton Pugh* (Melbourne: Hardie Grant Books, 2009)
Munro, Craig, *Wild Man of Letters: The Story of PR Stephensen* (St Lucia: UQP, 1984)
Munster, George, *A Paper Prince* (Ringwood: Viking, 1985)
Murphy, John, *Evatt: A Life* (Sydney: New South, 2016)
——*Imagining the Fifties: Private sentiment and political culture in Menzies' Australia* (Sydney: UNSWP, 2000)
Murray-Smith, Joanna, *Judgement Rock* (Camberwell: Penguin Books, 2002)
O'Leary, Zoe, *The Desolate Market: A biography of Eric Lambert* (Sydney: Edwards & Shaw, 1977)
Palmer, Vance, *The Legend of the Nineties* (Melbourne: MUP, 1954)
Persse, Michael Collins, *A Well-ordered Liberty: A Portrait of Geelong Grammar School 1855–1995* (Melbourne: Cliffe Books, 1995)
Phillips, AA, *The Australian Tradition: Studies in a Colonial Culture* (Melbourne: Cheshire, 1958)
Picot, James, *With a Hawk's Quill* (Meanjin Press, 1953)
Pi O, *Heide* (Artarmon: Giramondo, 2019)
Pirie, AA, *Commando Double Black: An Historical Narrative of the 2/5th Division Australian Independent Company, Later the 2/5th Cavalry Commando Squadron 1942–1945* (Sydney: 2/5th Commando Trust, 1993)
Poetry Australia, Francis Webb (1925–1973) Commemorative Issue, no 56 (Sep 1975)
Poynter, JR, and Carolyn Rasmussen, *A Place Apart: The University of Melbourne. Decades of Challenge* (Carlton: MUP, 1996)
Report of the Royal Commission on Espionage (Canberra: Government Printer, 1955)
Royal Commission on Espionage: Official Transcript of Proceedings (Sydney: Government Printer, 1955)
Ryan, Peter, *Fear Drive My Feet* (Ringwood: Penguin, 1992)
Sendy, John, *Comrades Come Rally* (West Melbourne: Nelson, 1978)
——*Ralph Gibson: An Extraordinary Communist* (Melbourne: Ralph Gibson Biography Committee, 1988)
Serle, Geoffrey, *From Deserts the Prophets Come: The Creative Spirit in Australia 1788–1972* (Melbourne: Heinemann, 1973)
——*Sir John Medley: A Memoir* (Carlton: MUP, 1993)
Shapcott, Thomas, *The Literature Board: A Brief History* (St Lucia: UQP, 1988)
Sheridan, Susan, *Nine Lives: postwar women writers making their mark* (St Lucia: UQP, 2011)
Smith, Vivian (ed.) *Letters of Vance and Nettie Palmer 1915–1963* (Canberra: NLA, 1977)
——(ed.) *Nettie Palmer: Her private journal 'Fourteen Years', poems, reviews and literary essays* (St Lucia: UQP, 1988)

Snowden, Betty, *Max Harris, with reason, without rhyme* (North Melbourne: Australian Scholarly Publishing, 2015)
Stephensen, PR, *The Foundations of Culture in Australia* (Sydney: George Allen & Unwin, 1986 [1936])
Strahan, Lynne, *Just City and the Mirrors: Meanjin Quarterly and the Intellectual Front 1940–1965* (Melbourne: OUP, 1984)
Taft, Bernie, *Crossing the Party Line: Memoirs of Bernie Taft* (Newham, Vic: Scribe, 1994)
Thompson, John, *The Patrician and the Bloke: Geoffrey Serle and the Making of Australian History* (Canberra: Pandanus Books, 2006)
Tregenza, John, *Australian Little Magazines 1923–1954* (Adelaide: Libraries Board of SA, 1964)
Turner, Ian, *The Australian Dream: a collection of anticipations about Australia from Captain Cook to the present day* (Melbourne: Sun Books, 1968)
——*Industrial Labour and Politics: The dynamics of the labour movement in Eastern Australia, 1900–1921* (Sydney: Hale & Iremonger, 1979)
——*In Union is Strength: A history of trade unions in Australia* (West Melbourne: Thomas Nelson, 1978)
——*Room for Manoeuvre: Writings on History, Politics, Ideas and Play* (ed. Leonie Sandercock and Stephen Murray-Smith) (Richmond: Drummond, 1982)
Walker, David, *Dream and Disillusion: A Search for Australian Cultural Identity* (Canberra: ANU Press, 1976)
——*Not Dark Yet: a personal history* (Artarmon: Giramondo, 2011)
Ward, Russel, *A Radical Life* (South Melbourne: Macmillan, 1988)
Watson, Don, *Brian Fitzpatrick: A Radical Life* (Sydney: Hale & Iremonger, 1978)
Webb, Francis, *Collected Poems* (Intro Toby Davidson) (Perth: UWAP, 2011)
Whiteoak, John, and Aline Scott-Maxwell (eds), *Currency Companion to Music and Dance in Australia* (Strawberry Hills: Currency Press, 2012)
Wilde, William H, Joy Hooton and Barry Andrews, *The Oxford Companion to Australian Literature* (Melbourne: OUP, 1985)
Wright, Judith (ed. Patricia Clarke), *Half a Lifetime* (Melbourne: Text Publishing, 1999)
Yarwood, AT, *Walers: Australian Horses Abroad* (Carlton: Miegunyah Press, 1989)

Booklets, articles and chapters from books and magazines

Andrews, Barry, 'The Federal Government as Literary Patron', *Meanjin* vol 41 no 1 (1982) pp 3–19
Ashbolt, Allan, 'The great literary witch-hunt of 1952', in Ann Curthoys and John Merritt (eds), *Australia's First Cold War 1944–53*, vol 1 *Society, Communism and Culture* (Sydney: George Allen & Unwin, 1984) pp 153–82
Barnes, John, 'Remembering the Palmers', *La Trobe Journal* no 83 (2009), pp 57–67
Bennett, Bruce, 'Australian Literature and the Universities', in SMS (ed.), *Melbourne Studies in Education 1976* (Carlton: Melbourne University Press, 1976) pp 106–56
Blainey, Geoffrey, Foreword to Brian Fitzpatrick, *The British Empire in Australia* (South Melbourne: Macmillan, 1969) pp vii–x
Carter, David, 'Coming Home after the Party: *Overland*'s First Decade', *Meanjin* vol 44 no 1 (1985) pp 462–96
Christesen, Nina, 'A Russian Migrant', in Patricia Grimshaw and Lynne Strahan (eds), *The Half Open Door* (Sydney: Hale & Iremonger, 1982), pp 54–77
Connolly, Cyril, 'Little Magazines', in *The Evening Colonnade* (London: David Bruce & Watson, 1973), pp 414–27
Davidson, Jim, Interview with Dorothy Hewett, *Sideways from the Page: The Meanjin Interviews* (Melbourne: Fontana/Collins) pp 184–208; with AA Phillips, pp 34–51
——'"Home" Becomes Away: Melburnians in Oxford in the 1920s', in Carl Bridge, Robert Crawford and David Dunstan (eds), *Australians in Britain: The Twentieth Century Experience* (Melbourne: Monash University ePress, 9.1-9.10)
——'Mr Whitlam's Cultural Revolution', *Journal of Australian Studies* no 20 (1987), pp 83–91
Davison, Graeme, 'Rethinking the Australian Legend', *Australian Historical Studies*, vol 43 no 3 (2012) pp 429–51
Fitzpatrick, Brian, *The Royal Commission on Espionage: A Commentary* (Melbourne: C.B. Christesen, 1955)
Green, Cliff, 'David Martin: Our Most Improbable Friend', *Overland* 141 (1995) pp 25–7

Green, Dorothy, 'Three Editors and the Status Quo', *Meanjin*, vol 44 no 2 (1985) pp 193–208
Hesketh, Rollo, 'AA Phillips and the "Cultural Cringe": Creating an "Australian Tradition"', *Meanjin* vol 72 no 3 (2013) pp 92–103
Hewett, Dorothy, excerpt from 'The Empty Room', an autobiography in progress, *Overland* 160 (2000) pp 4–10
Hope, AD, 'Vance Palmer Reconsidered', *Southerly* vol 16 no 4 (1955) pp 203–9
Indyk, Ivor, 'Vance Palmer and the Social Function of Literature', *Southerly*, vol 50 no 3 (1990) pp 346–58
Lucas, Robin, '"A fine ruddy mess": The publication of Nettie Palmer's *Fourteen Years*': *La Trobe Journal* 83 (May 2009) pp 69–75
Macartney, Frederick T, *The Increased Price of Liberty* (Black Rock: F Macartney, 1955)
McGregor, Craig, 'Pop Man, Political Man, and Just Plain Man', in *People, Politics and Pop: Australia in the Sixties* (Sydney: Ure Smith, 1968) pp 158–75
McLachlan, Noel, '*Meanjin* and Australia in the Fifties', *Arena* no 70 (1985) pp 92–103
McQueen, Humphrey, 'Rex Ingamells and Environmental Values', *Meanjin* vol 37 no 1 (1978) pp 29–38
Marginson, Max, in Hume Dow (ed.), *More Memories of Melbourne University: Undergraduate Life Since 1919* (Hawthorn: Hutchinson, 1985) pp 89–117
Moore, Nicole, 'Dorothy Hewett: Twentieth-century writer', *Overland* 169 (2002) pp 15–17
——'Jill-of-all-trades', interview with Dorothy Hewett, *Overland* 153 (1998), pp 34–41
Mortimer, Rex, 'The Benefits of a Liberal Education', *Meanjin* vol 35 no 2 (1976) pp 115–26
Papps, Phyllis, 'Barrett Reid: a charismatic chameleon', *La Trobe Journal* (May 2011), pp 136–48
Read, Sir Herbert, *Preface to Francis Webb: Collected Poems* (Sydney: A&R, 1969)
Smith, Graeme, 'Making Folk Music', *Meanjin*, vol 44 no 4 (1985) pp 477–90
Taft, Bernie, *Crossing the Party Line: Memoirs of Bernie Taft* (Newham: Scribe, 1994)
Tipping, Marjorie, 'Remembrance of Palmers Past', *Overland* 100 (1985), pp 10–18
Turner, Ian, 'My Long March', *Overland* 59 (1974), pp 23–40
——'Reflections on Violence', Introduction to David Williamson, *The Removalists* (Sydney: Currency Press, 1973), pp 3–8
Ward, Stuart, 'The Empire's New Clothes', *Griffith Review* 59 (2017), pp 125–30
Wright, Judith, 'Brisbane in Wartime', *Overland* 100 (1985) pp 64–8

Periodicals
(in addition to *Meanjin* 1940–1974 and *Overland* 1954–1988)
Brisbane High School Magazine, 1927–28
The Corian, 1934–1941
Melbourne University Magazine, 1947
Outlook, 1957–1960
Realist Writer, 1952–1954
Shop, 1945–1947

Thesis
Adam Carr, 'An Age of Certainty: Three Generations of Melbourne Radicals, 1870–1988' (PhD, University of Melbourne, 2001)

Archival and manuscript
National Archives of Australia
A56/11/43 ASIO: *Overland* Magazine
A6119/68-9, 280, ASIO: Stephen Murray-Smith
AA 6119/64/477, 6119/7/276-78 and AA6119/275, ASIO: CB Christesen
A463/2565 (1-5) CLF—Grant to *Meanjin* Magazine
A463/1967/2797 Meeting of Advisory Board and Committee of CLF, Canberra 1961
A463/1968/2578(2) CLF—Assistance to Literary Magazines—Policy
A 463/1968/3444 CLF—Combined Meetings of Committee and Advisory Board, 1961 to 1967
A463/1973/4908 Clement Christesen—General Representations
A1967/2797 Meeting of Advisory Board and Committee of CLF 1961
A3753/1972/89 CLF Meeting, Adelaide 1972
A3753/1972/ 2759(2) and /2761(2) Minutes of Meeting of Advisory Board
A3753/1972/2763 Minutes of Combined meetings of Committee & Advisory Boards 1955–61

National Library of Australia
MS 1174 Vance & Nettie Palmer Papers
MS 1945 Frank Dalby Davison
MS 1691 Judah Waten, Speech at Nettie Palmer's Funeral
MS 4965 Brian Fitzpatrick Papers
MS 5378 Nancy Keesing Papers
MS 5678 Dorothy Green Papers
MS 5781 Judith Wright Papers
MS 6184 Dorothy Hewett Papers
MS 6206 Ian Turner Papers
MS 6327 Laurence Collinson Papers
MS 6885 David Martin Papers

La Trobe Library, State Library of Victoria
LaT MS 8272 Stephen Murray-Smith Papers
LaT MS 6244 Rex Ingamells Papers
LaT MS 13047 KD Gott Papers
LaT MS 9160 AA Phillips Papers
LaT MS 12491 Phillips Family Papers
LaT MS 13339 Barrett Reid Papers

University of Melbourne Archives
2005.0004 *Meanjin*: CBC editorship
2002.0029 AR Chisholm Papers
Central Registry File 1999.0014/1966/404 Meanjin—Donations and Grants

Fryer Library, University of Queensland
CBC, 'Poetry in Queensland in 1940', in Appendix to QAAA Annual Report 1940
Grano, Paul, Comments on CBC broadcast [draft for '21 Lives'], FLUQ 2/380
Grano, Paul, letter to Father Hayes, 20 Mar 1964, FLUQ 2/3240
Hayes Papers, FLUQ 2/380, 5

University of Queensland Archives
Minutes of Professorial Board 1932–34
CBC Student Record card, UQA 5157

Barr Smith Library, University of Adelaide
MSS 92 H315p Max Harris Papers

Privately held
Stephen Murray-Smith, Diaries 1977–1988 (27 vols). Now with two Canadian Notebooks, 1971, transferred to State Library of Victoria
Stephen Murray-Smith, Private and confidential report to the Hon. Barry Jones concerning Australian operations in Antarctica; with appended Summary For the Information of the Director, Antarctic Division (Barry Jones)
Record, *Overland* Print Runs 1954–1962 (David Murray-Smith)
Excell, Patricia, 'Meanjin in the Fifties: A View from the Assistant Editorial Chair', paper presented at ASAL conference, 1985 (Excell)
——'Flying without Borrowed Plumes: Meanjin 1940–90', paper presented at ASAL Conference, 1990; notes by CBC on same (Excell)
Ray Marginson, SMS folder (Marginson)
Murray-Smith, Joanna, 'Eulogy for Nita', 28 June 2013 (David Murray-Smith)

Interviews
CBC by Hazel de Berg, 18 Nov 1969, NLA Tape 411-12
SMS by Hazel de Berg, 21 Nov 1969, NLA Tape 426-28
Colin Badger by Patricia Excell, Aug 1992 (Patricia Excell)
AR Chisholm by Lynne Strahan, 19 Feb 1980 (UMA 1984.0083.0001)
David Martin by Hazel de Berg, 6 Dec 1969, NLA Tape 443
Ted Harrington by SMS and Nita, 11 Jan 1955, NLA Tape 2277-13-52

JD interviews

Stuart Macintyre	11 Mar 2011
Nita Murray-Smith	24 Mar 2011, 29 May 2012
Patricia Excell	24 Aug, 14 Dec 2011, 27 Jan 2015
Larry Bagg	14 Nov 2011
John McLaren	23 Nov 2011
Ken Inglis	26 Nov 2011
Rodney Hall	8 Dec 2011
Vane Lindesay	20 Dec 2011
Ray Marginson	2 Feb 2012, 28 Jan 2015
Chris Wallace-Crabbe	3 Feb 2012
Beth Gott	21 Mar 2012
John Barnes	2 Apr 2012
Richard Selleck	17 Apr 2012
Fay Zwicky	22 Apr 2012 *(phone)*
Jill Anwyl	1 May 2012
Joan Grant	18 May 2012
David Murray-Smith	30 May 2012, 5 Mar 2014
Bruce Grant	31 May 2012
Robin Wallace-Crabbe	19 Aug 2012
Harry Heseltine	7 Sep 2012
John Besemeres	28 Sep 2012
Jim Hammerton	10 Dec 2012
Robert Newton	12 Dec 2012
Jessie Serle	26 June 2012
Barry Jones	15 May 2013
Joanna Murray-Smith	1 Aug 2013
Jenny Love	6 Aug 2013
Bernard Rechter	13 Aug 2013
John Bluthal	6 Feb 2014
Don Anderson	12 Feb 2014
Rick Amor	4 Mar 2014
Frank Moorhouse	29 Apr 2016
Cleeve Charles	16 Aug 2017
Neville Maxwell	19 June 2017
John Thompson	8 Apr 2019

Illustrations

The Christesens in their Brisbane garden, Clem as editor, c 1945, Judith Wright, Brian Vrepont, James Picot, Paul Grano, AD Hope MS 'Australia', Dorothy Green, Vance and Nettie Palmer at Eltham, Clem with SMS and Kylie Tennant, Stan Ostoja-Kotkowski with electronic designing unit, AA Phillips, Brian Fitzpatrick, Clem and Nina at Eltham 1975, all Meanjin Collection 2005.0004 series, University of Melbourne Archives, Baillieu Library.

Stephen Murray-Smith in the Loft, Youth Festival Budapest, the Murray-Smiths with Prague friend, Meanjin-Overland cricket match presentation, SMS wearing tin-foil crown, and CBC painting of Eltham landscape, all courtesy Cleeve Charles.

Stephen with Ian Turner, photo by Robert Newton.

David Martin, Geoffrey Serle (1961, 1967), sketches by Louis Kahan published in *Meanjin Quarterly*, courtesy of the estate of Louis Kahan.

Dorothy Hewett, photo by Merv Lilley, permission Kate Lilley.

Rounds of the kitchen, permission David Murray-Smith.

Fred Williams portrait of SMS, 1980, State Library Victoria, copyright Estate of Fred Williams.

Index

Note: Page references in **bold** refer to illustrations or captions.

THE MIEGUNYAH PRESS

This book was designed and
typeset by Cannon Typesetting
The text was set in 11½ point Adobe Garamond Pro
with 14½ points of leading
The text is printed on 80gsm woodfree
This book was edited by Richard McGregor

THE
MIEGUNYAH
PRESS